VideoHound's® Golden Movie Retriever

VideoHound's Vampires on Video

VideoHound's Complete Guide to Cult Flicks and Trash Pics

VideoHound's Sci-Fi Experience:
Your Quantum Guide to the Video Universe

VideoHound's Family Video Guide, 2nd Edition

The VideoHound & All-Movie Guide StarGazer

Toxic Fame:
Celebrities Speak on Stardom

If you liked VideoHound...

MusicHound™ Rock:
The Essential Album Guide

MusicHound Country:
The Essential Album Guide

CyberHound's™ Web Guide:
8,000 Sites with Bite

VideoHound's

VIDEO
PREMIERES

VideoHound's VIDEO PREMIERES

The Only Guide to
Video Originals
and
Limited Releases

Mike Mayo

VISIBLE
INK
PRESS

Detroit   New York   Toronto   London

Published by Visible Ink Press®, a division of Gale Research
835 Penobscot Bldg.
Detroit MI 48226-4094

Visible Ink Press and VideoHound are trademarks of Gale Research

Art Director: Mary Krzewinski
Cover photos: *Bloodfist 7,* © New Horizons Home Video; *Carried Away* and *Nature of the Beast,* © New Line Home Video. All rights reserved.

Library of Congress Cataloging-in-Publication Data

Mayo, Mike, 1948–
    Videohound's video premieres : the only guide to video originals and limited
releases / Mike Mayo.
        p. cm.
    Includes index.
    ISBN 0-7876-0825-4
    1. Motion pictures—Catalogs. 2. Video recordings—Catalogs.
    I. Title.
PN1998.M32   1997
016.79143'75—dc21   97-970
                                                                     CIP

ISBN 0-7876-0825-4
Printed in the United States of America
All rights reserved
10 9 8 7 6 5 4 3 2 1

A Cunning Canine™ Production

"If you don't have a good story to tell, you're dead."

—*John Alonzo, cinematographer*

Contents

Sidebars

Sidebars (cont.)

I It's Friday evening. On your way home from work, you stop at the corner video store to pick up a couple of movies for the weekend. The New Releases shelf, of course, is virtually empty. All the big hits have been rented—the latest from Kevin, Meryl, and Clint are gone. The only things left are unfamiliar titles with semi-famous stars.

What are these movies? How did they find their way onto videocassette? And, most important, are they any good?

Welcome to the world of Video Premieres.

A few of these are small serious films, both foreign and domestic, that had brief runs on the art-house circuit. Others are conventional "major motion pictures" that played briefly in the largest cities, but didn't make it to suburban multiplexes and rural audiences. Some are older movies that haven't been seen for decades. More of them are lower-budget genre films—the "B" movies (and "A" minuses) that have always been a staple of the industry.

But as the video market has grown, the larger studios are now creating more ambitious films, like Disney's *Aladdin and the King of Thieves,* specifically for the video marketplace. With the expansion of broadcast outlets, the various cable networks have become more actively involved in the production of mid-budget movies. These films often show up in video stores before they're broadcast, and a few even make the festival circuit.

Strict definitions are impossible. The lines that divide Video Premieres, "A" pictures, and made-for-TV movies are becoming increasingly blurred. And less important. Though some Video Premieres may have been advertised in a few markets, for most of us in the vast American hinterland between Broadway and Santa Monica Boulevard, they're unknown quantities.

As Peter M. Nichols noted in *The New York Times,* "Every now and then a film comes along—a 'terrific little movie' in word-of-mouth parlance—that needs to be savored in private. Out at the cineplex the action sagas, formula romances, and family epics sprawl across the big screen, but terrific little movies often aren't for dating or teenage boys. Psychologically charged and featuring grittier if lesser-known stars, they provoke second thoughts. Intimate and usually without elaborate special effects, they play well on the small screen."

ix

Video Premieres

That's the best kind of Video Premiere—films like Ang Lee's debut *Pushing Hands,* the cable-made thriller *Red Rock West,* or the festival hit *Bottle Rocket.*

The movie business being what it is, these films can turn a profit—and provide an evening's entertainment—without an American theatrical run and the incredible expenses that come with it. According to the most recent MPAA figures, it takes $54.1 million to release a feature: $36.4 million in negative costs, plus another $17.7 million for prints and advertising! The film industry is simply making more movies than conventional theatres can handle.

Remember Rule #1 of Video Premieres: The decision to send one film to the video store and another to theatres was made by the same people who brought you *Hudson Hawk, House of the Spirits,* and all of Pauley Shore's movies.

Of course, all Video Premieres are not created equal.

Even the most devoted fan will have to admit that many are lacking in one way or another, but that doesn't mean they're not fun. Everyone knows that a big budget doesn't guarantee success, and in the right hands, a low budget can deliver the goods. In the world of Video Premieres the ratio of good stuff to garbage is about what it is for theatrical releases— roughly one to nine. That means there are some real treats tucked away on the shelves of the video store.

And the best of bad Video Premieres tend to be energetically, wonderfully bad. Who, for example, can forget the moment in *Food of the Gods: Part 2* when mutant rats the size of Winnebagos attack the synchronized swim team to the strains of Beethoven's Ode to Joy?

Video Premieres reviews the significant releases. It doesn't cover everything; no single book could. This one attempts to separate the thoroughbreds from the goats, the dazzlers from the duds. Since the films arrive in stores without advance reviews or publicity, they're unknown quantities. Their boxes promise excitement, romance, thrills, and healthful weight-loss, and most of us rightly ignore those claims. Still, people watch and enjoy these movies. The first part of the reason is simple economics.

If you and your sweetie decide to go out to the multiplex for the evening, you're probably looking at $15-25 with popcorn. Add in dinner and the optional babysitter, and you're talking about real money. Then you do have a right to expect excitement, romance, thrills, and healthful weight-loss.

At the video store, you can pick up a double or triple feature from the back of the rack and still be in single figures. With liberal use of the fast-forward button, the investment of your irreplaceable time isn't that great either. And home video is where most people see most movies these days. In 1995 Americans spent $5.5 billion on theatre tickets. They spent almost three times that much, $15.4 billion, renting and buying videos. By the year 2000, theatrical boxoffice will be about $6 billion; home video $20 billion. (*Video Business* magazine, 9/20/96)

The second part of the reason is innovation. When you explore the world of Video

Premieres, you'll find that you're sometimes disappointed but seldom bored. These movies are lively! You're also likely to discover fine talent, mostly young, on the way up.

Look at Nicolas Cage in *Red Rock West* or the hilarious *Zandalee*, or virtually anything with Lance Henriksen, Adienne Shelley, Trevor Goddard, or Shannon Whirry. Director John Woo's brilliant Hong Kong films were first discovered by most Americans as Video Premieres, and at PM Entertainment Joseph Merhi and Richard Pepin make some of the most energetic action movies in the business.

To help both the perplexed innocent and the experienced videophile through this thicket of questionable taste, hidden gems, and unfortunate trash, *Video Premieres* includes:

- More than a thousand short reviews of the best and worst releases, including an explanation of the MPAA rating, if any.

- Quotes from key people in the business: directors, producers, studio heads, actors, actresses.

- A guide to guilty pleasures, and a scandalous 10-point rating scale or GPI, Guilty Pleasure Index, explained below.

- Separate lists of the best serious films, comedies, mysteries, thrillers, sleepers, etc.

- Lots of photographs and stills.

Judging Video Premieres is tricky. With big-budget mainstream films, it's easy. As Mr. Nichols observed, they fall into familiar categories—period pieces, dramas, action, youth, comedy. They're aimed at the widest audience possible and don't take many chances. Every year, it seems that the Oscar nominees become more and more predictable.

The best Video Premieres tend to be a lot quirkier and more individualistic. Because of that, these films are subject to even more disagreement among audiences than their Hollywood counterparts. Different viewers may well love and hate *The Pathfinder* or *Reflections in the Dark* or *Suture* for precisely the same reasons. That's what makes the field so much fun.

The rating system is the VideoHound's familiar 4-bones (𝄢𝄢𝄢𝄢) to WOOF!:

𝄢𝄢𝄢𝄢	Excellent. One of the best of its kind. Worth owning.
𝄢𝄢𝄢	Very good. Prime rental material.
𝄢𝄢	Average. For fans of the genre.
𝄢	Make sure the fast-forward button is working.
WOOF!	You have been warned.

(𝄢s indicate mixed emotions, second and third thoughts, free-floating indecision.)

Each review contains a brief description of the contents, including the usual suspects—nudity, violence, strong language—and such unique variations as "shrubbery impersonation," "frog abuse," "hand puppets," "excessive mucus"—whatever fits.

Guilty pleasures, by definition, contain strong language, sex, violence, nudity, etc., and so they are also rated on the 10-1 Guilty Pleasure Index (GPI) in addition to the bone system. In general terms, a film with a GPI of 9.0 or more should be rented only in a nearby town and under an assumed name. Films in the 8.9-8.1 range are so salacious that you should never admit that you've seen one, much less enjoyed it. 8.0-6.5 may be discussed with close friends. 6.4-5.0 are acceptable for mixed company. Anything below a 4.9 is tame enough to show to your mother.

The key ingredients of virtually all Video Premieres are surprise and solid story-telling. Since they don't depend on highly paid stars or expensive computer wizardry, the best of them provide that unexpected eye-opener, the stunning out-of-left-field performance, the plot twist that knocks you back on your sofa, the perceptive small effect you've never seen.

The best Video Premieres come from filmmakers who want to tell a good story, not to make a deal or to create a line of action figures to be merchandised at fastfood chains. Talking about the creation of his comedy *The Pompatus of Love,* writer/producer/star Jon Cryer said that he and his friends realized they were becoming caught up in the Hollywood game of Byzantine studio politics. Finally they decided to find financing themselves because they didn't want to "develop" the film, they wanted to **make** it.

Recently, while working on *VideoHound's Sci-Fi Experience,* I relearned an important truth about all movies. Categories really don't count for much. Viewers shouldn't dismiss a film because they perceive it to be a "genre piece"—science fiction, horror, whatever. A good movie is a good movie. If the filmmakers can create interesting characters to engage your imagination, conflicts that somehow ring true, and mix them with the proper amount of humor and intelligence, then chances are they'll tell a story you want to see. And that's what the movie business is and ought to be about, from megabudget blockbusters to Video Premieres.

They're out there at the video store. Finding them takes some work—all good things do. *Video Premieres* will help.

Finally, a note on the sidebar material. Over the years, I've interviewed a lot of people in the film and video business. Here they speak for themselves and their work in short quotations. In a separate section—"Video Voices"—some of the men and women who work behind the scenes present their opinions. No matter what position these actors, filmmakers, and executives occupy on the entertainment food chain, they share a desire to please their viewers. As director Sam Raimi said, "I live and die for the audience like a child that needs attention and approval. If they like it [my movie] I'll be stupidly happy."

The sidebars also contain some personal lists and ideas about Video Premieres that reflect the quirky nature of the business and the VideoHound's penchant for outrageous categorization.

And don't miss the various Hound's Favorite Sleepers lists. These are a quick guide to best in *Video Premieres.*

This book could not have been written without the help of a lot of people, particularly the publicists who work hard and deserve special mention:

Warren Betts, Sandi Bushnell, Janice Clifford, Audrey Davis, Frank Djeng, Evan Fong, Fritz Friedman, Vicki Greenleaf, Susan Hale, Ed James, Dana Kornbluth, Maria LaMagra, Linda Lew, Shawna Lynch, Mike Pascuzzi, Sue Procko, Rick Rhoades, Maryann Ridini, Noah Scalin, Ann Schwarz, Nicole Silverstein, Jonna Winnicki.

Many thanks, guys!

Also:

Deborah Shames at Deborah Films;

Michael Karaffa at New Line;

Beth Corets, Barry Leshtz and Jim Nagle at Playboy;

Mike Krause and Marcus Ticotin at Triboro;

Lloyd Kaufman at Troma;

John Ellis at The VERY BIG Motion Picture Co.;

Bruce Apar at *Video Business* magazine;

Marcelle Abraham at Walt Disney.

All of them have been generous with their time and their knowledge of home video. Again, many thanks.

Titles are arranged on a word-by-word basis, including articles and prepositions. Leading articles (A, An, The) are ignored in English-language titles; the equivalent foreign articles are not ignored (because so many people—not you, of course—don't recognize them as articles); thus, *A Better Tomorrow* appears in the Bs, but *La Vie de Boheme* appears in the Ls. Some other points to keep in mind:

Acronyms appear alphabetically as if regular words. For example, A.P.E.X. is alphabetized as "APEX."

Common abbreviations in titles file as if they were spelled out, so Dr. Alien will be alphabetized as "Doctor Alien" and Mr. Stitch as "Mister Stitch."

Movie titles with numbers (such as *84 Charlie Mopic*) are alphabetized as if the number was spelled out—so this title would appear in the Es as if it were "Eighty Four Charlie Mopic."

Sample Review

Each review contains up to 19 tidbits of information, as enumerated below. Please realize that we faked a bit of info in this review, because we couldn't find one single movie that coincidentally contained every single element that might appear in a review.

➊ Haunted

➋ Handsomely produced thriller from Francis Coppola's American Zoetrope company is reminiscent in look and atmosphere to *Brideshead Revisited*. It's also a ghost story. Maybe. The setting is 1928, at the Edbrook estate. That's where university professor and spiritualist debunker David Ash (Aidan Quinn) goes in answer to an old woman's cry for help. Something terrible is going on, she says. But, upon arriving, Ash is more interested in Christina (Kate Beckinsale), an uninhibited young woman who admires his book. Ash isn't so sure about her brother (Anthony Andrews) who claims, "We're all mad, you know." Based on James Herbert's novel. The script by Tim Prager, Robert Kellett, and director Lewis Gilbert combines a nostalgic evocation of the period with various sexy undercurrents and a teasing attitude toward the supernatural. The veteran Gilbert— *Alfie, Educating Rita, Shirley Valentine*—handles a complex story with a sure touch and manages to pull out a few more surprises when most viewers will think they've got everything figured out. In the end, this one's a solid hit that deserves a strong recommendation. **➌ AKA:** Lewis Gilbert's The Haunted. **➍** 🦴🦴🦴 **➎ GPI:** 0.0.

➏ *Mature subject matter, brief nudity, some violence.*

➐ **➑ ➒ ➓** 1995 (R) 108m/C **⓫** *GB* **⓬** Aidan Quinn, Kate Beckinsale, Anthony Andrews, Alex Lowe, Anna Massey, Geraldine Somerville, Victoria Shalet; *Cameos:* John Gielgud; **⓭ D:** Lewis Gilbert **⓮ W:** Lewis Gilbert, Bob Kellett, Tim Prager; **C:** Tony Pierce-Roberts; **M:** Debbie Wiseman. Mayo Medal '96: Best Picture. **VHS** *HMK*

⓯ **⓰** **⓱** **⓲ ⓳**

1. Title (see also Alternate Title below, and the "Alternate Titles Index")
2. Description/review
3. Alternate title (we faked it here)
4. One- to four-bone rating (or WOOF!), four bones being the ultimate praise
5. Guilty Pleasures Index (see page xii for an explanation)
6. Explanation of MPAA rating
7. Year released
8. MPAA rating
9. Length in minutes
10. Black and white (B) or Color (C)
11. Country in which the flick was produced (if other than the U.S.)
12. Cast, including cameos and voiceovers (V)
13. Director(s)
14. Writer(s)
15. Cinematographer(s)
16. Music composers/lyricists
17. Awards, including nominations (we made this up)
18. Format, including VHS and Laservideo/disk (LV)
19. Distributor code(s) (see also "Distributor List" and "Distributor Guide")

Across the Moon

A good ensemble is cast adrift in a fitful come-dy-drama about two young women (Elizabeth Pena and Christina Applegate) who follow their jailbird boyfriends (Tony Fields and Peter Berg) to the Mojave desert after said boyfriends' arrest, conviction, and incarceration in a remote prison. Stephen Schenck's script meanders aimlessly, introducing eccentric characters (played by the likes of Michael McKean, Burgess Meredith, and James Remar) and then doing nothing with them. The whole film is ridiculously overacted and the actors look far too prettified for their allegedly down-and-out characters. Overall, it's reminiscent of but not nearly as enjoyable as the sleeper, *Little Vegas*. 🎞

Profanity, violence, brief nudity, sexual content.

1994 **(R)** 88m/C Elizabeth Pena, Christina Applegate, Tony Fields, Peter Berg, James Remar, Michael McKean, Burgess Meredith, Jack Nance; *D:* Lisa Gottlieb; *W:* Stephen Schenck; *C:* Andrzej Sekula; *M:* Christopher Tyng, Exene Cervenka. **VHS** *HMD*

Adventures in Spying

Typical small-town teenager Brian McNichols (Bernie Coulson) is delivering newspapers when he spots Al Dorn (right-wing talk show host G. Gordon Liddy), a drug kingpin with a $50,000 price on his head. But everyone thinks that Dorn is dead, blown up by a car bomb. So with the help of Julie (Jill Schoelen), the new girl in town, Brian sets out to take Dorn's picture. The film relies on too many coincidences and contrived bits of business to keep the story moving, but kids who like contemporary adventures with a light *Hardy Boys* touch will enjoy it. 🎞🎞

Mild violence, strong language.

1992 **(PG-13)** 92m/C Jill Schoelen, Bernie Coulson, Seymour Cassel, G. Gordon Liddy, Michael Emil; *D:* Hil Covington; *W:* Hil Covington; *M:* James Stemple. **VHS** *NLC*

The Advocate

Curious legal thriller has a medieval setting. All of the cases referred to are real, and despite their bizarre quality, it's not hard to accept their reality. In France, circa 1400, idealistic young lawyer Colin Firth leaves the hectic pace and political games of Paris for a new practice in a small town. His more worldly and skeptical assistant (scene stealer Jim Carter) doesn't believe things will be so simple. The town already has a lawyer (Donald

Pleasence), and the courts have to answer to both church and secular authorities whose jurisdictions sometimes overlap and conflict. The central mystery concerns the murder of a Jewish boy and the arrival of a group of gypsies. The film doesn't have the dense historical texture of *The Name of the Rose* or *The Return of Martin Guerre,* but the plot is so tricky and intriguing that it's never boring. Recommended. By the way, this BBC production was the source of some controversy when it received an NC-17 rating from the MPAA. The offending scene, a bawdy bedroom romp, has been trimmed to an "R." *AKA:* The Hour of the Pig. 🌶🌶🌶

Nudity, sexual content, strong language, some violence.

1993 (R) 102m/C *GB* Colin Firth, Amina Annabi, Nicol Williamson, Ian Holm, Lysette Anthony, Donald Pleasence, Michael Gough, Harriet Walter, Jim Carter; *D:* Leslie Megahey; *W:* Leslie Megahey. **VHS, LV** *MAX, TOU*

After Midnight

One dark and stormy night, college students taking Psych 102—the Psychology of Fear—go to their professor's house to tell scary stories. One of their disgruntled classmates is lurking around outside with an axe. The subjects of their tales are familiar campfire fare: haunted house, pack of killer dogs, deranged killer. And then there's the framing device for the anthology which comes to a cop-out conclusion. Dialogue and production values are well above average. The pace is deliberately slow, a bit too slow really, but at least the film shows some originality and it keeps the bloody special effects to a minimum. 🌶🌶🌶

Violence, profanity.

1989 (R) 90m/C Marg Helgenberger, Marc McClure, Alan Rosenberg, Pamela Segall, Nadine Van Der Velde, Ramy Zada, Jillian McWhirter, Billy Ray Sharkey; *D:* Jim Wheat, Ken Wheat. **VHS** *FOX, MGM*

After School

Where but home video would you find a movie that tries to combine a squeaky-clean teen exploitation story with serious theological debates and a separate subplot involving

topless cavemen and cavewomen. (As Dave Barry would say here, I am not making this up.) The contemporary side of the action is set at a Florida college where student and non-believer Renee Coleman has a serious crush on her religion professor, Sam Bottoms, a priest. Their story, which could have turned into sexy fluff, is completely serious. To further complicate the situation, the Vatican has chosen Bottoms to represent the church at a televised debate with ex-priest Robert Lansing, whose best-seller questions the existence of God. That part is intercut with scenes involving a tribe of prehistoric folks. At times, their actions correspond with the modern stuff, but more often they're senseless and confusing. At no time are they at all believable. 🌶🌶

Toplessness, mature subject matter, profanity.

1988 (R) 90m/C Sam Bottoms, Edward Binns, Page Hannah, Renee Coleman, Dick Cavett, Robert Lansing; *D:* William Olsen. **VHS** *ACA*

Akira

Katsuhiro Otomo's 1987 film is the most famous work of Japanese animation, "manga," to arrive on these shores to date. It's a mythic adventure that borrows freely from such diverse sources as *The Wild One, Blade Runner, The Road Warrior,* and Stephen King's *Carrie.* The wildly complex, multilayered story begins 31 years after World War III in Neo-Tokyo, a chaotic place where an oppressive government rules in spite of massive civil unrest and organized, armed resistance. The primary heroes are two bikers, Tetsuo and Kaneda. The nature and identity of the title character are a mystery throughout. He (or it) could be a redeemer, or is it part of a military conspiracy? But beyond the dazzling and sometimes extremely violent action, this is a story of adolescence, of the stormy transit between childhood and adulthood. In the big scenes, where the focus may shift among as many as five characters, Otomo uses some dizzying perspective, taking full advantage of the freedom of animation. And in one dream sequence, he captures the reality of a nightmare as well as any film—live action or animated—ever has. Even though *Akira* is technically a "cartoon," it's too violent and too complicated for younger children to follow. For more mature kids, teenagers, and anyone who appreciates animation, *Akira* is a masterpiece. The laser version includes both the English and Japanese soundtracks, plus details about the story's evolution from 1,800-page comic book to feature film. ♫♫♫▽

Strong violence.

1987 124m/C *JP D:* Katsuhiro Otomo, Sheldon Renan; *W:* Katsuhiro Otomo, Izo Hashimoto; *C:* Katsuji Misawa. **VHS, LV** *STP, INJ, CRC*

Aladdin
and the King of Thieves

In the first three minutes Robin Williams impersonates Sylvester Stallone, Walter Cronkite, boxing promoter Don King, and Tin-kerbell. The rest doesn't maintain that frantic pace—it couldn't—but this one's still a hugely entertaining third (and final) installment in the series. As viewers of the first two films doubtless remember, the wedding of Aladdin (voiced by Scott Weinger) and Jasmine (Linda Larkin) has been postponed. As it approaches, our hero gets cold feet and worries about the father he never knew. At the same time, Cassim (John Rhys-Davies, sounding eerily like Sean Connery), King of the 40 Thieves, is planning to rob the palace. His target is the Oracle (CCH Pounder), a magical scepter. The pace matches the original with lots of fast-moving action, much of it staged underground. And again like the original, the film really kicks into overdrive whenever Robin Williams' "big blue guy" shows up. If he's not quite as inspired and hyperactive as he was before, he's still funny, inventive, and fun for both kids and adults. The same applies to the animation and the songs. Recommended. ♫♫♫

AKIRA. ©Orion Home Video.

1996 82m/C *D:* Tad Stone; *W:* Mark McCorkle, Robert Schooley; *V:* Robin Williams, Scott Weinger, Jerry Orbach, John Rhys-Davies, Gilbert Gottfried, Linda Larkin, CCH Pounder. **VHS** *DIS*

Alexa:
A Prostitute's Own Story

Title character Christine Moore is an expensive call-girl who agrees to tell her life story to playwright Kirk Baily. Her pimp objects. The plot provides few surprises, though it's told with a remarkable degree of realism, neither romanticizing nor glamorizing the sex-for-sale business. This one is similar to (but not as good as) 1987's *Street Smart*. *AKA:* Alexa. 🦴🦴🦴 **GPI: 4.9**

Mature subject matter, profanity, violence, sexual scenes, brief nudity.

1988 (R) 81m/C Christine Moore, Kirk Baily, Ruth Collins; *D:* Sean Delgado; *W:* Sean Delgado, Peggy Bruen. **VHS, LV** *ACA*

Alien Intruder

In the time-honored tradition of killer B's, this s-f vid combines a good cast with fair special effects and laughably flimsy models and sets. The plot has something to do with mysterious computer-generated siren Tracy Scoggins, who can drive men mad with passion. She's loose on a space ship with Billy Dee Williams, Maxwell Caulfield, and some other guys on a dangerous secret mission. They have lots of fights and shoot-outs and fantasy sequences. It's all handled with enough spirit and energy to please fans of bad movies. Everyone else should give it a pass. 🦴🦴 **GPI: 6.0**

Sexual material, nudity, strong language, violence.

1993 (R) 90m/C Billy Dee Williams, Tracy Scoggins, Maxwell Caulfield; *D:* Ricardo Jacques Gale. **VHS, LV** *PMH*

Alien Seed

At best, this low-budget s-f is no more far-fetched than Whitley Strieber's *Communion* or any of the other "alien abduction" tales that some people seem to take seriously. The tough heroine is well played by Heidi Paine. The plot is goofy from the first frame, but the flick delivers all the lively cheap thrills you want from an unpretentious, low-budget B-movie. 🎦🎦

Violence, profanity, brief nudity.

1989 88m/C Erik Estrada, Heidi Paine, Steven Blade; **D:** Bob James. **VHS** *AIP*

Alien Terminator

Simple low-budget rip-off of *Alien* posits generic "scientists" who have been locked in an underground experimental facility for two years. One of them invents a new killer species and promptly lets it escape. There's nothing to recommend this one beyond some gross-out effects that have been done better in many other flicks. 🎦

Nudity, violence, strong language, mild sexual content, drug use.

1995 (R) 78m/C Maria Ford, Kevin Alber, Rodger Halstead, Cassandra Leigh, Emile Levisetti; **D:** Dave Payne. **VHS** *NHO*

Aliens, Dragons, Monsters & Me: The Fantasy Film World of Ray Harryhausen

Video celebration of special effects genius Ray Harryhausen is based on an exhibit of his work at the Museum of the Moving Image in London. Also included is an affectionate analysis of Harryhausen's appeal by his friend Ray Bradbury. The story is told in rough chronological order, beginning when a Los Angeles teenager saw *King Kong* and his life was changed. During World War II, he continued his work with Frank Capra's film unit and even made a short propaganda film (included here) entitled "Guadalcanal." After the war, Harryhausen found that his tastes in fantasy and science fiction weren't shared by the larger movie-going public. Though much of his black-and-white work is respected and studied today, such films as *Mighty Joe Young, The Beast from 20,000 Fathoms, It Came from Beneath the Sea,* and *20 Million Miles to Earth* were relegated to drive-ins and double features in the 1940s and '50s. But then he and his long-time producer Charles H. Schneer made the bold leap to color and myth, and *The 7th Voyage of Sinbad* became the sleeper hit of 1958. After it came *The Three Worlds of Gulliver, Mysterious Island, Valley of Gwangi, The Golden Voyage of Sinbad,* and several others, including everybody's favorite, *Jason and the Argonauts.* Some were commercial hits; some weren't. All contain Harryhausen's wonderful creations—cyclops and griffins, bronze giants and moon men, sword-waving skeletons and flying horses, and perhaps best of all, dinosaurs and dragons. They often tower over their human counterparts on the screen, and they always have as much personality. The clips included will make you want to see the films and the critters again. Younger videophiles who are unfamiliar with Harryhausen's magic will become instant fans and demand another trip to the video store. This one's a delight. If only it were twice as long. 🎦🎦🎦🎦

Contains some violence.

1992 57m/C **W:** Richard Jones. **VHS, LV** *LUM, FUS*

Alligator Eyes

Part road movie, part mystery, part twisted romance, this film-festival sleeper defies any useful classification. It's the kind of movie that benefits enormously from the heady atmosphere of a festival and the weird mood that audiences achieve sometime between the cocktail hour and two in the morning. It works on video, too. The story begins when three friends take off for a beach vacation and meet blind hitchhiker Annabelle Larsen. Straight away, she begins to manipulate them, suggesting that they change their plans. When they don't come around, she uses more unusual and persuasive methods. At the same time, a car may be following them, and her stories about her psychiatrist grow more outlandish. Her talk of alligators becomes obsessive. To some tastes, the film is too talky. The charac-

ters have an unpleasant edge and the writing is so strange that it's impossible to judge the acting. Even if this one's exasperating at times, it is never boring. Director John Feldman has gone on to make the cult hit, *Dead Funny*. 𝄞𝄞♡

Strong language, brief nudity, sexual content, violence.

1990 (R) 101m/C Annabelle Larsen, Roger Kabler, Mary McLain, Allen McCullough, John MacKay; *D:* John Feldman; *W:* John Feldman; *M:* Sheila Silver. **VHS** *ACA*

Almost Dead

As supernatural thriller/comedies go, this is thin formula stuff, notable only for the presence of notorious bad girl Shannen Doherty. She plays a professor of abnormal psychology (yeah, right) who believes that her mother—dead these past four years after committing suicide by blowing up her motel room—has returned from the grave. Costas Mandylor is the cop who helps her sort it out. The silly story needs no comment. As for the humor, this is one of those movies that you alternately laugh at and with. 𝄞𝄞

Some violence, icky effects.

1994 92m/C Shannen Doherty, Costas Mandylor, John Diehl, William R. Moses; *D:* Ruben Preuss. **VHS** *MNC*

Almost Hollywood

Video's low-budget answer to *Swimming with Sharks* is an acidly affectionate parody of the movie business. Tony (Don Stuart) is an unashamedly sleazy producer of erotic thrillers. The company is suffering assorted accidents and setbacks, and his bread-and-butter product (video sequels) seems doomed until Playmate India Allen (a co-producer of this film who plays herself) is brought in by Tony's investors. She'll star in his next epic, and even agrees to fill in when the current leading lady is mysteriously murdered. But she'll have nothing to do with Tony's ersatz Indian director Abdu (Scott Apel). He protests,

"My vision includes pubic hair!" Writer/director Mike Weaver maintains a good sense of humor throughout. His portrait of the movie business as a world of sexist, treacherous slime isn't new, but then, some things don't change, no matter how large or small the budget. 𝄞𝄞𝄞

Comic nudity, sexual material, strong language, violence.

1995 100m/C India Allen, Don Stuart, Gregg Scott, Scott Apel, Lisa Buckles, Rachel Dyer; *D:* Michael Weaver. **VHS** *YHV*

Almost Pregnant

As you'd hope and expect, a comedy about infertility is often tasteless. It's not particularly funny, but then this isn't exactly great humorous material. Linda (Tanya Roberts) and Charlie (Jeff Conaway) can't conceive, and their doctor says that it's Charlie's fault. After attempting various medical remedies, they consider engaging a "surrogate," and the film becomes an unconventional bedroom farce. That's also when Joan Severance shows up, adding a welcome note of off-beat intelligence that helps considerably. An unrated version containing explicit scenes is also available. 𝄞𝄞

Nudity, sexual situations, strong language.

1991 (R) 90m/C Tanya Roberts, Jeff Conaway, Joan Severance, Dom DeLuise; *D:* Michael DeLuise; *W:* Fred Stroppel. **VHS, LV** *COL*

Amanda and the Alien

For the first half, this inventive s-f comedy is almost a "Clueless X-Files." The alien of the title looks like a horseshoe crab but can inhabit human bodies easily. Of course, that kills the host. Amanda (Nicole Eggert) is a smart, hip San Francisco girl—tattoos, navel ring, attitude—who takes pity on the creature because...well, because the cops and the feds are after him, or her, or it, whatever. Off they go, with Stacey Keach in pursuit. As long as writer/director Jon Kroll is revealing the two

main characters and their curious relationship, the film is sexy, with an odd snappy humor. Eventually though, it becomes a fairly tame chase flick, and isn't nearly as interesting. Still, for fans, it rates a qualified recommendation. By the way, this Showtime production is based on a Robert Silverberg story. 🦴🦴🦴

Strong language, sexual content, brief nudity, violence.

1995 (R) 94m/C Alex Meneses, Nicole Eggert, Michael Dorn, Stacy Keach, Michael C. Bendetti; *D:* Jon Kroll; *W:* Jon Kroll. **VHS** *REP*

The American Angels: Baptism of Blood

Here's a sensitive, thought-provoking examination of the high-pressure world of women's professional wrestling. Will the rookie, Luscious Lisa (Jan MacKenzie), make the team? Or will she be driven off by her arch-enemy, Magnificent Mimi (Mimi Lesseos)? And what about the dwarf who lives under the ring? This fictional wrestling story is just as realistic and believable as the real thing. There is, however, one moment in the big fight when the loud "CRUNCH" sound effect comes about a quarter-second before Luscious Lisa lands on Magnificent Mimi. The effect is diminished; but, hey, nothing is perfect, right? 🦴🦴🦴

Violence, profanity, brief nudity, sexual content.

1989 (R) 99m/C Jan MacKenzie, Tray Loren, Mimi Lesseos, Trudy Adams, Patricia Cavoti, Susan Sexton, Jean Kirkland, Jeff Lundy, Lee Marshall; *D:* Beverly Sebastian, Ferd Sebastian. **VHS, LV** *PAR*

American Dream

Initially, it appears that this Oscar-winning documentary will follow a conventional union-management conflict at the Hormel meatpacking plant in Austin, Minnesota, in the mid 1980s. But director Barbara Kopple isn't interested in the management side. Instead, she focuses on an increasingly bitter internecine struggle within the union itself, and that's a sad, sad story. Not surprisingly, the film is suffused with a strong anti-Reagan bias. But when he was president, Reagan never made any bones about his pro-business attitudes, so he's an insubstantial villain here. By extension, the executives of the Hormel company aren't such bad guys, either. They're simply using new labor laws to cut the best deal they can. The losers are the workers, their families, and their town, and most of the film focuses on them and their immediate problems. There it becomes a genuine tragedy where good people follow their best instincts to a disastrous conclusion. Kopple is such a skilled storyteller that this version of the "truth" is as compelling as the best fiction. If *American Dream* lacks the strong visual action and suspense of her earlier and similar work, *Harlan County, U.S.A.*, it's just as involving on a more personal, psychological level. Highly recommended. 🦴🦴🦴🦴

Contains some strong language.

1989 100m/C *D:* Barbara Kopple; *C:* Phil Parmet. Academy Awards '91: Best Feature Documentary; National Society of Film Critics Awards '92: Best Feature Documentary; Sundance Film Festival '91: Audience Award, Grand Jury Prize. **VHS, LV** *WAR, HBO, BTV*

American Roulette

Andy Garcia stars as the deposed poet/president of an unnamed Latin American country. He's trying to raise money in London while all sorts of folks—Soviets, Americans, death squads from back home—are trying either to buy him off or kill him. Kitty Aldridge says that she's trying to help him, but is she? The dialogue is sharp and abundant, and the relationship between the leads is surprisingly complex. Good performances all around, notably Robert Stephens as Screech, the sympathetic spy. By the way, the poetry is taken from the work of Pablo Neruda. 🦴🦴

Profanity, violence.

1988 (R) 102m/C *GB AU* Andy Garcia, Kitty Aldridge, Robert Stephens, Al Matthews, Susannah York; *D:* Maurice Hatton; *M:* Michael Gibbs. **VHS, LV** *VMK*

American Tiger

A foreword states: "The way that is the way is not the ordinary way. —Confucius (VI century BC)." Say what? The rest of the movie is a showcase—if that's the right word—for Olympic gymnast Mitch Gaylord and several other semi-professional actors. It's all about magic, topless dancers, televangelists, and other screwy goings-on in Miami. The ordinary effects are no help and neither is the needless trickiness. Overall, the production values are O.K., and the way that is the way stays mainly in the plain. **AKA:** American Rickshaw. 🦴🦴

Violence, nudity, sexual situations.

1989 (R) 93m/C Mitch Gaylord, Donald Pleasence, Daniel Greene, Victoria Prouty; *D:* Martin Dolman. **VHS** *ACA*

American Yakuza

Often silly shoot-'em-up certainly has its moments, particularly at the beginning, when director Frank Cappello tosses in some strong visual flourishes. Viggo Mortensen is a cop who impersonates an ex-con to infiltrate a Japanese gang in Los Angeles. The real point of the film is his relationship with the gang's leader, Ishibashi. The story owes some obvi-ous debts to John Woo's wonderful action movies with its emphasis on honor and loyalty; the big action scenes also show Woo's influence. The two leads are excellent, and if the long middle section hadn't bogged down in plot details, this one might have been a four-bone sleeper. As it is, the film is still better than average and it'll be interesting to see what Cappello does next. 🦴🦴🦴

Graphic violence, strong language, brief nudity, sexual content.

1994 (R) 95m/C Viggo Mortensen, Michael Nouri; *D:* Frank Cappello; *W:* Max Strom, John Allen Nelson. **VHS** *COL*

Amore!

Midlife wish fulfillment is the basis for this light musical fantasy. Investment banker Saul Schwartz (Jack Scalia) is successful but unhappy. Encouraged by his psychiatrist (James Doohan), he beams up from New York to start over as an actor in Hollywood. He shaves his beard, changes his name, and is reborn as Salvatore Guiliano III, an Italian heartthrob ready to take the movie business by storm. This big, sloppy movie is loads of fun if you're in the right frame of mind. It looks like writer/director Lorenzo Doumani knows a lot of people in the film industry and wrote quirky little parts for all of them. The result is an old-fashioned romantic comedy with a few songs. If the story lacks a certain polish, so what? Its heart is in the right place. Scalia is fine both as a ham actor and as a bearded broker; Kathy Ireland is less convincing as a sharp writer, though she doesn't embarrass herself, either. A genuine sleeper. 🦴🦴🦴

Mature subject matter, a little strong language, brief nudity.

1993 (PG-13) 93m/C Jack Scalia, Kathy Ireland, Elliott Gould, George Hamilton, Brenda Epperson, James Doohan, Katherine Helmond, Betsy Russell, Norm Crosby, Frank Gorshin; *D:* Lorenzo Doumani; *W:* Lorenzo Doumani. **VHS, LV** *PMH*

And God Created Woman

Curiously, the "unrated, uncensored" version of this screwball 1988 soap opera is two minutes shorter than the R-rated version. That's

somehow appropriate for a story of sex, politics, incarceration, and rock music in Arizona. Rebecca DeMornay is a prison escapee who hitches a ride in gubernatorial candidate Frank Langella's limo, but she winds up back in the slammer where she meets, woos (graphically), and marries carpenter Vincent Spano before she gets a parole and forms a rock band, and then for reasons too ridiculous to explain, refuses to sleep with her new husband and begins fooling around with the politico. No, the plot doesn't make any more sense on the tube than it does here on the page. It lacks the camp appeal of the original 1957 Brigitte Bardot film (also made by Roger Vadim), and it isn't nearly as funny (at least, not intentionally) as his fine black comedy, *Pretty Maids All in a Row.* But it does feature DeMornay at her sexiest and most elfin, and that's certainly worth something. Also available in an unrated version. 🦴🦴

Sexual activity, nudity, profanity.

1988 (R) 100m/C Rebecca DeMornay, Vincent Spano, Frank Lan-

gella, Donovan Leitch, Judith Chapman, Thelma Houston; **D:** Roger Vadim; **M:** Tom Chase, Steve Rucker. **VHS, LV** *VES, LIV*

...And God Spoke

This "mocumentary" is the *Spinal Tap* of low-budget movie making. Independent director Michael Riley is reaching for the brass ring with his epic independent production based on the Bible. There are still a few problems to be worked out with financing and casting, but his partner/producer Stephen Rappaport assures him that his vision will make it to the screen. Yes, they've had to scale back the script—Jesus is out—and the actress who's supposed to play Eve has a rather prominent tattoo, but they can work around that. Outside the studio system, low-budget filmmaking is a hand-to-mouth business. Nothing is certain; from the seemingly simple matter of who's in charge of the morning meeting to building an Ark. The more you know about the actual mechanics of film production, the better the movie is. But anyone with a taste for dry, deadpan humor will appreciate it. 🐾🐾🐾

Strong language, brief nudity.

1994 (R) 82m/C Michael Riley, Stephen Rappaport, Soupy Sales, Lou Ferrigno, Eve Plumb, Andy Dick, R.C. Bates, Fred Kaz, Daniel Tisman; *D:* Arthur Borman; *W:* Gregory S. Malins, Michael Curtis **VHS** *WFA*

Android

The special effects aren't too special, but the characters are terrific, particularly Dr. Daniel (Klaus Kinski), the maddest mad scientist you're ever likely to see, and Max 404 (Don Opper), an innocent, curious robot. Three escaped prisoners land on their space station, interrupting Dr. Daniel's plan to build a super-android. One of the visitors (Brie Howard) stimulates Max's questions about sex. Writer Opper turns in a performance worthy of Chaplin with more than a hint of his famous Little Tramp. He has that same wistful quality; especially in one scene when he's packing for a trip and carefully places a spare hand or two in his bags. 🐾🐾🐾

Mature subject matter, brief nudity.

1982 (PG) 80m/C Klaus Kinski, Don Opper, Brie Howard; *D:* Aaron Lipstadt; *W:* Don Opper. **VHS, LV** *MED*

Angel of Destruction

Low-budget revenge/martial arts flick scrapes the bottom of the action-adventure barrel. Even though the tropical locations and cheap hotel sets give it the look of trashy '60s drive-in fare, the film lacks the necessary energy, imagination, and style. Police detective (Maria Ford) avenges sister's (Charlie Spradling) murder by psycho (Jimmy Broome). The plot is thoughtless nonsense; the fight choreography is awkward and untrained. Despite the feminist plot elements, the violence against women is uncomfortably graphic. 🐾🐾

Language, violence, and sexuality.

1994 (R) 80m/C Maria Ford, Charlie Spradling, Jimmy Broome; *D:* Charles Philip Moore. **VHS, LV** *NHO*

Animal Instincts

The Mother of All Erotic Thrillers is one of the truly great guilty pleasures of our time. It's loosely based on that supermarket tabloid story about the call girl and her husband who kept a list of names and videotapes of her escapades with the rich and politically connected in a Florida town. Joanne (Shannon Whirry, in the role that made her a video star) is a bored housewife whose policeman husband (Maxwell Caulfield) discovers that he enjoys watching more than participation. Before this steamy tale is over, it has touched on most of your basic sexual proclivities including (but not limited to) powdered wigs and women in business suits. Director Gregory Hippolyte, the Orson Welles of soft core, is in top form, and that's recommendation enough for any fan. Also available in an unrated version. Followed by two sequels to date. 🐾🐾🐾 **GPI: 9.8**

Contains nudity, sexual subject matter, some strong language.

1992 (R) 94m/C Maxwell Caulfield, Jan-Michael Vincent, Mitch Gaylord, Shannon Whirry, Delia Sheppard, John Saxon, David Carradine; *D:* Alexander Gregory Hippolyte. **VHS** *ACA*

Animal Instincts 2

Average sequel repeats the key ingredients that made the original a hit in a more coherent plot about a woman who becomes involved with a voyeuristic neighbor. Like the first film, it uses the confessional—to a priest or a psychiatrist or perhaps someone else—as a framing device. If it lacks freshness, the filmmakers do understand one important fact about this kind of story. It's not really about sex; it's about sin, an infinitely more interesting subject. Also available in an unrated version. 🐾🐾🐾 **GPI: 8.2**

Sexual content, nudity, strong language, some violence.

1994 (R) 92m/C Shannon Whirry, Woody Brown, Elizabeth Sandifer, Al Sapienza; *D:* Alexander Gregory Hippolyte. **VHS, LV** *ACA*

"*I liked the script, thought there was a lot I could do with it. I thought it was an interesting character if done the right way. She was a sympathetic character but she could have played as a slut and that wouldn't have been interesting at all. But I really saw where it could go. I took it and the rest is history.*"

—Actress Shannon Whirry on *Animal Instincts.*

Animal Instincts 3: The Seductress

The glossy erotic series gets a tad studied in its third installment, minus original star Shannon Whirry. It's about a writer of dirty novels (Wendy Schumacher) living with a record producer (James Matthew) who pretends to be blind so he can "watch" her. Veteran producer/director Gregory Hippolyte tries some experimental techniques that don't interfere with his real intentions. 🐾🐾🐾 GPI: 9.0

Nudity, strong sexual content, language.

1995 **(R)** 92m/C Wendy Schumacher, James Matthew; *D:* Alexander Gregory Hippolyte. **VHS** *APX*

Another Chance

Comic misfire features sexy women and exotic cars. Philandering actor Bruce Greenwood falls in love with model Vanessa Angel but is seduced by supernatural temptress Barbara Edwards. He dies—sort of—and is given another chance to prove that he can be faithful, etc., etc. The thin storyline is padded with unfunny Hollywood jokes but the real problem is a glamorous cast that simply cannot act. Angel recalls Olivia Newton-John at her least expressive. She reads her lines as if English were her third language. 🐾

Sexual situations, brief nudity, profanity.

1988 **(R)** 99m/C Bruce Greenwood, Frank Annese, Jeff East, Anne Ramsey, Barbara Edwards, Vanessa Angel; *D:* Jerry Vint. **VHS, LV** *REP*

Another Pair of Aces: Three of a Kind

Made-for-television film is true to its roots with overly dramatic bad music and regular breaks for ads. But, as the box states, the tape "Includes NEVER BEFORE SEEN EROTIC FOOTAGE" and the Film Advisory Board Rating System says that it is "EXTREMELY MATURE" for "explicit sex and extreme nudity." That's a lot of hype for one short bedroom scene with Kris Kristofferson and Joan Severance. And what is "extreme" nudity, anyway? Formula story follows contemporary Texas Rangers Kristofferson and Rip Torn and con man Willie Nelson as they take on a group of wealthy right-wing vigilantes. The script has some good, funny moments for Willie and Rip. They walk away with the movie without breaking a sweat. 🐾🐾

Nudity, sexual content, violence.

1991 93m/C Willie Nelson, Kris Kristofferson, Joan Severance, Rip Torn, Dan Kamin, Ken Farmer; *D:* Bill Bixby. **VHS** *VMK*

Apartment Zero

One of the best sleepers in any video store, this haunting exercise in originality is a surprise from the first scene to the last. A serial killer is on the loose in Buenos Aires, 1988, and his work appears to be somehow related to the recently disbanded government-sponsored death squads. Or is something else going on? Adrian LeDuc (Colin Firth) runs a theatre that specializes in old movies. He's an eccentric young man, compulsively neat. A roommate is the last thing he wants, but financial straits demand it. Enter Jack Carney (Hart Bochner), a handsome American who instantly cracks Adrian's defensive shell. That's where the mysterious games begin. Jack is a manipulative charmer. To tippling old ladies, he is the rescuer of stranded cats. To an obnoxious lady's man, he's a drinking buddy. To the beautiful, lonely wife of a salesman, he's a Byronic lover. To the transvestite, he's a nonjudgmental friend. And to Adrian? Their relationship is more difficult to define. Though there is an undercurrent of homosexuality, nothing is overt and much is hidden about these two. Given Adrian's profession, the film is filled with film references, both blatant and oblique. *Blood Simple, Psycho,* and *Rear Window* figure prominently. Writer/producer David Koepp's story is subtle stuff. It contains no graphic violence or sexual scenes. Everything is nuance, suggestion. Important information comes through small visual touches. You have to watch it carefully to catch everything that's going on. And *Apartment Zero* is well worth watching carefully. In fact, it's worth watching carefully twice. ✦✦✦✧

Profanity, mature subject matter.

1988 (R) 114m/C *GB* Hart Bochner, Colin Firth, Fabrizio Bentivoglio, Liz Smith; *D:* Martin Donovan; *W:* Martin Donovan, David Koepp. **VHS, LV** *ACA, FCT, IME*

A.P.E.X.

Another shoot-'em-up set in a desolate dystopian future. The plot has to do with time-travelling killer robots and serves mostly to show off visual effects that range from fair to good. The best of them are reminiscent of *Predator* and *RoboCop*. True fans will note other similarities to *Damnation Alley* and *Mad Max*. The script doesn't follow through with all the tricky complications that the subject of time travel entails, but then these days, neither do big-budget theatrical releases. That's a shame because those details can raise so many interesting questions, and that's what the best science fiction is all about. The pace is slow and the big physical scenes tend to be stiffly staged. Newcomer Lisa Ann Russell has the inside track for the lead if anyone decides to film *The Gabriella Sabatini Story*. ✦✦

Violence, strong language.

1994 (R) 103m/C Richard Keats, Mitchell Cox, Lisa Ann Russell, Marcus Aurelius, Adam Lawson; *D:* Phillip J. Roth; *W:* Phillip J. Roth, Ronald Schmidt; *M:* Jim Goodwin. **VHS, LV** *REP*

Arcade

Charles Band's Full Moon label promises video originals with an emphasis on special effects and tightly written formula plots. This one's based on virtual reality video games. Though the plot doesn't mean much to those who are "game-impaired," the digital effects work well on the small screen. Young stars Peter Billingsley and Megan Ward are fine, and the whole film looks good. Well made escapism for those who appreciate the form. ✦✦

Strong language, graphic special effects, some violence.

1993 (R) 85m/C Megan Ward, Peter Billingsley, John de Lancie, Sharon Farrell, Seth Green, Humberto Ortiz, Jonathan Fuller, Norbert Weisser; *D:* Albert Pyun; *W:* David S. Goyer; *M:* Alan Howarth. **VHS** *PAR*

Arizona Dream

What a stinker! This is one of those tales that begins in obscurity—an extended dream sequence involving Eskimos, sled dogs, and snow—and descends into virtual chaos. Our narrator Axel Blackmar (Johnny Depp) is persuaded to leave a job tagging fish in New York (don't ask) to return to Arizona for his uncle Leo Sweetie's (Jerry Lewis) marriage to Millie (swimsuit mannequin Paulina Porizkova). (Stop for a frightening moment here to imagine the Nutty Professor himself in conjugal bliss with the *Sports Illustrated* supermodel.) No sooner has Axel arrived than he falls in love with an older woman (Faye Dunaway) who's even more eccentric than he is. What follows involves several threatened suicides, the construction of a flying machine, and lots of rambling pointless monologues meant to pass for philosophical musings. Bosnian director Emir Kusturica seems to have been aiming for a romantic comedy along the lines of *Like Water for Chocolate*, but the characters are uniformly distasteful. A waste of time and effort for all concerned. WOOF!

Strong language, subject matter, sexual material, brief nudity.

1994 (R) 119m/C Johnny Depp, Faye Dunaway, Jerry Lewis, Lili Taylor, Paulina Porizkova, Tricia Leigh Fisher, Vincent Gallo; *D:* Emir Kusturica; *W:* Emir Kusturica, David Atkins. **VHS** *WAR*

The Art of Dying

O.K., this may not be another *Silence of the Lambs*, but it's a better-than-average psycho killer movie. Wings Hauser, who also directed, plays a Hollywood cop helping runaways. The most recent threat to these kids is insane would-be film director Gary Werntz, who stages reenactments of scenes from horror movies using real bullets and chainsaws. Though the violence is graphic, it is restrained and leavened by humor. The performances are much better than you find in most B-movies, or most A-movies, for that matter. Kathleen Kinmont is very good as Hauser's mysterious girlfriend, but Mitch Hara, as the psycho's

"The biggest change in the last ten years is how home video has become an accepted part of our whole culture. VCRs are almost taken for granted. They're in over 85 percent of homes. The VCR has really become an extension of our lives. Just the extraordinary access that people have to movies has changed our whole perception of movies, and more recently, along the same lines, the desire to own and build collections of movies the same way in the past people have done with books and records and the like.

"As far as the next year, I think new technology is going to dramatically change—at least—people's perception of home entertainment. It's not [going] to change their use of it that quickly, but they're going to start to think about it a lot differently. And over the next five years they will probably start to change how they use home entertainment in terms of having even more control over it and more options. Over the last fifteen or 20 years, the VCR has been like training wheels for how people are going to personalize their entertainment options. You'll really be able to customize what you watch and listen to much more so than in the past.

"The CD was the beginning of that in the sense that you can program tracks in any order, and I think that's going to become a lot easier and more intuitive to do. Now very few people do that because it's a pain in the neck, but I think when it's more intuitive, people will actually become like disc jockeys, programming entertainment that combines sight and sound and other elements we don't even know about yet.

"I also believe it's a generational change. We're very fixed in our ways. We're linear in the way we use entertainment. We watch from point A to point B and that's the end of it. But video games have been the training wheels for the next generation and they'll want and expect to have a lot more control over what they listen to and watch, not simply selecting the particular title but changing the content to a certain degree."

—BRUCE APAR, EDITOR OF *VIDEO BUSINESS* MAGAZINE

---

flamboyant assistant, steals the movie from everyone else. ♫♫♫

Graphic violence, strong language, nudity, sexual situations.

1990 90m/C Wings Hauser, Michael J. Pollard, Sarah Douglas, Kathleen Kinmont, Sydney Lassick, Gary Werntz, Mitch Hara; **D:** Wings Hauser. **VHS, LV** *PMH*

At Play in the Fields of the Lord

At heart, this is the story of two men's efforts to "save" a tribe of Amazonian Indians, the Niaruna. Tom Berenger is a mercenary pilot who's engaged by the local authorities in a backwater town to scare the tribe off its land. Aidan Quinn, also newly arrived, is a devout missionary who wants to save Niaruna souls. Providing varying degrees of support are John Lithgow, Kathy Bates, Tom Waits, and Daryl Hannah. The pace is slow, too slow in places. Another maddening flaw is the on-again, off-again subtitles. Sometimes Indian dialogue is translated; other times it isn't. The subtitles begin and end capriciously within scenes, and have nothing to do with what other characters can or cannot understand. Based on Peter Matthiessen's 1965 novel, the story strongly echoes Conrad's *Heart of Darkness*. Both are about "civilized" men and women who go deep into the forest where they face horrors both external and internal. At three hours-plus, it's rough going, though more serious than standard home video fare. The second half is much better than the first. 🎵🎵🎵

Violence, nudity, strong language, some sexual content.

1991 **(R)** 186m/C Tom Berenger, Aidan Quinn, Kathy Bates, John Lithgow, Daryl Hannah, Tom Waits, Stenio Garcia, Nelson Xavier, Jose Dumont, Niilo Kivirinta; *D:* Hector Babenco; *W:* Hector Babenco, Jean-Claude Carriere; *M:* Zbigniew Preisner. **VHS, LV** *MCA*

Avanti!

It's easy to see why this uneven romantic comedy faded so quickly when it was made in 1971, and only recently reappeared on home video. Writer I.A.L. Diamond and director Billy Wilder have some trouble freeing their story from its roots on the stage, but once they do, the movie just gets better and better. Hard-charging, boorish Baltimore businessman Wendell Armbruster (Jack Lemmon) goes to Italy to bring home the body of his father. It appears that dad was killed in a car wreck at a resort hotel. Pamela Piggott (Juliet Mills), from London, meets him on the way and seems to know a lot about him. Her mother has died at the same hotel. Wendell is shocked when Carlucci (Clive Revill), the debonair hotel owner, tells him that the recently deceased couple were lovers. Yes, you know precisely where it's leading, but that's fine. These three characters are easy to like, particularly Pamela. Juliet Mills makes her a complete delight. As Lemmon's Ugly American is seduced by her and by Italy, the film draws you in. Comparisons to more recent films like *Shirley Valentine* and *Enchanted April* are well taken. 🎵🎵🎵

Mature subject matter, nudity, strong language.

1972 **(R)** 144m/C Jack Lemmon, Juliet Mills, Clive Revill, Edward Andrews, Gianfranco Barra, Franco Angrisano; *D:* Billy Wilder; *W:* I.A.L. Diamond, Billy Wilder. **VHS** *MGM*

The Baby Doll Murders

Two LAPD detectives, Benz (Jeff Kober, from TV's *China Beach*) and Brown (Bobby DiCicco), think that they've nabbed a serial killer who leaves a broken doll beside each of his victims. But their guy got off on a technicality and is now walking the street. When the killings begin again, they're ordered away from their suspect, and try to find new leads, possibly involving abortion. But Benz refuses to give up on his original gut belief, even when he finds new connections between the victims, until boss (John Saxon) and his live-in girlfriend (the fetching Melanie Smith), also a cop, show him the light. Director Paul Leder, still trying to live down the infamous title *I Dismember Mama*, doesn't do much better here. The pace is lazy and several scenes are padded with less-than-suspenseful shots of cars being parked and people walking down hallways. All in all, this one's an acceptable time-waster with a topical angle, but nothing more. 🎵🎵

Violence, nudity, sexual content.

1992 **(R)** 90m/C Jeff Kober, Melanie Smith, John Saxon, Tom Hodges, Bobby DiCicco; *D:* Paul Leder; *W:* Paul Leder. **VHS** *REP*

Back in Action

A standard-issue buddy picture. Roddy Piper plays a cop who joins forces with martial arts favorite Billy Blanks as a Special Forces veteran to save Blanks' sister from gangsters. The fight choreography is cliched, though there are some scenes where Piper really cuts loose with full Wrestlemania craziness. 🎵🎵

Violence, strong language, sexual content.

1994 **(R)** 93m/C Roddy Piper, Billy Blanks, Bobbie Phillips, Matt Birman, Nigel Bennett, Damon D'Oliveira, Kai Soremekun; *D:* Paul Ziller, Steve DiMarco; *W:* Karl Schiffman. **VHS, LV** *MCA*

Backfire!

Parody of Ron Howard's *Backdraft* is built on a screwy sexual role reversal. A boy (Josh Mosby) dreams of growing up to follow in his mother's footsteps as a firewoman,...er, firefighter, whatever. But he has to break the

B-Movies

A few years ago, the shelves of video stores were filled with cheap B-movies. Now they're filled with hideously expensive B-movies like *Terminator 2* and *Mission: Impossible*. Overall, the level of technical quality has risen substantially, but at heart, the B-movie hasn't changed. It's still about violence, sex, and craziness. Give the same story a multimillion-dollar budget and a big name star and it's treated seriously. Go figure.

ALLIGATOR EYES	IN A MOMENT OF PASSION
THE ART OF DYING	JACK BE NIMBLE
BAD LOVE	KILL ME AGAIN
BALLISTIC	LAST MAN STANDING (1995)
THE BANKER	LIVE WIRE
BLOOD AND SAND (1989 SHARON STONE VERSION)	LOVE IS A GUN
	MEN OF WAR
BLOOD TIES	MERIDAN: KISS OF THE BEAST
BOUND AND GAGGED: A LOVE STORY	MURDER WEAPON
	NEAR DARK
DARK ANGEL: THE ASCENT	ONE FALSE MOVE
DEAD FUNNY	PICASSO TRIGGER
DIAL HELP	POWWOW HIGHWAY
EMBRACE OF THE VAMPIRE	RE-ANIMATOR
EVEN HITLER HAD A GIRLFRIEND	RED ROCK WEST
	REPO MAN
FAIR GAME	SAINTS AND SINNERS
FIVE CORNERS	SLAM DUNK ERNEST
FUGITIVE X	STREETS
HOLD ME, THRILL ME, KISS ME	ZANDALEE

department's all-female tradition. It's really a *Naked Gun*-type spoof with appearances by swimsuit model Kathy Ireland, Robert Mitchum, the late Telly Savalas, and Shelley Winters. The combination of a modest budget and location shooting in Bayonne, NJ, gives the film a gritty look that's somehow appropriate. 𝄇𝄇𝄈

Bathroom humor, comic violence, strong language.

1994 (PG-13) 88m/C Josh Mosby, Kathy Ireland, Robert Mitchum, Shelley Winters, Telly Savalas; **D:** A. Dean Bell. **VHS** *APX*

Backlash: Oblivion 2

All of the raucous elements for the original outer space Western are back, with the addition of Maxwell Caulfield as a W.C. Fieldsian bounty hunter. Of all the inventive make-up and cosmetic effects, Julie Newmar's stretched-taut face is perhaps the most startling. The hammy overacting is an ensemble effort, as it was in the first film. Though limited, the stop-motion and morphing effects are pretty good. **AKA:** Oblivion 2. 𝄇𝄇

Strong language, mild violence, sexual material.

1995 (PG-13) 82m/C Andrew Divoff, Meg Foster, Isaac Hayes, Julie Newmar, Carel Struycken, George Takei, Musetta Vander, Jimmie F. Skaggs, Irwin Keyes, Maxwell Caulfield; **D:** Sam Irvin; **W:** Peter David; **M:** Pino Donaggio. **VHS, LV** *FLL*

Backstab

More video noir. Recently widowed architect Cliff Murphy (James Brolin) is picked up in a bar by a beautiful young woman (Isabelle Truchon) who claims that she's being bothered by a large, annoying fellow. They find themselves in the back seat of her car; one thing leads to another.... The next day they arrange to meet at her house where Cliff discovers the body of the guy who just bought his firm. From that moment, the logical lapses loom large. It's one thing to suspend your disbelief, but to enjoy this one, you've got to wrestle your disbelief into submission and lock it in the closet. The courtroom scenes in the second half are preposterous and an important part of the solution is obvious early on. The direction can't compensate for the transparent writing but the action moves well and the film retains an evocative autumnal sense. (It was made in Montreal and Boston.) 𝄇𝄇𝄈

Sexual content, violence, profanity, brief nudity.

1990 (R) 91m/C James Brolin, Meg Foster, Isabelle Truchon; *D:* Jim Kaufman. **VHS, LV** *MED, VTR*

Backstreet Dreams

Star Jason O'Malley also wrote and co-produced this story of an autistic boy, his shady dad, and the dedicated social worker who triumphs over all adversity. Dean (Jason O'Malley) is an enforcer for a loan shark. He refuses to accept the fact that his young son is autistic. When his wife (Sherilyn Fenn) leaves, Stevie Bloom (Brooke Shields) takes over. The writing is stiff and saccharine, and the characters are one-dimensional. Shields comes off better than anyone else, and that says a lot about the film. Good intentions don't make up for the flaws. 🦴🦴

Strong language, some violence.

1990 (R) 104m/C Brooke Shields, Jason O'Malley, Sherilyn Fenn, Tony Fields, Burt Young, Anthony (Tony) Franciosa, Nick Cassavetes, Ray "Boom Boom" Mancini; *D:* Rupert Hitzig; *W:* Jason O'Malley; *M:* Bill Conti. **VHS, LV** *VMK*

Bad Blood

How do you judge an action star? As a screen presence, Lorenzo Lamas is much less obnoxious than, say, Steven Seagal, plus he has much prettier hair with a more luxuriant ponytail. In this bargain basement actioner, he's Travis Blackstone, an ex-cop with a no-account younger brother. Said brother owes big bucks to a mob-controlled bank and comes to Travis to bail him out. Before it's all over, Travis's treacherous ex-girlfriend (Frankie Thorn) and treacherous current girlfriend (Kimberly Kates) are in the mix, too, along with his TV-addicted dad (familiar character actor John T. Ryan). As the rotund villain, Joe Son steals the flick. Director Tibor Takacs has obviously been watching his John Woo movies. Several of the big scenes attempt to copy Woo's inventive style, with careful choreography and good lighting. Too often, though, the graphic violence verges on sadism. 🦴🦴

Nudity, violence, and sexual content.

1994 (R) 90m/C Lorenzo Lamas, Hank Cheyne, Frankie Thorn, Kimberley Kates, Joe Son, John T. Ryan; *D:* Tibor Takacs. **VHS, LV** *WEA, LIV*

Bad Company

A well-cast thriller about industrial/political espionage finally misses the mark. Vic Grimes (Frank Langella) and Margaret Wells (Ellen Barkin) run a company of former spies who specialize in corporate dirty work. Nelson Crowe (Laurence Fishburn) is their latest recruit. All the cooler-than-thou cigarettes, shades, and tough talk make for a sleek surface, but everyone involved tries too hard, missing the point of mystery master Ross Thomas' script. It's also notable for one of the most gracelessly staged sex scenes ever committed to film. 🦴

Violence, sexual content, strong language, brief nudity.

1994 (R) 118m/C Ellen Barkin, Laurence "Larry" Fishburne, Frank Langella, Michael Beach, Gia Carides, David Ogden Stiers, Spalding Gray, James Hong, Daniel Hugh-Kelly; *D:* Damian Harris; *W:* Ross Thomas; *C:* Jack N. Green; *M:* Carter Burwell. **VHS, LV** *TOU*

Bad Love

Gritty naturalistic film earns more points as a character study than as a compelling drama. Viewers who understand that going in will enjoy this story of two losers searching for salvation in each other. Eloise (Pamela Gidley) is a secretary involved in a dead-end sexual relationship with her married boss (Joe Dallesandro). Lenny (Tom Sizemore) is a borderline alcoholic and dreamer who can't hold a job. Even his Uncle Bud (Seymour Cassel), a pawn shop owner who likes him, says that Lenny is "a no-good small-time hustler." Lenny and Eloise fall for each other immediately. Their rocky relationship is a search for love and employment. Writer George Gary gets these two characters exactly right. They're deeply flawed, and though there's an inevitability to their self-created predicaments, there's also something fascinating about them. Director Jill Goldman makes their low-rent Southern California world an important part of the

17

story. She's also careful with physical details. Note the way she subtly highlights small bruises on Eloise's ankle in a key scene. Given the current fashion in Hollywood, it's tempting to say that *Bad Love* is Quentin Tarantino without the stylistic excesses, but that's not really true. Though the film is fiction, it's really closer in substance to *In Cold Blood* and *The Executioner's Song*. ♫♫♫

Mature subject matter, strong language, some violence, sexual content, incidental nudity.

1995 (R) 93m/C Tom Sizemore, Pamela Gidley, Debi Mazar, Jennifer O'Neill, Margaux Hemingway, Richard Edson, Seymour Cassel, Joe Dallesandro; **D:** Jill Goldman; **W:** George Gary. **VHS** *APX*

Baja

Lance Henriksen has built an impressive body of work—first in films and now, increasingly, on video—playing memorable off-beat, edgy, intelligent, and potentially violent characters. His presence has raised many low-budget pictures from obscurity to cult status and outright popularity. But his best efforts aren't enough for this, a plodding, needlessly profane little crime movie. After a half-baked drug buy goes sour, Alex (Donal Logue) and Bebe (Molly Ringwald) hide out in desolate Baja, Mexico. She contacts her pill-popping dad (Corbin Bernsen) for dough, and he sends her estranged husband Michael (Michael Nickles) to fetch her. He hits town at the same time that a hitman (Henriksen) shows up. Who's the target? There's nothing wrong with writer/director Kurt Voss' story. The problem is the characters. They're all so ugly—either physically, psychologically, or both—that the sooner they're all run over by a bus, the better. As the film goes along, they do increasingly stupid things to keep the plot moving. It's really funny at all the wrong moments, and the viewer who makes it to the hare-brained ending will be hooting with unrestrained derision. ♫

Gratuitously strong language, violence, brief nudity, sexual content.

1995 (R) 92m/C Molly Ringwald, Lance Henriksen, Michael A. Nickles, Donal Logue, Corbin Bernsen; **D:** Kurt Voss; **W:** Kurt Voss; **C:** Denis Maloney; **M:** Reg Powell. **VHS, LV** *REP*

Ballistic

Marjean Holden is a real looker—there's no other word for it—and she's the best reason to see this low-budget martial arts movie. It could be the beginning of a fair series because she's such a spirited leading lady. Otherwise the film has a no-surprises plot and seen-it-before fight choreography. Policewoman Jesse Gavin's (Holden) father (Richard Roundtree) was framed for drug charges by corrupt cops years before. It's time to clear his name. The relaxed presence of fellow B-movie stalwarts Charles Napier and Sam Jones helps considerably. Again, though, the key is Marjean Holden who has that indefinable screen presence or "likeability" that can carry a picture. ♫♫♡

Violence, strong language, brief nudity, mild sexual content.

1994 (R) 86m/C Marjean Holden, Richard Roundtree, Sam Jones, Joel Beeson, Charles Napier; **D:** Kim Bass. **VHS, LV** *IMP, IME*

The Banker

What would happen if Jack the Ripper got a Sharper Image catalogue and an American Express Gold Card? He'd go out and buy all sorts of neat grown-up toys, like a crossbow with a laser sight, and use them to murder prostitutes. The title character, Spaulding Osbourne (Duncan Regehr), is a wealthy financier whose passions are primitive religions and "Snow White and the Seven Dwarfs." Really. The opening scene, strongly reminiscent of *Betty Blue,* is a stylish blend of eroticism and violence that sets the tone for the rest of the movie. His antagonists are familiar B-movie stereotypes. Robert Forster is the veteran streetwise cop (why don't we ever see streetstupid cops?) with a rookie partner and an ex-girlfriend (Shanna Reed) who's a TV newswoman. These three walking cliches threaten to sink the story in predictability, but Osbourne gets crazier and crazier (and funnier) as the film goes along. You're never quite sure what he's going to do next and so the second half pulls away from the formula. The whole production has an ultra-slick MTV look and a fast pace, making it a potent guilty pleasure. 🦴🦴🦴

Violence, nudity, sexual activity, strong language.

1989 (R) 90m/C Robert Forster, Jeff Conaway, Leif Garrett, Duncan Regehr, Shanna Reed, Deborah Richter, Richard Roundtree, Teri Weigel, E.J. Peaker; **D:** William Webb. **VHS, LV** *NO*

Bar Girls

Like so many play adaptations, this one hasn't completely escaped the stage. It's a fairly pedestrian romantic comedy that's more successful as propaganda than as entertainment. Its politico-dramatic point—that lesbians are just as jealous, loving, screwed up, and healthy as everybody else—is self-evident but labored. Loretta (Nancy Allison Wolfe) loves Rachel (Liza D'Agostino) who's attracted to J.R. (Camila Griggs) who seduces Loretta...etc., etc. Neither producer/writer Lauran Hoffman nor director Marita Giovanni can make the story work as a film. 🦴🦴

Mature subject matter, brief nudity, strong language.

1995 (R) 95m/C Nancy Allison Wolfe, Liza D'Agostino, Justine Slater, Paula Sorge, Camila Griggs, Pam Raines; **D:** Marita Giovanni; **W:** Lauran Hoffman; **C:** Michael Ferris. **VHS, LV** *ORI*

Based on an Untrue Story

Beautiful and talented perfume magnate Satin Chau (Morgan Fairchild) is tragically stricken with anosmia (loss of sense of smell) just as her newest scent, Puppy, makes its debut. Quel dommage! Her only hope is a nasal nerve transplant from one of her sisters, Velour (Ricki Lake) or Corduroy (Victoria Jackson) from whom she was separated at birth. She also must deal with her philandering boyfriend (Robert Goulet) and boss (Dyan Cannon, who still may have the best legs in Hollywood). Considering that its sights are set so low, this parody of TV is about as funny as it could be. But there's little to recommend it to anyone who's not familiar with the source material. And if you are familiar with the source material, you're watching way too much daytime TV when you could be watching videos. 🦴🦴

1993 90m/C Morgan Fairchild, Dyan Cannon, Victoria Jackson, Ricki Lake, Harvey Korman, Robert Goulet, Dan Hedaya; **D:** Jim Drake. **VHS** *FXV*

Basket Case 2

Fans know that the original *Basket Case* is one of the most bizarre exercises in low-budget excess ever committed to film or videotape. The sequel is an expensive production that ignores key aspects of the original and takes place mostly on clean well-lighted sets with a glossy "Hollywood" look. It's concerned with a nosy tabloid reporter and a group of physically deformed people. These guys look like refuges from the cantina bar sequence in *Star Wars* and are neither frightening nor believable. They're just silly masks. Until the conclusion, when writer/director Frank Henenlotter does manage to twist some kinks into the action, the plot ambles along without focus. It lacks the spirit and raw craziness that drove the original, and proves that more really can be less. Followed by a third. 🦴🦴

Violence, sexual content.

1990 (R) 90m/C Kevin Van Hentenryck, Annie Ross, Kathryn Meisle, Heather Rattray, Jason Evers, Ted Sorel, Matt Mitler; **D:** Frank Henenlotter; **W:** Frank Henenlotter; **M:** Joe Renzetti. **VHS, LV** *VTR, IME, SGE*

Battleground: Extreme Fighting

"Extreme" fighting is an essentially unregulated form of public entertainment that has moved such luminaries as George Will to, once again, predict the eminent collapse of Western civilization as we know it. This video seems to be an accurate, unvarnished recording of bouts that took place in Wilmington, NC. For all the controversy, it's relatively tame fare. The fighters don't gouge or bite; there are no ripped ears. It's more like Olympic wrestling—not the fake professional stuff—with submission holds. Considering the overall level of violence—both real and fictional—in American society, the reaction to this particular form of entertainment seems a little overstated. If the fights on this tape are representative of the norm, the potential for

serious injury to the combatants is less than it is for NFL linemen. 🎬🎬

Realistic violence, strong language.

1995 120m/C **VHS** *TRI*

Beach Babes from Beyond

Beach Babes from Beyond—what a great title! And the flick lives up to it. The text is taken from those wonderful, cheesy American International beach movies of the mid-'60s. The dumb jokes and generic rock soundtrack are the same. So are the semi-famous guest stars: Jacqueline Stallone, Don Swayze, Joey Travolta, Joe Estevez. The plot is also a venerable retread. How will the kids save Uncle Bud's beach house from the evil rich people? There are even lots of filler shots of young crowds dancing the frug and the bugaloo on the sand. The presence of Burt Ward, Robin on the *Batman* TV series, somehow closes the circle. The only differences are the bathing suits (much smaller) and the sexual content (much stronger, but on the soft-focus, romantic side). 🎬🎬🎬 **GPI: 8.5**

Nudity and sexual material.

1993 (R) 78m/C Joe Estevez, Don Swayze, Joey Travolta, Burt Ward, Jacqueline Stallone, Linnea Quigley, Sara Bellomo, Tamara Landry, Nicole Posey; **D:** Ellen Cabot. **VHS** *PAR*

Beanstalk

As the title indicates, this is a contemporary tongue-in-cheek variation on the famous story, though the elements are familiar stuff. Jack (J.D. Daniels) is the bright son of a single mom. They're threatened by the town banker (Richard Moll) who's about to foreclose on their mortgage, until Jack happens upon some magic beans. Said beans have been discovered by a mad scientist (Margot Kidder, virtually unrecognizable under a heavy costume). The Giant (Stuart Pankin) does not live in a castle. Instead, he, Mrs. Giant, and their daughter live in a celestial tract house, circa 1958. The broad humor and the obnoxious overacting are on the level of a live-action Saturday morning TV show. The jokes are for kids only. 🎬🎬

Mild violence.

1994 (PG) 80m/C J.D. Daniels, Margot Kidder, Richard Moll, Amy Stock-Poynton, Patrick Renna, Richard Paul, David Naughton, Stuart Pankin, Cathy McAuley; **D:** Michael Paul Davis; **W:** Michael Paul Davis; **M:** Kevin Bassinson. **VHS** *PAR*

The Beatles: The First U.S. Visit

A third to half of the black-and-white documentary is live (not lip-synced) musical numbers shot on the *Ed Sullivan Show* and in Washington, D.C. The rest is unstaged footage of four incredibly young guys going through the prosaic side of rock stardom. Riding in taxis and trains, waiting in hotel rooms, mugging for photographers, plugging their stuff with DJs, generally fooling around and killing time. The handheld cameras of David and Albert Maysles tell the story. There is no narration. For those who remember those times, it's an evocative piece of nostalgia. Those who are younger may well wonder how and why a few simple, catchy pop tunes generated such an uproar. A little explanation is in order: all this took place in February 1964, less than four months after the assassination of President Kennedy. The whole country was just beginning to recover from a profound state of shock. "The four moptops," as they were called, offered something fresh and different in appearance and sound. They were an innocent antidote to a national nightmare. And as they would show a year or so later in *A Hard Day's Night*—which is remarkably similar to this tape—they refused to take themselves seriously. In one way or another, virtually everybody took part in Beatlemania. But adolescent girls led the charge with a wave of adulation bordering on hysteria. This tape doesn't capture the scope and intensity of that moment. Instead it shows those heady days as they were, without any false sweetness. 🎬🎬🎬

1991 85m/B Paul McCartney, Ringo Starr, John Lennon, George Harrison, Ed Sullivan; **D:** David Maysles, Al Maysles. **VHS, LV** *MPI, BTV*

Beau Pere

French import is probably more controversial now than it was when it was made in 1981. The subject is the changing relationship between Remi (Patrick Dewaere), a 29-year-old man, and Marion (Ariel Besse), his 14-year-old stepdaughter, after the death of her mother. That's potentially explosive material, but director Bertrand Blier (who won an Oscar for Best Foreign Language Film in 1978 for *Get Out Your Handkerchiefs*) handles it deftly. He focuses on the two main characters, keeping the pace slow to examine their personalities. How do they handle grief? How do they deal with Marion's father? Can Remi handle Marion's emerging sexuality? Blier lets the details accumulate, and though the action moves leisurely, he spices it with unconventional techniques. In the opening scene, for example, we meet Remi where he works, playing piano in a classy hotel bar. He addresses the camera, telling us about himself, his lack of success, his frustrations. After that introduction, the film slips back into a traditional narrative. But at odd moments throughout, other characters turn and talk to the camera. It takes a skillful, confident filmmaker to use that technique effectively. In this case, it fits perfectly; it's the best way to tell this story. Blier's main point is that maturity doesn't necessarily have much to do with age. Remi is never going to grow up and will always lean on the strongest emotional support. Marion, on the other hand, may be inexperienced but she's not stupid. She's a strong-willed young woman who tends to get what she wants. Remi is really no match for her. Their relationship ends with an unusual but perfectly realistic and satisfying conclusion. In French with subtitles. *AKA:* Stepfather. 𝄞𝄞𝄞𝄞

Mature subject matter and brief nudity.

1981 125m/C *FR* Patrick Dewaere, Nathalie Baye, Ariel Besse, Maurice Ronet; *D:* Bertrand Blier; *W:* Bertrand Blier. Nominations: Cannes Film Festival '81: Best Film. **VHS** *MED, INJ*

Beauty School

Your basic guilty pleasure is about some sexy young criminals who are given a chance to reform themselves and lead productive lives as topless dancers. It's an extremely low-budget bawdy comedy that gains a lot through judicious speed watching. *AKA:* Sylvia Kristel's Beauty School. 𝄞𝄞 **GPI: 6.2**

Strong language, brief nudity, sexual activity, some violence.

1993 (R) 95m/C Sylvia Kristel, Kevin Bernhardt, Kimberly Taylor, Jane Hamilton; *D:* Ernest G. Sauer; *W:* Mike MacDonald, Merrill Friedman; *M:* Jonathan Hannah. **VHS, LV** *IMP*

Bedroom Eyes 2

This surprisingly enjoyable little sequel is a convoluted mystery about insider stock trading, the art business, infidelity, and madness. The late Chuck Vincent keeps the pace zipping right along. In the leads, video vet Wings Hauser, ex-Playmate of the Year Kathy Shower, and the indefatigable Linda Blair are letter perfect. The plot is purposefully similar to (and actually better than) the overrated *Fatal Attraction*. It's got a strong sense of humor and never lets common sense get in the way. Toward the end it may become too screwy, but that's nit-picking. 𝄞𝄞𝄞 **GPI: 9.4**

Mature subject matter, violence, sexual situations, brief nudity, profanity.

1989 (R) 85m/C Wings Hauser, Kathy Shower, Linda Blair, Jane Hamilton, Jennifer Delora; *D:* Chuck Vincent. **VHS, LV** *VMK, IME*

A Better Tomorrow

In the opening scene, the soundtrack is a tip-off to what director John Woo is up to. The music could have come straight from a spaghetti Western, and Woo tells this crime story about two brothers on opposite sides of the law with the same kind of exaggeration. The wildly complex plot is about counterfeiting, betrayal, and murder. Though the action is violent, it's not as crisply choreographed as it is in Woo's more recent work. Some of the humor slips into slapstick and that doesn't help the overall tone. Neither does the atrocious dubbing. But if you can overlook those flaws, you'll see another terrific performance by Chow Yun-Fat. The guy is simply one of the best actors in the business. He has an appeal that transcends boundaries of language and culture. With the right breaks, he could become the next Gerard Depardieu. Woo's

Real Life Is Real Life

John Woo is the legitimate cinematic heir to Sam Peckinpah. Many other directors have tried to recreate his violent visual poetry and they've usually come up with obvious imitations. Not John Woo. His stylized action pictures are genuine originals that easily cross national borders. Once viewers discover his work, Woo's films are as popular in Hoboken as they are in Hong Kong.

Woo's interest in movies began—as it did for most fans—as a child. His family left China in 1950, and he grew up in the Hong Kong slums. The riots he witnessed there had a strong and lasting impact on him. But it wasn't until he joined a local film society and discovered the wealth of American movies—from Martin Scorsese, Peckinpah and Sam Fuller to Fred Astaire, Gene Kelly, and Bob Fosse—that he realized what he wanted to do.

He began his career in 1969, first working with low-budget martial arts movies and then quickly moving up in the thriving local industry. As his films became more ambitious, his reputation grew with filmgoers and with critics. Films like *A Better Tomorrow* and *Hard-Boiled* attracted attention beyond the local audience, and then in 1993, *The Killer* achieved genuine cult status in this country.

In all of his best work, Woo combines elements of Western action films with the Asian tradition he calls "martial chivalry" and his own Christianity. Despite their graphic violence, his films have a strong spiritual side. That religious element is perhaps most obvious in *The Killer*. In comparison, *Hard-Boiled* has a stronger political subtext, concerning the Chinese takeover of Hong Kong which had caused Woo to emigrate to America.

Woo's subjects are usually cops and criminals. Chow Yun-Fat, a remarkably expressive actor, is one of his favorite leading men. (Woo himself appears as the bartender in *Hard-Boiled*.) His American debut, *Hard Target*—a retelling of *The Most Dangerous Game* with Jean-Claude Van Damme—isn't as successful as his previous films but it's still enjoyable. The thriller *Broken Arrow* is a boxoffice hit.

For action fans, Woo's films are a real treat that stand up well to repeated viewings. (Some day, film students may well write papers about his use of the color white in *A Better Tomorrow*.) The letterboxed laserdisc editions capture the full range of Woo's carefully choreographed action sequences. They also have more colorful translations into English.

When it comes to the content of his films, Woo is neither apologetic nor defensive, and he doesn't believe that his work causes violent behavior. "The audience can realize that the movie is a movie," he said in an interview, "Real life is real life."

philosophical interests are evident too. Even if *A Better Tomorrow* isn't the best place for the neophyte to discover John Woo—try *Hard-Boiled* or *The Killer* first—it's a lot of fun, and, for those who have acquired a taste for Hong Kong action, it's a treat. *AKA:* Yingxiong Bense. 🦴🦴🦴

Strong violence, language.

1986 95m/C *CH* Chow Yun-Fat, Leslie Cheung, Ti Lung; *D:* John Woo. **VHS** *REP, FCT*

Beyond Desire

Ray (William Forsythe) is an Elvisian ex-con who's just finished a 14-year stretch in the penitentiary. Rita (Kari Wuhrer) is the babe in the slinky little black dress who stops her red Corvette convertible to give him a lift on a lonely desert road. It's always been a fantasy of hers, she says, to pick up a guy who's fresh out of jail. Yeah, right. Las Vegas gangsters and

a bag full of money are also involved. Mystery fans won't have much trouble predicting most of the plot turns, and the action scenes aren't all they could be, either. But the leads are all you could ask for. Forsythe, who's also executive producer, brings his usual intensity, and Wuhrer, always in danger of falling out of her skimpy costumes, is convincingly sexy. 🗡🗡🗡 **GPI: 7.5**

Strong language, violence, nudity, sexual content.

1994 **(R)** 87m/C William Forsythe, Kari Wuhrer, Leo Rossi, Sharon Farrell, *D:* Dominique Othenin-Girard. **VHS** *LIV*

Beyond Forgiveness

Forget the hyperbolic title. This less-than-serious thriller often looks like a spaghetti Western, but it's based on a particularly nasty international rumor about children from underdeveloped countries being kidnapped and used as involuntary organ suppliers in richer nations. Thomas Ian Griffith is a Chicago cop who goes to Poland to avenge his brother's murder and uncovers a diabolical plot led by surgeon Rutger Hauer, who, as usual, seems to be having a grand time. Most of the action is senseless shoot-outs and artlessly staged explosions. The Polish locations give the film a different and semi-exotic atmosphere. 🗡🗡

Violence, mature subject matter, strong language, brief nudity.

1994 **(R)** 95m/C Thomas Ian Griffith, Rutger Hauer, John Rhys-Davies; *D:* Bob Misiorowski; *W:* Charles Cohen. **VHS, LV** *REP*

Beyond Innocence

Curious Australian import is one of three film versions of a French novel, *Devil in the Flesh*, by Raymond Radiguet. The first was a French film made in 1946. The 1986 Italian version is a poorly constructed and rather slow politico/sexual melodrama, noteworthy only for one explicit sexual scene. In this telling, the story of an affair between a student and an older married woman is simpler, more focused on believable characters, well played by Keith Smith and Katia Caballero. Though it's not explicit, it's just as erotic as the Italian film. It has the look and the deliberately measured pace that are usually associated with public television's *Masterpiece Theatre*; slow and sexy without being exploitative. 🗡🗡🗡

Nudity, sexual activity, mature subject matter, profanity.

1987 87m/C *AU* Keith Smith, Katia Caballero, John Morris; *D:* Scott Murray; *C:* Andrzej Bartkowiak. **VHS** *NO*

Bikini Bistro

Restaurateuse Amy Lynn Baxter's Nibble Vegetarian Cafe is doing rotten business until pal Marilyn Chambers suggests that the waitresses change costume. The rest of the film follows the drill. This one is unique in that it appears to have been shot on video using some curiously grainy special effects with slow-motion sequences in key scenes. Because of those, the film looks better if you fast forward *through* the good parts, not just *to* the good parts. Also available in an unrated version at 84 minutes. *AKA:* Marilyn Chambers' Bikini Bistro. 🗡🗡🗡

Nudity and sexual content.

1994 **(R)** 80m/C Marilyn Chambers, Amy Lynn Baxter, Joan Gerardi, Isabelle Fortea, John Altamura, Joseph Pallister; *D:* Ernest G. Sauer; *W:* Matt Unger. **VHS** *AVI*

The Bikini Car Wash Company

Strait-laced Midwesterner comes to L.A. to run his uncle's carwash. It's saved from bankruptcy when brainy beach babe Kristie Ducati brings in a group of her friends to work there. You can figure out the rest. Softcore fluff squarely aimed at the arrested adolescent sexual fantasies of your average male videophile; in other words, an archetypal bikini flick. *AKA:* California Hot Wax. 🗡🗡🗡 **GPI: 8.9**

Oodles of nudity, sexual content, strong language.

1990 **(R)** 87m/C Joe Dusic, Neriah Napaul, Suzanne Browne, Kristie Ducati; *D:* Ed Hansen. **VHS** *IMP*

The Bikini Car Wash Company 2

Should beach babe Kristie Ducati continue to run the carwash or should she become a corporate executrix with the big company that wants to buy her out? Will it be power suits or suds and thongs? Decisions, decisions, decisions. As silly sex comedies go, this one is shallow, silly, and suggestive—just as it should be. ⅃⅃⅃⅁ **GPI: 8.1**

Nudity, sexual content, strong language.

1992 **(R)** ?m/C Kristie Ducati, Suzanne Browne, Neriah Napaul, Rikki Brando, Greg Raye, Larry De Russy; *D:* Gary Orona; *W:* Bart B. Gustis; *M:* Michael Smith. **VHS, LV** *IMP*

Bikini Drive-In

Another fine example of an emerging home video sub-genre: the swimsuit flick. This one features a large cast of well-endowed and silicone-enhanced young women, led by Ashlie Rhey and Sara Bellomo. It's also got a script with more humor than most. At the titular ozoner, previews are shown for *Gator Babes* and *Goliath and the Cheerleaders* ("filmed in Italy where it really happened!"). Perhaps the subject matter made the movie a labor of love for prolific producer/director Fred Olen Ray. The film seems to have been made with a bit more care than most of his micro-budget wonders. And though he's not listed in the credits, one of the drive-in patrons looks and sounds suspiciously like director Robert Altman. Also available in an unrated verison. ⅃⅃⅃ **GPI: 8.0**

Sexual content, nudity, a little rough language.

1994 **(R)** 85m/C Ashlie Rhey, Richard Gabai, Ross Hagen, Sara Bellomo, Steve Barkett, Conrad Brooks; *D:* Fred Olen Ray. **VHS** *AVI*

Bikini Summer

When the character named Big Earl says "You got your ecology, you got your bikinis, and you got your beer," that pretty much says it all as far as this one is concerned. Star Shelley Michelle has acted as body double for Julia Roberts (in *Pretty Woman*) and many other

famous actresses. Followed by a sequel. ⅃⅃⅁
GPI: 7.2

Strong language, nudity, violence.

1991 90m/C David Millburn, Melinda Armstrong, Jason Clow, Shelley Michelle, Alex Smith, Kent Lipham, Kelly Konop, Carmen Santa Maria; *D:* Robert Veze; *W:* Robert Veze, Nick Stone; *M:* John Gonzalez. **VHS, LV** *PMH*

Biohazard

Think *Alien* set in Southern California and made on the cheap with a breezy sense of humor. The emphasis is on the silly, not the scary, particularly at the end when the outtakes and miscues are rolled. Note the replay of the gratuitous sex scene when Angelique Pettyjohn's blonde wig starts to slide slowly off during a torrid kiss. ⅃⅃

Silly violence, sexual content, brief nudity.

1985 **(R)** 84m/C Angelique Pettyjohn, Aldo Ray; *D:* Fred Olen Ray. **VHS** *MTX*

Biohazard: The Alien Force

Like the original, a 1985 alternative classic, this is a silly little thing about a monster played by a guy in the least-scary rubber suit you ever saw. It's obvious from the opening moments that the sequel is either going to be a wonderfully bad movie or a plain bad movie. It turns out to be both, but mostly plain bad. After all, amateurish acting, cheap sets, and lots of slime can accomplish only so much. ⅃

Strong language, violence, nudity, sexual material.

1995 **(R)** 88m/C Steve Zurk, Chris Mitchum, Susan Fronsoe, Tom Ferguson, Patrick Moran, John Maynard; *D:* Steve Latshaw. **VHS** *VMK*

Bix

For those who are only vaguely familiar with the man and his reputation, this video biography may work best as an overview of the early days of jazz. Though cornetist Bix Beiderbecke's life was short and sad, it didn't involve much conflict and, on its own, isn't really that interesting. Leon Bix Beiderbecke was born into a prosperous Midwestern family in 1903. He was a genuine musical prodigy who followed his natural inclinations to jazz, the most dynamic popular music of his day. Though his parents disapproved, he found work in a number of bands. Too many late nights and too much booze killed him in 1931. Writer/producer/editor/director Brigitte Berman tells his story through interviews with musicians (including Hoagy Carmichael), still photographs, period film footage, and the paintings of Edward Hopper. Of course, there's also the music—a lot of it—and that's the point. 𝄞𝄞𝄞

1990 116m/C *IT D:* Brigitte Berman; *W:* Brigitte Berman. **VHS** *PBY*

Black Day Blue Night

When Hallie (Mia Sara) catches her no-good husband with Rinda (Michelle Forbes) in a Utah desert motel, she pulls out a revolver. Curious circumstances force the two women onto the road together in Rinda's red Caddie ragtop where they run across hitchhiker Dodge (Gil Bellows) who has a heavy suitcase and the ugliest sideburns you've about ever seen. Meanwhile, police detective Quinn (J.T. Walsh) is on the trail of armored truck robbers who killed his old partner and made off with a million in cash. Veteran writer/director J.S. Cardone turns that premise into a lyrical Western noir, with slow pace and lots of smokey come-hither looks. The capable cast members are reworking familiar typecast roles. Though the action would be more effective if it had been cranked up about two stops on the weirdness scale, it is surprising all the way through. 𝄞𝄞𝄞

Violence, nudity, sexual material, strong language.

1995 (R) 99m/C Michelle Forbes, Mia Sara, Gil Bellows, J.T. Walsh; *D:* J.S. Cardone; *W:* J.S. Cardone. **VHS, LV** *REP*

Black Magic Woman

When an L.A. gallery owner (Mark Hamill) becomes involved with seductive stranger (Apollonia), his girlfriend and partner (Amanda Wyss) is not amused, particularly when an inexplicable illness strikes. The action is inventive enough, especially in a few spooky scenes, and the production values are first-

rate. But the actors are lame—it's not the glorious bad acting that can make B-movies so much fun; it's just plain old everyday bad acting. 𝄞𝄞𝄞

Strong language, violence, sexual content, brief nudity.

1991 (R) 91m/C Mark Hamill, Amanda Wyss, Apollonia, Abadah Viera, Larry Hankin, Victor Rivers, Bonnie Ebson; *D:* Scott Thomson, Deryn Warren; *W:* Gerry Daly; *M:* Randy Miller. **VHS** *VMK*

Black Rainbow

In rural North Carolina, bogus psychic Martha Travis (Rosanna Arquette) and her father (Jason Robards) travel the small-town circuit. When her predictions come true, a reporter (Tom Hulce) is interested. Writer/director Mike Hodges' script ranges from excellent to stilted. The performances are as good as you'd expect from Robards and Hulce, but Arquette's limitations are all too obvious in the big emotional scenes. The sets, soundtrack, and limited effects show how tight the budget was. The plot gets thinner, weaker, and more preposterous as it goes along. Those who don't think the whole subject is pure hokum will be intrigued by the premise, if not the resolution. 𝄞𝄞

Graphic violence, sexual content, strong content, brief nudity.

1991 (R) 103m/C Rosanna Arquette, Jason Robards Jr., Tom Hulce, Ron Rosenthal, John Bennes, Linda Pierce, Mark Joy; *D:* Mike Hodges; *W:* Mike Hodges. **VHS, LV** *VTR, FXV, MED*

Black Rose of Harlem

If only *Black Rose of Harlem* were as good as its title. Sadly, this low-budget video premiere is a formula flick with nothing to say about its historical setting. On the other hand, star Cynda Williams is remarkably beautiful and manages to do a lot with a stereotyped role. She's Georgia Freeman, a singer who turns the Congo Club into a goldmine in 1931. Mobster Costanza (Joe Viterelli) tries to take over from the black owners, but his righthand man Johnny Verona (Nick Cassavetes) falls hard for Georgia. The film's main problem is a budget that limits most of the action to one heavily

shadowed set. About the best that can be said of the boneheaded script is that it's equally insulting to both black and white characters. The action scenes are clumsy and the songs aren't going to make anyone forget Billie Holiday. Cynda Williams does her best to overcome those limitation but director Fred Gallo does her no favors with some atrocious lighting. **AKA:** Machine Gun Blues. ✇✇

Violence, strong language, sexual material, brief nudity.

1995 (R) 80m/C Cynda Williams, Nick Cassavetes, Joe Viterelli, Maria Ford, Lawrence Monoson, Garrett Morris, Richard Brooks; **D:** Fred Gallo. **VHS** *NHO*

Blade Runner

Taking a second, third, or fourth look at this s-f masterpiece, it's easy to see why the first audiences were disappointed with it. The premise is convoluted and shaky with necessary background information clumsily presented. Some of it is told twice. Some of it's dished out in pseudo-tough voiceover narration which is meant to smooth out the maddening plot. But the core of the film is Ridley Scott's brilliant realization of a future Los Angeles. It's violent, rainy, smoky, and dark; a multi-ethnic, multi-racial place where the wealthy live in cool luxury and everyone else fights for a little space and quiet away from the crowd and the constant barrage of advertising. That world is so believable that it gives the action an unusual amount of emotional power. And, as has been noted here before, after several viewings, the story actually makes sense. All of those have combined to make *Blade Runner* an enduring cult favorite. On tape and laserdisc, the film exists in three versions—the theatrical release, the "international cut," and the "director's cut." The versions vary in the amounts of graphic violence and voiceover narration they contain. The differences are subtle but significant to the film's most devoted fans. In his fine book, *Future Noir: The Making of Blade Runner*, Paul M. Sammon explains the differences among the six distinct theatrical and video releases in great detail. ✇✇✇✇

Graphic violence, brief nudity, strong language.

1982 (R) 122m/C Harrison Ford, Rutger Hauer, Sean Young, Daryl Hannah, M. Emmet Walsh, Edward James Olmos, Joe Turkel, Brion James, Joanna Cassidy, William Sanderson; **D:** Ridley Scott; **W:** Hampton Fancher, David Peoples; **C:** Jordan Cronenweth; **M:** Vangelis. Los Angeles Film Critics Association Awards '82: Best Cinematography; Nominations: Academy Awards '82: Best Art Direction/Set Decoration. **VHS, LV** *COL, WAR, NLC*

Blindfold: Acts of Obsession

Tabloid bad girl Shannen Doherty bares all, as it were, in this *Basic Instinct* wanna-be. She plays a woman whose demanding husband (Michael Woods) has suggested she see a psychiatrist (Judd Nelson) to save their failing marriage. Could hubby be connected with the serial killings that are going on? Her policewoman sister (Kristian Alfonso) wonders if the good doctor himself might be guilty of "perversive activity." Ms. Doherty is a sexy, albeit somewhat chunky, leading lady whose skills are well suited to the material. Video veteran Lawrence Simeone directs ably enough, though this one has more appeal as a curiosity than as a guilty pleasure. Also available in an unrated version. ✇✇✇ **GPI: 6.1**

Nudity, sexual content, strong language, mild violence.

1994 (R) 93m/C Shannen Doherty, Judd Nelson, Michael Woods, Kristian Alfonso, Shell Danielson, Drew Snyder; **D:** Lawrence L. Simeone; **W:** Lawrence L. Simeone; **M:** Shuki Levy. **VHS** *AVE*

Blondes Have More Guns

Troma parody of *Basic Instinct* and *Indecent Proposal* is typically trashy. Is blonde Montana (Elizabeth Key) the psycho chainsaw killer? What about her sister Dakota (Gloria Lusiak)? And why is that man dressed in a dog suit? (Hint: He's not the VideoHound.) Dimbulb detective Bates (Michael McGahern) is

"I'd rather be a killer than a victim."

—Harrison Ford in *Blade Runner.*

Cynda Williams in *Black Rose of Harlem.* ©New Horizons Home Video.

hot on the case. As Troma fans expect, the action is crude, raunchy, sexy, and unashamed. 🗡🗡🗡

Comic violence, sexual material, nudity, strong language.

1995 (R) 90m/C Michael McGahern, Elizabeth Key, Gloria Lusiak, Richard Neil; *D:* George Merriweather. **VHS** *TTV*

Blood & Donuts

Director Holly Dale uses a limited budget to excellent effect in this curious little Canadian horror comedy. It's the story of Boya (Gordon Currie), a Toronto vampire who's accidentally awakened after a 25-year nap and hangs out at a rundown coffee shop where Molly (Helene Clarkson) is a waitress. He's a romantic Byronic vampire who upsets a gangster's (David Cronenberg) plans to take over the neighborhood. Considering the recent excesses of the genre, the action is relatively restrained. The main irritant is Justin Louis as Earl, the cabbie. While everyone else is playing it straight, he grazes on every stick of scenery in sight. Even so, Dale has come up with some intelligent variations on familiar themes. 🗡🗡🗡

Violence, strong language.

1996 (R) 89m/C *CA* Gordon Currie, Justin Louis, Helene Clarkson, Fiona Reid, Frank Moore; *Cameos:* David Cronenberg; *D:* Holly Dale; *C:* Paul Sarossy. **VHS, LV** *LIV*

Blood and Sand

Young Juan (Christopher Rydell) is the hottest young matador in all Spain when he becomes smitten by the jet-setting Dona Sol (Sharon Stone). As his star rises, he forgets his wife and family, and the coquettish Dona Sol leads him into a life of recreational drugs and outdoor hanky-panky. Stone seems to be having a grand time and brings a bracing sense of humor to her villainous role. Rydell isn't so lucky. He is saddled with some truly laughable lines. And the big non-surprise ending is so overstated that it turns alleged tragedy into giggles. You'll be rooting for the bulls and Dona Sol all the way. 🗡🗡🗡 **GPI: 8.5**

Violence, strong language, nudity, sexual content.

1989 (R) 96m/C Christopher Rydell, Sharon Stone, Ana Torrent, Jose-Luis De Villalonga, Simon Andrew; *D:* Javier Elorrieta. **VHS, LV** *VMK*

Blood In...Blood Out: Bound by Honor

At three hours, this vid will test your patience. But on tape, you can break up the running time to suit your schedule, so that's not a big problem. And the story does deserve the extended treatment. Set in the 1970s and '80s, it's about three young Chicano cousins in Los Angeles. Miklo (Damian Chapa) has a white father, blond hair, and blue eyes, and because of that, he's the most ethnically chauvinistic of the three. With his tight tank top, pork pie hat, and suspenders, Paco (Benjamin Bratt) fits the stereotype of the tough, cocky kid. Cruz (Jesse Borrego), a talented painter, has the most promising future. Much of the action takes place in prison, where it has a frighteningly realistic feel. That authenticity carries over into the scenes filmed on location in East L.A. Though the entire production has the well-scrubbed look of a mainstream film—this one came from Disney's Hollywood Pictures—the neighborhoods and streets appear to be authentic. The story is by veteran mystery writer Ross Thomas, who knows how to keep things moving. Director Taylor Hackford focuses on the characters of the three protagonists and he's not afraid to let the pace move slowly while those are developed. At other times, particularly toward the end, he lets them spend a lot of time philosophizing. But that's all right; there's also compelling physical action then, reminiscent of *The Godfather*. *AKA:* Bound by Honor. 🗡🗡🗡

Graphic violence, raw language, sexual content, brief nudity.

1993 (R) 180m/C Damian Chapa, Jesse Borrego, Benjamin Bratt, Enrique Castillo, Victor Rivers, Delroy Lindo, Tom Towles; *D:* Taylor Hackford; *W:* Floyd Mutrux, Jimmy Santiago Baca, Jeremy Iacone; *M:* Bill Conti. **VHS, LV** *HPH, TOU*

Blood Relations

Imagine a Gothic *Body Heat* set in the dead of a Canadian winter. In an unhappy household, even lies aren't what they seem. An egomaniacal surgeon (Jan Rubes) may have killed his wealthy wife. His unstable son (Kevin Hicks) hasn't forgiven him. The son's manipulative girlfriend (Lydie Denier) looks like the dead woman, and his dying grandfather (Ray Walston) may be the kinkiest of them all. The games they play with and against each other in a snow-covered mansion become creepier and creepier until they reach a wonderfully nasty Grand Guignol conclusion. For fans of director Graeme Campbell's 1987 film, *Into the Fire*, it's more polished and controlled. 🗡🗡🗡∨ **GPI: 9.3**

Mature subject matter, nudity, violence, profanity.

1987 (R) 105m/C *CA* Jan Rubes, Ray Walston, Lydie Denier, Kevin Hicks, Lynne Adams; *D:* Graeme Campbell. **VHS, LV** *NLC*

Blood Relatives

Fans of Ed McBain's *87th Precinct* novels may surprised by this 1978 Canadian film. McBain writes realistic police procedurals marked by absorbing plots and deft characterization. Director Claude Chabrol captures both of those elements in his adaptation. The surprise for McBain's readers comes in the casting of Donald Sutherland as detective Steve Carella. (Burt Reynolds played Carella in the 1972 film *Fuzz*.) McBain's recurring theme of innocence warped into evil is strong throughout, and so is his dispassionate point of view. The plot revolves around a murder and a sexual relationship between cousins. Donald Pleasence and David Hemmings provide their usual excellent supporting work. Lisa Langlois and Stephane Audran are good too. *AKA:* Les Liens de Sang. 🗡🗡🗡

Profanity and strong subject matter.

1978 94m/C *CA* Lisa Langlois, Donald Sutherland, Stephane Audran, David Hemmings, Donald Pleasence, Laurent Malet, Micheline Lanctot, Aude Landry; *D:* Claude Chabrol; *W:* Claude Chabrol. **VHS** *BTV*

Blood Salvage

Welcome to *Motel Hell* country. This horror/comedy about organ transplants is cut from the same cloth as the cult classic. Filmed in rural Georgia, it's the story of Jake (Danny Nelson), who uses his tow-truck business as a front for an organ bank. He takes them from unwilling donors and sells them to unscrupulous doctors through middleman Ray Walston. Things are going fine for Jake and his two half-witted sons until he falls for April (Lori Birdsong), who's paralyzed from the waist down. Jake, a latterday Victor Frankenstein in coveralls, decides to help her. The writing, acting, and direction are several notches above average. Given the subject matter, the film has a high Yuck-factor, but the gross moments are played for laughs of the haunted house peeled-grapes-for-eyeballs variety. Also, the screen is filled with religious imagery and language that's somehow appropriate to this story of twisted love and sacrifice. 🗡🗡🗡

Yucky special effects, profanity.

1990 (R) 90m/C Evander Holyfield, Lori Birdsong, Danny Nelson, John Saxon, Ray Walston; *D:* Tucker Johnson. **VHS, LV** *TTC*

Blood Ties

A young man goes to L.A. to stay with relatives after his family is murdered. Christian vigilantes led by Bo Hopkins pursue him. The boy's kinfolk are a curious bunch. Though Hopkins' people think of them as "the undead," they prefer to be called "Carpathian-Americans." While some keep the old traditions, others, including our hero Harry (Patrick Bauchau), think "it's time we came out of the coffin." But uncle Eli (Salvator Xuereb) warns that if they go public, that's "when the pogroms begin." The rest involves conflicts between the elders and the young Carpathian-Americans who live in loft apartments, ride motorcycles, engage in sexy dance numbers, and generally act like refugees from *Melrose Place*. The film never gets too serious and since it comes from Roger Corman's New Horizons organization, it looks terrific. Director Jim McBride has a lot of fun with well-worn

horror movie themes. He tinkers with the conventions of the genre, and indulges in some timely social satire. At the same time, it's a slick, sexy horror movie with a sense of humor. ♫♫♫

Violence, strong language, sexual content, fleeting nudity.

1992 84m/C Harley Venton, Patrick Bauchau, Kim Johnston-Ulrich, Michelle Johnson, Jason London, Bo Hopkins, Grace Zabriskie, Salvator Xuereb; *D:* Jim McBride; *W:* Richard Shapiro. **VHS** *NHO*

Bloodfist

Early effort by Don Wilson—before he became "The Dragon"—is a solid, economically constructed little B-movie with good Philippine locations, excellent sets, and a no-frills martial arts plot: revenge for brother's murder. The cast features several championship-winning tournament fighters. The onscreen bouts and training sequences are fairly effective. In

these first films, Wilson shows hints of the star quality that drives his best work. ♫♫♫

1989 (R) 85m/C Don "The Dragon" Wilson, Rob Kaman, Billy Blanks, Kris Aguilar, Riley Bowman, Michael Shaner; *D:* Terence H. Winkless. **VHS** *MGM*

Bloodfist 2

Sequel follows the drill with more Philippine locations and a cast of trained tournament fighters. The key plot element of the original—our hero's single-kidney status—has been lost. The story is another standard for the genre: kidnapped kickboxers forced to fight. Joe Mari Avellana is a good villain and Wilson turns it on for the fight scenes. Many sequels have followed, each wandering farther from the initial premise. ♫♫

1990 (R) 85m/C Don "The Dragon" Wilson, Maurice Smith, James Warring, Timothy Baker, Richard Hill, Rina Reyes, Joe Mari Avellana; *D:* Andy Blumenthal. **VHS** *MGM*

Bloodfist 7: Manhunt

By number 7, the series has lost all contact with the original concept. The only connection is Don Wilson, who plays a mysterious loner who picks up the wrong woman (Jillian McWhirter) in a biker bar, and finds himself pursued by corrupt cops and other bad guys. The story has some noirish elements but it quickly becomes a chase flick shot on familiar Southern California locations. In some ways, this one's similar to David Heavener's *Fugitive X* but with a stronger anti-authoritarian attitude. 8 looms. 🦴🦴

Martial arts violence, strong language.

1994 (R) m/C Don "The Dragon" Wilson, Jillian McWhirter, Jonathan Penner, Rick Dean; *D:* Jonathan Winfrey. VHS *NHO*

Bloodknot

To call this one *The Last Seduction*-lite gives it too much credit, but it's still a fair suspense film with a feminine slant. From the get-go, we know that Connie Alexander (Kate Vernon) has it in for some or all of the Reaves family. She arrives in their sleepy Southern town (actually Canada), and persuades everyone that she's the fiancée of the eldest son, recently killed while he was stationed overseas. Mom (Margot Kidder) takes some work, but her son Tom (Patrick Dempsey) is easy. His girlfriend Julie (Krista Bridges) doesn't buy the act for a second. Writer Randy Kornfield manages to slip a few surprises into the formula story, but director Jorge Montesi never establishes the right mood of edginess, and in the key roles the acting is flat. 🦴🦴

Strong language, violence, sexual content, nudity.

1995 (R) 98m/C Patrick Dempsey, Kate Vernon, Margot Kidder, Craig Sheffer, Krista Bridges; *D:* Jorge Montesi; *W:* Randy Kornfield; *C:* Philip Linzey; *M:* Ian Thomas. VHS *PAR*

Bloodlust: Subspecies 3

The Transylvanian locations are about all that this sequel has going for it. *3* is the weakest of the *Subspecies* series, though the gooey effects will appeal to hardcore fans. (See reviews of *Subspecies* and *Bloodstone* for more information.) *AKA:* Subspecies 3. 🦴🦴🦴

Gooey special effects, violence, brief nudity.

1993 (R) 83m/C Anders Hove, Kevin Blair, Denice Duff, Pamela Gordon, Ion Haiduc, Michael DellaFemina; *D:* Ted Nicolaou; *W:* Ted Nicolaou. VHS, LV *PAR*

Bloodsport 2: The Next Kumite

The most remarkable thing about this video sequel is the resemblance that star Daniel Bernhardt bears to Jean-Claude Van Damme on the box art. On the tape itself, they're not quite so similar but the two films are pretty much the same. Both are about the Kumite, a big martial arts tournament, and both feature lots of fights with loud swoopy-crunchy sound effects. The bouts, choreographed by Philip Tan and directed by Alan Mehrez, are alternately realistic, comic, graceful, and staged. For fans, this one's not up to the best of the recent Hong Kong imports but young Bernhardt has the build and the moves to make it in action movies. He gets good support from James Hong, Pat Morita, and bad guy Ong Soo Han. 🦴🦴

Martial arts violence.

1995 (R) 87m/C Daniel Bernhardt, Ong Soo Han, Noriyuki "Pat" Morita, James Hong; *D:* Alan Mehrez. VHS *FEI*

Bloodstone: Subspecies 2

The good-vampire/bad-vampire bit was the premise of the original *Subspecies,* and it ended with both characters temporarily out of commission. The sequel begins with some really yucky Grand Guignol scenes wherein bad vamp Radu (Anders Hove) is, as it were, recapitated. For those who came in late, Radu is this grotesque dude who's having one long bad hair day—not to mention bad face, bad hands, bad drool. We're talking serious personal hygiene problems. Again, there's nothing too original about the plot. The good vampire's American girlfriend (Denice Duff) steals the Bloodstone, a supernatural lava light, and heads for Bucharest. (Like the original, it was made in Romania.) The rest contains enough

imaginative, grotesque effects to keep even the most jaded fan happy and nauseous. **AKA:** Subspecies 2. 🐾🐾🐾

Bloody effects, strong language, brief nudity.

1992 (R) 107m/C Anders Hove, Denice Duff, Kevin Blair, Michael Denish, Pamela Gordon, Ion Haiduc; **D:** Ted Nicolaou; **W:** Ted Nicolaou. **VHS, LV** *PAR*

Blown Away

Think *Body Heat* with the Hardy Boys, Nancy Drew, and several explicit but unimaginative love scenes. Kinky, but somehow, not quite... right. Two brothers (Coreys Feldman and Haim) work at a fancy Western ski resort where Megan (Nicole Eggert) is the spoiled daughter of the owner. This one also features Gary Farmer, a fine character actor who's been woefully underutilized since his debut in *Powwow Highway*, one of the truly great video premieres. 🐾🐾

Nudity, strong sexual content and language, some violence.

1993 (R) 91m/C Nicole Eggert, Corey Haim, Corey Feldman, Gary Farmer; **D:** Benton Spencer. **VHS, LV** *LIV*

Blue

Seen individually, the films in Krzysztof Kieslowski's *Three Colors* trilogy are remarkable, ambitious works. Taken together, they form a real masterpiece—multilayered, rewarding, and remarkably entertaining. Kieslowski was a director of prodigious talents, the equal of Scorsese in his technical skills. He could combine sound, music (here by Zbigniew Preisner), character, and striking images; both big breathtaking shots and closely observed individual details. And he could use them in service of serious, timely stories. All three of these revolve around beautiful women—really beautiful. The titles refer to the colors of the French flag and the ideas they symbolize: blue for liberty, white for equality, and red for fraternity. *Blue* is about Julie (Juliette Binoche), whose husband and daughter are killed in a car accident, thereby "freeing" her from her past. In *White*, Karol's (Zbigniew Zamachowski) marriage to Parisienne Dominique (Julie

Delpy) disintegrates, and he must return to Poland just as the country is undergoing profound political and social change. *Red* concerns the developing relationship between Valentine (Irene Jacob), a model, and a retired Judge (Jean Louis Trintignant) in Geneva. The films are respectively a drama, a picaresque comedy, and a romance, though they're so unconventional that those definitions mean little. A courtroom scene and a disaster are the only two overlapping points. Instead of focusing on strong narratives, Kieslowski is more concerned with moments that mirror or complement each other: coffee being absorbed into a sugar cube, a woman swimming in a pool at night, a street musician's song, breaking glass. The colors themselves are equally important. Kieslowski often washes the entire screen with red, blue, or white. Doctoral theses could and certainly will be written about the literal and symbolic uses of color in the films. But that's for scholars, not videophiles. Any viewer who wants something more intelligent and substantial than mainstream Hollywood has to offer should take a look. And if Kieslowski's films aren't in your favorite video store, find a rent-by-mail organization. They're well worth the extra effort and would make a first-rate weekend video festival. (By the way, the trilogy can be seen in any order—and each stands alone—but the chronological order is *Blue, White, Red,* and the last film is the most emotionally satisfying.) **AKA:** Three Colors: Blue; Trois Coleurs: Bleu; Bleu. 🐾🐾🐾🐾

Mature subject matter, a little strong language, sexual content, brief nudity.

1993 (R) 98m/C *FR* Juliette Binoche, Benoit Regent, Florence Pernel, Charlotte Very; **Cameos:** Emmanuelle Riva; **D:** Krzysztof Kieslowski; **W:** Krzysztof Piesiewicz, Krzysztof Kieslowski; **C:** Slawomir Idziak. Cesar Awards '94: Best Actress (Binoche), Best Film Editing, Best Sound; Los Angeles Film Critics Association Awards '93: Best Score; Venice Film Festival '93: Best Actress (Binoche), Best Film; Nominations: Golden Globe Awards '94: Best Actress—Drama (Binoche), Best Foreign Language Film, Best Original Score. **VHS, LV** *TOU*

Blue Desert

After two sexual attacks, comic book artist Lisa Roberts (Courteney Cox) leaves New York for a little desert town. One of the first people she meets is Randall (Craig Sheffer), a scroungy, motorcycle-riding oddball. He seems nice enough, but he has an unusual intensity that suggests he might be a distant cousin of Charles Manson. An attentive deputy (D.B. Sweeney) advises her not to trust him and promises to keep a close eye on the trailer where she's living. One of the guys is a psychopath. Chances are you'll figure out which one it is a little too soon, and at key moments Lisa is unrealistically stupid. But, like Sam Peckinpah's *Straw Dogs,* the film focuses on the paranoia any outsider can feel in a small community. While this is no masterpiece, it's an overachieving piece of work made with excellent production values and a good cast. 🎜🎜🎜

Violence, language, sexual content, brief nudity.

1991 (R) 98m/C D.B. Sweeney, Courteney Cox, Craig Sheffer, Philip Baker Hall, Sandy Ward; *D:* Bradley Battersby; *W:* Bradley Battersby, Arthur Collis; *M:* Jerry Goldsmith. **VHS** *ACA*

Blue Iguana

Highly stylized remake of *A Fistful of Dollars* (itself a remake of Akira Kurosawa's *Yojimbo*) was filmed in Mexico. It combines a *Miami Vice* look with 1950s cool: lots of pastel-colored buildings, unshaven guys in ice-cream suits, two-tone shoes, and big-finned Caddies. The script is a purposeful collection of cliches. Jessica Harper is one of the less psychotic bad guys; Tovah Feldshuh and Dean Stockwell are two crooked I.R.S. agents. Everyone onscreen hams it up shamelessly. In the end, this one's slightly similar to Walter Hill's *Streets of Fire,* but it doesn't take itself seriously for a second. Nothing but fun if you're in the right mood, unwatchable if you're not. 🎜🎜🎜

Graphic violence, strong language, and suggestive sexual content.

1988 (R) 88m/C Dylan McDermott, Jessica Harper, James Russo, Dean Stockwell, Pamela Gidley, Tovah Feldshuh; *D:* John Lafia. **VHS, LV** *PAR*

Blue in the Face

Patchwork feature was cobbled together with leftovers from Wayne Wang's theatrical fea-

ture, *Smoke.* It uses the same sets and some of the same cast, notably Harvey Keitel as Augie. He's the central character in a loose succession of comic vignettes, scenes, and interviews. Mira Sorvino, Lily Tomlin, Madonna, Malik Yoba, Michael J. Fox, and Giancarlo Esposito show up for cameos that appear to be largely unscripted. The main subjects are Brooklyn and Belgian waffles. Overall, it's too quirky, episodic, and improvised for a theatrical film, but those same qualities serve it well on video. Fans of the cast and the filmmakers will enjoy watching what sometimes seems more like outtakes than finished performances. 🎜🎜🎜

Strong language, brief nudity.

1995 (R) 83m/C Harvey Keitel, Lou Reed, Michael J. Fox, Roseanne, Jim Jarmusch, Lily Tomlin, Mel Gorham, Jared Harris, Giancarlo Esposito, Victor Argo, Madonna, Keith David, Mira Sorvino, Malik Yoba; *D:* Wayne Wang, Paul Auster; *W:* Wayne Wang, Paul Auster. **VHS, LV** *TOU*

Blueberry Hill

Trapped in a 1950s California mountain town, 16-year-old Ellie Dane (Jennifer Rubin) dreams of music and city lights, but her weird mother Becca (Carrie Snodgress) won't hear of it. She won't even allow a radio or telephone in their house. Becca's problems go back to the night her husband was killed, the same night that Ellie was born. He got drunk and drowned after he'd been out messing around. All that comes from the prologue. But the one-note characters take an hour and a half to work through it. Throughout the action is too talky and the pace is choppy. The forced conclusion doesn't ring true, and one embarrassingly bad love scene near the end is completely out of place. The credits suggest the film may be partly autobiographical. Maybe that's the problem. 🎜🎜

Profanity and one brief love scene.

1988 (R) 93m/C Jennifer Rubin, Carrie Snodgress, Margaret Avery; *D:* Strathford Hamilton. **VHS** *FOX*

Body Chemistry

Though its debts to *Body Heat* and *Fatal Attraction* are too obvious, this is still a good

thriller in its own right. Sex researcher Dr. Claire Archer (Lisa Pescia) puts some strong moves on her married colleague Dr. Redding (Marc Singer). When things go bad, they really go bad. The performances and production values (including Gary Plumeri's music) are above average. The inventive and often weirdly funny script works through believable characters. Pescia's ball-buster extraordinaire is right up there with the best of the killer babes. ♫♫♫ **GPI: 8.0**

Mature subject matter, sexual content, brief nudity, violence, strong language, performance art.

1990 **(R)** 84m/C Marc Singer, Mary Crosby, Lisa Pescia, Joseph Campanella, David Kagen; **D:** Kristine Peterson; **W:** Jackson Barr, Thom Babbes; **C:** Phedon Papamichael. **VHS, LV** *COL*

Body Chemistry 2: Voice of a Stranger

On the series scale, *2* is about 70 percent as enjoyable as the original, which isn't bad for a sequel. Dr. Archer (Lisa Pescia), the lethal sex therapist, is plying her trade on the radio and messing with an ex-cop's (Gregory Harrison) already screwed-up psyche. The script isn't nearly as tight, but the humor is intact and Pescia's villainous performance make up for a lot. Look for Jeremy Piven and director John Landis in cameos. ♫♫♫ **GPI: 5.9**

Mature subject matter, sexual material, nudity, violence, strong language.

1991 **(R)** 84m/C Gregory Harrison, Lisa Pescia, Morton Downey Jr., Robin Riker; **Cameos:** Jeremy Piven, John Landis; **D:** Adam Simon. **VHS, LV** *COL*

Body Chemistry 3: Point of Seduction

Femme fatale radio psychologist Claire Archer (Shari Shattuck)—a sort of sexually explicit Dr. Joy Brown—has left a trail of dead male conquests behind her on her rise to stardom. Producer Alan Clay (producer Andrew Stevens) thinks it's perfect material for a made-for-TV movie, and his actress wife Beth (Morgan Fairchild) will do anything to play Claire's part. But Claire doesn't want her life turned into tabloid TV trash. Sure, she admits that she's a tramp, but a girl has to maintain standards, doesn't she? Stevens is an established video veteran on both sides of the camera. So is low-budget auteur Jim Wynorski. They put every penny they spent on the screen and they got professional support from Robert Forster, Chick Vennera, and Stella Stevens, Andrew's mom. For a sequel to a sequel, this one's O.K., and it was followed by yet another. ♫♫♫ **GPI: 7.7**

Sexual material, nudity, strong language, and violence.

1993 **(R)** 90m/C Shari Shattuck, Andrew Stevens, Morgan Fairchild, Robert Forster, Chick Vennera, Stella Stevens; **D:** Jim Wynorski. **VHS, LV** *NHO*

Body Chemistry 4: Full Exposure

4 uses the premise and title of the remarkably long-lived series about a radio talkshow host as the basis for a low-voltage legal thriller. It appears that our heroine Dr. Claire Archer (Shannon Tweed) has murdered our hero Alan Clay (Andrew Stevens, who also produced), and so has to hire lawyer Simon Mitchell (Larry Poindexter) to defend her. Veteran Karen Kelly's script is a convoluted contraption that's impossible to follow, but with this kind of movie, that's not necessarily a problem. I suspect she put it together so that Claire can engage in some reverse sexual harrassment that's really funny. Director Jim Wynorski and the rest of the production team have long track records in the genre. They bring competence to the project, along with a certain sameness. Also available in an unrated version. 🦴🦴 **GPI: 7.2**

Nudity, sexual material, strong language, violence.

1995 (R) 89m/C Shannon Tweed, Larry Poindexter, Andrew Stevens; *D:* Jim Wynorski; *W:* Karen Kelly. **VHS, LV** *NHO*

Body Language

It's another babe-from-hell suspense flick, following the nanny in *Hand That Rocks the Cradle,* the mistress in *Fatal Attraction,* etc. This time, it's the secretary (Linda Purl) who's out to do in her executrix boss (Heather Locklear). No surprises. 🦴🦴

Strong language, brief nudity, sexual activity, some violence.

1992 (R) 93m/C Heather Locklear, Linda Purl, Edward Albert, James Acheson; *D:* Arthur Seidelman; *W:* Dan Gurskis, Brian Ross; *C:* Hanania Baer. **VHS** *PAR*

Body of Influence

Beverly Hills psychiatrist (Nick Cassavetes) advises cop (Richard Roundtree) in his search for a serial killer. Could it be that Shannon Whirry, who's suffering from intense sexual fantasies, has something to do with the murders? Seems likely, but that doesn't stop the good doctor from joining her for some extracurricular activity. Director Andrew Gregory Hippolyte (AKA Andrew Garroni) and Whirry have made some of the best guilty pleasures. This one's among them. Slickly produced, unashamedly trashy entertainment. Followed by a sequel. 🦴🦴🦴 **GPI: 8.0**

Sexual content, nudity, strong language.

1993 (R) 96m/C Nick Cassavetes, Shannon Whirry, Sandahl Bergman, Don Swayze, Anna Karin, Catherine Parks, Diana Barton, Richard Roundtree; *D:* Alexander Gregory Hippolyte; *W:* David Schreiber. **VHS** *ACA*

Body Shot

Photographer Mickey Dane (Robert Patrick) is so fascinated by rock star Chelsea that he roots through her garbage. That makes him a natural choice to shoot a series of suggestive pictures of Chelsea lookalike (Michelle Johnson). When the original turns up dead, he's been framed. Noirish voiceover is used to good effect, and the presence of B-movie veterans Kenneth Tobin and Charles Napier doesn't hurt either. Beware the circling camera cliche. Patrick is known best as Arnold Schwarzenegger's implacable antagonist in *T2* and he brings the same intensity to this part. A tricky cut above the norm. 🦴🦴🦴

Strong language, violence, sexual content, brief nudity.

1993 (R) 98m/C Robert Patrick, Michelle Johnson, Charles Napier, Kenneth Tobin; *D:* Dimitri Logothetis; *W:* Robert Strauss. **VHS, LV** *TRI*

Body Snatchers

For sheer paranoia, Abel Ferrara's take on the famous s-f tale may not be as suspenseful as Don Siegel's original, but it's better than Philip Kaufman's 1978 remake. The inventive special effects are about as skin-crawly as any you'll see these days. They involve soft, gently probing little tendrils that do absolutely revolting things. The setting is a Southern military base and sullen teenager Marti Malone (Gabrielle Anwar) hates it. She doesn't much care for her dad (Terry Kinney), stepmom (Meg Tilly), or little brother (Reilly Murphy) either. The only thing she likes is a handsome chopper pilot (Billy Wirth). Of course, they're all potential pod fodder. In the first part of the film, director Ferrara uses a funereal pace to turn the ordinary into the ominous. It's an effective way to build tension until the icky effects kick in. On the minus side, he overuses the shortcut of panning his camera through walls between rooms. It's a technique that rudely reminds viewers they're watching a movie when they should be getting into the action, and toward the end, the plot makes a misstep

or two. But judged against the rest of the film, those are minor flaws. 🦴🦴🦴

Icky special effects, violence, strong language, brief nudity.

1993 (R) 87m/C Gabrielle Anwar, Meg Tilly, Terry Kinney, Forest Whitaker, Billy Wirth, R. Lee Ermey, Reilly Murphy; *D:* Abel Ferrara; *W:* Stuart Gordon, Dennis Paoli, Nicholas St. John; *C:* Bojan Bazelli; *M:* Joe Delia. **VHS, LV** *WAR*

Body Strokes

Curious little video original attempts to combine soft-core eroticism with character development. The story concerns a burned out artist's (Bobby Johnson) lack of inspiration that parallels his troubled marriage. Will the presence of two new models turn things around? Deliberately paced and overall, more serious than spicy. Also available in an unrated version at 95 minutes. 🦴🦴 **GPI: 6.8**

Nudity, sexual content, strong language.

1995 (R) 85m/C Bobby Johnson, Kristen Knittle, Catherine Weber; *D:* Dixie Beck. **VHS** *APX*

Bootleg

Terrorists, brutish cops, politics, rock music, surrogate motherhood, bootleg tapes, and two or three sinister subplots are all involved in a senseless thriller. Our hero is a saxophone-playing detective (John Flaus) who bears a strong resemblance to Gene Hackman. The action is odd and surreal at times, and throughout, it's slowly paced and darkly lit. Viewed purely as an exercise in style, the Aussie vid will hold your attention, if you're in the mood. For full-tilt action scenes or Hitchcockian suspense, try something else. 🦴🦴

Profanity, mild violence, brief nudity.

1989 82m/C *AU* Ray Meagher, John Flaus; *D:* John Prescott. **VHS** *AIP*

Bottle Rocket

Wes Anderson's feature debut is one of the most enjoyable sleepers in the video store.

Given the film's loosely plotted unpredictability, comparisons to *Fargo* are inevitable, but this one's much lighter, funnier, and easy-going. As it begins, young Anthony (Luke Wilson) has just released himself from a mental institution. His friend Dignan (co-writer Owen C. Wilson), a would-be criminal mastermind, is waiting for him with big plans. Before they can become the terror of Dallas, they must invite their rich pal Bob (Robert Musgrave) to join the gang. (Bob's got a car.) The trio's on-again-but-mostly-off-again adventures as outlaws take a sharp turn when Anthony meets Inez (the luminous Lumi Cavazos from *Like Water for Chocolate*). Co-writer/director Wes Anderson first told the story as a short film, which became a hit at the Sundance Festival. That attracted the attention of Hollywood producers, including James Brooks, and the film expanded to feature length. Though it didn't fare so well in a limited theatrical release, this is the kind of warm, offbeat character piece that's going to be an enduring favorite on home video. (By the way, the score is terrific.) Don't miss it. 🦴🦴🦴🦴

A little strong language, subject matter, some violence.

1995 (R) 91m/C Owen C. Wilson, Luke Wilson, Robert Musgrave, Lumi Cavazos, James Caan, Teddy Wilson, Andrew Wilson, Jim Ponds; *D:* Wes Anderson; *W:* Owen C. Wilson, Wes Anderson; *C:* Robert Yeoman; *M:* Mark Mothersbaugh. MTV Movie Awards '96: Best New Filmmaker Award (Anderson). **VHS, LV** *COL*

Boulevard

Jennifer (Kari Wuhrer) leaves her abusive husband and catches the first Trailways from her backwater Canadian burg to Toronto. He follows. Ola (Rae Dawn Chong), a kind-hearted but tough-minded hooker, takes Jennifer in off the streets. Writer Andrea Wilde and director Penelope Buitenhuis take a gritty, objective view of prostitution, neither exploiting, glamorizing, nor condemning it out of hand. (That's not to say their film doesn't have its racy moments.) The main flaw is Lou Diamond Phillips, who might have based his perfor-

ROBERT PATRICK IN *BODY SHOT*. ©TRIBORO ENTERTAINMENT GROUP.

mance as a pimp on Gary Oldman in *True Romance*. Ethnic stereotypes are insulting enough on their own, but when actors of other races affect broad accents and mannerisms, the result is latter-day blackface. The female characters are much more fully developed, believable, and engaging, and the focus stays mostly on them. Comparisons to *Ruby in Paradise* and *Exotica* aren't out of place. ♫♫♫

Mature subject matter, nudity, violence, strong language.

1994 **(R)** 96m/**C** Kari Wuhrer, Rae Dawn Chong, Lou Diamond Phillips, Lance Henriksen, Joel Bissonnette; *D:* Penelope Buitenhuis; *W:* Andrea Wilde, Rae Dawn Chong; *M:* Ian Thomas. **VHS, LV** *LIV*

Bound and Gagged: A Love Story

The box copy promises "not your average insane road movie," and it's not exaggerating. Instead, this is a romantic comedy about attempted suicide, spouse abuse, lesbianism, and kidnapping, which may not sound like funny stuff, but it can be. Leslie (Ginger Lynn Allen) is pretty much fed up with her loutish husband Steve (Chris Mulkey). She has become involved in a relationship with Elizabeth (Elizabeth Saltarrelli), a free spirit with a short fuse. Elizabeth thinks that she knows what's best for everyone, including her friend Cliff (Chris Denton), who's so tormented by memories of his own unfaithful wife (Mary Ella Ross) that he has barely survived an unsuccessful suicide. Without giving away the game, Elizabeth winds up heading west from Minneapolis in an aging Chrysler with a mute Cliff riding shotgun, Leslie bound and gagged in the back, and Steve in hot pursuit. The film isn't always as funny as it's trying to be, but that's a small flaw. For the most part, this one has the natural performances and spontaneous, unexpected quality that a good road movie needs. It also has a strong feel for the landscape. In that respect it's right up there with *Powwow Highway,* maybe the best road movie of recent years. Writer/director Daniel Appleby has won several prizes from such august bodies as the American Film Institute and the National Endowment for the Arts, but don't let that put you off. This is a first-rate little sleeper. ♫♫♫

Mature subject matter, nudity, sexual material, strong language.

1993 **(R)** 96m/**C** Ginger Lynn Allen, Karen Black, Chris Denton, Elizabeth Saltarelli, Mary Ella Ross, Chris Mulkey; *D:* Daniel Appleby; *W:* Daniel Appleby; *M:* William Murphy. **VHS, LV** *TRI*

A Boy Called Hate

The title character (Scott Caan) is a juvenile car thief who inadvertently rescues a young woman (Missy Crider) as she's being attacked by Elliott Gould. Shots are fired and the two obnoxious kids are on the run across a gritty, sun-blasted Western landscape. O.K., that's a legitimate premise, but these two are such selfish and fundamentally uninteresting characters that the rest of the film really doesn't matter. The script is incessantly and needlessly profane. Writer/director Mitch Marcus tells the simple story at a leaden pace and so the protagonists' transformation is too little too late for anyone who's made it to the last reel without hitting the fast-forward button. ♫

Strong language, violence, sexual content.

1995 **(R)** 98m/**C** Scott Caan, Missy Crider, Elliott Gould, Adam Beach; *Cameos:* James Caan; *D:* Mitch Marcus; *W:* Mitch Marcus; *C:* Paul Holahan. **VHS** *PAR*

Boyfriends & Girlfriends

Parisiennes Blanche (Emmanuelle Chaulet) and Lea (Sophie Renoir) have just met and become friends. Lea is sort of living with her boyfriend Fabien (Eric Viellard); Blanche is attracted to his handsome friend Alexandre (Francois-Eric Gendron) even though everyone says they're wrong for each other. It takes almost two mostly uneventful hours for these four to get their romantic attachments sorted out. They lead fairly ordinary middle-class lives punctuated by discussions about love, friendship, and happiness; they doubt themselves, they make mistakes, they cry, they wish they had longer vacations. Throughout, Eric Rohmer's style is relaxed and confident, but the film sneaks up on you. The characters are so likable and real that it's easy to become involved with their problems. The subtitled story is told simply, without a musical soundtrack, on starkly uncluttered sets and locations. The pace is appropriately languid for a summer story. And though it seems unfocused, the film builds to a brilliant conclusion—a cross-purpose confrontation scene that's a near-perfect ending to a delightful comedy. *AKA:* My Girlfriend's Boyfriend; Ami de Mon Ami. ♪♪♪▽

A little profanity and mature subject matter.

1988 (PG) 102m/C **FR** Emmanuelle Chaulet, Sophie Renoir, Eric Viellard, Francois-Eric Gendron; **D:** Eric Rohmer; **W:** Eric Rohmer. **VHS, LV** *ORI, INJ*

Brain Damage

Frank Henenlotter's second low-budget feature about a boy and his pet monster is also a visceral anti-drug horror-comedy. The critter is a grotesque little parasite that looks like a cross between a prune and a catfish. It feeds on brains (human or animal) and is capable of injecting its host with a highly addictive hallucinogen. This thing is called Aylmer, or Elmer, and in one of the film's strangest moments, it launches into an a cappella version of that old Glenn Miller favorite, *Elmer's Tune.* Yes, Aylmer can sing and it can also talk; in fact, it can be quite persuasive. It comes into the possession of a young man, Brian (Rick Herbst), and, as it begins to gain control of him, Aylmer argues that it's all right for him to kill people, as long Brian isn't directly involved. Or, as he puts it, "Part of my talent, Brian, is to spare you any unpleasantness." And of course, there's plenty of unpleasantness to be spared. The violence is graphic (and often reminiscent of David Cronenberg's *Rabid*), outlandish, and comic. There's also a strong sexual element to the story, though it's played mostly for laughs. Beyond the Grand Guignol horror, *Brain Damage* has some serious things to say about addiction, about how it changes a person, and about how it can kill or hurt others. This one isn't as striking or as original as Henenlotter's first effort, but for fans of *Basket Case*, it's a must-see. ♪♪♪

Graphic violence, profanity, brief nudity, sexual content.

1988 (R) 89m/C Rick Herbst, Gordon MacDonald, Jennifer Lowry; *Cameos:* Kevin Van Hentenryck; **D:** Frank Henenlotter. **VHS** *PAR*

The Brave Little Toaster

Based on Thomas Disch's novella, this is the inspiring story of five household appliances and their search for their beloved Master. They've been left alone in a vacation cabin for years, but they still love the boy who used them. Young Blanky (the voice of Timothy E. Day), an electric blanket, was probably closest to him and misses him most. Kirby (Thurl Ravenscroft), the gruff and grumpy vacuum cleaner, won't admit to such sentimental nonsense. Lampy (Tim Stack) and Radio (Jon Lovitz) squabble like two excitable adolescents. Toaster (Deanna Oliver), more mature and sensible than the rest, is their natural leader. She misses the boy too—he used to make faces at his reflection on her bright side as he ate breakfast—but she is content, if not happy, organizing the others to keep the cabin clean. Then one day, a "For Sale" sign appears in the front yard. Though their mobility is limited, they decide they must leave the safety of the cabin and make their way through the unknown forest and into the city where Master lives. The animation style is close to the Warner Bros. cartoons of the early 1950s with bright, clean, stylized shapes. Under Jerry Rees' direction, the action moves so quickly that even the youngest viewers won't become bored. But some scenes may frighten them, and they will miss some of the humor. Radio, with his fondness for old broadcasts of baseball games and political speeches, has most of the best lines and Lovitz makes the most of them. In both the visuals and the dialogue, the film is filled with inventive wit. When he's feeling particularly puckish, Radio refers to Toaster as "slothead." Fans of good animation who don't have ready access to a toddler shouldn't be ashamed to rent this one for themselves, and parents who don't watch it with their kids are making a big mistake. It deserves a place on the shelf beside *Dumbo,*

Toy Story, and your favorite collection of Bugs Bunny cartoons. 🦴🦴🦴

1988 90m/C D: Jerry Rees; **V:** Jon Lovitz, Phil Hartman, Timothy E. Day, Thurl Ravenscroft, Tim Stack, Deanna Oliver. **VHS, LV** DIS, TOU, FCT

Breathing Fire

Charlie (Jonathan Ke Quan from *Indiana Jones and the Temple of Doom*) is the adopted Vietnamese son of a bank robber, but Charlie doesn't know that. He and his American brother are your average goofy teenaged kickboxers. They're caught up in a silly plot involving hidden gold bars, a slice of ceramic pizza, a young girl on the run from dear old dad's gang, a restaurant run by midgets, and a dozen or so slow-motion fight scenes. "Bolo" Yeung, so wonderfully villainous in other martial arts movies, does his usual fine work as one of the bad guys. And, yes, fans, once again he makes his pectoral muscles dance the boogaloo. 🦴🦴

Martial arts violence, some strong language.

1991 (R) 86m/C Bolo Yeung, Jonathan Ke Quan, Jerry Trimble; **D:** Lou Kennedy. **VHS** IMP

Brenda Starr

Made in 1986, this stinker sneaked shamefully onto home video some years later without a theatrical release. Such things are inevitable, even for movies as wretched as this. There's no other way to describe it; the movie is just a mess. The script is a hash of nonsensical elements that have nothing to do with each other. The part about the cartoonist who's sucked into his own strip is particularly out of place. The rest has something to do with a mad scientist in the Amazon jungle. The producers might have made something of it if they'd stayed with a simple adventure storyline, but they aren't capable of the basic stuff of narrative filmmaking. Though the story is supposed to be set in 1948, there's no historical detail. The attempts at physical humor are lame, and in two shots you can see the rails of the track for the camera dolly. *Brenda Starr* may well be the worst big-budget movie ever

to appear as a video premiere, and that puts in some very bad company, indeed. WOOF!

Strong language, overall incompetence.

1986 (PG) 94m/C Brooke Shields, Timothy Dalton, Tony Peck, Diana Scarwid, Nestor Serrano, Jeffrey Tambor, June Gable, Charles Durning, Eddie Albert, Henry Gibson, Ed Nelson; **D:** Robert Ellis Miller; **W:** James David Buchanan. **VHS** COL

Bride of Re-Animator

Even in Grand Guignol horror movies, more can be less. This sequel to the 1985 cult masterpiece goes too far in all the wrong directions. Of course, the prosthetic special effects are graphic, but severed body parts have been so overused that they don't even have the power to shock any more. The strong, flippant humor of the first film has become studied, though star Jeffrey Combs gives it his best. But the worst part of this sequel—as Annie Wilkes from *Misery* might say—is that they didn't get the cockadoodie story right. Characters who were clearly dead and/or squashed in the original are brought back without explanation. No, logic is not a prime consideration in cheap horror movies, but that kind of sloppiness is still an insult to fans. Also available in an unrated version. WOOF!

Graphic special effects, violence, strong language, sexual situations.

1989 (R) 99m/C Jeffrey Combs, Bruce Abbott, Claude Earl Jones, Fabiana Udenio, Kathleen Kinmont, David Gale; **D:** Brian Yuzna; **M:** Richard Band. **VHS, LV** LIV

The Bride with White Hair

Expensive Hong Kong epic is so visually ambitious that it loses something on the small screen. It's a magical tale of warring clans. Ye Hong (Leslie Cheung, who looks a lot like Johnny Depp) is the young warrior prince who falls in love with his enemy, Wolf Girl (Brigitte Lin Ching Hsia). Their story mixes operatic overstatement with soaring Shakespearian plot turns and real emotional depth. Director Ronny Yu works with a large cast on unbelievably evocative sets. The action scenes employ flying effects and highly stylized fights and swordplay. The stuntwork owes more to dance than to conventional martial arts films.

Fans of Hong Kong movies really have to see this one. It's a huge step forward. ☑☑☑▽

Violence, some sexual material.

1993 92m/C **HK** Leslie Cheung, Brigitte Lin Ching Hsia; **D:** Ronny Yu. **VHS** *TAI*

Broadcast Bombshells

Thoroughly silly little low-budget sex comedy has an attractive cast—Amy Lynn Baxter, Debbie Rochon, Elizabeth Heyman—and a sense of humor. The setting is a TV station where nothing is meant to be taken seriously. A first-rate guilty pleasure that delivers on its limited promises. Also available in an unrated version. ☑☑▽ **GPI: 8.9**

Nudity, sexual content, strong language, comic violence.

1995 (R) 83m/C Amy Lynn Baxter, Debbie Rochon, Elizabeth Heyman; **D:** Ernest G. Sauer. **VHS** *AVI*

Broken Trust

Sweet blonde Erika (Kimberly Foster) inherits her uncle's estate, much to the distress of her evil sister Paula (Kathryn Harris, who looks like a voluptuous Reba McIntire). Erika won't follow the advice of her ambitious but dumb husband (Nick Cassavetes) or her ambitious but smart lawyer (Edward Albert) who, like just about everyone else, is having an affair with Paula. Who then is trying to drive poor Erika crazy? Only the sheriff (Don Swayze) believes her, but he could be part of the plot too. At least the cheesy video soap has an intentional sense of humor and that counts for a lot. ☑☑▽

Strong language, violence, brief nudity, sexual content.

1993 85m/C Kimberly Foster, Nick Cassavetes, Kathryn Harris, Don Swayze, Edward Albert, Wendy MacDonald; **D:** Rafael Portillo. **VHS** *MNC*

Brother's Keeper

Filmmakers Joe Berlinger and Bruce Sinofsky tell a true story as if it were a murder mystery, establishing characters and setting, squeezing out clues and key information at a measured pace, then finally ending with an emotional courtroom denouement filmed as it happened. The four Ward brothers had spent their entire lives on their central New York farm. Childlike, largely uneducated, and possibly retarded, they lived in a squalid two-room shack without running water. Then in June 1990, the oldest, Bill Ward, died in his sleep. Was it congestive heart failure, or did Delbert Ward put his sick and fragile brother out of his misery by smothering him? Or, as the authorities would intimate later, did something much more sinister happen? In any case, after the state police questioned the brothers for several hours without the presence of an attorney, they got a confession from Delbert. That's when the people of Munnsville rallied to support the three men who had little if any idea what was happening to them. Particularly in the early scenes, Berlinger and Sinofsky—who produced, directed, and edited—make it clear that these three old guys were deeply frightened by the intrusions of the larger world on their insulated lives. Without the help of their community, the legal system could have accused and convicted the Wards of anything. As the wheels of justice ground forward, Berlinger and Sinofsky got much closer to the brothers. They came to understand that part of rural New York, and captured it on film. The score by Jay Unger and Molly Mason, whose music was such an important part of the PBS series *The Civil War*, is just as effective here. More importantly, the Wards become real individuals beyond the stereotyped country bumpkins. At the same time, a critical viewer has to wonder just how much the cameras affected the events as they unfolded. Berlinger and Sinofsky weren't the only ones who were interested. Local stations, network magazine shows, and tabloid TV all gave the story considerable coverage, and doubtless played a part in its outcome. And one footnote: *Brother's Keeper* received funding from both PBS and the National Endowment for the Arts. Keep it in mind the next time a candidate for public office tries to use the NEA as a whipping boy. This is the kind of film that's driven by commitment, and could never be made within the conventional studio system.

Video Premieres

It deserves wide distribution. And if viewers who wouldn't normally consider a "documentary" will give this one a try, they'll be happily surprised. 🦴🦴🦴▽

Contains some strong language, mature subject matter, scenes of animal slaughter.

1992 104m/C **D:** Joe Berlinger, Bruce Sinofsky; **M:** Jay Unger, Molly Mason. National Board of Review Awards '92: Best Feature Documentary; New York Film Critics Awards '92: Best Feature Documentary; Sundance Film Festival '92: Audience Award. **VHS, LV** *FXL, BTV*

Bugged!

Microbudget horror/s-f comedy is grainy and often amateurish, though it tries to make virtues of its flaws. Filmmaker and star Ronald K. Armstrong works with an all-black cast to tell a silly B-movie story. A long, too-talky introduction sets up your basic science-gone-bad plot. Armstrong plays an exterminator who's called in to clean up poet Divine Hill's (Priscilla Basque) house. Little do the guys at Dead & Buried Pest Removal know that the insecticide in their tanks is actually the genetic superjuice Clemol C-83, which turns normal roaches and crickets into vicious superbugs. The cheap effects and the violence are more silly than scary. Armstrong bucks the current trend by keeping the levels of violence and language well within the limits of his PG-13 rating. 🦴🦴

Strong subject matter, mostly comic violence.

1996 (PG-13) 80m/C Ronald K. Armstrong, Priscilla Basque, Jeff Lee, Derek C. Johnson, Billy Graham; **D:** Ronald K. Armstrong; **W:** Ronald K. Armstrong; **C:** S. Torriano Berry; **M:** Boris Elkis. **VHS** *TTV*

Bulletproof Heart

Mark Malone's offbeat thriller is an intelligently written and effective combination of comedy and drama. Mick (Anthony LaPaglia) is a dapper hitman who's suffering a crisis of faith. His long dark night of the soul has brought him to ask, "What is the meaning of meaning?" Yes,

the humor is intentional, but the tone shifts smoothly to more serious matters. Mick's bumbling assistant Archie (Matt Craven) is trying to win his job back, after botching their last assignment, when George (Peter Boyle), a midlevel Mafioso, asks Mick for a rush job. There's a woman (Mimi Rogers) who must be removed immediately. Why? Well...it's hard to say exactly, but this is going to be easy. She's expecting Mick and wants to die. What? Director Malone paces the film like a stage play, stretching out two-character scenes and emphasizing dialogue over action. And this is a talky film, much like *Pulp Fiction* in that area. It's also unpredictable and suspenseful all the way to an offbeat conclusion that doesn't attempt to answer every question. *Bulletproof Heart* is well acted, handsomely produced, and enjoyable. Recommended to those in the mood for a mystery with a psychological bent. **AKA:** Killer. 🦴🦴🦴

Strong language, some violence, sexual material, brief nudity.

1995 (R) 96m/C Anthony LaPaglia, Mimi Rogers, Peter Boyle, Matt Craven, Monika Schnarre, Joseph Maher; **D:** Mark Malone; **W:** Gordon Melbourne. Mark Malone; **C:** Tobias Schliessler; **M:** Graeme Coleman. **VHS, LV** *REP*

Burial of the Rats

This Russian-American cable production is a throwback to those terrific Hammer films of the 1950s and '60s. It has the same look and cheeky attitude toward its "classic" horror source. The wacky tale begins in the 1860s with young aspiring writer Bram Stoker (Kevin Alber) being abducted by ruthless swordfighting lesbian feminist rat-worshippers in black leather thong bikinis. Madeleine (Maria Ford) and the rest serve the Queen of Vermin (Adrienne Barbeau) whose aim is to unseat the male power structure of the village of St. Cecile. Just as soon as her minions finish the topless modern dance routine. The pace is quick, and the humor is intentional. Great stuff for drive-in fans. **AKA:** Roger Corman

RONALD K. ARMSTRONG AND PRISCILLA BASQUE IN *BUGGED!* ©TROMA TEAM VIDEO.

Presents Burial of the Rats; Bram Stoker's Burial of the Rats. 🦴🦴🦴

Violence, nudity, sexual content.

1995 (R) 77m/C Adrienne Barbeau, Maria Ford, Kevin Alber; **D:** Dan Golden. **VHS** *NHO*

Burndown

This bozo has something to do with a serial murderer and an inactive nuclear power plant, but it's impossible to watch without a functioning fast-forward button. The pace is leaden; the script is filled with amateurish dialogue and even though the action is supposed to be set in Florida, the actors speak with unplaceable accents. Heroine Cathy Moriarty sounds like she phoned in her performance from Fairbanks. **WOOF!**

Violence, profanity, suggestive material.

1989 (R) 97m/C Cathy Moriarty, Peter Firth; **D:** James Allen. **VHS, LV** *NO*

Cabin Fever

Deborah Shames' first short feature is unashamed eroticism for women. It's a simple, two-character story about an older woman (Belinda Farrell) on sabbatical in a remote cottage, the younger handyman (Judd Dunning) who's working there, and the physical relationship that develops between them. Writer/director Shames has a background in serious educational films and Disney television documentaries. She knows the business of filmmaking well enough to have spent a limited budget wisely. The 45-minute story is told with solid, if not lavish production values. It's sexy, not explicit, with an emphasis on lusty romanticism and humor—a fine introduction to Shames' subsequent features, *The Hottest Bid* and *The Voyeur.* 🦴🦴🦴

Nudity and sexual material.

1993 45m/C Belinda Farrell, Judd Dunning; **D:** Deborah Shames; **W:** Deborah Shames. **VHS** *DEB*

Caged Heat 2: Stripped of Freedom

The original *Caged Heat* has earned a measure of fame as the debut of director Jonathan Demme. The sequel isn't likely to repeat, though it's certainly lively enough. CIA agent Amanda (Jewel Shepard) gets herself locked up in the tropical Rock Island Prison to rescue Princess Marga (Chanel Akiko Hirai). Veteran Vic Diaz repeats his familiar role as the warden. Pamella D'Pella takes over for Pam Grier. From the 1970s to the '90s, this particular school of exploitation has evolved (if that's the right word) to embrace feminist sisterhood and to de-emphasize sex and nudity. Anxious fans must wonder: Is this progress? 🦴🦴

Language, nudity, violence, and sexual situations.

1994 **(R)** 84m/**C** Jewel Shepard, Chanel Akiko Hirai, Pamella D'Pella, Vic Diaz; **D:** Cirio H. Santiago. **VHS, LV** *NHO*

Caged Heat 3000

Though the box copy makes the dubious boast that "*Caged Heat 3000* takes the women-in-prison genre to a whole new level," it must refer to a whole new low. With the exception of the star and a couple of others, this is the most unattractive cast—male and female—ever assembled for a bad movie. It's also a whole new level of cheapness, with silly sets and costumes made from plastic sheeting. Fans know that this kind of exploitation can overcome its shortcomings with outrageous humor and inventiveness—not this time, though. Also available in an unrated version. 🦴

Nudity, violence, strong language, sexual content.

1995 **(R)** m/**C** Cassandra Leigh, Debra Beatty, Robert J. Ferilli, Kena Land; **D:** Aaron Osborne. **VHS** *NHO*

Cannibal! The Musical

This feature began as a stage play at the Uni-

Caged Heat 2: Stripped of Freedom. ©New Horizons Home Video.

Cannibal Women in the Avocado Jungle of Death

Who could not love a title like this? It's a parody of the John Milius brand of chest-thumping, macho adventure movie. "Respected middle-of-the-road feminist" and ethno-historian Dr. Hunt (Shannon Tweed) is hired to go into the dangerous Avocado Jungle, located just east of Los Angeles, and find out what happened to Dr. Kurtz (Adrienne Barbeau), who disappeared there. Was she killed by the man-hating Piranha Women, or has she gone native and joined them? Some of the jokes are obvious, but the comedy is more inventive and intelligent than a lot of big-budget films. Tweed underplays the cool comedy effectively. Writer/director J.D. Athens (actually J.F. Lawton, writer of *Pretty Woman* and *Under Siege*) didn't have much of a budget to work with, but he came up with the kind of sassy little satire that makes home video as much fun as it is. 🦴🦴🦴

Brief toplessness, profanity, mild violence.

1989 (PG-13) 90m/C Shannon Tweed, Adrienne Barbeau, Karen Mistal, Barry Primus, Bill Maher; *D:* J.F. Lawton; *W:* J.F. Lawton. **VHS, LV** *PAR*

Capone

When FBI agent Michael Roarke (Keith Carradine) puts a dent in Al Capone's (Ray Sharkey) organization, the gangster goes after his wife (Jayne Atkinson) and kids. But the stronger threat turns out to be a seductive speak-easy waitress (Debrah Farentino). At its best, the script by Tracy Keenan Wynn shows how morally ambiguous those times were, when everyone broke the law. On the street level, the cops and the crooks were less adversaries than guys who called each other by first names and knew that they were playing the same game. Elliot Ness and J. Edgar Hoover are presented as self-promoting publicity seekers. The late Ray Sharkey turns Capone into a rabid villain straight out of a *Batman* movie, but it's somehow appropriate to the story. Carradine, a severely underrated actor,

versity of Colorado. Now it has become a Troma movie, proving that sometimes the system works. The subject is Alferd Packer (Juan Schwartz), who was convicted of cannibalism in 19th century Colorado. (Didn't the students at UC once vote to name the new dining hall after him?) Though this is 100 percent pure Troma with unapologetically cheesy ambiance and effects, the film is also true to its undergraduate roots with smart, irreverent, cheerfully tasteless humor. Writer/director Trey Parker uses a cheeky attitude to compensate for an inexperienced cast and whatever-works locations and sets. 🦴🦴🦴

Violence, subject matter.

1996 (R) 105m/C Ian Hardin, Jason McHugh, Matt Stone, Trey Parker, Juan Schwartz; *D:* Trey Parker; *W:* Trey Parker. **VHS** *TTV*

plays Roarke as an ordinary man trying to do his job. Veteran Michael Pressman uses the locations to create a strong sense of time and place. This one is not one of the great gangster pictures, but it takes an unusual angle on a familiar story. 🦴🦴🦴

Strong language, violence, brief nudity, sexual content.

1989 (R) 96m/C Ray Sharkey, Keith Carradine, Debrah Farentino, Jayne Atkinson; *D:* Michael Pressman; *W:* Tracy Keenan Wynn. **VHS, LV** *VMK*

Caribe

John Savage, as a British (?!) agent in Belize, provides voiceover narration that sounds like *Apocalypse Now,* but in the action scenes the film tries to look like *Miami Vice.* That's an uncomfortable mix for a non-thrilling tropical thriller about guns and drugs and general craziness and stuff like that. Most of the flick is slow and predictable, but sometimes it loses control and begins to resemble an Oliver North fantasy of Contras and bad guys. Toward the end, the action becomes more violent and a little sick. 🦴🦴

Violence, profanity, sexual situations.

1987 (R) 90m/C John Savage, Kara Glover, Stephen McHattie, Sam Malkin; *D:* Michael Kennedy. **VHS, LV** *LIV, VES*

Carnosaur

The title sequence—some really disgusting stuff apparently filmed in a real chicken processing plant—sets the tone for your basic mad-scientist plot with several environmental twists. Dr. Jane Tiptree (Diane Ladd), the mad scientist in question, has been up to something nefarious out in the Nevada desert. It has to do with nasty but unseen critters who attack chickens. If the dinosaur effects created by John Buechler and Magical Media Industries aren't as realistic and convincing as Spielberg's Jurassic monsters, they're not all bad, either. In fact, they're much more believable than you'd normally find in more expensive productions. But they're not the only point to the film. Writer/director Adam Simon has a wicked sense of humor that gets consistently stronger and more crazed as the movie goes along. Toward the end, it becomes downright Strangelovian. *Carnosaur* is such an energetic B-movie treat that it's probably worth a trip to the back of the rack to find Simon's earlier work, *Brain Dead* and *Body Chemistry 2.* 🦴🦴🦴🦴

Graphic violence, strong language.

1993 (R) 82m/C Diane Ladd, Raphael Sbarge, Jennifer Runyon, Harrison Page, Clint Howard, Ned Bellamy; *D:* Adam Simon; *W:* Adam Simon; *M:* Nigel Holton. **VHS** *NHO*

Carnosaur 2

The real inspiration for this sequel isn't *Jurassic Park* but James Cameron's *Aliens.* The mutant-chicken dinosaurs from the first film are back and looking for more human Happy Meals in a super-secret government installation that's about to blow up. Tick, tick, tick. Overall, the acting is better than average and the dialogue has that gritty quality that made Cameron's early work so much fun. Director Louis Morneau keeps things moving quickly enough that the plot lapses and less-than-stellar special effects aren't fatal. 🦴🦴

Violence, strong language.

1994 (R) 90m/C John Savage, Cliff DeYoung, Arabella Holzbog, Ryan Thomas Johnson; *D:* Louis Morneau. **VHS, LV** *NHO*

Caroline at Midnight

Reporter Clayton Rohner is working on a hot story about police corruption when he gets a

---

telephone call from an old girlfriend who died in a mysterious car crash years before. That gets him hooked up with a vicious cop (Timothy Daly) and his abused wife (Mia Sara). Travis Rink's script is unusually tight and complicated, and director Scott McGinnis did a lot with a limited budget. He made a solid sleeper. ♫♫♫

Violence, strong language, drug use, sexual content, nudity.

1993 (R) 92m/C Clayton Rohner, Mia Sara, Timothy Daly, Judd Nelson, Virginia Madsen, Zach Galligan; *D:* Scott McGinnis; *W:* Travis Rink. **VHS, LV** *NHO*

Carried Away

"What can I say? I'm a bad man. Sometimes it's fun to be bad." That's Joseph Svenden (Dennis Hopper), 47, explaining his affair with Catherine Wheeler (Amy Locane), 17. It's not a flippant line; it's an accurate description of what's going on in Bruno Barreto's adaptation of Jim Harrison's novel, *Farmer.* The setting is a bleak, wintry Midwest where Joseph teaches at a two-room school. Rosalie (Amy Irving) teaches in the other room. She and Joseph have a comfortable "arrangement" until Catherine arrives. Actually, everyone in Howardsville plays their expected roles—the doctor (Hal Holbrook), Joseph's dying mother (Julie Harris), even Catherine's father (Gary Busey). Brazilian Barreto seems comfortable with this uniquely American—almost Faulknerian—material. In most of the important scenes he uses a strong horizontal light to emphasize the flat landscape. While telling the highly charged story, he values honesty over discretion, leaving himself open to charges of exploitation. But that's not his point. The film is sexy, well acted, and not without humor. Hopper proves again that he can be effective in an understated dramatic role. *AKA:* Acts of Love. ♫♫♫

Mature subject matter, nudity, sexual content, language, some violence.

1995 (R) 105m/C Dennis Hopper, Amy Locane, Gary Busey, Hal Holbrook, Amy Irving, Julie Harris, Christopher Pettiet, Priscilla

Pointer, Gail Cronauer; *D:* Bruno Barreto; *W:* Ed Jones; *C:* Declan Quinn; *M:* Bruce Broughton. **VHS, LV** *NLC*

Cartel

Star Miles O'Keeffe is a graduate of the Clint Eastwood school of unemotional squinting. Even in the action scenes of this nutty thriller, he moves and talks like a 45 rpm record played at 33. It's all about drug smuggling in small planes, corruption, jail breaks, and revenge. Too slow and brutal. Look for B-movie veterans William Smith and Don Stroud. ♫♫

Graphic violence, profanity, brief nudity.

1990 (R) 106m/C Miles O'Keeffe, Don Stroud, Crystal Carson, William Smith; *D:* John Stewart; *C:* Thomas Callaway. **VHS, LV** *IME*

A Case for Murder

Chicago lawyer Jack Hammet (Peter Berg) has a reputation for winning "Hail Mary" criminal cases, but his ethics, both professional and personal, are questionable. When one of his colleagues is killed and the man's widow (Belinda Bauer) is accused of the murder, Jack takes on her defense. Assisting him is the new girl in town, Kate Weldon (Jennifer Grey), whose career contains a few question marks, too. That's a good, ambiguous premise for the script by Pablo Fenjves and director Duncan Gibbins. Though the pace drags, the film works through the characters. They're a complex, unconventional bunch, particularly Jack. Is he an ambitious and ruthless flawed hero? Is he a womanizing jerk or something much worse? That calculated uncertainty raises this one above the normal level of the genre. ♫♫♫

Strong language, sexual content, violence.

1993 (R) 94m/C Peter Berg, Jennifer Grey, Belinda Bauer; *D:* Duncan Gibbins; *W:* Duncan Gibbins, Pablo F. Fenjves. **VHS, LV** *MCA*

Castle Freak

Straightforward Gothic horror flick even contains a night shot of said castle with a single

ALFERD PACKER (JUAN SCHWARTZ), CANNIBAL, PREPARES TO DINE IN *CANNIBAL! THE MUSICAL.* ©TROMA TEAM VIDEO.

window lit, just like you used to see behind the lady in the negligee on the covers of paperback romances. In standard fashion, the story begins with the Reillys—father John (Jeffrey Combs), mother Susan (Barbara Crampton), and blind daughter Rebecca (Jessica Dollarhide)—going to the Italian castle they've inherited. The title character, in desperate need of a manicure and a makeover, is locked in the basement. Who is he? What is he doing there? Director Stuart Gordon establishes a creepy mood and punctuates it with some sharp humor. He also comes up with a wild finale, but nothing here equals the shameful delights that Gordon, Combs, and Crampton reached in their camp classic *Re-Animator.* 🐾🐾🐾

Graphic violence, sexual content, nudity, strong language.

1995 (R) 90m/C Jeffrey Combs, Barbara Crampton, Jonathan Fuller, Jessica Dollarhide; *D:* Stuart Gordon; *W:* Dennis Paoli; *C:* Mario Vulpiani; *M:* Richard Band. **VHS, LV** *FLL*

Cat Chaser

George Moran (Peter Weller) owns a low-budget Miami Beach motel. On vacation, he runs into an old acquaintance (Kelly McGillis) and they begin a high-octane affair. The problem is her husband, a wealthy deposed dictator who'll kill both of them if he finds out. Complicating matters further are a boozy drifter (Frederic Forrest), a none-too-honest cop (Charles Durning), and a suitcase full of cash. The plot is fairly faithful to Elmore Leonard's novel—he co-wrote the script—and director Abel Ferrara (famous for the cult hits *Ms. 45* and *The King of New York*) seems to have understood the mood and quirky unpredictability of the novel. But where did the ridiculous, third-person voiceover narration come from? In an interview, Leonard said that he knew this film had been made and been released in England. He also thought that some kind of narration had been added, but he had nothing to do with it. 🐾🐾🐾

Nudity, sexual content, strong language, graphic violence.

1990 97m/C Kelly McGillis, Peter Weller, Charles Durning, Frederic Forrest, Tomas Milian, Juan Fernandez; *D:* Abel Ferrara; *W:* Elmore Leonard, Jim Borrelli; *M:* Chick Corea. **VHS** *VES*

Cellblock Sisters: Banished Behind Bars

They're sexy siblings in the slammer. Yes, they're "Cellblock Sisters"! Separated as children, May (Gail Harris) and April (Annie Wood) are reunited but find themselves locked up with the wonderfully evil Manny (Jenna Bodnar). Director Henri Charr is an old hand at this particular brand of exploitation. He keeps the action quick, silly, and breezy. It's the contemporary video equivalent of 1950s and '60s drive-in fare. 🗡🗡🗡

Violence, strong language, nudity, sexual content, shower scenes.

1995 (R) 95m/C Gail Harris, Annie Wood, Ace Ross, Jenna Bodnar; *D:* Henri Charr. **VHS** *PMH*

Century

In the England of 1900, old rules and conventions are falling away and new ideas are being tested. Paul Reisner (Clive Owen), the son of a Rumanian Jewish emigrant (Robert Stephens), leaves his country home to work with Professor Mandry (Charles Dance) at a new medical research institute in London. Paul is immediately attracted to Clara (Miranda Richardson), a bright young lab assistant. At first, Paul's intelligence and curiosity serve him well with Mandry. Those same qualities also lead to curious conflicts and even more curious resolutions. Writer/director Stephen Poliakoff (*Close My Eyes*) has said that the film is loosely based on experiences of his grandfather. Perhaps because of that, parts of the story have the feel of truth, though that's not Poliakoff's point. He's interested in the characters, and these are believable, interesting, and extremely well portrayed. A genuine sleeper for fans of *Masterpiece Theatre* historical drama. 🗡🗡🗡

Mature subject matter, nudity, sexual content.

1994 (R) 112m/C *GB* Clive Owen, Charles Dance, Miranda Richardson, Robert Stephens, Joan Hickson, Lena Headey, Neil Stuke; *D:* Stephen Poliakoff; *W:* Stephen Poliakoff; *C:* Witold Stok; *M:* Michael Gibbs. **VHS** *PGV*

Chameleon

An enjoyable, almost-too-much star turn by Anthony LaPaglia is the main attraction here. He plays an undercover cop whose traumatic past may have driven him over the edge of sanity. Investigating a drug/money-laundering ring, he submerges himself so deeply in the roles he assumes that his boss Kevin Pollak becomes worried. The rest of the plot is standard movie thriller stuff, a little slow and, at the end, cliched, but LaPaglia's performance overcomes the flaws. 🗡🗡🗡

Violence, strong language.

1995 (R) 108m/C Anthony LaPaglia, Kevin Pollak, Melora Hardin, Wayne Knight; *D:* Michael Pavone; *W:* Dave Allen Johnson, Michael Pavone; *C:* Ross Berryman; *M:* John Debney. **VHS** *AVE*

Charleen and Backyard

Fans of Ross McElwee's *Sherman's March* should take a look at two of his earlier short films available on one tape. "Charleen" is a 1978 portrait of Charleen Whisnant, who's so prominent in *Sherman's March*. In that film, she's the mother figure who's trying to get McElwee married to the Mormon girl. She's also a well-known writer, poet, and teacher in Charlotte, N.C. The cliche "larger-than-life" doesn't begin to describe the original "Designing Woman." She's funny, smart, bawdy, bursting with life, and wonderfully melodramatic. She prepares for a poetry "performance," argues with her boyfriend, has troubles with her teenaged daughter, worries about getting older, talks about her past with Ezra Pound, and frets over work and money. McElwee's fans will recognize his no-frills, handheld style immediately. He uses the same close-up camera, and is more than willing to sacrifice the visual element of film if something interesting is being said. More important, he demonstrates the same dry, deadpan humor that brightens the sometimes slow action. The

same holds true for his 1976 film, "Backyard." It's about a homecoming as he revisits his home in Charlotte after a stay in the North. The main characters are his family, and, yes, that looks like the famous MG from *Sherman* in one shot near a garage. Without Charleen Whisnant's commanding presence, "Backyard" will probably seem slow and pointless to viewers who aren't familiar with McElwee's other work. It does have something of a plot, though, and again, that understated McElwee humor. The conclusion is surprisingly strong and touching. ♫♫♫

Contains some scenes of surgery.

1978 95m/C *D:* Ross McElwee. **VHS** *ICA*

Cheyenne Warrior

Glamor girl Kelly Preston isn't at all persuasive as Rebecca Carver, a pregnant pioneer woman doing the best she can to prepare for winter after her husband is killed. Her only ally—and she doesn't trust him much—is Soars Like a Hawk (Pato Hoffmann), the title character. The villains include vengeful Pawnee Indians and Kearney (Rick Dean), an evil Irishman who revels in his own wickedness. Despite budget limitations, director Mark Griffiths evokes the sense of space and the loneliness of the West as well as Clint Eastwood did in *Unforgiven*. Most of the action seems fairly realistic, too, though Michael Druxman's script only hints at the overt racism of the times. ♫♫♫

Violence, strong language, mature subject matter.

1994 **(PG-13)** 90m/C Kelly Preston, Pato Hoffmann, Bo Hopkins, Dan Haggerty, Charles Powell, Rick Dean, Clint Howard; *D:* Mark Griffiths; *W:* Michael B. Druxman. **VHS, LV** *NHO*

China Moon

Kyle Bodine (Ed Harris) is the best homicide detective in Brayton, Florida. He's got a lot to teach his rookie partner (Benicio Del Toro). But neither of them are a match for Rachel Munro (Madeleine Stowe), the abused wife of Rupert (Charles Dance), an all-around rat, albeit a wealthy rat. You can take it from there. Writer Roy Carlson's story isn't exactly filled with surprises, but who cares? It covers

familiar *Body Heat* ground competently enough, and if Harris and Stowe don't generate William Hurt-Kathleen Turner fireworks, they will keep your attention. Director John Bailey is best known as a cinematographer (*In the Line of Fire, Ordinary People*), so a strong visual style, particularly in the night scenes, often supersedes substance. ♫♫♫

Strong language, sexual content, brief nudity, violence.

1991 **(R)** 99m/C Ed Harris, Madeleine Stowe, Benicio Del Toro, Charles Dance; *D:* John Bailey; *W:* Roy Carlson; *M:* George Fenton. **VHS, LV** *ORI*

Chopper Chicks in Zombietown

Troma strikes again! The title says it all as a female motorcycle gang tries to keep a little town being from overrun by the living dead. The general level of humor is established by jokes involving a dwarf and a busload of blind orphans. Even the gory special effects are fairly tame. Flesh-eating zombie stuff has been done so often that it's not even disgusting any more, though this flick may set a record for living-dead decapitations. ♫♫

Violence, strong language.

1991 **(R)** 86m/C Jamie Rose, Catherine Carlen, Lycia Naff, Vicki Frederick, Kristina Loggia, Martha Quinn, Don Calfa; *D:* Dan Hoskins; *W:* Dan Hoskins. **VHS, LV** *COL, NLC*

Chuck Amuck: The Movie

Chuck Jones was responsible for many of the wonderful Warner Bros. cartoons of the 1940s-'60s. He didn't invent Bugs Bunny and Daffy Duck, but he refined them and made them the characters they are today. He sums them up perfectly when he says, "Bugs is an aspiration. Daffy is a realization." His most famous original creations—Pepe LePew, the Coyote and Roadrunner—receive star treatment here. Writer/producer/director John Needham touches lightly on Jones' childhood and early professional career. He also gives a quick overview of the development of a cartoon from storyboard ideas to finished product. But

most of the film is devoted to a fascinating drawing lesson. The camera literally peeks over Chuck Jones' shoulder as he makes pencil sketches of his characters and talks about them in detail. He shows, for example, how all Warner Bros. animated figures have the same basic body shape and how it varies. He explains why the Coyote's knees and elbows look a certain way, and notes that Bugs had either four or six whiskers, depending on the budget of the particular cartoon. Needham follows the example Jones set in his autobiography of the same title and is quick to give credit where it is due. While Chuck Jones is the genius who came up with many of the original ideas, those couldn't have been realized without the contributions of designer Maurice Noble, artist Mike Maltese and, of course, the vocal work of Mel Blanc. They receive special recognition. Without ever resorting to schmaltz or sentimentality, *Chuck Amuck: The Movie* is a fine, overdue tribute to a filmmaker whose work has often been dismissed as kid stuff by critics. Audiences of all ages have always known better. A must-see (maybe even a must-own) for any animation fan. 𝄞𝄞𝄞𝄞

Contains no offense material.

1991 51m/C Chuck Jones; **D**: John Needham; **W**: John Needham. **VHS** *WAR, FCT*

Ciao, Professore!

Lina Wertmuller's updated *To Sir, With Love* has a distinct Italian flavor. Loosely based on a best-selling book of elementary-school student essays, the film is about Marco Sperelli (Paolo Villaggio), a teacher who's sent to Corzano, a small town in southern Italy. He finds an empty classroom. The kids are all out working; the principal doesn't care; and effective control of the whole school has been turned over to a janitor who charges students for toilet paper. In short, Marco's work is cut out for him. His education and urban background don't count for much as he does whatever he can to get the kids—a gang of cute, foul-mouthed ragamuffins—into their seats and teach them something. Much of the conflict is based on the deep-seated mistrust and suspicion that exist between the prosperous northern part of the country and the poorer and less sophisticated south. The key to the film is the winning performance by Villaggio, the popular equivalent of Tim Allen on Italian television and film. He's a thoroughly engaging hero, a rotund teddy-bear who holds his own even when surrounded by his pint-sized co-stars. The lack of a strong plot gives director/co-writer Wertmuller time to make the setting more than a backdrop for the action. The place becomes the key to the human characters, and the characters are a delight. *AKA:* Io Speriamo Che Me La Cavo. 𝄞𝄞𝄞

Strong language, subject matter.

1994 (R) 91m/C *IT* Paolo Villaggio, Isa Danieli, Ciro Esposito; **D**: Lina Wertmuller; **W**: Leo Benvenuti, Piero De Bernardi, Alessandro Bencivenni, Domenico Saverni, Lina Wertmuller. **VHS, LV** *MAX*

Circuitry Man

In a stylishly bleak future that borrows freely from *Blade Runner, Mad Max,* and *Max Headroom,* people have been driven underground by pollution. A tough loner (Dana Wheeler-Nicholson) and an emotional robot (Jim Metzler) are on the run from a group of gonzo bad guys. Plughead (Vernon Wells) likes to experience other people's pain, and Yo-yo (Barbara Alyn Woods) is a tough-talking gangster. The main problems are a leaden pace and apparent ignorance of basic storytelling techniques. But the acting is above average, the characters are interesting, and beneath the gritty surface, there's a strange likable quality to the film. Followed by an unnecessary sequel. 𝄞𝄞𝄞

Violence, strong language, sexual material.

1990 (R) 85m/C Jim Metzler, Dana Wheeler-Nicholson, Lu Leonard, Vernon Wells, Barbara Alyn Woods, Dennis Christopher; **D**: Steven Lovy; **W**: Steven Lovy; **M**: Deborah Holland. **VHS, LV** *COL*

Class of Nuke 'Em High 2: Subhumanoid Meltdown

Why are the students at Nuke 'Em High acting so strangely? Where did the Godzilla-sized

squirrel come from? What does Professor Holt (Lisa Gaye) have hidden in her Marge Simpson hairdo? What's wrong with Victoria's (Leesa Rowland) navel? Why can't handsome but dumb-as-a-post Roger (Brick Bronsky) get a date? Troma devotees will be delighted; all others will be disgusted. Even judged by the studio's own loose standards, this one is a high watermark in overall cheesiness. Followed by another sequel. 🦴🦴🦴

Strong language, nudity, violence.

1991 **(R)** 96m/**C** Lisa Gaye, Brick Bronsky, Leesa Rowland; **D:** Eric Louzil. **VHS, LV** *VTR, MED, FXV*

Class of Nuke 'Em High 3: The Good, the Bad and the Subhumanoid

Irreverent, free-wheeling Troma schlock comedy targets environmentalism, political satire, potty jokes, and sex, all in wonderfully poor taste. Though it was crushed by a giant mutant Godzilla-like squirrel at the end of *Part 2,* Tromaville's state-of-the-art student-run nuclear power facility has reopened, and it's up to Adlai Smith (Brick Bronsky in three roles) to save the town, the school, and his girlfriend (Lisa Star) from the evil Prof. Holt (Lisa Gaye), she of the Marge Simpson hair. Troma films being the acquired taste that they are, *Nuke 'Em High 3* is probably best left to the initiated. Neophytes should work up to it through the first two, and be warned, the producers promise (or threaten) *Class of Nuke 'Em High 4: Battle of the Bikini Subhumanoids.* 🦴🦴

Nudity, comic sexual content and violence, humor.

1994 **(R)** 103m/**C** Brick Bronsky, Lisa Gaye, Lisa Star; **D:** Eric Louzil; **W:** Lloyd (Samuel Weil) Kaufman. **VHS** *TTV*

Class of '61

Can a video original make the Civil War seem real to a young audience? This one focuses on the contradictions, divided loyalties, and hypocrisies that existed in both North and South. The story begins with the firing on Fort Sumter and ends at the battle of First Manassas. It follows three West Point cadets (Clive Owen, Dan Futterman, and Joshua Lucas) who choose sides and live or die with those choices. Writer Jonas McCord tries to capture the spirit of those terrible times in the dialogue, and so many of the characters in a large cast climb on soapboxes to deliver political proclamations. Realistic or not, those moments are hard for today's audiences to accept. McCord also uses the racial language of the times and that's even more shocking. The overlapping differences and similarities between North and South are equally difficult to dramatize. How does a filmmaker show confusion without being confusing? Director Gregory Hoblit doesn't always succeed, despite technical advice from Shelby Foote. The battle scenes appear to have been filmed with help from re-enactors, so they have an authentic feel,

though they never come close to the believability and emotional power of *Glory*. Stephen Spielberg is listed as executive producer, and the film has the polished look of mid-budget studio production. Given the curious structure of the story, and the many loose ends left unresolved, it feels like the first part or chapter of a longer work. The next installment will probably be better. ♫♫

Contains strong racial language, some violence.

1992 95m/C Dan Futterman, Clive Owen, Joshua Lucas, Sophie Ward, Laura Linney, Andre Braugher, Len Cariou, Dana Ivey, Scott Burkholder, Niall O'Brien, Christien Anholt, Paul Guilfoyle, Beverly Todd, Ed Wiley, Sue-Ann Leeds; **D:** Gregory Hoblit; **W:** Jonas McCord; **C:** Janusz Kaminski. **VHS** *MCA*

A Climate for Killing

In the desert near a small southwestern town, a woman's body is found with head and hands missing. For personal reasons, the coroner (Katherine Ross) knows the victim's identity.

CLASS OF NUKE 'EM HIGH 3: THE GOOD, THE BAD AND THE SUBHUMANOID. ©TROMA TEAM VIDEO.

The problem is that she had been declared dead 16 years before in a murder-suicide. That sounds more confusing than it really is. The characters carry the weight of this story. Writer/director J.S. Cardone got good performances from a seasoned cast, and the production values belie what must have been a fairly low budget. The story is told well with a satisfying resolution, and that's what most mystery fans are looking for. 🗡🗡🗡

Strong language, violence, brief nudity.

1991 (R) 104m/C Steven Bauer, John Beck, Katharine Ross, Mia Sara, John Diehl, Phil Brock, Dedee Pfeiffer, Lu Leonard, Jack Dodson, Eloy Casados; *D:* J.S. Cardone; *W:* J.S. Cardone; *M:* Robert Folk. **VHS, LV** *MED*

Close My Eyes

Incest is a difficult subject, and this English film deals with it about as successfully as any popular entertainment could. As children, Natalie (Saskia Reeves) and her brother Richard (Clive Owen) weren't close, and they see each other only occasionally as adults. That changes after she marries Sinclair (Alan Rickman). To his credit, writer/director Stephen Poliakoff handles the material seriously. He's interested in the emotional side of the characters and their situation. The film is uncomfortable, not exploitative. It's also a bit slow. At first, the pace is languid; the siblings seem little more than fuzzy, self-absorbed characters. When Rickman shows up, sparks fly. He turns in the same kind of winning performance that made him so successful in *Die Hard* and *Robin Hood, Prince of Thieves,* though here he's completely sympathetic. He generates the most interest in this romantic triangle, and for a time, the uncertain relationship among the three is interesting and suspenseful. Then, right in the middle, the plot takes a huge illogical turn—the kind that makes you laugh at the characters for being so foolish—and the film never completely recovers. 🗡🗡🗡

Mature subject matter, brief nudity, strong language.

1991 (R) 105m/C *GB* Alan Rickman, Clive Owen, Saskia Reeves; *D:* Stephen Poliakoff. **VHS** *ACA*

Close to Eden

This nominee for the Best Foreign Language Film Oscar is a comedy that will be difficult for many Western viewers to appreciate. The setting is Mongolia where, after a slow and confusing introduction, a shepherd and a Russian road builder become friends. Though the performances are very good, the cultural differences both between the characters and between the characters and American audiences are so vast that the humor is hard to catch. I, for one, pretty much lost interest when a sheep was slaughtered, skinned, and cooked on camera. Yes, I admit there's a certain hypocrisy at work when a carnivorous video writer objects to watching the reality behind his own lunch, which he happened to be eating at the time. But the death of an animal is not entertainment and there's nothing in either the box art or copy, or the rating (PG!) to indicate that the film is going to be so graphic. *AKA:* Urga. 🗡🗡

Onscreen animal slaughter, strong language, sexual content.

1990 (PG) 109m/C *RU* Baoyinhexige, Badema, Nikita Mikhalkov; *D:* Nikita Mikhalkov; *W:* Rustam Ibragimbekov; *M:* Eduard Artemyev. Venice Film Festival '91: Best Film; Nominations: Academy Awards '92: Best Foreign Language Film. **VHS** *PAR, FCT*

The Club

The kids at Eastern High School have decided to hold their prom in a castle and to dress up in Renaissance costumes, giving the rest of the action the atmosphere of a Hammer movie. Beyond the usual adolescent angst of loneliness and breaking up is hard to do, etc., there are other problems. One of the chaperones is a serial murderer, and at the stroke of midnight, time stops. Someone on the dance committee has a lot of explaining to do. Six kids and the aforementioned chaperone find that everyone else has disappeared. One of them (Matthew Ferguson) is carefully made up to look like Johnny Depp, and another (Joel Wyner) is a dead ringer for Jim Carrey. He injects a manical sense of humor to the second half of the film that almost makes up for the predictable Gothic scares. The story is similar to Sam Raimi's *Evil Dead,* but this variation on the standard dead-teenager plot lacks the out-of-control pace and crazed energy that make Raimi's films so much fun. 🎜🎜

Graphic effects, violence, strong language, sexual content, brief nudity.

1994 (R) 88m/C Kim Coates, Joel Wyner, Andrea Roth, Rino Romano, Zack Ward, Kelli Taylor, Matthew Ferguson; *D:* Benton Spencer; *W:* Robert Cooper; *M:* Paul Zaza. **VHS, LV** *IMP*

Cold Comfort

Consider a strange little Canadian backwater somewhere between Lake Wobegon and Twin Peaks. That's where a disturbed father kidnaps a lover for his daughter on her 18th birthday. As the unstable dad, Maury Chaykin looks like John Candy playing Norman Bates. He's so creepy and surprising that he dominates the film. Margaret Langrick, as his daughter, and Paul Gross, as the kidnapped travelling salesman, fade into the wallpaper when Chaykin cuts loose. The story's roots on the stage are evident in the slow stretchs, but most of the time, director Vic Sarin keeps the action moving. The violence and sexual content of the material are handled with restraint. For comparative purposes, this one is similar to an odd 1972 film, *The Strange Vengeance of Rosalie,* and Stephen King's *Misery.* 🎜🎜🎜

Mature subject matter, profanity, brief nudity, some violence.

1990 (R) 90m/C *CA* Margaret Langrick, Maury Chaykin, Paul Gross; *D:* Vic Sarin. **VHS** *REP*

Cold Sweat

Dark, tongue-in-cheek humor lifts this crime thriller/ghost story above the expected levels of either genre. The main players are a hitman (Ben Cross) haunted by the ghost of a recent victim, a financially strapped businessman (Dave Thomas), his faithless wife (Shannon Tweed), and their drug-dealer (Adam Baldwin). The plot moves along in standard fashion for about an hour and then comes thoroughly unhinged in the last act. Like so many Canadian productions, the film has a bleak look and a standard plot that's twisted into

unexpected directions. Not to all tastes but quirky. 🎜🎜

Nudity and sexual material, some violence.

1993 (R) 93m/C *CA* Ben Cross, Shannon Tweed, Adam Baldwin, Dave Thomas; *D:* Gail Harvey; *W:* Richard Beattie. **VHS** *PAR, VTR*

Coldfire

O.K., this cop flick isn't veteran Wings Hauser's finest moment, but it's still worth a look. The mechanics of the plot, about a highly addictive and lethal new drug, are overly familiar. Some talented character actors, particularly Addison Randall as the villain, keep the movie interesting. 🎜🎜

Profanity, violence, nudity.

1990 (R) 90m/C Wings Hauser, Kamar Reyes, Robert Viharo, Gary Swanson, Addison Randall; *D:* Wings Hauser. **VHS, LV** *PMH*

The Colony

Thriller rises above its made-for-TV roots, but it doesn't rise quite high enough. Rick Knowlton (John Ritter) has had it with city life—carjackings, bad schools, etc.—when he's unexpectedly invited to live in The Colony, an exclusive and expensive security-conscious subdivision up in the hills above the ocean. He designs security systems and his company has just cut a deal with Phillip Denning (Hal Linden), the billionaire behind the development. Once Rick and his wife (Mary Page Keller) and computer-whiz daughter move in, they find that paradise is something more than it's cracked up to be. Are they living in the Stepford Subdivision, and giving up their freedom for an enhanced "quality of life"? Seen simply as an exercise in suspense, the film does most of the right things. At its best, though, it begins to explore the appeal of fascism. After all, the Nazis didn't attract converts by telling them that they'd be joining a movement that would become synonymous with evil. No. They promised safety, the companionship of likeminded, upright neighbors, and good things for the kids. If you disagree with that, what's wrong with you? Casting Linden and

Lassie's mom June Lockhart as the Colony's main boosters is inspired, but the film too quickly settles into familiar grooves. Had writer/director Rob Hedden's ideas been fully developed, the film might have been a grand sleeper. *ᗒᗕᗒ*

Mature subject matter, mild violence, strong language.

1995 (PG-13) 93m/C John Ritter, Hal Linden, Mary Page Keller, Marshall Teague, Frank Bonner, Michelle Scarabelli, June Lockhart, Todd Jeffries, Alexandra Picatto, Cody Dorkin; *D:* Rob Hedden; *W:* Rob Hedden. **VHS** *MCA*

Color of Night

Anyone who takes this wacky flick seriously will detest it. But those who see it as a parody of *Basic Instinct* thrillers will be wonderfully entertained. (The presence of B-veterans Lance Henriksen and Brad Dourif is the tip-off.) Bruce Willis plays a psychiatrist trying to solve the murder of a fellow shrink who was killed by one of his patients. The rest is a mix of racy sex scenes, hammy overacting, and ridiculous pop psychology. Only Ruben Blades, as a detective, seems to have understood how silly the material really is. The video version contains about 20 minutes more footage than the theatrical release. It shows a bit more skin—including blink-and-you'll-miss-it male nudity—and makes the already convoluted plot a little more so. Definitely not for kids, but a must for guilty-pleasure fans. Also available in an unrated version. *ᗒᗕᗒ* **GPI: 9.1 (NC-17), 7.5 (R)**

Graphic violence, sexual activity, nudity, strong language.

1994 (R) 136m/C Bruce Willis, Jane March, Scott Bakula, Ruben Blades, Lesley Ann Warren, Lance Henriksen, Kevin J. O'Connor, Andrew Lowery, Brad Dourif, Eriq La Salle, Jeff Corey, Shirley Knight, Kathleen Wilhoite; *D:* Richard Rush; *W:* Matthew Chapman, Billy Ray, Richard Rush; *M:* Dominic Frontiere. Golden Raspberry Awards '94: Worst Picture; Nominations: Golden Globe Awards '95: Best Song ("The Color of the Night"); Golden Raspberry Awards '94: Worst Actor (Willis). **VHS** *HPH*

Come See the Paradise

In L.A.'s Little Tokyo, 1936, Jack McGurn (Dennis Quaid) finds work at Mr. Kawamura's (Sab Shimono) Japanese movie theatre and falls in love when he meets his boss's stunning daughter Lily (Tamlyn Tomita). Their rocky courtship and marriage, over her family's disapproval, survives until the outbreak of World War II and the infamous internment of immigrant Japanese and Nisei, first generation children who were American citizens. The biggest problem with the film is its lack of balance. The main focus is on the love story, and while that's handled well, it's not nearly as interesting as the larger story of the Kawamura family, Lily's parents and her brothers and sisters. Some of the early scenes in the Japanese community are reminiscent of the best moments of the first two *Godfather* films. Writer/director Alan Parker does a wonderful job of capturing the spirit and mood of large social gatherings. He's even able to let the characters speak Japanese without subtitles and still get across the sense of what they're saying and doing. Their conflicts and the raw injustice they endured are the stuff of good drama, but that's not what persuades studio executives to finance multi-million dollar pictures. They want marketable stars. To satisfy conventional wisdom, Parker almost made two movies, one about the family and another about the couple. Instead, he got one long (two hours plus) slow one. Quaid and Tomita are appealing actors, but we've seen their story before. Details of life in the camp are sketched in quickly and the ending of both stories has a let's-get-this-over-with feeling. *ᗒᗕᗒ*

Strong language, mild sexual content.

1990 (R) 135m/C Dennis Quaid, Tamlyn Tomita, Sab Shimono, Shizuko Hoshi, Stan Egi, Ronald Yamamoto, Akemi Nishino, Naomi Nakano, Brady Tsurutani, Pruitt Taylor Vince, Joe Lisi; *D:* Alan Parker; *W:* Alan Parker; *M:* Randy Edelman. **VHS, LV** *FOX, FCT, CCB*

Commercial Mania

TV commercials from the 1950s and '60s are presented without comment or explanation. They're wonderfully funny, but the important thing to keep in mind about these ads is not that in the past we were so gullible that we bought this line of foolishness; it's that we're still so gullible and buy new lines of foolishness. Nothing on this tape is any more ridiculous than, say, a Michelob Dry beer or Infiniti ad. The pitchmen may have sharpened their techniques but they haven't changed them. Younger viewers who have never seen these 30-second wonders will probably laugh their fannies off at "21 percent fewer cavities with Crest" and the Anacin ads that show grown women having mini-breakdowns. Those old enough to recall the originals will feel a certain nostalgia for some of them. Remember that incredibly round, brown voice that promoted Pall Mall cigarettes with the words, "outstanding...and they are mild" and the great communicator himself, Ronald Reagan, proclaiming the benefits of Boraxo soap. ♫♫♫

Contains no objectionable material.

1986 60m/B VHS *RHI*

Communion

Most people probably know the outlines of Whitley Strieber's story and the other "alien abduction" tales that have surfaced since. In 1987, Strieber had established a successful career as an author of horror novels—*The Wolfen, The Hunger,* and others—when he wrote *Communion.* In that book, and in its sequel *Transformation,* he claimed that he had been repeatedly abducted by alien beings who performed extremely unpleasant examinations or experiments on him, and then somehow caused him to forget what had happened. In the film adaptation, Christopher Walken is perfectly cast in the lead. His innate strangeness serves him well in an unusual role. Lindsay Crouse turns in her normal arid, understated performance. Director Philippe Mora, who also made *Howling II: Your Sister Is a Werewolf,* produced the film with Strieber and gives the production a glossy, slightly stylized look. The pace is measured, reinforcing the "realism" of the story. Given the nature of Strieber's claims of truthfulness and the lack of any substantiating evidence, the viewer is forced to choose among three explanations: 1) Strieber is telling the truth. All of this actually happened to him and to the hundreds of others who have virtually identical stories. 2) Strieber is lying. He's a canny novelist who realized that he could tap into public curiosity and credulity to turn a tidy profit. 3) Strieber has hallucinated the experiences. In interviews, he has claimed that this is what he meant to say all along. In the end, those who already accept the "truth" of these stories will probably appreciate *Communion* more than others. Doubters will not be convinced, and the loopy ending will leave everyone else with a strong desire to throw something at the TV. ♫♫

Profanity and mature subject matter.

1989 (R) 103m/C Christopher Walken, Lindsay Crouse, Frances Sternhagen, Joel Carlson, Andreas Katsulas, Basil Hoffman; *D:* Philippe Mora; *M:* Eric Clapton. VHS, LV *NO*

Contagion

A salesman (John Doyle) sees a young woman being attacked at night on a lonely road. He's assaulted by the same deranged Aussie rubes. Escaping, he stumbles through the woods to a mysterious, brightly lit house where gramophone music from the '20s is playing. He meets a strange millionaire named Bael and two beautiful women who offer him unlimited money, power, and sex. Delirious, he leaves and later doesn't know whether the house was real or a dream. Unfortunately, the resolution of that ambiguity isn't as interesting as its unfolding; the second half is much weaker than the first. Director Karl Zwicky establishes a mysterious, unpredictable mood at the beginning, with strong echoes of *Deliverance* and *The Texas Chainsaw Massacre.* But he can't maintain it all the way through. ♫♫

Violence, sexual content, nudity, profanity.

1987 90m/C *AU* John Doyle, Nicola Bartlett, Roy Barrett, Nathy Gaffney, Pamela Hawksford; *D:* Karl Zwicky. VHS, LV *NO*

The Conviction

This Italian meditation on sexual harassment begins on a deliberately uncertain note and maintains a tone of ambiguity throughout. Sandra (Claire Nebout, who looks a lot like Sandra Bernhard) and Lorenzo (Vittorio Mezzogiorno) find themselves locked inside a public art museum for the night. Are they there on purpose? Did he follow her? Is she trying to

"The world is getting so small that it would be nice to meet someone new."

—CHRISTOPHER WALKEN MUSES ON EXTRATERRESTRIAL LIFE IN *COMMUNION.*

59

(Andrzej Seweryn) launches into a long discussion of the nature of sex. When he goes home at night, his wife (Grazyna Szapolowska) tells him that he doesn't know what he's talking about. He's wrong to be so sympathetic to Sandra's case, and she's leaving him. After that, things get seriously strange. Writer/director Marco Bellocchio (*Devil in the Flesh*) doesn't differentiate between "reality" and dreams. For the purposes of his story, they're the same, and he doesn't care to resolve the problems he raises, either. Bellocchio is much more interested in careful shadings of difference, not the simple black-and-white issues. If there is a conclusion, it's that men and women are different. Men are far too logical to understand what women want and expect of us. We just don't get it—never have and never will—so why bother? But, we men can't allow ourselves to give in to the animal side of our nature, even though that's what women really want us to do when they say they don't, and if we pretend to understand, we'll only get in more trouble. Got that? Anyone looking for titillation or physical action of any sort will be disappointed. Those with a taste for a more stylized approach—a little like Antonioni in places—should give it a try. 🦴🦴🦴

Mature subject matter, brief nudity, some strong language (subtitled).

1995 92m/C Claire Nebout, Vittorio Mezzogiorno, Andrzej Seweryn, Grazyna Szapolowska; *D:* Marco Bellocchio; *W:* Marco Bellocchio. VHS *ORI*

The Cook, the Thief, His Wife & Her Lover

Peter Greenaway's highly stylized tale of greed, gluttony, hate, and love was the first film to receive an NC-17 rating. The story contains so many bizarre elements and deliberate excesses that cutting it down to an R would have been like trying to make a skateboard out of a sportscar. That might be possible, but the result probably wouldn't work very well. At the same time, it has nothing in common with conventional X-rated adult films and shouldn't be shelved with them, either. Even on the small screen, where many of Greenaway's

seduce him? It's hard to say. In any case, they talk. Waxing philosophical as people in high-minded Italian movies are wont to do, he seduces her with art criticism. (The sexual scenes are as posed and unrealistic as dance, presented in long, static shots.) Later, he tells her that he has the keys to the building. She then charges him with rape. His trial takes up the last hour of the film, and it's not a typical courtroom confrontation. Instead, the D.A.

Video Premieres

visual flourishes are diminished, the film is a feast of bizarre characters in exotic costumes, big splashes of thick primary colors, and expressionistic sets. Michael Gambon, as Albert the repulsive thief, has an actor's dream of a role. It's filled with blustery speeches and outsized emotions. Gambon devours it with villainous relish (and ketchup and chocolate sauce and anything else he can cram into his maw). Helen Mirren is, as ever, coolly beautiful as his wife who takes a bookish lover (Alan Howard) at the restaurant where they eat every night. With Michael Nyman's music providing a hypnotic background, Greenaway's camera glides through the action giving the film a strong dream-like quality. It's an unsettling mix of the beautiful and the repugnant; strongly recommended for adult viewers with a taste for the challenging. 𝄞𝄞𝄞

Intense violence, strong language, sexual content, nudity, general principle.

1990 (NC-17) 123m/C *GB* Richard Bohringer, Michael Gambon, Helen Mirren, Alan Howard, Tim Roth; *D:* Peter Greenaway; *W:* Peter Greenaway; *M:* Michael Nyman. **VHS** *VMK*

A Cop for the Killing

Definitely not another cop shoot-'em-up, despite the title. Writer Philip Rosenberg tells the story of an LAPD narcotics squad (played by Steven Weber, Susan Walters, Harold Sylvester, and Charles Haid) led by Lt. Wiltern (James Farentino). They're an effective and closely knit unit until one of them is killed in a drug bust that goes bad. The real focus of the film is not on the violence of their work, but on the emotional toll it takes, particularly on Wiltern. Veteran director Dick Lowry neither glosses over nor sensationalizes the physical action. He's much more interested in its effects on the survivors and on those who commit violent acts. Though police officers have become familiar stereotypes in popular entertainment, these are treated seriously. If the cast lacks star power, it's an ensemble of accomplished character actors who do uniformly excellent work. In many ways the film is similar to the French film, *L.627,* but with a stronger plot. 𝄞𝄞𝄞

Violence, strong language.

1994 (R) 95m/C James Farentino, Steven Weber, Charles Haid, Susan Walters, Harold Sylvester; *D:* Dick Lowry; *W:* Philip Rosenberg. **VHS** *NHO*

Coup de Torchon

Bertrand Tavernier's 1981 adaptation of Jim Thompson's novel, *Pop. 1280,* is set in a dusty little French West Africa hamlet, July, 1938. The local police chief, Lucien Cordier (Phillipe Noiret), lets everybody push him around—the local crooks, his wife (Stephane Audran), her live-in lover—everybody. But then a colleague shows Lucien just how much power he really has, and the lamb becomes a wolf. That transformation is more internal than external, and Tavernier tells the story as a droll, deadpan comedy. The casting is dead-on. With his comfortable paunch and unshaven hang-dog mug, Noiret is a Gallic Matthau. As his sometimes mistress, Isabelle Huppert is every bit as memorable. Beyond the humor, though, this is a grim film noir about the ultimate betrayal: self betrayal. Yes, it is a little long and slow in the telling, but it's still fascinating and unpredictable all the way through. Required viewing for noir fans. *AKA:* Clean Slate. 𝄞𝄞𝄞𝄞

Strong language and racial epithets (subtitled), brief nudity, violence.

1981 128m/C *FR* Philippe Noiret, Isabelle Huppert, Guy Marchand, Stephane Audran, Eddy Mitchell, Jean-Pierre Marielle; *D:* Bertrand Tavernier; *W:* Bertrand Tavernier. Nominations: Academy Awards '81: Best Foreign Language Film. **VHS** *HMV*

The Courtyard

New York architect Jonathan (Andrew McCarthy) moves into the Shangri-La apartments in L.A. to finish his first important commission—a mini-mall. But all is not serene in La-La Land. The air-conditioner doesn't always work; the super (Vincent Schiavelli) is a prickly bird; the lovely Lauren (Madchen Amick) seems to be attracted to Jack but she's keeping secrets; an absentee neighbor has a loud TV; a guy in the next building has just been stabbed to death and detective Steiner (Cheech Marin) thinks Jack may have done it. Director Fred Walton is an old hand at light

comic mysteries, and he does a fine job with a solid cast, classy production values, and a witty script by Wendy Biller and Christopher Hawthorne. Take a look. 🦴🦴🦴

Mature subject matter, some violence, strong language, sexual content, brief nudity.

1995 (R) 103m/C Andrew McCarthy, Madchen Amick, Richard "Cheech" Marin, Vincent Schiavelli; **D:** Fred Walton; **W:** Wendy Biller, Christopher Hawthorne. **VHS** *REP*

Cover Me

Playboy Entertainment's first feature-length entry in the "erotic thriller" genre is notable for a relatively high-powered cast—Rick Rossovich, Paul Sorvino, Corbin Bernsen, Elliot Gould. The story concerns a policewoman (Courtney Taylor) trying to capture a cross-dressing serial killer. The film is well-acted and competently constructed, though there's not much to distinguish it in an already crowded field. 🦴🦴

Nudity, sexual content, strong language, violence.

1995 (R) 94m/C Courtney Taylor, Rick Rossovich, Paul Sorvino, Elliot Gould, Corbin Bernsen; **D:** Michael Schroeder; **W:** Steve Johnson. **VHS** *PAR*

The Crawlers

Your basic low-budget drive-in creature feature appears to have been made somewhere in the Pacific northwest. Could it be that the managers of the local nuclear plant have been dumping their radioactive waste out in the woods? Is that what's causing tree roots to become wriggling monsters that attack the townspeople? There's hardly a serious moment in this one, and the special effects aren't particularly special. Fans of the genre who are in the mood for a chuckle will get their money's worth. 🦴🦴

Unpersuasive violence, language.

1993 (R) 94m/C Jason Saucier, Mary Sellers; **D:** Martin Newlin; **W:** Dan Price, Martin Newlin. **VHS** *COL*

The Crew

The conformity police, those guardians of popular entertainment who demand that all feature films fit into a recognizable genre or form, must have been asleep at the switch when this one slipped through. After a static, discomforting introduction, the scene shifts to Miami where a yacht sets out for Bimini. Philip (Viggo Mortensen), a wealthy aggressive lawyer, is the boat's owner and captain. His younger "trophy" wife (Sam Jenkins) and his friend Alex (John Philbin) are also aboard, along with Philip's sister Jennifer (Pamela Gidley) and her troubled husband Bill (Donal Logue). Before long, they acquire two more passengers, Timothy (Jeremy Sisto) and Camilla (Laura Del Sol) who may be up to something illegal, though that's not clear. At first, it appears that director Carl-Jan Colpaert is going to tell a story of sexual intrigue in the Caribbean. Then the tone shifts when weapons are drawn and the film becomes a hostage drama, but that changes too, and.... The ensemble cast does excellent work with good, surprising material. Sisto makes Tim a complex, hermaphroditic character who has a letter-perfect soft Southern drawl and "smooth, silky skin just like Catherine Deneuve." From beginning to end, *The Crew* is a deliberately unconventional and often humorous film that knocks down expectations as soon as they've been established. 🐾🐾🐾🐾

Strong language, mature subject matter.

1995 (R) 99m/C Viggo Mortensen, Jeremy Sisto, Pamela Gidley, Donal Logue, Laura Del Sol, Grace Zabriskie, John Philbin, Sam Jenkins; *D:* Carl Colpaert; *W:* Carl Colpaert. VHS *LIV*

Crime Lords

None-too-bright L.A. cops (Martin Hewitt and director Wayne Crawford) break up a Hong Kong auto-theft syndicate in this off-beat comic thriller. There are only a few dozen monstrous holes in the plot, but Crawford keeps the action moving at a brisk pace; the production values are first rate and the big finish is a real corker. Also, Susan Byun turns in a sexy performance as a moll with a dragon tattooed on her thigh. Light-weight James Bondish fluff. 🐾🐾🐾

Strong language, graphic and bloody violence, and brief nudity.

1991 (R) 96m/C Wayne Crawford, Martin Hewitt, Susan Byun, Mel Castelo, James Hong; *D:* Wayne Crawford. VHS *ACA*

Crimebroker

Australian import reworks *The Thomas Crown Affair* with the sexual roles reversed. Judge Holly McPhee (Jacqueline Bisset) moonlights as a criminal mastermind. When she's not dispensing justice, she's planning robberies for a gang of thieves. She doesn't participate herself; the thrill is strictly vicarious. Dr. Gin Okazaki (Massaya Kato) is the Japanese criminologist brought in by the local cops to help with the rash of heists. It doesn't take the good doctor long to figure things out. His reaction is unconventional. Director Ian Barry and writer Tony Morphett tell a good story. The film was made with a respectable budget and production values. The real attraction, though, is Jacqueline Bisset. She still looks as good as any actress of her generation, and she's more attractive than many who are younger and more popular now. Even if her range is somewhat limited, she's perfect for this part and brings a welcome star "presence" to the film. 🐾🐾🐾

Strong language, sexual content, violence.

1995 (R) 93m/C AU Jacqueline Bisset, Massaya Kato; *D:* Ian Barry; *W:* Tony Morphett. VHS *APX*

Criminal Hearts

Terrific little road-action movie has lots of surprises and laughs. Rafe (Kevin Dillon) robs a desert roadside joint of dubious legitimacy. Kelli (Amy Locane) is driving from Los Angeles to Phoenix to find out if her fiance is two-timing her when Rafe's motorcycle conks out. She gives him a lift, and from that beginning, writer/director Dave Payne spins out a wild story that manages somehow to be simultaneously fast-paced and full of talk. Good interesting talk. The heroes are likeable, fully dimensional characters, and they're matched by M. Emmet Walsh and James Michael Mac-Donald as two excellent, scene-stealing villains. The film has a strong feeling for place—the Arizona desert—and a nasty, none-too-subtle sense of humor. All in all, it's a first-rate debut. Whatever Payne does next, I'll watch. 🐾🐾🐾

Violence, strong language, brief nudity, sexual content.

1995 (R) 92m/C Kevin Dillon, Amy Locane, Morgan Fairchild, M. Emmet Walsh, James Michael MacDonald; *D:* Dave Payne; *W:* Dave Payne. VHS *AVE*

The Criminal Mind

Formula thriller vaults from simple incompetence to alternative classic in a series of breathtaking strides. Nick (Frank Rossi) and Carlo (Ben Cross) are the sons of an assassinated Mafia chief. Carlo goes into the family business; Nick becomes a D.A. The loopy plot contains flashbacks within flashbacks, a dozen or so ridiculous but somehow predictable twists, and perhaps the most inept chase scene imaginable. The acting ranges from Rossi's shy mumbling to Cross's hysterical rants. When this hambone cuts loose, watch out! The supporting cast, including Lance Henriksen and Tahnee Welch, is better but the script is hopeless. Still, for unintentional laughs, this one gets full marks. 🐾🐾

Violence, strong language, sexual content, brief nudity.

1993 **(R)** 93m/C Ben Cross, Frank Rossi, Tahnee Welch, Lance Henriksen, Joseph Ruskin, Lynn-Holly Johnson; *D:* Joseph Vittorie; *W:* Sam A. Scribner. **VHS** *COL*

Criminal Passion

Tough cop Mel Hudson (Joan Severance), who favors men's clothes (including two-tone wingtips), has a problematic personal life and has a no-nonsense professional attitude. She's working on a series of sexual murders, and though all the clues point to suave millionaire Connor Ashcroft (Allen Nelson, who also co-wrote and -produced), she thinks he's kinda cute. Toss in an unstable girlfriend and a string of ex-lovers and the formula is complete for *Basic Instinct* with the sexes reversed. Director Donna Dietch handles the proceedings well enough, though the action scenes are clumsily staged. Joan Severance, a familiar face in the genre, gets more than she should from the thin material. Also available in an unrated version. 🎬🎬

Violence, sexual material, nudity, strong language.

1994 **(R)** 98m/C Joan Severance, Allen Nelson; *D:* Donna Dietch; *W:* Allen Nelson. **VHS** *VMK*

Cronos

An aging alchemist has "skin the color of marble in moonlight." What a beautiful image. Guillermo Del Toro's elegant horror film is completely unlike any that have been produced in this country for years. It's reminiscent of David Cronenberg's early work, though Del Toro's use of special effects is much more restrained. Where Cronenberg might have exploded a human head onscreen, Del Toro will use a glittering golden needle with fiendish delight. The story begins with a 14th century alchemist's invention of the Cronos Device, a bejeweled gizmo that confers immortality upon the owner—immortality with a price. In present-day Mexico City, it falls into the possession of Jesus Gris (Federico Luppi), an aging antiques dealer who's devoted to his young granddaughter Aurora (Tamara Shanath). De la Guardia (Claudio Brook), a crippled and corrupt millionaire, owns the instruction manual for said gizmo and has been searching for it for years. He sends his mercurial nephew (Ron Perlman) to Gris' shop, and from that moment on, the plot defies description. The film's quirky humor has a strong Felliniesque edge, and compared to American horror movies, the pace is almost stately. There are also some genuinely tender moments, to go along with those that are utterly revolting. Writer/director Del Toro has a masterful visual style. He tells the story through a series of slow, vivid nightmare images. More importantly, he got a winning performance from his star: Federico Luppi has the engaging charm of a Jimmy Stewart. He's the kind of actor that audiences warm to instantly, and so the film is much more involving than it sounds. Some of the scenes between him and Tamara Shanath are really touching. 🎬🎬🎬

Strong special effects, violence, language.

1994 **(R)** 92m/C *MX* Federico Luppi, Ron Perlman, Claudio Brook, Tamara Shanath; *D:* Guillermo Del Toro; *W:* Guillermo del Toro; *M:* Ian Deardon. **VHS, LV** *VMK*

Cross Country

Journeyman director Paul Lynch's 1983 road movie became a cult hit in the early years of the home video revolution. Michael Ironside plays Roersch, a cop who suspects that ad man Evan Bley (Richard Beymer, from *West Side Story*) has killed a woman. Bley is crossing the continent in his Mercedes with a couple (Nina Axelrod and Brent Carver) who are up to no good. As Roersch gets closer, the trio in the Mercedes play sexual power games of uncertain motives and expectations. At its best, the film keeps you off balance, wondering who the bad guy (or bad girl) is, and the ending curiously predates *Thelma and Louise.* 🎬🎬

Violence, sexual content, brief nudity, strong language.

1983 **(R)** 95m/C *CA* Richard Beymer, Nina Axelrod, Michael Ironside, Brent Carver; *D:* Paul Lynch; *W:* Logan N. Danforth. **VHS, LV** *NLC*

The Crossing Guard

On one level, it's easy to see why this grim drama didn't catch on in its limited theatrical release. The story of two parents' reaction to the death of a child is nobody's idea of a good time at the movies. And "a good time at the movies" is what we've come to expect all films to be. Freddy (Jack Nicholson) hangs out in strip joints, drinks too much, and is obsessed with revenge. His ex-wife Mary (Anjelica Huston) goes to group therapy sessions and works through her grief. Then Booth (David Morse), the drunk driver who killed their daughter, is released from prison. Freddy decides to kill him. Those are the bare bones of writer/director Sean Penn's story. At the film's best, Penn and Nicholson are able to make Freddy's dislocation, anger, and frustration seem absolutely real. As characters, Booth and Mary are almost as strong, but the film belongs to Nicholson. He's the focus. For the most part, Penn handles things well; he makes mistakes in little things—over-relying on cigarettes as props at the big emotional moments, and stretching too far for an ending that will strike some as false. But even if it's not perfect, the film is still worth watching, particularly for fans of the cast. By the way, Bruce Springsteen's theme, *Missing*, isn't up there with *The Streets of Philadelphia*, but it's way better than *Dead Man Walking*. 𝄢𝄢𝄢

Strong language, some violence, brief nudity.

1994 (R) 111m/C Jack Nicholson, Anjelica Huston, David Morse, Robin Wright, Robbie Robertson, Piper Laurie, Richard Bradford, John Savage, Priscilla Barnes, Kari Wuhrer; *D:* Sean Penn; *W:* Sean Penn; *C:* Vilmos Zsigmond; *M:* Jack Nitzsche. Nominations: Golden Globe Awards '96: Best Supporting Actress (Huston); Independent Spirit Awards '96: Best Supporting Actor (Morse); Screen Actors Guild Award '95: Best Supporting Actress (Huston). **VHS, LV** *TOU*

The Crude Oasis

What's going on at "The Crude Oasis"? Could it be a conventional mystery? Or a paranoid woman's troubled view of her Midwestern world? In any case, writer/director Alex Graves creates a hypnotic atmosphere that *Twin Peaks* aimed for but never sustained. And Graves does it honestly, finding real creepiness in the ordinary details of everyday life. Karen Webb's (Jennifer Taylor) clinical depression may have returned, or she may be reacting to her husband's (Robert Peterson) blatant faithlessness when she becomes attracted to a young service station attendant (Aaron Shields). But he has already appeared in her dreams. The rest is methodically paced and subtly surprising. Viewers who also like the original *Vanishing, Positive I.D.,* and *Suture* should make a point of finding this one. 𝄢𝄢𝄢𝄢

Strong language, mature subject matter.

1995 (R) 82m/C Jennifer Taylor, Aaron Shields, Robert Peterson, Mussef Sibay, Lynn Bieler, Roberta Eaton; *D:* Alex Graves; *W:* Alex Graves; *C:* Steven Quale. **VHS** *PAR*

Crusoe

Loosely based on Daniel Defoe's novel, this version begins in Tidewater, Virginia, 1808. Crusoe (Aidan Quinn) is a slave trader who's first seen chasing a runaway. He's ship-wrecked when he pushes his luck, trying to make one more ocean crossing to buy slaves before winter sets in. He fetches up on an island (in reality one of the Seychelles, which may have the most photogenic beaches on the planet). What follows is virtually a silent film as Crusoe makes a life for himself alone. His only companion, for a time, is a scene-stealing mongrel dog. There is no Friday character, but later a warrior (well played by Ade Sapara) arrives. He's better equipped to deal with the island than Crusoe is. That, of course, is the film's point: the slave trader coming to understand equality. It's a valid, commendable theme, but in this slow telling, it's also a tedious theme. The script by Walon Green (*The Wild Bunch*) is, necessarily, focused on only one man for most of the story. As played by Quinn, Crusoe isn't that compelling a character. We follow what he does with a certain curiosity, but there's seldom any suspense or emotional involvement with what's happening. Director Caleb Deschanel does little to heighten the tension either. He's more interested in making the island world complete and believable, as he did when he was cinematographer on *The Black Stallion*. 🎵🎵♥

Violence.

1989 (PG-13) 94m/C Aidan Quinn, Ade Sapara, Jimmy Nail, Timothy Spall, Colin Bruce, Michael Higgins, Shane Rimmer, Hepburn Grahame; *D:* Caleb Deschanel; *W:* Walon Green, Christopher Logue; *M:* Michael Kamen. VHS, LV *NO*

Curse 2: The Bite

A young fellow takes an ill-advised shortcut through a government installation in the desert. He's bitten on the hand by a nuclear snake. Jamie Farr gives him the wrong antidote and then his whole arm turns into a snake! His girlfriend is not amused. Followed by two sequels to date. 🎵🎵

Violence, profanity, sexual subject matter, and grotesque effects involving mouths.

1988 (R) 97m/C Jill Schoelen, J. Eddie Peck, Jamie Farr, Savina Gersak, Bo Svenson; *D:* Fred Goodwin. VHS *TWE*

Curse of the Crystal Eye

Undernourished adventure aims to imitate *Raiders of the Lost Ark* and Disney's *Aladdin*, and flops. The story opens with an incoherent desert battle where it's impossible to tell who's attacking whom, who wins, or why any of the people involved are doing what they're doing. The scene then shifts to an urban battleground, though the action doesn't make any more sense. The acting is amateurish; the pace is uneven. Be sure your fast-forward button is fully operational. 🎵

Violence, special effects.

1993 (PG-13) 90m/C Jameson Parker, Cynthia Rhodes, Mike Lane, David Sherwood, Andre Jacobs; *D:* Joe Tornatore. VHS *NHO*

The Custodian

Realistic Australian police drama comes close to a Joseph Wambaugh novel in its portrayal of men (and a few women) who are tested by a variety of temptations. James Quinlan (Anthony LaPaglia) is an honest cop who comes to realize that his honesty is cold comfort in today's world. His refusal to accept any extra money or favors has destroyed his marriage, and when he sees how well his friend and partner Frank (Hugo Weaving) is living, he questions his values. Is he principled, or is he naive? At times, it may seem that writer/director John Dingwall lets the pace move a little slowly and stretches too far with some of his stylistic flourishes. This is a film about complexity and choices—how they are made and what they mean later—so it works through the characters, and the cast is near perfect. LaPaglia makes Quinlan's introspection interesting and tense. He gets strong support from Weaving, Barry Otto, and Essie Davis, who makes a memorable debut as a young waitress. The Australian accents are a little hard to understand at times, but *The Custodian* is still one of the best sleepers in the video store. 🎵🎵🎵

Strong language, violence, brief nudity, sexual content.

1994 (R) 110m/C AU Anthony LaPaglia, Hugo Weaving, Barry Otto, Bill Hunter, Kelly Dingwall, Gosia Dobrowolska, Essie Davis; Naomi Watts; *D:* John Dingwall; *W:* John Dingwall. VHS, LV *ACA*

Cyber Ninja

Elements of a samurai movie are recycled with inventive s-f hardware (including swords with bullets and a flying house) and the outrageous style of *Godzilla*, and they're wrapped up in a plot that makes no sense at all. The key is pace, a relentless rat-a-tat-tat that seldom slows. The original film was directed by Keita Amemiya; the English-language adaptation is credited to Carl Macek. One or both of them did good work with a tale of rival warlords, mercenaries, a captive princess, a guy whose brother was killed in an early battle and, of course, the title character, a mysterious man-machine of ambiguous loyalties. Enjoy the special effects, the stuntwork, and the carefully choreographed fight scenes. Don't expect logic. 🦴🦴❤

Contains wild comic book violence.

1994 80m/C *JP* Hanbel Kawai, Hiroki Ida; *D:* Keita Amemiya. **VHS** *FXL*

Cyber-Tracker

Few things in the video world are as certain as PM Entertainment releases. Whenever the plot of one of these low-budget wonders is in danger of slowing down, something explodes or burns. In other words, you get a big bang for your rental buck. This one's no exception. In many respects it's a standard issue shoot-'em-up. But with this kind of movie, story is less important than style. Don "The Dragon" Wilson is on Senator Dilly's security team. But the evil lawmaker is ready to turn the California legal system over to computers that establish guilt or innocence without trials and robot "trackers" to dispense instant justice. Two things set the *Terminator* knock-off apart from other action flicks. First, the story has some concerns for civil liberties, as opposed to the kneejerk fascist authoritarianism so common to the genre. Second, the film benefits considerably from Wilson's always welcome presence. 🦴🦴❤

Graphic violence, strong language.

1993 (R) 84m/C Don "The Dragon" Wilson, Richard Norton, Joseph Ruskin, Abby Dalton, John Aprea; *D:* Richard Pepin. **VHS, LV** *PMH*

Cyber-Tracker 2

Don Wilson is a cop in near-future L.A. where the police are aided by virtually indestructible armed robot "trackers." The bad guys have created their own outlaw trackers that can assume any identity. (Shades of *T2*.) Villainous versions of our hero and heroine (Stacie Foster) are committing dastardly acts, and something blows up or crashes or is shot about every five minutes. All the action and gun violence is handled with such cartoonish energy that it's neither offensive nor sadistic. But you do have to wonder why everybody spends so much time shooting at these robots when they know that bullets can't hurt them. Oh well, it's still silly fun for fans. 🦴🦴❤

Violence.

1995 (R) 97m/C Don "The Dragon" Wilson, Stacie Foster, Stephen Burton. **VHS** *PMH*

CyberSex Kittens

As the title indicates, this one is a soft-core s-f comedy with an adolescent mindset. The gimmick is a cheesy computer cap that turns women into willing playthings for the guys who are in control. If one second of the film were even half-way serious it would be offensive but there's no danger of that. This is a semi-professional, shot-on-video production notable for its cheerfulness and a plump cast, both male and female. 🦴

Nudity and sexual material.

1995 80m/C Shannyn Smedley, Hal Wamsley, Alex Cohen; *D:* Kirk Bowman; *W:* Kirk Bowman. **VHS** *ROM*

Cyberzone

Futuristic shoot-'em-up revels and glories in its own inadequacies. In 2077, 50 years after the big quake turned Phoenix into a beach town, New Angeles is an underwater city that's run by the 21st century equivalent of the Christian Coalition—no alcohol, no gambling, no drugs, in short...no sin. That's why smuggler Burt Hawks (Matthias Hues) is trying to bring in four "pleasure droids," female robots programmed to please and padded with sili-

cone. Grungy bounty hunter Jack Ford (Marc Singer) is hired to bring them back and he's teamed up with the fastidious Beth Enright (Rochelle Swanson). Prolific producer/director Fred Olen Ray quotes liberally from *For a Few Dollars More*, particularly at the end. This is strictly tongue-in-cheek material and possibly the first of a series. ♫♫♫

Nudity, violence, strong language, sexual content.

1995 (R) 90m/C Marc Singer, Matthias Hues, Rochelle Swanson; *D:* Fred Olen Ray. **VHS** *NHO*

The Dallas Connection

Fans of Andy Sidaris flicks know what to expect:

• Sexy, powerful women in slinky outfits

• Vintage cars and souped-up power boats

• Shower scenes every 12 to 15 minutes

• Lots of exotic weapons and explosions

• Neat radio-controlled toys

• Heroes who are so thick-headed they couldn't pour lemonade out of a boot

The plot, such as it is, has to do with secret agents Bruce Penhall and Mark Barriere; dressed-to-thrill assassins Julie Strain, Julie K. Smith, and Wendy Hamilton; satellites and meteor showers; but it's really unimportant. Sidaris films exist in their own universe and the things that would ruin other movies—wooden acting, nonsensical story—are precisely what make these archetypal guy flicks so wonderful, so unpredictable...so Sidarian! ♫♫♫♫

Nudity, sexual material, and mild violence.

1994 (R) 90m/C Julie Strain, Samantha Phillips, Julie K. Smith, Wendy Hamilton, Bruce Penhall, Mark Barriere; *D:* Drew Sidaris. **VHS** *MNC*

Dance Me Outside

The young people on an Ontario Indian reservation see a future of pointless drunkeness ahead, and so they mostly don't think about it. They don't know how to talk to each other either, and whenever they begin to get close, they back off immediately. That's good stuff for any coming-of-age story, but it's too tough

a subject for this film to deal with. The focus shifts to Anglo-Indian conflicts where it's cartoonish at best, racist at worst. But before long, director Bruce McDonald shifts gears again and, for a little while, the film is a crime story about the murder of a young girl. The pieces fit together poorly and never amount to much. ♫♫

Mature subject matter, some strong language, violence.

1995 (R) 87m/C *CA* Ryan Black, Adam Beach, Michael Greyeyes, Lisa Lacroix; *D:* Bruce McDonald; *W:* Bruce McDonald, Don McKellar, John Frizzell. Genie Awards '95: Best Film Editing. **VHS, LV** *APX*

The Dangerous

Problem Number One: Explain the title. "The Dangerous" what? "Dangerous" is an adjective, not a noun. But perhaps the producers were using it as a subtle tip-off for Problem Number Two: Linguistic curiosities within the film itself. (More about them presently.) The story is about brother and sister ninja assassins who come to New Orleans from Japan to avenge the death of their sister at the hands of drug dealers. At the same time, a guy named Davalos (Robert Davi) is blackmailed into working with a cop (Michael Pare). Are you following this so far? Good. Problem Number Three: Who is Davalos? What does he have to do with anything or anyone else in the movie? Don't ask me. I had to read the press material to figure out the plot and still don't get it. But that's all right. Also involved are Elliott Gould as a film projectionist; John Savage as half of a knife-wielding pair of assassins who seem to have learned their moves at the Bolshoi ballet; O.J.'s ex-squeeze Paula Barbieri as a hooker; and Joel Grey as an informant with a bizarre accent. The credits state that writer Rod Hewitt co-directed with Maria Dante and perhaps that explains the nutty excesses. The violence is graphic, imaginative, filled with continuity mistakes, and so preposterous that it's silly. So are the acting and dialogue, in both Japanese and English, resulting in Problem Number Four: Near the end, when one noble character has been mortally wounded at the New Orleans Art Museum, he explains as he expires, "I have always believed that if a man has been a true warrior when he dies, those around him can feel a wind from his body." Two interpretations came to mind immediately—one spiritual and one intestinal and maybe that's what the title refers to. *The Dangerous* is one of those alternative gems that's full of wind and other things. 🦴🦴

Violence, strong language, brief nudity, sexual material.

1995 **(R)** 96m/C Robert Davi, Michael Pare, Paula Barbieri, Elliott Gould, John Savage, Joel Grey; **D:** Maria Dante, Rod Hewitt; **W:** Rod Hewitt. **VHS, LV** *ORI*

Dangerous Game

The main character in this first-rate Australian suspense film is a mentally unstable motorcycle cop, Murphy (Stephen Grives). He's obsessed with a group of college students who are, he thinks, out to get him. Most of the action takes place in a huge department store where the kids and their enemy find themselves trapped for the night. The setting does give the action the claustrophobic intensity of *Die Hard,* but director Stephen Hopkins quotes other films, too, most obviously *The Most Dangerous Game* and James Whale's *Frankenstein.* Judged simply as a thriller, this one is a winner. The production values are excellent; terrific sets and superb photography from Peter Levy. The cat-and-mouse action is inventive and involving, but Hopkins never resorts to explicit violence. In that respect, the film is admirably restrained. But the best and most effective parts are the characters. The young people here may look a little too perky and cute, but they still have depth and recognizable personalities. The real surprise is Murphy. Like Karloff's Monster, he manages to be frightening and sympathetic at the same time. Murphy is insane, and his madness is frightening but it's often aimed at himself. In short, the character is a fascinating contradiction. From beginning to end, Grives' performance is convincing and touching. 🦴🦴🦴

Violence, strong language, mild sexual content.

1990 **(R)** 102m/C *AU* Miles Buchanan, Sandy Lillingston, Kathryn Walker, John Polson, Stephen Grives; **D:** Stephen Hopkins. **VHS, LV** *ACD*

Dangerous Heart

A drug dealer (Timothy Daly) sets out to seduce a cop's widow (Lauren Holly) in a potentially enjoyable suspense flick that fades toward the end. The performances are good and the situation is tense. But thin production values show through when the focus shifts to the allegedly seedy side of Oakland, California. And Daly's two semi-comic henchpersons (Alice Carter and Joe Pantoliano) are fun but out of place. Toward the end, they're a real distraction. 🦴🦴

Strong language, violence, subject matter.

1993 **(R)** 93m/C Timothy Daly, Lauren Holly, Jeffrey Nordling, Alice Carter, Joe Pantoliano; **D:** Michael Scott; **W:** Patrick Cirillo. **VHS, LV** *MCA*

Dangerous Indiscretion

Smart young ad man C. Thomas Howell meets the enigmatic beauty Joan Severance in a Seattle grocery store. One-night stand turns into affair. Then he learns that she's married to Malcolm MacDowell, a powerful businessman who wants to hire the ad agency. O.K., in most neo-noir vids, this is where the lovers conspire to knock off hubby, but here.... If director Richard Kletter stretches credulity in the second half of the story, it's a forgivable sin. In terms of setting and tone, this one's similar to *Disclosure,* though it's much more involving, tense, and sexy. (Kletter knows how to shoot a hot love scene.) 🦴🦴🦴

Mature subject matter, sexual content, brief nudity, violence, strong language.

1994 **(R)** 81m/C Joan Severance, C. Thomas Howell, Malcolm McDowell; **D:** Richard Kletter; **W:** Richard Kletter, Jack Tarpon; **M:** Richard Gibbs. **VHS** *PAR*

Dangerous Love

Sloppy, embarrassingly bad thriller (?) about computer dating has the mentality and construction of a grade-Z slasher flick. How did

1987 (R) 96m/C Lawrence Monoson, Brenda Bakke, Peter Marc, Elliott Gould, Anthony Geary; **D:** Marty Ollstein. **VHS** *MED*

The Hound's Favorite Sleepers: Chick Vids

The Hound sincerely hopes that serious feminists and other linguistically correct individuals will not be offended by the phrase "chick vid." It's a derivation of "chick flick" and is used to describe films that have an extra appeal to women. Anyone familiar with the titles on this list will realize instantly that they are all over the political-social-geographic-sexual-orientation map. The Hound has wide-ranging tastes in Video Premieres and goes wherever his sensitive nose leads him. That also applies to "The Hound's Favorite Sleepers: Guy Vids" (please see page 188).

THE BRIDE WITH WHITE HAIR	PUSHING HANDS
THE CRUDE OASIS	QUEEN MARGOT
DARK ANGEL: THE ASCENT	RADIO INSIDE
DEAD FUNNY	REFLECTIONS IN THE DARK
DOUBLE HAPPINESS	ROSALIE GOES SHOPPING
FLIRTING	SISTER, MY SISTER
THE HAWK	SLEEPWALK
LILY WAS HERE	SOLITAIRE FOR 2
MADAME BOVARY	THE SORCERESS (1955)
MURIEL'S WEDDING	THE TALL GUY
MY FAMILY	TIME INDEFINITE
NINA TAKES A LOVER	TRULY, MADLY, DEEPLY
POSITIVE I.D.	WHEN NIGHT IS FALLING

Elliot Gould and Anthony Geary find themselves stuck in it? Oil up the fast-forward button. WOOF!

Brief nudity, violence, profanity.

Dangerous Touch

Everyone involved with this one seems to have realized that they were slumming. And well they should have. Auteur Lou Diamond Phillips' film opens with a scene blatantly based on the most salacious moment of Julia Phillip's Hollywood tell-all book, *You'll Never Eat Lunch in This Town Again*. From there, the story of a Los Angeles therapist (Kate Vernon) who becomes involved with a mercurial stranger (Phillips) gets even more sordid, kinky, and sleazy. Somehow though, it's not as sordid, kinky, and sleazy as it's trying to be. Kate Vernon is no Sharon Stone and Phillips is no Mickey Rourke. Curiously, once the film gets past all the overheated hubba-hubba, it actually becomes more interesting. 🦴🦴

Mature subject matter, sexual content, nudity, strong language, violence.

1994 (R) 101m/C Lou Diamond Phillips, Kate Vernon, Andrew Divoff, Donna Ekholdt; **D:** Lou Diamond Phillips. **VHS, LV** *VMK*

A Dangerous Woman

Murder, sex, politics, and Tupperware. This wildly unfocused film revolves around a child-like, possibly mentally disabled woman (Debra Winger) who cannot lie. Both she and her aunt (Barbara Hershey) fall under the spell of silver-tongued handyman (Gabriel Byrne). Director Stephen Gyllenhaal and writer/producer Naomi Foner (his wife) capture the small-town atmosphere and tell the story well. The film's primary strength and weakness is Winger. She's made up to be deliberately unattractive, redefining frumpy. At times her character borders on Lily Tomlin's famous Edith Ann. At other times, she seems absolutely believable and right, but still so intense that some viewers will be put off. 🦴🦴

Strong language, violence, sexual content.

1993 (R) 93m/C Debra Winger, Barbara Hershey, Gabriel Byrne, David Strathairn, Chloe Webb, John Terry, Jan Hooks, Paul Dooley, Viveka Davis, Richard Riehle, Laurie Metcalf; **D:** Stephen Gyllenhaal; **W:** Naomi Foner; **M:** Carter Burwell. Golden Globe Awards '94: Best Actress—Drama (Winger). **VHS, LV** *MCA*

The Dark

A creepy, creepy premise, an overdeveloped sense of humor, and a deep streak of humanism make this horror flick a sleeper. The main characters are a half-mad ex-FBI agent (Brion James), a doctor (Stephen McHattie) on a mission, a sympathetic waitress (Cynthia Belliveau), an understanding gravedigger (Jaimz Woolvett), and the monstrous creature who lives under the cemetery and eats bodies. Robert C. Cooper's script follows the rules for the genre and gives fans what they want to see. But it goes a step farther and gives all of the characters—including the monster—more depth than you usually find in horror flicks. 🦴🦴🦴

Violence, subject matter, strong language, brief nudity and sexual content.

1994 (R) 90m/C Brion James, Jaimz Woolvett, Cynthia Belliveau, Stephen McHattie; *D:* Craig Pryce; *W:* Robert Cooper. **VHS, LV** *IMP*

Dark Angel: The Ascent

Director Linda Hassani makes a memorable debut with a horror film of humor, imagination, intelligence and, perhaps even wisdom. It begins beneath the surface of the Earth, literally in hell—the fire and brimstone hell of Hieronymus Bosch where the souls of sinners suffer eternal pain. The place is run by fallen angels, some of whom still worship God even though they have been banished from his presence. These, after all, are rebellious angels, and none more than Veronica (Angela Featherstone) who dreams of the world above. When a friend tells her about an unguarded cavern that leads to the surface, she's outta there. Up she pops, buck naked, from a manhole cover in the middle of an unnamed city where things are just as nasty and dangerous as they are back home. And to make it worse, humans don't recognize sin for what it is, and don't punish it. The mugger gets away; the corrupt cop is still on the job; the mayor who builds his career attacking welfare moms is re-elected. Matthew Bright's script borrows bits from such diverse sources as *Splash, Death Wish,* and *The Exorcist,* but it's neither derivative nor predictable. Even the most jaded horror fan will be surprised by some of the twists. Fuzzbee Morse's score steals blatantly and effectively from Bernard Herrmann. 🦴🦴🦴

Violence, strong language, nudity, sexual content.

1994 (R) 83m/C Angela Featherstone, Charlotte Stewart, Nicholas Worth, Daniel Markel, Michael C. Mahon, Milton James; *D:* Linda Hassani; *W:* Matthew Bright; *M:* Fuzzbee Morse. **VHS** *PAR*

Dark Before Dawn

The dubious premise of this conspiracy thriller appears to be corporate control of wheat farms. Solid production values and a strong sense of place are undercut by clumsy construction relying on cliches and implausibilities. Unfortunately, those mistakes show up in the opening scenes when a suspense film has to seduce you into believing its intrigues. 🦴

Violence and profanity.

1989 (R) 95m/C Doug McClure, Sonny Gibson, Ben Johnson, Billy Drago, Rance Howard, Morgan Woodward, Buck Henry, Jeffery Osterhage, Red Steagall, John Martin, Gary Cooper; *D:* Robert Totten. **VHS, LV** *VES, LIV*

Dark Breed

Creepy alien transformation effects, a *Predator*-inspired monster, and some remarkable stunt driving are the main attraction here. Jack Scalia is the soldier in charge when a space shuttle crashes—in a nice variation on the standard lovers-lane opening—and the titular critters emerge. PM films are known for high-octane action and this one delivers; the performances, particularly by Jonathan Banks as an infected astronaut and Robin Curtis as a pathologist, are a solid cut above average. So are the production values and the nice little riff on the famous "toast" scene from *Five Easy Pieces.* 🦴🦴🦴

Graphic violence, language, creepy effects.

1996 (R) 104m/C Jack Scalia, Jonathan Banks, Robin Curtis, Donna W. Scott; *D:* Richard Pepin. **VHS** *PMH*

How to Find 'Em

O.K., you've been scanning and skimming these reviews, and you've dog-eared a few pages, noted some titles that look interesting. But they're not at the video store down the street. What to do?

First—ask. The people behind the counter generally know their inventory. Different stores use different classification systems, so don't assume that you will know exactly where to look. After all, is *Powwow Highway* a drama or a comedy?

But what if the store doesn't have the tape and doesn't plan to buy a copy? How can you see it?

Check the store's policy on special orders. Most stores will do something. The drug stores, department stores, and convenience stores that carry tapes as a sideline aren't likely to be equipped to handle a special search, but businesses that specialize in tape rentals and sales will make an effort to find unusual titles.

The catch is that in most cases, they'll search for a film only if you're willing to buy it. (Feature-length films on tape usually run between $10 and $85 these days.) If you just want to rent the film to see it one time, most stores aren't likely to invest too much time and effort in finding it. If there's a sudden surge of interest in a particular title and several customers request it, all that changes, of course.

Again, policies on searches for individual titles vary from store to store, so it's a good idea to check with several different ones.

But suppose you try all of the local sources and come up with nothing. What then?

There are several national chains that deal in tape rentals through the mail. I've contacted two of them. They're more expensive than local stores. For spur of the moment, impulse rentals, they're not convenient, and they don't have every title either. They do carry films that you won't find in some stores and considering the service they offer, their prices are not exorbitant.

Home Film Festival (1-800-258-3456) is based in Scranton, PA. Facets Multimedia (1-800-331-6197) is a Chicago outfit. Both specialize in foreign films, independent productions, and documentaries. Membership fees change but they tend to be reasonable ($20-25), and so are the rental fees. Both operations work primarily with major credit cards, but Facets has a special arrangement for people who prefer to pay by check.

Those more interested in renting, specifically in renting the more obscure and outrageous films, can try Video Vault (1-800-VAULT66) of Alexandria, VA. As the cover of the catalog proudly states, "Guaranteed Worst Movies in Town!!" Mail order rental memberships begin at $15, and for $19.95 plus return shipping you can get three movies for a weekend. Video Vault's selections are strong in horror, science fiction, fantasy, exploitation, cult, and "mondo" (i.e. bizarre non-fiction). The Vault also has movies for sale.

For sales of American feature-length films, Movies Unlimited (1-800-4MOVIES) in Philadelphia is the biggest and best-known distributor in the country with three catalogs: general, laser, and adult.

Norman Scherer's Video Oyster (145 W. 12th St., New York, NY 10011; 212-989-3300) specializes in out-of-print tapes. Scherer is an iconoclast who speaks his mind. He publishes a regular catalog, prefers to handle his business through the mail, and does not accept credit cards.

For purchases of hard-to-find tapes, contact A Million and One World-Wide Videos at 1-800-849-7309 or fax 1-800-849-0873. It's a specialized search service, and is priced accordingly, though no money changes hands until terms have been agreed upon.

Video Library is a Philadelphia rent-by-mail outfit with an impressive list of titles in four catalogs: American and International Cinema, Special Edition, Family, and Alternative (i.e. non-explicit) Adult. There's no membership fee; only a credit card number for security. A single rental is $8 for one tape, $6 each for two or more plus shipping (approximately $4.50) for three nights. I recently rented the rare 1974 Richard Lester *The Three Musketeers* without a hitch. For more information contact Video Library at 1-800-669-7157 (7157 Germantown Ave., Philadelphia, PA 19119, or on the web at http://www.vlibrary.com).

For sales, try Thomas Video (810-280-2833; 122 S. Main St., Clawson, MI 48017). Owner Jim Olenski describes it as "the arty store in town," and offers a ten percent discount on all new tape sales. The store specializes in laserdiscs, foreign, underground, cult, and other esoteric fare, and it has a large selection of used tapes for sale. Inquiries are welcome.

The Dark Dancer

Your basic soft-core erotic thriller, made and set in Texas, is a little less coherent than most. The indefatigable Shannon Tweed plays Dr. Margaret Simpson, respected professor of feminist studies by day, masked stripper by night. The framing device is more interesting than the cliched story. Also available in an unrated version. 🐾

Violence, strong language, nudity, sexual content.

1995 (R) 7m/C Shannon Tweed, Lisa Pescia, Francesco Quinn, Jason Carter, D. Robert Burge. VHS TCE

Dark Secrets

Artsy skin flick presents a conservative woman (Monique Parent) who's seduced by a millionaire into giving in to her sexual proclivities. More accurately, there are skin flick parts and artsy parts with very little overlap. Toward the end, the action goes about as far as it can without wandering into hardcore territory. Also available in an unrated version. 🐾🐾

Nudity, strong sexual content.

1995 (R) 90m/C Monique Parent, Julie Strain, Justine Carroll; D. John Bowen. VHS APX

Dark Side of Genius

L.A. art critic Finola Hughes falls hard for artist Brendan Fraser even though he killed a model years before and is still obsessed by the woman. Director Phedon Papamichael tosses in the requisite plot twists and keeps things moving fairly well. In visual terms, though, he aims for (and gets) a trashy, paint-stained shabbiness. The studio-loft set looks like it ought to be scrubbed down with a wire brush and strong soap, and Fraser seems right at home there. He plays the part as a seedy, sweaty, lank-haired Andre Agassi of the artsy set. Tom Hiel's elegant classical score is completely at odds with the images on the screen and deserves special mention. 🐾🐾

Nudity, sexual material, and mild violence.

1994 (R) 86m/C Finola Hughes, Brendan Fraser, Glenn Shadix, Moon Zappa, Patrick Richwood, Seymour Cassel; D. Phedon Papamichael; W. Fred Stroppel; C. Phedon Papamichael; M. Tom Hiel. VHS PAR

Dark Tide

Straw Dogs in the tropics. Unhappily married Chris Sarandon and Brigitte Bako harvest sea snakes for venom until boat captain Richard Tyson falls for her. The location shooting is effective, but the film is curiously put together. The first half is sexy and romantic, but it abruptly shifts gears and becomes graphically violent and ugly. The two sides of the film aren't properly balanced, making this one less than it could have been. Also available in an unrated version. 🐾🐾

Violence, sexual content, strong language, brief nudity.

1993 (R) 92m/C Brigitte Bako, Richard Tyson, Chris Sarandon; D. Luca Bercovici. VHS, LV VMK

Darkman 2: The Return of Durant

"I choose to live on as a creature of the shadows—as Darkman!" So says brilliant scientist Peyton Westlake in a sequel that recalls the great Universal horror series of the 1930s (particularly *The Invisible Man*). Evil villain Durant (Larry Drake) has chosen to live on, too, even though he was turned to toast in the helicopter crash at the end of the first film. But villains as good as Durant are hard to come by, so he miraculously survived and has been in a coma. Now, he's back and meaner than ever. Meanwhile, Westlake (Arnold Vosloo ably taking over for Liam Neeson) is still working on a formula for synthetic skin. Director/cinematographer Bradford May captures the energy, black humor, and comic book spirit of Sam Raimi's original, but this one lacks that extra spark and attention to small details that mark the best of Raimi's work. 🐾🐾🐾

Strong language, violence.

1994 (R) 93m/C Arnold Vosloo, Larry Drake, Kim Delaney, Renee O'Connor, Rod Wilson; D. Bradford May; W. Steven McKay, Chuck Pfarrer; C. Bradford May; M. Randy Miller. VHS, LV MCA

Darkman 3: Die Darkman Die

Third entry in the series adds new characters and conflicts to the premise. As fans know, Dr. Peyton Westlake (Arnold Vosloo), horribly disfigured in the first movie, is searching for a formula for synthetic skin. The stuff he's got is temporary but it does allow him to look briefly like anyone else including new bad guy, drug dealer Peter Rooker (Jeff Fahey, who has a grand time). Under Bradford May's direction, the pace is crisp and the action has a deliciously nasty edge with beheadings and self-administered spinal surgery. What's lacking is the brilliantly sharp individual detail that Sam Raimi brought to the original. 🦴🦴🦴

Violence, strong language.

1995 (R) 87m/C Arnold Vosloo, Jeff Fahey, Darlanne Fluegel, Nigel Bennett, Roxann Biggs-Dawson; *D:* Bradford May; *W:* Mike Werb; *M:* Randy Miller. **VHS, LV** *MCA*

Dawn of the Dead

The director's cut of what many consider to be George Romero's finest horror film is 11 minutes longer than the theatrical release (also available on video). Horror fans should know, however, that they haven't been missing any extra violence or gore. The film was never rated by the MPAA. It was simply tightened up a bit because theatre owners thought that at two-hours plus it was too long. For the target audience, that extra length is a treat. Romero's story of horror, politics, and consumerism has aged well. The violence is no longer shocking; gory effects have progressed (if that's the right word) so far that these simple shootings and such seem almost primitive. The rest of the action—mostly set in a huge shopping mall—is suspenseful, intelligent, and surprisingly funny at times. This one is easily the best of Romero's *Dead* trilogy, and it gets the right treatment here with a remastered, letterboxed print and soundtrack, plus a second tape with theatrical trailers. 🦴🦴🦴

Graphic violence, strong language.

1978 137m/C David Emge, Ken Foree, Gaylen Ross; *D:* George A. Romero; *W:* George A. Romero. **VHS, LV** *VTR*

Dead Air

Imitation is the most sincere compliment, and Clint Eastwood's *Play Misty for Me* is the object. Soulful late-night DJ Gregory Hines has a female fan who kills any woman who gets close to him. Though he tries to persuade the police that he wants to help, they're suspicious of a similar incident in his past. Writer David Amann and director Fred Walton stretch credulity beyond conventional limits, but Hines is excellent and that's enough to keep most videophiles interested and guessing. 🦴🦴🦴

Mature subject matter, some violence, sexual material.

1994 (PG-13) 91m/C Gregory Hines, Debrah Farentino, Gloria Reuben, Beau Starr, Laura Harrington, Michael Harris, W. Earl Brown, Veronica Cartwright; *D:* Fred Walton; *W:* David Amann; *M:* Dana Kaproff. **VHS, LV** *MCA*

Dead Beat

Curious little misfire makes a valiant attempt to be different. At first, it appears to be straightforward nostalgia—a story of teenagers in Albuquerque, 1965. The narrator is Rudy (Balthazar Getty), but the main character is Kit (Bruce Ramsay), a narcissistic Elvis wannabe who romances and discards Martha (Sara Gilbert) and Donna (Meredith Salenger) in short order. The ultimate object of Kit's affections is Kristen (Nastasha Gregson Wagner), the banker's mad blonde daughter. When she shows up, the story takes a surreal turn. Their tumultuous relationship is roughly equal parts *Twin Peaks*, *Pulp Fiction*, and *American Graffiti*, but without their style or originality. Director Adam Dubov manages a few good moments but neither the script nor the earnest young cast quite measure up. In the end, the film isn't nearly as weird as it's trying to be, or as it needs to be. 🦴🦴

Mature subject matter, strong language, brief nudity.

1994 (R) 94m/C Bruce Ramsay, Natasha Gregson Wagner, Balthazar Getty, Meredith Salenger, Sara Gilbert, Deborah Harry,

Max Perlich, Alex Cox; *D:* Adam Dubov; *W:* Adam Dubov. **VHS** *WEA, LIV*

Dead Certain

Blue-light special *Silence of the Lambs* has scuzzy cop Francesco Quinn on the trail of a serial killer. He's sure that Brad Dourif is somehow involved despite ironclad alibis. Throughout, the screen is filled with ugly characters who are made up to look even uglier and are photographed in the ugliest conditions. The action contains graphic drug use and bloody violence. Toward the end, the half-baked script places children in jeopardy in an absolutely unconscionable manner. **WOOF!**

Rated R for violence, drug use, nudity, language, and general principle.

1992 **(R)** 93m/**C** Brad Dourif, Francesco Quinn, Karen Russell, Joel Kaiser; *D:* Anders Palm; *W:* Anders Palm. **VHS** *HMD*

Dead Cold

Fine little thriller gets the most out of a modest budget. It's one of those tricky films that works through uncertainty. For the first hour or so, every character's actions are open to several interpretations. The basic situation—minus a few key pieces of information—is this: Screenwriter Eric Thornsen (Chris Mulkey) and his wife Alicia (Lysette Anthony, who also co-produced) are taking a second honeymoon at a remote mountain cabin. Kale Beacham (Peter Dobson) is a semi-menacing, uninvited guest. Somebody wants somebody else dead. Maybe. With this kind of material, the set-up is invariably more complex and interesting than the pay-off, but the second half is above average. The level of violence is appropriate to the story and so's the humor. 🎵🎵🎵

Mature subject matter, strong language, violence, sexual content, brief nudity.

ANDREW MCCARTHY AND ELIZABETH PENA IN *DEAD FUNNY.* ©A-PIX.

1996 (R) 91m/C Lysette Anthony, Chris Mulkey, Peter Dobson, Alina Thompson, Michael Champion; *D:* Kurt Anderson; *W:* Richard Brandes. **VHS, LV** *LIV*

Dead Funny

Inspired, quirky comic mystery manages to combine genuine laughs and spooky, nightmarish moments without diminishing the effect of either. For comparative purposes, think of *Desperately Seeking Susan* and *The Gun in Betty Lou's Handbag*, but this one's an original. Vivian (Elizabeth Pena) returns from work to her messy apartment, half-painted in a rainbow of colors and filled with the debris of last night's party. If that weren't enough, her boyfriend Reggie (Andrew McCarthy) is dead in the kitchen. There's a samurai sword in his chest and, no, this isn't another of his practical jokes. Vivian and her ditzy, none-too-sober friend Louise (Paige Turco) "reason" that they've got to figure out who did it before they call the police. The script by director John Feldman and Cindy Oswin then moves back and forth in time, filling in the details of the yearlong relationship between Viv and Reggie and slipping back into the present. The device works well, particularly when Viv's Women's Support Group shows up for a meeting. It all arrives at a neatly twisted ending. Feldman was also responsible for the video cult hit *Alligator Eyes.* ✍✍✍✎

Mature subject matter, strong language, sexual content, brief nudity.

1994 (R) 91m/C Elizabeth Pena, Andrew McCarthy, Paige Turco, Blanche Baker, Lisa Jane Persky, Michael Mantell; *D:* John Feldman; *W:* Cindy Oswin, John Feldman; *M:* Sheila Silver. **VHS, LV** *APX*

Dead On

Video noir might have been called *Strangers on a Plane* but any resemblance to Hitchcock ends right there. Matt McCoy is a commercial pilot whose shrewish wife owns the airline. Shari Shattuck has an abusive, inconvenient husband. They meet one night in an airport hotel bar, and one thing graphically leads to another, until she explains her ideas about perfect murders where strangers trade vic-

tims. Three weeks later, wifey disappears. Though the script contains the necessary red herrings, most experienced mystery fans will be one step ahead of writer April Wayne. Still, her characters work, and director Ralph Hemecker has a good visual sense, making effective use of light, color, and abstract shapes. The actors don't embarrass themselves either. They know what the material is and handle it appropriately. Also available in an unrated version. ✍✍✍ **GPI: 8.8**

Sexual material, nudity, strong language, violence.

1993 (R) 87m/C Matt McCoy, Shari Shattuck, David Ackroyd, Tracy Scoggins, Thomas Wagner; *D:* Ralph Hemecker; *W:* April Wayne. **VHS, LV** *ORI*

Dead Right

Under its 1968 title *If He Hollers, Let Him Go,* this one was famous for singer/star Barbara McNair's nude scenes, also seen in the pages of *Playboy* magazine. Today it could be shown virtually uncut on network television, but the years have not dimmed its craziness. Considering the racial/political turmoil of the times, it's an appropriate piece of bad pop entertainment that takes the anger and outrage that black Americans felt at institutionalized racism, and turns it into schlock, glorious B-movie schlock. Falsely accused of rape and murder, Raymond St. Jacques breaks out of prison and finds himself trapped in a screwloose plot. Don't miss Paula Prentiss' deranged cameo as a shotgun-toting crazy lady. Writer/producer/director Charles Martin never let logic or common sense get in the way of this blatant, hokey nonsense. He created an alternative masterpiece and an embarrassment for all concerned. ***AKA:*** If He Hollers, Let Him Go. ✍✍✍

Rated R for fleeting nudity, mild profanity, general principle.

1968 (R) 105m/C Raymond St. Jacques, Dana Wynter, Kevin McCarthy, Barbara McNair, Paula Prentiss; *D:* Charles Martin; *W:* Charles Martin. **VHS** *PSM*

Deadly Desire

While it's no *Body Heat*, this thriller has most of the right moves. If the conclusion gives itself away too soon, the ride is still a lot of fun. As usual, the story is set in California and it begins with a triangle. There's abused wife Kathryn Harrold, rich husband Will Patton who spends a lot of time on the road, and ex-cop turned security guard Jack Scalia who installs their security system and patrols the neighborhood. You can take it from there. Charles Correll's direction is stylishly understated. The script by Jerry and Tobi Ludwig doesn't break any new ground, but the characters are unusually well developed and well acted. Made-for-cable with extra footage added for tape version. *ᐱᐱ𝒱*

Sexual content, brief nudity, violence.

1991 (R) 93m/C Jack Scalia, Kathryn Harrold, Will Patton, Joe Santos; *D:* Charles Correll; *W:* Jerry Ludwig, Tobi Ludwig. VHS PAR, HHE

Deadly Embrace

In many ways, this early effort from low-budget veteran Dave DeCoteau (directed under his nom-de-video Ellen Cabot) set the mold for the "erotic thriller." It's a simple story of infidelity and videotape with characters who have become veritable archetypes—the wealthy neglectful husband, beautiful bored wife, younger man—played by actors who have gone on to busy careers in the field. By current standards, the production values are rough, but that's O.K. This one would have been right at home on a 1970s drive-in screen. *ᐱᐱᐱ*

Subject matter, sexual content, brief nudity, strong language, some violence.

1988 (R) 82m/C Jan-Michael Vincent, Jack Carter, Ty Randolph, Linnea Quigley, Michelle (McClellan) Bauer, Ken Abraham; *D:* Ellen Cabot. VHS PSM

Deadly Possession

Handsome Australian suspense film is not as compelling as director Craig Lahiff's sleeper hit *Fever*. Instead, it's more an homage to Hitchcock; from Frank Strangio's music to a somewhat predictable ending that reworks one of the master's most famous twists. The setting's a music school where a young woman is attacked one night and thrown from a high window. Kate (Penny Cook) is a student there and at first the police suspect her ex-husband, but she believes his outlandish alibi. The plot moves slowly with individual shots carefully composed in large balanced areas of primary colors. The script by Lahiff and producer Terry Jennings is filled with serious literary and musical references. Before it's over, sexual roles and stereotypes have shifted. A striking visual treat. *ᐱᐱᐱ*

Violence, mature subject matter.

1988 99m/C *AU* Penny Cook, Anna-Maria Winchester, Liddy Clark, Olivia Hamnett; *D:* Craig Lahiff; *W:* Craig Lahiff, Terry Jennings; *M:* Frank Strangio. VHS, LV LIV, VES

Deadly Sins

So-so Gothic thriller is set in a rural Catholic girl's school described by the characters as "a place of terrible secrets" and "a hotbed of sexual repression." It's up to the new cop in town (David Keith) to solve a series of murders and disappearances, with the help of a nun (Alyssa Milano) who might not be a nun. For much of the film, it's uncertain whether it's a horror film or a mystery, but that doesn't matter. Director Michael Robison will do anything for a scare and he overuses the smoke machines for cheap atmospherics, or maybe the smoke is coming from the hotbed. *ᐱᐱ𝒱*

Mature subject matter, sexual content, nudity, violence, strong language.

1995 (R) 98m/C David Keith, Alyssa Milano, Terry David Mulligan, Corrie Clark; *D:* Michael Robison; *W:* John Langley, Malcolm Barbour. VHS AVE

Deadly Weapons

This installment in Joe Bob Briggs' "Sleaziest Movies in the History of the World" series features the incredible 73-32-36 Chesty Morgan, and, yes, the title refers to the first number. Chesty, you see, has to avenge the murder of her lover and so she goes after the Mafia hit men with her awesome natural talents, and smothers them to death. Must be seen to be believed. *ᐱᐱ*

Vast toplessness, mild violence.

cessors with characters named John Carpenter, Sam Raimi, and Scott Ridley. Great stuff for fans. 🦴🦴🦴

Violence, strong language.

1995 (R) 99m/C Brad Dourif, Ely Pouget, William Hootkins; **D:** Stephen Norrington; **W:** Stephen Norrington. **VHS, LV** *VMK*

Death Magic

Ultra-low-budget horror was made in Tucson, Arizona. Producer/writer/director Paul E. Clinco appears to have assembled a group of amateur and semi-pro actors, some Old West re-enactors, and filmed his vengeful-ghost story on whatever locations were available. Sound quality and lighting are poor to marginal. At first the overwritten story is reminiscent of the original *Dark Shadows* soap opera, but it devolves into mystical mumbo jumbo and gory special effects, some of which seem to have been achieved through fingerpaints. The guys keep their clothes on; the women mostly don't. The one bright spot involves an older woman who has trouble remembering her lines. She plays a cop and the movie gets better every time she shows up. 🦴🦴

Sexual scenes, nudity, violence, bloody special effects.

1992 93m/C Anne Coffrey, Keith DeGreen, Jack Dunlap, Danielle Frons, Norman Stone; **D:** Paul E. Clinco; **W:** Paul E. Clinco. **VHS** *NO*

Death Spa

A cast of B-movie regulars is stranded in a well-produced but really silly story about a haunted health club. The prosthetic special effects are too ridiculous to be frightening and the pace is far too slow. Even so, the worst moments are funny. 🦴🦴

Also available in an unrated version; both contain brief nudity, violent effects, profanity.

1987 (R) 87m/C William Bumiller, Brenda Bakke, Merritt Butrick; **D:** Michael Fischa. **VHS** *MPI*

December 7th: The Movie

A radically abbreviated version of John Ford's "lost" film won an Oscar in 1943 but the full-

---

1970 (R) 90m/C Chesty Morgan, Harry Reems; **D:** Doris Wishman. **VHS** *SLZ*

Death Machine

This video premiere puts lots of big-budget big-screen s-f to shame. It too is solidly in the *Terminator* tradition of hard-edged action with a satiric side. In a near-future setting, corporate executive Hayden Cale (Ely Pouget) tries to fire mad scientist Jack Donte (Brad Dourif, at his inspired inimitable best). Seems Jack has invented a killer gizmo and, when he learns that his services are no longer wanted, he lets it loose in the headquarters building. This monster is essentially Robo-Raptor, an impressive collection of razor-sharp hardware and loud metallic sound effects. Writer/director Stephen Norrington and his effects crew do really nice work, keeping the action inventive and quick with a fair degree of suspense. Norrington tips his hat to his cinematic prede-

length feature, a fascinating piece of wartime propaganda, made a belated debut as a video original. The film was co-directed by Ford and cinematographer Gregg Toland, who also wrote the strange script. Even though Ford had reservations about the project, he helped Toland make the movie as part of Hollywood's war effort. The Navy was not so enthusiastic when it saw the result, and demanded that references to official unpreparedness be censored. The 84 minute running time became 34 minutes. In the restored video version, some Japanese language scenes have been subtitled, and the picture is remarkably sharp for film that's almost 50 years old. The story itself is a fascinating combination of propaganda, travelogue, fiction, history, allegory, and inspiration. On Dec. 6, 1941, Uncle Sam (Walter Huston) arrives in Hawaii. He's taking a vacation from the international worries that plague him, but his conscience, Mr. C. (Harry Davenport), won't let him relax. He warns the isolationist Sam that the Japanese are up to no good, even implying that Japanese-American children in Hawaii are spies. After an inconclusive foreign policy debate, Sam falls asleep to frightening nightmares. Though the following attack was recreated on the Twentieth Century-Fox backlot, it's remarkably realistic, and the supernatural aftermath is a properly bizarre ending to a unique piece of work. Curiously, the government was probably right to censor the film. The full-length version is so heavy handed and preachy that it's ineffective propaganda. But on video now, it provides an intriguing glimpse into America's wartime mentality and the sense of outrage that motivated and united a diverse country. 🗡🗡🗡

Contains no objectionable material.

1991 82m/B Walter Huston, Harry Davenport; *D:* Gregg Toland, John Ford; *W:* Gregg Toland; *C:* Gregg Toland. **VHS** *KIT, CPM, FUS*

Deconstructing Sarah

The title character (Shiela Kelley) is a hotshot advertising executive with a secret life. To those who know her, she's a proper businesswoman who's good at her job, dates suitable men, and seldom orders anything stronger than Perrier and lime to drink. But Sarah also has a taste for the wild side. Some nights she dyes her hair red, slinks into tight dresses, and heads for the closest biker bar where her drink of choice is tequila with Johnnie Walker back. While they're setting up the conflicts, writer Lee Rose and director Craig Baxley keep things moving with admirable trickiness. The characters are realistic and properly enigmatic, but the beginning is stronger than the conclusion. The second half falls back on silly visual cliches—the guy hiding in the backseat of the car—and lame dialogue. 🗡🗡

Mature subject matter, brief nudity, language, violence.

1994 (R) 92m/C Rachel Ticotin, Sheila Kelley, A. Martinez, David Andrews, John Vickery, Jenifer Lewis, Dwier Brown, Peter Jason; *D:* Craig R. Baxley; *W:* Lee Rose; *M:* Tom Scott. **VHS** *MCA*

Deep Red

The subject is immortality. The structure is a chase with a genuinely mad scientist hunting for a little girl and her mother. In a role reminiscent of *The Terminator*, Michael Biehn plays a burnt out bodyguard who accepts a questionable assignment and finds himself under attack by killer milkmen. He also provides the voiceover narration that explains D. Brent Mote's complicated story. Veteran director Craig Baxley handles the action crisply, and makes effective use of a limited special effects budget. Several well-placed touches of humor help a lot, though the s-f elements of the plot aren't expanded as fully as they might have been. Recommended for s-f fans. 🗡🗡🗡

Violence.

1994 (R) 85m/C Michael Biehn, Joanna Pacula, John de Lancie; *D:* Craig R. Baxley; *W:* D. Brent Mote. **VHS, LV** *MCA*

Def by Temptation

Writer/director/producer/music supervisor/star James Bond III has managed to make a horror/comedy that's actually frightening and funny. The monster here is the Temptress (Cynthia Bond, no relation to JBIII), who "wants to remain in the fallen lustful state of existence...incarnate in the flesh." She picks men up in a bar, takes them back to her loft, and they're never seen again. What a revoltin' development! Her real prey is a young divinity student undergoing a crisis of faith. Bond makes several critical observations about male sexual irresponsibility. To one degree or another, the victims deserve their fate. But the best part of the story is its strong traditional moral sense, something that has been noticeably lacking in recent horror films. There are some rough moments in the script and the low budget shows through in some of the locations, but those are small flaws. This remarkable debut is one of the best and most original horror films anyone has made in years. 🎵🎵🎵

Strong language, sexual content, violence, brief nudity.

1990 **(R)** 95m/C James Bond III, Kadeem Hardison, Bill Nunn, Samuel L. Jackson, Minnie Gentry, Rony Clanton, Cynthia Bond; *D:* James Bond III; *W:* James Bond III. **VHS, LV** *SGE, IME*

Delta Heat

Anthony Edwards is a Los Angeles narcotics detective whose partner is killed in the French Quarter. Lance Henriksen, a one-handed ex-cop, is the only person who'll give him any help. They hate each other at first sight—that's what the formula demands—but before long, they're busting up bad guys and bonding to beat the band. Throughout, the stars handle the light material with tongues firmly in cheeks. Edwards is sporting two of the ugliest sideburns you'll ever see, and they're no better than his hideous suits in orange, green, and olive. If you don't figure out who the bad guy is the second he shows up, you haven't been watching many cop movies. But again, who cares? Director Michael Fischa is having fun with this stuff. In the city, he captured a good sense of the Quarter and the Garden District, and when the action moves out to the bayous and swamps, it's not as cliched as it could have been. The soundtrack features music by Rockin Dopsie and the Zydeco Twisters. 🎵🎵🎵

Violence, strong language, brief nudity.

1992 **(R)** 91m/C Anthony Edwards, Lance Henriksen, Betsy Russell, Linda Dona, Rod Masterson, John McConnell, Clyde Jones; *D:* Michael Fischa. **VHS** *ACA*

A Demon in My View

In a way, this German-English co-production can be seen as a coda to Anthony Perkins' career because he plays yet another variation on the archetypal serial killer, Norman Bates. Arthur Johnson (Perkins) has lived for more than 20 years in an aging London apartment. He stays on while other tenants come and go, and when the pressures of memory become too great, he strangles young women. Writer/director Petra Haffter does a fine job of adapting Ruth Rendell's novel to the screen and revealing the inner workings of Arthur's fevered psyche. She also captures the uneasy moral texture of Rendell's fiction. Rendell doesn't write about brave heroes, guilty villains, and innocent victims. Her world is much more complex and dangerous than that. Almost all of the violence and physical action is suggested or shown quickly. The most frightening moment—and it's a real skin crawler—involves nothing more threatening than a safety pin. Even so, this is the spookiest psychological horror film to hit the video stores since the original *The Vanishing* and *Monsieur Hire*. 𝄞𝄞𝄞

Mature subject matter, sexual content, language, violence.

1992 (R) 98m/C Anthony Perkins, Sophie Ward, Stratford Johns; **D:** Petra Haffter; **W:** Petra Haffter. **VHS, LV** *VMK, MOV*

Demon Keeper

Cheesy guilty pleasure benefits hugely from liberal use of the fast-forward button. This Zimbabwean production is a supernatural variation on the *Ten Little Indians* plotline. Isolated mansion, dark and stormy night, group of strangers who quickly become murder victims. The differences here are two psychics (Dirk Benedict and Edward Albert) and a monster who's obviously a guy in a scaly suit with a skull on his jockstrap. It's fun if you're in the mood for a really bad movie. Otherwise, forget it. 𝄞 **GPI: 6.2**

Ridiculous violence, strong language, brief nudity, sexual content.

1995 (R) 90m/C Edward Albert, Dirk Benedict; **D:** Joe Tornatore. **VHS** *NHO*

Demonstone

Philippine import is either a screwloose supernatural adventure or an allegory on the local political situation. Whichever, it's the story of a spirit that rises from the dead, possesses the body of TV newswoman Nancy Everhard, and tries to destroy an important family. The storyline could hardly be more far-fetched, but Jan-Michael Vincent and R. Lee Ermey handle the physical action well enough. Director Andrew Prowse seldom lets the pace get too slow and he made good use of dozens of locations; the film has a strong sense of place. Despite the obvious weaknesses, it's lively and engaging. **AKA:** Heartstone. 𝄞𝄞
GPI: 7.9

Strong language, some violence, brief nudity and sexual situations.

1989 (R) 90m/C *PH* R. Lee Ermey, Jan-Michael Vincent, Nancy Everhard; **D:** Andrew Prowse. **VHS, LV** *FRH*

Dennis Potter: The Last Interview

Potter, creator of such off-beat productions as *Pennies from Heaven, The Singing Detective,* and *Lipstick on Your Collar,* died from pancreatic cancer. A few weeks before his death, he sat down with British television producer Melvyn Bragg to talk about his life and his work. At the time, Potter knew the end was close and had to sip from a flask of liquid morphine to balance pain and consciousness. This tape is his testament. He talks about everything from smoking—"It's easier to pull a gun in America than a cigarette out of your pocket."—to God—"a rumor, if you like." But he's mostly concerned with politics, the decline of the British press, his own writing both past and present, and his life. Throughout, his calm sense of purpose is unshakable. He's at peace with his dead father—how many men can say that?—and with himself. There's no self-pity or recrimination. Instead, he's a man who is completely free and unafraid to speak his mind. And his most important point, the one that he states as strongly as he can, is to live in the moment, to appreciate the present as fully as you can because nothing else is certain. That may be simple wisdom but it's worth repeating and Potter states it with rare eloquence. 𝄞𝄞𝄞𝄞

Contains some strong language.

1994 70m/C *GB* **D:** Tom Poole. **VHS** *TVC*

Descending Angel

Despite an impressive cast, this is something of a disappointment. Part of the problem lies in the daddy-was-a-Nazi plot that was also used in *The Music Box*. George C. Scott and Diane Lane do their best—and that's very good—but the story is predictable and the drab Midwestern locations don't help either. 𝄢𝄢

Violence, sexual situations, nudity.

1990 (R) 96m/C George C. Scott, Diane Lane, Eric Roberts, Mark Margolis, Vyto Ruginis, Amy Aquino, Richard Jenkins, Jan Rubes; *D:* George C. Scott, Jeremy Paul Kagan; *W:* George C. Scott. VHS, LV *HBO*

Desire

Literary love story follows a French girl (Greta Scacchi) who falls for a Scottish fisherman (Vincent D'Onofrio). Can an intellectual and a working man find happiness together? It's tough. On their first date she quotes Matthew Arnold. Then a few years later she discovers existentialism and after that she becomes a feminist college professor. Over the years and through various marriages and children, they find time for the occasional long weekend of passion together in scenic locales. Writer/director Andrew Birkin takes the story and the characters seriously, but it's not particularly compelling. The lovers remain distant and their allegedly overpowering desire seems forced. 𝄢

Sexual content, language.

1993 (R) 108m/C Greta Scacchi, Vincent D'Onofrio; *D:* Andrew Birkin; *W:* Andrew Birkin. VHS *ACA*

Desire

Thriller takes a conventional premise for a "tough" detective story and switches the sexes. (It's done all the time in fiction these days, but virtually never on film.) Lauren Allen (Kate Hodge) is an ex-cop turned security analyst for Lantel Cosmetics. Desire is the company's newest perfume. Sales take a predictable dive when several young women are found murdered and doused with it. Did the company president (Deborah Shelton) steal the formula for the scent from designer Gordon Lewis (Martin Kemp)? In time-honored detective fashion, Lauren becomes personally involved when she investigates Lewis. Writer/director Rodney MacDonald is more comfortable with characters and with his cast than with the mystery elements, which are handled clumsily. Still, this one has its moments. 𝄢𝄢𝄢

Contains some violence, nudity, sexual material, strong language.

1995 90m/C Kate Hodge, Martin Kemp, Deborah Shelton, Robert Miranda; *D:* Rodney MacDonald; *W:* Rodney MacDonald. VHS *MNC*

Desperate Prey

Claudia Karvan is a tough self-centered street kid who knows how to play the game until she witnesses the murder of a prominent lawyer and tapes the killing. Catherine McClements is an idealistic lawyer who wants to help her. The premise is so unusual that it takes some effort to get into the action, and that's made even more difficult by the often impenetrable Aussie accents. But writer/director Danny Vendramini knows how to create striking scenes and good characters. He got thoroughly believable performances from his two leads, and as long as the action is focused on them, this is a good female buddy picture. I can't claim to have completely understood the conclusion, but that's O.K., too. Overall, the movie works. 𝄢𝄢𝄢

Violence, strong language, subject matter.

1994 (R) 102m/C AU Claudia Karvan, Catherine McClements, Holly Butler; *D:* Danny Vendramini; *W:* Danny Vendramini. VHS *APX*

Desperate Remedies

Quirky New Zealand import is so stylized that it's bound to irritate more viewers than it delights. But obviously that's what Stewart Main and Peter Wells (who co-directed and -wrote) intended. The whole film was made on sets—no exteriors—with wildly exaggerated make-up, colors, camera angles, sound effects, acting...everything. As for the story—imagine the Fellini version of an overripe Dickens novel. In a 19th century seaport town being flooded with immigrants, business-woman Dorothea Brook (Jennifer Ward-Lealand) has a host of problems. Her opium-addicted sister Rose (Kiri Mills) is involved with the totally unsuitable and nasty Frazer (Clifford Curtis). The oily and unscrupulous Poyser (Michael Hurst) wants to marry Dorothea to gain control of her money and to advance his political career, though he's not at all certain about Dorothea's relationship with her "servant" Ann Cooper (Lisa Chappell). Meanwhile, Dorothea haunts the docks looking for a man, and when she spies pouty-lipped Lawrence Hays (Kevin Smith), she thinks she's found him. Toss in a few more subplots, add a fistful of rubies, and stir vigorously. For loose comparative purposes in a visual sense, think of *Absolute Beginners*, *Ballroom Dancing*, and *The Cook, the Thief, His Wife & Her Lover*, but this one's more operatic and grandiose than any of them, and it's got a much better ending. 🦴🦴🦴

Mature subject matter, sexual content, brief nudity, drug use.

1993 (R) 92m/C NZ Jennifer Ward-Lealand, Kevin Smith, Lisa Chappell, Michael Hurst, Kiri Mills, Clifford Curtis; D: Stewart Main, Peter Wells; W: Stewart Main, Peter Wells; C: Leon Narbey; M: Peter Scholes. VHS PAR

Devil in the Flesh

This story of a teenager's affair with an older woman received a lot of attention for its one explicit sexual scene, but that doesn't alter the fact that the other 98 percent of the film is a stodgy mix of misogyny and politics. Writer/director Marco Bellocchio manages to make young lust boring. On tape, it's available in two versions, rated X and R. In either case though, it's little more than a skin flick with shallow artistic pretensions; i.e., a late-'80s answer to *I Am Curious Yellow*. **AKA:** Il Diavolo in Corpo. 🦴

Nudity, sexual situations, profanity.

1987 (R) 110m/C IT Maruschka Detmers, Federico Pitzalis; D: Marco Bellocchio; W: Marco Bellocchio. VHS, LV ORI, INJ

Dial Help

Alternative classic boasts top-drawer production values, special effects, and a plot of soaring silliness. Italian telephones are possessed by spirits and try to communicate with an English model (Charlotte Lewis). The evil telephones also sneak up on unsuspecting victims. Toward the end, director Ruggero Deodato creates one brilliant moment of slapstick supernatural eroticism when the telephones call Lewis and seduce her into putting on her sexiest underwear (including high heels). Then she hops into a tub full of sudsy green water and writhes around while her phone serenades her with the Italian version of the 1,001 Strings performing *Unchained Melody*. Video fans, it doesn't get any better than this! 🦴🦴🦴🦴 **GPI: 9.5**

Mature subject matter, profanity, violence, and don't-blink-or-you'll-miss-it nudity.

1988 (R) 94m/C IT Charlotte Lewis, Marcello Modugno, Mattia Sbragia, Victor Cavallo; D: Ruggero Deodato. VHS PSM

Digger

Coming of age drama tries to do too much. When his parents separate, Digger (Adam Hann-Byrd from *Little Man Tate*) is sent to live with his aunt and uncle and reluctantly makes friends with the imaginative Billy (Joshua Jackson). Writer Rodney Gibbons and director Robert Turner treat the conflicts of youth with the proper seriousness, and that's a problem. The action is talky, slow, and hard to follow. Young viewers who aren't immediately hooked by the Pacific Northwest scenery may give up in frustration before the story really gets moving. Once it does, it attempts to cram in every possible adolescent emotion and crisis: disease, divorce, death, abandonment, unrequited love. On the other hand, the acting is first rate, particularly from the two leads, and most of the time they sound like real kids. For those who stick with it, the story has a strong emotional ending. 🦴🦴🦴

Contains a little mild sexual humor.

1994 (PG) 92m/C Adam Hann-Byrd, Olympia Dukakis, Leslie Nielsen, Joshua Jackson, Barbara Williams, Timothy Bottoms;

The Hound's Favorite Sleepers: Coming of Age

"Coming of Age" is, at best, a nebulous term. In the context of these Video Premieres, it refers to films about characters who, at any age, come to realize who and what they are. And since the Hound calculates such matters in dog years, what do the numbers mean, anyway?

Bottle Rocket	My Family
Coup de Torchon	The Pompatus of Love
Double Happiness	Powwow Highway
Flirting	Radio Inside
Five Corners	Streets
King of the Hill	There Goes My Baby
Muriel's Wedding	The Year My Voice Broke

D: Robert Turner; *W:* Rodney Gibbons; *M:* Todd Boekelheide. **VHS** *PAR*

Digital Man

Umpteenth post-apocalyptic s-f action movie is about an army patrol composed of humans and cyborgs (who think they are human) on the trail of the titular Matthias Hues, a super-cyborg who totes a quintuple-barreled rocket gun. The main attractions are effective use of desert locations, fairly good effects, and a little cornball humor. Director Phillip J. Roth keeps things moving well enough but, as is so often the case in the genre, the action degenerates into characters wearing silly shoulder pads and waving absurdly large weapons. For fans only.

Violence, strong language, fleeting nudity.

1994 (R) 95m/C Ken Olandt, Adam Baldwin, Ed Lauter, Matthias Hues, Kristen Dalton, Paul Gleason; *D:* Phillip J. Roth; *W:* Phillip J. Roth, Ronald Schmidt. **VHS** *REP*

Dillinger and Capone

Strange little cross-pollination combines the plot of a B-movie with the techniques of an experimental film. The key is a trio of tongue-in-cheek bravura performances by Martin Sheen and F. Murray Abraham in the title roles and Stephen Davies in support. In this version of the story, Dillinger wasn't killed in front of the Biograph Theatre in Chicago. It was somebody else; Public Enemy Number One retired to a farm in Bakersfield, CA, and got married. Years later, Capone, syphilitic and more than half mad, forces Dillinger back into action for one last job. Director Jon Purdy (*Reflections in the Dark*) makes the most of a limited budget and gets his stars fully into the spirit of the piece. And, he uses lots of Tommyguns.

Violence, strong language.

1995 (R) 95m/C Martin Sheen, F. Murray Abraham, Catherine Hicks, Stephen Davies, Don Stroud, Clint Howard; *D:* Jon Purdy; *W:* Michael B. Druxman. **VHS, LV** *NHO*

Dinosaur Island

Co-producers/directors Jim Wynorski and Fred Olen Ray have a combined track record of more than 30 alternative classics, and here they set a new low for themselves. Virtually everything about the flick has a recycled look to it, from the familiar locations to the tryannosaurus who also appeared in *Carnosaur*. This time out, he looks like he'd be more at home overlooking a miniature golf course. As the title and advertising promise, it's mindless, sexy fluff about an uncharted island populated by the titular critters and curvy babes in leather bikinis. **GPI: 4.4**

Nudity, sexual activity, unconvincing violence.

1993 (R) 85m/C Ross Hagen, Richard Gabai, Antonia Dorian, Peter Spellos, Tom Shell, Griffin Drew, Steve Barkett, Toni

Naples; *D:* Jim Wynorski, Fred Olen Ray; *W:* Bob Sheridan, Christopher Wooden. VHS *NHO, HVL*

Diplomatic Immunity

In your basic revenge movie, a suave and sadistic South American Nazi pervert kills a Marine's daughter. Claiming "diplomatic immunity," he goes home to Paraguay. The Marine follows and lots of stuff blows up. There are no big surprises, but Bruce Boxleitner gets the most out of his stereotyped hero and Billy Drago is well cast against type as a burnt-out cynic. ⚂⚂⚀

Violence, strong language, and brief nudity.

1991 (R) 95m/C Bruce Boxleitner, Billy Drago, Meg Foster, Robert Forster; *D:* Peter Maris. VHS, LV *FRH, IME*

Discretion Assured

Brazilian thriller has a good cast and an overly complicated story that simply doesn't know when to stop. Michael York is a businessman who's having an affair with his partner's deranged, possessive wife. He's also got the hots for Elizabeth Gracen, a real knockout who may be setting him up. At the same time, someone is embezzling money from the company. Toss in a murder or two and a world-weary detective and you've got everything you need for a hyperventilating soap opera-mystery. The best part is Jennifer O'Neill's gleefully maniacal performance. The film looks great with exotic locations, a strong sense of humor—always a welcome addition—and a twist ending. Recommended for those in the mood for something decidedly different. ⚂⚂⚂

Mature subject matter, strong language, violence, brief nudity.

1993 (R) 97m/C Michael York, Jennifer O'Neill, Dee Wallace Stone, Elizabeth Gracen; *D:* Odorico Mendes. VHS *MNC*

Do or Die

Another slickly made Sidaris exercise in non-acting, nudity, and model airplanes. (Yes, model airplanes.) The superspy plot is just an excuse to get several overdeveloped young actors and actresses together onscreen. Sidaris'

movies tend to look like Al Capp's *Li'l Abner* comic strips on film, with big dumb guys being outfoxed by big aggressive women. ⚂⚂⚀

Strong language, nudity, violence.

1991 (R) 97m/C Erik Estrada, Dona Speir, Roberta Vasquez, Noriyuki "Pat" Morita, Bruce Penhall, Carolyn Liu, Stephanie Schick; *D:* Andy Sidaris; *W:* Andy Sidaris. VHS, LV *COL*

Dr. Alien

Wesley the nerd (Billy Jacoby) becomes Wesley the ladykiller overnight after alien Judy Landers gives him a shot of experimental stuff. Director David DeCoteau generally avoids the smutty, snickering humor that infects most B movies in this pleasant little s-f/teen comedy. Landers isn't exactly Judy Holliday, but she's got more comic talent than her blonde airhead image indicates. ⚂⚂

Nudity, sexual situations, and profanity.

1988 (R) 90m/C Billy Jacoby, Olivia Barash, Stuart Fratkin, Troy Donahue, Arlene Golonka, Judy Landers; *D:* David DeCoteau. VHS, LV *PAR*

Doctor Mordrid: Master of the Unknown

Standard good sorcerer (Jeffrey Combs) vs. bad sorcerer (Brian Thompson) tale borrows freely from Marvel's Dr. Strange and other more unusual sources, notably the novels of Ira Levin and John D. MacDonald. The special effects highlight is the big stop-motion animation finale, a fight between prehistoric skeletons in a natural history museum. One of Full Moon's more ambitious efforts. ⚂⚂⚂

Brief nudity, violence, special effects, language.

1990 (R) 89m/C Jeffrey Combs, Yvette Nipar, Jay Acovone, Brian Thompson; *D:* Albert Band, Charles Band; *M:* Richard Band. VHS *PAR*

Document of the Dead

In 1978, Roy Frumkes interviewed director George Romero on the set of *Dawn of the Dead*. Ten years later, he interviewed Romero again on the set of *Two Evil Eyes*. Parts of those interviews have been combined with scenes from other Romero films to create a revealing if uncritical portrait of the man and his work. When Frumkes judges Romero's work artistically, he tends to rely on film school cliches. But when he turns his attention to the filmmaking process, the work is fascinating. He follows *Dawn* from the beginnings of Romero's script, through the preproduction work, the location filming in a huge shopping mall, and finally the editing and distribution of the film itself. Frumkes focuses on the nuts-and-bolts side of the business: lighting, make up, special effects, and stunts. On the set of *Two Evil Eyes,* Frumkes films three takes of one seemingly simple special effects shot. Recommended for those interested in the real work that creates "movie magic." 𝕯𝕯𝕯

Contains special effects violence.

1990 83m/C *D:* Roy Frumkes. VHS *HTV*

The Dogfighters

Rowdy Wells (Robert Davi) is a blue-light special James Bond; Ben Gazzarra is the spook who dragoons him into a European mission to intercept stolen plutonium from slick bad guy Lothar (Alexander Gudunov). Both the dialogue and the acting are stilted, and in any given scene, at least one character will do something really really stupid to keep the plot wobbling along. That plot is no more ridiculous than your average Schwarzenegger epic, with lively chases and an interesting setting. 𝕯𝕯

Violence, strong language, brief nudity.

1995 (R) 96m/C Robert Davi, Alexander Godunov, Ben Gazzara, Lara Harris; *D:* Barry Zetlin; *W:* Sean Smith, Anthony Stark; *C:* Levie Isaacks; *M:* Jimmie Haskell. VHS, LV *LIV*

Dollman Vs. Demonic Toys

For the uninitiated, Dollman (Tim Thomerson) is a foot-tall tough detective from another world who's stranded on Earth. The Demonic Toys are possessed by an evil spirit. Also tossed into the mix is a sexy nurse (Melissa Behr) who was shrunk in *Bad Channels.* For a plot, the diminutive good guys and bad toys duke it out in a warehouse. Despite some vio-

lence and rough language, this one is aimed at younger videophiles and they'll like it. 𝕯𝕯𝖁

Violence, strong language.

1993 (R) 84m/C Tim Thomerson, Tracy Scoggins, Melissa Behr, Phil Brock, Phil Fondacaro; *D:* Charles Band; *W:* Craig Hamann; *M:* Richard Band. VHS *PAR*

The Dolphin

As a Brazilian legend puts it, a dolphin is transformed into a man when the moon is full. He seduces the women and scares off the fish, much to the dismay of the local male population. Writer/director Walter Lima's tale veers wildly in tone from restraint and heavily atmospheric scenes, to humor that borders on slapstick, to screaming emotionalism. For someone unfamiliar with the conventions of South American films, it's difficult to tell when the action is meant to be realistic, supernatural, psychological, or a mixture of all three. In any case, this one is decidedly different, the kind of thing you're not going to find anywhere but on home video and well worth a look for those interested in something out of the ordinary. 𝕯𝕯𝖁

Contains brief nudity, mild sexual content, strong language.

1987 95m/C *BR* Carlos Alberto Riccelli, Cassia Kiss, Ney Latorraca; *D:* Walter Lima Jr.; *W:* Walter Lima Jr. VHS *FXL, INJ, FCT*

Don't Do It

Ensemble cast takes realistic, funny look at love in the mid-'90s. Waitress Alicia (Sarah Trigger) is pregnant. Her current live-in beau Robert (James Marshall) might be the father, or it might be former flame Dodger (James LeGros) but now he is tentatively involved with Suzanna (Heather Graham) who's carrying a torch for Charles (Esai Morales) who, at that very moment, is putting some serious moves on Michelle (Sheryl Lee) but she hasn't gotten over Robert yet. Meanwhile, Balthazar Getty and Alexis Arquette cruise around discussing love and life when they're not calling old girlfriends. Got all that? Actually, writer/director Eugene Hess makes it hold together pretty well. Even though most of the action consists of couples sitting around talking, there's enough two-timing, lies, and hanky-panky for six weeks of a soap opera. Hess has a good sense of comic timing and he got the right mix of humor and seriousness. He also winds things up with a clever ending. Whatever he does next ought to be worth a look. 🎞🎞🎞

Strong language, sexual humor and situations.

1994 (PG-13) 90m/C James Marshall, James LeGros, Sheryl Lee, Esai Morales, Alexis Arquette, Balthazar Getty, Sarah Trigger, Heather Graham; **D:** Eugene Hess; **W:** Eugene Hess **VHS** *TRI*

Don't Talk to Strangers

Someone's threatening divorced mom Shanna Reed and her son. His dad (Terry O'Quinn) is a cop who's possibly psychotic, probably alcoholic, and certainly jealous of the new mystery man (Pierce Brosnan) in his ex's life. The first half or so is fairly predictable, but still involving. Then in the middle, the plot takes the wildest turn imaginable. Some major logical lapses follow, but by then the story has wandered so far afield it hardly matters. Acceptable diversion for the dedicated mystery fan. 🎞🎞🎞

Rated R for no reason I could see; subject matter, probably.

1994 (R) 94m/C Pierce Brosnan, Shanna Reed, Terry O'Quinn; **D:** Robert Lewis; **W:** Neill D. Hicks, Jon George, Nevin Schreiner. **VHS, LV** *MCA*

Double Happiness

Because the main characters are Chinese immigrants and their children, it's easy to compare this delight to *The Joy Luck Club,* but writer/director Mina Shum's debut is a more simple and straightforward coming-of-age story. Jade (Sandra Oh) is an inexperienced but talented young actress. She lives

BALTHAZAR GETTY AND ALEXIS ARQUETTE IN *DON'T DO IT.* ©TRIBORO ENTERTAINMENT GROUP.

at home with her parents (Stephen M.D. Chang and Alannah Ong) and her little sister Pearl (Frances You) while she auditions for roles and practices alone in her room. (Jade as Blanche DuBois is wonderful.) Her folks tolerate her ambitions but want nothing more than for her to marry a nice Chinese boy—preferably a doctor. That's the film's central conflict, the ultra-conventional parents vs. the dutiful but increasingly independent daughter. It's a familiar story but Mina Shum tells it with refreshing vigor. She's not one-sided, and takes pains to see all perspectives, making good use of the onscreen "interview" technique to let the characters explain themselves. But the film belongs to Sandra Oh. Her voice, energy, and screen presence are reminiscent of a young Jamie Lee Curtis. I look forward to whatever she and Mina Shum choose to do next. A sequel would be terrific. 🎜🎜🎜🎝

Mature subject matter, sexual content, strong language.

1994 (PG-13) 81m/C *CA* Sandra Oh, Stephen Chang, Alannah Ong, Frances You, Johnny Mah, Keith Callum Rennie; *D:* Mina Shum; *W:* Mina Shum; *C:* Peter Wunstorf. Genie Awards '94: Best Actress (Oh), Best Film Editing; Nominations: Genie Awards '94: Best Director (Shum), Best Film. **VHS, LV** *TTC, NLC*

Dracula (Spanish Version)

The famous Spanish version of the 1931 horror classic was made simultaneously, on the same sets, at night. It shares the same flaws and strengths. By today's standards, the pace is slow but the film is so richly atmospheric— even more than the English version—that it's still a treat. If Carlos Villarias lacks Bela Lugosi's presence, Lupita Tovar is a delightful (and sexy) heroine. Required viewing for serious horror fans. 🎜🎜🎜

Contains some sexual content.

1931 104m/B Carlos Villarias, Lupita Tovar, Eduardo Arozamena, Pablo Alvarez Rubio, Barry Norton, Carmen Guerrero; *D:* George Melford; *W:* Garrett Fort. **VHS** *MCA*

Dracula Rising

Art restorer Stacy Travis is commissioned to go to Europe to work on an old painting. There she finds that Christopher Atkins, the Byronic figure she met at an L.A. art show, is a vampire. But, hey, he's handsome, he's single, and he says he loves her. His brother Doug Wert thinks he should kill her. Does she really want this guy for an in-law? The budget is anemic; the cast is young, attractive, and stiff. 🦴🦴

Violence, bloody effects, brief nudity, sexual content.

1993 (R) 85m/C Christopher Atkins, Stacy Travis, Doug Wert; *D:* Fred Gallo. **VHS** *NHO*

Dragon Fury 2

Even judged as a micro-budget martial arts flick, this one's still pretty thin beer. Something is lacking when our heroine (Cathleen Ann Gardner) tries to show how tough she is by throwing her sword into a stuffed fish mounted on the wall. The fact that the first half of the film seems to have been lit with one 60 watt bulb doesn't help either. 🦴

Contains martial arts violence, brief nudity.

1996 90m/C Mike Norris, Robert Chapin, Cathleen Ann Gardner, Cole Andersen, Walter O'Neill, Kayla Murphy; *D:* Bryan Michael Stoller; *W:* Parker Bostwick. **VHS** *SLI*

Dragonard

Low-budget exercise in historical kinkiness and torture has a Caribbean setting. Our hero, Patrick Warburton, is a Scottish fellow who backed the wrong side in a revolt and has been condemned to slavery. He's bought by an evil plantation owner; the estate's mistress falls for him (she's not really married to the other guy) and so does Eartha Kitt, the local madame. Then the slaves rebel and the volcano erupts...oops, sorry, there is no volcano. Instead, there's Oliver Reed at his hammiest and that's better than a volcano. He rolls his eyes and orates in a gravelly Scottish dialect thicker than oat bran. In other movies that might be a flaw but it's welcome in this one because everyone else seems to be read-

ing cue cards. Throughout, this one is so clumsy and goofy that it's like an Italian gladiator movie with costumes from the wrong period. 🦴🦴

Violence, brief nudity, and sexual activity.

1988 (R) 93m/C Eartha Kitt, Oliver Reed, Annabel Schofield, Patrick Warburton; *D:* Gerard Kikoine; *W:* R.J. Marx. **VHS** *WAR*

Dragonworld

Live-action fantasy from Charles Band's Moonbeam label is a solid hit with kids. It's about a Scottish boy, his pet dragon, and the greedy businessman who wants to turn the critter into the main attraction at the titular theme park. As is always the case with Band films, the plot follows a familiar formula; the special effects are fine; and the production values look great. The target audience will watch it over and over. 🦴🦴🦴🦴

Mild violence.

1994 (PG) 86m/C Sam Mackenzie, Courtland Mead, Brittney Powell, John Calvin, Andrew Keir, Lila Kaye, John Woodvine; *D:* Ted Nicolaou; *W:* Ted Nicolaou, Suzanne Glazener Naha; *M:* Richard Band. **VHS** *PAR*

Dream Horse

This independent release is aimed at girls, ages three to nine, but any kid who's fascinated by horses will enjoy it. The producers use a simple fictional framework and a little animation to present information about various breeds and such. The tone is light, never lecturing, and though the animals are presented at their most handsome—these are virtual equine centerfolds—the film doesn't become too sentimental or cute, either. Certain little girls (and their parents and grandparents know who they are) will watch this one about 1,200 times before they get tired of it. 🦴🦴🦴

No offensive material.

1995 40m/C **VHS** *SHA*

Dream Lover

Ray (James Spader) has just been taken to the cleaners in a divorce. He lets it happen; that's the kind of passive fellow he is. Then he meets

Lena (Madchen Amick), a provocative, seductive young woman who might be perfect for him. He certainly wants to believe so. But what about the contradictions in her stories about her past and other unexplained curiosities? First-time director Nicholas Kazan handles the material with a soft touch, dodging cliches and telling the story through the characters. He got fine performances from his leads, two of the most attractive actors in the business these days. He gave this mystery the same cynical edge that made his script for *Reversal of Fortune* so unnerving. That quality is nowhere more apparent than at the end, which will strike some as a step too far and others as just right. All in all, this one's so neatly put together that it really shouldn't be shelved with all the other "erotic thrillers" in the video stores. Also available in an unrated version. ♫♫♫

Nudity, strong sexual content, language, violence.

1993 (R) 103m/C James Spader, Madchen Amick, Frederic Lehne, Bess Armstrong, Larry Miller, Kathleen York, Blair Tefkin, Scott Coffey, William Shockley, Clyde Kusatsu; **D:** Nicholas Kazan; **W:** Nicholas Kazan; **M:** Christopher Young. **VHS, LV** *PGV*

Driven to Kill

Knowing too much about this loopy story would spoil the fun. The key elements are an alcoholic dentist, his wife, $4 million in stolen cash, an unreliable station wagon, and two rival gangs. All of them collide on a lonely desert highway. It's half thriller, half comedy, with considerable overlap. ♫♫♫

Contains violence and profanity.

1990 90m/C Jake Jacobs, Chip Campbell, Michele McNeil; **D:** John Gazarian. **VHS** *PMH*

Drug Runners

Energetic action flick about D.E.A. agents and Mexican gangsters puts the "shoot" back in shoot-'em-up. The voice dubbing is so wonderfully bad that between gunshots, the cast sounds like they belong in an Italian gladiator flick. The inspiration seems to have been the non-stop action films of John Woo, but director Alan Kukowski doesn't have Woo's touch. ♫♫

Graphic gun violence, strong language, mild sexual content.

1988 86m/C Aldo Ray; **D:** Alan Kukowski. **VHS** *ORP*

Dust Devil

In terms of tone and style, this African import is similar to *Candyman*. Both try to tell a horror story within a realistic contemporary political context, and both feature well developed characters. Chelsea Field is running away from her abusive husband when she picks up hitchhiker Robert Burke in the Namibian desert. She should have been tipped off by his ugly sideburns. He's the title character, a spiritual creature who is endlessly rejuvenated by ritual murder. But this demon kills only people who have reached spiritual despair—those who are about to commit suicide—and he even develops an emotional attachment to them. The only person who has any understanding of what he's doing is black policeman Zakes Mokae. Writer/director Richard Stanley tends to get too tricky and inventive for his own good toward the end, and at times the film threatens to become a spaghetti Western. But it's still a cut above the norm. Recommended for horror fans. ♫♫♫

Graphic violence, sexual content, brief nudity, strong language.

1993 (R) 87m/C Robert John Burke, Chelsea Field, Zakes Mokae, Rufus Swart, John Matshikiza, William Hootkins, Marianne

Saegebrecht; *D:* Richard Stanley; *W:* Richard Stanley; *M:* Simon Boswell. **VHS** *PAR*

Easy Wheels

A voiceover narrator tells us that one day while he was riding his Harley and thinking existential thoughts, our hero Paul LeMat felt "a rift in the delicate fabric of the universe and found himself staring into the dark heart of destiny." A vision sends him and his gang, the Bourne Losers, on a quest to "locate evil, destroy it, and find a great light beer." Off they go to Iowa, the land of She Wolf (Eileen Davidson), who was raised by Iowa wolves. Yes, it's all just as silly and frivolous as it sounds, but without that mile-a-minute, joke-a-second speed that makes the *Airplane* and *Naked Gun* comedies such fun. 🦴🦴

Profanity and comic violence.

1989 94m/C Paul LeMat, Eileen Davidson, Marjorie Bransfield, Jon Menick, Mark Holton, Karen Russell, Jami Richards, Roberta Vasquez, Barry Livingston, George Plimpton; *D:* David O'Malley; *W:* Ivan Raimi, Celia Abrams, David O'Malley; *M:* John Ross. **VHS, LV** *FRH*

Ebbtide

Given Aussie director Craig Lahiff's track record, this one is something of a disappointment. As a screwy thriller, it has some moments of prime weirdness, but those are outweighed by an absolutely ridiculous legal angle. It's a plotline that begins with some realism but disintegrates midway through and doesn't even attempt to recover. Harry Hamlin plays an amoral lawyer who rediscovers his conscience during a suit involving a boy's death due to environmental poisoning. Judy McIntosh is the femme fatale who's part of a complex conspiracy. Imagine a shaky combination of *Body Heat* and *The China Syndrome*. This one isn't nearly as good as Lahiff's brilliant sleeper, *Fever.* 🦴🦴

Strong language, nudity, sexual material, violence.

1994 (R) 90m/C Harry Hamlin, Judy McIntosh, Susan Lyons, John Gregg, Frankie J. Holden; *D:* Craig Lahiff; *W:* Robert Ellis, Peter Goldsworthy. **VHS** *PAR*

Ebony Tower

Laurence Olivier is a famous artist who lives with a much younger mistress, the delightful Greta Scacchi. Of course, the star is excellent, but this is a restrained performance. The film is a mood piece, deliberately Impressionist with lush soft-focus landscapes of the French countryside and a bit of nudity in a picnic skinny-dipping scene. Understated adaptation of John Fowles' novel was made for Britain's Grenada Television. 🦴🦴🦴

Brief nudity, sexual content.

1986 80m/C *GB* Laurence Olivier, Roger Rees, Greta Scacchi, Toyah Wilcox, *D:* Robert Knights, *M:* Richard Rodney Bennett. **VHS** *NO*

Echoes of Paradise

When Maria (Wendy Hughes) learns that her politician husband has been cheating on her, she leaves the kids with him and heads for Thailand. She finds a beachhouse and a Balinese dancer (John Lone) and sets herself free. Director Phillip Noyce is able to communicate volumes of information in short, simple scenes. An early sequence at a party, where Maria realizes what her husband has done, could be put in film textbooks. It's a brilliant bit of Hitchcockian economy. The script has a strong, exotic Somerset Maugham quality. **AKA:** Shadows of the Peacock. 🦴🦴🦴

Mature subject matter, sexual scenes, and profanity.

1986 (R) 90m/C *AU* Wendy Hughes, John Lone, Rod Mullinar, Peta Toppano, Steve Jacobs, Gillian Jones; *D:* Phillip Noyce. **VHS, LV** *ACA*

Ed and His Dead Mother

Wow, what a title! Doesn't it make you want to run down to the video store and snatch it off the shelf? Actually, the black comedy is better than you might expect, but it's disappointing for fans of director Jonathan Wacks' *Powwow Highway*. Succumbing to Mr. Powell's (John Glover) slick Midwestern salesmanship, Ed (Steve Buscemi) agrees to have his departed mother (Miriam Margolyes) brought back from the dead. Uncle Benny (Ned Beatty), who'd

"*Shield that 'gator—no regrets later!*"

—UNCLE BENNY'S
SEXUAL ADVICE TO
HIS NEPHEW IN
*ED AND
HIS DEAD MOTHER.*

rather be spying on the comely new neighbor (Sam Jenkins), thinks it's a bad idea. Given Mom's sudden penchant for cannibalism and chainsaws, he's probably right. The satiric targets (family values, consumerism, corporations) are well chosen but the tone isn't quite right. Imagine a sketch on *The Carol Burnett Show* gone somehow terribly awry. 🗡🗡

Mature subject matter, language, brief nudity.

1993 (PG-13) 85m/C Ned Beatty, Steve Buscemi, John Glover, Miriam Margolyes, Sam Jenkins; *D:* Jonathan Wacks; *W:* Chuck Hughes. **VHS, LV** *FXV*

Ed Wood: Look Back in Angora

Ed Wood is generally considered to be the worst filmmaker ever to work in Hollywood. That's an ambitious claim but the films back it up. From *Plan 9 from Outer Space* to the semi-autobiographical transvestite drama *Glen or Glenda?*, Wood's work has stood the test of time and derisive critics. He came to Hollywood after World War II with a genuine passion for filmmaking and absolutely no ability. His work, as this documentary points out, is not simply bad in the ways that low-budget schlock is so often bad; it's wonderfully bad in unexpected ways, particularly the infamous Ed Wood dialogue. At random moments, his characters tend to launch into flights of convoluted philosophical fantasy that leave the viewer in speechless amazement. Several of his friends and co-workers are interviewed here, and they all agree that his lack of talent was matched by an engaging personality. Everybody liked Ed Wood and felt sorry about the sad end that he met. Happily, the film strikes just the right tone, a mixture of wonder, admiration, and humor with appropriate tongue-in-cheek narration by *Laugh-In*'s Gary Owens. 🗡🗡🗡

Brief nudity, sexual content.

1994 51m/C *D:* Ted Newsom; *W:* Ted Newsom. **VHS** *AVE*

Eddie and the Cruisers

This off-beat rock drama barely caused a ripple in its theatrical release, but went on to become one of home video's original cult hits. The title refers to an early '60s rock group clearly patterned on Bruce Springsteen and the E Street Band. (In the opening shot, a banner reading "Spring" is obvious in the top right corner of the screen.) Eddie (Michael Pare) mysteriously disappeared on the eve of fame. Though the pace is sluggish and the storyline thin, the film boasts a fine derivative soundtrack and good performances by Tom Berenger and Ellen Barkin. 🗡🗡🗡

A little rough language, drug use.

1983 (PG) 90m/C Tom Berenger, Michael Pare, Ellen Barkin, Joe Pantoliano, Matthew Laurance; *D:* Martin Davidson; *W:* Martin Davidson, Arlene Davidson; *C:* Fred Murphy. **VHS, LV** *MVD, NLC*

Eddie and the Cruisers 2: Eddie Lives!

Canadian-made sequel rehashes the key elements of the original, actually reusing considerable footage (without the participation of stars Tom Berenger and Ellen Barkin). The script is even more leaden than the first, and the acting is no better. Still, the music's not bad. 🗡🗡

Strong language, mild sexual content.

1989 (PG-13) 106m/C *CA* Michael Pare, Marina Orsini, Matthew Laurance, Bernie Coulson; *D:* Jean-Claude Lord; *W:* Charles Zev Cohen; *M:* Leon Aronson. **VHS, LV** *CCB, IME*

Edge of Sanity

Hungarian production is a droll retelling of Robert Louis Stevenson's most famous story with some distinctly modern twists. In this version, Henry Jekyll (Anthony Perkins), a proper and respectable Victorian physician, first suffers a childhood sexual trauma that haunts him in nightmares. Then, while experimenting with anesthetics, he invents crack cocaine and becomes addicted. His eyes redden; his hair becomes lank and stringy; his complexion turns white and pasty. Instead of checking himself into the Betty Ford clinic or doing a Cosmo make-over, he becomes the evil Jack Hyde. Yes, Jack, as in Jack the Ripper. Director Gerard Kikoine manages to maintain a solid sense of atmosphere reminiscent of the best Hammer films in its evocation of the time. Perkins' inspired, kinky performance contains echoes of Norman Bates and so he underplays the wilder moments. Also available in an unrated version. 🎞️🎞️🎞️

Violence, drug use, sexual activity, nudity.

1989 (R) 85m/C *GB* Anthony Perkins, Glynis Barber, David Lodge, Sarah Maur-Thorp; *D:* Gerard Kikoine. **VHS, LV** *NO*

The Efficiency Expert

Gentle, offbeat Australian comedy will probably strike some viewers as a subdued delight, while others will scratch their heads and wonder what the point is. Title character Anthony Hopkins is used to dealing with the complexities and hard economic realities of the business world. But when his partner uses some of their findings to manipulate a union-management negotiation, he begins to question his work. Is there any human value to the cold statistics he gathers? Some of the subplots are predictable, but the scenes between Hopkins and Alwyn Kurts, as an amiable factory owner, have a genuine warmth to them. Overall, director Mark Joffe makes the picture work by sustaining a wry, good-humored mood and a 1960s setting. You won't laugh out loud, but you'll probably smile, and there's a lot to be said for that. **AKA:** Spotswood. 🎞️🎞️🎞️

A little strong language.

1992 (PG) 97m/C *AU* Anthony Hopkins, Ben Mendelsohn, Alwyn Kurts, Bruno Lawrence, Angela Punch McGregor, Russell Crowe, Rebecca Rigg, Toni Collette; *D:* Mark Joffe; *W:* Andrew Knight, Max Dann; *M:* Ricky Fataar. **VHS** *PAR, BTV*

84 Charlie Mopic

The story of one Vietnam reconnaissance patrol is told as it is recorded by 84 Charlie Mopic (Byron Thomas), a cameraman who goes out with the patrol to shoot a training film. All of the action is seen through his lens; all of the sound comes through his microphone. A newly arrived, ambitious career officer L.T. (Jonathon Emerson) dreamed up the film project and tries to act like he's in charge. Everyone knows, though, that the sergeant,

O.D. (Richard Brooks), "a walking razor blade," is the real leader. Easy (Nicholas Cascone) has less than a month to go before his tour is finished and he never lets anyone forget it. Pretty Boy (Jason Tomlins) is much quieter. Hammer (Christopher Burgard) is a gung-ho fire-breather, and the older Cracker (Glen Morshower) is the group's father figure. At various times, each of them addresses the camera and talks about why he is in Vietnam, and what he thinks about what he is doing there. Writer/director and veteran Patrick Duncan's limited point of view works perfectly on video for several reasons. First, he handles it so well that it's not intrusive. It's the right way to tell this story because it keeps your attention focused so tightly on these characters. All of the unfamiliar actors turn in thoroughly persuasive performances; Brooks and Morshower are outstanding. On the other hand, those self-imposed restrictions deny the story the dramatic depth and scope of films like *Platoon* and *Apocalypse Now*. But in showing what the war was like on an individual level and in allowing the viewer to experience it vicariously and viscerally, this may be the strongest film yet to come out of Vietnam. 🎞️🎞️🎞️🎞️

Graphic violence, profanity.

1989 (R) 95m/C Richard Brooks, Christopher Burgard, Nicholas Cascone, Jonathon Emerson, Glen Morshower, Jason Tomlins, Byron Thomas; *D:* Patrick Duncan; *W:* Patrick Duncan; *C:* Alan Caso; *M:* Donovan. **VHS, LV** *COL*

Electra

Rising Phoenix-like from its celluloid ashes, the spirit of Ed Wood, Jr., is reborn in *Electra,* a gloriously nutty "erotic" s-f tale. The humor is, I think, completely intentional with cheesy effects, sets, and atrocious acting played for alternative laughs. A convoluted exposition establishes young Billy Duncan's (Joe Tab, who's a dead ringer in face, voice, and hairdo for novelist Michael Chabon) semi-super powers inherited from chemist dad. The other key players are his girlfriend (Katie Griffin), his lusty stepmother (Shannon Tweed), and the Strangelovian Roach (Sten Eirik), a maniac who wants to steal the secret formula with the help of his two henchwomen (Lara Daans and

Dyanne DiMarco) in their leather bustiers and thigh-high boots. Director Julian Grant attempts to imitate the soaring fight choreography of Hong Kong magical action movies, but it's hard to soar very high on a bare-bones budget. *ᛚᛚ*

Silly violence, nudity, sexual material, strong language.

1995 85m/C Shannon Tweed, Joe Tab, Sten Eirik, Katie Griffin, Lara Daans, Dyanne DiMarco; **D:** Julian Grant. **VHS** *NHO*

Elves

Christmas horror movie is perhaps not as offensive as some slasher Santa flicks, but it's close. The title critters (unconvincing, stiff models) are the result of experiments by aging Nazis living in America. Perhaps the most surprising aspect of the film is the rating. Despite considerable profanity, a sick sexual angle involving incest and rape, graphic violence, and full nudity in a scene in which a woman is electrocuted in a bathtub, the MPAA ratings board thought it deserved a PG-13. Without question, it should have been an R. Not for the whole family. *ᛚ*

Profanity, violence, nudity, sexual situations

1989 (PG-13) 95m/C Dan Haggerty, Deanna Lund, Julie Austin, Borah Silver; **D:** Jeffrey Mandel. **VHS** *AIP*

Embrace of the Vampire

Virginal college student Alyssa Milano is pursued by vampire Martin Kemp. For reasons never explained, he needs her to recharge his batteries. Director Anne Goursaud certainly knows how to steam things up. Her approach ranges from bodice-ripper romanticism to *90210* stereotypes to artfully posed eroticism. Forget about coherence or logic. Also available in an unrated version. *ᛚᛚ*

Nudity, strong sexual content, violence, strong language.

1995 (R) 92m/C Alyssa Milano, Martin Kemp, Harrison Pruett, Charlotte Lewis; **Cameos:** Jennifer Tilly; **D:** Anne Goursaud; **W:** Halle Eaton, Nicole Coady, Rick Bitzelberger; **M:** Joseph Williams. **VHS, LV** *TTC, IME*

Empire Records

Though it's more or less doomed from the start, this teen-vid manages a degree of success. The problem: it's an establishment film about anti-establishment heroes, and the engaging young cast is less than completely convincing. The title refers to a music store; manager Joe (Anthony LaPaglia) is the only adult on the payroll. His staff is made up of adolescents, each poised on the brink of a total emotional breakdown at any moment. One steals the day's receipts and takes off for Atlantic City. Another has decided to profess his love to a co-worker at precisely 1:37, but she has chosen that day to give herself to a visiting pop star (Maxwell Caulfield) who's there to sign records. Not to mention the potential suicide, the shoplifter, the headbanger, and the floozie. Will they be able to keep the evil Music Town franchise from taking over their funky store? Director Allan Moyle keeps things moving briskly but the film lacks the inspired anarchy that powered his cult hit *Pump Up the Volume*. Even so, teenaged videophiles shouldn't be put off if the subject sounds interesting. *ᛚᛚᛚ*

Strong language, sexual content, drug use.

1995 (PG-13) 91m/C Anthony LaPaglia, Rory Cochrane, Liv Tyler, Renee Zellweger, Johnny Whitworth, Robin Tunney, Ethan Randall, Maxwell Caulfield, Debi Mazar; **D:** Allan Moyle; **W:** Carol Heikkinen; **C:** Walt Lloyd. **VHS** *WAR*

Endless Descent

Remember all those underwater monster movies that were released a few years ago— *The Abyss, Deepstar Six,* and a few others? This one was in that litter, and it's actually not bad. The sub Siren II is sent to investigate the disappearance of the original Siren and, to nobody's surprise, they find something evil lurking on the ocean floor. R. Lee Ermey is the by-the-book commanding officer; Jack Scalia is the ship's designer; Deborah Adair is his estranged wife. Several others are on hand, too, but few make it to the last reel. The pace is brisk and the critter is fun. **AKA:** La Grieta. *ᛚᛚᛚ*

Language, graphic effects.

1990 (R) 79m/C *SP* Jack Scalia, R. Lee Ermey, Ray Wise, Deborah Adair, Ely Pouget; *D:* J. Piquer Simon; *W:* David Coleman. VHS, LV *LIV*

Ernest Goes to School

This comedy is, without question, the finest film vehicle for Jim Varney's Ernest P. Worrell, or something to that effect. Ernest, the commercial character turned leading man, is the janitor of Chippewa Falls High School. In his efforts to close the school, the evil superintendent demands that all employees earn their diplomas. Two mad scientists use Ernest as a guinea pig in their "Sub-Atomic Brain Accelerator" and turn him into a Worrellian Carl Sagan. Most of the laughs come from pure Three-Stooges slapstick and Varney's patented comedic shtick. It's everything an Ernest fan could ask for, and everything that drives the rest of the world crazy. 🦴🦴🦴

Comic violence.

1994 (PG) 89m/C Jim Varney, Linda Kash, Bill Byrge; *D:* Coke Sams. VHS *MNC*

Eternity

This nutball video attempts to connect reincarnation, big business, television, and world peace. The opening shot—Jon Voight riding his horse toward a castle that looks like it came straight from the Magic Kingdom—sets the tone for the rest of the film. Yes, as Yogi so aptly stated, it's deja vu all over again, as liberal weenie brother Voight struggles against macho fascist brother Armand Assante throughout the centuries. In pseudo-medieval times, they're princes. In the present, Voight is a Phil Donahue-clone and Assante is a greedhead zillionaire. The cast also includes oatmeal huckster Wilford Brimley, ex-Four Season Frankie Valli, and sexy soap star Eileen Davidson. The script by Voight, executive producer Dorothy Paul, and director Steven Paul is both earnest and simpleminded. It's the kind of thing that Shirley MacLaine, Jane Fonda, and Donald Trump might have come up with if they broke into a case of cheap wine one night. 🦴

Profanity, sexual content, brief nudity, mild violence.

1990 (R) 122m/C Jon Voight, Armand Assante, Wilford Brimley, Eileen Davidson, Kaye Ballard, Lainie Kazan, Joey Villa, Steven Keats, Eugene Roche, Frankie Valli, John P. Ryan; *D:* Steven Paul; *W:* Jon Voight, Dorothy Paul, Steven Paul. VHS *ACA*

Even Hitler Had a Girlfriend

This independent production has achieved a rarefied cult status on video. It's one of those inspired films that clearly comes from the heart and makes a virtue of its low budget. The reason: Marcus Templeton (Andren Scott). Think Travis Bickle from *Taxi Driver* without the weapons and the attitude. Marcus is an overweight, sexually frustrated Omaha security guard. He sits around his crackerbox apartment watching the X-rated cable channel, wishing he had some female companionship, and reading the religious tracts that are slipped under his front door. When it all gets to be too much for him, he peels the plastic wrapper on another Slim Jim. Then he discovers out-call escort services and everything changes...but nothing changes. The box copy proclaims "99 percent true" and that's easy to believe. Beyond the leering (and self-aware) exploitation angle, David Manning's script is a perceptive examination of loneliness—one of the most moving and funny you'll ever see. Director Ronnie Cramer gives the film the rough-edged look, irreverence, and unpredictability of a '70s drive-in flick. And that's exactly the way the story ought to be told. Followed by a sequel of sorts. 🦴🦴🦴

Considerable nudity, sexual material, strong language, mild violence.

1991 90m/C Andren Scott; *D:* Ronnie Cramer; *W:* David Manning. VHS *SEP*

Excessive Force

On one level, *Excessive Force* is little more than your basic martial-arts movie. In fact, the beginning is so formulaic it resembles one of those action parodies on *The Simpsons* TV series. Thomas Ian Griffith (who also wrote

The Hound must admit that this is another less-than-strictly defined category. Some of these might be called thrillers, others mysteries, still others are psychological suspense stories. Each of them has at least one crime at the heart of the plot.

APARTMENT ZERO	ORGANIZED CRIME & TRIAD BUREAU
COUP DE TORCHON	
FALL TIME	PEEPING TOM
FEVER	POSITIVE I.D.
HARD-BOILED	RED ROCK WEST
THE HAWK	REFLECTIONS IN THE DARK
INNOCENT VICTIM	STORYVILLE
KILL ME AGAIN	STREETS
THE KILLER	SUTURE
L.627	SWEET KILLING
MR. FROST	UNDER SUSPICION
ONE GOOD TURN	THE VANISHING
	THE WRONG MAN (*1993*)

winter light. At its best moments, this Illinois production is reminiscent of *The Fugitive*. 🦴🦴

Graphic violence, strong language, brief nudity.

1993 (R) 87m/C Thomas Ian Griffith, Lance Henriksen, James Earl Jones, Charlotte Lewis, Tony Todd, Burt Young, W. Earl Brown; *D:* Jon Hess; *W:* Thomas Ian Griffith; *C:* Donald M. Morgan; *M:* Charles Bernstein. **VHS, LV** *NLC, IME*

Excessive Force 2: Force on Force

Standard shoot-'em-up, kick-'em-up features a female protagonist and a bit more imagination than most. Stacie Randall is the glamourpuss martial artiste who takes on a renegade U.S. Army death squad. The fight scenes range from pretty good to so-so. It's obvious that Ms. Randall's training isn't equal to that of the top male stars in the field, but working with the right people, she could become just as effective onscreen. 🦴🦴

Violence, strong language, mild sexual content.

1995 (R) 105m/C Stacie Randall, Dan Gauthier, Jay Patterson, John Mese; *D:* Jonathan Winfrey; *W:* Mark Sevi; *C:* Russ Brandt; *M:* Kevin Kiner. **VHS, LV** *NLC, IME*

The Executioners

Though it's technically a sequel to *The Heroic Trio*, with the female stars playing the same characters, this one bears little resemblance in either plot or tone to the first film. It's your basic feminist science-fiction Hong Kong magical martial arts action epic. Co-directors Johnny To and Ching Siu Tung never let logic get in the way of their bizarre story about a false messiah in a corrupt post-apocalyptic world that must be saved by the three super-heroines. Key characters appear without introduction or explanation; grotesque sentimentality runs amok; and the plot defies any logical explication. But the overall energy level and mad imagination put American movies to shame. One caveat: *Executioners* goes so far beyond the conventions of Western filmmaking that it's probably not the best place for the uninitiated to discover Hong Kong cinema. But for fans—Wow! 🦴🦴🦴

the script) is honest cop Terry McCain who cavalierly tortures suspects until they tell him what he wants to hear. His boss (Lance Henriksen) is not amused, even though everyone knows that gangster DiMarco (Burt Young) is guilty of just about everything. Director Jon Hess shows no real flair for the pedestrian fight scenes, but he does create a believably textured Midwestern atmosphere with gray

Graphic violence, strong language.

1993 100m/C *HK* Anita Mui, Michelle Yeoh, Maggie Cheung; **D:** Johnny To, Ching Siu Tung. **VHS, LV** *TAI*

The Expert

Enthusiastically pro-death penalty revenge picture was made in Nashville. Jeff Speakman is the counter-terrorism "expert" whose sister is murdered by a psychopath in a needlessly brutal scene. From that premise, the story wanders down some weird sidestreets, finally ending in a near-empty prison. It becomes so unusual that even the most jaded videophile will have trouble predicting what's going to happen next. Speakman handles the physical action well enough, and gets solid support from James Brolin, Elizabeth Gracen and, in a surprise cameo, Jim Varney. 🦴🦴🦴

Violence, subject matter, language.

1995 (R) 92m/C Jeff Speakman, James Brolin, Michael Shaner, Alex Datcher, Wolfgang Bodison, Elizabeth Gracen, Red West, Jim Varney; **D:** Rick Avery; **W:** Max Allan Collins; **C:** Levie Isaacks; **M:** Ashley Irwin. **VHS** *ORI*

The Experts

One of the most famous cold war urban myths told of a little town in the Russian hinterlands where everyone spoke English and the KGB trained their insidious spies. Fast forward to the 1980s, but the town is still stuck in the '50s, until the Russkies trick the hip but none-too-bright John Travolta and Arye Gross into bringing them up to speed with new technology and fashion. For every good joke about kids who've never heard a Walkman, there are two thudballs. Near the middle, Travolta and Kelly Preston (as a Soviet spy) perform what must be the ugliest dance number ever put on film. It's bad enough to make your VCR spit out the tape. 🦴🦴

Profanity, sexual situations, bad dancing, mild violence.

1989 (PG-13) 94m/C John Travolta, Arye Gross, Charles Martin Smith, Kelly Preston, James Keach, Deborah Foreman, Brian Doyle-Murray; **D:** Dave Thomas; **W:** Nick Thiel, Eric Alter; **M:** Marvin Hamlisch. **VHS, LV** *PAR*

Exposure

Peter Coyote is an American photographer in Rio De Janeiro who finds himself in the middle of a baroque yet half-baked plot. It all has to do with knife-fighting, a serial killer, a missing computer disk, and a bunch of rich guys who are up to no good. Watchable, but in the end, nothing special. 🦴🦴

Violence, strong language, brief nudity, sexual content.

1991 (R) 105m/C Peter Coyote, Amanda Pays, Tcheky Karyo; **M:** Todd Boekelheide. **VHS** *HBO*

Eye of the Stranger

Imagine a contemporary *High Plains Drifter* combined with the sensibility of a fantasy beer commercial. The title character, writer/director/producer David Heavener, is a nameless guy in a leather jacket and black T-shirt who squints and postures a lot. He wanders into the corrupt little town of Harmony and sets about cleaning it up. The problem is unintentional humor. For example, when he first appears, the stranger fires up a smoke by striking a kitchen match somewhere under his leather jacket. What are we supposed to think of this? That he's got steel wool chest hair? A really bad rash? That it's way past time to wash that T-shirt? 🦴🦴

Strong language, violence, brief nudity, sexual content.

1993 (R) 96m/C David Heavener, Sally Kirkland, Martin Landau, Don Swayze, Stella Stevens, John Pleshette, Joe Estevez, Thomas F. Duffy; **D:** David Heavener; **W:** David Heavener; **M:** Robert Garrett. **VHS** *MNC*

Eyes of an Angel

John Travolta is a Rocky-esque loser who's hanging on by his fingernails in Chicago. To support his ten-year-old daughter, he goes to work as a bagman. At the same time, she has befriended a wounded Doberman (Tripoli). When things go wrong on the job, they head for L.A. The rest of the story could be described as Quentin Tarantino's *Lassie*. Director Robert Harmon is particularly effec-

tive in scenes that take the dog's point of view on Chicago streets. He also got believable performances from his three protagonists. Travolta has as much to work with here as he had in *Pulp Fiction* and the role is much more realistic. He makes a deeply flawed character sympathetic. ⨴⨴⨴

Rough language, some violence.

1991 (PG-13) 91m/C John Travolta, Elie Raab, Jeffrey DeMunn; *D:* Robert Harmon. **VHS, LV** *LIV*

The Fable of the Beautiful Pigeon Fancier

Based on a story by Gabriel Garcia Marquez and set in the Brazil of 1892, this myth-like film describes the romance between aristocratic dilettante Ney Latorraca and Claudia Ohana, the beautiful young wife of a musician. Mozambican director Ruy Guerra creates a dreamlike setting from large simple shapes, stark landscapes, and primary colors, reducing the tale to its elemental pieces. By North American entertainment standards, the action is slow, and the subtitled dialogue is unrealistic. These characters seem to talk constantly. But once you get past those preconceptions and focus on the characters, the film is fascinating. Its mix of humor, surrealism, and earthiness is reminiscent of good Fellini. *AKA:* Fabula de la Bella Palomera. ⨴⨴⨴

Contains nudity, sexual material, mild violence.

1988 73m/C SP Ney Latorraca, Claudia Ohana, Tonia Carrero, Dina Stat, Chico Diaz; *D:* Ruy Guerra. **VHS, LV** *FXL, FCT, INJ*

Faces

John Cassavetes' 1968 drama has a strong reputation despite (or perhaps because) it has been seen so infrequently outside of larger cities. It looks like a documentary—grainy black and white, naturalistic lighting, harsh sound, almost no music, improvisational dialogue. The slow action often meanders plotlessly, like non-fiction. The focus is on four

lonely characters: a troubled married couple (John Marley and Lynn Carlin), a good-time-girl of a certain age (Gena Rowlands), and a surfer-stud (an impossibly young Seymour Cassel). Today, the film is more interesting as a portrait of the social and sexual mores of the late 1960s than as conventional entertainment. The people themselves are an unsympathetic quartet. With their forced laughter and not-so-quiet desperation, they're off-putting—but still fascinating at the same time. Even those who appreciate the avant-garde will probably find this one tough going for almost two full hours before it arrives at a payoff, but their determination will be rewarded. Judged by any standard, it's unusual. ⨴⨴⨴

Mature subject matter, some strong language.

1968 (R) 129m/B John Marley, Lynn Carlin, Gena Rowlands, Seymour Cassel, Val Avery, Dorothy Gulliver, Joanne Moore Jordan, Fred Draper, Darlene Conley; *D:* John Cassavetes; *W:* John Cassavetes; *C:* Al Ruban; *M:* Jack Ackerman. National Society of Film Critics Awards '68: Best Screenplay, Best Supporting Actor (Cassel); Nominations: Academy Awards '68: Best Screenplay, Best Supporting Actor (Carlin), Best Supporting Actress (Cassel). **VHS** *FXL*

Fair Game

What is insanely jealous businessman Greg Henry to do when his girlfriend Trudie Styler jilts him? Why, he locks her in her spacious apartment with an irate mamba, of course. Wouldn't you? The action is so well photographed and staged that you can suspend your disbelief until the end, when it does go too far. A welcome streak of unexpected humor runs throughout, but Giorgio Moroder's here-comes-the-snake music is more irritating than frightening. The surprise in this one is Henry's unhinged villain. He is a scene-stealing delight. ⨴⨴⨴

Profanity, subject matter.

1989 (R) 81m/C Greg Henry, Trudie Styler, Bill Moseley; *D:* Mario Orfini; *M:* Giorgio Moroder. **VHS, LV** *VMK*

Fall Time

Despite a ferociously offbeat quality, this "thriller" is a strong, compelling story. In late '50s rural Wisconsin, three teenaged pals (Jason London, Jonah Blechman, and David Arquette) decide to pull a silly prank, a fake murder in front of a smalltown bank where Carol (Sheryl Lee) is a teller. On the same day, Florence (Mickey Rourke) and Leon (Stephen Baldwin) are planning to rob the bank. The two actions take place at almost the same time, and from that moment on, nothing goes as planned. The tone shifts between the dark threat of violence and equally dark humor with a constant undercurrent of ambivalent sexuality. Though much of the focus is on the kids, the bad guys steal the show. Baldwin is a mercurial, cliche-spouting ex-con. Rourke is perfectly cast as a pompadoured philosopher in the world's ugliest leather jacket. The characters are believably capable of anything and that's what gives the film its unpredictability. The ending is just about perfect. Paul Warner makes a strong directorial debut. Comparisons to Quentin Tarentino's *Reservoir Dogs* are not out of place. *AKA:* Falltime. 🐾🐾🐾

Mature subject matter, violence, strong language, sexual material.

1994 (R) 88m/C Mickey Rourke, Stephen Baldwin, Jason London, David Arquette, Jonah Blechman, Sheryl Lee; *D:* Paul Warner; *W:* Steve Alden, Paul Skemp; *C:* Mark J. Gordon. VHS, LV *LIV*

Fandango

Kevin Costner's fans who are familiar only with his theatrical films should take a look at this early effort, which has earned cult fav status. It's a loose-jointed story about college students on a 1971 trip across Texas. If writer/director Kevin Reynolds' isn't always successful, this road movie is lively, funny, and touching. 🐾🐾🐾

Mild profanity.

1985 (PG) 91m/C Judd Nelson, Kevin Costner, Sam Robards, Chuck Bush, Brian Cesak, Elizabeth Daily, Suzy Amis, Glenne Headly, Pepe Serna, Marvin J. McIntyre; *D:* Kevin Reynolds; *W:* Kevin Reynolds; *M:* Alan Silvestri. VHS *WAR*

Far from Home

Divorced dad Matt Frewer is on vacation with his teenaged daughter Drew Barrymore. She's none too happy about visiting a series of national parks—she's just discovered boys— but she's even less happy when they run out of gas in the desert burg of Banco, Nevada. Everyone they meet there is cheap, rude, and nasty. There is one cute guy, but it looks like he's a psycho. What a drag. Any movie that's dealing with teen sexuality is walking a fine line and this one is never exploitative. At the same time, though, it doesn't make much sense. Director Meiert Avis establishes an eerie, almost *Twilight Zone* atmosphere, and the idea of the isolated town where something has gone wrong appeals to the xenophobic streak in all of us. 🐾🐾

Brief nudity, sexual situations, graphic violence, profanity.

1989 (R) 86m/C Matt Frewer, Drew Barrymore, Richard Masur, Karen Austin, Susan Tyrrell, Anthony Rapp, Jennifer Tilly, Andras Jones, Dick Miller; *D:* Meiert Avis; *M:* Jonathan Elias. VHS, LV *LIV, VES*

Far Out Man

Even though it lasts for 84 minutes and has fictional characters and a minimal storyline, this isn't really a film. It's a loose collection of skits, bits of business, animation, and improvisation, all revolving around Tommy Chong's drug-based humor. To say that it's loose and sloppy is a ridiculous understatement. Compared to this, *Up in Smoke* looks like *Citizen Kane.* Apparently the auteur invited all of his family and friends to take part in a story about an unreconstructed freak who hasn't adjusted to life in the '90s. A lot of them said yes. Most of the comedy is based on disgusting food and drug use. It might be funny with

the proper pharmacological adjustment, but that's not likely. **WOOF!**

Gross humor, rough language, drug use, brief nudity, sexual content.

1989 (R) 84m/C Thomas Chong, Rae Dawn Chong, C. Thomas Howell, Shelby Chong, Martin Mull, Paris Chong, Paul Bartel, Judd Nelson, Michael Winslow, Richard "Cheech" Marin; *D:* Thomas Chong; *W:* Thomas Chong. **VHS, LV** *COL*

Fast Food

Jim Varney is fast-food baron Wrangler Bob Bundy and the laughs are as tough and tasteless as a $2.00 steak. Don't expect much from this one-joke effort about a barbecue sauce that is also an aphrodisiac. 🐾🐾

Mature subject matter, mild sexual content, profanity.

1989 (PG-13) 90m/C Jim Varney, Clark Brandon, Tracy Griffith, Randal Patrick, Traci Lords, Kevin McCarthy, Michael J. Pollard; *D:* Michael A. Simpson; *W:* Clark Brandon. **VHS, LV** *FRH*

Fast Money

Reworking a perennially popular Hollywood theme—the adventurous woman teamed up with the shy guy—turns into a fair romantic chase. Francesca (Yancy Butler) is a professional car thief; Jack (Matt McCoy) is a naive reporter. The two of them wind up in Reno with a suitcase full of cash and other stuff that gangsters and corrupt cops want back. The chases are energetic and more inventive than cliched. Both leads do good work, and they're upstaged by supporting actors John Ashton and Trevor Goddard as the main bad guys. Goddard is a fine Australian actor who's due for stardom. 🐾🐾🐾

Violence, language.

1996 (R) 93m/C Yancy Butler, Matt McCoy, John Ashton, Trevor Goddard, Andy Romano, Carole Cook, Patrika Darbo; *D:* Alexander Wright; *W:* Alexander Wright; *C:* Thomas Jewett. **VHS** *ORI*

Fatal Charm

Christopher Atkins is on trial for several murders when teenager Amanda Peterson falls for him. She simply can't believe that anyone "that

gorgeous" could rape and kill young women. The fact that her divorced mom Mary Frann is fooling around with creepy James Remar (who played a sicko killer in *48 HRS*) might have something to do with her reaction, and then there's the town's sheriff, Andy Robinson (who played the sickest sicko killer of them all in *Dirty Harry*). The courtroom scenes are absolutely ludicrous. The dream sequences and the scenes in the girls' shower are pure exploitation, and the whole cast overacts shamelessly. Credit for the histrionics must go to the infamous Alan Smithee, the pseudonym that directors are allowed to hide behind when projects goes seriously awry. 🐾🐾

Violence, sexual content, brief nudity.

1992 (R) 90m/C Christopher Atkins, Amanda Peterson, Mary Frann, James Remar, Andrew (Andy) Robinson, Peggy Lipton; *D:* Alan Smithee; *W:* Nicholas Niciphor. **VHS** *ACA*

Fatal Instinct

Don't be fooled by the derivative title. This is a low-intensity mystery about the world's dumbest policeman, Michael Madsen, who (surprise, surprise) falls for beautiful blonde suspect Laura Johnson. Yes, this same material has been the subject of numerous recent thrillers, but none of them have been so slow, unimaginative, or cliched. Also available in an unrated version at 95 minutes. **WOOF!**

Violence, strong language, sexual material, and nudity.

1992 (R) 93m/C Michael Madsen, Laura Johnson, Tony Hamilton; *D:* John Dirlam. **VHS** *NLC, COL*

Fatal Past

In the present, Costas Mandylor is a mobster's bodyguard; Kaisa Figura is the mobster's paramour. They had the same relationship in medieval Japan where a feudal lord was the third point in the triangle. Way back when, it ended with ritual suicide and other unpleasantness. Will it be repeated in the present? Unfortunately, that premise is undone by a static pace and director Clive Fleury's inability to handle action. 🐾🐾🐾

Mature subject matter, violence, strong language, brief nudity.

1994 **(R)** 85m/C Costas Mandylor, Kaisa Figura; *D:* Clive Fleury; *W:* Richard Ryan. **VHS** *PAR*

Fatal Skies

Alternative classic is gloriously inept—a B-movie that wallows in its own badness. Timothy Leary—yes, *that* Timothy Leary—leads a cast of the acting-impaired in a nutty story of environmental destruction and political corruption. It begins with this message: "The story you are about to see is a work of fiction, but it is based on true events. The names and places have been changed to protect the innocent and to make the story more tragic." This tragedy is all about a bunch of teenaged parachutists who drop in on a toxic waste dump where 55-gallon barrels routinely blow up. Leary and his two henchmen drive them away, but the plucky kids (whose average age looks to be about 30) persevere. 🎞🎞🎞

Laughable violence, unpersuasive special effects, profanity, fleeting nudity.

1990 88m/C Timothy Leary, Veronica Carothers, Michael Esposito; *D:* Thomas Dugan; *W:* Thomas Dugan. **VHS** *AIP*

Fatally Yours

Sometimes sheer lunacy can accomplish what skill and talent cannot, and an otherwise unremarkable video becomes an alternative gem. That's the case with *Fatally Yours*, a multigenerational gangster reincarnation flick. A black-and-white sequence—which will be repeated in its entirety for slow learners—introduces Jon (Rick Rossovich) and Sara (Sarah MacDonnell) and her father's (George Lazenby) gang in 1928. Flash forward to the present where Jon is Danny who's married to Patti (Annie Fitzgerald), daughter of Pauley (Roddy MacDowall), an alcoholic compulsive gambler who owes big bucks to a ruthless contemporary gangster. The moment that Jon sees a dilapidated old house once owned by the gangster from the past, he knows he must have it, setting in motion a plot that beggars description. It's almost impossible to say how

much of the humor is intentional. Is a line like "Jon McGregor had a passion for his work. Accounting was to be his life." meant to be funny? Probably. And how about the bizarre finale where it's revealed that almost every character is a reincarnation of someone else, and sometimes the wires get crossed? It's a real howler. MacDowall overacts ferociously throughout while Rossovich plods through with complete earnestness. When it's all over, this one is certainly different and it's never boring. 🎞🎞🎞

Contains violence, strong language, bad Italian accents, sexual material, nudity.

1995 90m/C Rick Rossovich, George Lazenby, Roddy McDowall, Sage Stallone, Sarah MacDonnell, Annie Fitzgerald; *D:* Tim Everitt. **VHS** *MNC*

Fate

The Three Stooges do *Moonstruck* in an amateurish romantic comedy about a couple of attractive kids. The most curious thing about this one is that it appears to have been a Paul family production. Stuart wrote, directed, and starred. Hank Paul and Dorothy Koster Paul share producing and writing credits. That kind of family shows through in the sweet story, too. 🎞🎞

Some strong language, subject matter.

1990 **(PG-13)** 115m/C Cheryl Lynn, Stuart Paul, Kaye Ballard, Susannah York; *D:* Stuart Paul; *W:* Dorothy Paul. **VHS** *ACA*

Fatherland

Made-for-cable political thriller isn't nearly as complex and moving as its source material, Robert Harris' fine novel, but it's still worth a look. In Berlin, 1964, after Germany has won World War II, Rutger Hauer is the SS detective whose murder investigation leads him into government secrets on the eve of a visit by a new American President. Miranda Richardson is the journalist who helps him. Director Christopher Menaul follows the rules of the thriller formula and generates a fair amount of suspense, though the conclusion has a hurried feeling. More importantly, the story does justice to its subject without reducing Nazis to

stick-figure villains. Flaws and all, above average. ✔✔✔

Contains strong language, violence.

1994 106m/C Rutger Hauer, Miranda Richardson, Peter Vaughan, Jean Marsh, Michael Kitchen, John Woodvine, John Shrapnel, Clare Higgins; *D:* Christopher Menaul; *W:* Stanley Weiser, Ron Hutchinson; *C:* Peter Sova; *M:* Gary Chang. **VHS** *WAR*

The Fearless Vampire Killers

The video edition of Roman Polanski's 1967 horror-comedy is a full-length "director's version." Longer doesn't necessarily mean better, though. In Polanski's take on the stylish Hammer horror films of the period, the sets and costumes are lavish. So are the camerawork and acting. Today's audiences will find the pace a little slow and Polanski's humor sometimes forced. The film has its moments—Ferdy Mayne is an excellent vampire—but it's no *Young Frankenstein*. **AKA:** Pardon Me, Your Teeth Are in My Neck; Dance of the Vampires. ✔✔✔

Contains mild violence, sexual material.

1967 98m/C *GB* Jack MacGowran, Roman Polanski, Alfie Bass, Jessie Robbins, Sharon Tate, Ferdinand "Ferdy" Mayne, Iain Quarrier; *D:* Roman Polanski, *W:* Roman Polanski, Gerard Brach. **VHS, LV** *MGM*

Femalien

This is about as hot as non-hardcore erotica gets. It's a simple s-f themed film about the title character (Vanessa Taylor) who comes to California from outer space to discover what human physical sensations feel like. Director Cybil Richards also made the slick *Virtual Encounters*. This one has equally high production values, despite a modest budget. Perhaps the key lies with director of photography "Allen Smitty," possibly a variation on the "Alan Smithee" pseudonym used by directors who don't want their names associated with a film. Maybe this man (or woman) was moonlighting. ✔✔✔ **GPI: 9.3**

Contains strong sexual content, nudity.

1996 (R) 90m/C Vanessa Taylor, Jacqueline Lovell, Matt Schue; *D:* Cybil Richards; *C:* Allen Smitty. **VHS, LV** *AFE*

Femme Fatale

This odd romantic mystery might have been the subject for a Ross MacDonald novel. Colin Firth is a burned-out Los Angeles artist who has become, of all things, a park ranger. Things change when he meets and marries Lisa Zane. Then as suddenly and mysteriously as she appeared, she disappears. Armed only with the few things he thinks he knows about her, he goes back to the city to find her. What gradually emerges is a portrait of a troubled young woman who may have been involved with drug trafficking, pornography, and even, gasp, performance art. Firth's role has undertones of the character he played in the cult hit *Apartment Zero*. **AKA:** Fatal Woman. ✔✔✔

Strong language, some violence, subject matter.

1990 (R) 96m/C Colin Firth, Lisa Zane, Billy Zane, Scott Wilson, Lisa Blount; *D:* Andre Guttfreund; *W:* John Brancato. **VHS, LV** *REP*

Femme Fontaine: Killer Babe for the C.I.A.

Breathes there a videophile who could not love this title? And, happily, the film itself lives up (or down as the case may be) to that title. Femme (the multi-hyphenated producer-director-writer-star-and all-round-auteur Margot Hope), hitwoman extraordinaire, wants to find out what happened to her daddy. Skinheads, neo-Nazis, Asian gangsters, and soft-core porn producers get in the way, but not for long. All in all, this one's a Troma throwback to those wonderful *Ginger* movies, the drive-in exploitation staples from the 1970s that have become cult hits on video. ✔✔✔

Violence, nudity, strong language, sexual content.

1995 (R) 93m/C Margot Hope, James Hong, Arthur Roberts, Catherine Dao, David Shark, Kevin Fry, Harry Mok; *D:* Margot Hope; *W:* Margot Hope; *C:* Gary Graver; *M:* Gardner Cole. **VHS** *TTV*

Ferocious Female Freedom Fighters

Troma tries its hand at Woody Allen's *What's Up, Tiger Lily?* Producer/writer Charles Kaufman took a low-budget Japanese martial arts movie, threw out the voice track, and added English dialogue that has nothing to with the original story. In the middle of an involved fight scene, a character will say, "You know, as a rule, you should never refreeze sea bass." The cast features an Asian Elvis lookalike and a snake who has some very good lines. Obviously, this unusual comedy is funny only if you're in the mood for it. 🦴🦴

Comic violence and sexual humor.

1988 **(R)** 74m/C Eva Arnaz, Barry Prima; **D:** Jopi Burnama; **W:** Charles Kaufman. **VHS, LV** *MED, IME*

The Feud

Adaptation of Thomas Berger's indescribable novel is the story of two '50s families who become caught up in a needless dispute that involves more posturing than action. The main attraction is Reverton (Rene Auberjonois), a comic villain whose name should be listed with the greats: Captain Hook, Dr. Strangelove, etc. Fearful, feisty, crafty, and stupid, Reverton is a little man who believes that the whole world is conspiring against him. But armed with his pistol and handcuffs, he refuses ever to back down, sallying forth bravely and madly, always ready to tell other people what to do. Auberjonois' performance is a tour de force. For one of the strangest literary triple-features imaginable, take a look at this one along with the two other adaptations of Berger novels, *Little Big Man* and *Neighbors*. 🦴🦴🦴

Profanity, some violence, subject matter.

1990 **(R)** 87m/C Rene Auberjonois, Ron McLarty, Joe Grifasi, David Strathairn, Gale Mayron; **D:** Bill D'Elia; **W:** Bill D'Elia. **VHS** *VMK*

Fever

Tough cop Bill Hunter watches a drug deal go sour in the desert. At the same time, his bored young wife Mary Regan is engaged in an affair with Gary Sweet, a shallow, selfish lover. The other important elements are a suitcase full of money, the train out of town, and another suspicious policeman. That's all anyone should know about this Aussie noir because it's so logical, yet still so surprising. John Emery's script follows Joe Bob Briggs' first rule for drive-in classics—any character can die at any time—straight through to a neat, neat ending. If the cast lacks the surface glamour we see so often in Hollywood movies, then they're largely unfamiliar and unpredictable to American viewers. We haven't seen them in other roles; we don't know how they've been typecast or how their characters will react to pressure. And director Craig Lahiff keeps these characters under pressure. He does it visually. *Fever* is virtually a silent film; the narrative moves through images and action, not dialogue. Strongly recommended. 🦴🦴🦴🦴

One intense sexual scene, violence, and profanity.

1988 **(R)** 83m/C *AU* Bill Hunter, Gary Sweet, Mary Regan, Jim Holt; **D:** Craig Lahiff; **W:** John Emery. **VHS, LV** *ACA*

Final Equinox

From the forgettable title to the tinny synthetic score to the boring fight at the end, *Final Equinox* is a mistake. It's an s-f shoot-'em-up with minimal special effects about an alien artifact that looks like half of an aluminum softball bat. Not much is done with that side. Writer/director Serge Rodunsky is more interested in gunfights involving his hero (Joe Lara), a lank-haired dude in leather britches, and a dozen or so bad guys suffering equally bad hair days. There's nothing here that fans haven't seen before. The sheer nuttiness of the proceedings can overcome the other flaws, but don't miss the bejewelled Village-People-refugee outfit that villain Martin Kove sports in the last reel. 🦴🦴

Contains violence, strong language, brief nudity, sexual material.

1995 90m/C Martin Kove, Joe Lara, David Warner; **D:** Serge Rodunsky; **W:** Serge Rodunsky. **VHS** *MNC*

Video Premieres Noir

Film noir may be the all-time favorite cinematic genre for scholars, reviewers, and fans. For all three, it's easy to understand why.

The intellectual can dissect these films and find the most popular themes of serious contemporary literature and art—alienation, loss of faith, societal disintegration, and dozens of other angst-riddled notions. For reviewers and other serious students of film, the form provides a rich visual terrain. Even the worst films noir are enjoyable for their heightened use of light and dark as they turn "reality" into the stuff that dreams are made of. And fans like noir for the simple reason that these movies tell complicated, interesting stories with memorable characters and unusual endings.

More importantly, films noir are about a subject that has universal popularity: Sin.

BACKSTAB	INNER SANCTUM
BLACK DAY BLUE NIGHT	LOVE, CHEAT & STEAL
BODY SHOT	NIGHT RHYTHMS
COUP DE TORCHON	OUT OF THE RAIN
DEAD ON	POSITIVE I.D.
DEADLY DESIRE	RED ROCK WEST
FEVER	THE UNDERNEATH
HOURGLASS	

On one level, almost all these movies are crime stories, but it's crime with a difference. In a good film noir one or more of the characters will decide to do the wrong thing—not just to break the law but to sin—knowing that he or she probably won't get away with it but going ahead anyway. The motivation is usually lust, greed, or a combination of the two. The results are seldom what we expect, but as these twisted characters are pursuing their goals, the viewer can—for a long moment in the darkness—identify with and share those wicked choices.

Who among us, after all, hasn't fantasized about getting rid of the curvy blonde's husband and running off with her? Or of diddling the company's books and embezzling the year's profits? Of course we know we won't do it—at least most of us won't—so we enjoy watching someone else try and that's what noir is all about.

Final Impact

Like all good martial arts movies, this one's a simple story that sticks close to established formulas and still contains some nice surprises. The action scenes are well choreographed by Eric Lee, and the fights are relatively realistic, not sadistic. Young contender Jeff Langton searches out a burnt-out kickboxing master Lorenzo Lamas to help him train against villain Mike Worth, who took the master's championship, not to mention his wife. Also on hand is the master's current girlfriend, Kathleen Kinmont, to provide the voice of reason. These characters are unusually believable and well-developed for the genre, and the film is aimed equally at male and female audiences; the big scenes are focused on well developed, semi-dressed, good-looking young guys who are as flatteringly photographed as any calendar girls. *ƊƊƊ*

Fight scenes.

1991 **(R)** 99m/C Lorenzo Lamas, Kathleen Kinmont, Mimi Lesseos, Kathrin Lautner, Jeff Langton, Mike Worth; *D:* Joseph Merhi, Stephen Smoke; *M:* John Gonzalez. **VHS** *PMH*

Final Mission

Something is going wrong with the virtual reality experiments that fighter pilot Billy Wirth is conducting. Could it involve his shady superiors Corbin Bernsen and Steve Railsback or the gorgeous Elizabeth Gracen who falls for the dumbest pick-up line ever at a gas station? The limited budget shows through whenever the action moves out of the sky and onto the ground, and the script is transparently simple. For fans, the main attractions are computer effects and above-average aerial footage. 🐾🐾

Strong language, violence, brief nudity, sexual content.

1993 **(R)** 91m/C Billy Wirth, Corbin Bernsen, Elizabeth Gracen, Steve Railsback; *D:* Lee Redmond. **VHS, LV** *VMK*

Final Notice

Adaptation of Jonathan Valin's Harry Stoner mystery is an embarrassment for all concerned, save jazzman Tom Scott whose score is pretty good. Everything else stinks. Gil Gerard is too old and chubby and well-dressed for Stoner, and Melody Anderson, as the librarian heroine, is even worse. But given the sloppy script, can they shoulder all the blame? Valin's books are good and they deserve better. WUUF!

Contains some profanity and violence.

1989 91m/C Gil Gerard, Steve Landesburg, Jackie Burroughs, Melody Anderson, Louise Fletcher, David Ogden Stiers, Kevin Hicks; *D:* Steven Hilliard Stern; *W:* John Gay; *M:* Tom Scott. **VHS, LV** *PAR*

Fires Within

A good cast works with an intriguing, timely story and comes up with nothing. Greta Scacchi is a Cuban refugee who has made a life for herself and her daughter in Miami. For eight years, her husband (Jimmy Smits) has been a political prisoner. In the meantime, she has become romantically involved with Vincent D'Onofrio, the fisherman who rescued her. Then Castro has a change of heart. Will Smits adjust to life in Florida? Or will he rejoin the activists who want him to help with an invasion of the homeland? Those questions, along with the love triangle, are given obligatory treatment by director Gillian Armstrong. Everyone involved seems to have been going through the motions. Armstrong even lets key characters' heads move out of the frame at key moments. Though the immigrants' conflicts are central to the story, the film never really gets inside Miami's Cuban community. Too bad. 🐾

Mature subject matter, profanity, brief nudity, and sexual content.

1991 **(R)** 97m/C Jimmy Smits, Greta Scacchi, Vincent D'Onofrio; *D:* Gillian Armstrong; *W:* Cynthia Cidre. **VHS** *MGM*

First Degree

Though the characters are familiar crime movie stereotypes, the plot takes enough unexpected twists to keep you watching. Investigating the murder of philanthropist Andrew Pine, NYPD detective Rick Mallory (Rob Lowe) promptly falls for the dead man's widow Hadley (Leslie Hope). Was Pine killed by gangsters who'd loaned him money to keep his financial empire afloat, or did Hadley have something to do with it? Ron Base's script provides several answers before it's over. Throughout, director Jeff Woolnough maintains a cool, almost cold attitude toward the characters. It's unusual but appropriate. There's really no one to empathize or identify with in this one. It's more a matter of style and reversal of expectations that might have been crafted to fit Lowe's clean-cut bad boy image. 🐾🐾🐾

Mature subject matter, strong language, violence, incidental nudity.

1995 **(R)** 98m/C Rob Lowe, Leslie Hope; *D:* Jeff Woolnough; *W:* Ron Base. **VHS** *PGV*

Fist of Honor

Rocky-esque Sam Jones doesn't like working for a loan shark but he's trying to save up enough to buy a home for himself and his fiancee, Joey House. The rest is a complex tangle of gang wars, double crosses, and fight scenes; half martial arts flick, half *Godfather*-lite. Old pros Harry Guardino, Abe Vigoda, and Nicholas Worth turn in savvy supporting

work. Model Joey House is a real looker, and not a bad actress either. The real surprise though is Jones. It's easy to believe that he's a kind-hearted lug who's easily tricked and left holding the bag. This one's a cut above the norm for action flicks. 🗡🗡🗡

Violence, strong language, brief nudity.

1992 (R) 90m/C Sam Jones, Joey House, Harry Guardino, Nicholas Worth, Frank Sivero, Abe Vigoda, Bubba Smith; *D:* Richard Pepin; *W:* Charles Kanganis. **VHS** *PMH*

Fist of the North Star

The live-action version of the famous Japanese animated feature stays true to its roots. The film was made completely on sound stages—no exteriors—and both the violence and the acting are slightly stylized. The story is archetypal post-apocalyptic martial arts material. Two fighting schools are led by the brave Kenshiro (Gary Daniels) and the evil Shin (Costas Mandylor). Julia (Isako Washio) is the woman they both want. Chris Penn is the bad guy with a bubbling brain and Malcolm McDowell is the levitating master who has decreed that the two schools must never fight each other. Yes, it's all pure hokum, but it's passionate, fiercely realized hokum. In every sense it's much more enjoyable that director Tony Randel's *Hellraiser II.* Because his background is in horror, the fight choreography was handled by Winston

Omega, star Gary Daniels' martial arts teacher. Overall, the film is visually inventive, well acted, and funny in the right places. Despite the R-rating, the violence isn't too strong for kids who like martial arts. 🗡🗡🗡

Violence, strong language.

1996 (R) 102m/C Gary Daniels, Costas Mandylor, Christopher Penn, Julie Brown, Malcolm McDowell, Melvin Van Peebles, Isako Washio; *D:* Tony Randel; *W:* Tony Randel; *C:* Jacques Haitkin. **VHS** *BMG*

Five Corners

Comedy-drama is strong willed, unconventional, and constantly surprising. The title refers to the neighborhood in the Bronx where all of the action takes place. The time is 1964, but this is not another exercise in misty-eyed nostalgia. The key elements are a recently paroled psychotic criminal (chillingly played by John Turturro), the girl (Jodie Foster) he tried to rape years before, and her reluctant protector (Tim Robbins, at his youthful best) who has decided to dedicate his life to non-violence. A couple of penguins, glue-sniffing girls, and a mysterious archer are also important. John Patrick Shanley's script may not be as instantly likable as his Oscar-winning *Moonstruck,* but it's just as sharp and funny. And sometimes unnerving. Director Tony Bill has a deft touch with setting and off-beat action. (By the way, watch the closing credits carefully; a fine bit of comic business takes place behind them.) 🗡🗡🗡

Profanity and violence.

1988 (R) 92m/C Jodie Foster, John Turturro, Todd Graff, Tim Robbins, Elizabeth Berridge, Rose Gregorio, Gregory Rozakis, Rodney Harvey, John Seitz; *D:* Tony Bill; *W:* John Patrick Shanley; *C:* Fred Murphy; *M:* James Newton Howard. Independent Spirit Awards '89: Best Actress (Foster). **VHS** *MGM*

Flesh Gordon 2: Flesh Gordon Meets the Cosmic Cheerleaders

The original *Flesh Gordon* is one of the great guilty pleasures. This one isn't nearly as much fun but it is notable for rude, scatological humor. In recent years, Americans have become so obsessed with not offending each other—as groups and as individuals—that we're becoming bland and homogenous. Not this spirited little flick. It begins with jokes about flatulence and a sport called "codball," and then it becomes seriously tasteless. And that's what guilty pleasures are all about. Also available in an unrated version. 🙸🙸🙸 **GPI: 9.3**

Strong language, nudity, sexual content, comic violence.

1990 **(R)** 98m/C *CA* Vince Murdocco, Tony Travis, William Dennis Hunt, Robyn Kelly; *D:* Howard Ziehm. **VHS** *NHO*

Fleshtone

Despite the sexy box art, this is an improbable little mystery. L.A. artist Martin Kemp is so lonely and innocent that he answers an ad in the personals and then actually believes that a woman he meets through a 900-number is telling the truth when she describes her fantasies and says she loves him. After the standard soft-core fantasy stuff, the story picks up steam. Kemp has an intense screen presence and writer/director Harry Hurwitz comes up with absolutely the right ending to an uneven plot. Also, credit Mark Stock for the pictures that are so important to the mood. Flawed? Yes, but after it's over, this one has some odd staying power. Unrated version also available at 98 minutes. 🙸🙸🙸

Nudity, sexual content, strong language, mild violence.

1994 **(R)** 91m/C Martin Kemp, Lise Cutter, Tim Thomerson; *D:* Harry Hurwitz; *W:* Harry Hurwitz. **VHS, LV** *PSM*

Flirting

John Duigan's funny, touching coming-of-age story is one of the best sleepers in your video store. It lacks the "name" stars—and attendant studio hype—that draw audiences. Instead, it has all the fundamentals of a really good movie: likeable, fully developed characters dealing with universal conflicts in an unusual setting. It's Australia, 1965. Young Danny Embling (Noah Taylor) is an outsider at a snotty, traditional private school. His fellow students are a mostly thick-headed lot with a strict pecking order. Smart, dark-complected, and smaller than the rest, Danny is near the bottom. At night, after the house master has administered canings with the ill-concealed zeal of a self-righteous bully, Danny lies awake and stares across the lake at the girl's school. That's where Thandiwe (Thandie Newton) finds herself almost as ostracized as Danny. She's black, and, like Danny, a romantic who reads Camus and Sartre. Their attraction to each other is completely natural. So are the barriers that will be thrown up by the adolescents and adults who surround them. The supporting cast is filled with instantly recognizable characters who cross cultural boundaries—the jock who looks like he's 35 when he's 16; the kid who's almost in the "in crowd" but laughs too loud at the wrong moments. Nicole Kidman is perfectly cast as the cool blonde cutie—there's one in every school—who rules the female population and has considerable power over the boys. If all of this sounds a little familiar to some viewers, it's because *Flirting* is a sequel to another fine Australian film, *The Year My Voice Broke.* And according to the production notes, writer/director Duigan plans a third look at Danny's journey through adolescence. By the way, even though the MPAA, in its wisdom, has given this one an R-rating for its realistic, delicately handled sexual content, it's much more appropriate for teenagers than a lot of the PG and PG-13-rated crap that Hollywood passes off on them. 🙸🙸🙸

Sexual content, mild violence, strong language.

1989 **(R)** 100m/C *AU* Noah Taylor, Thandie Newton, Nicole Kidman, Bartholomew Rose, Felix Nobis, Josh Picker, Kiri Paramore, Marc Gray, Joshua Marshall, David Wieland, Craig Black, Leslie Hill; *D:* John Duigan; *W:* John Duigan. Australian Film Institute '90: Best Film. **VHS, LV** *VMK, BTV*

Floundering

James LeGros is aimlessly adrift in Los Angeles. Unemployed and lacking in ambition, he's prone to circular philosophical discussions with friend John Cusack, while dealing with his brother Ethan Hawke's paranoid fantasies and

problems in detox, and his girlfriend Lisa Zane's casual infidelities. Anything more in the way of plot synopsis would be pointless because the story is about 50 percent realistic, 50 percent metaphorical, and 100 percent politically naive. Writer/producer/director Peter McCarthy blames all of the problems of southern California on one character: an authoritarian parody of former L.A. police chief Daryl Gates. It's a curious and unnecessary flaw. With its shadings of impending apocalypse, the film is strongly reminiscent of *Repo Man,* which McCarthy produced. 🗡🗡🗡

Strong language, sexual humor and situations, violence.

1994 (R) 97m/C James LeGros, Ethan Hawke, Steve Buscemi, John Cusack, Lisa Zane, Sy Richardson; *D:* Peter McCarthy; *W:* Peter McCarthy. **VHS** *APX*

Food of the Gods: Part 2

Any film that ends with mutant rats the size of Winnebagos attacking the synchronized swim team, which is doing its routine to a disco version of Beethoven's "Ode to Joy," has to be worth at least a look. Unfortunately, that grand finale is the best thing about this low-budget horror sequel based on genetic research. *AKA*. Gnaw Food of the Gods 2. 🗡🗡

Violence, profanity, brief nudity, sexual scenes, synchronized swimming.

1988 (R) 93m/C Paul Coufos, Lisa Schrage; *D:* Damian Lee; *W:* E. Kim Brewster. **VHS, LV** *AHV*

A Fool and His Money

When aggressive young adman Morris Codman (Jonathan Penner) loses his job, he is inspired by God (George Plimpton) to found a new religion. Actually the Supreme Being, who appears via late-night television and immoderate amounts of whiskey, is vague on the details, but our boy charges ahead anyway, basing this new faith on old-fashioned selfishness and embroidering the "greed is good" cliche into gospel. Toss in some marketing and glib front man Gerald Orange, and Morris is on his way. His girlfriend Sandra Bullock disagrees. Literary celebs Tama Janowitz and the late Jerzy Kosinski appear in cameos. It's obvious that writer/director/co-producer Daniel Adams was working on a shoestring budget. The acting ranges from acceptable to poor, and the pace is much too slow. Some of the religious satire works; more often it comes across as heavy handed. 🗡🗡

Strong language, subject matter.

1988 (R) 84m/C Jonathan Penner, Sandra Bullock, Gerald Orange, George Plimpton; *Cameos:* Tama Janowitz, Jerzy Kosinski; *D:* Daniel Adams; *W:* Daniel Adams. **VHS** *VMK*

Forbidden Sun

Offbeat, handsome production is notable mostly for its unusual plot that has to do with American women gymnasts training at a school on Crete. Director Zelda Barron lets the focus wander from conflicts between the conservative Greek islanders and the more easygoing athletes, to an affair that school mistress Lauren Hutton is having, to rock musicians on a nearby island, to the gamy Greek myths about the Minotaur. Not surprisingly, the ending is as unconvincing as it is silly. 🗡🗡

ᴏᴘᴛ: 5.5

Mature subject matter, sexual situations, violence, brief nudity.

1989 (R) 88m/C Lauren Hutton, Cliff DeYoung, Renee Estevez; *D:* Zelda Barron. **VHS, LV** *ACA*

Forbidden Zone: Alien Abduction

Despite the title, *Forbidden Zone: Alien Abduction* is extremely slick, extremely romanticized eroticism meant primarily for a female audience. If a bunch of English grad students and *X-Files* fans got together to share their fantasies, this might be the result. It's all about three friends (Darcy Demoss, Pia Reyes, and Meredyth Holmes) who discover that they've each experienced "missing hours" involving a guy (Dumitri Bogmaz) who looks a lot like the comic book character Submariner. The remarkable thing about the film is director Lucian Diamonde's attention to photographic detail, down to the level of skin pores and individual hairs. Also available in an unrated version. 𝄢𝄢𝄢

Nudity, sexual content, a little strong language.

1996 (R) 90m/C Darcy Demoss, Pia Reyes, Dumitri Bogmaz, Carmen Lacatus, Alina Chivulescu, Florin Chiriac, Meredyth Holmes; *D:* Lucian S. Diamonde; *W:* Vernon Lumley; *C:* Adolfo Bartoli; *M:* Reg Powell. **VHS** *AFE*

The Force

Conventional L.A. cop yarn has a loopy New Age twist. When veteran detective Des Flynn (Gary Hudson) is murdered by sinister forces, his spirit relocates in the body of rookie patrolman Cal Carner (Jason Gedrick). After some psychic sorting out, the two form a "partnership" to find the killer. They get help from Cal's partner Erin (Cyndi Pass) and Des' widow Sara (Kim Delaney) who are more than a little skeptical about this two-mind/one-body thing. Overall, director Mark Rosman does acceptable work with thin material and an attractive cast. 𝄢𝄢

Violence, strong language, fleeting nudity.

1994 (R) 94m/C Jason Gedrick, Gary Hudson, Cyndi Pass, Kim Delaney; *D:* Mark Rosman. **VHS, LV** *REP*

The Forgotten One

Searching for inspiration, widowed novelist Terry O'Quinn moves to Denver and buys an old Victorian house that's haunted by the fetching Blair Parker. Neighbor Kristy McNichol helps him find answers. O.K., the story does have the logic problems that plague most supernatural stories, but beyond that, this is one spooky, sexy ghost movie. O'Quinn brings the same tightly wrapped unpredictability to this role that made *The Stepfather* so memorable. Throughout, the formula aspects of the genre are kept to a minimum, and the special effects are atmospheric and effective. 𝄢𝄢𝄢

Nudity, sexual content, violence, profanity.

1989 (R) 89m/C Kristy McNichol, Terry O'Quinn, Blair Parker, Elisabeth Brooks; *D:* Phillip Badger. **VHS, LV** *ACA*

Fortunes of War

Labor of love wears its humanistic politics on its sleeve in an attempt to combine an Eric Ambler/Graham Green plot of intrigue and double-dealing with a conventional action framework; gunfights, explosions, chases, etc. A visual quote from *Apocalypse Now* at the beginning sets the mood. On the Thai-Cambodian border, Matt Salinger (also the film's producer) is a burnt-out relief worker who allows himself to be hooked into a scheme hatched by Canadian diplomat Michael Ironside: transport a truckload of medical supplies to a Cambodian warlord, bring back a million dollars in gold bars. Mark Lee's script treats the characters and the situation seriously. It is a little preachy at times—I think it earns the right to be—and the conventional "Hollywood" ending is weak. Recommended for fans of *84 Charlie Mopic* and *A Midnight Clear*, though it's not quite as successful as either of those. 𝄢𝄢𝄢

Contains some violence, strong language, sexual situations.

1994 107m/C Matt Salinger, Michael Ironside, Haing S. Ngor, Sam Jenkins, Martin Sheen, Michael Nouri; *D:* Thierry Notz; *W:* Mark Lee. **VHS, LV** *COL*

Four Days in November

Combining black-and-white news footage with carefully unsensationalized re-creations, this documentary from producer David L. Wolper tells the "official" version of the assassination of John F. Kennedy. It's an effective rebuttal to the exaggerations and outright lies of more sensational versions of those terrible events. First, it explains why Kennedy went to Texas, then proceeds chronologically to the killing, the frantic action that followed on several fronts, the memorial services and funeral, and the reaction worldwide. It does not go into the details, real or suspected, but in terms of emotion, the film is one hundred percent accurate. It describes and shows the confusion, the sense of disbelief and dislocation that we all felt then. As David Frost said at the time, "It was the most unexpected piece of news one could possibly imagine." Perhaps

Video Premieres

the most astonishing aspect of this version of the story is the way the Dallas police paraded Lee Harvey Oswald through their headquarters in front of the cameras. In its portrayal of Kennedy himself, the film never strays from rose-colored "Camelot" nostalgia, showing the handsome, boyish president with a lovely wife and adorable kids. 🎜🎜🎜

Contains no objectionable material.

1964 123m/B D: Mel Stuart; **M:** Elmer Bernstein. **VHS** *MGM*

Frame Up

In an updated *High Noon,* sheriff Wings Hauser defies the local millionaire whose spoiled son has killed a man. The film has a solid understanding of smalltown sociology, and the characters are well written and well acted. At the same time, the mechanics of the plot are clumsy and the beginning is stronger than the conclusion. 🎜🎜🎜

Violence, strong language and brief nudity.

1991 (R) 90m/C Wings Hauser, Bobby DiCicco, Frances Fisher, Dick Sargent, Robert Picardo; **D:** Paul Leder. **VHS, LV** *REP*

Frankenhooker

James Lorinz is a "bioelectrotechnician" whose fiancee Patty Mullen is killed in a tragic lawn mower accident. But he manages to salvage a few key body parts. If he can just find donors for the rest, he's sure he can recreate her. Late one night he heads for Times Square. Like Frank Henenlotter's overlooked *Brain Damage,* this one is strongly, even violently anti-drug. Though parts of the story are so grotesque they make Henenlotter's own cult hit *Basket Case* look like *Mary Poppins,* they're exaggerated for comic effect. The real surprise here is Mullen, an ex-Penthouse model who turns out to be an accomplished comedienne. Also available in an unrated version. 🎜🎜🎜

Contains graphic violence, strong language, nudity, sexual situations.

1990 (R) 90m/C James Lorinz, Patty Mullen, Charlotte J. Helmkamp, Louise Lasser; **D:** Frank Henenlotter. **VHS, LV** *SGE, FCT*

Freakshow

Anthology of short horror films was made in South Carolina. The framing device is a carnival sideshow where two teens listen to scary stories told by Gunnar Hansen (without his "Leatherface" mask from *Texas Chainsaw Massacre*). Naturally, they're fairly graphic tales about revenge, cannibalism, and such with a grisly sense of humor along the lines of the old E.C. Comics. The production values are a bit on the thin side and the pace is slow, but the films get better. "The Mummy" has a slight Poe quality and it stars Veronica Carlson, familiar to fans for her work in Hammer horror films of the 1960s, and still looking terrific. 🎜🎜🎜

Violence, strong language, brief nudity.

1995 (R) 102m/C Gunnar Hansen, Veronica Carlson, Brian D. Kelly, Shannon Michelle Parsons; **D:** William Cooke, Paul Talbot. **VHS** *AVI*

Freddie the Frog

This curious animated feature is probably too offbeat and "European" for young American audiences. It boasts some high-powered voice talent—James Earl Jones, Nigel Hawthorne, and Ben Kingsley in the lead—and a loosely wrapped excuse of a plot. The story begins as a fairy tale about a French frog (insert your own joke here), then turns into a James Bondish spy spoof when our hero grows to human size and becomes Agent FRO7, and for those hearty few who make it to the last reel, it finally becomes a science-fiction musical. Throughout, the animation is no better than fair and the film tells too much while showing too little. **AKA:** Freddie as F.R.O.7. 🎬

1992 **(G)** 72m/C *GB D:* Jon Acevski; *W:* Jon Acevski, David Ashton; *V:* Ben Kingsley, Nigel Hawthorne, James Earl Jones, Jenny Agutter, John Sessions, Brian Blessed, Billie Whitelaw, Jonathan Pryce, Phyllis Logan, Michael Hordern. **VHS** *MCA*

Friend of the Family

Soft-core *Beverly Hills 90210* finds sexy Shauna O'Brien as a houseguest to a dysfunctional family of ultra-rich Californians. Acting as a combination Ann Landers and the Happy Hooker, she helps each of them—from spoiled daughter Lisa Boyle, to long-suffering dad C.T. Miller and stepmother Griffin Drew—overcome their sexual problems and accept themselves for who they are. Like all Andrew Garroni productions it's highly polished and the people are pretty, even if their acting abilities are limited. That's not exactly the point. Also available in an unrated version. **AKA:** Elke. 🎬🎬🎬

Sexual content, nudity, and a little rough language.

1995 98m/C Shauna O'Brien, C.T. Miller, Griffin Drew, Lisa Boyle; *D:* Edward Holzman. **VHS** *TRI*

Friends, Lovers & Lunatics

Unfunny romantic comedy features unpleasant, unattractive characters. Daniel Stern is a misunderstood artist who chases his ex-girlfriend and her new beau into the middle of the Canadian woods. On the way, he runs across Deborah Foreman who's running from her nutty boyfriend Page Fletcher. Toward the middle, one character asks the revealing question: "Is this some kind of sick joke?" The answer is, "Yes, but not the kind where you laugh at the end." Bingo. **AKA:** Crazy Horse; She Drives Me Crazy. 🎬

Profanity.

1989 87m/C *CA* Daniel Stern, Deborah Foreman, Sheila McCarthy, Page Fletcher, Elias Koteas; *D:* Stephen Withrow. **VHS, LV** *FRH, IME*

Fright House

The spirit of legendary master Ed Wood, Jr., lives on in this alternative classic. The tape contains two short films that make absolutely no sense. The first, "Fright House," has something to do with a coven of chubby topless witches, a guy who does stand-up comedy on a picnic table, a monster that lives in a fireplace, and an abandoned school. The second, "Abadon," examines the horrors of bad plumbing, art school, and moldy bathrooms. Several of the characters look so much alike that it's hard to tell what's going on, but who cares? The amateurish acting and the relentless parade of horror cliches are the real attractions here. Destined for cult greatness and a place of honor in the Bad Movie Hall of Fame. 🎬🎬🎬

Graphic violence, grotesque special effects, strong language, brief nudity, and sexual content.

1989 **(R)** UNRm/C Al Lewis, Duane Jones; *D:* Len Anthony. **VHS** *NO*

From Beyond

Unfortunately, the team that made the brilliant cult hit *Re-Animator* isn't quite as successful with this loose adaptation of an H.P. Lovecraft tale about interdimensional travel via the "Praetorius Resonator" which stimulates the pineal gland. Again, the film is filled with all sorts of imaginative prosthetic special effects, beginning with an exploding head and then moving farther afield. The sexual side of the action isn't as graphic or as strange as it was in the first film. Rats. 🎬🎬🎬

Mature subject matter, violence, grotesque special effects, sexual content.

1986 **(R)** 98m/C Jeffrey Combs, Barbara Crampton, Ted Sorel, Ken Foree, Carolyn Purdy-Gordon, Bunny Summers, Bruce McGuire; *D:* Stuart Gordon; *W:* Dennis Paoli, Brian Yuzna; *M:* Richard Band. **VHS, LV** *LIV, VES*

1996 (R) 98m/C Wendy Schumacher, Jay Richardson; *D:* Fred Olen Ray; *W:* Dani Michaeli, Sean O'Bannon. **VHS** *APX*

Fugitive X

Imaginative and imitative action flick is yet another variation on *The Most Dangerous Game* theme. Writer/producer/director/star David Heavener is an ex-cop with a tragic past (paralyzed wife, dead daughter) who is set upon by a bunch of rich guys with Armanis and Uzis. A grandly gory and funny opening sets the tone. The action is set on familiar low-rent L.A. locations. Between the rote chases and gunfights, the atmosphere has an eerie dreamlike quality, most obviously in the *Pulp Fiction* rip-off scene. This one earns points for energy; loses points for cliches. 🐾🐾🐾

Violence, strong language, brief nudity, sexual content.

1996 97m/C David Heavener, Richard Norton, Lynn-Holly Johnson, William Windom, Chris Mitchum, Robert Z'Dar; *D:* David Heavener; *W:* David Heavener. **VHS** *SLI*

Funny

The ultimate "talking head" movie is simply people telling jokes, about 80 of them in 80 minutes. The famous and the not-so-famous sit or stand in front of Brian Ferren's camera and tell stories; some funny and some not. The level of humor is established in the opening credits when the executive producers are listed as Benjamin Dover and Seymour Butts. As for the gags themselves, generally, the ones from real people (as opposed to celebrities) are the best. Bartender Susan Agranoff has terrific comic timing. Naturalist Roger Caras' long joke about the lion, the mouse, and the giraffe doesn't have a great punchline but he's such a good storyteller that it's one of the best moments on the disc. The interplay between actor Peter Boyle and his young daughter, Lucy, as they read moose jokes from a book is wonderful; again, the material itself isn't that funny—she is. It's obvious that she absolutely cannot believe that her father is doing this in front of a camera and her mortification is wonderful. 🐾🐾🐾

Fugitive Rage

Veteran video schlockmeister Fred Olen Ray has come up with something of an overachiever with this hybrid revenge/women's-prison flick. Two reasons: (1) some snappy dialogue in Dani Michaeli and Sean O'Bannon's script, and (2) a gritty performance by Wendy Schumacher in the lead. She's Tara McCormick, who takes matters into her own hands when mobster Tommy Stompanato (Jay Richardson) is found not guilty of her sister's murder. Toward the end, the action becomes unfocused and cliched, with the obligatory shower scene, but it's still a cut above the usual exploitation fare. 🐾🐾🐾

Graphic violence, nudity, sexual content, strong language.

Disclaimer states, "Parental Warning: This disc contains gratuitous nudity, profanity and something to offend almost everyone."

1992 80m/C *D:* Brian Ferren. **LV** *WEA*

The Further Adventures of Tennessee Buck

The title character borrows freely from Indiana Jones and 'Crocodile' Dundee, and star David Keith, directing himself, seems to be having a grand time. The film was made in Sri Lanka, flatteringly shown at its greenest and most picturesque, and co-stars ex-Playmate of the Year Kathy Shower. This is exactly the kind of silly movie that benefits most from the presence of an ex-Playmate. All of your favorite jungle flick cliches reappear. The action is a little violent and a little sexy—never ever serious. 🦴🦴🦴

Violence, nudity, strong sexual content.

1988 **(R)** 90m/C David Keith, Kathy Shower, Brant Van Hoffman; *D:* David Keith; *M:* John Debney. **VHS, LV** *MED, VTR*

Future Force

RoboCop ripoff stars David Carradine doing a bad John Wayne imitation as a chubby-cheeked and tired-looking bounty hunter. The chases are tepid, the effects aren't special, and in some scenes the synchronization of lip movement with dialogue isn't even close. Give the flick a few points for being so bad that it's kind of fun, but it's recommended only to true fans of alternative video fare who are not afraid to use the fast-forward button liberally. 🦴🦴

Violence, profanity, brief nudity.

1989 **(R)** 90m/C David Carradine, Robert Tessier, Anna Rapagna, William Zipp; *D:* David A. Prior. **VHS** *AIP*

Future Shock

Anthology of three loosely connected short films has nothing to do with Alvin Toffler's book. The first is about a wealthy woman (Vivian Schilling, also one of the writers) who is either paranoid or well informed. When her husband leaves her alone overnight in their huge house, she fantasizes about a pack of wolves lurking outside. Is she delusional? Is someone trying to frighten her? Or is she reacting to the violence and horror that she sees on the evening news? In part, the film is a nice combination of elements: the traditional Gothic heroine in her nightgown caught up in a science-fiction story. Schilling is one of the most interesting people working in home video and she manages to put a different spin on the proceedings. The film works better as a black comedy than as a thriller, but it's still worth a look. The second part, "The Roommate," is fast-forward material. The third, "Mr. Petrified Forest," is less ambitious than the first but it may be more successful. It's a wry, offbeat story of a man who appears to be having a near-death experience. Despite the flaws, director Eric Parkinson shows that he knows what he's doing and can juggle different tones. Also available in an unrated version. 🦴🦴🦴

Some violence and language. (The unrated version contains one exploding head special effect.)

1993 **(PG-13)** 93m/C Bill Paxton, Vivian Schilling, Brion James, Martin Kove; *D:* Eric Parkinson, Matt Reeves, Oley Sassone; *W:* Vivian Schilling. **VHS** *HMD*

> **"**'d like to be known as the female Van Damme. The problem is we haven't had a real female action star who can pull in the clientele, because...it's hard to sell—there aren't many women who can do it and do it well and who can act. Women want to see it; men want to see it and it's pretty much untapped right now.
>
> "Until I got into martial arts, I felt like a victim, and it's amazing how much you can do [to defend yourself]. There's a lot of soft tissue on the body. If I'm really in danger, I could rip your eyes out. It's not hard — I could do it right now. Women just don't know that."
>
> —Actress Wendy Schumacher, star of *Fugitive Rage*

Video Premiere Documentaries

Unlike public TV, video originals almost never expect you to watch something that's not fun just because it's good for you. That's just as true for documentaries as it is for conventional features. When it comes to non-fiction, video can provide some wonderful stuff. These tapes are usually (but not always) on the edge of respectability. In its own way, each is fascinating.

AMERICAN DREAM	HUGH HEFNER: ONCE UPON A TIME
BIX	
BROTHER'S KEEPER	THE INLAND SEA
CHUCK AMUCK: THE MOVIE	MYSTERIES OF PERU
DENNIS POTTER: THE LAST INTERVIEW	THE REAL RICHARD NIXON
	TIME INDEFINITE
DOCUMENT OF THE DEAD	VISIONS OF LIGHT: THE ART OF CINEMATOGRAPHY
ED WOOD: LOOK BACK IN ANGORA	
	WISECRACKS
GEORGE STEVENS: A FILMMAKER'S JOURNEY	

tic reason, and Karen Medak steals the second half as a down-on-her-luck actress. At his worst moments, writer/director John Ryman comes across as a would-be Woody Allen who uses talk in place of action. In the end, though, the film's humor and unpredictability earn it a recommendation for those in the market for something different. 🦴🦴🦴

Strong language, some violence, sexual content.

1992 (R) 97m/C Dwier Brown, Kelsey Grammer, Susan Walters, Karen Medak; *D:* John Ryman; *W:* John Ryman; *C:* Philip Lee; *M:* Stephen Barber. **VHS** *PAR*

Gator Bait 2: Cajun Justice

Sequel to a 1976 drive-in classic is a feminist/rural revenge tale. Newlyweds Tray Loren and Jan MacKenzie are tormented by half-witted, light-beer-swilling psychos. These guys are so scummy, they make the mangy rednecks in *Deliverance* look like Rhodes scholars. The difference here is that sexual violence is depicted in all its ugliness. It's meant to be repellent and has nothing to do with soft-core fantasies. The film still follows all the rules of the form, and so it is recommended mostly for fans of the genre. 🦴🦴🦴

Graphic violence, nudity, profanity, sexual content.

1988 (R) 101m/C Jan MacKenzie, Tray Loren, Paul Muzzcat, Brad Kepnick, Jerry Armstrong, Ben Sebastian; *D:* Ferd Sebastian, Beverly Sebastian; *W:* Ferd Sebastian, Beverly Sebastian. **VHS, LV** *PAR*

Galaxies Are Colliding

Offbeat little drama is enjoyable and off-putting in about equal amounts. On the eve of his wedding, Adam (Dwier Brown) is having serious doubts, not just about his future, but about everything. World hunger, god, the afterlife, salvation—all the biggies. Why then is he wandering, stupefied, through the Mojave desert? And why are his friends at his funeral? For much of the picture, Adam is a blank slate that the other characters bounce monologues and ideas off of. Kelsey Grammer provides the voice of sweet-tempered atheis-

George Stevens: A Filmmaker's Journey

All right, any tribute to a father from his son isn't going to be completely objective, but this one certainly is enjoyable. Stevens Jr. combines scenes from his father's professional work with personal footage he shot with his own camera to tell the story of a life. Most of the personal film was taken while Stevens was working for the Army in World War II, and it's the only color cinematic record we have of D-Day and possibly the only color film that was made of the liberation of Paris and the horrors of the concentration camps. When the focus returns to Hollywood, it shows the business at its best, from *Shane* to *Giant*. The film also goes beyond the facts of biography to find subtle insights into the human mind. At Dachau, Stevens came to the realization, so often overlooked, that under the wrong circumstances, each of us can be monstrously evil. He says, "I see myself being capable of arrogance and brutality.... That's a fierce thing—to discover in yourself that which you despise the most." 🦴🦴🦴🦴

Contains graphic wartime horror.

1984 110m/C George Stevens, Katharine Hepburn, Cary Grant, Joel McCrea, Fred Astaire, Ginger Rogers, Warren Beatty; *D:* George Stevens Jr.; *M:* Carl Davis. **VHS** *PME, FCT, BTV*

George's Island

In the opening scene, comical pirates bury treasure, and several of them are killed; one is beheaded. But that bit of bloodless violence is finished quickly and the rest of this Canadian film is an engaging supernatural comedy of kids vs. stuffy adults. Ten-year-old George (Nathaniel Moreau) lives with his crusty old grandfather Capt. Waters (Ian Bannen) in a shanty by the water. When George repeats granddad's wild tales of pirates and ghosts in school, it's the last straw for his Pecksniffian teacher, Miss Birdwood (Sheila McCarthy). She and Mr. Droonfield (Maury Chaykin), a social worker, try to put George in a foster home. It all ends on Halloween night with a long chase, encounters with ghosts, and a satisfying resolution where just desserts are handed out to everyone—good and bad. Overall, the performances are good. So are the limited special effects. And even though this is a kid's movie, the humor is fairly sophisticated. Very young viewers, who probably wouldn't sit through any feature-length movie, won't care for this one, but for everyone else, it's fun. 🦴🦴🦴

Some violence, a little salty language.

1991 (PG) 89m/C Ian Bannen, Sheila McCarthy, Maury Chaykin, Nathaniel Moreau, Vicki Ridler, Brian Downey, Gary Reineke; *D:* Paul Donovan; *W:* J. William Ritchie; *M:* Marty Simon. **VHS, LV** *COL, NLC*

The Getaway

The video release of this unnecessary remake doesn't merit much notice. But fans of guilty pleasures should know that it comes in two video versions: along with the R-rated theatrical release, there's an unrated version with a racier love scene between stars Alec Baldwin and Kim Basinger. It appears late in the story and, in terms of character and pace, it makes more sense than the original cut. 🦴🦴 **GPI: 7.1**

Graphic violence, strong language, sexual content, brief nudity.

1993 (R) 110m/C Alec Baldwin, Kim Basinger, James Woods, Michael Madsen, Jennifer Tilly, David Morse; *D:* Roger Donaldson; *W:* Walter Hill, Amy Holden Jones; *C:* Peter Menzies Jr.; *M:* Mark Isham. Nominations: MTV Movie Awards '94: Most Desirable Female (Basinger). **VHS, LV** *MCA*

Ghost in the Shell

Though it's been compared to *Akira*, this slick feature lacks the epic scope and energy of that masterpiece of Japanese animation. Based on Shirow Masamune's manga (graphic novel/comic book) it's a sophisticated s-f adventure about identity, secret agents, and the relationship between humans and machines. Yes, comparisons to *Blade Runner* are in order. The overly ornate and unfinished plot suggests that this is the first part of a larger work with several important but vague concepts at the center. Director Mamoru Oshii sets a slow, moody pace with long introspective scenes, exaggerated lighting, and evocative music. Some of the noir-tinged images are breathtaking. 🦴🦴🦴

Contains violence, nudity.

1995 75m/C *JP D:* Mamoru Oshii. **VHS** *CPM*

Ghosts Can't Do It

Yes, Bo-watchers, once again John Derek has cast his wife as the central character in a full-length movie of breathtaking incompetence. It's the story of the undying love between a larger-than-life zillionaire, Scott (Anthony Quinn, who doesn't seem nearly as embarrassed as he should), and his child bride, Bo.

As the story opens, they're herding cattle on their Wyoming ranch (these scenes are an excuse for Bo to put on her cowgirl outfits with lots of fur and fringe and to prance around on her horsey in the snow). Then Scott has a heart attack and decides to kill himself. Bummer. His spirit returns in time for the funeral where he hears the preacher say, "What is life? It is the breath of the buffalo in the wintertime." He then advises his widow that she should take a little time off to smell the buffalo breath at their favorite vacation spot in the Maldive Islands. That sets the stage for the obligatory naked-on-the-beach scene where Bo proves that she hasn't been neglecting her sit-ups. From there, it's off to fun-filled Hong Kong where she meets Donald Trump—yes, the real Donald Trump—who isn't embarrassed either, but that's probably to be expected. Though Bo's shortcomings as an actress have been thoroughly cataloged, it should be noted that she has perfected the blank, wide-eyed stare to a degree that few other starlets have achieved. In their prime, the other Mrs. Dereks, Linda Evans and Ursula Andress, certainly gave it a good shot, and Demi Moore has made a career on it, but none of them have mastered the complete vacancy that Bo projects. With the right lighting, she can look like the first thought has yet to penetrate her smooth skull. Maybe someday she'll be cast as a mute nudist who spends her time silently savoring the buffalo breath. With a little luck, she could waltz down the aisle past Meryl and Barbra to pick up her Oscar. Hey, if Cher could do it.... 🐾

Brief nudity.

1990 (R) 91m/C Bo Derek, Anthony Quinn, Don Murray, Leo Damian, Donald Trump; *D:* John Derek. Golden Raspberry Awards '90: Worst Picture, Worst Actress (Derek), Worst Director (Derek). **VHS, LV** *COL, TTC*

Ginger Ale Afternoon

Though it's advertised as a sexy farce, this is a slowly paced story about an unpleasant, bickering couple: a very pregnant wife and her unemployed husband. They sit around outside their mobile home—he with a T-shirt wrapped around his head—and quarrel and threaten

each other in bad Southern accents. There's nothing interesting or attractive about either character. In fact, they're so realistically irritating that the temptation to hit the fast-forward button is almost impossible to resist. WOOF!

Profanity and subject matter.

1989 (R) 88m/C Dana Anderson, John M. Jackson, Yeardley Smith; *D:* Rafal Zeilinski; *W:* Gina Wendkos; *M:* Willie Dixon. **VHS, LV** *ACA, IME*

The Girl in a Swing

Sexual obsession overtakes staid young English antiques dealer Rupert Frazer when he meets mystery woman Meg Tilly whose accent is even more mysterious. She is a professional translator who talks in stilted dialogue that sounds like it was translated from German to French to English. She says "graffel" for "gravel," "afreebotty" for "everybody" and "broins" for "brains," making this one a nobroiner for afreebotty. 🐾

Strong language, some violence, brief nudity, sexual situations.

1989 (R) 119m/C Meg Tilly, Rupert Frazer, Elspet Gray, Lynsey Baxter, Nicholas Le Prevost, Jean Both; *D:* Gordon Hessler. **VHS, LV** *HBO*

The Girl with the Hungry Eyes

Independent production is solidly on the Ed Wood side of the horror spectrum. It's hard to tell whether auteur Jon Jacobs means for his film to be so unhinged, but it certainly is. Loosely based on Fritz Lieber's famous short story, it's about a Miami vampire (Christina Fulton) who's brought back to life by a South Beach hotel. (As Dave Barry would say, I swear I am not making this up.) The hotel commands her to find a key and a deed so that it will not be demolished to make room for a parking lot. In the process, she meets Carlos (Isaac Turner), a photographer who's in trouble with drug thugs. With her eyes wildly rolling like speed-crazed pinballs, Fulton is almost indescribable; she makes Elvira, Mistress of the Dark, look like Katherine Hepburn. Jacobs uses sim-

ple reverse motion camera tricks to complement her excesses, though in some scenes, the quality of both lighting and sound are so poor as to make the proceedings unintelligible. ✂✂

Violence, strong language, brief nudity, sexual content.

1994 (R) 84m/C Christina Fulton, Isaac Turner, Leon Herbert, Bret Carr, Susan Rhodes; **D:** Jon Jacobs; **W:** Jon Jacobs; **M:** Paul Inder. **VHS** *COL*

The Glass Cage

Lively B-movie fare about spies, crooked cops, and drug smugglers has a nice New Orleans setting and first-rate production values. Yeager (Richard Tyson) is a burnt-out ex-CIA agent who knows he's home when he wanders into a French Quarter strip joint and sees his old flame Jackie (Charlotte Lewis), now the paramour of the vicious club owner. Eric Roberts strolls through another of his patented likeable bad guy roles as detective Montrechet. Director Michael Schroeder makes full use of locales and he keeps things moving briskly. ✂✂✂

Violence, mutilation, drug use, brief nudity, sexual material, strong language.

1996 (R) 96m/C Charlotte Lewis, Richard Tyson, Eric Roberts, Stephen Nichols, Joseph Campanella, Richard Moll, Maria Ford, Lisa Marie Scott; **D:** Michael Schroeder. **VHS** *ORI*

The Glass Shield

Sleeper, based in part on a true story, takes a realistic and morally complex look at law enforcement. J.J. (Michael Boatman) arrives fresh from the police academy as the only black officer in a division of a Southern California Sheriff's department. The first images on the screen are of comic book cops bravely chasing bad guys. J.J. quickly learns that the reality of the job is quite different. There's racism, both overt and hidden, from his superiors (Richard Anderson, M. Emmet Walsh, Michael Ironside) and fellow officers. Then there are the pressures to remain loyal to the department, even when he's asked to do things that are illegal or wrong. When a young black man (Ice Cube) is arrested for no reason and then framed for another crime, J.J. has to decide which side he's on. His only ally is Deborah (Lori Petty), a fellow rookie who's also a woman and a Jew. At times, writer/director Charles Burnett makes things look too slick and polished, when the story would have been more effective with a layer of *Hill St. Blues* grittiness, and the bad guys are too one-dimensional. For the most part, though, Burnett is successful in making J.J.'s hard decisions seem real and important, and they're what the film is really about. Burnett also deserves credit for telling the story without using any profanity, and he keeps the violent content to a minimum. As far as the language is concerned, that may be unrealistic for these characters, but it somehow strengthens the performances. Recommended, flaws not withstanding. ✂✂✂

Mature subject matter, violence.

1995 (PG-13) 109m/C Michael Boatman, Lori Petty, Michael Ironside, M. Emmet Walsh, Ice Cube, Richard Anderson, Elliott Gould; **D:** Charles Burnett; **W:** Charles Burnett; **C:** Elliot Davis; **M:** Stephen James Taylor. **VHS, LV** *TOU*

Glitch!

Bonehead burglars Will Egan and Steve Donmyer break into producer Dick Gautier's mansion, but before they can abscond with his TV, they learn that a hundred starlets are on their way to take screen tests for roles in the upcoming epic, *Sex and Violence*. Should they take what's behind Door Number Three, or hang around and pass themselves off as Hollywood bigshots? What follows is accurately described by Julia Nickson-Soul as "tasteless, exploitative, full of adolescent humor and sleazily preoccupied with T&A." Starlets in and out of bikinis pop into hottubs, gangsters show up and are attacked by a model helicopter, and there's even a bizarre swordfight between a stereotyped (but very funny) gay guy and a lady in sexy underwear. It ends with a sharp send-up of the "legitimate" movie business, and the closing credits contain lots of Pythonesque bits. Not to all tastes, but its

Bikini Flicks

Curiously, in the few years that the form has existed, the bikini movie has already developed a formula as rigid as the sonnet.

All of these video premieres below have the word "bikini" or "beach" in the title and their plots are identical. A young person inherits or agrees to help a friend with a failing business which a villain is also trying to obtain. The addition of bikini-clad babes to the enterprise in question (car wash, off-road guide service, drive-in theatre, etc.) causes a financial windfall and an epidemic of what writer Dave Barry calls "Lust-Induced Brain Freeze" among the local male population. The bad guy is foiled and each of the primary characters walks off into the sunset with the partner of his or her choice. (*Bikini Summer 2* boldly breaks from the formula by having the heroines raise money for the homeless.)

The roots of this video sub-genre can be found in those wonderful American-International Annette Funicello-Frankie Avalon beach movies of the 1960s. These days, the swimwear is smaller, and the sex is more explicit. The general level of intelligence hasn't changed at all. We're talking sun, surf, silicone, and spandex.

BEACH BABES FROM BEYOND	BIKINI DRIVE-IN
BIKINI BISTRO	BIKINI SUMMER
THE BIKINI CARWASH COMPANY	GREAT BIKINI OFF-ROAD ADVENTURE
THE BIKINI CARWASH COMPANY 2	

Golden Gate

This American Playhouse production is an intergenerational mystery with a strong political side. Matt Dillon plays an FBI agent who becomes so caught up in the anti-communism of the 1950s that he persecutes a Chinese immigrant. Years later, he falls for the man's daughter (Joan Chen). The central conflict between his professional and personal lives is effectively set out, but the tone varies from scene to scene, and the film tries to do too much with a limited budget. Strong well-drawn characters overcome some but not all of the flaws. 🎭🎭

Strong language, sexual content, violence.

1993 (R) 101m/C Matt Dillon, Joan Chen, Bruno Kirby, Teri Polo, Tzi Ma, Stan Egi, Peter Murnik; *D:* John Madden; *W:* David Henry Hwang; *C:* Bobby Bukowski; *M:* Elliot Goldenthal. **VHS, LV** *TOU*

A Good Day to Die

Maddening Western is alternately bad and good in almost every way. The production looks great—it was filmed in Canada—but while some of the writing is excellent, some stinks. The same goes for the acting and the overall tone. Gypsy Smith (Sidney Poitier) is a gunfighter and cavalry scout. In a too-long introduction, he introduces Corby, an Indian boy, to Rachel, daughter of a troubled pioneer couple (Michael Moriarty and Farrah Fawcett). After a fadeout that looks like a commercial break (and reveals the film's TV roots), the young people grow up and are played by Billy Wirth and Joanna Going. From that point, the story follows two lines as Gypsy helps a group of black settlers found a new community, and Corby and Rachel continue a star-crossed romance. The connection is Hornbeck (Hart Bochner), a wealthy racist and Rachel's fiance. Some stretches of the action are appallingly clumsy, but once all the elements are in place, the story gathers the melodramatic speed of a good potboiler. The last half is lots of fun with some surprising twists. Veteran director David Greene has had a long career in film

slapstick space-cadet humor makes it great stuff for fans of alternative video. 🎭🎭🎭

Nudity, mild sexual content, and bawdy dialogue.

1988 (R) 88m/C Julia Nickson-Soul, Will Egan, Steve Donmyer, Dan Speaker, Dallas Cole, Ji Tu Cumbuka, Dick Gautier, Ted

and television (*Roots*). He's short on flashy visual style, long on straight ahead narrative. **AKA:** Children of the Dust. ⚔⚔▽

Violence, strong sexual material.

1995 (R) 120m/C Sidney Poitier, Michael Moriarty, Joanna Going, Billy Wirth, Regina Taylor, Hart Bochner, Shirley Knight, Robert Guillaume, Farrah Fawcett; **D:** David Greene; **W:** Joyce Eliason; **M:** Mark Snow. **VHS** *VMK*

Goodnight, Sweet Marilyn

This curiosity purports to tell the "truth" about the death of Marilyn Monroe, as revealed by her platonic friend, Mesquite (Jeremy Slate). He begins on the last night of her life, shifts to biographical flashbacks about the beginnings of her career, and then returns to her death. The younger Norma Jean Baker is played by Paula Lane; the older Marilyn by *Hee Haw* veteran Misty Rowe. Considering that they are supposed to be portraying a bad actress, they're fine. Describing her personality and her life, the film doesn't have anything new to say. When the focus turns to her death, it is more difficult to judge. Fact, fiction, fictionalized fact, and speculation are presented without differentiation. All the stories about her association with the Kennedy brothers are tossed in, along with flat statements that she was about to reveal all. Since we have only Mesquite's word for what "really" happened, it is impossible to prove or disprove anything. Hey, it works for Oliver Stone. Whatever the truth or lack of it, the film has the feeling of a story that's been told over and over again late at night in smokey bars, and has grown more richly detailed with each retelling. Did it come from a seed of truth or from an unfulfilled dream, or does that matter? ⚔⚔▽

Contains profanity, violence, mature subject matter, brief nudity.

1989 (R) 100m/C Paula Lane, Jeremy Slate, Misty Rowe; **D:** Larry Buchanan. **VHS** *NO*

Grand Tour: Disaster in Time

Well-made science fiction echoes *Back to the Future*. Jeff Daniels is a widower who lives with his daughter (Ariana Richards) in a small New England town. He's converting their Victorian house into an inn when the enigmatic Madame Iovine (Marilyn Lightstone) makes him an offer he can't refuse. Even though the house isn't ready for guests, he agrees to take in a busful of strange travelers. They're not your average tourists; their passports have curious stamps and an X-ray reveals that one of them, Mr. Quish, has something odd inside his head. It's a good, tricky story with fairly impressive special effects and fine acting. S-f films based on characters and ideas are rare these days. ⚔⚔⚔

Some violence, sexual content.

1992 (PG-13) 98m/C Jeff Daniels, Ariana Richards, Emilia Crow, Jim Haynie, Nicholas Guest, Marilyn Lightstone, George Murdock; **D:** David N. Twohy; **W:** David N. Twohy. **VHS, LV** *ACA*

Grandma's House

As the title indicates, this horror film has a solid premise based on the same primal fears that give fairy tales their power. After the loss of their parents, Eric Foster and Kim Valentine go to live with their grandparents in a rural California town. When odd things begin to happen in and around the house, they suspect that the two older people are hiding something. Loose ends abound and the story won't stand up to any serious examination, but the pace is so quick that the cliches and flaws aren't too obvious. Overall, the film works well without elaborate effects or a retreaded plot. More importantly, it's suspenseful without being overly violent. When the protagonists are children, that's a significant distinction. ⚔⚔⚔

Profanity and violence.

1988 (R) 90m/C Eric Foster, Kim Valentine, Brinke Stevens, Ida Lee; **D:** Peter Rader. **VHS, LV** *ACA*

Great Bikini Off-Road Adventure

Earnest little video makes a heartfelt plea for wilderness preservation and girls in tiny swimsuits. Off-the-shelf plot has to do with an

evil developer trying to pry loose Duke Abbey's (Floyd Irons) Utah desert land. There's just not enough money in Jeep tours to pay the rent. So Duke asks his niece (Lauren Hays) and her pal (Avalon Anders) to help out. The rest is unequal parts innocent cheesecake, frivolous comedy, good scenery, and more references to the works of novelist and environmentalist Edward Abbey. 🗡🗡🗡

Nudity, strong language, mild sexual content.

1994 (R) 90m/C Avalon Anders, Lauren Hays, Floyd Irons, Laura Hudspeth, Dan Frank; *D:* Gary Orona. **VHS, LV** *IMP, IME*

The Great St. Louis Bank Robbery

Rarely seen curiosity from 1959 rates a footnote in the history of popular film. It's one of Steve McQueen's first leading roles, and his character can be seen as a prototype for the alienated loner hero that would make him a star. The film itself is a black-and-white fact-based crime drama with murky psychological undercurrents. McQueen is George Fowler, a college dropout who's recruited as a driver for a bank job. While the older gang members are career criminals—with lawyer's bills to pay— George thinks that the job is going to be a one-time thing, his ticket back to a life of respectability. The film itself follows two lines of action. One is an almost documentary recreation of the robbery. Seen as a snapshot of American city life in the late 1950s—what the bars, automobiles, and hotels looked like—it's fascinating. When the filmmakers delve into the histories of their characters, they're on less solid footing. Perhaps the more restrictive times forced them to be circumspect about sexual motivations, but there are enough Oedipal conflicts and repressed urges at work to fill a textbook. The violence, on the other hand, is remarkably realistic. On balance, the film earns a solid recommendation for McQueen fans, particularly those who think they've seen all of his work. (By the way, the title listed on the screen is simply *The St. Louis Bank Robbery*.) 🗡🗡🗡

Contains some violence.

1959 86m/B Graham Denton, David Clarke, James Dukas, Steve McQueen, Molly McCarthy; *D:* Charles Guggenheim. **VHS** *IVY*

Grim

As low-budget horror movies go, *Grim* is about average. It's not at all frightening because the premise is so ludicrous and the organ music in the soundtrack is so melodramatic. The title character, a guy in a silly monster suit, lives in caverns beneath a new subdivision and communicates telepathically with certain above-ground residents before he chops them up and worships the devil. Or something; I couldn't figure out that part. The characters have no depth, and the whole thing becomes far too gory; again, though, it's too ridiculous to be offensive. 🗡

Gory violence, strong language.

1995 (R) 86m/C Emmanuel Xuereb, Tres Handley, Peter Tregloan; *D:* Paul Matthews. **VHS, LV** *APX*

The Gun in Betty Lou's Handbag

Why would mild-mannered Betty Lou Perkins (Penelope Ann Miller) confess to a murder? She's a happily married smalltown librarian. Was she really rubbing out a Mafia stool pigeon at the local No-Tell motel while she was supposed to be leading the three-year-old story hour? Of course not. But she did find the murder weapon, and when she tried to tell her policeman husband about it, he was too busy to listen. That's the story of Betty Lou's life. She's just not assertive enough. Nobody pays any attention to her. Once she confesses, though, the spotlight's on her. And, hey, it's not so bad. Her transformation from mouse to vamp is dynamite. The action moves crisply and the small-town characters have a believability that Hollywood seldom achieves. In other hands, this material could easily have been too cute, too feminine in the most limiting sense of the word, but that's never a consideration. Recommended. 🗡🗡🗡

Violence, language.

1992 (PG-13) 99m/C Penelope Ann Miller, Eric Thal, Alfre Woodard, Cathy Moriarty, William Forsythe, Julianne Moore, Xander Berkeley, Michael O'Neill, Christopher John Fields; *D:* Allan Moyle; *W:* Grace Cary Bickley; *M:* Richard Gibbs. **VHS, LV** *TOU*

The Gunrunner

Early Kevin Costner effort is a muddled crime drama set in Montreal, 1926. He plays an idealist just returned from China who wants to help the revolution that's going on there by sending guns back. But first, he becomes embroiled in a family squabble, bootleg booze, kidnapping, and ransom. It takes a long time (far too long) to set up those conflicts and the action slogs along at a lethargic pace. 🔪🔪

Contains sexual content, violence, profanity.

1984 (R) 92m/C *CA* Kevin Costner, Sara Botsford, Paul Soles; *D:* Nardo Castillo. **VHS, LV** *VTR, HHE*

Guns

Andy Sidaris—the Ingmar Bergman of low-budget, high-quality home video—has come up with another winner. It's a fast-paced James Bondish adventure set in Hawaii and Las Vegas. The action has most of the elements of a well-made plot, but not enough to get in the way. As usual, Sidaris tosses in lots of sexy women and imaginative grown-up toys; sort of like Victoria's Secret meets the Sharper Image. This one has more humor than some of his work, particularly some really good bawdy one-liners. 🔪🔪🔪 **GPI: 8.0**

Nudity, violence, sexual material.

1990 (R) 95m/C Erik Estrada, Dona Speir; *D:* Andy Sidaris; *W:* Andy Sidaris. **VHS, LV** *COL*

Guns of Honor

Confusing Western is no better than the senseless title. The setting is Mexico, 1866, where ex-Confederate, French, Mexican, and U.S. government forces are somehow at cross purposes. The writing and acting are atrocious all around, and the violence is needlessly graphic. **WOOF!**

Graphic violence, language, rape.

1995 (R) 95m/C Christopher Atkins, Juergen Prochnow, Martin Sheen; *D:* David Lister. **VHS** *VMK*

The Guyver

By-the-numbers comic book tale turns the physical and emotional upheavals of puberty into heroic fantasy. The title refers to a bio-mechanical suit of armor that gives the wearer superhuman powers. In the original Japanese "manga," the hero is Sho, an overachieving high school student. He's fallen in love and that pressure, on top of his school work, has taken its toll. He wants to do the right things, but the harder he works, the more he seems to fall behind. Then he finds the Guyver gizmo. Weird creatures called Zoanoids want it too. Fans of Japanese animation know that lots of fights and transformations will ensue. The editing is quick, moving the story back and forth in time to keep the viewer guessing. The animation is much more detailed than conventional TV cartoon fare. While it may not be up to the highest standards set by Disney and Warner Bros., it's very very good. (The material is too violent to recommend it to younger audiences.) Comparisons to the American version, reviewed next, reveal some interesting differences. 🔪🔪🔪

Violence, strong language.

1989 60m/C *D:* Koichi Ishiguro; *W:* Yoshiki Takaya. **VHS** *USR*

The Guyver

American live-action version simplifies the plot of the Japanese animated series. It changes the tone and the characters considerably, and loses a lot in the process. This time our hero is Sean (Jack Armstrong), a dimbulb college student with a microscopic attention span. Much of the action is comic, in a silly Three Stooges way, but it's much too gory for kids, and the whole production is remarkably clumsy and amateurish. Co-directors Steve Wang and Screaming Mad George manage to make their live-action version more cartoonish than the animated one. Here the Zoanoids are guys in rubber suits and they look just like guys in rubber suits. Of course, this isn't the

hero? Possibly. It is true that we don't see many news stories about overworked high school students in this country. That doesn't mean they don't exist. Given the overall ineptitude of the American *Guyver*, it's more likely that filmmakers simply got their characters wrong, just like they got so much else wrong. Forget the national differences. This kind of pop entertainment is about universal themes that travel well and translate easily. These two versions of *The Guyver* tell us more about the differences between Japanese and American filmmakers than they do about the differences between Japanese and American teenagers. (Followed by a sequel.) 🦴

Graphic violence, strong language.

1991 (PG-13) 92m/C Mark Hamill, Vivian Wu, David Gale, Jeffrey Combs, Michael Berryman, Jack Armstrong; *D:* Steve Wang, Screaming Mad George. **VHS** *COL, NLC*

H. P. Lovecraft's Necronomicon: Book of the Dead

This collection of three short horror films loosely based on Lovecraft stories is notable for high production values and some deliciously nasty special effects. The first entry is virtually a vignette about drowning; the second features David Warner as a man with a peculiar affliction involving cold temperatures; and the third is an ambitious Grand Guignol so bizarre it defies description. As a group the three—and the framing device with Jeffrey Combs as Lovecraft—avoid the graphic sadism that infects so much contemporary horror while delivering the gruesome excesses that fans of the genres demand. They will be delighted. **AKA:** Necronomicon. 🦴🦴🦴

Bloody violence, strong language, some sexual content, general principle.

1996 (R) 96m/C Bruce Payne, Belinda Bauer, Bess Meyer, David Warner, Signy Coleman, Richard Lynch, Dennis Christopher, Jeffrey Combs; *D:* Brian Yuzna, Shusuke Kaneko, Christophe Gans; *W:* Brian Yuzna, Christophe Gans, Brent Friedman, Kazunori Ito; *C:* Gerry Lively, Russ Brandt; *M:* Joseph Lo Duca, Daniel Light. **VHS, LV** *NLC*

first time Hollywood has taken a good concept from abroad and mucked it up, and it won't be the last. Much more interesting is the choice and treatment of the protagonists, and what, if anything, those characters tell us about the cultures they represent. Sho is the kind of kid you'd love to have living next door. He's not some Goody Two-Shoes who'll do anything to please his parents and teachers. Instead, he's ambitious but innocent. He makes mistakes, lets his emotions get the best of him sometimes, and he's not above lying when he has to. Sean, on the other hand, is a likable dolt, much like Bill and Ted, Wayne and Garth, et al. Apparently, we're supposed to admire and side with him because the antagonists are so nasty and evil. Did the American filmmakers think that their target audience would be threatened by or unable to identify with an intelligent

Hail Mary

Jean-Luc Godard's take on the Gospels is an allegory, of sorts, about a contemporary virgin birth. This Mary plays basketball; her dad owns a gas station; Joseph drives a taxi. Though the film was banned and condemned by various religious groups, it's difficult to see what all the fuss is about. This is typically pretentious French surrealism. Godard tosses in lots of shots of the moon and trees and pastures and lakes and such. Several different theories concerning the origins of life are batted about, and the characters tend to speak like people always do in subtitled French movies, spouting angst-ridden pronouncements—"with you, silence can be unbearable"—and the odd untranslatable thudball—"those ants are strictly the invisible man." Francophiles may be intrigued, but everyone else will be reaching for the fast-forward button. *AKA:* Je Vous Salue Marie. WOOF!

Contains nudity, profanity, French symbolism.

1985 107m/C *FR SI GB* Myriem Roussel, Thierry Rode, Philippe Lacoste, Manon Anderson, Juliette Binoche, Johan Leysen; *D:* Jean-Luc Godard; *W:* Jean-Luc Godard. VHS, LV *LIV, VES, INJ*

Happy Together

Lively comedy is done in by a formula script and overly bright performances. Patrick Dempsey and Helen Slater are east-coast freshmen at a west-coast college. The computer mistakenly makes the bookish writer and the zany actress roommates. How will their love-hate relationship resolve itself? You get one guess. As youthful and cute as they are, the two leads still look about ten years too old for their characters. Dempsey is annoying but Slater is so abrasively perky that it's painful. ⚐

Brief nudity, mature subject matter, profanity.

1989 (PG-13) 102m/C Helen Slater, Patrick Dempsey, Dan Schneider, Marius Weyers, Barbara Babcock; *D:* Mel Damski; *M:* Robert Folk. VHS, LV *LIV*

JOHN WOO DIRECTING A SCENE FROM *HARD-BOILED.*
©FOX LORBER HOME VIDEO.

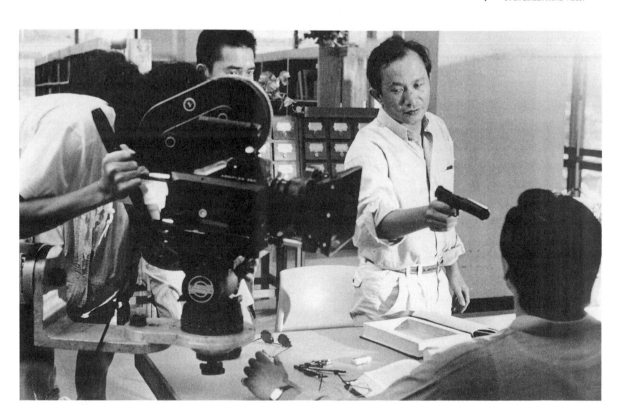

Hard-Boiled

A masterpiece of action. John Woo has been widely praised for *The Killer,* and less so for *Hard Target* and *Broken Arrow.* This one is his best to date. Woo's frequent star Chow Yun-Fat plays a tough Hong Kong cop who's out to shut down a gun-running operation. Two rival gangs are fighting for control of the business, and Tony Leung is an undercover cop working for one of them. Like Sam Peckinpah, Woo is more interested in elaborately choreographed action sequences, and the moral after effects of violence. Where Peckinpah's outlaws are at the end of their lives—and know it all too clearly—Woo's policemen are caught up in the middle of Byzantine schemes that are played out in a bizarre, no-limits plot. Those two sides of the film come together in a long, impossible-to-describe finale set in a hospital and involving dozens of characters. The best moments of *Die Hard, Under Siege,* and *Speed* pale in comparison. In visual terms, this is one of Woo's most ambitious and inventive works. He uses freeze frames and various speeds of slow motion to punctuate key moments. (By the way, Woo has a small but important supporting role as the bartender.) By American standards, the violence is extreme, but Woo has such a strong vision that it doesn't seem sadistic or excessive. Some of the credit for that should go to Chow Yun-Fat. He has an expressive face that can convey the full range of emotions that cross cultural lines. The Criterion laserdisc edition contains both dubbed and subtitled soundtracks, and it's letterboxed to include the entire frame. For Woo's fans, the disc is a must-see. It's that much better. ***AKA:*** Lashou Shentan. ♪♪♪♪

Contains graphic violence, strong language.

1992 126m/C *HK* Chow Yun-Fat, Tony Leung, Philip Chan, Anthony Wong, Teresa Mo, John Woo; *D:* John Woo; *W:* Barry Wong; *M:* Michael Gibbs. **VHS, LV** *ORI, FCT*

Hard Bounty

While the feminist Western *Bad Girls* was a critical and popular fiasco, this one's not bad. The plots are more or less identical; the production values about the same; the acting is certainly no worse and in the video premiere, the humor is intentional. It's obvious from beginning to end that this story of prostitutes rebelling against patronizing patriarchs is the stuff of a B-movie. That's what *Bad Girls* was supposed to be, but somewhere in the filmmaking process, it tried to become "a major motion picture." Director Jim Wynorski and company avoided such delusions and came up with a completely serviceable little timewaster. ♪♪♪

Nudity and sexual content.

1994 (R) 90m/C Matt McCoy, Kelly Le Brock, Rochelle Swanson, Felicity Waterman, Kimberly Kelley; *D:* Jim Wynorski. **VHS** *TRI*

Hard Choices

Good-old-druggies from the Tennessee mountains decide to rob a pharmacy. They're stupid, selfish guys who deserve whatever they get after they're caught. But what about the youngest (Gary McCleery) who's only 15 and stayed in the truck? A social worker (Margaret Klenck) with more empathy than sense comes to care for him and when he's tried as an adult, she decides she has to act. Writer/director Rick King does a terrific job with these realistic characters and avoids conventional sentimentality and romanticism. Based on a true story and well worth seeking out. ♪♪♪♪

Violence, sexual material, strong language, brief nudity.

1984 90m/C Margaret Klenck, Gary McCleery, John Seitz, John Sayles, Liane Curtis, J.T. Walsh, Spalding Gray; *D:* Rick King; *W:* Rick King. **VHS** *BAR, ORI, WAR*

Hard Evidence

Fair thriller based on familiar elements. Trent Turner (Gregory Harrison) is a real estate developer who's having an affair with Dina (Cali Timmins), a young woman moonlighting as a drug courier. She persuades him to mix pleasure and business on a weekend jaunt to Vancouver. After the deal goes sour, his wife Madelyn (Joan Severance) figures out that he's up to something. The rest of William Martell's script involves a blackmail plot that any seasoned mystery fan will see straight through. As video premieres go, the production values are about average; the performances are better. ♫♫

Mature subject matter, violence, sexual content, brief nudity, strong language.

1994 (R) 100m/C Gregory Harrison, Joan Severance, Cali Timmins, Andrew Airlie, Nathaniel DeVeaux; *D:* Michael Kennedy; *W:* William Martell; *C:* Bruce Worrall; *M:* Barron Abramovitch. **VHS** *AVE*

Hard Justice

Though the box copy compares *Hard Justice* to John Woo's action films, it's really just another gun movie, fairly slickly made, about guys with bulging muscles and large caliber weapons. Most of the story is set in a prison where ATF agent Nick Adams (David Bradley) goes undercover. Veteran Charles Napier is the evil warden. Overall, the production values are excellent, the acting is so-so, and the fight choreography is about average for the genre. ♫♫

Graphic violence, strong language.

DAVID BRADLEY AS NICK ADAMS IN *HARD JUSTICE.*
©NEW LINE HOME VIDEO.
ALL RIGHTS RESERVED.

1995 **(R)** 95m/C David Bradley, Charles Napier, Yuji Okumoto, Vernon Wells; **D:** Greg Yaitanes; **W:** Nicholas Amendolare, Chris Bold; **C:** Moshe Levin; **M:** Don Peake. **VHS, LV** *TTC*

Hard Ticket to Hawaii

In the minds of some fans, this is Andy Sidaris' masterpiece. It has everything you could ask of an alternative classic: lame-brained sportscasters, transvestites, female bodybuilders, an assassin on a skateboard, a quadruple-barreled bazooka, a lethal frisbee, and the fakiest fake snake ever to appear on video. The finest moment in the film comes near the end when, in one prolonged scene, the meanest bad guy is shot, speared, stabbed, and snakebit! It's that strange combination of unpredictability and fast-paced physical comedy that makes Sidaris' films so much fun. This kind of B-movie is perfect fare for home video where convenience and a low price tag are more important than the big screen image, or the seriousness of the subject matter. ♫♫♫ **GPI: 6.5**

Nudity, sexual content, violence, some strong language.

1987 **(R)** 96m/C Ron Moss, Dona Speir, Hope Marie Carlton, Cynthia Brimhall; **D:** Andy Sidaris. **VHS** *BAR, ORI, WAR*

Hard to Die

Since Meryl Streep, Glenn Close, Joan Plowright, Vanessa Redgrave, and Emma Thompson weren't available, director Jim Wynorski hired five lesser-known babes to play the leads in this action-horror-slasher-parody. They're doing inventory for the Acme Lingerie Co. in an empty skyscraper with only the hulking Orville Ketchum and an evil spirit for company. (The evil spirit was supposed to be delivered to Forrest J. Ackerman, famous editor of *Famous Monsters of Filmland,* who shows up in a pleasant cameo.) Of course, our heroines get dirty, so they have to take showers and put on fancy underwear before someone or something starts stalking them. If one frame of the film were halfway serious, it might be offensive, but this is the kind of comedy where someone is shot a couple of hundred times with a machine gun, falls down, then pops up a few seconds later. It has every-

thing fans of bad movies love—atrocious acting, dumb jokes, lots of action, cheap sets, and a complete lack of good taste and moral rectitude. **AKA:** Tower of Terror. ♫♫♫

Graphic silly violence, strong language, shower scenes.

1990 77m/C Robin Harris, Melissa Moore, Debra Dare, Lindsay Taylor, Bridget Carney, Forrest J. Ackerman, Orville Ketchum; **D:** Jim Wynorski. **VHS** *NHO*

Haunted

Handsomely produced thriller from Francis Coppola's American Zoetrope company is reminiscent in look and atmosphere to *Brideshead Revisited.* It's also a ghost story. Maybe. The setting is 1928, at the Edbrook estate. That's where university professor and spiritualist debunker David Ash (Aidan Quinn) goes in answer to an old woman's cry for help. Something terrible is going on, she says. But, upon arriving, Ash is more interested in Christina (Kate Beckinsale), an uninhibited young woman who admires his book. Ash isn't so sure about her brother (Anthony Andrews) who claims, "We're all mad, you know." Based on James Herbert's novel. The script by Tim Prager, Robert Kellett, and director Lewis Gilbert combines a nostalgic evocation of the period with various sexy undercurrents and a teasing attitude toward the supernatural. The veteran Gilbert—*Alfie, Educating Rita, Shirley Valentine*—handles a complex story with a sure touch and manages to pull out a few more surprises when most viewers will think they've got everything figured out. In the end, this one's a solid hit that deserves a strong recommendation. ♫♫♫

Mature subject matter, brief nudity, some violence.

1995 **(R)** 108m/C *GB* Aidan Quinn, Kate Beckinsale, Anthony Andrews, Alex Lowe, Anna Massey, Geraldine Somerville, Victoria Shalet; **Cameos:** John Gielgud; **D:** Lewis Gilbert; **W:** Lewis Gilbert, Bob Kellett, Tim Prager; **C:** Tony Pierce-Roberts; **M:** Debbie Wiseman. **VHS** *HMK*

Haunted Summer

Like *Amadeus,* this ambitious period piece attempts to treat famous figures as real, flesh and blood human beings. Its subjects are the great Romantic poets, Shelley and Byron, and Mary Shelley, author of *Frankenstein*. The year is 1816 when all of them lived together for a time in Byron's Swiss villa. In this version of their story, they're hardly the people we learned about in 11th grade English class. Shelley is fond of morphine cocktails, skinny-dipping, and spitballs. Byron prefers smoking opium. He's also a sexual tyrant who carries on overlapping affairs with partners of both sexes. It's all just too too decadent. It's also too too slow and there's the matter of the humor, some of which may or may not be intentional. Note this exchange between Byron and Shelley.

"Well, Shelley, is we poets or ain't we?"

"We is, God help us."

"Then let us poetize...."

If all of this seems more than a little familiar, it's because Ken Russell handled exactly the same material in his wonderfully weird horror comedy *Gothic*. 🎬

Brief nudity, drug use, subject matter, and sexual scenes.

1986 (R) 106m/C Alice Krige, Eric Stoltz, Philip Anglim, Laura Dern, Alex Winter; *D:* Ivan Passer; *W:* Lewis John Carlino. VHS, LV *MED*

The Hawk

Helen Mirren turns in another flawless performance in this BBC psychological mystery. She's Annie Marsh, a middle-class wife and mother whose husband Steven (George Costigan) may be murdering young women. The film is carefully shaded with convincing and contradictory details. Annie might be reasonably suspicious or her own troubled past could be betraying her. To further complicate matters, Steven's brother (Owen Teale) and mother (Rosemary Leach) are the original in-laws from hell. Don't be put off by the accents, the occasional cliches, and unfamiliar slang. The story is strong and the last 15 minutes are full of surprises. 🎬🎬🎬

Strong language, subject matter, violence.

1993 (R) 84m/C *GB* Helen Mirren, George Costigan, Owen Teale, Rosemary Leach; *D:* David Hayman; *W:* Peter Ransley; *M:* Nick Bicat. VHS *ACA*

Head of the Family

If this tongue-in-cheek horror-comedy were a little quicker out of the gate, it might have been a cult hit. Unfortunately, it doesn't get weird enough until the second half. The title character, Myron (J.W. Perra), is literally the "head" of the Stackpool family. In fact, he's nothing but an oversized head on a tiny wizened body, and he's psychically linked with his three subnormal siblings. They live in the faux-Southern Gothic hamlet of Nob Hollow. When Lance (Blake Bailey), a local restaurateur, learns the Stackpool family secrets (there are others), he and his lover Lorretta (Jacqueline Lovell), a drug dealer's wife, decide to put the squeeze on the head, as it were. Toward the end, producer/director Robert Talbot approaches his model—the wonderful *Motel Hell*—but this one isn't quite as kinky. Even so, successful series have been based on less. Don't be surprised if a sequel shows up. 🎬🎬🎬

Strong subject matter, sexual content, nudity, language.

1996 (R) 82m/C Blake Bailey, Jacqueline Lovell, Bob Schott, J.W. Perra, Diane Colazzo, James Jones; *D:* Robert Talbot. VHS *AFE*

Heart and Souls

In synopsis, this neat romantic fantasy sounds terrible. It begins in 1959 when Thomas Reilly is born. At precisely that moment, Alfre Woodard, Charles Grodin, Kyra Sedgwick, and Tom Sizemore are killed in a bus accident. They become young Thomas's guardian angels. He can hear and see them until, for reasons best left unexplained, they choose to disappear. When Thomas grows up to become hard-charging young executive Robert Downey, Jr., the four spirits return. They're destined to finish their lives' work through him before they're carried off to wherever. Yes, it's schmaltzy, contrived, overdone, derivative, and...terrific. 🎬🎬🎬

Strong language, some violence.

1993 (PG-13) 104m/C Robert Downey Jr., Charles Grodin, Tom Sizemore, Alfre Woodard, Kyra Sedgwick, Elisabeth Shue, David Paymer; **D:** Ron Underwood; **W:** Brent Maddock, S.S. Wilson, Gregory Hansen, Erik Hansen; **M:** Marc Shaiman. **VHS, LV** *MCA, BTV*

Heart of Midnight

The box art—actress Jennifer Jason Leigh laced into a backless black leather dress—indicates that this is an erotic thriller. Actually, it's an anti-erotic thriller about destructive sexual impulses, and it's carefully calculated not to arouse viewers. Leigh is a young woman of brittle emotions who inherits the Midnight nightclub from her uncle. Peter Coyote is a cop who's overly familiar with the place's history as a sex club. When she's alone in the building at night, she dresses in her uncle's clothes and wanders through the strange rooms. She imagines that someone hiding under the floors and within the walls is watching her. Writer/director Matthew Chapman tells the story in such a stylized, elusive way that it's difficult to say exactly what's happening. Is this (a) a serious thriller, or (b) a disturbed young woman's prolonged hallucination, or (c) a muddled mess, or (d) all of the above? Chapman will sacrifice clarity and suspense for unusual or startling images, but he does manage to create an unpleasant atmosphere of sordidness. The twisted weirdness is slightly reminiscent of Brian DePalma's *Sisters,* and the creepy ending echoes Hitchcock's *Marnie.* When it's over, you'll want to clean the heads on your VCR. 🗡🗡🗡

Mature subject matter, violence and profanity.

1989 (R) 93m/C Jennifer Jason Leigh, Brenda Vaccaro, Frank Stallone, Peter Coyote, Gale Mayron, Sam Schacht, Denise Dumont; **D:** Matthew Chapman; **W:** Matthew Chapman; **M:** Yanni. **VHS, LV** *NO*

Hearts of Fire

This stinker sat on the shelf for several years before it found its way onto tape. It's easy to see why. Supposedly a realistic look at the world of rock music, the film is filled with lame humor, atrocious acting, insipid music, and unsympathetic characters. Bob Dylan plays an aging rock legend who has turned his back on stardom. But his spirit is renewed in a small Pennsylvania town when he hears Fiona, turnpike tollbooth girl by day, rock singer by night. Dylan looks like a haggard Harpo Marx and even though he's playing a character based on himself, he's not convincing. Our heroine is supposed to be effervescent and irrepressible, but she comes across as immature and irritating. Similar material was handled more realistically in Paul Schrader's *Light of Day,* and much more successfully all around in the Beatles' *A Hard Day's Night.* 🗡

Strong language, violence, brief nudity, and sexual content.

1987 90m/C Bob Dylan, Fiona, Rupert Everett, Julian Glover; **D:** Richard Marquand; **W:** Joe Eszterhas; **M:** John Barry. **VHS, LV** *ORI, WAR*

Heaven & Earth

In 16th century Japan, feudal lords Takaai Enoki and Masahiko Tsugawa are the two biggest dogs on the block, so to speak. The political situation is so chaotic that war between them is inevitable. The two leaders are not so much individual characters as historical or mythic archetypes in this epic. The battles are somewhat stylized, photographed from a distance through long lenses that compress the action. Director Haruki Kadokawa is more interested in color, movement, and image than in realistic combat. He fills the screen with carefully staged waves of figures—ranks of advancing infantry: hundreds of horsemen dressed in black armor attacking and mingling with their opponents in red armor. Nary a drop of blood is shown; this is cinematic chess. When the focus shifts away from the battlefield, Kadokawa indulges his taste for striking visuals even more fully. His camera lingers on a forest of blossoming dogwoods, slowly follows a single figure walking across a dark winter beach, and waits patiently as lancers emerge from thick mountain fog. The film was made in Japan and western Canada where the pristine landscapes have seldom been presented more handsomely. 🗡🗡🗡

Battle scenes.

1990 (PG-13) 104m/C *JP* Masahiko Tsugawa, Takaai Enoki, Atsuko Asano, Tsunehiko Watase, Naomi Zaizen, Binpachi Ito; *D:* Haruki Kadokawa. **VHS, LV** *LIV, INJ*

Hedd Wyn

In 1917, "the fourth year of the Great War," Ellis Evans (Huw Garmon) wins the Welsh national poetry competition. At the time, he's a solider in the trenches. "Hedd Wyn" is his pseudonym. The film, based on fact, is the story of his young manhood. On one level, it looks like a top drawer *Masterpiece Theatre* production with a focus on the rural landscape and strongly defined, fundamentally good characters. Director Paul Turner and writer (and poet) Alan Llwyd make their anti-war sentiments unequivocally clear. Though their use of Welsh dialogue (subtitled) is key to the film, the guttural speech sounds rough and unpleasant at first. The final third is much more compelling. 🗡🗡🗡

Contains some male nudity, sexual material, violence.

1992 123m/C *GB* Huw Garmon, Catrin Fychan, Ceri Cunnington, Judith Humphreys, Llio Silyn; *D:* Paul Turner; *W:* Alan Llwyd; *C:* Ray Orton; *M:* John E.R. Hardy. Nominations: Academy Awards '92: Best Foreign Language Film. **VHS** *FXL*

Heidi Fleiss: Hollywood Madam

The seamy underside of the film business is such familiar territory that any sort of expose shouldn't surprise anyone, but this video tabloid is still an eye-opener. The noirish documentary manages to be just as sleazy as its subject, perhaps even sleazier (though opinions will differ on that one). Most people probably know that Heidi Fleiss was arrested for pandering in 1993. She ran a prostitution ring with a client-list that included some of the movies' more important names. A year after the arrest, producer/director/narrator

HUW GARMON AND JUDITH HUMPHREYS IN *HEDD WYN.*
©FOX LORBER HOME VIDEO.

Nick Broomfield arrived in Tinseltown from England with a camera and a pocketful of cash. He was prepared to buy the story of anyone who had inside knowledge of the case—anyone from hookers to ex-police chief Daryl Gates (who picks up his cash payment on camera). In doing so, he simply underscores what everyone else in the film understands: money is the only thing that counts in that town. The main players are Fleiss herself, a flint-hard chippie; Ivan Nagy, an ex-lover who swears he didn't introduce her into the business; and the aging Madam Alex, Fleiss' convicted competition. Taken as a group, they're about as distasteful a bunch as any you'll ever see—and that includes Broomfield, who dives into their world with unseemly enthusiasm for his often inconclusive interviews. Their vapid story is filled with back-biting, lies, and self-serving evasions. In the end, the only person involved who retains any integrity is porn star Ron Jeremy who neither hides what he does nor tries to make himself more important than he is. Though the tape is undeniably compelling and watchable, it's also so sordid that you'll want to clean the heads on your VCR as soon as it's over. 𝄢𝄢𝄢

Contains strong subject matter, language, nudity.

1995 10m/C **D:** Nick Broomfield. **VHS** *DMG*

Hellgate

Unintentionally funny horror flick is a variation on the old ghostly hitchhiker story. You know it...the one that ends "and he found his sweater on her tombstone." The seductive spook lives in a ghost town full of refugees from one of George Romero's *Living Dead* movies. The plot is nothing more than an excuse to trot out unconvincing but gory special effects. On the positive side, the bad ensemble acting from a no-name cast is inspired. And any movie with a monster goldfish can't be all bad. Fun for an appreciative crowd that's ready to laugh. 𝄢𝄢

Bloody special effects, profanity, brief nudity.

1989 (R) 96m/C Abigail Wolcott, Ron Palillo; **D:** William A. Levey. **VHS, LV** *VMK*

Henry: Portrait of a Serial Killer

Loosely based on crimes reportedly committed by Henry Lee Lucas, this is one of the most disturbing and frightening horror films anyone has ever made. (Lucas, like Ted Bundy, is an accomplished liar who has confessed to some 600 murders and later denied them.) Chillingly underplayed by Michael Rooker, Henry is an illiterate drifter who moves from job to job, and kills at random. Though he claims to have been abused as a child, that doesn't explain him. Neither does the sexual element that some of the murders contain. Killing is simply something he does without emotion or pleasure. Director John McNaughton tells the story with a deliberately flat, documentary style: stark naturalistic lighting and acting, Midwest locations, grainy color, limited music. Originally given an X rating for violence and subject matter, the film has been released on tape without a rating. It is definitely not for kids, and older audiences looking for titillating violence or elaborate effects will be disappointed. In terms of onscreen acts of violence, *Henry* contains only a tiny fraction of the lurid excesses of a *Friday the 13th* or *Elm St.* flick. But *Henry* is a real nightmare and these suggested horrors—including an unexpected ending—are much more terrifying than graphic cinematic schlock. 𝄢𝄢𝄢

Contains exceptionally strong violence, profanity, brief nudity.

1990 90m/C Michael Rooker, Tom Towles, Tracy Arnold; **D:** John McNaughton; **W:** Richard Fire, John McNaughton. **VHS, LV** *MPI*

The Heroic Trio

The rules are different for Honk Kong action movies. The narrative conventions and storytelling techniques are so unusual that Western viewers have trouble following the anything-can-happen plots. But these films are so energetic and imaginative that those plots are mostly unimportant. This one's a crazed tale of a supernatural being, kidnapped cannibal babies, cops, computers, and three magical heroines—Wonderwoman, Thief Catcher, and Invisible Girl, played by Anita Mui, Maggie Cheung, and Michelle Yeoh. The stunt choreography is almost impossible to describe, and it really shouldn't be. Surprise counts for a lot. The action scenes are graphic with beheadings and such, but it takes place in such an unrealistic context that the violence doesn't seem excessive. Martial arts fans who are tired of the same old kicks and spins should definitely give this one a try. ✄✄✄

Contains violence, strong language.

1993 87m/C *HK* Michelle Yeoh, Maggie Cheung, Anita Mui, Anthony Wong; *D:* Ching Siu Tung, Johnny To. **VHS, LV** *TAI*

The Hidden 2

Sequel to the cult s-f hit rehashes key elements of the original with young lovers as the protagonists. The story's the same—good alien (Raphael Sbarge) MacLachlan (apparently named after Kyle who played the char-

acter in the first film) chases a body-trading bad alien while romancing Juliet (Kate Hodge). Curiously, the look, tone, and theme of the film mirror TV's *X-Files*. The main flaw is the graphic violence, which becomes numbingly repetitive. ✄

Graphic violence, strong language, some sexual content.

1994 (R) 91m/C Raphael Sbarge, Kate Hodge, Michael Nouri; *D:* Seth Pinsker; *W:* Seth Pinsker; *M:* David McHugh. **VHS, LV** *NLC, IME*

Hidden City

Strangely constructed conspiracy thriller stars Charles Dance and Cassie Stuart as an odd couple who stumble across some old film that may tell an incomplete story about an abduction and a government cover-up. The unusual plot contains strong hints of *Max Headroom* and, in the end, is less than completely satisfying. The acting, the intelligent writing, and

the engaging relationship between the two main characters are the real attractions. 🗡🗡

Contains profanity, violence.

1987 **112m/C** Charles Dance, Cassie Stuart, Alex Norton, Tusse Silberg, Bill Paterson; *D:* Stephen Poliakoff. **VHS** *COL*

Hidden Obsession

Heather Thomas is the vacationing TV newsbabe. Jan-Michael Vincent, who lives in a nearby cabin, is either a lovestruck cop or a psycho killer, but it could be the escaped convict who's knocking off the supporting cast. You don't need three guesses. 🗡🗡

Strong language, brief nudity, sexual activity, some violence.

1992 (R) **92m/C** Heather Thomas, Jan-Michael Vincent, Nicholas Celozzi; *D:* John Stewart; *W:* David Reskin. **VHS, LV** *MCA*

High Stakes

Sally Kirkland turns in a persuasive performance as a working girl who's trying to get out of the business. She's a tough woman who made mistakes and finds herself in more trouble when she plays Good Samaritan to stockbroker Robert LuPone. Her best efforts are undermined by a story that runs out of gas about 30 minutes too soon. The film's dark, grainy look doesn't help either. 🗡🗡🗡 **GPI: 5.0**

Mature subject matter, violence, profanity, brief nudity.

1989 (R) **86m/C** Sally Kirkland, Robert LuPone, Richard Lynch, Sarah Gellar, Kathy Bates, W.T. Martin; *D:* Amos Kollek. **VHS, LV** *VMK*

Highlander: The Final Dimension

This is a fitting third chapter in the goofball sword-and-sorcery series. Like the first two, it's built around excellent but uninspired special effects, bad acting, and a story that doesn't even attempt to make sense. The "exclusive director's cut!" video contains some sexual material left out of the theatrical release. *AKA:* Highlander 3: The Magician; Highlander 3: The Sorcerer. 🗡🗡

Contains graphic violence, strong language, sexual content, nudity.

1994 **99m/C** Christopher Lambert, Mario Van Peebles, Deborah Unger, Mako; *D:* Andrew Morahan; *W:* Paul Ohl; *M:* J. Peter Robinson. **VHS, LV** *TOU*

Highway to Hell

Standard low-budget horror comedy is notable only for its high-powered cast, including Patrick Bergin as the devil who kidnaps Kristy Swanson. Even though the plot is a crackpot variation on the myth of Orpheus and Eurydice, this one's too sloppy and too studied to be a prime guilty pleasure. Toward the end it does have a few moments. 🗡🗡

Violence, strong language, sexual material, and nudity.

1992 (R) **93m/C** Patrick Bergin, Adam Storke, Chad Lowe, Kristy Swanson, Richard Farnsworth, C.J. Graham, Lita Ford, Kevin Peter Hall, Pamela Gidley, Brian Helgeland; *Cameos:* Gilbert Gottfried; *D:* Ate De Jong. **VHS** *HBO*

Hit the Dutchman

This period gangster picture is told with the brash foolishness of a good comic book. Veteran producer/director Menahem Golan has put together a B-movie version of *The Godfather* that copies Coppola's original all the way down to the imitation Nino Rota score. It's a combination of sharp one-liners—"Take your brother to the hospital and have them sew his nose back on."—and wild characterizations of Dutch Schultz, Legs Diamond, and Mad Dog Coll. The story is an interesting mix of Irish, Jewish, and Italian conflicts, and since the film was made in Moscow, it has a genuinely different look to it. This one's a sleeper. 🗡🗡🗡

Contains sexual material, nudity, strong language, and violence.

1992 (R) **116m/C** Bruce Nozick, Sally Kirkland, Will Kempe; *D:* Menahem Golan. **VHS** *VMK*

Hold Me, Thrill Me, Kiss Me

Marriages don't get off to a much rockier start than they do here. Before the wedding is over, Eli (Max Parrish) and Twinkle (Sean Young) are fighting. Things get out of hand and, well...he sort of shoots her and steals her Porsche and a sack of cash. On the lam, Eli winds up in the El Monte Hide-Away trailer park where his life becomes hopelessly entangled with voracious topless dancer Andrea Naschak, and her virginal sister Adrienne Shelly. The rest of the loose comedy wanders into several unpredictable areas. Overall, give writer/director Joel Hershman credit for originality and irreverence. And he got solid performances from a motley cast, particularly Naschak, a former porn star who makes a brassy debut on legitimate video. Also available in an unrated version. 🐾🐾🐾

Sexual humor, strong language, violence, brief nudity.

1993 (R) 92m/C Max Parrish, Adrienne Shelly, Andrea Naschak, Sean Young, Diane Ladd, Bela Lehoczky, Ania Suli; *Cameos:* Timothy Leary; *D:* Joel Hershman; *W:* Joel Hershman. **VHS** *LIV*

Hollywood Hot Tubs 2: Educating Crystal

Lightweight comedy combines the best of *Porky's* with the best of *Wall Street.* (How's that for an odd couple?) Jewel Shepard plays an allegedly brainless bimbo who saves the family hottub business from unscrupulous entrepreneurs by going to business school. 🐾🐾 **GPI: 8.5**

Strong language, some violence, brief nudity, sexual situations.

1989 (R) 103m/C Jewel Shepard, Patrick Day, Remy O'Neill, David Tiefen, Bart Braverman; *D:* Ken Raich. **VHS, LV** *CCB*

Hologram Man

Futuristic action flick is an unapologetic rip-off *Demolition Man,* and almost as much guilty fun. California becomes a warzone where the corporate bosses at Cal Corp. aren't much better than the gangs. Thug Evan Lurie (who also co-wrote and -produced) is sentenced to "hologramatic reprogramming," i.e., they separate his personality from his physical body. But his henchman William Sanderson (the veteran s-f B-movie character actor who specializes in henchmen) hotwires the computer, and Lurie is reborn as an indestructible electronic "virtual" villain. Actually, he looks like a grainy late-'50s color TV broadcast, but that's O.K. 🐾🐾🐾

Violence, strong language, brief nudity.

1995 (R) 96m/C Joe Lara, Evan Lurie, William Sanderson, Tiny Lister, Michael Nouri, John Amos; *D:* Richard Pepin; *W:* Evan Lurie; *M:* John Gonzalez. **VHS, LV** *PMH*

Homicidal Impulse

A gullible lawyer. A sultry blonde. A dead older lover. Is it Madonna's *Body of Evidence?* No, it's a video premiere that's even more outrageous, inventive, and fun than the Material Girl's cinematic romp on the wild side. Assistant D.A. Scott Valentine lacks the "killer instinct" to win the big cases. When his sexy and ruthless new assistant (Vanessa Angel) decides to help advance his career, sparks fly. For the first 40 minutes or so, the film chugs along without any real surprises, beyond some enthusiastic love scenes involving body doubles and salad dressing. But then something bizarre happens (too bizarre to describe without spoiling the fun) and this little movie gets seriously, audaciously weird. Also available in an unrated version at 86 minutes. 🐾🐾🐾

Violence, nudity, sexual activity, strong language, subject matter.

1992 (R) 84m/C Scott Valentine, Vanessa Angel; *D:* David Tausik. **VHS** *LIV*

Hong Kong '97

Formula shoot-'em-up is brightened by an ensemble cast of familiar character actors and excellent Far East locations in Honk Kong and the Philippines. Robert Patrick is a corporate assassin who kills a corrupt Chinese general on the eve of the Red Chinese takeover of the city. In short order, he's betrayed and finds himself on the run with his friends Tim Thomerson and Brion James, doing an excellent mushmouthed British mumble. Whenever the plot slows, a dozen armed extras jump out of the woodwork to attack our heroes, and gunfights ensue. These are a pale imitation of John Woo's brilliantly choreographed action scenes. 🦴🦴🦴

Violence, nudity, strong language, subject matter.

1994 (R) 99m/C Robert Patrick, Ming-Na Wen, Brion James, Tim Thomerson; *D:* Albert Pyun. **VHS, LV** *VMK*

Hostile Intentions

The premise of your basic babes-behind-bars exploitation flick is twisted together with an unapologetically feminist-liberal attitude. Nora (Tia Carrere) and Maureen (Tricia Leigh Fisher) take their pal Caroline (Lisa Dean Ryan) to Tijuana for a final fling before her marriage. They run into the wrong house party, corrupt rapacious cops, jail—you know the drill...most of the drill, anyway. The differences here come from writer/director Catherine Cyran's well-developed, non-stereotypical characters, and excellent performances from the three leads. Ignore the idiotic title. 🦴🦴🦴

Violence, rape, strong language, brief nudity.

1995 (R) 90m/C Tia Carrere, Lisa Dean Ryan, Tricia Leigh Fisher, Carlos Gomez; *D:* Catherine Cyran; *W:* Catherine Cyran. **VHS** *AVE*

The Hottest Bid

This is the sexy comedy that *Exit to Eden* tried to be—romantic, bawdy, comfortable with itself, and "adult" in the real sense of the word. Featuring an unfamiliar cast of men and women who look like real people—not starved, sculpted, and siliconed Hollywood fantasy bodies—it's about two romances that begin at a charity auction. Though the film lacks the complexity of most studio releases, producer/director Deborah Shames makes a virtue of simplicity, emphasizing familiar, realistic settings. She handles the material with confidence, and even tosses in a few experimental touches. But as has been the case with her previous work (*Cabin Fever*, *The Voyeur*), she emphasizes character over technical slickness, and she got excellent performances from her two leads, Gwen Somers and Dennis Matthews. The feminine perspective she brings to the overworked genre of erotic video is refreshing. By the way, the smoky vocals on the soundtrack are by that '70s pop icon, Maria Muldaur, of "Midnight at the Oasis" fame. 🦴🦴🦴

Considerable nudity, sexual material.

1995 92m/C Gwen Somers, Dennis Matthews; *D:* Deborah Shames; *W:* Deborah Shames. **VHS** *DEB*

Hourglass

Until the last 20 minutes or so, this is a fair noirish thriller with a few sharp touches. The humor is bright and unexpected, and the characters are well-observed, but the budget's on the thin side and the plot is familiar. It has to do with Michael Jardine (C. Thomas Howell, who also directed and co-wrote), L.A. fashion honcho. His Hourglass clothing company is about to get an infusion of Japanese money and he's on top of the world. Then he bumps into the exotic Dara (Sofia Shinas), and bumps into her again...and again. As she leads him on, other parts of his life suffer. To reveal any more would spoil the fun, but getting back to those last 20 minutes, let's just say that some women will really enjoy them. In fact, they could generate an unusual cult following. It's also worth noting that Howell, who's done a lot of work in video premieres, plays skillfully with several conventions of the medium. And within the limitations of his budget, he creates some striking visuals. 𝄞𝄞𝄞

Mature subject matter, sexual content, violence, strong language, brief nudity.

1995 (R) 91m/C C. Thomas Howell, Sofia Shinas, Ed Begley Jr., Timothy Bottoms, Anthony Clark; *D:* C. Thomas Howell; *W:* C. Thomas Howell, Darren Dalton; *C:* John Lambert; *M:* Chris Saranec. **VHS, LV** *LIV*

The House of Usher

South African howler bears only a passing resemblance to the master's short story. Until the overly violent conclusion, it's a Gothic romance. There's the big spooky house—complete with hidden passages—and the plucky heroine (Romy Windsor) who's prone to wandering the halls late on dark and stormy nights, while dressed in her peignoir and carrying a candle. There's the dark, brooding older guy (Oliver Reed) who owns the joint, and there's even someone locked in the attic. Whenever the action flags, the scenery falls down as the house allegedly collapses. *AKA:* Edgar Allen Poe's House of Usher. 𝄞𝄞

Strong violence, sexual situations.

1988 (R) 92m/C Oliver Reed, Donald Pleasence, Romy Windsor; *D:* Alan Birkinshaw; *W:* Michael J. Murray; *M:* Gary Chang. **VHS, LV** *COL*

How to Get Ahead in Advertising

Scathing black fantasy/satire targets advertising and consumerism. Hotshot British ad man Richard E. Grant brags to a group of his younger co-workers that he can sell anything, that he can create a desire for any product. But, alone in his office, he has no ideas for promoting a new acne cream. He becomes so frustrated by this failure of imagination that he suffers a bizarre emotional breakdown and a weird boil appears on his neck. Is it controlling him, or is it part of his madness? Unfortunately, the film is more interesting for its social criticism than for the characters or their situation. Despite some fiendishly funny and mad moments, the film is a victim of its own unrelieved cynicism. 𝄞𝄞𝄞

Profanity, grotesque special effects.

1989 (R) 95m/C GB Richard E. Grant, Rachel Ward, Susan Wooldridge, Mick Ford, Richard Wilson, John Shrapnel, Jacqueline Tong; *D:* Bruce Robinson; *W:* Bruce Robinson; *M:* David Dundas, Rick Wentworth. **VHS, LV** *VTR*

How U Like Me Now?

Slice of contemporary life looks at six black adults in Chicago. These people aren't cliches—they don't deal drugs or shoot each other—but they never come fully alive as characters, either. Darnell Williams is an underemployed and unambitious young man who's living with Salli Richardson, an executive who wants something more out of her life. When it comes to visions of the future, they're not on the same page. When her gay friend and hairdresser Byron Stewart shows her a way out, she takes it. Their friends have other problems. Daniel Gardner can't see beyond the next party. Raymond Whitefield, believing that image is everything, has created a fragile fantasy world around himself. Daryll Roberts (who also wrote, produced, and directed) is the militant nationalist, filled with black pride, who can't persuade the others to join his causes. Roberts deserves a lot of credit for showing that all black people in movies aren't a *Menace II the 'Hood,* but they need to be presented in more compelling situations; their conflicts, personalities, and motivations explored more deeply. So, even if *How U Like Me Now* falls short of the mark, it's so right minded and well intentioned that it's worth a look for anyone who's interested in the subject. 𝄞𝄞

Strong language, sexual subject matter.

1992 (R) 109m/C Darnell Williams, Salli Richardson, Daniel Gardner, Raymond Whitefield, Debra Crable, Jonelle Kennedy, Byron Stewart, Charnele Brown, Daryll Roberts; *D:* Daryll Roberts; *W:* Daryll Roberts; *M:* Kahil El Zabar, Chuck Webb. **VHS, LV** *MCA*

"Even in feature films, there's almost never any playfulness to a sexual scene. There's an intensity, there's a seriousness, but there's not a playfulness. That's why I do the films."

—DEBORAH SHAMES, PRODUCER/DIRECTOR OF *THE HOTTEST BID.*

137

Howling II: Your Sister Is a Werewolf

Sequel has none of the wit or inventive special effects of the original, though it is fun in its own dumb way. The subtitle—"Your Sister Is a Werewolf"—sets the tone for unintentional humor. Alleged star Sybil Danning is onscreen for only a few minutes and has to play her big love scene while sprouting fur, but she does have one great B-movie moment where she rips her dress off. She does it so well that the filmmakers elected to repeat it during the closing credits—not once, not twice, not thrice, but ten—count 'em...ten—times. Is that art or what? Followed by several sequels. 🦴🦴

Violence, nudity, sexual content.

1985 (R) 91m/C *FR IT* Sybil Danning, Christopher Lee, Annie McEnroe, Marsha Hunt, Reb Brown, Ferdinand "Ferdy" Mayne; **D:** Philippe Mora; **W:** Gary Brandner. **VHS, LV** *REP*

Howling III: The Marsupials

Truly imbecilic horror comedy is an alternative masterpiece for anyone who can put up with its fractured sensibility. For those who aren't on the right wavelength, it's unwatchable. Jerboa (Imogen Annesley) is a psychic Australian werewolf who leaves the country for the big city and straightaway lands a role in a cheap horror flick. Then there's the toothy defecting Russian ballerina who suffers from a similar condition. The ludicrous writing, acting, and editing suggest that the humor is meant to be a parody of bad movies. But, can a movie parody itself? 🦴

1987 (PG-13) 94m/C *AU* Barry Otto, Imogen Annesley, Dasha Blahova, Max Fairchild, Ralph Cotterill, Leigh Biolos, Frank Thring Jr., Michael Pate; **D:** Philippe Mora. **VHS, LV** *LIV*

Howling IV: The Original Nightmare

The Roman numeral is the only link to the sharp 1981 Joe Dante/John Sayles horror-comedy. (For those who are keeping score, *II* was a European flick subtitled "Your Sister Is a Werewolf" and *III*, an Australian production about shape-changing marsupials that has developed something of a cult following.) The plot for *IV* contains all the right ingredients for decent cheap-thrill: novelist recovering from nervous breakdown goes to the country to relax and hears strange animal noises at night. Why are the locals so strange? Is her husband part of their conspiracy? Is he fooling around with the sultry shopkeeper in town? Why is she having visions of a short nun? There's no suspense to any of these goofy goings-on. The whole thing is almost saved by some really bad acting, but fans have seen better. 🦴🦴

Gory special effects, violence, profanity, brief nudity, and one sexual scene.

1988 (R) 94m/C Romy Windsor, Michael T. Weiss, Antony Hamilton, Susanne Severeid, Lamya Derval; **D:** John Hough. **VHS, LV** *LIV*

Hugh Hefner: Once Upon a Time

Even those who disagree with and disapprove of Hugh Hefner have to admit that he has been one of the most influential Americans in the second half of this century. This quickly paced video documentary examines his personality and eventful career. Beginning in 1953 with the first issue of *Playboy*, the one featuring the famous calendar shot of Marilyn Monroe, Hefner turned a magazine into an empire. As he sees it, "the adolescent dreams that I turned into reality are the adolescent dreams of an entire society...very American dreams." It's hard to argue with that observation, but there's got to be more to Hefner's success. After all, there were magazines with pictures of naked women before *Playboy* appeared, and there have been several thousand since, but none of them have achieved the national prominence that Hefner reached. According to the film, there are two reasons. First, Hefner had the right idea at the right time. America was growing rapidly in the post-war years, and with prosperity came change. In pictures and later in text, *Playboy* was part of that massive societal change. For better or worse, it led the first charge in the sexual revolution. Second, and more important, Hefner was driven to succeed. In the tradition of Horatio Alger, he dedicated his life to his work. To use today's business cliche, he "micromanaged" the magazine. Fueled by ambition and dexedrine, he worked incredibly long hours, and became consumed by every detail of every issue, writing long detailed memos to his staff. Then in 1959, he decided to live the fantasy life he had created. This is also when he began to assume a key, if not pivotal role in the fantasy lives of millions of American men and boys, yours truly included. Even fantasy lives have their rough spots, though, and Hefner's has been no exception. The film doesn't avoid the bad times that came later. In the end, it's a fascinating, stranger-than-fiction story—the kind of unusual material that's perfect for the medium of home video. 🦴🦴🦴

Contains brief nudity, a little strong language.

1992 91m/C Hugh Hefner; **D:** Robert Heath. **VHS, LV** *UND, BTV*

The Hunchback of Notre Dame

1982 TV production of the famous story isn't as lavish as the 1939 Charles Laughton film, but it's still terrific. The key is the casting. Lesley-Anne Down is at her loveliest as the gypsy Esmeralda. Derek Jacobi's Dom Claude Frollo has the right combination of villainy and love. Anthony Hopkins, nearly unrecognizable under the makeup, is a memorable Quasimodo. The ending is weak, but most of the script stays close to Victor Hugo's romantic masterpiece. This is a grand story of love and adventure in an exotic medieval setting. It's probably too complicated for very young viewers, but kids who enjoy spectacle and can understand the emotions involved will be fascinated. **AKA:** Hunchback. 🦴🦴🦴

Contains no objectionable material.

1982 (PG) 102m/C Anthony Hopkins, Derek Jacobi, Lesley-Anne Down, John Gielgud, Tim Pigott-Smith, Rosalie Crutchley, Robert Powell; **D:** Michael Tuchner. **VHS** *VMK*

The Hunting

Strange little Australian import is pretentious, inept, and heavy-handed. Secretary Kerry Armstrong is swept off her feet by billionaire John Savage. What's to be done about her husband? In case you can't figure out what the film is about, it begins with a close-up of a moth fluttering around a candle flame. And since that might be too subtle for some viewers, the image is repeated at regular intervals for the next 90 minutes. WOOF!

Egregious symbolism, subject matter, brief nudity, sexual content, violence, strong language

1992 (R) 97m/C AU John Savage, Kerry Armstrong, Guy Pearce, Rebecca Rigg; **D:** Frank Howson; **W:** Frank Howson. **VHS** *PAR*

Husbands and Lovers

Italian adaptation of Alberto Moravia's novel is the story of Stefan (Julian Sands), his wife Alina (Joanna Pacula), and her lover Paolo (Tcheky Karyo). Though Stefan and Alina have an "open marriage," he decides that he'd like to close it up a little when she announces that she'll spend every weekend with Paolo at his ugly mansion. Potentially enjoyable B-movie material often stops dead while these fatuous characters deliver boring speeches about relationships and their innermost thoughts and emotions. What sets this one apart from most video originals is the unusual amount of male nudity. Also available in an unrated version. 🦴🦴

Nudity, sexual situations, strong language, no real violence.

1991 (R) 91m/C IT Julian Sands, Joanna Pacula, Tcheky Karyo; **D:** Mauro Bolognini; **W:** Sergio Bazzini; **M:** Ennio Morricone. **VHS** *COL*

I Don't Buy Kisses Anymore

Bernie (Jason Alexander) is 30, addicted to chocolate, overweight, and still living at home with his mother in Philadelphia. Then he meets Theresa (Nia Peeples) at the bus stop. She's a graduate student and sometimes singer, a woman who's as outgoing and confi-

also has an interesting plot built on the characters' personalities and some good acting. It's about the competitive relationship that develops between Suzanne (Lisa Boyle), a sexually adventurous ad woman, and Michael (Ken Steadman), her new boss. The film boasts expensive production values, with attractive sets and cast polished to airbrushed perfection, and a kinky mind set. Director Moctezuma Lobato has a future in the field. Also available in an unrated version. 𝄞𝄞𝄞 GPI: 8.9

Nudity, strong sexual content, language, mild violence.

1995 **(R)** 95m/C Lisa Boyle, Ken Steadman; **D:** Moctezuma Lobato. **VHS, LV** *APX*

I Love N.Y.

Love isn't easy for Mario (Scott Baio), a photographer from Little Italy, and Nicole Yeats (Kelley Van Der Velden), the daughter of an egotistical actor. This sleeper makes good use of New York locations. The young leads do first-rate work playing likable characters that have a remarkable amount of depth to them. (Many big-budget Hollywood movies don't understand their main characters nearly as well as this one does.) The story resorts to a few cliches, which are particularly noticeable toward the end, but that's not a major flaw. The rest of the cast—Jerry Orbach, Virna Lisi, Jennifer O'Neill, and Christopher Plummer—provide solid support. By the way, according to the credits, this one was written and directed by "Alan Smithee," the standard pseudonym used by directors when they're dissatisfied with the finished work. In this case, the credit should go to coproducer Gianni Bozzacchi. 𝄞𝄞𝄞

Profanity, brief nudity, sexual content.

1987 **(R)** 100m/C Scott Baio, Kelley Van Der Velden, Christopher Plummer, Jennifer O'Neill, Jerry Orbach, Virna Lisi; **D:** Gianni Bozzacchi, Alan Smithee; **W:** Gianni Bozzacchi, Alan Smithee; **M:** Bill Conti. **VHS, LV** *HHE, OM*

dent as Bernie is shy and uncertain. The road to romance is unusually (and unnecessarily) rough. They're believable, fully realized individuals, and as long as the focus stays on them, the film works fairly well. But the story wanders into lengthy, pointless subplots, and the slow pace sucks the energy out of the narrative. The characters are so engaging, they deserve better. 𝄞𝄞

Mature subject matter.

1992 **(PG)** 112m/C Jason Alexander, Nia Peeples, Lainie Kazan, Lou Jacobi, Eileen Brennan, Larry Storch, Arleen Sorkin; **D:** Robert Marcarelli; **W:** Jonnie Lindsell; **M:** Cobb Bussinger. **VHS** *PAR*

I Like to Play Games

Erotic thriller pushes the limits of the genre about as far as they'll go. Actually, this one

Ice

Traci Lords and Phillip Troy, wife-and-husband cat burglars, steal $60 million in diamonds from a Mafia honcho and then find themselves caught in the middle of an internecine war between families. The plot is every bit as silly as it sounds. Whenever it threatens to get boring, something blows up or someone is shot or cars chase each other. Good stuntwork, special effects, and production values make this one a fair little time-waster. 🦴🦴🦴

Strong language, violence.

1993 **(R)** 91m/C Traci Lords, Phillip Troy, Zach Galligan, Jorge Rivero, Michael Bailey Smith, Jamie Alba, Jean Pflieger, Floyd Levine; *D:* Brook Yeaton; *W:* Sean Dash. **VHS, LV** *PMH*

Iced

"You know, one of those flicks where the only time you watch the screen is if there's someone naked or someone getting killed, or both." That self-descriptive line of dialogue pretty much sums up this little low-budget horror about a psycho-in-ski-mask dispatching thirty-somethingers at a ski cabin. Whenever the movie threatens to make sense, it runs into trouble. But while it larks along with lethal hottubs, hidden bear traps, and the like, we've got alternative video at its laughable best. 🦴🦴

Contains nudity, fairly strong sexual content, violence, profanity.

1988 86m/C Debra Deliso, Doug Stevenson, Ron Kologie, Elizabeth Gorcey, Alan Johnson; *D:* Jeff Kwitny. **VHS** *PSM*

Idaho Transfer

Peter Fonda's sober-sided science-fiction film is about time travel, government repression, and ecological disaster. It was made on a minuscule budget with modest effects and a mostly non-professional cast. Before Fonda arrives at a leaden downbeat ending, he presents the future as a post-apocalyptic camping trip without any suspense or tension. (By the way, the last words of the film, "Esto Perpetua," are the state motto of Idaho: "May she endure forever.") **AKA:** Deranged. 🦴🦴

Contains mild violence.

1973 **(PG)** 90m/C Keith Carradine, Kelley Bohanan; *D:* Peter Fonda. **VHS** *MPI, FCT*

Identity Crisis

Low-budget comedy has the loose-jointed, spontaneous quality of producer/director Melvin Van Peebles' late '60s work, *Watermelon Man* and *Sweet Sweetback's Baadasssss Song.* Missing from his son Mario's script are the violence and racial anger that made those films cult hits. This one's a screwball farce about two souls inhabiting the same body. When gay French designer Yves Malmaison (Richard Fancy) is murdered by his crooked partner, a bag-lady/witch transfers his spirit into the body of Chilly D (Mario Van Peebles), an aspiring young New York rapper. But only one consciousness can control the body. After a blow to the head, they trade places. Of course, for the rest of the movie Chilly/Yves gets conked on the noggin about every ten minutes or so. That's the source of the comedy, and Mario Van Peebles has a grand time with the dual role; imagine a combination of *La Cage Aux Folles* and *Trading Places.* There aren't many surprises in the plot, but the senior Van Peebles tells the story with a machine-gun pace, using lots of flashy quick cuts, unusual camera angles, and a combination of various tints of color and black-and-white footage. Budget restraints show through in the locations, occasional harsh lighting, and rough sound. Look for the elder Van Peebles as the police detective, TV producer Stephen Cannell as the coroner, and don't miss Shelly Burch, behind the welder's mask, as Roxy, the virgin mudwrestler. 🦴🦴🦴

Profanity, bawdy humor.

1990 **(R)** 98m/C Mario Van Peebles, Ilan Mitchell-Smith, Nicholas Kepros, Shelly Burch, Richard Clarke, Richard Fancy, Stephen J. Cannell; *Cameos:* Melvin Van Peebles; *D:* Melvin Van Peebles; *W:* Richard Rothstein, Mario Van Peebles. **VHS, LV** *ACA*

Illegal Entry: Formula for Fear

Promising little suspenser begins with the wonderful bad acting that makes B-movies so much fun. It's about a teenaged girl whose scientist parents are murdered for the secret

formula. Whatever credibility the story might have goes down the drain when we learn that the folks keep a huge open tub of hydrochloric acid in the basement. Watch that first step. 🔪🔪🔪

Strong language, brief nudity, sexual activity, some violence.

1993 88m/C Sabryn Gene't, Barbara Lee Alexander, Gregory Vignolle, Arthur Roberts, Carol Hoyt; **D:** Henri Charr; **W:** John B. Pfeifer. **VHS** *PMH*

Illegal in Blue

Most of the erotic elements in this "erotic" thriller appear to have been grafted on. The main characters are an honest cop (Dan Gauthier) accused of corruption by his corrupt superiors, and a sexy torch singer (Stacey Dash) suspected of murdering her rich husband. The tricky plot may not be as tightly wrapped as it ought to be, but the film does come to a nicely cynical conclusion, and it has a sense of humor. Dash's spirited performance

helps a lot, too. Also available in an unrated version. 🔪🔪🔪

Nudity, sexual content, violence, strong language.

1995 (R) 94m/C Dan Gauthier, Stacey Dash, Louis Giambalvo, Michael Durrell, David Groh; **D:** Stu Segall; **W:** Noel Hynd; **M:** Steve Edwards. **VHS, LV** *ORI*

Illicit Behavior

Wildly complicated thriller is cut from the same cloth as the big-budget theatrical release *Internal Affairs*. It's about a Los Angeles cop (Jack Scalia) whose wife (Joan Severance) is either a victim or a manipulator. He and his partner (James Russo) are already in trouble with an internal affairs guy (Robert Davi), who meets the missus and is more interested than he should be. The overheated plot contains enough infidelities, lies, shouting matches, deceptions, and dirty dealings to keep your average soap opera cooking for a month. Special credit should go to Ms. Severance and her body double. Seen simply as video popcorn, this is grand trashy fun, and it doesn't pretend to be anything else. Also available in an unrated version at 104 minutes. 🎞🎞🎞 **GPI: 8.8**

Strong sexual content, nudity, violence, strong language.

1991 (R) 101m/C Joan Severance, Robert Davi, James Russo, Jack Scalia, Kent McCord; *D:* Worth Keeter. **VHS** *PSM*

Illicit Dreams

Veteran Andrew Stevens directs and stars as a building contractor drawn by supernatural powers into a romance with a stranger (Shannon Tweed) who has been dreaming about him. The problem: she's married to a corrupt and ruthless rich guy (Joe Cortese). Stevens' mother Stella shows up in a nice supporting role as a fortune teller who claims that "psychokenetic teleportation" is at work. Stevens has been in the business long enough to know how to tell a well-constructed story and to make the most of a modest budget. This one does what it means to do. Any resemblance to *Ghost* is completely intentional. Also available in an unrated version. 🎞🎞🎞

Sexual content, nudity, and a little rough language.

1994 (R) 93m/C Shannon Tweed, Andrew Stevens, Joe Cortese, Stella Stevens; *D:* Andrew Stevens. **VHS** *REP*

I'm Dangerous Tonight

Supernatural hokum is loosely based on a Cornell Woolrich story. The gimmick here is an Aztec ceremonial cloak that releases the darker side of anyone wearing it. That causes a few off-screen murders and such, but then the cloak falls into the hands of college student Madchen Amick. She tailors it into a dropdead red party dress, and, PRESTO!, the innocent undergrad becomes a femme fatale reincarnation of Rita Hayworth in *Gilda*. That's the finest moment, though the rest of the movie benefits considerably from fine supporting work. This one was made for the USA cable network and so Tobe Hooper's direction is restrained. 🎞🎞🎞

Inexplicably rated R, for subject matter and drug use, I guess.

1990 (R) 92m/C Madchen Amick, Corey Parker, R. Lee Ermey, Mary Frann, Dee Wallace Stone, Anthony Perkins; *D:* Tobe Hooper; *W:* Alice Wilson. **VHS** *MCA*

Improper Conduct

Unapologetic exploitation is just another leering bit of low-budget soft-core video. But—surprise, surprise—it's also a remarkably accurate portrayal of sexual harassment in the workplace. That side of director Jag Mundhra's story takes a sharp look at the complex sexual politics that are played out in an office and the ways in which a male power structure has stacked the deck in its favor. Boss (Stuart Whitman) brings his son-in-law (John Laughlin) in from New York to take over an L.A. ad agency. Tahnee Welch is a young woman who has a problem with booze and makes bad decisions when she's drunk, and her reputation makes her an obvious mark for her predatory new supervisor. After he attacks her, she takes him to court. The rest is more or less standard retribution, implausibly meted out by Lee Ann Beaman, as a vengeful sister. It's a shame that the film changes course so radically in midstream. The first half is often effective, particularly when it focuses on the inner workings of a small office. Mundhra is a seasoned veteran of video originals. He knows how to keep a plot moving and, when he's not catering to his audience's baser instincts, he can create believable characters in realistic situations. Also available in an unrated version. 🎞🎞🎞

Mature subject matter, sexual content, brief nudity, strong language, some violence.

1994 (R) 95m/C Steven Bauer, Lee Ann Beaman, John Laughlin, Kathy Shower, Tahnee Welch, Nia Peeples, Stuart Whitman, Adrian Zmed, Patsy Pease; *D:* Jag Mundhra; *W:* Carl Austin. **VHS** *MNC*

Impulse

Lottie (Theresa Russell) is an L.A. vice cop who works undercover, impersonating prostitutes and drug addicts. She's good at her work but the rest of her life is a mess: her credit card accounts are dangerously overdue; her boss (George Dzundza) is a true rat; and her romantic relationships have been a string of disas-

ters. D.A. Jeff Fahey brings her into an elaborate sting operation and his interest in her is soon more personal than professional. Initially, Lottie doesn't know how to react. She is so involved with the intrigue and trickery of her work that she is sometimes unsure which side she's on. Russell, at her sexiest, handles this complex role deftly, turning in better work than she did in *Black Widow*. Unfortunately, the plot hinges on a fantastic coincidence that's hard to accept; the denouement resorts to clichés; and the ending is suspect. Those flaws aren't as troubling as they might be because actress-turned-director Sondra Locke has a sure touch with action sequences and the erotic scenes, and, most importantly, she understands Lottie. 𝄞𝄞𝄞

Graphic violence, sexual content, profanity, brief nudity.

1990 **(R)** 109m/**C** Theresa Russell, Nicholas Mele, Eli Danker, Charles McCaughan, Jeff Fahey, George Dzundza, Alan Rosenberg, Lynne Thigpen, Shawn Elliott; *D:* Sondra Locke; *W:* John DeMarco, Leigh Chapman; *M:* Michel Colombier. **VHS, LV** *WAR*

In a Moment of Passion

Here's one of those wild videos that's so bizarre, flamboyant, and atrocious that it transcends conventional definitions of good and bad. Tammy (Chase Masterson), a stuntwoman and aspiring actress, is doubling for Krista (Vivian Schilling), the evil starlet, until she, Tammy, is sent overseas to train a German actor to ride a horse. But before she arrives, the actor—Werner, by name—is murdered by a psychotically jealous flunky (Maxwell Caulfield) who assumes Werner's identity and his Porsche. Are you with me so far? Tammy and the fake Werner meet at a horse farm owned by unctuous millionaire Joe Estevez and run by Greta, the Teutonic lesbian. Of course, other people involved with the movie and with the real Werner stop by to visit and all of them suffer uniformly unfortunate results. What sets this one apart from your run-of-the-mill video soap is writer/producer/director Zbigniew Kaminski's complete misunderstanding of the material. First there's the inappropriate music. It's loud, ominous, melodramatic stuff that could have come straight from a low-budget 1950s s-f flick. It pops up for no reason at the oddest moments. Then there's Caulfield's "British" accent, which must be heard to be believed. Finally, at the end of the movie, right when everything should be winding up, Krista, the evil starlet, reappears and bursts into song! The closing credits suggest that this is a German-Polish American production, so perhaps there was some lack of communication. In any case, as unintentional comedy, this one goes right off the scale. 𝄞𝄞𝄞 **GPI: 7.7**

Strong language, violence, brief nudity, sexual content.

1993 **(R)** 100m/**C** Maxwell Caulfield, Chase Masterson, Vivian Schilling, Julie Araskog, Joe Estevez, Robert Z'Dar; *Cameos:* Jeff Conaway; *D:* Zbigniew Kaminski; *W:* Zbigniew Kaminski, Charles Haigh. **VHS** *HMD*

In the Blood

Producer George Butler (*Pumping Iron*) turns his attention to a safari. His point of view is openly pro-hunting, embracing the quasi-mystical male-bonding lore that surrounds the hunt. The film's star is his son Tyssen, and the leader is Robin Hurt, a professional hunter. Their trip is a rough recreation of a similar journey taken by Theodore Roosevelt and his son Kermit in 1909 (footage from that excursion, provided by the Smithsonian, is intercut with the modern film). Roosevelt's presence is a central thread of the storyline; his great-grandson is with Butler's safari and so is his rifle, which was refitted by London gunsmiths. The modern narrative follows two groups of hunters: one is after a "trophy" Cape Buffalo; the other tries to kill a huge crocodile that has been preying on Masai livestock. Judged as a portrait of the vanishing African wilderness, the film looks like a National Geographic special with teeth, claws, leeches, and spoor. The country is as violent and brutal as it is beautiful. As one character notes, "No animal in Africa dies of old age." In the last ten minutes, Butler achieves his main goal by showing the viewer what this kind of hunting is like. If he romanticizes one side of the activity, he still presents it effectively. He is not going to change anyone's mind. Those who see hunting as an excuse for guys to play with toys that go "Boom" and to hang around outside and get dirty probably won't be swayed by Butler's emotional arguments. And the film will strike animal-rights advocates as the equivalent of pornography. 𝄐𝄐𝄐

Violence and subject matter.

1989 (PG) 90m/C VHS, 8mm *FCT*

In the Cold of the Night

Jeff Lester's unsettling dreams seem to be coming true. All right, he does sleep on a lighted waterbed and he has a taste for pineapple pizza, which might explain them, but then he meets a mysterious woman (Adrienne Sachs) who played a part in one of his dreams. That's a familiar premise, but it's developed into an interesting and reasonably credible conclusion with first-rate production values. The film looks better than many theatrical releases. Though the thriller does feature some surrealistic love scenes, the real charge is provided by Peggy Lee's "Fever" on the soundtrack. Also available in an NC-17 version. 𝄐𝄐𝄐

Violence, strong language, nudity, sexual content.

1989 (R) 112m/C Jeff Lester, Adrienne Sachs, Shannon Tweed, David Soul, John Beck, Tippi Hedren, Marc Singer; *D:* Nico Mastorakis. VHS, LV *REP*

In the Kingdom of the Blind the Man with One Eye Is King

Would-be Scorsese film about New York gangsters, punks, and crooked cops lacks the Scorsese genius. When a Mafia elder is killed, Tony C (William Petersen) calls in a favor from Al (writer/director Nick Vallelonga), an NYPD detective. Al's young brother Mick (Quinn Duffy) is involved. So are Papa Joe (Paul Winfield), a Harlem gangster trying to cut a deal with the Italians; Jack Ryan (Michael Biehn), boss of the Irish mob; and Moran (Leo Rossi), a sadistic cop who's eager to kill somebody. The initial crime leads to a long dark night of the soul for all concerned. Unfortunately, the film is simultaneously complex, static, and talky. It also seems bound by the conventions and limitations of the stage with extended scenes of stiff confrontations. These are long-winded (really long-winded), overly dramatic set pieces in which about as many lines are screamed as are spoken. Likewise, much of the acting looks like it's meant for the theatre, not the screen, with loud voices and exaggerated gestures. Because his cast is so feverishly dismantling the scenery, Vallelonga tends to keep his camera at a distance from the characters. Without minimizing those criticisms, the film still earns a qualified recommendation. It's got soul and passion, and those count for something. 𝄐𝄐𝄐

Strong language, violence, brief nudity.

1994 (R) 99m/C Nick Vallelonga, William L. Petersen, Michael Biehn, Paul Winfield, James Quarter, Quinn Duffy, Leo Rossi; *D:* Nick Vallelonga; *W:* Nick Vallelonga. VHS *AVI*

In the Realm of the Senses

Famous (some would say notorious) Japanese film about violent sexual obsession is such an intense, graphic, and disturbing experience that it was banned at the 1976 New York Film Festival. On tape, it carries the warning that it

is intended for adults only. And the truth of the matter is that many adults will be repulsed. Based on incidents that occurred in Tokyo in 1936, this is the story of the sexual relationship that develops between a young businessman, Kichi-San (Eiko Matsuda), and Sada (Tatsuya Fuji), an ex-prostitute. Their affair moves from simple sex to a virtual exchange of identities and finally to a sort of mutual death wish. It is difficult to describe the intense atmosphere that director Nagisa Oshima creates. The film contains graphic sexual acts and explicit violence that makes "splatter" horror films seem as childish and silly as they really are. *Realm* is a sensual horror story. The foreign setting—white-painted geishas, the droning atonal music that sounds so harsh to Western tastes, the flowing robes and stark sets—gives the story a vivid, nightmarish surrealism. It's not another *I Am Curious, Yellow*—i.e., boring political claptrap masquerading as "erotic art." Neither is it a piece of cheap exploitation that's taken on serious airs. It's a demanding work that is so extreme it will never find a large mainstream audience. It should also be noted that for all its excesses and successful attempts to shock, *Realm* is far too long. By the end, what was once outrageous has become tedious. Recommended for videophiles with strong stomachs and a taste for the truly unusual. 🦴🦴🦴

Contains graphic scenes of violence and sexual activity.

1976 (NC-17) 105m/C *JP FR* Tatsuya Fuji, Eiko Matsuda, Aio Nakajima, Meika Seri; *D:* Nagisa Oshima. **VHS** *FXL, CVC*

In Too Deep

Like most Australian imports, this one's watchable even when it's inept. Mack (Hugo Race) is a sick, vicious punk. Wendy (Santha Press), a shop owner and would-be singer at the Cafe Noir, is obsessed with him. Her 15-year-old sister Jo (Rebekah Elmaloglou) has just hit town and is looking for trouble. Miles (John Flaus), a bone-weary cop, knows that political trouble is imminent. For the first half, while the numerous conflicts are being sorted out, the film is fascinating. But when it has to start making sense, it succumbs to unintentional humor. Though Wendy is singing-impaired, that doesn't stop her from massacring several jazz standards. At the same time, the writers couldn't decide whether they wanted to make *Body Heat, Lady Sings the Blues,* or *All the President's Men.* They threw in elements of all three and the result is about as mixed as you'd expect. 🦴🦴🦴

Nudity, sexual content, violence, language.

1990 (R) 106m/C *AU* Hugo Race, Santha Press, Rebekah Elmaloglou, John Flaus, Dominic Sweeney; *D:* Colin South. **VHS** *PAR*

Incident at Deception Ridge

Fair little woodland adventure flick opens with a variation on that great aerial shot of the prison from *The Shawshank Redemption.* It's quickly apparent that this one isn't tackling such an ambitious project, but it is a nice beginning and the rest of the film moves along smartly with some good moments. Jack Bolder (Michael O'Keefe) has just been released from prison somewhere in Washington state. While he's waiting for a bus, two thugs (Miguel Ferrer and Ian Tracey) kidnap a woman (Linda Purl) and force her bank manager husband Jack David (Ed Begley, Jr.) to steal the ransom. To reveal much more would give the game away. 🦴🦴🦴

Mild violence.

1994 (R) 94m/C Michael O'Keefe, Ed Begley Jr., Linda Purl, Miguel Ferrer, Colleen Flynn, Michelle Johnson, Ian Tracey; *D:* John McPherson, John McPherson; *W:* Ken Hixon, Randy Kornfield; *C:* David Geddes. **VHS, LV** *MCA*

The Incredibly True Adventure of Two Girls in Love

Despite its propagandistic overtones, this offbeat comic romance manages to deal fairly with its title characters. Those are Randy (Laurel Holloman), a confirmed lesbian at 17, and Evie (Nicole Parker), who's uncertain about many things but is still attracted to Randy. Further complicating the situation, Randy is poor and white while Evie is well-heeled and black. Their road to romance is rocky, indeed. Writer/director Maria Maggenti allows the story to veer wildly between absolutely accurate depictions of mercurial adolescent emotion and ridiculous overacting in contrived scenes that wouldn't be out of place in a bad soap opera. She uses simple, effective filmmaking techniques to move the low-budget action along, and she gets complex, believable performances from her two young stars. On the other hand, her obvious sexual politics, never far from the surface, aren't likely to win over any converts. *JJJ*

Mature subject matter, sexual content, nudity, strong language.

1995 (R) 95m/C Laurel Holloman, Nicole Parker, Kate Stafford, Stephanie Berry; *D:* Maria Maggenti; *W:* Maria Maggenti. **VHS** *NLC*

Independence Day

He (David Keith) has just come back home to Mercury, Texas; she (Kathleen Quinlan) is ready to leave, feeling suffocated by the small town. Of course, they fall in love. Their families are a believable and important part of the story, involving car races, comedy, an intense feeling of place, physical violence, and even stronger emotional violence. Dianne Wiest turns in a super supporting performance that previews the work she's done more recently. Unfairly dismissed as a "woman's picture," it's developed a strong following on tape. *AKA:* Follow Your Dreams. *JJJ*

Mature subject matter, strong language, violence.

1983 (R) 110m/C Kathleen Quinlan, David Keith, Frances Sternhagen, Dianne Wiest, Cliff DeYoung, Richard Farnsworth, Josef Sommer, Cheryl "Rainbeaux" Smith; *D:* Robert Mandel; *M:* Charles Bernstein. **VHS** *WAR, CCB*

The Inland Sea

On one level, the subject is Seto Naikai, a body of water bordered by three of Japan's four large islands and containing hundreds of smaller islands. But this meditative documentary is also about travel and the nature of the expatriate. Donald Ritchie, an American living in Japan, narrates the film that recreates a journey he took 30 years before. His humor is dry and sharp. So are his observations on Japanese culture past and present, his gloomy predictions for the future, and his ideas on sex and religion. Particular credit has to go to the other creative people responsible for the film—cinematographer Hiro Narita, composer Toru Takemitsu, and director Lucille Carra. They seem to have been perfectly attuned to Ritchie's particular point of view. Their combination of word, image, and sound sustains a mood of intelligent wonder, regret, and speculation for almost an hour. *The Inland Sea* is a superb film, strongly recommended even for those who don't normally watch non-fiction. *JJJJ*

Contains no objectionable material.

1993 56m/C Donald Ritchie; *D:* Lucille Carra; *C:* Hiro Narita; *M:* Toru Takemitsu. **VHS, LV** *BTV, PME, HMV*

The Inner Circle

Stalin's Moscow—1939. Ivan Sanshin (Tom Hulce) is a young soldier who has just married Anastasia (Lolita Davidovich) when there's a knock on their apartment door. Without explaining where they're going—or if he'll be coming back—the KGB men whisk him away. But Ivan is lucky (maybe). He has been chosen to be Stalin's personal projectionist, and he keeps the job for decades. From that fly-on-the-wall point of view, the film examines the seductive workings of a totalitarian bureaucracy. Stalin himself (convincingly played by Alexandre Zbruev) comes across as a fatherly, Reaganesque figure, admired and even loved by those like Ivan who hate his government.

At the same time, Anastasia tries to rescue a young girl whose parents were victims of one of Stalin's purges. Eventually, she comes to the attention of KGB-head Beria (Bob Hoskins), the smoothest and most ruthless of Stalin's men. Russian writer/director Andrei Konchalovsky said that he meant the film to be a social study. He wanted to show "a state of terror, psychological rape by the state," and that's exactly what he's done. *The Inner Circle* was filmed in Russia, and has a grim, grainy Kafkaesque look. To think of it as the other side of *Dr. Zhivago* is close to the mark. No, this is not conventional entertainment. The movie means to make viewers uncomfortable, and so it's difficult to watch. That said, its historical truths are undeniable. And the continuing political instability in that part of the world shows that the larger questions the film poses concerning the relationship between individuals and governments are still relevant. 🕭🕭🕭

Mature subject matter, sexual content, strong language.

1991 (PG-13) 122m/C Tom Hulce, Lolita Davidovich, Bob Hoskins, Alexandre Zbruev, Maria Baranova, Feodor Chaliapin Jr, Bess Meyer; *D:* Andrei Konchalovsky; *W:* Andrei Konchalovsky, Anatoli Usov; *M:* Eduard Artemyev. **VHS, LV, 8mm** *COL*

Inner Sanctum

The steamy hubba-hubba scenes are about all that this guilty pleasure has to offer. It's a pseudo noir hash about a hypochondriac wife (Valerie Wildman), her philandering husband (Joseph Bottoms), his mistress (Margaux Hemingway), and a live-in nurse (Tanya Roberts). Nobody on either side of the camera seems to have cared much about the disposable plot, which is just as well. The non-acting is glorious. Also available in an unrated version. 🕭
GPI: 8.5

Both Unrated and R-rated versions contain nudity, sexual content, strong language, some violence.

1991 (R) 87m/C Tanya Roberts, Margaux Hemingway, Joseph Bottoms, Valerie Wildman, William Butler, Brett Clark; *D:* Fred Olen Ray. **VHS, LV** *COL*

Innocent Lies

Screwy mystery can't decide whether it's crass exploitation or serious art, and so delivers neither the deep satisfaction of the former nor the embarrassed joy of the latter. Instead, writer/director Patrick Dewolf offers up gobs of art-deco style and a certain studied kinkiness. The year is 1938; the place, "somewhere on the French coast." The irritable and irritating Inspector Cross (Adrian Dunbar), a British police detective, goes there for a cockeyed murder investigation. It all has to do with an aristocratic family led by a Fascist sympathizer (Joanna Lumley) and her spoiled children (Stephen Dorff and Gabrielle Anwar). A loose subplot involves the historical setting but that really has little importance. Dewolf is more interested in semi-sordid depravity. The whole thing looks like an episode of *Masterpiece Theatre* about Brits gone bad, but not quite bad enough. As a thriller, the story is too arty to be taken seriously, and the characters are so unpleasant and essentially unattractive that you can't care about them. The deranged lu-lu of an ending is almost enough to redeem the rest, but that's a close call. For fans of this sort of thing only. 🕭🕭

Mature subject matter, violence, language, brief nudity.

1995 (R) 88m/C *FR GB* Adrian Dunbar, Stephen Dorff, Gabrielle Anwar, Joanna Lumley; *D:* Patrick Dewolf; *W:* Kerry Crabbe, Patrick Dewolf; *C:* Patrick Blossier; *M:* Alexandre Desplat. **VHS** *PGV*

Innocent Victim

Ruth Rendell is one of the best mystery writers in the business. Her work tends to be lumped together with Agatha Christie's and Dorothy Sayers' simply because she's British. That's where the similarity ends. In their own way, her novels are as harsh and violent as any "tough guy" fiction. This creepy thriller, based on *Tree of Hands,* captures the spirit of her work and her fascination with the darker selfish side of love. The subject matter is potent stuff, a mother's reaction to the death of her child. Benet Archdale (Helen Shaver) is shattered by the unexpected death of her

Firth) is a hustling chauffeur and would-be agent; Carol (Katie Hardie) is the kidnapped boy's less-than-grief-stricken mother; Barry (Paul McGann) really does love the boy and wants to be his father. These characters are perceptively written and acted. Credit to the screenplay by Gordon Williams and director Giles Foster. From its opening image of a stained-glass serpent and apple tree to its conclusion, *Innocent Victim* is unpredictable and unsettling. **AKA:** The Tree of Hands. 🐾🐾🐾

Mature subject matter, profanity, sexual content, some violence.

1990 (R) 100m/C Lauren Bacall, Helen Shaver, Paul McGann, Peter Firth, Kate Hardie; *D:* Giles Foster; *W:* Giles Foster, Gordon Williams. VHS *ACA*

Inside Out

New Yorker Jimmy Morgan (Elliott Gould) is so afraid of the world outside that he refuses to leave his apartment. It's not that big a problem, though. He's so well-heeled that he can afford to have everything he needs brought to him. His only connections with the rest of the world are the telephone and cable TV. Not even his daughter or best friend (Howard Hesseman) can persuade him to take one step outside. But Jimmy has been losing heavily to his bookie and his business partner has started to keep things from him. Agoraphobia is an interesting premise and generally the action isn't too claustrophobic. At the same time, though, Jimmy is such a self-pitying weenie that it's hard to work up much sympathy for him. 🐾🐾

Strong language, drug use, sexual content.

1991 (R) 87m/C Elliott Gould, Jennifer Tilly, Howard Hesseman, Beah Richards, Timothy Scott, Sandy McPeak, Dana Elcar, Meshach Taylor, Nicole Norman; *D:* Robert Taicher; *W:* Robert Taicher. VHS *HMD*

Inside Out

The short films in this anthology are all about sex. That's not surprising; it's a Playboy production. What is surprising is the humor. Despite the advertising, which stresses the *Twilight Zone* quality of some of the films, most of them are really funny. The writing is

young son. She's an American writer living in London. The presence of her half-mad mother Marsha (Lauren Bacall) is little comfort. Just as Benet is beginning to recover, Marsha impulsively kidnaps a blond little boy who resembles the dead child. The premise may sound outlandish but it's no stranger than the daily headlines, and its development...well, that's the point. Overall the acting is excellent. Though Bacall is a little overt at times, Shaver is completely convincing. The secondary characters almost steal the film: Terence (Peter

sharp and there's a strong feminist perspective to the best ones. Viewers looking for the traditional air-brushed Playmate-types will be disappointed. All of these films have the look of high-budget student productions. Most have small casts and only one or two sets. Several have O. Henry endings. The focus is on character. "The Other Half" is a fine through-the-looking-glass story. "The Leda" reworks an s-f concept that's been around for decades. "My Secret Moments" may be the funniest of the bunch and "The Diaries" is certainly the sexiest. 🦴🦴🦴

Contains nudity, strong sexual content.

1992 90m/C D: Lizzie Borden, Adam Friedman, Tony Randel, Richard Shepard, Linda Hassani, Alexander Payne, Jeff Reiner. **VHS, LV** *UND*

Inside Out 2

Second installment in Playboy's anthology series contains nine stories that range in length from seven to 12 minutes. "I've Got a Crush on You" is an inventive one-joke sight gag taken to a wonderful extreme. "There's This Traveling Salesman, See" is, as you might expect, about the title character and the farmer's daughter. "Profiles In Cleavage" is a mock documentary. Using the same techniques that Woody Allen pioneered in *Zelig,* it's the black-and-white biography of stripper Busty Gusty (Kitten Natividad). The film traces her life from her humble beginnings in the 1940s to her professional success and fame—she even dated Albert Einstein—and, of course, her inevitable fall and resurrection as one of America's early feminist heroines. The best and wittiest story is Joe Frank's "The Hitchhiker," a complex shaggy-dog story with a terrific ending. 🦴🦴🦴

Contains nudity, sexual activity, strong language.

1992 (R) 90m/C Francesca "Kitten" Natividad; **D:** Nigel Dick, Martin Donovan, Linda Hassani, Tony Randel, Yuri Sivo, John Wentworth. **VHS, LV** *UND*

Intent to Kill

Despite the dubious distinction of being the first film rated NC-17 for violence, not sex, this is still an off-the-shelf cop picture with a high body count, broad ethnic stereotypes, dozens of onscreen shootings, and well staged action sequences. Traci Lords stars as police detective Vickie Steward, a virtual "Dirty Harriet" who takes no guff from any guy: not her live-in boyfriend, not South American drug gangsters, not date-rapists, not sexual harassers. Before the end of the movie, all of those and several more get their comeuppance from her. Director Charles Kanganis got a spirited performance from his star. She's able to make her aggressive, in-your-face feminism believable. Despite an over reliance on cliches, this one's fast and violent enough to satisfy fans of the genre. 🦴🦴

Violence, strong language. (Also available in a less violent unrated version. Go figure.)

1992 (NC-17) 93m/C Traci Lords, Yaphet Kotto, Kevin Benton, Michael Foley; **D:** Charles Kanganis; **W:** Charles Kanganis. **VHS, LV** *PMH*

Interceptor

Aerial thriller with s-f elements is notable for its slow pace and preposterous plot. Terrorists led by Juergen Prochnow decide to steal two Stealth fighters from a C5-A transport plane while it's in flight. Andrew Divoff is the brave, cardboard fighter jock. Elizabeth Morehead is the transport pilot. The most far-fetched moments are two murders by Perrier and toilet flush, and the hijacking itself. The flying scenes, which seem to have been done largely with models and computer effects, are much better, though they're not going to make anyone forget *Top Gun* or even *Iron Eagle III,* for that matter. 🦴

Violence, strong language.

1992 (R) 92m/C Juergen Prochnow, Andrew Divoff, Elizabeth Morehead; **D:** Michael Cohn; **W:** John Brancato. **VHS, LV** *VMK*

Intervista

Fellini's last film was released on video just a few weeks before he died. It's a fitting and poignant farewell, combining fiction and autobiography with that wry humor Fellini was so famous for. Toward the end there's a

and Bryce Walton has the look and slow pace of a spaghetti Western with cliched dialogue and grotesque characters. The film starts on a low note and goes steadily downhill. The bounty hunter Barstow (Bruce Dern) is the narrator. The first story is about an outlaw (Dylan McDermott) who falls in love with a prostitute (Helen Hunt). The second concerns two women (Mariel Hemingway and Lisa Pelikan) who are trapped in a cabin by a snow storm and a pack of wolves. In the third, Barstow finds his prey. The middle story, potentially the strongest, fails because the two characters are, by turns, unpleasant, boring, and insipid. You'll be pulling for the wolves all the way. More troubling is the way director Sam Pillsbury handles the graphic violence. He seems to be taking sadistic delight in some scenes and that makes the film more than a little sickening. 🦴

Graphic violence, strong language.

1992 (R) 89m/C Bruce Dern, Mariel Hemingway, Helen Hunt, Dylan McDermott, Lisa Pelikan, Andrew (Andy) Robinson; *D:* Sam Pillsbury; *W:* Dick Beebe, Marjorie David, Gordon Dawson. **VHS** *MCA*

Into the Fire

Four-character/one-dog study of lust and murder is basically *Body Heat* in the north woods. We've got young drifter Lee Montgomery, abusive husband Art Hindle, abused and possibly crazy wife Susan Anspach, and sexy waitress Olivia D'Abo, and, of course, the pooch. They're all stuck out in a small snow-covered town and a failing hotel, and by the time everyone's been introduced, we know that some of them are trying to kill the others, and they're all messing where they shouldn't be messing. Director Graeme Campbell does earn some points for sheer guilty-pleasure audacity, but in the end, *Into the Fire* isn't quite as sleazy or nearly as involving as you'd like it to be. 🦴🦴

Brief nudity, sexual content, violence, profanity.

1988 (R) 88m/C *CA* Susan Anspach, Art Hindle, Olivia D'Abo, Lee Montgomery; *D:* Graeme Campbell. **VHS** *LIV, VES*

ALIEN AUTOPSY—FACT OR FICTION? ROBERT DIEDERMANN, A. THOMAS SMITH, AND HANS BACHMAN EXAMINING BURNSIC, THE CORPSE, IN *INVADER*. COURTESY OF JOHN ELLIS.

wonderful moment when Marcello Mastroianni and Anita Ekberg recreate their famous dance in the fountain from *La Dolce Vita.* For fans of "the maestro," that scene is worth the price of a rental all by itself. In Italian with English subtitles. *AKA:* Federico Fellini's Intervista. 🦴🦴🦴

Contains some strong language, sexual references.

1987 108m/C *IT* Marcello Mastroianni, Anita Ekberg, Federico Fellini, Sergio Rubini, Lara Wendell, Antonio Cantafora, Antonella Ponziani, Maurizio Mein, Paola Liguori, Nadia Ottaviani; *D:* Federico Fellini; *W:* Federico Fellini, Gianfranco Angelucci; *C:* Tonino Delli Colli; *M:* Nicola Piovani. **VHS** *TRI*

Into the Badlands

Collection of three short supernatural tales, based on stories by Will Henry, Marcia Muller,

Into the Sun

The aerial footage is the key to this acceptable little time-waster. The leads do fair work with thin roles, and some of the humor has a fine edge. Anthony Michael Hall plays an overbearing, none too bright actor who hangs around with a real fighter jock Michael Pare to research an upcoming role. Fans have seen worse and much better. 𝄞𝄞♪

Violence and language.

1992 **(R)** 101m/C Anthony Michael Hall, Michael Pare, Terry Kiser, Deborah Maria Moore; *D:* Fritz Kiersch; *W:* John Brancato. **VHS, LV** *VMK*

Invader

In the Virginia countryside, one group of soldiers inexplicably massacres another. McCall (Hans Bachman), a reporter for a sleazy tabloid is sent to find (or to invent) a story about UFOs and Martians. But he and army investigator Harry Anders (A. Thomas Smith) find that there is something to the nutty theory. In some respects, this is a B-movie that could have been made in the 1950s. It's an imaginative story with a strong streak of humor, often tongue in cheek. At the same time, the script has rough spots, the acting isn't all that it might be, and the special effects aren't consistent. Still, as any fan knows, those come with the territory. Bachman and Smith do good work in the leads and the important effects involving a Stealth fighter and stop-motion models are fine. 𝄞𝄞♪

Strong language, some violence.

1991 **(R)** 95m/C Hans Bachman, A. Thomas Smith, Rich Foucheux, John Cooke, Robert Diedermann, Allison Sheehy, Ralph Bluemke; *D:* Phillip Cook. **VHS, LV** *VMK*

Iron Maze

Gimmicky tale with international implications is set in a dying Pennsylvania steel town near Pittsburgh. It looks like Barry (Jeff Fahey) has killed Sugita (Hiroaki Murakami). It might be because the wealthy Japanese man had plans to turn the empty steel mill into a theme park, or perhaps Barry's affair with Sugita's wife (Bridget Fonda) was behind it. In a long series of contradictory flashbacks, the sheriff (J.T. Walsh) slowly learns what really happened. It's a device that wears thin before it should, but the characters are intriguing throughout. Fahey is a convincing Springsteenian hero. Murakami is equally sympathetic, and Walsh, a character actor who usually plays heavies, does very good work. Writer/director Hiroaki Yoshida captures the sense and gritty feel of the place well, too. 𝄞𝄞♪

Violence, strong language, sexual content.

1991 **(R)** 102m/C Jeff Fahey, Bridget Fonda, Hiroaki Murakami, J.T. Walsh, Gabriel Damon, John Randolph, Peter Allas; *D:* Hiroaki Yoshida; *W:* Tim Metcalfe. **VHS, LV** *ACA*

Irresistible Impulse

Jag Mundhra has made a name for himself with "erotic thrillers," some very good, some routine. *Irresistible Impulse, Tainted Love,* and *Twisted Passion* were economically made back to back to back with overlapping casts. Only *Irresistible Impulse* adds anything to the genre. It's a loosely wrapped story of a sleazy real estate agent (Doug Jeffrey) who allows himself to be entangled in a wild scam with femme fatale Lee Anne Beaman who, in *Tainted Love,* is a tough cop looking for a serial killer who may be rich guy Jeffrey who, in *Twisted Passion* is a cop who arrests a psycho. *Tainted* and *Twisted* depend on uninspired cliches. *Irresistible* has several surprises and is well-photographed by Howard Wexler. 𝄞𝄞𝄞

Sexual scenes, nudity, violence, strong language.

1995 107m/C Doug Jeffrey, Lee Anne Beaman, Kathy Shower; *D:* Jag Mundhra. **VHS** *YHV*

Istanbul

The location and the characters are the best part of this poorly constructed thriller. The muddled plot concerns two tourists (Timothy Bottoms and Twiggy) who visit Istanbul with their daughters. It has something to do with a videotape in their possession. Several key coincidences seem to be involved too, but I have to admit that I never figured it all out. The story is almost half over before you learn

> *"For someone who doesn't watch a lot of films, I have a deep love and passion for them."*
>
> —ANTHONY MICHAEL HALL, STAR OF *INTO THE SUN*.

how some of the major characters are related to each other. That's realistic enough—though dramatically flawed—and for the most part, the characters act believably. The slightly seedy but exotic quality of the city makes it an effective setting. This one's interesting and different, in both the good and bad senses of the words. *AKA:* Istanbul, Keep Your Eyes Open. 🎞🎞

Mature subject matter, profanity, some violence.

1990 (PG-13) 88m/C *TU SW* Robert Morley, Timothy Bottoms, Twiggy; *D:* Mats Arehn. **VHS, LV** *IME*

Jack and Sarah

From the box art to the casting to the story, it's obvious that the producers of *Jack and Sarah* were hoping to recreate the success of *Four Weddings and a Funeral.* But that elusive cinematic chemistry has to begin with a solid script, and this film has one big strike against it. The subject is death and grieving, and the approach is sometimes comic, sometimes dramatic, sometimes uncomfortable. Jack's (Richard E. Grant) wife (Imogen Stubbs) dies giving birth to their daughter Sarah. He falls into drunken depression, unable to have anything to do with the baby or his half-renovated London townhouse. Before long, of course, he comes around and hires Amy (Samantha Mathis), an enthusiastic but completely inexperienced nanny. That side of the story contains few surprises, and the baby stuff is equally familiar. The saving grace is another brilliant supporting performance from Sir Ian McKellen as William, an unexpectedly versatile alcoholic. Overall, writer/director Tim Sullivan got good performances from an able cast. Combined with the London locations, they give the film an undeniable attractiveness. And despite the formulaic nature of the material, it's enjoyable enough to earn a qualified recommendation. 🎞🎞🎞

Mature subject matter, strong language.

1996 (R) 110m/C *GB* Richard E. Grant, Samantha Mathis, Ian McKellen, Judi Dench, Cherie Lunghi, Eileen Atkins, Imogen Stubbs; *D:* Tim Sullivan; *W:* Tim Sullivan; *C:* Jean-Yves Escoffier; *M:* Simon Boswell. **VHS** *PGV*

Jack Be Nimble

Gothic horror tale from New Zealand has been properly compared to Stephen King's work and to *Heavenly Creatures,* though it's much darker and more frightening. Jack (Alexis Arquette) and his sister Dora (Sarah Smuts-Kennedy) are taken from their parents as children and raised in separate homes. She goes to middle-class suburbia; he winds up in a rural hellhole more intense and vividly realized than anything that's come out of Hollywood recently. His tortured upbringing there turns him into a rebellious, unstable young man who's driven to find his lost sister. By then she has begun an affair with Teddy (Bruno Lawrence), who understands her on an unusually sympathetic level. And that is all anyone should know about the plot. The story is told through grim, grainy images. Though the film is violent, it's not particularly explicit. It doesn't need to be. A single scene of believable domestic violence can be much more powerful than all the pyrotechnics in a summer blockbuster. Garth Maxwell is an imaginative filmmaker who really knows what he's doing. Despite its obviously limited budget, the film is strong stuff, building to an unpredictable finish that's not for everyone. 🎞🎞🎞🎞

Mature subject matter, some violence, brief nudity, sexual material.

1994 (R) 93m/C *NZ* Alexis Arquette, Sarah Kennedy, Bruno Lawrence; *D:* Garth Maxwell; *W:* Garth Maxwell; *M:* Chris Neal. **VHS** *TRI*

Jack-O

The video equivalent of a suburban Halloween spook house is a low-budget horror comedy that emphasizes laughs over scares. And like any good spook house, it's also a loving evocation of the season. The opening nursery rhyme, "Mr. Jack will break your back and cut off your head with a whack, whack, whack" sets the tone. The bloody effects are about the least realistic you'll ever see, and the hoary plot revolves around a warlock who's resurrected as a pumpkin-headed slasher. Young Ryan Latshaw is fine as the trick-or-treating hero. He shares the screen with a host of horror veterans led by John Carradine and Cameron Mitchell (appearing posthumously in recycled footage), Dawn Wildsmith, Linnea Quigley, and Brinke Stevens, who ham it up happily. If it weren't for one long and deliberately gratuitous shower scene, this one would be recommended for kids. Instead, it's aimed more at nostalgic drive-in fans. 🦴🦴🦴

Silly violence, brief nudity, strong language.

1995 (R) 90m/C Linnea Quigley, Ryan Latshaw, Cameron Mitchell, John Carradine, Dawn Wildsmith, Brinke Stevens; **D:** Steve Latshaw. **VHS, LV** *TRI, IME*

Jailbait

Teenager Renee Humphrey runs away to the mean streets of L.A. Young vice cop C. Thomas Howell tries to save her from herself. Half the story is about a poorly defined "white slave" operation and is too ridiculous to comment on. But the film also takes a coldly realistic look at a kid's life on the streets—eating out of dumpsters, women urinating on the sidewalk. That part's meant to be frightening and it is. Also available in an unrated version. 🦴🦴🦴

Mature subject matter, sexual content, strong language, brief nudity, mild violence.

1993 (R) 100m/C C. Thomas Howell, Renee Humphrey; **D:** Rafal Zielinski; **W:** Robert Vincent O'Neil. **VHS** *PAR*

Jamon, Jamon

Earthy, bawdy story of young lovers Penelope Cruz and Jordi Molla has a bright satiric streak that shows up at the most surprising times. And the ending is so unexpected and so offbeat that it's almost a comic tragedy. When Cruz becomes pregnant, Molla's mom hires a mercenary hunka-hunka burnin' funk to seduce the girl away from her little boy. Of course, nothing works out exactly as planned. But writer/director Bigas Luna is up to something more than a conventional sex farce. An undercurrent of social commentary often rises to the surface, though the film is not overtly political. Despite the cultural differences, it's easy to imagine the same story being set in this country—in the rural South or the rustbelt North. It would be more difficult, if not impossible, to translate Luna's ribald barnyard humor and that's the most enjoyable part of the film. Also, sound is important to the film, and the stereo reproduction on this tape is exceptional. Also available in an unrated version. **AKA:** Ham Ham. 🦴🦴🦴

Nudity, strong language, sexual content and humor, comic violence, and lots of other stuff.

1993 95m/C *SP* Penelope Cruz, Anna Galiena, Javier Bardem, Stefania Sandrelli, Juan Diego, Jordi Molla; **D:** Bigas Luna; **W:** Bigas Luna, Cuca Canals; **M:** Nicola Piovani. **VHS, LV** *ACA*

Jefferson in Paris

Bloated bio-vid is slow, long, humorless, poorly acted, overinflated with self-importance and—worst of all—BOR-INNNG! Of its many problems, the most obvious is the casting of Nick Nolte as Thomas Jefferson. True, he bears a slight physical resemblance to Jefferson and his performance is about as stiff, lifeless, and bland as many statues of the author of the Declaration of Independence. When Nolte speaks, you sense that he's stepping up onto an imaginary pedestal. After a pointless introduction, the setting shifts to Paris, 1784-1789, when Jefferson was ambassador to France. Though that was one of the most eventful moments in world history, virtually nothing happens in the film. While countries are being born and teetering on the brink of revolution, Jefferson worries about his daughter's (Gwyneth Paltrow) religious beliefs and his unconsummated relationship with Greta Scacchi, another diplomat's wife. As Sally Hemmings, the slave some claim had children by Jefferson, Thandie Newton is simply appalling. She seems to have based her florid performance on Butterfly McQueen in *Gone with the Wind*. The rest of the cast wanders through a forest of accents—American South, French, English, Italian—picking one or more as it suits. WOOF!

Mature subject matter.

1994 (PG-13) 139m/C Nick Nolte, Greta Scacchi, Gwyneth Paltrow, Thandie Newton, Jean-Pierre Aumont, Seth Gilliam, Todd Boyce, James Earl Jones; **D:** James Ivory; **W:** Ruth Prawer Jhabvala; **M:** Richard Robbins. **VHS, LV** *TOU*

Jekyll and Hyde

Tepid retelling of Stevenson's famous story never gets to the heart of it. Michael Caine plays the good doctor and his brutal alter-ego. The first part of the film follows the familiar plot, but it twists when he falls in love with his sister-in-law (Cheryl Ladd). Then for a time, the film focuses on Victorian values and mores, complete with egregious overacting from all concerned. When it returns to Mr. Hyde, the film becomes a standard mid-budget monster flick with a surprise ending that's no surprise. The transformation effects are nothing special, and the Hyde makeup is about the same. He looks like a lumpy onion with a bad attitude. In her own way, Ladd doesn't fare much better. She has to wear a bustle that is truly remarkable. Hit the pause button when that astonishing appendage appears. 🎬🎬

Mature subject matter, violence, sexual content.

1990 (R) 100m/C Michael Caine, Cheryl Ladd, Joss Ackland, Ronald Pickup, Kim Thomson, Lionel Jeffries, Kevin McNally, Lee Montague; *D:* David Wickes; *W:* David Wickes. **VHS** *VMK*

Jezebel's Kiss

Like *Wild Orchid,* this is a grandly atrocious guilty pleasure. Katherine Barrese, the titular heroine and possibly an amnesiac, unlocks the guilty secrets in a small town's past. Malcolm McDowell's hammy overacting as an unscrupulous land developer is indescribable, and his big bedroom scene is the film's strangest moment. Naked, he is as pink and plump as a huge boiled shrimp. 🎬🎬🎬 **GPI: 7.5**

Sexual activity, brief nudity, violence, strong language.

1990 (R) 96m/C Meg Foster, Malcolm McDowell, Meredith Baxter, Everett McGill, Katherine Barrese; *D:* Harvey Keith; *W:* Harvey Keith. **VHS, LV** *COL*

Joey Breaker

From his slicked-back Pat Reilly hair and Italian suits to his unshakable self-confidence, Joey (Richard Edson) is a deal-maker. He's an entertainment agent, an operator; take away his phone and you'd kill him. When Joey has to meet people face to face, things get a little trickier. At first, it appears that Joey wouldn't know a real emotion if it bit him. At the same time, he's so transparent in his insincerity that there's a certain honesty to his character. The film is at its best when Joey is at work. Writer/director/co-producer Steven Starr was an agent with William Morris in New York, so many of the details have that unmistakable ring of reality. The game playing, the calculated deal making, the setbacks and repositioning—that's an agent's life. When Joey "gets religion," as it were, he's not nearly as interesting a character. Most of the film is an enjoyable glimpse into a world that most of us will never know. Starr manages to de-glamorize the entertainment business without trashing it, as so many "behind the scenes" stories do. No, this movie isn't as deep, as slick, or as angry as *The Player,* but it's certainly as entertaining. 🎬🎬🎬

Strong language.

1993 (R) 92m/C Richard Edson, Cedella Marley, Erik King, Gina Gershon, Philip S. Hoffman, Fred Fondren; *D:* Steven Starr; *W:* Steven Starr; *M:* Paul Aston. **VHS** *PAR, FCT*

Johnny 100 Pesos

It's easy to compare Gustavo Graef Marino's fact based crime film to *Dog Day Afternoon,* but the Chilean production is a genuine original. It takes such neat, unexpected twists that almost any synopsis would be a mistake. Let's just say that it concerns a botched robbery and leave it at that. The main characters are young Johnny Garcia (Armando Araiza) and Glorita (Patricia Rivera), a sexy older woman. The first act could be used as a textbook example for the establishment of character and conflict. Director/co-writer Graef-Marino sets things up brilliantly without a single false step. Then when the initial suspense fades, he expands the scope of the film to include a realistic political dimension. At the same time, he punches up the action with dry, ribald humor. 🎬🎬🎬

Strong subject matter, strong language (subtitled), sexual content, brief nudity.

1996 (R) 95m/C Armando Araiza, Patricia Rivera, Willy Semler, Sergio Hernandez; *D:* Gustavo Graef-Marino; *W:* Gustavo Graef-Marino, Gerardo Caceres; *C:* Jose Luis Arredondo; *M:* Andres Pollak. **VHS** *FXL*

The Josephine Baker Story

At a low point near the end of her long life, Josephine (Lynn Whitfield) writes a confessional letter to her many adopted children, trying to explain and make sense of her eventful life: her tumultuous loves, the fortunes earned and lost (for a time she was the richest black woman in the world), and her life-long fight against racial prejudice. Born to a poor family in St. Louis, 1906, she is a natural performer. Her humor and vitality lead her to success in vaudeville. Like so many American artists and performers in the 1920s, she goes to France and finds a new world. "The first time a white waiter served me and called me 'Ma'am,' I nearly died," she says. "I fell in love with Paris that day." She becomes a sensation with the famous (or infamous) topless "Banana Dance." But her career is really based on her bright personality, humor, and the indefinable "presence" of a true star. Whitfield and director Brian Gibson capture that side of the woman without sugarcoating her. Josephine Baker is impulsive, ambitious, and sometimes self-destructive. She's also generous, loving, and impractical. The script is cliched and stilted at times, but the compelling story and performances overcome the rough spots. This one's a rare treat. If the times and the subject are of any interest, don't miss it. ✐✐✐✐

Brief nudity, strong language.

1990 **(R)** 129m/**C** Lynn Whitfield, Ruben Blades, David Dukes, Craig T. Nelson, Louis Gossett Jr., Kene Holliday, Vivian Bonnell; **D:** Brian Gibson; **M:** Ralph Burns. Emmy Awards '91: Best Actress (Whitfield), Best Director (Gibson). **VHS** *HBO, FCT*

The Journey of August King

Some spectacular North Carolina mountain scenery easily upstages a wooden cast and a

PATRICIA RIVERA AND ARMANDO ARAIZA IN *JOHNNY 100 PESOS.* ©FOX LORBER HOME VIDEO.

> **"I**n Hong Kong, everybody knows me at the censorship board* and they give me a lot of respect. They also realize that my kind of action and violence is very artistic. So if there's any problem with a certain scene, they'll give me a certain point where to cut. They're also concerned about doing the cut without hurting the movie. For example, in a certain scene if a character kills a guy with ten bullets, well, the censor will ask me, 'John, if you could cut out three bullets...,' or in another scene if you could cut down the sound effects.' "
>
> *—*JOHN WOO, DIRECTOR OF *THE KILLER*

slowly paced story in this historical drama. In 1815, the title character (Jason Patric) is a young widower who helps a runaway slave (Thandie Newton) elude her obsessed owner (Larry Drake). The pace is slow, and while the accents and phrasings may be historically accurate, they're still off-putting. Australian director John Duigan seems emotionally distant from the material, and the performances are impenetrably self-absorbed. *JV*

Violence, mature subject matter.

1995 (PG-13) 91m/C Jason Patric, Thandie Newton, Larry Drake, Sam Waterston; *D:* John Duigan; *W:* John Ehle; *C:* Slawomir Idziak; *M:* Stephen Endelman. **VHS, LV** *TOU*

Judge

Imaginative Japanimation posits divine retribution for human crimes. And if supernatural forces are going to go into the courtroom, then there have to be metaphysical lawyers. The key players are a treacherous corporate executive, an unassuming office worker who can transform himself into a magical creature, and the New-Age ambulance chaser who represents the latter before the former. The animation is on a par with the rest of the genre, and beyond the quirky premise, so is the telling of the story. In Japanese with English subtitles. *JJ*

Violence, strong language, some sexual material.

1991 50m/C JP *D:* Hiroshi Negishi. **VHS** *CPM*

Jungleground

Wrestler Roddy Piper is a cop who's forced by a drug gang to make his way across an urban wasteland before dawn. If he doesn't, they kill his girlfriend (Torri Higginson). It's a variation on Walter Hill's fine action film, *The Warriors,* with inventiveness, colorful characters, and humor. Even in the quieter moments, Piper seems at ease—that's a trick that other action stars, such as Arnold and Jean-Claude, haven't completely mastered—and in one nice bit of comic business, he even manages a fine Elmer Fudd imitation. *JJJ*

Violence, strong language.

1995 (R) 90m/C Roddy Piper, Torri Higginson, Peter Williams; *D:* Don Allan; *W:* Michael Stokes. **VHS, LV** *TRI*

Kill Me Again

As soon as the credits start to roll, William Olvis' simple music sets a strong *Body Heat* mood and the rest of the film lives up to it. The key elements are sketched in quickly: Faye (Joanne Whalley-Kilmer), an impetuous, greedy young woman; Vince (Michael Madsen), her unstable lover; and Jack Andrews (Val Kilmer), a Reno private detective who's no smarter than he absolutely has to be. At the center of the triangle is a stolen briefcase full of money. The story is properly complicated and filled with unexpected turns, though fans may see the conclusion coming. That's a minor quibble, though. Director John Dahl has a strong visual sense, capturing the seedier side of Reno and the stark beauty of the high mountains. Latter-day James M. Cain material at its best. *JJJ*

Violence, profanity, sexual material.

1989 (R) 93m/C Val Kilmer, Joanne Whalley, Michael Madsen, Jonathan Gries, Bibi Besch; *D:* John Dahl; *W:* John Dahl, David Warfield; *M:* William Olvis. **VHS** *MGM*

The Killer

In a beautiful candlelit Catholic church, hitman Jeff (Chow Yun-Fat) accepts a contract from the local Hong Kong mob. When his contact asks if he believes in God, Jeff answers in a dreamy voice, "I've seen no evidence, but I like the peace in here." Cut from that elegiac beginning to one of the most violent (and inventive) shoot-outs ever put on film, and director John Woo is off on a wild cerebral action film that has won legions of fans. Jeff accomplishes his job, and in the process, blinds a beautiful young singer, Jenny (Sally Yeh). He becomes obsessed by her condition and his own guilt. At the same time, though, his employers are betraying him, and a dedicated policeman (Danny Lee) is hot on his trail. The rest of the plot careens along like a runaway truck. The big scenes make *Lethal Weapon* look like *The Care Bears*, but this isn't an exercise in mindless violence. It's a story about friendship, loyalty, platonic love, and religious faith. With lots of automatic weapons and a hundred or so onscreen shootings. The tape version is available in both dubbed and subtitled editions; the Criterion laserdisc is formatted in the original widescreen image. It also contains commentary by Woo, and several extra features devoted to Hong Kong action movies and stars. Available in English-language and subtitled versions. **AKA:** Die Xue Shuang Xiong. 🦴🦴🦴🦴

Contains graphic violence, strong language.

1990 (R) 110m/C *HK* Chow Yun-Fat, Sally Yeh, Danny Lee, Kenneth Tsang, Chu Kong; **D:** John Woo; **W:** John Woo. **VHS, LV** *FXL, RTV, FCT*

Killer Inside Me

Deputy Lou Ford (Stacy Keach) knows that his small Montana town is corrupt, and that the rich mine owner runs things, but he works within the system to change it and to keep the peace. As the film unfolds, we come to understand that Ford is troubled and, as seen through flashbacks, the dimensions of his illness keep growing. Keach is an undervalued actor and this is one of his most effective and controlled performances. Based on a Jim Thompson novel. 🦴🦴🦴

Mature subject matter, violence, sexual material, strong language.

1976 (R) 99m/C Stacy Keach, Susan Tyrrell, Tisha Sterling, Keenan Wynn, John Dehner, John Carradine, Don Stroud; **D:** Burt Kennedy; **W:** Robert Chandlee. **VHS** *WAR*

Killer Looks

To spice up the marriage, Phil (Michael Artura) has his wife Diane (Sara Suzanne Brown) tease and lead on strange men. When she has these guys right where she wants them, he interrupts, pretending to be the outraged husband. Then they run into Mickey (Len Donato), who's more than willing to play by their rules. At the same time, Phil wants to go farther. If the filmmakers had stuck with that idea and followed those three characters (and their obsessions), this might have been a four-bone wonder. For the most part, the acting and production values are excellent, and the first half of the story generates some suspense. Unfortunately, the film gets sidetracked with irrelevant soft-core fantasy stuff involving glamorous lesbians and the like. At their worst, those scenes verge on unintentional comedy and the whole thing runs out of steam well before the story is over. So it goes. Also available in an unrated version at 97 minutes. 🦴🦴

GPI: 9.1

Sexual content, nudity, strong language, some violence.

1994 (R) 87m/C Michael Artura, Sara Suzanne Brown, Len Donato; **D:** Toby Phillips. **VHS, LV** *IMP*

Killing for Love

"A group of film people get trapped in the mountains. They get naked and they get dead." From that self-synopsis, you can tell that *A Killing for Love* is a video rehash of Agatha Christie's oft-filmed *Ten Little Indians*. This one has more plot than most and it's well photographed by Howard Wexler. Also available in an unrated version at 90 minutes. 🦴🦴

Sexual material, nudity, violence, strong language.

1995 (R) 81m/C Jay Richardson, Alex Demir, Lisa Haslehurst, Brandy Sanders; **D:** Mike Kesey; **W:** H.M. Johnson. **VHS** *ORI*

King of New York

Ultra-violent gangster story begins with Frank White's (Christopher Walken) release from prison and follows his rise back to the top of the underworld heap, and, naturally, his fall.

The action is stylish and slow throughout, and the big scenes have the unrealistic visual quality of a music video. The main attraction here is Walken's performance. It's one of his most bizarre and that's about as bizarre as you'll ever want to see. The film also faithfully obeys Rule # 1 of the gangster movie: any character making a call from a public phone will be killed while in the booth. 𝄞𝄞𝄞

Raw language, graphic and bloody violence, and brief nudity.

1990 (R) 106m/C Christopher Walken, Laurence "Larry" Fishburne, David Caruso, Victor Argo, Wesley Snipes, Janet Julian, Joey Chin, Giancarlo Esposito, Steve Buscemi; **D:** Abel Ferrara; **W:** Nicholas St. John; **C:** Bojan Bazelli; **M:** Joe Delia. **VHS, LV** *LIV*

King of the Hill

Steven Soderbergh has turned A.E. Hotchner's memoir of growing up in the 1930s into a film that's nostalgic but never sentimental. His polished evocation of the time is first-rate, but the real spark is young Jesse Bradford who does masterful work in the lead. He's 12-year-old Aaron Kurlander, who's doing all he can to hold his family together during the dark days of Depression-era St. Louis. His father (Jeroen Krabbe) is something of a dreamer who has trouble holding onto a job. His mother's (Lisa Eichhorn) illness has put more strains on the family, so they've had to send his younger brother Sullivan (Cameron Boyd) to live with relatives. Aaron finds himself on his own at a residential hotel. He's an imaginative, resourceful young man, and he's got his hero Lester (Adrien Brody), a bold Jewish radical, to look after him. Across the hall there's Mr. Mungo (Spalding Gray), whose liaisons with Lydia (Elizabeth McGovern) introduce Aaron to the mysteries of sex. Don't miss Aaron's introductory essay, the marbles game, the bellboy's (Joseph Chrest) routine with a match, and a wonderful scene when Lester and Aaron save a car. Cliff Martinez's terrific score brings it all together. Look for this one. It's one of the best bets in your video store. 𝄞𝄞𝄞𝄞

Strong language, some violence.

1993 (PG-13) 102m/C Jesse Bradford, Jeroen Krabbe, Lisa Eichhorn, Karen Allen, Spalding Gray, Elizabeth McGovern, Joseph Chrest, Adrien Brody, Cameron Boyd, Chris Samples, Katherine

Heigl, Amber Benson, John McConnell, Ron Vawter, John Durbin, Lauryn Hill, David Jensen; **D:** Steven Soderbergh; **W:** Steven Soderbergh; **M:** Cliff Martinez. Nominations: Cannes Film Festival '93: Best Film. **VHS, LV** *MCA*

Kiss Daddy Goodnight

Uma Thurman is the main attraction in this impoverished low-budget thriller. She plays a young woman who poses as a prostitute. She picks up men in bars, goes home with them, spikes their drinks, and robs them. Her friend (Paul Dillon) has returned to New York and is trying to find another old friend to start a band. Their two stories eventually meander to a mutually flat conclusion. The action is underlit, dark, and ugly; the acting is amateurish; the soundtrack is discordant and much of the dialogue is unintelligible. Is this art or incompetence? It's hard to say and not really worth the effort. **WOOF!**

Violence, profanity, sexual situations.

1987 (R) 89m/C *DK* Uma Thurman, Paul Dillon, Paul Richards, David Brisbin; **D:** P.I. Huemer; **C:** Bobby Bukowski. **VHS** *ACA*

Kiss Me a Killer

Contemporary Latino retelling of *The Postman Always Rings Twice* isn't as intense as the original. The key elements are an older guy who owns a bar, his younger (and ambitious) wife, and the musician who plays there and brings them more business. Do you need to know any more? 𝄞𝄞

Mature subject matter, brief nudity.

1991 (R) 91m/C Julie Carmen, Robert Beltran, Guy Boyd, Ramon Franco, Charles Boswell; **D:** Marcus De Leon; **W:** Marcus De Leon. **VHS, LV** *COL*

Kiss Me Deadly

Reviewers and critics are supposed to love this cult rarity. The French New Wave guys went ga-ga over it, and it's quoted in *Pulp Fiction*, but I've always had problems with it. First, what does the title mean? In context, what is "deadly"? An appellation or an adverb? Should we read it along the lines of *Kiss Me Sweetly* or *Kiss Me, Fred*? The lack of a comma would indicate the former but neither interpretation makes much sense. And that, at least, is completely appropriate. Robert Aldrich's 1955 adaptation has almost nothing to do with Mickey Spillane's novel. By turns, the film is overstated, overacted, overdirected, and senseless. It's stylishly photographed throughout, and the sets and costumes are fine examples of '50s kitsch. The loosely woven plot involves a woman on the run from an asylum. Mike Hammer (Ralph Meeker) gives her a lift but can't save her when her pursuers catch them. Before it's over, most of the genre's cliches—booby trapped cars, mysterious keys, treacherous blondes, etc.—have been trotted out, but they're not meant to be taken seriously. The tongue-in-cheek ending proves that. Looking back on the film now, it's interesting to note that it predicts answering machines, aerobic exercise, and phone sex. Still, for my money, *Kiss Me Deadly* is nothing more than an interesting curiosity. Watchable as it often is—and it plays well on video—the whole is still considerably less than the sum of the parts. 🔪🔪🔪

Contains some violence.

1955 105m/B Ralph Meeker, Albert Dekker, Paul Stewart, Wesley Addy, Cloris Leachman, Strother Martin, Marjorie Bennett, Jack Elam; *D:* Robert Aldrich; *C:* Ernest Laszlo. **VHS, LV** *MGM, FCT*

Kiss Me, Stupid!

Many fans looked forward to this "lost" Billy Wilder comedy for a long time. The film had only a limited theatrical release when it was made in 1964. The critics dismissed it, and it disappeared quickly. But over the years, it developed a sort of phantom reputation for being racy and risque. A few people said it had been unjustly slighted and no one could argue because hardly anyone had seen it. Most of Wilder's other work came to home video quickly, but *Kiss Me, Stupid* stayed on the shelf. Unfortunately, the critics were right. This one is virtually unwatchable. Dean Martin plays himself, sort of, at his smarmiest. He's Dino, a Las Vegas lounge lizard, who stops for gas and cigarettes in the little town of Climax—yeah, right—home to struggling song writers Orville (Ray Walston) and Barney

(Cliff Osmond). They sabotage Dino's car so he'll have to spend the night and listen to their stuff, but they have to keep him away from Orville's wife (Felicia Farr). To do that, they pay the town "cocktail waitress" Polly (Kim Novak) to impersonate her and keep Dino occupied. From that less-than-scintillating premise, the story, based on a play, dissolves steadily and slowly, very very slowly. This bow-wow is more than two hours long. The muddy black-and-white photography doesn't make it move any faster. As for racy and risque, imagine a tame episode of *Married...With Children*. **WOOF!**

Mature subject matter.

1964 (PG-13) 126m/B Dean Martin, Kim Novak, Ray Walston, Felicia Farr, Cliff Osmond, Barbara Pepper, Doro Merande, Howard McNear, Henry Gibson, John Fiedler, Mel Blanc; *D:* Billy Wilder; *W:* Billy Wilder, I.A.L. Diamond; *C:* Joseph LaShelle; *M:* Andre Previn. **VHS, LV** *MGM*

Knock Outs

New low for cheap exploitation is so poorly made that it's unwatchable without liberal use of the fast-forward button. The plot has to do with a sleazy photographer and the ongoing conflicts between a sorority and a gang of bike babes. Sounds like fun, doesn't it? But bad non-acting, grainy shot-on-video images, and wall-to-wall ineptitude on both sides of the camcorder undermine any cheap thrills. You really don't want to know how bad it is. **WOOF! GPI: 2.1**

Nudity, sexual subject matter, some strong language.

1992 90m/C Chona Jackson, Cindy Rome, Brad Zutaut, Leigh Betchley; *D:* John Bowen. **VHS** *HMD*

Kovacs!

Some of these clips from Ernie Kovacs' TV routines are a little slow, some are rough and grainy, but all of them are worth seeing again. Jokes, concepts, and bits of business that he thought up have been recycled countless times on *Rowan and Martin's Laugh In, Saturday Night Live*, MTV, and *The Benny Hill Show*. His influence can even be seen in Steven Spielberg's *Close Encounters of the Third Kind*

Letterboxing

Letterboxing has become the subject of some controversy in the ongoing evolution of home video.

For those unfamiliar with the term, letterboxing is one method by which widescreen theatrical films are made to fit the squarish dimensions of a TV screen. The roots of the issue go back to the 1950s when Hollywood studios, threatened by the sudden popularity of network television, came up with CinemaScope and other widescreen formats to compete.

It was a logical response. Early TV broadcasts were black and white, small, and fuzzy. By contrast, movies became larger than life. The width-to-height ratio of a TV screen was (and still is) approximately 1:1. A CinemaScope image is 2.55:1 or 2.35:1, depending on the type of sound used. Today, most films are made with Panavision equipment, which, while not as extreme as CinemaScope, is still wider than a TV screen.

There are four ways to fit one of these films on a TV screen:

(1) Squeeze the picture. This method is often employed during the opening credits. In many cases, you won't notice it, but if there's action behind the words, you'll see it. Take a look at the first few minutes of *Where Eagles Dare* and watch the cast and credits scroll up over an impossibly square airplane.

(2) Cut off the edges. In making the transfer from 35mm or 70mm film to video, keep the focus on the middle of the image. That's why you often miss Alfred Hitchcock's appearance in *To Catch a Thief.* He's sitting on the bus beside Cary Grant, but he's not close enough to the center of the frame.

(3) Pan and scan. During the transfer, an editor follows the most important part of the action by shifting the focus of the video image. That's what's done with most films and it usually gets the necessary visual information across, but not always. In *Silverado,* only one of the participants in the climactic gunfight is visible.

(4) Letterbox the image. Place horizontal strips of black or gray at the top and bottom of the screen, shrinking the overall size of the original image but remaining faithful to the dimensions.

Until recently, letterboxing has been rare, but that's changing. Letterboxing has become the prestige format for film-to-video conversion.

Some films, *North by Northwest* for example, are available in both letterboxed and pan-and-scan versions. Further confusing the issue, some films, like *Inside Daisy Clover,* are strictly letterboxed to the 2.55:1 ratio while others, like John Wayne's *The Alamo* are only slightly boxed, with narrow strips at the top and bottom of the screen. All tapes and discs that use the process will state "letterboxed" or "widescreen edition" somewhere on the front of the box or sleeve.

But what does letterboxing mean to the video audience?

For most movies, not much. Let's face it; most of the stuff that shows up in theatres and on video is junk. Some of it's good junk, but it's still junk, and letterboxing doesn't change that. How much, after all, are we missing by not seeing the pristine original of *Flashdance*?

But a good film—made by someone who uses the whole frame to tell the story—does lose something. The pan-and-scan *Lawrence of Arabia* isn't as strong as the letterboxed version, and neither can compete with the theatrical experience.

For the individual viewer, it boils down to screen size. Don't try to watch a strictly letterboxed film on a 13" portable; your mother told you not to sit that close to the screen. With a larger set, though the difference is still noticeable, the picture is watchable. And genuinely good films do deserve the best treatment available.

In the end, the question is: What are you asking of your home video equipment? If you're trying to create a "home theatre," letterboxed tapes and discs are worth your attention. Particularly on laserdisc, they are the clearest and most carefully handled transfer from film to video.

But if you use home video as inexpensive, convenient entertainment, letterboxing probably won't do much for you (and the kids will hate it).

and Woody Allen's *Zelig*. All of the most famous moments are included: the Nairobi Trio, commercial parodies, the bathtub bits, the Dutch Masters ads, Kovacs' version of the "1812 Overture," and of course the gravity-defying table. A few of the funniest parts will be familiar to only the most devoted fan. The martini-swilling, ad-libbing poet Percy Dovetonsils is wonderful, and the sight of ballet dancers performing Swan Lake in gorilla suits and tutus is beyond description. 🗡🗡🗡

Contains no objectionable material.

1971 85m/C Ernie Kovacs. **VHS** *RHI, OM*

Kung Fu Rascals

Slapstick comedy is aimed squarely at martial arts fans. Filmmaker Steve Wang (star/writer/producer/editor/director, etc.) worked with an extremely low budget and made every penny count. Most of the film is run-of-the-mill, juvenile martial action, but it ends with a long special effects sequence that's just astonishing. Our three heroes—Chen (Wang), Lao Zo (Troy Fronin), and Repo (Johnnie Saiko Espiritu)—are young warriors who are closer to Larry, Mo, and Curly than Bruce Lee. They've stolen a treasure map to "the power most big" from the evil Bamboo Man. He has dispatched his porcine henchman Raspmutant, the Mad Monk, to get it back. When all else fails, Bamboo summons the giant Nio-Titan. That's where the film becomes so inventive. Nio-Titan is a ponderous stone giant who's almost as impressive as Talos, the bronze man in Ray Harryhausen's *Jason and the Argonauts*. But Wang couldn't afford stop-motion animation effects. Instead, he used a man (Ed Yang) in costume, unusual lenses, and forced perspective to create the illusion that Nio-Titan is 30 feet tall. Even when you know the tricks, it works. As for the rest of the film, it's made for a young audience, with lots of "schwing" sound effects and potty jokes. 🗡🗡🗡

Comic violence, juvenile bathroom humor.

199? (PG-13) 90m/C Troy Fronin, Johnnie Saiko Espiritu, Steve Wang, Edward Yang; *D:* Steve Wang; *W:* Steve Wang. **VHS** *YHV*

L.627

Lulu (Didier Bezace) is a Paris narcotics cop who moonlights on weekends videotaping weddings. At work, he's frustrated by the size of the job he's got to do and the lack of resources. Forget computers; these cops get by with manual typewriters and carbon paper. The civil service bureaucracy surrounding the narcotics department is maddeningly inefficient, and his superiors care only about statistics. The human cost of crime means nothing to them. But that's the part of it that keeps the veteran Lulu from resigning. Though he's fairly happily married, he also has a complex friendship with Cecile (Lara Guirao), an HIV-positive prostitute and drug addict. (The title refers to an AIDS test that all suspects brought in on narcotics charges have to take.) Their relationship is the thread that runs throughout Bertrand Tavernier's long episodic film. The acting style is low key and naturalistic, reflecting the overall tone of the film. There are no big crimes to be solved; not a single shot is fired onscreen. Instead, there are only the small and all too rare victories of the individual over the odds. The film is in French with clear subtitles, so it's not for everyone, but it is the kind of serious, non mainstream work that's perfect for home video. 🗡🗡🗡

Contains strong language, violence, nudity.

1992 145m/C *FR* Didier Bezace, Jean-Paul Comart, Cecile Garcia-Fogel, Lara Guirao, Charlotte Kady, Jean-Roger Milo, Philippe Torreton, Nils Tavernier; *D:* Bertrand Tavernier; *W:* Bertrand Tavernier, Michel Alexandre; *M:* Philippe Sarde. **VHS** *KIV*

L.A. Goddess

Real comedy is mixed with unintentional laughs in the tale of stuntwoman Kathy Shower who's writing a script. When high-powered producer David Heavener learns about it, he invites her to spend a few weeks at his mansion where she can write in peace and quiet. He swears that he's interested in her story, not her body. Sure he is. This one could have been a low-budget combination of *The Player* and *The Stuntman* but gloriously bad acting and a really slow pace undermine that comparison. Still, for those who know anything

about how the movie business works, it's a tongue-in-cheek Hollywood fantasy. Also available in an unrated version. 🦴🦴🦴 GPI· 5 0

Nudity, sexual content, strong language.

1992 (R) 92m/C Kathy Shower, Jeff Conaway, David Heavener, Wendy McDonald, Joe Estevez, James Hong; **D:** Jag Mundhra; **W:** Jerry Davis. **VHS** *PSM*

La Pastorela

Imagine a slightly surrealistic amateur Christmas pageant in a *Wizard of Oz* framework. Gila (Karla Montana) is a contemporary Mexican-American teenager suffering the universal problems of adolescence. Her large family doesn't understand her. She has to help out too much around the house. There's never enough money, etc., etc. After a bump on the head, she finds herself with the shepherds on their way to Bethlehem. They become the focus of a battle between the forces of God, as represented by the Archangel Michael (Linda Ronstadt), and the demons of Hell, led by comedian Paul Rodriguez and aided by Cheech Marin. It's every bit as unusual and unpredictable as the casting suggests. Writer/direc-

tor Luis Valdez (*La Bamba*) mixes religion with rough, ribald humor, but he's never sacrilegious or irreverent. And despite the offbeat approach, this isn't a spoof, either. It's a comedy with inexpensive special effects and a fine soundtrack from Los Lobos. The entire production was handled with more enthusiasm than sophistication, and that's what makes it so much fun. 🦴🦴🦴

Contains some scary, supernatural stuff.

1992 80m/C Linda Ronstadt, Richard "Cheech" Marin, Paul Rodriguez, Karla Montana, Don Novello, Robert Beltran, Freddy Fender, Falco Jimenez; **D:** Luis Valdez; **W:** Luis Valdez. **VHS** *BMG, MVD, RIN*

La Vie de Boheme

This one's an amiable 1993 updating of the story that's already provided the basis for the opera *La Boheme* and the Broadway hit *Rent*. It's about three scruffy, engaging artists—Marcel (Andre Wilms), a writer; Schaunard (Kari Vaananen), a composer; Rodolfo (Matti Pellonpaa), a painter—and Rodolfo's sometimes girlfriend Mimi (Evelyne Didi) in Paris. Their quasi-episodic stories are beautifully filmed in black and white. Writer/producer/director Aki Kaurismaki lets the pace flow slowly, and the notable absence of music heightens the European sensibility. The dry humor is sometimes silly, sometimes completely charming, sometimes touching. Look for directors Sam Fuller and Louis Malle in cameos. **AKA:** Bohemian Life. 🦴🦴🦴

Contains some strong language.

1993 100m/C Matti Pellonpaa, Andre Wilms, Kari Vaananen, Jean-Pierre Leaud, Samuel Fuller, Louis Malle, Evelyne Didi, Christine Murillo, Laika, Carlos Salgado, Alexis Nitzer, Sylvie van den Elsen, Gilles Charmant, Dominique Marcas; **D:** Aki Kaurismaki; **W:** Aki Kaurismaki. **VHS** *FXL*

L.A. Wars

Micro-budget action flick revolves around a gang war with ex-cop Vince Murdocco romancing a don's daughter (Mary Zilba). Lots of shoot-outs and fight scenes ensue, but these aren't really martial arts. They're more martial crafts, often involving overweight guys with massive wobbling love handles and tight tanktops. 🦴🦴

Violence, strong language, sexual material, brief nudity.

1994 (R) 94m/C Vince Murdocco, Mary Zilba, A.J. Stevens, Rodrigo Obregon; *D:* Martin Morris, Tony Kandah. **VHS** *MNC*

Lady in Waiting

A killer is preying on prostitutes, and police detective Michael Nouri has more interest in the case than he should—his infidelities with some of these working girls destroyed his first marriage. But now he thinks that his ex-wife's new husband may be behind the murders. Boss William Devane doesn't buy it, but ex-madame Meg Foster says he's on the right track. Where does femme fatale Shannon Whirry fit in? Though most of the cops are pure stereotype, Nouri's flawed character has his moments. In the end, this one is a competently made time-waster with slick production values. Also available in an unrated version. 🦴🦴🦴 **GPI: 7.0**

Violence, sexual material, nudity, strong language.

1994 (R) 85m/C Michael Nouri, Shannon Whirry, William Devane, Karen Kopins, Crystal Chappell, Robert Costanzo, Meg Foster, Charles Grant; *D:* Fred Gallo. **VHS** *AVE*

Ladykiller

Burnt-out detective Mimi Rogers meets wealthy, charming John Shea through a dating service. He's also handsome and attentive, but, darn it, all the clues point to his being another of those pesky psychotics. Or is he just married? What's a single woman to do these days? The script has more wit and suspense than most genre films, and as always, Rogers is excellent. 🦴🦴🦴

Mature subject matter, strong language.

1992 (R) 92m/C Mimi Rogers, John Shea, Alice Krige, Tom Irwin; *D:* Michael Scott; *W:* Shelley Evans. **VHS, LV** *MCA*

Lake Consequence

More heavy-breathing eroticism from video auteur Zalman King, who's built a successful career in the soft-core marketplace. This one's

a fantasy about young mom Joan Severance who falls asleep in a trailer. Workman Billy Zane carries her off and helps her get in touch with her feelings and other parts of herself. It's all too serious, atmospheric, and coy. Also available in an unrated version at 90 minutes. 🦴🦴 **GPI: 6.0**

Strong language, brief nudity, sexual activity, some violence.

1992 (R) 85m/C Joan Severance, Billy Zane, May Karasun; *D:* Rafael Eisenman; *W:* Zalman King, Melanie Finn, Henry Cobbold; *M:* George S. Clinton. **VHS, LV** *REP*

The Land Before Time 2: The Great Valley Adventure

This sequel was one of the first large-scale studio efforts to establish a video series on a theatrical release. It's also proved to be one of the more successful with simple animation and strong characters. The songs are thin and the whole thing is really too sappy for older kids. But younger viewers will like the adventure story and the simple morals about responsibility and obedience. Following installments have actually improved. 🦴🦴

1994 (G) 75m/C *D:* Roy Allen Smith. **VHS, LV** *MCA*

The Land Before Time 3: The Time of the Great Giving

Animated sequel has everything its young audience wants to see: familiar characters, colorful animation, simple conflicts, O.K. songs. The dinosaur tale begins with a brief lesson about evolution and then follows its saurian heroes—Littlefoot, Sara, Ducky, Spike, and Petry—as they venture forth from the Great Valley into the Mysterious Beyond to find water. The story teaches lessons about conservation, tolerance, and parenting, but those are laid in so painlessly that the kids won't mind. Fans of the first two will love it. 🦴🦴🦴

1995 (G) 71m/C *D:* Roy Allen Smith. **VHS, LV** *MCA*

The Land Before Time 4: Journey Through the Mists

The adventures of Littlefoot, Sara, Spike, and the rest continue in a by-the-numbers sequel that will entertain young fans of the series. With their new pal Ally, the little dinos set off to find the "nightflowers" that will cure grandpa longneck's illness. The messages about friendship are simple; the animation is O.K. with bright colors and mediocre songs. *♪♪*

1996 74m/C *D:* Roy Allen Smith. **VHS, LV** *MCA*

Landslide

Cross-pollinated genre effort combines amnesia and town-with-a-secret tale. Bob Boyd (Anthony Edwards) lost his memory years before in a car crash that killed most members of the influential Trinovant family, leaving control of the local economy to the villainous Matterson family. Bob comes back with an assumed identity (and an ugly crewcut), determined to find out what really happened, and why the Mattersons are trying to buy up all of the nearby forest land. Joanna Cassidy, as an evil Matterson daughter, steals the show. The script is stilted and cliched, and the pace is far too slow. As the title promises, though, it does end with some good special effects. Based on a Desmond Bagley novel. *♪♪*

Some strong language, mild violence.

1992 (PG-13) 95m/C Anthony Edwards, Tom Burlinson, Joanna Cassidy, Melody Anderson, Ronald Lacey, Ken James, Lloyd Bochner; *D:* Jean-Claude Lord. **VHS, LV** *REP*

Lap Dancing

With the critical and commercial failure of *Showgirls,* desperate moviegoers wondered if there would ever be a sensitive and perceptive portrayal of topless dancing on film. The answer is a resounding "Yes!" This video original has all the sex and sleaze of its big-budget counterpart plus a sense of humor. Take a look. Also available in an unrated version at 93 minutes. *♪♪♪* **GPI: 8.6**

Nudity, sexual material, strong language.

1995 (R) 90m/C Lorissa McComas, Tane McClure, C.T. Miller, Kim Dawson, Michael Wates; *D:* Mike Sedan; *W:* K.C. Martin. **VHS, LV** *TRI*

Laser Moon

After a promising beginning, this generic B-movie contains no real surprises. Traci Lords is less than convincing as yet another cop on the trail of yet another serial killer. Fans have seen the same thing done with more intelligence and style elsewhere. *♪*

Violence, strong language, sexual material, nudity.

1992 90m/C Traci Lords, Crystal Shaw, Harrison Leduke, Bruce Carter; *D:* Bruce Carter. **VHS** *HMD*

Last Call

Overly complicated, poorly written caper picture involves land swindles, performance art, and secrets buried deep in the past. Some of the voice dubbing is so bad it sounds like an Italian gladiator flick. Stars William Katt and Shannon Tweed seem to have realized what they were dealing with and so they don't exactly stretch their thespian abilities to the limit. Her performance art routines and their hyperventilating bedroom scenes are as imaginative and ridiculous as any on videotape. Also available in an unrated version. 🐕🐕 **GPI: 9.0**

Strong language, sex, violence, nudity.

1990 (R) 90m/C William Katt, Shannon Tweed, Joseph Campanella, Stella Stevens, Matt Roe; *D:* Jag Mundhra. **VHS** *PSM*

The Last Hit

Grant (Bryan Brown) is a sniper/assassin whose career goes back to Vietnam. But when his boss fingers retired lawyer Harris Yulin, Grant finds that he can't carry out the job. Instead, he falls for the scenic New Mexico landscape and buys a house from a widow (Brooke Adams). They're all set to close when he finds that his intended victim is her father. From there, the plot really gets ridiculous. The pace is pokey; the story never gets into the details of long-range shooting or a sniper's psychology; and there's no spark between the leads. 🐕

Strong language, some violence.

1993 (R) 93m/C Bryan Brown, Brooke Adams, Harris Yulin; *D:* Jan Egleson; *W:* Walter Klenhard, Alan Sharp; *M:* Gary Chang. **VHS, LV** *MCA*

The Last Hour

Gangsters hold Shannon Tweed hostage until her husband returns stolen mob millions. Her ex, a cop, comes to the rescue. Low-budget *Die Hard* wannabe is notable for narrative incompetence—the opening sequence contains flashbacks of scenes that took place moments before—and sadistic violence. When our hero and a bad guy shoot it out in an artist's studio, wildly colored paints and bullets fly everywhere. That's fine, but the scene ends with the bad guy standing in front of a white wall where he is shot repeatedly, and bright red blood splashes across the white surface in large abstract shapes. When the twitching body finally falls, the survivor makes a crack about the wall being "his best work." This indicates, apparently, that the whole thing is supposed to be funny. It isn't. It's needlessly sadistic and repulsive, and the MPAA felt it deserved an R-rating. Why is this kind of graphic sadism acceptable for a teenaged audience "with accompanying parent or guardian," while an NC-17 film with a few seconds of simulated sexual activity is not? **WOOF!**

Sadism, strong language, nudity.

1991 (R) 85m/C Michael Pare, Shannon Tweed, Bobby DiCicco, Robert Pucci; *D:* William Sachs. **VHS, LV** *ACA*

Last Man Standing

In this near-perfect video action flick, the first reel alone may set a record for shattered glass and exploding cars—and these aren't the usual junker Mavericks and Pintos. We're talking BMWs and 'vettes biting the dust before it's over. Honest detective Kurt Bellmore (Jeff Wincott) and his banker wife (Jillian McWhirter) go up against corrupt cops and vicious crooks led by the despicable Snake Underwood (Jonathan Fuller). Veteran action director Joseph Merhi keeps things moving at a machine gun pace with some terrific stuntwork. If the cast lacks star power, all the leads do fine work and the whole film is a lot more enjoyable than many of its big-screen counterparts. Think Michael Mann's *Heat* on amphetamines. 🐕🐕🐕½

Graphic violence, strong language, brief nudity, sexual content.

1995 (R) 96m/C Jeff Wincott, Jillian McWhirter, Jonathan Banks, Steve Eastin, Jonathan Fuller, Michael Greene, Ava Fabian; *D:* Joseph Merhi; *W:* Joseph Merhi; *M:* Louis Febre. **VHS** *PMH*

The Last Movie

In 1969, Dennis Hopper played a key role in the creation of the "youth wave" of filmmakers with *Easy Rider*. Then he almost killed it off single-handedly in 1971 with this experimental film that was released in only a few theatres and almost universally panned. It then sat on the shelf for decades before it made a belated debut on video. And that's exactly where it should be seen. It's an artsy stream-of-consciousness film-within-a-film-within-a-film contraption about the making of a Western about Billy the Kid in Peru. Auteur Hopper sometimes plays a stuntman named Kansas. At other times he seems to be himself directing

"I like thrillers. You can still do a very good-looking Rear Window with a good but unknown actor. The cost will be a very small fraction without compromising the presentation of the story. If you try to do a big action movie for a small budget, it's going to look cheesy because you've got to make compromises somewhere."

—Jag Mundhra, director of *Last Call*.

Video Premieres

the movie you're watching. Actually, he invited a whole bunch of his friends—including Peter Fonda, Kris Kristofferson, Sam Fuller, Michelle Phillips, and a few dozen others—down to Peru where they played music and fooled around in front of the cameras and went to fiestas and altered their consciousnesses. Footage of them having a fine old time is intercut with the loosely told story of Kansas and a local prostitute, and scenes from the Billy the Kid movie. As he did in *Easy Rider,* Hopper captured some spectacular landscapes and more or less let the plot take care of itself. After a time, the film almost makes its own kind of ridiculous sense, but that's not really the point. You either appreciate this one for its stylistic excesses and inventiveness, or you don't. Comparisons to Hopper's work several years later in *Blue Velvet* are not out of place. *AKA:* Chinchero. 🦴🦴🦴

Nudity, sexual scenes, profanity, violence.

1971 **(R)** 108m/**C** Dennis Hopper, Julie Adams, Peter Fonda, Kris Kristofferson, Sylvia Miles, John Phillip Law, Russ Tamblyn, Rod Cameron, Samuel Fuller, Michelle Phillips; *D:* Dennis Hopper; *W:* Stewart Stern; *M:* Kris Kristofferson. VHS *NO*

Last Rites

A stylish woman walks down a New York sidewalk and enters a ritzy hotel where a man gives her a silenced automatic and a room key. She catches her husband in flagrante and plugs him right where it hurts the worst. Her ex-hubbie's sweetie, Angela (Daphne Zuniga), escapes and eventually takes refuge with a priest, Father Michael (Tom Berenger), an old pal of the perforated philanderer! Before it's over, the plot has become so convoluted, with most of the important characters related by blood or marriage, that it's impossible to follow. And then there's the matter of Father Michael's fight to resist temptations of the flesh in several intense but coy sexual scenes. The unusual mixture of religion, ritual, imagery, sex, and violence will certainly be enough to offend some devout Catholics. Had the film been more effective and more believable, it might be offensive to other religious persuasions too. But, alas, it's just a quirky

misfire; interesting at times and finally disappointing. 🦴🦴

Brief nudity, strong sexual content, violence, profanity.

1988 **(R)** 103m/**C** Tom Berenger, Daphne Zuniga, Chick Vennera, Dane Clark, Carlo Pacchi, Anne Twomey, Paul Dooley, Vassili Lambrinos; *D:* Donald P. Bellisario; *W:* Donald P. Bellisario; *C:* David Watkin; *M:* Bruce Broughton. VHS, LV *FOX*

The Last Samurai

Veteran cast easily surpasses the script in an uneven adventure thriller. Japanese corporate titan Endo (John Fujioka) goes into the African wilderness to check on an arms deal and to find evidence of an ancestor, a missionary who tried to bring Buddhism to Africa and disappeared there. Transportation is provided by chopper pilot Johnny Congo (Lance Henriksen), a self-destructive Vietnam vet. After a lengthy (too lengthy) introduction, they find themselves held hostage by a local general (James Ryan). The action scenes are fairly effective, but those arrive late and they're interrupted by long stretches of pseudo-philosophical discourses on honor that degenerate into nutty sloganeering. Some good scenery and the usual solid performances by Henriksen and Fujioka are the film's strengths. (Note Henriksen's neat business with the top of the Scotch bottle.) 🦴🦴🦴

Violence, strong language, brief nudity.

1990 **(R)** 94m/**C** Lance Henriksen, John Saxon, Henry Cele, Arabella Holzbog, John Fujioka, James Ryan, Duncan Regehr, Lisa Eilbacher; *D:* Paul Mayersberg. VHS *AVI*

The Last Word

Newspaper columnist Martin Ryan (Timothy Hutton) is the toast of Detroit. He hangs out with suave gangsters (Chazz Palminteri) and beautiful strippers (Michelle Johnson) until his pal Doc (Joe Pantoliano) suggests that Martin turn his best-selling book into a screenplay which he, Doc, will produce. Once the action moves west, it's notable mostly for cameo appearances by Richard Dreyfuss, Cybill Shepherd, and Jimmy Smits. The Hollywood conflicts are standard stuff, energetically presented, but the dramatic conclusion is a revelation that's much too strong for this kind of movie. Still, give writer/director Tony Spiridakis credit for ambition and attempting to tell a serious, entertaining story of the *Get Shorty* school. ✔✔✔

Strong language, violence, subject matter, brief nudity.

1995 **(R)** 95m/C Timothy Hutton, Joe Pantoliano, Michelle Burke, Chazz Palminteri, Tony Goldwyn, Michelle Johnson; *Cameos:* Richard Dreyfuss, Cybill Shepherd, Jimmy Smits; *D:* Tony Spiridakis; *W:* Tony Spiridakis. **VHS** *VMK*

The Lawnmower Man

The central story here is a loose retelling of *Frankenstein*. Jobe Smith (Jeff Fahey) is a slow-witted handyman whose brain power is boosted by exposure to Dr. Angelo's (Pierce Brosnan) experiments in virtual reality. The home video version is 30 minutes longer than the theatrical release with more special effects and a fully developed, coherent story. Its well-deserved popularity has elevated the video above cult status and into the realm of a solid mainstream hit. The plot has almost nothing to do with King's short story—he had his name removed from the title—but the tone is faithful to his fictional territory of small towns, bullies, kids, cruelty, abuse, ominous government agencies, and, of course, a big pyrotechnic finale. Followed by a sequel. ✔✔✔

Contains violence, strong language, sexual content, nudity.

1992 **(R)** 108m/C Jeff Fahey, Pierce Brosnan, Jenny Wright, Mark Bringleson, Geoffrey Lewis, Jeremy Slate, Dean Norris; *D:* Brett Leonard; *W:* Brett Leonard, Gimel Everett; *C:* Russell Carpenter. **VHS, LV** *COL, FCT, MOV*

Leapin' Leprechauns!

Michael Dennehy (John Bluthal) lives in an old Irish castle atop Fairy Hill (actually Romania, but so what?) where the "little people" live—male leprechauns and female fairies. But Michael's grown son who lives in Denver wants to build a theme park on the family estate; something lamely called Ireland-Land. So off Michael goes, with four pint-sized stowaways in his luggage, for an American visit. Only his granddaughter Melanie (Erica Nicole

Hess, the cutest little redhead to grace the screen in years) can see these magical tricksters. The pleasant little fantasy-comedy has lots of slapstick and food-throwing, always a crowd-pleaser with the small fry. The hammy overacting may well drive adults from the TV room, but the kids will love it. They'll also love the bright, lively score; music is an often overlooked area where Band productions always shine, and this one is no exception. ✔✔✔

Comic action and some spooky stuff.

1995 **(PG)** 84m/C Grant Cramer, John Bluthal, Sharon Lee Jones, Gregory Edward Smith, Sylvester McCoy, James Ellis, Godfrey James, Tina Martin, Erica Nicole Hess; *D:* Ted Nicolaou; *W:* Ted Nicolaou, Michael McGann. **VHS** *PAR*

Les Patterson Saves the World

Raunchy Aussie satire makes Benny Hill look like Noel Coward. Barry Humphries (before his incarnation as Dame Edna) is the Australian ambassador who offends oil-rich Abu-Nivea in a truly tasteless scene that employs several cans of beans and a cigarette lighter. The rest of the coarse comedy revolves around a plot to conquer the world. With his rubbery face and hideous mid 1970s shoes, Humphries is the driving force. He provides some colorful, inventive swearing and frantic energy that's slightly (but only slightly) reminiscent of the early Jerry Lewis. ✔✔✔

Strong language, rough humor, bawdy slapstick.

1990 **(R)** 105m/C *AU* Barry Humphries, Pamela Stephenson, Thaao Penghlis, Andrew Clarke, Joan Rivers; *D:* George Miller; *C:* David Connell. **VHS** *HMD*

Liebestraum

Nick (Kevin Anderson) comes to a small unfamiliar town to be near his dying mother (Kim Novak, who still looks good even when she's supposed to be seconds away from the reaper). He's surprised to meet an old college pal, Paul (Bill Pullman), whose company is about to demolish an old cast iron building. Nick wants to explore and write about the historically significant structure. Paul's unhappy

effects, while not up to *Star Wars* standards, are remarkably good. For a stay-at-home evening's entertainment, this one's a good bet. ♫♫♫

Contains some violence.

1993 90m/C Ron Silver, Robert Loggia, CCH Pounder, Stan Shaw, Adam Storke, Jessica Tuck, Kelli Williams, Ed Gate; *D:* Ron Silver; *W:* M. Jay Roach, Pen Densham. **VHS, LV** *CAF*

Lily in Winter

Off-beat Christmas story about race and family relations has nothing new to say about either. Right before Christmas 1957, clumsy circumstances force housekeeper Lily Covington (Natalie Cole) to flee the household where she works in New York for her mother's (Marla Gibbs) home in rural Alabama. Michael (Brian Bonsall), the young son of her employers, tags along. Yes, it's a pretty far-fetched premise and it doesn't fetch any closer as it goes along. The film looks like it was made on a studio back lot and neither the performances nor the conflicts are strong enough to overcome the flimsy production values. It's enough to make you wonder why veteran director Delbert Mann signed on in the first place. About all the film has going for it is the clichéd sweetness of the season ♫♫♫

Mild violence.

1994 (PG) 120m/C Natalie Cole, Brian Bonsall, Dwier Brown, Cecil Hoffmann, Marla Gibbs, Monte Russell, Rae'ven Kelly, Salli Richardson, James Pickens Jr., Matthew Faison; *D:* Delbert Mann; *W:* Robert Eisele; *C:* Charles Mills; *M:* David Shire. **VHS** *MCA*

Lily Was Here

Belgian film takes so many unexpected turns that revealing almost anything about the plot would spoil it. The title character, played without a single false step by Marion Van Thijn, is a young pregnant woman who has to make some difficult decisions when it appears that the entire world is conspiring to make her life miserable. For one long sequence near the beginning, the film is almost a psychological horror story, along the lines of Polanski's *Repulsion*. Then it changes and becomes something like *Thelma Without Louise*.

wife, Jane (Pamela Gidley), offers to take pictures. Style is everything here. Think *Barton Fink* meets *Body Heat*. The lighting is atmospheric; the characters look like they just stepped out of a music video. (If you'd had the mousse concession on this production, you'd be in high clover now.) The story itself is underwritten and overdirected. The characters say so little and the action is so studied that it's often hard to tell what's going on. But, hey, it looks great. In some ways, this is almost a movie of a movie. At its worst moments, it becomes unintentionally funny. At best, it gets full marks for weirdness, and the ending may be tongue in cheek. Also available in an unrated version at 116 minutes. ♫♫♪

Strong sexual content, language, some violence.

1991 (R) 109m/C Kevin Anderson, Bill Pullman, Pamela Gidley, Kim Novak; *D:* Mike Figgis; *W:* Mike Figgis. **VHS, LV** *MGM*

Lifepod

Loose adaptation of Hitchcock's 1944 *Lifeboat* begins at a full run with the explosion of an interplanetary cruise ship. A few survivors manage to escape in a poorly equipped lifepod, and are beset by a series of disasters. Who's the saboteur? Actor Ron Silver, making a credible debut behind the camera, keeps the action moving at a good clip, and the ensemble cast does solid professional work. The

Throughout, an atmosphere of believability makes it seem like a true story. Despite some flaws involving minor characters and the cultural differences that sometimes intrude, it's easy to get deeply involved in this all-too-human film. 🗡🗡🗡

Brief nudity, sexual content, violence, harsh language.

1989 (R) 110m/C Marion Van Thijn, Thom Hoffman, Adrian Brine, Dennis Rudge; *D:* Ben Verbong; *W:* Ben Verbong, Sytze Van Der Laan, Willem Jan Otten. **VHS** *INJ*

Linda

Thriller based on John D. MacDonald's novella retains his vivid characters and atmosphere, and, for fans, several references to other works in John D.'s canon. The tight plot revolves around Paul Cowley (Richard Thomas), his wife Linda (Virginia Madsen), and their new neighbors (Ted McGinley and Laura Harrington). The four of them go off for a beach vacation where things quickly turn weird and nasty. The cast is fine, and again the show is stolen by the bad girl. Virginia Madsen is one of the best in the business and she really gets a lot out of this role. 🗡🗡🗡

Violence, mature subject matter.

1993 (PG-13) 88m/C Virginia Madsen, Richard Thomas, Ted McGinley, Laura Harrington; *D:* Nathaniel Gutman; *W:* Nevin Schreiner; *M:* David Michael Frank. **VHS** *PAR*

The Lion, the Witch and the Wardrobe

In this first volume of his Chronicles of Narnia, C.S. Lewis recast the tenets and mythology of Christianity as a fairy tale. Four children—Peter, Edmund, Susan, and Lucy, or "the sons of Adam and the daughters of Eve," as they're called—discover a passageway through an old wardrobe into the kingdom of Narnia. The White Witch rules the land where it's "always winter and never Christmas," until the great lion Aslan returns. This animated feature is faithful to Lewis' original; much of the dialogue comes straight from the book. Though the animation isn't up to the highest standards, the characters are complex and have more depth than you often find in cartoons, or in live action films, for that matter. The story is fascinating and intense, dealing with death, sin, sacrifice, and redemption. It may be more than some younger viewers can handle, but this is a particularly good tape for parents to watch with their kids and to talk about later. 🗡🗡🗡

Some violence.

1979 95m/C *D:* Bill Melendez. **VHS** *BTV, REP*

Lipstick Camera

Ambitious young Omy (Ele Keats) wants to be a TV news photographer. Her idol is cynical cameraman Brian Wimmer. To impress him, she borrows a tiny "lipstick camera" from her friend Corey Feldman and the three of them are caught up in a possible murder with a mysterious German (Terry O'Quinn) and a woman (Sandahl Bergman) who claims to be his wife. Though the mechanics of the plot take up too much time, the main characters are handled remarkably well. Feldman takes what could have been a so-so supporting role and turns it into a believable and sympathetic character. Keats does a lot with the lead, too. How much is Omy willing to sacrifice for her budding career? She's a complex character, one with more depth than you normally see in a protagonist, male or female. 🗡🗡🗡

Nudity and sexual material, some violence.

1993 (R) 93m/C Ele Keats, Brian Wimmer, Corey Feldman, Sandahl Bergman, Terry O'Quinn; *D:* Mike Bonifer; *W:* Mike Bonifer. **VHS, LV** *TRI*

Lipstick on Your Collar

Dennis Potter's ambitious musical fantasy was made for British television, but don't count on seeing it broadcast anywhere in this country. With straitlaced conservatives guarding the public morality, no network public or private would touch this funny, sexy, irreverent miniseries. But conventional TV's loss is home video's gain; this is what your VCR was made for. The series, available on three two-hour tapes, is a musical fantasy with an occasional-

1994 360m/C GB Ewan McGregor, Giles Thomas, Louise Germaine, Giles Thomas, Douglas Hershall; D: Renny Rye; W: Dennis Potter. VHS TVC, NEW

Lisa

Conventional thriller features another mass murderer—those guys are far too popular in escapist entertainment these days—but the main focus is on the relationship between a mother and her 14-year-old daughter. Lisa (Staci Keanan) is a bright 14-year-old who's beginning to realize the mysteries of sex. She and her best friend have developed a game of following "stud muffins," attractive older men they watch from afar and sometimes annoy on the telephone. Though Lisa and her mom, Katherine (Cheryl Ladd), are open about most things, Lisa hasn't told her about this game. Katherine, a single mother, is very strict about boys. No dating until Lisa turns 16. For Lisa, the situation is bleak but bearable until she runs into Richard (D.W. Moffett), and enters an anonymous telephone relationship with him. Superficially, he's the studliest muffin of them all, but he's also the infamous Candlelight Killer. How gross! If the story sounds vaguely familiar, it is. William Castle's 1965 thriller *I Saw What You Did* uses several of the same plot devices. But the characters seem real and the conclusion is exciting. 🐾🐾🐾

Profanity, mild violence, subject matter.

1990 (PG-13) 95m/C Staci Keanan, Cheryl Ladd, D.W. Moffett, Tanya Fenmore, Jeffrey Tambor, Julie Cobb; D: Gary Sherman; W: Karen Clark. VHS FOX

Little Heroes

"Heartwarming" story of a girl and her dog is well-intentioned but unwatchable. It's obvious from the opening scenes that the dog, Fuzz (Hoover), has no interest in Charley (Raeanin Simpson) or anyone else. He only has eyes for his trainer who was standing just off camera. True, Hoover is no worse than any of his human counterparts but I hope he didn't give up his day job for a career in show business. Even the amateurish acting—human and canine—could have been forgiven if the filmmakers hadn't committed the one unforgiv-

---

The Hound's Favorite Sleepers: Guilty Pleasures

ANIMAL INSTINCTS	HARD TICKET TO HAWAII
THE BANKER	IN A MOMENT OF PASSION
DIAL HELP	MERIDIAN: KISS OF THE BEAST

ly firm grip on reality. The setting is London, 1956, as the Suez Canal crisis looms. In a small intelligence department of the War Office, Pushkin scholar Francis Francis (Giles Thomas) arrives from rural Wales to translate Russian. The more experienced Pvt. Hopper (Ewan McGregor, from *Shallow Grave*) tries to show him the ropes. But just when the story threatens to become a boring politico-historical tale, these mid-level civil servants break into a lip-synced version of "Little Bitty Pretty One," complete with a very naked blonde angel in the background. Then the lovely Sylvia (Louise Germaine) appears. She's an archetypal '50s blonde bombshell. Francis is smitten, and fortunately, she lives right upstairs. Unfortunately, she's married to the violent Cpl. Barry (Douglas Hershall). Beyond the fantasy scenes—which might have been the Russ Meyer version of *How to Succeed in Business*—the whole production has that wonderful off-center quality that Potter's so justly famous for. The supporting cast will be familiar to fans of British film and television. In the end, Potter's tale is about a lot of things—cold war politics, rock music, class, theatre—but it's mostly about love, hopeless love, and all the craziness that it involves. 🐾🐾🐾

Strong subject matter, nudity (gratuitous and otherwise), sexual scenes, scatological humor.

able sin in children's entertainment. They talk down to their audience and oversimplify characters so foolishly that even the youngest, most uncritical kids will get bored with this one. 🦴

1991 (G) 78m/C Raeanin Simpson, Katherine Willis, Keith Christensen; *D:* Craig Clyde; *W:* Craig Clyde; *M:* John McCallum. **VHS** *HMD*

Little Vegas

Offbeat, leisurely paced comedy-drama revolves around the quirky residents of a trailer park in the Nevada desert. At the center is Carmine (Anthony John Denison), a recovering alcoholic who's trying to do the right thing by his young son and the memory of an old lover (Anne Francis). The main problem is a plot that tends to be cliched, sentimental, and hard to follow. But those flaws aren't as serious as they sound. The characters are more important, and they're played by an outstanding ensemble cast: John Sayles, Catherine O'Hara, Jerry Stiller, Michael Nouri, Jay Thomas, and P.J. Ochlan. Add a vivid sense of place and a good heart and you've got a fine little sleeper. 🦴🦴🦴

Strong language, subject matter, brief nudity.

1990 (R) 90m/C Michael Nouri, Jerry Stiller, John Sayles, Anthony John Denison, Catherine O'Hara, Bruce McGill, Anne Francis, Bob(cat) Goldthwait, Jay Thomas, P.J. Ochlan; *D:* Perry Lang; *W:* Perry Lang; *M:* Mason Daring. **VHS, LV** *COL*

Live Wire

Sheer imagination transforms a standard political thriller into a real treat. The setting: Washington, D.C. The gimmick: Exploding Senators. That's right, politicians who inexplicably blow up. Initially, FBI bomb disposal expert Danny O'Neil (Pierce Brosnan) is mystified. What could cause a seemingly harmless elected official to detonate? Only an international terrorist (Ben Cross) knows for sure. Danny has other problems; his estranged wife Terry (Lisa Eilbacher) has been seeing a particularly slimy character, Sen. Travers (Ron Silver). Danny hates Travers, but has to protect him anyway, lest the senator from Florida go ballistic—literally. At its best, the film has a keen comic edge

reminiscent of *The Manchurian Candidate*. The leads give properly tongue-in-cheek performances. Director Christian Duguay made excellent use of some unusual Washington locations. And overall, the film has a high-budget polish that would put many theatrical releases to shame. What more can you ask of a video premiere? Also available in an unrated version at 87 minutes. 🦴🦴🦴

Violence, strong language, nudity, sexual activity.

1992 (R) 85m/C Pierce Brosnan, Ben Cross, Ron Silver, Lisa Eilbacher; *D:* Christian Duguay; *W:* Bart Baker. **VHS** *COL, NLC*

Live Wire: Human Timebomb

Despite the title, the sequel isn't nearly as much fun as the original, a loopy thriller about exploding Senators. This one's an action flick set in Florida and Cuba about an FBI agent (Bryan Genesse) who gets a "bio-chip" implanted in his head by longhaired bad guy Joe Lara. It's all really silly, fast paced, and well staged, with lots of stuff that goes BOOM! The generic score doesn't help. 🦴

Violence, strong language, brief nudity.

1995 (R) 98m/C Bryan Genesse, Joe Lara; *D:* Mark Roper; *W:* Jeff Albert; *C:* Rod Stewart; *M:* Itai Haber. **VHS** *TTC*

Living to Die

Wings Hauser plays Nick Carpenter, a burned-out retired police detective. When gangster Asher Brauner is caught up in a blackmail scam, he asks Carpenter for help. Against his better judgment, Nick agrees and then compounds his mistake by falling for femme fatale Maggie (Darcy Demoss), who was part of the con job. The plot is inventive, if a bit outlandish at times with unexpected humor and nonstereotyped characters. As director, Hauser keeps the action moving well; the fights are visceral without being overly graphic. The supporting performances are good, with Brauner's unhinged mobster stealing the show. Just as importantly, the film has a fine sense of place, showing both the garish neon

night and the sun-faded low-rent side of Las Vegas. ✍✍✍

Profanity, violence, nudity.

1991 (R) 84m/C Wings Hauser, Darcy Demoss, Asher Brauner, Arnold Vosloo, Jim Williams; *D:* Wings Hauser. VHS *PMH, HHE*

Lobster Man from Mars

It's hard to parody a bad movie without becoming a bad movie, but this one is O.K. Overall, it isn't laugh-out-loud funny, but it has its moments, notably when a tough, metaphor-spouting private detective shows up. He doesn't have much to do with the story; he just provides needless voiceover narration. The presence of such old pros as Tony Curtis, Patrick MacNee, and Roddy McDowall gives the low-budget production an air of class that it desperately needs, as does Deborah Foreman, the suitably plucky heroine. She deserves better. ✍✍✍

Mild violence and profanity.

1989 (PG) 84m/C Tony Curtis, Deborah Foreman, Patrick MacNee, Roddy McDowall, Tommy Sledge, Billy Barty, Phil Proctor; *D:* Stanley Shiff. VHS, LV *LIV*

Lock 'n' Load

Colorado production rises above its shoe-string budget. It's a far-fetched tale of veterans and mind control that recalls *The Manchurian Candidate* and *Jacob's Ladder*. It's slow in the unwinding—people spend far too much time on such simple business as getting in and out of cars—and sometimes predictable. But writer/director David Prior deserves some credit for creating realistic, flawed, multi-dimensional characters. One good character is worth a hundred effects and this movie has several. If the young cast is inconsistent, they're believable in the important scenes. ✍✍✍

Contains mild violence, strong language.

1990 (R) ?m/C Jack Vogel, Renee Cline, Perry Roberts; *D:* David A. Prior; *W:* David A. Prior. VHS, LV *AIP*

Lone Justice 2

Bill Wittliff, the writer/producer of *Lonesome Dove,* was aiming at the same serious tone and scope here, but he fell short of the mark. For those who missed *1,* hero Ned Blessing (Brad Johnson) is a semi-outlaw who hightails it out of Mexico one step ahead of angry pursuers. With his friend Crecencio (Luis Avalos), a doctor, he returns home to find his family gone and the nasty Borgers terrorizing the town. Straightaway, the two of them set about righting wrongs, defending the defenseless, etc., etc. Brenda Bakke is the traditional hooker-with-a-heart-of-gold, and Wes Studi appears in a too-brief supporting role. Though the characters are fairly well developed, a dreary pace bogs them down. Wittliff and director Jack Bender chew much more than they bite off. They also use evocative but intrusive music to give emotion to scenes that have none. The film appears to have been produced as a mini-series—the open ending strongly suggests a *3*—so the story is tailored to the small screen. *AKA:* Ned Blessing: The Story of My Life and Times. ✍✍✍

Contains some violence, strong language.

1993 (PG-13) 93m/C Brad Johnson, Luis Avalos, Wes Studi, Bill McKinney, Brenda Bakke, Julius Tennon, Richard Riehle, Gregory Scott Cummins, Rob Campbell, Rusty Schwimmer; *D:* Jack Bender; *W:* William D. Wittliff. VHS *TRI*

Lonely in America

Young Indian Arun (Ranjit Chowdhry) immigrates to New York to work at one of his uncle's magazine stands, but a slick conman (Robert Kessler) persuades him to leave his family and move up in the business world. While some of the physical humor works, an equal amount doesn't, and the acting ranges from amateur to effective. When the film turns to the cultural conflicts that Arun must wrestle with, it becomes much more interesting. The immigrant experience is inherently fascinating, rich in conflict and strong emotions. Chowdhry is able to make Arun a sympathetic and engaging protagonist, someone you enjoy spending time with. Even when the film itself isn't as good as it might be, he's excellent. Director Barry Brown, known best as Spike Lee's editor, shows that he can work well behind the camera, too. This is light comic material, and he doesn't try to make too much of it. 𝄢𝄢𝄢

Mild sexual content, strong language.

1990 96m/C Ranjit Chowdhry, Adelaide Miller, Robert Kessler, Melissa Christopher, David Toney, Tirlok Malik; *D:* Barry Brown; *W:* Barry Brown, Satyajit Joy Palit. **VHS** *ACA*

The Long Goodbye

Robert Altman's version of Raymond Chandler's most ambitious novel is in part a serious detective film and in part a spoof of detective films. That's an uncomfortable combination. Veteran screenwriter Leigh Brackett (*The Big Sleep*) did an admirable job of compressing events, and she even managed to retain some of Chandler's romanticism. Some viewers have questioned the changes she made in the ending, but it is more dramatically satisfying than Chandler's. The main problems are the casting of Elliott Gould as Philip Marlowe and the attempts by him and Altman to turn Chandler's loner detective into a laid-back '60s hero (the film was made in 1973). Marlowe's often-used throwaway line, "It's O.K. with me," shows how disengaged he is from the rest of the characters and their problems. The supporting cast is excellent. Sterling Hayden is wonderful as a boozy, pompous novelist and so is Nina Van Pallandt as his wife. Baseball player Jim Bouton does a good job as Marlowe's friend Terry Lennox, and director Mark Rydell is terrific as a mad gangster (he'll remind you of Roman Polansky in *Chinatown*). The dark, grainy texture of the film will put off many viewers, and even Altman's fans will admit that this is not his best effort. But this one hasn't been available in an uncut form since its first, limited theatrical release, so, flaws and all, *The Long Goodbye* is recommended. 𝄢𝄢𝄢

Strong language, violence, brief nudity.

1973 (R) 112m/C Elliott Gould, Nina Van Pallandt, Sterling Hayden, Henry Gibson, Mark Rydell, David Arkin, Warren Berlinger, Jim Bouton; *Cameos:* Arnold Schwarzenegger, David Carradine; *D:* Robert Altman; *W:* Leigh Brackett; *C:* Vilmos Zsig-

mond; *M:* John Williams. National Society of Film Critics Awards '73: Best Cinematography. **VHS, LV** *MGM, FCT*

Long Road Home

Period piece earns points for a strong understated starring performance and an effective evocation of Depression-era California. It loses points for an overly emotional supporting cast and the wrong ending. In 1937, banged-up cowboy Ertie Robertson (Mark Harmon) moves his family from Texas to California. Looking for work picking whatever's in season, they arrive at Titus Wardlow's (Leon Russom) huge farm as union organization is on the rise. When Ertie stands up for his family's rights, he's labeled a "communist agitator." For a time, the film does a good job of dramatizing a time of massive social upheaval. The earthy, dirty browns and grays recall the great WPA rural photography of Walker Evans and others. But when it's time to wrap things up, the conclusion is far too neat and easy. 𝄢𝄢

Strong language, violence.

1991 (PG) 77m/C Mark Harmon, John Evans, Adam Horovitz, Lee Purcell, Leon Russom, Donald Sutherland, Morgan Weisser; *D:* John Korty. **VHS** *NHO*

Love & Murder

Low-octane Canadian import follows photographer (Todd Waring) who accidentally films a woman's death, involving him and his girlfriend (Kathleen Lasky) with a serial murderer. At various times the film is supposed to be a suspense story, a realistic character study, and a comedy. The combination of photography and murder is an obvious and crude knock-off of Hitchcock's *Rear Window*. Even in the action scenes, the pace is dreary and far too much time is devoted to long, static dialogue scenes, an obvious and accurate knock-off of bad Woody Allen. 𝄢

Mature subject matter, strong language.

1991 (R) 87m/C *CA* Todd Waring, Kathleen Lasky, Ron White, Wayne Robson; *D:* Steven Hilliard Stern. **VHS** *HMD*

Love, Cheat & Steal

Decent little noir-ish thriller of the *Body Heat* school succeeds through savvy casting. John Lithgow is the semi-prodigal son who's just returned home to a small California town to take over his father's (Dan O'Herlihy) bank. He brings along a lovely young wife (Madchen Amick) he met on holiday in Mexico. She, however, has another husband, Eric Roberts. He's a bank robber who's in prison because she abandoned him after a botched job. He sees her picture on the society page and we learn that the bank has sizeable unexplained cash deposits on hand. You can guess where it's all headed though you may not predict all the twists. Throughout, the production values are first rate. If the performances aren't inspired, they're properly understated. Lithgow, as usual, steals the show. 🔪🔪🔪

Violence, sexual content, strong language, brief nudity.

1993 (R) 95m/C Eric Roberts, Madchen Amick, John Lithgow, Richard Edson, Donald Moffat, David Ackroyd, Dan O'Herlihy; *D:* William Curran; *W:* William Curran. **VHS** *COL*

Love Is a Gun

The distributor calls this a "psychological thriller" and that loose definition is probably as accurate as any. It's a curious little film reminiscent of a good episode of the original *Twilight Zone*. For almost an hour and a half, writer/director David Hartwell manages to maintain an eerie "what's going on?" atmosphere, and he manages it despite several moments of grand unintentional humor. Jack Hart (Eric Roberts) has just moved to Los Angeles and landed a job as a police photographer. He suffers from vivid nightmares involving suicide. Live-in girlfriend Isabel (called Eliza Garrett in the press material and Eliza Roberts in the credits) has her doubts about Jack because he's a rat, an immature rat, when it comes to his personal life. He dangles an official engagement in front of Eliza but refuses to take the final step. Then he finds some photographs in his locker at work—intense, violent images of a woman in a bride's dress. The pictures mysteri-ously fade away but Jack's interest in the woman doesn't. She's Jean (Kelly Preston), and it doesn't take her long to make a move on Jack. He, of course, succumbs without a fight. For a time, he bounces between Jean and Isabel like a hormone-crazed pinball. All the while, his nightmares are getting worse. The is-it-real-or-is-it-a-dream? gimmick has been overused in recent years but Hartwell gives it some refreshing twists. He also generates suspense by artfully intercutting between key scenes, particularly at the end, which is too nutty for words. Those directorial touches elevate the film above the level of the genre—whatever genre that might happen to be. The same cannot be said of the acting. Eliza Garrett-Roberts is fine, even when she really cuts loose. Kelly Preston is lackadaisical and unfocused, though her body double contributes enthusiastically to the love scenes. Eric Roberts has built his career on unappealing characters, and this is one of his juiciest. In the big emotional moments he can appear so apoplectic that it looks like his face is about to fly off his head. At other times, when he's excited and confused, his resemblance to Jerry Lewis is pronounced. In the end, this wacky mystery somehow overcomes its excesses. Whatever Hartwell does next ought to be worth a look. 🔪🔪🔪

Violence, sexual content, brief nudity, strong language.

1994 (R) 107m/C Eric Roberts, Kelly Preston, Eliza Garrett, R. Lee Ermey; *D:* David Hartwell; *W:* David Hartwell. **VHS, LV** *VMK*

Love Letters

Jamie Lee Curtis is an NPR classical music DJ who finds her mom's old love letters while she's engaged in a hot affair with married James Keach. Despite the serious treatment of the subject matter (or perhaps because of it), the film is slow going. Monotonous voiceover narration doesn't help, either. **AKA:** Passion Play; My Love Letters. 🔪🔪

Mature subject matter, nudity, sexual content, strong language.

1983 (R) 102m/C Jamie Lee Curtis, Amy Madigan, Bud Cort, Matt Clark, Bonnie Bartlett, Sally Kirkland, James Keach; *D:* Amy Holden Jones. **VHS, LV** *LIV, VES, IME*

Love Matters

Though it's attempting to be a serious drama about couples dealing with adultery, this irritating little movie is simply slow and trite, and it looks like a filmed play. Tom (Griffin Dunne) and Julie (Annette O'Toole) are friends of Jeff (Tony Goldwyn) and Deborah (Kate Burton). Late one night, Deborah calls and says that Jeff has been missing for three days. At interminable length, he shows up drunk with his new girlfriend (Gina Gershon) in tow and asks if they can stay the night. Beyond a couple of bizarrely athletic sexual scenes, it's all talk, talk, talk. Also available in an unrated version at 103 minutes. **WOOF!**

Sexual material, nudity, strong language, and violence.

1993 (R) 97m/C Griffin Dunne, Tony Goldwyn, Annette O'Toole, Gina Gershon, Kate Burton; *D:* Eb Lottimer; *W:* Eb Lottimer; *M:* Simon Boswell. **VHS, LV** *REP*

Love Potion #9

Nerdish biochemist Paul (Tate Donovan) visits Madame Ruth (Anne Bancroft), who tells him that his love life stinks and gives him "love potion #8." Just a taste of it, she says, will make his voice irresistible to women. Whatever he says, they'll do. He takes the potion to Diane (Sandra Bullock), a biochemist as socially impaired as he is, for analysis. What are they to do then but test it on themselves? At this point, most video premieres would turn into soft core male fantasies, but writer/producer/director Dale Launer is really more interested in what this power does to Diane. How would a shy young woman react when suave Italians in Armani suits start following her around and buying her diamonds? When princes hang on every word she says? The script makes a few missteps toward the middle, but that's unimportant. The last 20 minutes redeem those slips. The leads are good, particularly Sandra Bullock in an early role that shows what she can do. 🎞🎞🎞

Sexual content, language.

1992 (PG-13) 96m/C Tate Donovan, Sandra Bullock, Mary Mara, Dale Midkiff, Hillary Bailey Smith, Dylan Baker; *Cameos:* Anne Bancroft; *D:* Dale Launer; *W:* Dale Launer. **VHS, LV** *FXV*

Lovers' Lovers

Rodnunsky family affair—starring, written, and directed by Serge; music by Pierre; produced by Albert; photographed by James—strikes out on all counts. It appears to be a romantic comedy, possibly autobiographical, about west-coast couples. The long introductory sequence at a party is boring, boring, boring. **WOOF!**

Nudity, sexual content, strong language, mild violence.

1994 90m/C Serge Rodnunsky, Jennifer Ciesar, Cindy Parker, Ray Bennett; *D:* Serge Rodnunsky; *W:* Serge Rodnunsky; *C:* James Rodnunsky; *M:* Pierre Rodnunsky. **VHS, LV** *TRI*

The Loves of a Wall Street Woman

Virginia Beach doesn't look at all like Manhattan, but it's the setting for a story of high-powered stock broker Brenda Baxter's (Tara Buckman) unethical rise to the top of the heap. And instead of doing his investigative journalism for the *Wall Street Journal*, stud muffin reporter Alex Russell (Charlie Edwards) works for *The Virginian-Pilot*. Otherwise, there are no surprises in the story. *AKA:* High Finance Woman. 🎞🎞 **GPI: 8.1**

Nudity, sexual subject matter, some strong language.

1989 (R) m/C Tara Buckman, Charles Edwards; *D:* Joe D'Amato. **VHS** *TSR*

Lurkers

What a repulsive little movie! The first part is focused on the emotional and psychological abuses that cause horrible nightmares in a little girl. Childhood fears are the source of almost all horror stories, but this presentation is unnecessarily brutal and ugly. Hey, that's what the fast-forward button is for. **WOOF!**

Grand Guignol Video

The *New Shorter Oxford English Dictionary* defines "Grand Guignol" as "[Fr. (=Great Punch), the name of a theatre in Paris] A dramatic entertainment in which short horrific or sensational pieces are played successively." In more general terms, the phrase is applied to the kind of entertainment that will do anything to scare and/or gross out its audience. The connections between 19th century French theatre and contemporary home video are too obvious for comment, and "Grand Guignol" horror has found new life on tape. Here are a few examples:

Basket Case 2	Luther the Geek
Blood Relatives	Pit & the Pendulum
Blood Salvage	Re-Animator
Bloodstone	Red Blooded American Girl
Brain Damage	
Castle Freak	Urotsukidoji
Frankenhooker	Witchboard 3: The Possession

Violence, subject matter, profanity, nudity, sexual content.

1988 (R) 90m/C Christine Moore, Gary Warner, Marina Taylor, Carissa Channing, Tom Billett; *D:* Roberta Findlay. VHS *MED*

Lurking Fear

Transylvanian locations don't really work for an adaptation of one of horror master H.P. Lovecraft's better stories. The film is supposed to be set in America and several scenes just don't look right. Also Lovecraftians will be appalled at the liberties that were taken. It's been turned into a crime movie, with lots of shoot-'em-up violence and grotesque special effects. That was not what HPL had in mind. Still, for today's horror fans who like lots of gore, the production values are solid. 🦴🦴

Violence, strong language, gooey special effects.

1994 (R) 78m/C Jon Finch, Blake Bailey, Ashley Lauren, Jeffrey Combs, Paul Mantee, Allison Mackie, Joe Leavengood, Vincent Schiavelli; *D:* C. Courtney Joyner; *W:* C. Courtney Joyner; *M:* Jim Manzie. VHS, LV *PAR*

Luther the Geek

Bizarre little independent production has earned itself a strong underground reputation. For those who think the word "geek" is only applied to nerdy guys, it actually refers to carnival performers who bite the heads off of live animals, usually chickens in this country. That's what the title character does. He's also a homicidal maniac who sets his sights on a rural Midwestern farm house. The result might have been titled *The Chainsaw Massacres of Madison County*. Director Carlton Albright aims for that same Grand Guignol combination of sex and violence. 🦴🦴🦴

Contains graphic bloody violence, nudity, sexual material, strong language.

1990 90m/C Edward Terry, Joan Roth, J. Jerome Clarke, Tom Mills, Stacy Haiduk; *D:* Carlton J. Albright. VHS *DAP*

M. Butterfly

The short review is *The Crying Game* in China, but that's not really fair because *The Crying Game* is a thriller. Though the two films share many elements—sexual role reversals, political intrigue, betrayal—*M. Butterfly* is an opera. Its sense of reality is less important than its sweeping passions. Like any opera, it's challenging, larger than life, and something of an acquired taste. In Beijing, 1964, Rene Gallimard (Jeremy Irons) is an accountant at the French embassy. He's a dry, tidy, unimaginative fellow until the night he hears Song Liling (John Lone) singing arias from *Madame Butterfly*. Not knowing that in Chinese opera, women's roles are portrayed by men, Rene believes Song is a woman. Offstage, he dresses and acts as a woman, and Rene becomes obsessed with him/her. They embark on a relationship that defies description. And even though the film is based on a true story, it also defies credibility at times. Without going into unsavory details, Rene doesn't figure out what's going on, and even believes that he is the father of Song's child. But, this is cinematic opera. Individual details—even those central to the story—don't mean as much as the overall effect of the piece. And from the animated opening credits to the violent conclusion, director David Cronenberg maintains his reputation as one of today's most unorthodox filmmakers. He and Irons create the same dense atmosphere that made *Dead Ringers* so creepy and hard to define, and Lone fits in perfectly. Though his role, unlike Jaye Davidson's, does not depend on audience deception, he makes Song a believable character. 🐾🐾🐾

Mature subject matter, sexual content, brief nudity, violence.

1993 **(R)** 101m/C Jeremy Irons, John Lone, Ian Richardson, Barbara Sukowa, Vernon Dobtcheff, Annabel Leventon, Shizuko Hoshi, Richard McMillan; **D:** David Cronenberg; **W:** David Henry Hwang; **M:** Howard Shore. **VHS, LV** *WAR*

Madame Bovary

Emma Bovary is one of the great heroines of fiction and Isabelle Huppert plays her flawlessly as a woman betrayed by her own passions and the men who use her. In an exceptionally faithful adaptation of Flaubert's novel, director Claude Chabrol recreates the world of 19th century France with vivid accuracy. From a rural wedding to a fancy dress ball to social life in the larger cities, the film looks like a moving Impressionist painting. Not that it's romantic or visually appealing— neither Flaubert nor Chabrol had those in mind. Instead, the film creates a growing atmosphere of sad inevitability. Even if you know what's going to happen to Emma, it's impossible not to become involved with her story. 🐾🐾🐾🐾

Mature subject matter.

1991 **(PG-13)** 130m/C **FR** Isabelle Huppert, Jean-Francois Balmer, Christophe MaLavoy, Jean Yanne; **D:** Claude Chabrol; **W:** Claude Chabrol; **M:** Matthieu Chabrol. Nominations: Academy Awards '91: Best Costume Design. **VHS, LV** *REP, INJ, BTV*

The Maddening

Wretched little suspense/horror movie is more distasteful than frightening. At core, it's a hostage story about a delusional couple (Burt Reynolds and Angie Dickinson at their all-time hammiest) who kidnap a young woman (Mia Sara) and her little girl. Though the material isn't handled as pure exploitation, it contains some out-of-place humor and considerable graphic violence specifically aimed at women and children. That is not entertainment. **WOOF!**

Mature subject matter, violence, strong language, brief nudity.

1995 **(R)** 97m/C Burt Reynolds, Angie Dickinson, Mia Sara, Brian Wimmer; **D:** Danny Huston. **VHS, LV** *VMK*

Magic in the Mirror

Kidvid works with a standard theme and gives it an effective if limited treatment. Young Mary Margaret (Jaime Renee Smith) has the traditional busy parents who don't understand her rich fantasy life until she finds her way to the other side of her grandmother's antique mirror. There she meets the comical "Mirror Minders" and their feathered enemies, big tea-drinking ducks. The makeup effects aren't bad; director Ted Nicolaou cut quantity, not quality. Imagine Dorothy and two Munchkins. First of a series. 🐾🐾🐾

1996 **(G)** 86m/C Jaime Renee Smith, Kevin Wixted, Saxon Trainor, David Brooks, Godfrey James; **D:** Ted Nicolaou; **W:** Frank Dietz, Ken Carter Jr.; **C:** Adolfo Bartoli; **M:** Richard Kosinski. **VHS** *PAR*

The Magic Sword

Time has been kind to low-budget legend Bert I. Gordon's fantasy. The simple story has to do with a brave young knight (Gary Lockwood) out to rescue a princess (Anne Helm) with the help of his mom (Estelle Winwood), a witch, and her magic mirror. Evil magician (Basil Rathbone) has a dragon on his side. The effects are rudimentary, but they're part of the fun. So is the silly acting. 🐾🐾🐾

No objectionable material.

1962 80m/C Basil Rathbone, Estelle Winwood, Gary Lockwood, Anne Helm; *D:* Bert I. Gordon. **VHS** *MGM, MRV, VYY*

The Maid

Throwback to the Rock Hudson-Doris Day romantic comedies works well on video. Anthony Wayne (Martin Sheen) is a hotshot investment banker with a breezy attitude and an unconventional approach to life. Impulsively he accepts a new job and moves from New York to Paris. Having a month to kill before his job starts, he signs on as a domestic for Nicole Chantrelle (Jacqueline Bisset). The first thing he discovers is her hellion daughter (Victoria Shalet). The second thing he discovers is that Nicole works for the firm he will be joining. If you've seen any of those old hidden-identity comedies, you know how the complications are going to be spun out, and you know exactly how it's going to end—well, almost exactly. Sheen and Bisset share a talent for this spun-sugar material, so its familiarity is welcome. 𝄞𝄞𝄞

Mild profanity.

1990 (PG) 91m/C Martin Sheen, Jacqueline Bisset, Jean-Pierre Cassel, James Faulkner, Victoria Shalet; *D:* Ian Toynton. **VHS, LV** *MED, VTR*

Malibu Express

The California setting and an inept hero (he can't shoot) make this one of Sidaris' silliest. An enthusiastic female supporting cast makes it one of his sexiest. For his fans it's required viewing. 𝄞𝄞𝄞 **GPI: 8.8**

Nudity, sexual content, violence, some strong language.

1985 (R) 101m/C Darby Hinton, Sybil Danning, Art Metrano, Shelley Taylor Morgan, Niki Dantine, Barbara Edwards; *D:* Andy Sidaris. **VHS** *MCA*

The Man in the Attic

Fact-based historical thriller doesn't live up to its considerable potential. It begins in California, 1930, where murderer Edward Broder (Neil Patrick Harris) arranges a jailhouse interview with a reporter to explain his side of things. Flashback to Milwaukee, 1910, where Edward works in Mr. Heldmann's (Len Cariou) factory, and promptly falls for the boss's wife, Krista (Anne Archer). She reciprocates and, as the title indicates, finds a place for him in her life. Though the production values are more than adequate, the film lacks two key elements—humor and sex. It does come close, however. When the two lovers start living out her fantasies—that he's the slave boy who'll do anything his queen desires—she has him moving furniture in the next scene. More seriously, neither Anne Archer nor her body double project the sexual magnetism of a believable femme fatale. Director Graeme Campbell handled similar material more effectively in *Blood Relations* and *Into the Fire*. 𝄞𝄞

Mature subject matter, brief nudity, sexual content, some violence.

1994 (R) 97m/C Anne Archer, Neil Patrick Harris, Len Cariou, Alex Carter; *D:* Graeme Campbell; *W:* Duane Poole, Tom Swale; *M:* Lou Natale. **VHS** *PAR*

Man of the Year

Dirk Shafer's autobiographical comedy is a quirky "mockumentary." Shafer was *Playgirl* magazine's 1992 Man of the Year. He recreates his 15 minutes of fame as a male sex symbol through a series of fictional recreations, vignettes, and tapes of his various TV talk show guest shots. The central event is the obligatory "dream date" with a lucky reader, but Shafer's real subject is his personal life and the eventual revelation of his homosexuality. The combination of non-fiction and drama is not completely successful. Yes, it's a funny story, but it doesn't have the element of surprise that you find in the best documentaries. The actors playing real characters tend to overplay their roles shamelessly, and the film has a strong stench of condescension toward many of the female characters. Of course, Shafer presents himself in the best possible light. The joke—if that's the right word for the premise—wears thin by the end and the overly emotional conclusion is weak. Even so, Shafer deserves some credit for originality and an economic, no-frills style. He also got a disarming performance by Vivian Paxton, his friend and co-conspirator. 🎬🎬🎬

Mature subject matter, a little strong language.

1996 85m/C Dirk Shafer, Vivian Paxton, Claudette Sutherland, Michael Ornstein; **D:** Dirk Shafer; **W:** Dirk Shafer; **C:** Stephen Timberlake; **M:** Peitor Angell. **VHS** *FXL*

The Man Who Fell to Earth

Moviegoers who have seen Nicolas Roeg's s-f masterpiece only in its theatrical form really haven't seen it. The print that played in American theatres was 118 minutes long. The 139-minute version is available on tape and the two-disk Voyager laser version is letterboxed and transferred to video with absolute clarity. The full-length film shows that Roeg was decades ahead of his time. The filmmaking techniques that were once so confusing and challenging have become commonplace; you can see them every day in commercials and music videos. But Roeg's quick-cut, overlapping sound and image, non-linear, multimedia, time-splitting approach made an unusual story all that more difficult to understand. On one level, though, the plot is simplicity itself. A man who calls himself Thomas Jerome Newton (David Bowie) arrives on Earth from another planet. Capitalizing on his advanced technologies, he secures valuable patents and amasses a huge fortune. His mission is to bring water to his desert home, but before he can accomplish that, he is seduced by the luxuries of his success, and the government takes an interest in his activities. The other key players in his story are Farnsworth (Buck Henry), a homosexual patent lawyer who helps Newton; Bryce (Rip Torn), a lecherous college professor whose life oddly parallels Newton's; and Mary-Lou (Candy Clark), a hotel maid who becomes Newton's Significant Other. That story is less important than the film's ideas about success, love, betrayal, and other thorny issues of the human condition. It can be seen as an allegory on success—New-

ton as a billionaire, Bowie as a pop star—and how it can become a trap. That's why the casting of the lead was so perfect. Bowie had already created an image of otherworldly, ambivalent sexuality around himself. Even without gaudy special effects, it's easy to accept him as an alien. And in the end, the movie is about being alien—isolated and different from the people around you. All of us have felt it and can empathize with the emotion, but the film also shows the other side of alienation, the self-serving side. Bowie's Newton is also saying, "I am so intelligent, talented, brilliant (pick one or more), that everyone else must take care of me while I create, compose, save the world (pick one or more)." Compared to many movies of the 1970s, this one has aged gracefully. The previously unseen material, much of it sexual and weirdly comic, makes the story easier to understand. The videodisk liner notes indicate the sequences that were altered or eliminated in the theatrical release. The supplemental section on the disk itself further explains the changes that the American distributors demanded. On a separate audio track, Roeg, Bowie, and Henry comment on the film. 🎵🎵🎵🎵

Contains nudity, sexual material, strong language.

1976 **(R)** 139m/C *GB* David Bowie, Candy Clark, Rip Torn, Buck Henry, Bernie Casey; *D:* Nicolas Roeg. **VHS, LV** *COL*

Man with a Gun

Crazed crime film has such a well-developed sense of humor that it's almost a comedy, but moody atmosphere is really more important. This one's got enough of that for a dozen thrillers. It's all about a hitman (Michael Madsen) who's caught up with scheming mobsters (Robert Loggia and Gary Busey) and a runaway wife (Jennifer Tilly) who's got blackmail on her mind. Before it's over, multiple betrayals, identical twins, and lots of gunfire have come into play. Director David Wyles gets the expected professional work from his ensemble cast, complemented by George Blondheim's smokey score and Freddy Hubbard's trumpet. 🎵🎵🎵

Violence, strong language, sexual content.

1995 **(R)** 100m/C Michael Madsen, Jennifer Tilly, Gary Busey, Robert Loggia, Ian Tracey, Bill Cobbs; *D:* David Wyles; *W:* Laurie Finstad-Knizhik; *C:* Jan Kiesser; *M:* George Blondheim. **VHS** *HMK*

The Man with the Perfect Swing

This wonderful little sleeper will play well with golfers, but even those who, like me, think that smacking a little white ball across overly landscaped pastures is a waste of real estate can appreciate it. Writer/director Mike Hovis avoids all the cliches that plague sports movies. At no point in this one do you care about the sinking of a putt or the winning of a match. Instead, it's about characters—believable, engaging people we've all met. Anthony "Babe" Lombardo (James Black) is a glad-handing middle-aged jock whose glory days are long gone. But he's a good golfer and his long-suffering wife Susan (Suzanne Savoy) loves him. They're getting by with his selling golf doo-dads, dreaming up schemes, and borrowing cash from friends. Then Babe invents the perfect golf swing. Like the Internet, it's a great idea, but how do you make money with it? Hovis is clearly telling a story he loves. The film appears to have been made on location in Texas, and so it's got a lived-in look that fits the story. The details have a ring of hard truth. The two leads couldn't be better. James Black has a sure comic touch and a strong resemblance to Lou Costello. 🎵🎵🎵

Contains strong language, brief nudity.

1995 94m/C James Black, Suzanne Savoy, Marco Perella, James Belcher, Richard Bradshaw; *D:* Michael Hovis; *W:* Michael Hovis; *C:* Jim Barham; *M:* Paul English. **VHS** *MNC*

Married People, Single Sex

At first, this seems to be a serious story about troubled relationships, but it's so poorly told as to be virtually unwatchable. The main flaw is frantic, claustrophobic camerawork, whipping back and forth among several characters in a small room. The technique didn't work when Woody Allen used it in *Husbands and Wives* and it's no better here. It is, however, easily overcome with the fast-forward button. Astonishingly, followed by a sequel. Also available in an unrated version. **WOOF!**

Sexual material, nudity, strong language, violence.

1993 (R) 110m/C Chase Masterson, Joseph Pilato, Darla Slavens, Shelley Michelle, Wendi Westbrook, Robert Zachar, Samuel Mongiello, Teri Thompson; *D:* Mike Sedan; *W:* Catherine Tavel. **VHS** *TRI*

Mascara

Bert (Michael Sarrazin) is a police superintendent. Chris (Derek De Lint) is a costume designer. Gaby (Charlotte Rampling) goes to the opera with Bert and immediately falls for Chris. The body of this Belgian-Dutch-French co-production concerns murder, transsexuals, transvestites, and free-floating kinkiness. Much of the action is so deliberately posed and arch that it's not meant to be taken seriously. Substance is deliberately subordinated to style, darlings, but the film manages to sustain a strong mood and that's the real point. 🎬🎬🎬

Rated R for nudity, sexual situations, profanity, subject matter, violence, and general principle.

1987 (R) 99m/C BF Derek De Lint, Charlotte Rampling, Michael Sarrazin; *D:* Patrick Conrad. **VHS** *WAR*

Masque of the Red Death

Remake of Roger Corman's 1964 original is curiously slow and dispirited though fairly faithful to Poe's story. Prince Prospero (Adrian Paul) tries to defeat the plague of the Red Death by bringing all of his noble pals inside and sealing the gates of the city. He imports a few comely peasant wenches for entertainment and also invites his old teacher, Machiavel (Patrick Macnee). Prospero is a dark, brooding sort who's prone to sophomoric philosophical reflection when he's not paying more attention than he should to his sister Lucretia (Tracy Reiner). He worries about Life and Death and the Duty of the Prince and stuff like that. Though the film has all the right elements—inexpensive but atmospheric sets; silly costumes, wigs, and dialogue; swordfights; boiling oil to pour on the peasants—it lacks the two key ingredients that made the Corman

movies so enjoyable: speed and lack of self-consciousness. Those films zipped along at a fast pace, and never for a moment did they take themselves seriously. Corman produced this *Masque* but it lacks his touch. 🎬🎬

Violence, sexual content, brief nudity.

1989 (R) 83m/C Patrick Macnee, Jeffery Osterhage, Adrian Paul, Tracy Reiner, Maria Ford; *D:* Larry Brand; *W:* Larry Brand, Daryl Haney. **VHS, LV** *MGM, IME*

Masseuse

When Kirsty's (Griffin Drew) dirty rotten no-good two-timing fiance Jack (Tim Abell) tries to swindle her, she gets all the revenge she wants and then some. Most of the action is strictly within the limits of the soft-core genre. What sets this one apart is its humor and spirited feminist attitude. Fans, look for a cameo by Brinke Stevens. Also available in an unrated version. 🎬🎬🎬 **GPI: 7.9**

Sexual content, nudity, comic violence.

1995 (R) 90m/C Griffin Drew, Monique Parent, Tim Abell; *Cameos:* Brinke Stevens; *D:* Daniel Peters. **VHS** *TRI*

A Matter of Honor

Affectionate if jejune undergraduate melodrama is a well-intentioned amateur effort about, of all things, college rugby. The film was written and produced by Craig Cosgrove and seems to have been produced primarily at the University of North Texas in Denton. With grainy color and lots of starkly illuminated locations, the production values are barely acceptable, even for video. The central character is John Bull (Jackson Bostwick), an allegedly old-fashioned history professor who lectures in blue jeans and open collar shirts (no tie). He's also the rugby coach and foe of arch villain Nick Raider (Allen Arkus), who disgraced the team years before. Raider is a thoroughly ridiculous caricature and the crackpot conflict between the two is embarrassing. 🎬

Contains mild sports violence, strong language, mature subject matter.

1995 (PG) 95m/C Jackson Bostwick, Allen Arkus, Rebecca Gray, David Michie; *D:* Frederick P. Watkins; *W:* Craig Cosgrove. **VHS** *AVI*

"We are driven by fear because frankly [films] are products, and now more than ever, they are products that very quickly have to establish brand identity and consumer awareness. We have this fear because there is so much product out there, when there are 500 movies a year being released in various shapes and forms, the consumer is pretty aware of the fact that every weekend there are three or four or five new choices."

—CHRIS PULA, PRESIDENT OF NEW LINE MARKETING

Me and the Mob

Jimmy Corona (James Lorinz) is a struggling writer who lacks inspiration and support. His agent brushes him off with, "Ask not what your agent can do for you, but what you can do for your agent." Then his avaricious girlfriend (Sandra Bullock, in a small but funny cameo) walks out on him. Bottomed out, Jimmy says yes when his uncle (Tony Darrow) offers him a job in the family business, collecting loan payments the old-fashioned way, making unrefusable offers and getting rid of "enemies," so to speak. But before he gets his feet wet, the cops are after him to inform on his new associates. Too often the action is talky and slow, but Jimmy's a good character and Lorinz is an effective deadpan comedian. Chalk this one up as an over-achieving ultra-low-budget comedy for gangster flick fans. 🗡🗡🗸

Strong language, mild violence, comic sexual content.

1994 (R) 85m/C James Lorinz, Tony Darrow, John Costelloe, Sandra Bullock, Anthony Michael Hall, Stephen Lee, Ted Sorel; *Cameos:* Steve Buscemi; *D:* Frank Rainone; *W:* James Lorinz, Frank Rainone. **VHS** *AVI*

Meet the Feebles

Destined to be confused with *Meet the Hollowheads,* this import will appeal to the same audience that has a taste for the bizarre and ugly. In fact, the film is a comedy of the grotesque that's so outrageous it will immediately offend most viewers. It's essentially a nasty parody of *The Muppet Show,* with a troupe of puppets and other creatures involved in the production of a variety show. But the overweight star Heidi the Hippo and her lover/boss Bletch the Walrus are thoroughly debauched variations on Miss Piggy and Kermit. The problems they face range from sexually transmitted diseases to drug dealing and mass slaughter. The puppetry is inventive but crude, and the humor involves vile material that extends well beyond some crude racial stereotypes. Director Peter Jackson (*Heavenly Creatures, Frighteners*) has certainly refined his style since this 1989 effort. The film's main problem lies in the subject of its parody. This kind of humor is at its best when it attacks pomposity. But the Muppets have never taken anything, including themselves, seriously and there's a strong streak of Marx Bros. anarchy to their humor. They're much more effective comedians than these Feebles, though not nearly as offensive. And that's the real point. 🗡🗡

Contains graphic puppet depictions of bodily functions, sexual acts, violence, strong language, bathroom humor.

1989 94m/C *NZ D:* Peter Jackson; *W:* Peter Jackson, Danny Mulheron, Frances Walsh. **VHS** *MTH*

Meet the Hollowheads

Imagine a combination of *PeeWee's Playhouse* and Terry Gilliam's *Brazil.* Throw in the nastier bits of *The Addams Family* and *Married...With Children.* This exercise in gaudy style will not appeal to all tastes. It's a mean-spirited parody of family sit-coms set in a fantasy world where everything is connected by tubes. Henry Hollowhead (John Glover) works for United Umbilical, the tube utility. His boss is the evil Mr. Crabneck (Richard Portnow). One night, Henry invites him home for dinner, to the horror of his wife Miriam (Nancy Mette). His kids Cindy (a young and obnoxious Juliette Lewis) and Bud (Matt Shakman) don't care. They're off to a concert while Mom tries to figure out how to stretch the gooey tentacles she had planned for a main course to serve five instead of four. When Cindy asks if she can use some "softening jelly" for her big night out, her mother refuses, saying she's too young. (Nothing in the film is specific; the tentacles, jelly, and such are generically grotesque.) The excesses don't quite mesh with the slapstick, absurdist humor. Somehow, it all seems more studied and less spontaneous than it should be. This kind of weirdness can't be faked; it has to come from the heart. 🐾🐾

Mild violence and nonspecific offensiveness.

1989 (PG-13) 89m/C John Glover, Nancy Mette, Richard Portnow, Matt Shakman, Juliette Lewis, Anne Ramsey; *D:* Tom Burman; *W:* Tom Burman. **VHS, LV** *MED, IME*

Men of Respect

Shakespeare's *Macbeth* is retold as a contemporary gangster story. After the obligatory opening massacre, a weird psychic tells Mike Battaglia (John Turturro) and his pal Bankie Como (Dennis Farina) that they have bright futures. Well, Mike's is better than Bankie's, but things are definitely not looking good for Padrino Charlie D'Amico (Rod Steiger). When Mike's ambitious wife Ruthie (Katherine Borowitz) hears that he's been promoted, she gets big ideas and suggests that they invite Charlie over for dinner. Anyone familiar with the original knows what's coming. These near-cartoon characters are so overstated and overacted that they make Mario Puzo's mobsters look like Campfire Girls. The only cast members to survive with any dignity are Peter Boyle, as an Irish gangster, and comedian Steven Wright, who has a hilarious cameo. Don't miss the famous sleepwalking scene, and take note of Mike's exit line. Both contain grand moments of unintentional humor that are almost worth the price of a rental by themselves. For an evening's entertainment at home, you could do much worse. Also, strange as it may sound, this isn't the first time the Bard's tragedy has been translated to this genre. A 1955 British film, *Joe Macbeth*, did exactly the same thing. 🐾🐾🐾

Paint-blistering language, graphic and bloody violence, brief nudity.

1991 (R) 113m/C John Turturro, Katherine Borowitz, Peter Boyle, Dennis Farina, Chris Stein, Steven Wright, Stanley Tucci, Rod Steiger; *D:* William Reilly; *W:* William Reilly; *C:* Bobby Bukowski. **VHS, LV, 8mm** *COL*

Men of War

Judging by the box art, this appears to be just another formula shoot-'em-up, but a glance into the fine print of the credits reveals that it's something more. First, the script was co-written by John Sayles; second it was directed by Perry Lang, who's often worked with Sayles as an actor and writer. Sayles is known best these days for his own serious work—*Matewan, Lone Star*—but he got his start in the business writing low-budget flicks for Roger Corman. Sayles knows how to tell a story quickly and economically, and that's exactly what he does here. In terms of moving the plot along, there's barely a wasted frame of film or word of dialogue. That story concerns ex-Special Forces mercenary Nick Gunner (Dolph Lundgren) who's recruited off a snowy Chicago street to put together a team to destabilize the government of a small island somewhere in the China Sea. His slick corporate employers are coy about their reasons. No matter. Gunner reluctantly accepts and, in a sequence pulled straight from *The Seven Samurai,* gathers the usual motley crew of colorfully off-beat characters. Before they reach the island, they run afoul of Gunner's old enemy Keefer (Trevor Goddard), a scenery-chomping, bare-chested villain who really cuts loose and steals the film. The humanism that's always so strong in Sayles' work is much in evidence. Lundgren has grown as an actor and is effective in the lead. He gets a lot of help from a fine supporting cast including B.D. Wong, Zeus "Tiny" Lister, Charlotte Lewis, Kevin Tighe, and Catherine Bell. In his previous directorial effort, *Little Vegas*, Lang showed an affinity for character-based comedy. Here he seems just as comfortable with action scenes played out on a human scale, and delivers everything that fans of the genre want to see. 🐾🐾🐾

Strong language, violence, brief nudity, sexual content.

1994 (R) 102m/C Dolph Lundgren, Charlotte Lewis, B.D. Wong, Anthony John Denison, Tim Guinee, Don Harvey, Tiny Lister, Tom Wright, Kevin Tighe, Trevor Goddard, Catherine Bell; *D:* Perry Lang; *W:* John Sayles, Ethan Reiff, Cyrus Voris; *C:* Ronn Schmidt; *M:* Gerald Gouriet. **VHS, LV** *TOU*

Meridian: Kiss of the Beast

This unapologetic bodice-ripper is one of home video's great guilty pleasures. American Catherine Bomarzini (Sherilyn Fenn) has just returned to the family estate in Italy, a palatial spread filled with oversized sculptures. In short order, she and her best friend Gina (Charlie Spradling) fall in with a traveling carnival led by a dark magician (Malcolm Jamieson). After a wild night of carousing, a fearsome lionlike critter shows up in the boudoir, and then.... Before it's all over, an evil dwarf, a ghost or two, a legend, and a Renaissance painting have been tossed into the mix. Sherilyn Fenn handles the lead with the right combination of seriousness and flip pancy. Staying true to the spirit of the genre, she gets dolled up in antique dresses (complete with several pounds of jewelry), wanders through miles and miles of mysterious corridors, and swoons at all the appropriate moments. The plot makes no more sense than it absolutely has to, but that's not a big deal. The pace is brisk and despite its derivative roots, the film is inventive. 𝄞𝄞𝄞 **GPI: 9.5**

Nudity, sexual content, mild violence.

1990 (R) 90m/C Sherilyn Fenn, Malcom Jamieson, Hilary Mason, Alex Daniels, Phil Fondacaro, Charlie Spradling; *D:* Charles Band; *W:* Dennis Paoli; *M:* Pino Donaggio. **VHS, LV** *PAR*

A Midnight Clear

Keith Gordon, probably best known as the young protagonist in Brian DePalma's *Dressed to Kill,* makes an impressive debut as writer/director of this passionate, intelligent anti-war film based on William Wharton's novel. It's mid-December 1944, the Ardennes Forest, in either France, Luxembourg, or Belgium, no one's really sure which. The six surviving members of an intelligence and reconnaissance patrol know only that they've been sent to a house in the forest to see if there's anything to the rumors of a German counterattack. Maj. Griffen (John C. McGinley), operating under the mistaken idea that military intelligence has something to do with human intelligence, has assigned the smartest young men under his command to the patrol. There used to be 12 of them, but, as our narrator, Will Knott, says, intelligence doesn't count for much in war. Knott (Ethan Hawke) is the nominal leader of the group. But Avakian (Kevin Dillon) really knows more about soldiering. The oldest of the group, Mother (Gary Sinise) is half mad. Only Stan (Arye Gross), who's Jewish, is really gung-ho to fight. Miller (Peter Berg) is ready for the war to be over, and Father (Frank Whaley) refuses to admit that the unit is part of the army. When they arrive at the house in the middle of the snow-covered woods, they find that the Germans are indeed in the area. But these Germans aren't the enemy they're used to fighting. The characters and the premise make the film sound like any number of formula WWII flicks, but just the opposite is true. This is not the story of a group of kids from different parts of the country who are tested in battle and become a fighting unit. It's about frightened young men who have virtually no understanding of what they're doing, and only the vaguest idea about why. The film's anti-authoritarian political slant is similar to *Catch-22* (the novel, not the movie), and the references to *King of Hearts* are hard to miss. But *A Midnight Clear* stands on its own without comparison. In the last third of the film, when the story becomes much more intense and unpredictable, Gordon adds a strong religious element. Throughout, the film has an eerie, cold dreamlike quality that creates an effective mood. Viewers looking for lots of firepower and heroic action should give this one a pass. That's not the point. But if you're in the mood for a fine serious drama with a first-rate young cast, don't miss it. 𝄞𝄞𝄞𝄞

Strong language, violence.

1992 (R) 107m/C Peter Berg, Kevin Dillon, Arye Gross, Ethan Hawke, Gary Sinise, Frank Whaley, John C. McGinley, Larry

Joshua, Curt Lowens; *D:* Keith Gordon; *W:* Keith Gordon; *M:* Mark Isham. **VHS, LV** *COL, PMS*

Midnight Heat

Washed-up quarterback and recovering alcoholic Tyler Gray (Tim Matheson) does all the wrong things when he has an affair with the team owner's toothsome wife (Mimi Craven) and then involves himself in said owner's murder. The cliched title is the tipoff. From beginning to end, Meredith Preston's script is remarkably predictable. According to the timer on the VCR, I figured it out before the ten-minute mark. 🦴🦴

Sexual scenes, nudity, language, some violence.

1995 (R) 97m/C Tim Matheson, Stephen Mendel, Mimi Craven; *D:* Harvey Frost; *W:* Meredith Preston. **VHS** *AVE*

Midnight Tease

Stripper flicks make up a sizeable and usually boring part of the video business. When they appear on the big screen, they're seldom any better and there they tend to be overpriced and overhyped. This video premiere actually has some interesting characters, created by writer Daniella Purcell, and good moments. Samantha (Cassandra Leigh) is a cynical, emotionally troubled stripper who's having nightmare fantasies about killing her customers and co-workers. She might be reliving a horrible childhood trauma or she might be acting it out. The resolution isn't nearly as intriguing as the theatrical sleeper, *Exotica,* but it's a lot more fun than Demi Moore's *Striptease.* 🦴🦴🦴

Contains nudity, sexual situations, violence, strong language.

1994 87m/C Cassandra Leigh, Rachel Reed, Edmund Halley, Ashlie Rhey, Todd Joseph; *D:* Scott Levy. **VHS, LV** *NHO*

Midnight Tease 2

Who's bumping off ecdysiasts? Jennifer (Kimberly Kelley) goes undercover—metaphorically—on the runway to find her sister's killer. Considering the general level of quality in the stripper-flick subgenre, this one's a notch or two above average, but it's not even close to the sleeper, *Stripteaser,* or the original. 🦴🦴

Contains nudity, sexual situations, violence, strong language.

1995 94m/C Kimberly Kelley, Tane McClure, Ross Hagen; *D:* Richard Styles. **VHS** *NHO*

A Million to Juan

A good heart can make up for a lot in real life and in home video. In many ways, this is a run-of-the-mill low-budget comedy about immigrant life in East Los Angeles. But comedian Paul Rodriguez—who stars and directs—has an engaging screen presence. He also has a fine cast to work with, and he tells a good story, based on his own characters and a Mark Twain tale. Juan Lopez (Rodriguez) is an ambitious widower who has problems with the Immigration Service, despite the efforts of his pretty case worker Olivia (Polly Draper). Then an anonymous benefactor gives him a check for a million dollars...with strings attached. Those strings involve timely questions of community, responsibility, materialism, and greed. The combination of drama and humor is effective, even though the film wears its emotions on its sleeve. 🦴🦴🦴

A little rough language, mature subject matter.

1994 (PG) 105m/C Paul Rodriguez, Polly Draper, Pepe Serna, Bert Rosario, Jonathan Hernandez, Gerardo, Victor Rivers, Edward James Olmos, Paul Williams; *Cameos:* Tony Plana, Ruben Blades, Richard "Cheech" Marin, David Rasche, Liz Torres; *D:* Paul Rodriguez; *W:* Francisca Matos, Robert Grasmere. **VHS** *PSM*

Mind Games

Dana (Edward Albert) and Rita (Shawn Weatherly) have been considering a separation. With their ten-year-old son Kevin (Matt Norero), they set off on an RV-vacation, hoping that a tour of the California coast will help them solve their problems. Instead, they run into a seductive sociopath, Eric (Maxwell Caulfield), who insinuates himself into their group and then begins to experiment with them. It's a gripping idea for a film. Writer Kenneth Dorward has created four fully developed, believable characters, and a situation

The Hound's Favorite Sleepers: Guy Vids

As opposed to "Chick Vids," which usually focus on perceptive analysis of individual and group characters, and a certain sensitivity to emotional content, "Guy Vids" tend to be coarser, more violent, and more keenly appreciative of bad taste and things that really shouldn't be discussed in polite company, which is not to say that they're not sensitive in their own way. At least, that's how the Hound sees it.

AKIRA	LES PATTERSON SAVES THE WORLD
ANIMAL INSTINCTS	
THE BANKER	MEN OF WAR
THE CROSSING GUARD	NOTHING BUT A MAN
84 CHARLIE MOPIC	THE POMPATUS OF LOVE
FALL TIME	POWWOW HIGHWAY
HARD-BOILED	RECKLESS KELLY
HARD TICKET TO HAWAII	ROMPER STOMPER
THE KILLER	THE SIEGE OF FIREBASE GLORIA
LAST MAN STANDING	
	THE STREET FIGHTER

that becomes more and more tense as it unfolds. The main problems are an obviously limited budget, unconvincing acting from Weatherly and Norero, and a slack pace. On the positive side, Caulfield is very good, and the ending is unusual and more than a little disturbing. 🦴🦴

Intense domestic violence, sexual situations.

1989 (R) 93m/C Edward Albert, Shawn Weatherly, Matt Norero, Maxwell Caulfield; *D:* Bob Yari; *W:* Kenneth Dorward. **VHS** *FOX, HHE*

Mindfield

Canadian conspiracy thriller about illegal government psychiatric experiments is something of a sleeper. Though the pace is slow and the action is oddly quiet, the film still works well. Director Jean-Claude Lord effectively captures the city of Montreal in winter. He gets the details right; the grittiness of city snow, the crunching sound of footsteps. The performances are unusually effective, too. Michael Ironside, usually seen as a villain, is a fine protagonist and Christopher Plummer, one of the best character actors in the business, adds his usual fine touch. 🦴🦴🦴

Violence, profanity, sexual material.

1989 (R) 91m/C *CA* Michael Ironside, Lisa Langlois, Christopher Plummer, Stefan Wodoslowsky, Sean McCann; *D:* Jean-Claude Lord. **VHS, LV** *NO*

Minute Movie Masterpieces

Collection of clips from 30 excellent and not-so-excellent films combines plot summaries with irreverent voiceover narration. As the copy on the box puts it, "This crash course in classic cinema packs over 100 viewing hours and four decades of movie magic—into just 30 minutes!" The sharp little attack on cinematic seriousness is right on target with Olivier's *As You Like It*, Fritz Lang's *Metropolis*, Hitchcock's *The Lady Vanishes*, Welles' *The Stranger*, Capra's *It's a Wonderful Life*, and the lesser films, all in public domain now. It's refreshing to see someone tweak immortals like Shakespeare and Maugham. More importantly, this tape highlights the virulent racism that runs through the work of D.W. Griffith. Credit goes to director Cliff Knotes (yeah, right) and to writer and editor David Starns, who also narrated with Judith Silinsky. 🦴🦴🦴

Contains no objectionable material.

1989 30m/C David Starns, Judith Silinsky; *D:* Cliff Knotes; *W:* David Starns. **VHS** *RHI*

Miracle Mile

Eccentric, dreamlike film is almost impossible to describe without giving the game away. It's a suspense film that begins with a short lecture on cosmic evolution taking us from the creation of the universe until now. Then in a leisurely paced introduction, the attractive protagonists meet each other and fall in love. Harry (Anthony Edwards) is a trombone player; Julie (Mare Winningham) is a waitress. Writer/director Steve DeJarnatt manages to create a growing sense of uneasiness bordering on menace in the first part of the film. That mood builds subtly and effectively until Harry answers a ringing public telephone outside an all-night diner. It's four in the morning; the panicked young man on the other end claims to be in a missile silo in North Dakota. He says that he's been ordered to fire his missiles in 50 minutes. In an hour and a half, the retaliatory strike will hit Los Angeles. Is it a joke, a mistake, a hoax, a false alarm, or the truth? If you're willing to accept the coincidental nature of the device, it taps into our collective nightmares about a nuclear holocaust and makes for an absorbing suspense story. But by the same token, if you accept it, you cannot accept many of the foolish things that the main characters do. Their unbelievable actions keep the plot chugging along, but they strain credulity well past the breaking point. Everything else about the film is so good that its flaws are all the more glaring. Anthony Edwards and Mare Winningham are up to form. The entire production seems to have been washed in pastel colors that give an unusual texture to the characters and settings. In the end, this is a risky film. Even those who admire it will have to admit that it's not completely successful, but I still recommend it and look forward to seeing what DeJarnatt does next. 𝄞𝄞𝄞

Profanity, violence, brief nudity.

1989 (R) 87m/C Anthony Edwards, Mare Winningham, John Agar, Denise Crosby, Lou Hancock, Mykelti Williamson, Kelly Jo Minter, Kurt Fuller, Robert DoQui, Danny De La Paz; *D:* Steve DeJarnatt; *W:* Steve DeJarnatt; *M:* Tangerine Dream. **VHS, LV** *HBO*

Mirage

So-so variation on Hitchcock's masterpiece *Vertigo* has a Southern California setting. As it begins, police detective Randazzo (James Andronica, who also wrote the script) drags his old pal Matty Juarez (Edward James Olmos) out of the bottom of a tequila bottle. Even though Matty has a terrible failure in his past that explains the drunkenness, Randazzo wants him to follow a wealthy woman (Sean Young) who's suffering from severe multiple-personality disorder. Seems that prim and respectable Jennifer wigs out from time to time and becomes Shannon, who hangs out and dances topless in biker bars. Andronica's dialogue is often cliched, and director Paul Williams brings no real style to the action. In the leads, Olmos and Young look a little worse for the wear. He's beefy; she really cuts loose in the nutcase scenes, and gets to do lots of other actressy stuff, though to say anything about that would give the game away. The ending is appropriately tongue in cheek. 𝄞𝄞

Strong language, some violence, brief nudity, sexual content.

1994 (R) 106m/C Edward James Olmos, Sean Young, James Andronica, Paul W. Williams; *D:* Paul W. Williams; *W:* James Andronica. **VHS** *MCA*

Mirror Images

Sex and politics mix in the wacky tale of twin sisters, one the repressed wife of a politician, the other a stripper. Guess which one decides to live the other's life? Again, the production values are better than the script or the acting, and judged as a guilty pleasure, this one isn't quite tawdry enough. Imagine a video mix of the racier parts of *The New Republic* magazine and the editorial content of *Penthouse*. Also available in an unrated version. 𝄞𝄞 **GPI: 8.2**

Nudity, sexual content, violence, strong language.

1991 (R) 94m/C Delia Sheppard, Jeff Conaway, Richard Arbolino, John O'Hurley, Korey Mall, Julie Strain, Nels Van Patten; *D:* Alexander Gregory Hippolyte. **VHS** *ACA*

Mirror Images 2

Shannon Whirry has carved out an odd little niche for herself. She has made several highly successful video premieres in which she plays an outwardly respectable woman who takes a graphic walk on the wild side and explains it

all to a psychiatrist. I suppose the psychological stuff is meant to give a patina of respectability to the soft-core exploitation. She carries on gamely here as Terrie and Carrie, good girl and bad girl twins. There are no surprises, but she and director Gregory Hippolyte give their fans what they want to see. Also available in an unrated version. 🦴🦴 **GPI: 9.1**

Sexual material, nudity, strong language, violence.

1993 92m/C Shannon Whirry, Luca Bercovici, Tom Reilly; **D:** Alexander Gregory Hippolyte. **VHS** *ACA*

Mirror, Mirror

Interesting little horror film has a strong feminist angle. The gimmick is a huge old supernatural mirror that bridges generations and dimensions. (Or something to that effect; the details aren't spelled out.) The setting is a small town where oddball newcomer Megan (Rainbow Harvest) is having a hard time adjusting to high school. She finds herself captivated by the antique mirror left in the bedroom of her new house. As she spends more time with it, terrible things begin to happen to those who torment her at school. The script—written by four women, one of them director Marina Sargenti—borrows liberally from *Beetlejuice*, *The Amityville Horror*, *Carrie*, and several other Stephen King works. Throughout, the male characters are either well-meaning oafs or pawns who are manipulated by

their evil girlfriends. At its best, the film avoids blatant violence and instead uses blood as a metaphor. Toward the end, the action degenerates into hand-in-the-disposal special effects. Even so, it's more ambitious than most low-budget horror movies. Fans should definitely take a look. Followed by a so-so sequel. 🦴🦴🦴

Violence, strong language, brief nudity.

1990 (R) 105m/C Karen Black, Rainbow Harvest, Kristin Datillo, Ricky Paull Goldin, Yvonne De Carlo, William Sanderson; **D:** Marina Sargenti; **W:** Marina Sargenti. **VHS, LV** *ACA*

Mirror, Mirror 2: Raven Dance

When a movie opens with a tattooed skinhead band playing at a Catholic orphanage for no audience, you know that plot doesn't count for much. And that's as it should be. The effects are everything in this one: they range from a guy in a silly rubber suit to some really good and inventive work done with lights and computers. The violence is too outlandish to be offensive. There are lots of veterans—Roddy McDowall, Sally Kellerman, William Sanderson, Veronica Cartwright—on hand, and the continuity errors are part of the fun, too. 🦴🦴

Wild special effects, violence, strong language.

1994 (R) 91m/C Tracy Wells, Roddy McDowall, Sally Kellerman, Veronica Cartwright, William Sanderson, Lois Nettleton; **D:** Jimmy Lifton; **W:** Jimmy Lifton, Virginia Perfili. **VHS, LV** *ORP*

Mr. Frost

Taut, understated thriller has a serious subject and a streak of sly humor. Frost (Jeff Goldblum) is an extremely polite, intelligent, and charming mass murderer. For two years, he has been institutionalized and has refused to speak. Nothing is known about the man: he has no birth certificate, no driver's license. He will not explain why he committed 24 brutal killings or reveal anything about himself. Inspector Detweiler (Alan Bates), who arrested him, has come to believe that Frost is Satan, Evil incarnate. Frost's new psychiatrist,

Dr. Day (Kathy Baker), doesn't accept such metaphysical explanations. She is the only person Frost will talk to; she sees him as a challenge to her training. But the more she learns about Frost, the more she suspects that Detweiler may be right. Frost can perform astonishing physical tricks, and he has a frightening effect on the patients and doctors around him. He seems to know things he shouldn't. Is he a lunatic who can do some interesting sleight of hand? A manipulator? The personification of evil? Or something else? The film is working with some of the same philosophical conflicts that intrigued novelist Walker Percy: questions about the nature of God and evil; faith and rationality; the relationship between the spiritual and the physical. The violence is mild and Frost's hideous crimes are never shown. The ambiguity that makes the film so appealing may keep it from finding a wide audience. It is thoughtful, in the best sense of the term, and that's seldom a quality that leads to commercial or cult success. 🦴🦴🦴

Profanity, mild violence, subject matter.

1989 (R) 92m/C Jeff Goldblum, Kathy Baker, Alan Bates, Roland Giraud, Jean-Pierre Cassel; **D:** Phillip Setbon; **W:** Phillip Setbon, Brad Lynch. **VHS** *FCT, IME*

Mr. Stitch

Stylized updating of *Frankenstein* starts slow and never generates any real energy. Much of it takes place on a nearly empty white set where the proverbial mad scientist (Rutger Hauer) has created a sexless patchwork man (Wil Wheaton) who combines all races and genders—a sort of off-the-shelf Michael Jackson. After some lengthy discussions of innocence and religion, the plot, such as it is, kicks in. That has to do with sinister government plots, half-hearted chases, and a sympathetic psychologist (Nia Peeples). Producer/director/writer Roger Avary also co-wrote *Pulp Fiction* but you'd hardly guess it on the basis of this Franco-American effort. It's really more akin to George Lucas' student film-turned-feature *THX-1138.* 🦴🦴

Mature subject matter, violence, strong language.

1995 (R) 98m/C Rutger Hauer, Wil Wheaton, Nia Peeples, Taylor Negron, Ron Perlman, Michael Harris; *Cameos:* Tom Savini; **D:** Roger Roberts Avary; **W:** Roger Roberts Avary. **VHS** *AVE*

Mob Boss

The overstated humor in this gangster parody comes from the same vein as *The Naked Gun* and several of the bits have been baldly lifted from *The Benny Hill Show.* When the aging Don Anthony (William Hickey) is shot by bungling assassins (Jack O'Halloran and Brinke Stevens, who prefers to be called a "hitperson"), he sends for his long lost son, Tony (Eddie Deezen), and installs the bumbler as the new boss. The rest of the cast is filled with B-movie veterans whose faces are recognizable, even if their names are not. The humor is rude slapstick, sight gags, and exaggerated sound effects. Deezen is truly a geek's geek, but, for my money, he's often far too reminiscent of Jerry Lewis. The pace is quick, the jokes are crude, and the women are sexy. In short, a video winner. 🦴🦴🦴

Nudity, humorous sexual content, profanity.

1990 (R) 93m/C Eddie Deezen, Morgan Fairchild, William Hickey, Stuart Whitman, Jack O'Halloran, Brinke Stevens; **D:** Fred Olen Ray. **VHS** *VMK*

Monika

Harry (Lars Ekborg) is a shy, bookish kid; Monika (Harriet Andersson) is, as they used to say, "fast." Once she sets her sights on him, the rest is almost inevitable. They fall in love, run away on a boat, spend an idyllic summer together, have a baby, get married, and then their problems really start. Even in its brightest moments, this is a somber, naturalistic story, but it's told with sharp, memorable black-and-white images: the boat receding across smooth water, the girl running across a field. The soundtrack is fuzzy at times and some of the night scenes blur into inky shadows, so this one is recommended mostly for hard-core Bergman fans. **AKA:** Summer with Monika. 🦴🦴🦴

Contains brief nudity and mature subject matter.

1952 96m/B SW Harriet Andersson, Lars Ekborg, John Harryson, Georg Skarstedt, Dagmar Ebbesen, Ake Gronberg;

The Killer Babe

These days, if you watch many movies—either in theatres or on tape—you'd think that the most dangerous criminals in America are attractive young white women.

Forget drug kingpins, terrorists, and gangsters; they're impotent wimps compared to Killer Babes. These women are sexy, ruthless, smart, manipulative, and murderous. Why, though, have they become so popular on the silver screen and the video store?

First, a little history:

The Killer Babe's foremothers were created by novelist James M. Cain in the 1930s and '40s. Cora in *The Postman Always Rings Twice* and Phyllis in *Double Indemnity* were brought to the screen by Lana Turner and Barbara Stanwyck in good films that considerably water down Cain's eroticism, but retain the women's strong characters and essential natures. They're sexually adventurous, and willing to break the law when it suits their needs.

Writer/director Lawrence Kasdan and actress Kathleen Turner certainly had them in mind when they created Matty Walker in *Body Heat* (1981). She, singlehandedly, is the link between the prototypes and today's Killer Babe who was born in the late 1980s. Like her precursors, Matty is an attractive woman who uses a lover to get rid of an inconvenient husband, and, with a little luck, turn a tidy profit in the process.

But there are two important differences between Matty and Cain's women. First, Matty is always one step ahead of her hapless accomplice. As she tells William Hurt, in the film's best line, "You're not very bright. I like that in a man." Second, Matty gets away with it. That's right. She's resourceful; she really applies herself and perseveres against the odds and a male-dominated legal system. Finally, she triumphs.

All right, she's not a perfect role model, but she marks a significant shift in female characters. Despite the monotonous criticism of conservatives, American movies tend to be strictly moralistic. Virtue is rewarded and sin is punished, and that's more true for women than for men. The hero can be a real rascal, but as long as he straightens out by the last reel, his transgressions can be forgiven. Not so with the con-

> ## The Killer Babe in Video Premieres
>
> **BODY CHEMISTRY**
>
> **BODY CHEMISTRY 2: VOICE OF A STRANGER**
>
> **BODY CHEMISTRY 3: POINT OF SEDUCTION**
>
> **BODY CHEMISTRY 4: FULL EXPOSURE**
>
> **FEMME FONTAINE: KILLER BABE FOR THE C.I.A.**
>
> **HOMICIDAL IMPULSE**
>
> **KILL ME AGAIN**
>
> **MORTAL PASSIONS**
>
> **PLAY NICE**
>
> **POSITIVE I.D.**
>
> **THE STRANGER**

ventional heroine. She's expected to retain a certain purity, despite the circumstances.

Not the Killer Babe.

The Killer Babe is an effective and frightening character because she tempts and threatens viewers on a uniquely personal level. She attacks the basic unit of society: the family. Her motivation is usually more complex than simple monetary gain, and with the easing of society's strictures against divorce, an unhappy marriage alone isn't enough for the Killer Babe to spring into action.

She engages the hero—and by extension, the audience—on the most intimate terms, disrupting the home and threatening blood relations. In other words, she literally wants to get you where you live.

In recent years she's been popular on the big screen, but the Killer Babe has really come into full flower, as it were, on home video. The cult favorite *Positive I.D.*, for example, takes many of the conventions of a Killer Babe mystery, turns them inside out, and twists them into a devilishly original and unpredictable story. It's an independent production that you can find tucked away on the back shelves of some video stores. Writer/director Andy Anderson's film has developed a small but devoted following, and deserves to be much more widely known.

Of course, Hollywood slavishly imitates success, and that's why there have been so many of these movies recently. But something else is going on here, too.

The Killer Babe, in her many incarnations, provides a focus for all of the confusion, resentment, anger, and discomfort that many men and women feel about women's roles in society. Simultaneously attractive and menacing, she's a figure who keeps audiences off-balance.

In the context of movies and videos, off-balance also means interested. Audiences are intrigued by this character because they don't know what she's going to do. Even at her worst—her most derivative and exploitative—the Killer Babe combines the two elements of drama that have been proven crowd-pleasers since the ancient Greeks. They called them *eros* and *thanatos*. To us, they're sex and violence. When a combination works, viewers are willing to stick with it.

D: Ingmar Bergman; W: Ingmar Bergman; M: Les Baxter.
VHS HMV, CVC, TPV

Monolith

S-f shoot-'em-up begins with a fair premise but falls apart completely in the second half. Tucker (Bill Paxton) and Flynn (Lindsay Frost) are stereotyped L.A. plainclothes cops who despise each other. They're working on a curious case involving a Russian scientist, but before they can question the woman she's spirited away by a spooky, arrogant government guy (John Hurt) from an intelligence agency. Their boss (Louis Gossett, Jr.) is no help. Will these maverick cops let that stop them? Of course not. The actors do better work than they have to. But there's little they can do to rescue the derivative story which borrows freely from the collected works of Stephen King, and the familiar characters.

Graphic gun violence, strong language.

1993 (R) 96m/C Bill Paxton, Lindsay Frost, John Hurt, Louis Gossett Jr.; **D:** John Eyres; **W:** Stephen Lister. **VHS, LV** MCA

Moon 44

With its hulking sets, strange lighting, and overall fatalism, this one owes a lot to *Blade Runner*. The subject is a corporate war over mineral rights on a mining planet. Solid cast handles the familiar material with more talent than it deserves. The special effects, involving futuristic helicopters, are the real star anyway. Pay as little attention as possible to the tissue-thin plot.

Violence, strong language.

1990 (R) 102m/C GE Malcolm McDowell, Lisa Eichhorn, Michael Pare, Stephen Geoffreys, Roscoe Lee Browne, Brian Thompson, Dean Devlin, Mechmed Yilmaz, Leon Rippy; **D:** Roland Emmerich. **VHS, LV** LIV, IME, BTV

Moontrap

Independently produced s-f flick never rises above its low-budget limitations. The dubious selling point is the presence of Walter Koenig, better known as Mr. Chekov, in a plot taken straight from the old pulp magazines; a space opera about bug-eyed monsters and rogue robots that have been hiding on the moon. The action in the second half is disjointed and silly. Besides the robots, there's this woman running around on the moon and she's wearing a space suit with a commode seat around the neck. She and Koenig engage in what has to be the most preposterous sex scene ever put on videotape. Throughout the acting is amateurish and stiff; the effects are acceptable but limited. Hardcore fans may find a hoot or two, but that's about it.

Gratuitous nudity, pointless profanity, unconvincing violence.

1989 92m/C Walter Koenig, Bruce Campbell, Leigh Lombardi; **D:** Robert Dyke. **VHS, LV** MOV, IME

Moral Code

Independently produced first-contact tale has moments, but it's undone by a budget that's too meager for its ambitious story, and a low-intensity script. When an alien craft mysteriously appears in space, the ship Gallant Fox is the only one close enough to meet it. Capt. Travis (Trevor Goddard) and his officers Lopez (Stacie Randall) and Ganz (Roddy Piper) examine the ship slowly (too slowly) and cautiously. An inventive plot twist forces them to make some key decisions concerning their relationship with the new arrivals. The most immediate problems are unpersuasive sets, dim lighting, and an overall lack of the sense of mystery and anticipation that this particular kind of s-f depends on. On the other hand, the cast is talented, and the film does have a sense of humor that will appeal to fans of *Mystery Science Theater 3000*.

Mild sexual content, some violence.

1996 90m/C Trevor Goddard, Stacie Randall, Roddy Piper, Holly Fields, Veronica Bird, Gage Sheridan, Redge Mahaffey; **D:** Redge Mahaffey; **W:** Redge Mahaffey. **VHS** SHE

Mortal Passions

Traditional exercise in femme fatale machinations follows Emily (Krista Errickson), the scheming cocktail waitress, as she works to get rid of weak husband Todd (Zack Galligan).

But she'd like to hold onto the fortune she could realize from the sale of his family mansion. Then fiercely protective older brother Berke (Michael Bowen) shows up, but he and Emily have a history, too. And what about the safety deposit box full of cash? From that duplicitous premise, the film tries to get seriously weird, and it almost succeeds. About midway through, the action reaches a strong moment of confrontation. If the scene had been done right, it would fuse all the moving parts in your VCR. But good taste, alas, prevails. The conclusion is arbitrary and silly. Sheila Kelley steals the film as an impoverished actress who is thinking of turning her talents to interior design. ♫♫♪ **GPI: 5.8**

Sexual content, violence, brief nudity, profanity.

1990 (R) 96m/C Zach Galligan, Krista Errickson, Michael Bowen, Luca Bercovici, Sheila Kelley, David Warner; *D:* Andrew Lane. **VHS** *FOX*

Mortal Sins

Strange comic mystery involves two feuding televangelists in New York City. The plot has to do with drug use and sexual shenanigans, and contains no surprises. There are no characters here either, only stereotypes: the Southern flimflam preacher, the New York detective, the Italian-American girlfriend. The only bright spot in the film is the all-too-brief appearance of Anthony LaPaglia. ♫

Drug use, violence, sexual content, brief nudity.

1990 (R) 85m/C Brian Benben, Anthony LaPaglia, Debrah Farentino; *D:* Yuri Sivo. **VHS** *ACA, FXV*

The Mosaic Project

After a long, kooky chase scene, this low-budget adventure/comedy becomes a curious hybrid of *Dumb and Dumber, True Lies,* and one of those "Yes, I am" Bud commercials. Two beer-swilling bozos (Jon Tabler and Ben Marley) have microchips implanted in their heads and become super-spies. The pace lags with pointless shots of people walking to one side of a room and then back to the other. The big scenes are more interesting, and since the violence and sexual activity are played down while the comic angle is played up, this one could be fun for older kids. It looks like it might've been made as a pilot for a syndicated TV series. ♫♫

Violence, strong language, one sexy dance.

1995 (R) 89m/C Jon Tabler, Ben Marley, Joe Estevez; *D:* John Sjogren. **VHS** *MNC*

A Mother's Prayer

Made-for-cable movie is an obvious labor of love. AIDS is not a subject that's going to shake loose big bucks at any boxoffice, and this film doesn't sugarcoat its subject. It's sometimes hard to watch, sometimes preachy, and too earnest. But its arrival on home video still merits some mention. The film is based on a true story about Rosemary Holmstrom, a New York widow who discovered she had AIDS. Once she'd accepted her condition, she set about to find someone to take care of her eight-year-old son T.J. after her death. That's pretty grim subject matter and star Linda Hamilton doesn't pretty it up. In a telephone interview, she said that she concentrated on physical characteristics—speech patterns, dress, extreme weight loss—to play the role. That's easy to believe; as her character's health deteriorates, she becomes realistically gaunt. There's none of the dewy soft-focus treatment that films use so often on fatal diseases. This is rough, uncompromising stuff. The real Rose Holmstrom died just before the production began filming in New York, but there's no overt sentimentality. She's shown as a flawed, often angry and contrary woman who's trying to do the right thing despite a lot of uncertainty. Linda Hamilton and the film's producers have already won awards from the cable industry and they've been nominated for Golden Globes. Win or lose, *A Mother's Prayer* is one of those rare films that was made because someone—writer/executive producer Lee Rose—demanded that it be made. Now it'll find an audience on home video. ♫♫♪

Mature subject matter, salty language, some domestic violence.

1995 (PG-13) 90m/C Linda Hamilton, Noah Fleiss, Bruce Dern, Kate Nelligan, S. Epatha Merkerson, Corey Parker, Jenny O'Hara, RuPaul; *D:* Larry Elikann; *W:* Lee Rose. **VHS** *MCA*

Murder Story

Dutch teenager Tony Zonis (Alexis Denisof) is a budding novelist who manages to meet his idol, mystery writer Willard Hope (Christopher Lee). Tony follows Hope's example of creating plots by combining seemingly random newspaper stories and stumbles onto a conspiracy involving an unnamed but sinister American intelligence agency, a murder, and two suspicious fires. The cast is attractive and capable enough, so younger viewers will probably forgive the film's glaring mistakes. Its underlying message—that committed kids can challenge and triumph over cynical adults who refuse to take them seriously—will, I hope, always find a receptive audience. 🦴🦴🦴

Violence, profanity.

1989 (PG) 90m/C Christopher Lee, Bruce Boa, Alexis Denisof; *D:* Eddie Arno, Markus Innocenti; *W:* Eddie Arno. **VHS, LV** *FHS, ACA*

Murder Weapon

Legendary low-budget video premiere reverses all of the conventions of the slasher flick. In this one, the heavy-breathing killer is stalking young guys. Recently released from a psychiatric institution, our heroines Dawn (Linnea Quigley) and Amy (Karen Russell) have, perhaps unadvisedly, gone off their medications. They invite several guys over to their house for an afternoon of beer and whatever. In flashback scenes, their psychiatrist (*Carol Burnett Show* veteran Lyle Waggoner) tries to explain the root of their problems, while, one by one, the guys disappear. There's no real suspense, and the imaginative killings are so illogical and unrealistic that the graphic prosthetic special effects don't even have much immediate shock value. They're just bloody and silly. The film never tries to be anything more than low-budget escapism and it succeeds at that quite admirably. 🦴🦴🦴 **GPI: 8.6**

Contains nudity, strong sexual content, violence, ridiculous effects, torn T-shirts.

1990 (R) 90m/C Linnea Quigley, Karen Russell, Lyle Waggoner; *D:* Ellen Cabot; *W:* Ross A. Perron. **VHS, LV** *NO*

Muriel's Wedding

It's easy to see why this off-beat Aussie flick has attracted a devoted but small following. It isn't really a comedy, isn't really a romance, isn't really a musical. For want of a better category, call it a coming-of-age story with music and costumes that might have been left over from *Priscilla, Queen of the Desert.* Muriel (Toni Collette) is an overweight romantic from the backwater burg of Porpoise Spit. She obsessively craves a big fancy wedding, but her chances don't look good. Her dad's a crooked womanizing politician and he's the most sympathetic member of the family. After a long quirky introduction, Rhonda (Rachel Griffiths) convinces Muriel to move to Sydney and everything changes, sort of. But just when you think you've got the film figured out, writer/director P.J. Hogan shifts gears and changes direction completely. It's unconventional and off-putting. In fact, the whole thing would probably fly apart if the two leads weren't so strong. And they're nothing less than terrific. 🦴🦴🦴

Mature subject matter, strong language, sexual material.

1994 (R) 105m/C *AU* Toni Collette, Bill Hunter, Rachel Griffiths, Jeanie Drynan, Gennie Nevinson Brice, Matt Day, Daniel Lapaine; *D:* P.J. Hogan; *W:* P.J. Hogan; *M:* Peter Best. Australian Film Institute '94: Best Actress (Collette), Best Film, Best Sound, Best Supporting Actress (Griffiths); Nominations: Australian Film Institute '94: Best Director (Hogan), Best Screenplay, Best Supporting Actor (Hunter), Best Supporting Actress (Drynan); Golden Globe Awards '96: Best Actress—Musical/Comedy (Collette); Writers Guild of America '95: Best Original Screenplay. **VHS, LV** *MAX*

Mute Witness

The first half of this inventive thriller is about as suspenseful as anything that's been put on film in recent years. Writer/director Anthony Waller sets his scene quickly and puts his heroine Billy Hughes (Marina Sudina) in a tough spot. She's a mute American special effects technician working on a cheap horror flick in Moscow. Mistakenly locked in the huge studio one night after filming has finished, she sees something she shouldn't. That act leads to an extended white-knuckle chase through

the building. It's a brilliant set piece, told with almost no dialogue, and that's a large part of Waller's point. Billy cannot speak; the American members of the crew can't understand their Russian co-workers and that lack of communication leads to suspicion on all sides. Waller also manages to add some fresh twists to the is-it-real-or-is-it-a-movie gimmick that's so popular these days in films-within-films. Unfortunately, the second half begins with an emotional misstep that's necessary to keep the plot moving and the rest of the film isn't nearly as strong as the beginning. Throughout, however, Waller mixes suspense and humor effectively, and he got fine performances from an unknown cast. (Don't miss a surprising uncredited guest star as the villain.) For Anthony Waller, this is a striking debut. Recommended. 𝄪𝄪𝄪

Violence, brief nudity, strong language.

1995 (R) 100m/C *GB* Marina Sudina, Fay Ripley, Evan Richards, Oleg Jankowskij, Igor Volkow, Sergei Karlenkov; *Cameos:* Alec Guinness; *D:* Anthony Waller; *W:* Anthony Waller; *C:* Egon Werdin; *M:* Wilbert Hirsch. **VHS, LV** *COL*

My Family

Multigenerational tale of the Sanchez family begins with Jose's (Eduardo Lopez Rojas) journey from rural Mexico to Los Angeles in 1926 "when the border was a line in the dirt." He meets and marries Maria (Jenny Gago), and the rest deals with their children: our narrator Paco (Edward James Olmos), Chucha (Esai Morales), Toni (Constance Marie), Jimmy (Jimmy Smits), and Memo (Enrique Castillo). Their episodic conflicts are realistic, based in differences of age and culture, and though they may seem heavy-handed at times, they're always emotionally honest, neither apologizing for the characters nor condemning them. The best moments are a curbside mambo lesson, an exciting knife fight, and a nicely handled romance between Smits and Elpidia Carrillo, as an immigrant in immediate need of a husband. Because the film covers so much ground in time and number of characters, it's uneven. But it's also the kind of engaging story that has the appeal of a good soap opera. You come to care about these people

and you want to know what's going to happen to them. 𝄪𝄪𝄪𝄪

Strong language, violence, sexual content, brief nudity.

1994 (R) 126m/C Jimmy Smits, Esai Morales, Eduardo Lopez Rojas, Jenny Gago, Elpidia Carrillo, Lupe Ontiveros, Jacob Vargas, Jennifer Lopez, Scott Bakula, Constance Marie, Enrique Castillo, Edward James Olmos; *D:* Gregory Nava; *W:* Gregory Nava, Anna Thomas; *C:* Edward Lachman; *M:* Pepe Avila, Mark McKenzie. Nominations: Academy Awards '95: Best Makeup; Independent Spirit Awards '96: Best Actor (Smits), Best Supporting Actress (Lopez). **VHS, LV** *NLC, TTC*

My Life's in Turnaround

Autobiographical comedy combines freewheeling "gen-x" sensibility with a New York setting. Eric Schaeffer and Donal Lardner Ward co-produced, -wrote, -directed, and -starred in the story of performance artists Splick and Jason who decide to turn their less-than-illustrious careers into a movie. As they see it, to break into the film business you don't need talent or a script or cameras or any of that stuff—you just need meetings. And so they set out to get them. They'd also like girlfriends, being, as they are, two of the Big Apple's more colorful neurotics. At various times, Phoebe Cates, Martha Plimpton, and Casey Siemaszko become "attached" to the guys' unfunded project, and John Sayles shows up for a sharp cameo as a sleazy producer. But in the business, there's always the danger of "turnaround," where yesterday's absolutely guaranteed sure thing becomes today's abandoned project. If Schaeffer and Ward had taken any of the material too seriously, it would have fallen flat. But they keep the energy level cranked up and the whole film has an intelligent, made-on-the-fly quality that serves it well. 𝄪𝄪𝄪

Strong language, sexual humor, fleeting nudity.

1994 (R) 84m/C Eric Schaeffer, Donal Lardner Ward, Lisa Gerstein, Dana Wheeler-Nicholson, Debra Clein, Sheila Jaffe; *Cameos:* Casey Siemaszko, John Sayles, Martha Plimpton, Phoebe Cates; *D:* Eric Schaeffer, Donal Lardner Ward; *W:* Eric Schaeffer, Donal Lardner Ward; *M:* Reed Hays. **VHS** *AVI*

Mysteries of Peru

This two-tape set was produced for British television in the mid-1980s. It's focused on the "lost" civilizations of the pre-Inca Chimu culture, and the more famous lines on the Nazca desert. Most people were probably introduced to those mysterious drawings by Erich von Daniken's book *Chariots of the Gods* and other wildly speculative works. Producer/director Peter Spry-Leverton demolishes those wacky theories in the first twenty minutes. In doing so, he raises other serious questions that are even more fascinating and enigmatic. First though, he explains the basics. He uses the familiar aerial shots to show the lines and huge drawings of animals and geometrical shapes. He goes on to explain how the lines are created—an easy process accomplished by disturbing different colored layers of the desert surface. After that, he turns to the possible reasons behind these markings. Much of that part of the film concerns Maria Reiche, a German mathematician who has spent 40 years studying and mapping the lines. Her presence and the rigor of her life and work give the story a human dimension that's often lacking in this kind of popular anthropology. When Spry-Leverton turns to questions of who drew the lines and why, he may not have as much solid evidence to back up his answers, but he is just as persuasive. It's not giving away too much to reveal that the ancient Nascans had an affinity for a particular psychedelic cactus that produces hallucinations of flight. His real answers, though, are much more complex with a serious religious meaning. The second tape, "Enigma of the Ruins," lacks the immediate dramatic hook of the first, but it's just as intriguing. What happened to the large pre-Inca cities and the huge irrigated, terraced fields that produced food for the people who lived there? How could a people who had no written language have been so sophisticated with mathematics and engineering? "Enigma" does not completely succeed in revealing who these ancient Peruvians were and how their society worked. Though some of their traditions and rituals have survived until today—in altered but recognizable forms—it's clear that in many basic ways, they were not at all like us. As Spry-Leverton puts it, they were "people highly intelligent, but whose minds worked in ways vastly different from ours." Overall, this documentary

is weighted more toward the National Geographic's approach than the National Enquirer's. At the same time, the subject lends itself to a deep sense of mystery and no matter how commonplace the reality behind that mystery may be, the tapes are never boring. Also, the stark beauty of the high Peruvian desert is captured vividly. ✶✶✶

Contains no objectionable material, beyond some sexually explicit archeological artifacts.

1993 100m/C *D:* Peter Spry-Leverton. **VHS** *ATS*

The Naked Country

Australian import looks like it was made for television with a quick pace that's geared toward regular commercial breaks and typically overdone TV music. That said, the story, based on a Morris West novel, is about an intense clash of cultures between aboriginal Australians and the ranchers who intrude on their land. It's 1955 in North Queensland, Australia. Rancher Lance Dillon (John Stanton) is having a lot of trouble with his work, his wife Mary (Rebecca Gilling), and the local tribesmen with whom he's supposed to share the land. The tribe resorts to magic and ritual murder to settle its own problems, and the film turns into a fine, surprising tale of wilderness survival. To their credit, the filmmakers don't take sides. Neither the ranchers nor the aborigines are sanctified or demonized. Both are selfish; both make mistakes; both struggle to survive. The action is violent, particularly in the second half, but it's never exploitative. ✶✶✶

Graphic violence, strong language, mild sexual content, incidental nudity.

1985 (R) 90m/C *AU* John Stanton, Rebecca Gilling, Ivar Kants; *D:* Tim Burstall; *M:* Bruce Smeaton. **VHS** *HMD*

Naked Souls

Talk about truth in titling! *Naked Souls* has more gratuitous nudity than any video that's hit the store shelves in recent memory. Though superbabe Pamela Anderson Lee gets top billing, she has to share the screen with

National Lampoon's Favorite Deadly Sins

When it comes to film comedy, the name "National Lampoon" has come to symbolize mediocrity and this trio of short films is no exception. "Greed," with Joe Mantegna and Cassidy Rae is a broad parody of movies-of-the-week and Hollywood; "Anger" features Andrew Dice Clay doing his loud schtick; and "Lust" is a take-off on *Rear Window* from director/star Denis Leary. Individually and as a group, they're unfunny. WOOF!

Contains strong language, brief nudity, comic violence.

1995 (R) 99m/C Joe Mantegna, Denis Leary, Annabella Sciorra, Andrew Dice Clay, Cassidy Rae, Brian Keith, William Ragsdale, Farrah Forke, Tanya Pohlkotte; *D:* Denis Leary, David Jablin; *W:* Michael Barrie, Jim Mulholland, Lee Biondi, Ann Lembeck. **VHS** *REP*

Nature of the Beast

Neatly gruesome little character study/road movie features solid performances from two of the best actors in the video business. Jack (Lance Henriksen) is a paunchy traveling salesman type. Adrian (Eric Roberts) is a spooky hitchhiker. They meet out in the remote California desert, miles away from the interstate, where a madman is chopping up people. At the same time, a million bucks-plus is missing from a Las Vegas casino. What does Adrian have in his daypack? Why is Jack so protective of his locked briefcase? Writer/director Victor Salva uses a deliberately slow pace and edgy characterizations to maintain suspense. With a couple of exceptions, he does a good job. Henriksen and Roberts have built their careers on quirky, colorful roles and these are two of their best. Henriksen is particularly strong—he also gets credit as "creative consultant"—and his performance carries the story over several rough spots. But not the opening. It begins with that irritating cinematic convention of someone hiding in the backseat of a car. It's a trite, overused trick, and while it may have had some justification in the days of Conestoga wagons and

several other buck nekkid cuties. They, however, are part of black-and-white flashbacks. She's the full-color sweetie of a young scientist (Brian Krause) whose genetic experiments run into trouble when he gets funding from an aging millionaire (David Warner). Seems the old guy has an eye for Pam and he's figured out a way to switch bodies with her beau. Despite fine production values and acceptable acting, the whole thing barely qualifies as formula s-f. As an excuse for blatant ogling, it gets full marks. 🦴🦴🦴 GPI: 9.1

Nudity, sexual material, some violence, strong language.

1995 (R) 90m/C Pamela Anderson, Brian Krause, Clayton Rohner, Justina Vail, David Warner; *Cameos:* Dean Stockwell; *D:* Lyndon Chubbuck; *W:* Frank Dietz; *C:* Eric Goldstein; *M:* Nigel Holton. **VHS** *WEA*

motorized land yachts, today it's a mark of lazy writing. 🦴🦴🦴

Mature subject matter, violence, strong language, sexual material.

1994 (R) 91m/C Eric Roberts, Lance Henriksen, Brion James; *D:* Victor Salva; *W:* Victor Salva. **VHS, LV** *NLC*

Near Dark

It's easy to see why Kathryn Bigelow's poorly released solo directorial debut became one of the first cult hits on video. It's an inventive combination of horror film and Peckinpah homage. The big action scenes—a long fight in a bar, a shootout in a recreational vehicle—are brilliant. It's alternately funny, frightening, and erotic. The plot revolves around a young man who's seduced and kidnapped by a gang of vampires (though that word is never used) who travel the Southwest in stolen cars at night. The ending is comparatively weak. 🦴🦴🦴

Graphic violence, strong language.

1987 (R) 95m/C Adrian Pasdar, Jenny Wright, Bill Paxton, Jenette Goldstein, Lance Henriksen, Tim Thomerson, Joshua Miller; *D:* Kathryn Bigelow; *W:* Kathryn Bigelow, Eric Red; *M:* Tangerine Dream. **VHS, LV** *HBO, IME*

Nemesis

Shoot-'em-up combines elements of *The Road Warrior* with an Oliver Stone conspiratorial mindset. The loosely woven story has to do with secret agent Olivier Gruner, who hunts down renegade cyborgs until he gets sick of his work and becomes a freelance "information cowboy." He operates in the bleak, sun-blasted futurescape that's typical for this kind of movie. The ridiculous violence and stylized look of the characters—sunglasses, long overcoats, ugly haircuts, European accents, dozens of exotic automatic weapons—could have come straight from the pages of a comic book. Action vet Albert Pyun keeps things moving quickly, if pointlessly. 🦴🦴

Graphic violence, strong language, nudity.

1993 (R) 95m/C Olivier Gruner, Tim Thomerson, Cary-Hiroyuki Tagawa, Merele Kennedy, Yuji Okumoto, Marjorie Monaghan, Nicholas Guest, Vincent Klyn; *D:* Albert Pyun; *W:* Rebecca Charles; *M:* Michael Rubini. **VHS, LV** *IMP, UND*

Nemesis 2: Nebula

Sequel in title only is notable for the presence of bodybuilder Sue Price, who looks like she could benchpress Rush Limbaugh without breaking a sweat. The gonzo plot pops in and out of three separate time frames before the title appears on the screen! It has to do with a future-past-present war between machines and people, and a genetically enhanced superbaby who's hunted by a Predator-inspired creature. Good effects and desolate desert landscapes. 🦴🦴

Violence, strong language, brief nudity.

1994 (R) 83m/C Sue Price, Tina Cote, Earl White, Jahi JJ Zuri, Traci Davis; *D:* Albert Pyun. **VHS** *IMP*

Nemesis 3: Time Lapse

By part three, the minimal plot provides little more than a framework for some nifty visual effects involving lights and "bubble" distortions. A pudgy Tim Thomerson morphs into a golden robot character that looks like the result of an unholy union between an Oscar statuette and a Power Ranger. Even judged by the relaxed standard of the genre, the general level of acting in this one makes Jean-Claude Van Damme look like Laurence Olivier. "4" is on the way. 🦴🦴

Violence, language, one naked backside.

1995 (R) 91m/C Sue Price, Tim Thomerson, Norbert Weisser, Xavier DeClie, Sharon Bruneau, Debbie Muggli; *D:* Albert Pyun; *W:* Albert Pyun; *C:* George Mooradian; *M:* Tony Riparetti. **VHS** *IMP*

The Nest

Killer mutant cockroaches that take over a small resort island. That's the plot, but the overall Yuck! factor is high with lots of icky special effects, assorted creepy crawly critters, and the cast is better than you'd expect, especially Terri Treas, as the scientist who turns out to be a little kinky for her bugs. The story gets funnier and grosser as it goes along; in short, giving fans everything they could ask for. 🦴🦴🦴

Violence, gooey special effects, profanity.

1988 **(R)** 89m/C Robert Lansing, Lisa Langlois, Franc Luz, Terri Treas, Stephen Davies, Diana Bellamy, Nancy Morgan; **D:** Terence H. Winkless; **W:** Robert King; **M:** Rick Conrad. **VHS** *MGM*

Netherworld

Typically slick Full Moon production has to do with reincarnation, magic, and such on a plantation in the Louisiana backwater. The film has an odd waking nightmare quality that's really chilling in its best moments. Some of the effects are ingenious, but the show is stolen by character actor Robert Burr as a deliciously decadent, Edsel-driving lawyer. Also, the Edgar Winter blues score is terrific. Watch all the way through the end of the credits for a nice final joke. *ひひひ*

Strong language, nudity, violence.

1990 **(R)** 87m/C Michael C. Bendetti, Denise Gentile, Anjanette Comer, Holly Floria, Robert Burr; **D:** David Schmoeller; **W:** Billy Chicago; **M:** Edgar Winter. **VHS, LV** *PAR*

Neurotic Cabaret

Texas production begins a little slowly, describing the troubles that would-be director and acting teacher Nick (Dennis Worthington) encounters as he tries to find financing for his movie, *Space Pirates*. The situation becomes so desperate that his girlfriend Terri (Tammy Stone) goes to work as an exotic dancer to raise money for the film. About then, it all takes a hard left turn and becomes a dandy screwball comedy. The key ingredients are a pair of snakes whose venom causes unusual hormonal changes, a briefcase that's supposed to be full of money, an actor with such strict religious beliefs that he cannot say certain words, and a cure for baldness. All right, it's not *Bringing Up Baby*, but parts of it are laugh-out-loud funny. Interestingly, the story was co-written by producer/editor/director John Woodward and Tammy Stone, who also served as executive producer. Obviously they didn't have much money for sets, costumes, and such, but they do have the right touch for this kind of humor. Re-edited and retitled *Good Girl, Bad Girl*. *ひひひ*

Contains brief nudity, strong language.

1990 90m/C Edwin Neal, Tammy Stone, Dennis Worthington; **D:** John Woodward; **W:** John Woodward, Tammy Stone. **VHS** *AIP*

Never on Tuesday

Stultifying comedy revolves—ever so slowly—around two teenagers who are stuck in the middle of the desert with a beautiful California blonde. Remember: your VCR has a fast-forward button. WOOF!

Profanity, brief nudity.

1988 **(R)** 90m/C Claudia Christian, Andrew Lauer, Peter Berg; *Cameos:* Charlie Sheen, Emilio Estevez; **D:** Adam Rifkin; **W:** Adam Rifkin. **VHS, LV** *PAR*

Never Say Die

Low-voltage South African actioner gets full points for inventiveness, if not logic. A somnambulant Billy Drago is the messianic cult leader who has visions of Jonestown and Mt. Carmel dancing in his head. He's also an ex-Green Beret. As it happens, his old pal Frank Zagarino lives just down the river from his compound and is ready to leap into action when a visiting congressman is killed, and FBI agents botch the ensuing raid. Actually, the religious elements are just the premise for a standard chase/fight flick. The clunky plot depends on wild coincidence at almost every key point. Director Yossi Wein keeps things moving quickly but again, like everyone else in the field these days, he's following in John Woo's footsteps. Fans aren't going to mistake his work for the original. *ひひ*

Violence, strong language.

1994 **(R)** 99m/C Frank Zagarino, Billy Drago, Todd Jensen, Jennifer Miller, Robin Smith; **D:** Yossi Wein; **W:** Jeff Albert; **M:** Wendy Oldfield, Adrian Levy. **VHS, LV** *TTC, NLC*

The New Age

This Hollywood comedy is so filled with self-loathing that any viewer outside of California has to wonder why it was made. But then, why do people make all sorts of comedies? Many moviegoers might have thought that writer/director Michael Tolkin had got all the bile out of his system with *The Player* and *The*

Rapture. But no; he was just warming up. The protagonists here (Peter Weller and Judy Davis) are a deliberately unsympathetic and often unattractive trendy couple whose success and materialism are only one paycheck deep. Finding themselves out of work, they set about to maintain their lifestyle. The first order of business is to throw a party. It's an embarrassing affair, complete with former and current lovers, and banal advice from guru (Patrick Bauchau). The film skates along both sides of a line between serious contemporary drama and satire. And it probably is an accurate portrait of shallow, fatuous people whose self-importance deserves to be skewered. It's also profoundly creepy in a couple of key scenes toward the end, but those aren't nearly enough to recommend the film. Weller always gives his characters a brittle edge, and Judy Davis is as abrasive here as she was in Woody Allen's *Husbands and Wives.* In short, these two are about as engaging as a couple of neurotic Chihuahuas. When scorn is the primary emotion that the central characters and their problems are supposed to evoke, it's difficult to become involved. Or to keep your finger away from the fast-forward button. All right, any film that has both Adam West (Batman), as Weller's father, and Samuel L. Jackson, as a high-pressure salesman, can't be all bad—but this one certainly comes close. 🦴

Mature subject matter, strong language, sexual content, brief nudity.

1994 (R) 106m/C Peter Weller, Judy Davis, Adam West, Patrick Bauchau, Corbin Bernsen, Jonathan Hadary, Samuel L. Jackson, Patricia Heaton, Audra Lindley, Paula Marshall, Maureen Mueller, Bruce Ramsay, Sandra Seacat, Susan Traylor; *D:* Michael Tolkin; *W:* Michael Tolkin, Mark Mothersbaugh. **VHS, LV** *WAR*

New Crime City: Los Angeles 2020

Futuristic action flick borrows blatantly from *The Road Warrior* and *Escape from New York.* Hero Rick Rossovich is an ex-cop named Ricks who's got a date with the gas chamber. Seems he ran afoul of the totalitarian authorities in 2020 for helping out the criminal inhabitants of New Crime City, a portion of L.A. that's been walled off from the rest. A delightfully evil military type (Stacy Keach) sends Ricks into the place to fetch a virus that's been developed by a local warlord (Rick Dean). Ricks' only assistance comes from Darla (Sherrie Rose), a gutsy heroine. Overall, the pace is pokey and, with the exception of Keach, the acting is no better than so-so. The film does have an effective post-apocalyptic look and enough unusual quirks, including an aggressive anti-organized religion streak, to keep you interested. 🦴🦴

Violence, strong language, sexual content, nudity.

1994 (R) 95m/C Rick Rossovich, Stacy Keach, Sherrie Rose, Rick Dean, *D:* Jonathan Winfrey; *W:* Rick Rossovich. **VHS, LV** *NHO*

Nexus

Cheerfully unapologetic copy of *Flash Gordon* steals both the plot and the cornball campiness. It could slip right into the *Mystery Science Theater 3000* rotation without missing a step. In this Prague production, Ming the Merciless has become the evil Tarn (Oliver Tobias), who appears to have gold battery terminals on top of his head; Flash is now Athor (Jeremy Gilley) and Dale is Zilia (Christina Goyanes). Most of the effects are done with models and miniatures. Save one fleeting nude scene, it'd be recommended for teens (who'll still like it a lot). 🦴🦴🦴

Brief nudity, silly violence.

1996 93m/C Oliver Tobias, Jeremy Gilley, Christina Goyanes, Oona Kirsch; *D:* Jose Maria Forque; *W:* Alvaro Forque; *M:* Daniel Jones. **VHS** *YHV*

Night Angel

Tons of fun! The setting is a fashion magazine; the title character is Lilith (Isa Andersen), a female demon who returns to seduce and destroy. Most of the time she looks like any other skinny fashion model, but when she turns up the heat, she changes. Her mascara looks like it was applied with a pallet knife and she grows shiny black stick-on nails that are about three inches long. When she goes after her victims, she's so trashy she

video of a guy watching a video and fast-forwarding to the good parts. Also available in an unrated version. ***AKA:*** Hidden Vision. 🦴🦴 **GPI: 7.5**

Sexual material, nudity, violence, profanity.

1990 (R) 95m/C Andrew Stevens, Tanya Roberts, Warwick Sims, Cooper Huckabee; *D:* Emilio P. Miraglio; *W:* Tom Citrano. **VHS, LV** *PSM*

Night Eyes 2

For those who came in late and missed the original, Andrew Stevens is back in a simplified version of same situation, this time opposite Shannon Tweed. Overall, the film has fair production values and it's not without humor, much of it intentional. Shannon Tweed does not giggle in the overwrought love scenes—not even the one where Stevens rubs raspberries all over her—which is the mark of a true professional. Also available in an unrated version. 🦴🦴🦴 **GPI: 7.8**

Nudity, sexual content, violence, strong language.

1991 (R) 97m/C Andrew Stevens, Shannon Tweed, Tim Russ, Richard Chaves, Gene Silva; *D:* Rodney McDonald. **VHS** *PSM*

Night Eyes 3

More naughtiness about video surveillance cameras and all the voyeuristic things that can be done with them. For the third telling of a well-worn formula flick, this one begins well enough but becomes predictably violent and incoherent by the end. Also available in an unrated version at 101 minutes. 🦴🦴 **GPI: 6.0**

Strong language, nudity, sexual content, some violence.

1993 (R) 97m/C Andrew Stevens, Shannon Tweed, Tracy Tweed, Tristan Rogers; *D:* Andrew Stevens; *W:* Andrew Stevens, Michael W. Potts. **VHS** *PSM*

Night Hunter

This attempt to combine martial arts with horror relies too heavily on the former. Perhaps that's to be expected with Don "the Dragon" Wilson as Jack Cutter, vampire hunter. He gets help from World Inquisitor tabloid reporter Raimy Baker (Melanie Smith), as he goes after

makes Madonna look like Mother Theresa. Director Dominique Othenin-Girard makes the film campy, flashy, and slick; the action peaks in the long phantasmagorical dream sequence. 🦴🦴🦴

Brief nudity, sexual content, wild special effects, violence, profanity.

1990 (R) 90m/C Isa Anderson, Linda Ashby, Debra Feuer, Helen Martin, Karen Black; *D:* Dominique Othenin-Girard; *W:* Joe Augustyn. **VHS, LV** *FRH*

Night Eyes

First entry in the successful video series has to do with security guard Andrew Stevens, who is watching Tanya Roberts in the middle of a nasty divorce from a rock star. He agrees to help hubbie's lawyer dig up some dirt, but then he falls for her. Before it's over, the story has become wildly complicated and illogical, and the telling of it is filled with visual cliches. Admittedly though, it is strange to watch a

Jacqueline Tournier (Maria Ford, the hardest working woman in home video) and her undead pals. Wilson has the presence to carry the simple story. The contemporary vampire concept has been handled much more imaginatively in several other recent videos. This one's an energetic low-budget effort that might be the first in a series from Roger Corman's production company. 🦴🦴🦴

Violence, strong language.

1995 (R) 86m/C Don "The Dragon" Wilson, Melanie Smith, Nicholas Guest, Maria Ford; *D:* Rick Jacobson. **VHS** *NHO*

A Night of Love

"1920 Central Europe. After the fall of great Empires, new governments appeared, taking themselves very seriously. Life became hard for revolutionaries." That's the premise for a comedy of politics and sex, a combination that may be a little hard to handle. The film is too gleefully licentious for serious cineastes and too funny and smart for the pure exploitation crowd. But somewhere in the wide world of home video, it ought to find an appreciative audience. The setting is the little mountain town of Waldheim where the King has scheduled a publicity visit. Avanti (Alfred Molina) is his frontman. Svetlana (Camilla Soeberg), daughter of a prominent local family, is plotting an assassination. Both of them are more interested in pleasures of the flesh than affairs of state. The bawdy sexual scenes could have come from Chaucer or D.H. Lawrence, and, like the politics, they're treated with nose-thumbing irreverence. This movie is incorrect in just about every way imaginable. I am really ashamed of myself for not being more offended. By the way, this 1987 U.S./then-Yugoslavia production had a limited theatrical run under the title *Manifesto*. **AKA:** Manifesto. 🦴🦴🦴

Nudity, sexual content, violence, strong language, rough humor.

1987 (R) 97m/C Alfred Molina, Camilla Soeberg, Eric Stoltz, Gabrielle Anwar; *D:* Dusan Makavejev. **VHS** *ORI, FXL*

Night of the Cyclone

Misfired mystery is done in by poor writing and wooden acting. Kris Kristofferson is a Chicago cop whose teenaged daughter is beginning a career as a professional model. When she doesn't return from a Caribbean assignment, he goes after her and finds that she has fallen in love with a shady local painter. Intentions were better than execution here. The characters could have been more than stereotypes and the conflict does have some complexity to it, but basically, everyone involved seems to have been going through the motions. And the music could have come from a 1950s TV show. Another strong candidate for the fast-forward button. 🦴🦴

Sexual content, violence, brief nudity.

1990 (R) 90m/C Kris Kristofferson, Jeffrey Meek, Marisa Berenson, Winston Ntshona, Gerrit Graham; *D:* David Irving. **VHS, LV** *REP*

Night of the Demons

Director Kevin Tenney told essentially the same story in *Witchboard*. Both are about a group of people trapped in a haunted house and then graphically murdered by supernatural forces. Of the two, this is the more lively, grotesque, and imaginative. The unrated version scores high on the Yuck-scale. 🦴🦴

Graphic violence, grotesque special effects, strong language, brief nudity, sexual content.

1988 (R) 92m/C Linnea Quigley, Cathy Podewell, Alvin Alexis, William Gallo, Mimi Kinkade, Lance Fenton; *D:* Kevin S. Tenney; *W:* Joe Augustyn. **VHS, LV** *REP*

The Night of the Following Day

Relatively obscure 1968 kidnapping thriller was radically re-edited (i.e. chopped apart) for American television and hasn't been available as it was meant to be seen since its initial limited release. Though it is still a seriously flawed film, it's a real treat for Brando fans. He's at his youthful best here and in some ways, his performance can be seen as a dry run for *Last Tango in Paris*, which came five years later. A young woman (Pamela Franklin) arrives at Paris' Orly Airport and is met by a sinister chauffeur (Marlon Brando). Without

1969 (R) 93m/C Marlon Brando, Richard Boone, Rita Moreno, Pamela Franklin, Jess Hahn, Jacques Marin, Gerard Buhr, Hughes Wanner; **D:** Hubert Cornfield; **W:** Robert Phippeny, Hubert Cornfield. **VHS** MCA, FCT

The Hound's Favorite Sleepers: Horror/Fantasy

CRONOS	MIRACLE MILE
DARK ANGEL: THE ASCENT	NEAR DARK
	NIGHTSCARE
HAUNTED	RED BLOODED AMERICAN GIRL
HEART AND SOULS	
JACK BE NIMBLE	SLEEPWALK
LA PASTORELA	SOULTAKER
LIPSTICK ON YOUR COLLAR	TRULY, MADLY, DEEPLY
MERIDIAN: KISS OF THE BEAST	

Night Rhythms

The hero of this noir-tinged mystery is a talk-radio host (Martin Hewitt) whose field is sexual fantasies. Imagine a combination of Rush Limbaugh and Dr. Ruth...no, wait; don't imagine that. It's sick. Anyway, this guy is framed for murder, etc, etc. As is so often the case with director Gregory Hippolyte's eroticism, the plot is senseless; the acting is so-so; and the production values are first rate. Also available in an unrated version. 🎭🎭🎭 **GPI: 9.1**

Violence, strong language, sexual material, nudity.

1992 (R) 99m/C Martin Hewitt, Delia Sheppard, David Carradine, Terry Tweed, Sam Jones, Deborah Driggs, Julie Strain; **D:** Alexander Gregory Hippolyte. **VHS, LV** IMP, MOV

Night Train to Venice

Lively, semi-realistic thriller seldom makes a lick of sense. Hugh Grant plays a writer who seems to be researching neo-Nazis. At least a bunch of skinheads follow him onto the Orient Express, and they appear to want a computer disk and his manuscript. While they're all rushing for the train, we're also seeing flashbacks and flashforwards involving a little girl in danger of falling from a high railing, her actress mother Tahnee Welch, a malevolent Malcolm McDowell who controls the skinheads, and an angry woman and girl in white who are probably ghosts. And just in case anyone is getting bored with all this, sometimes the skinheads turn into Dobermans. Go figure. Strong, unsettling images are more important than a coherent plot. The best moments bring to mind the hypnotic, hallucinatory mood of *Zentropa*. The acting varies between naturalistic and wooden. The score sounds like it was lifted from a cheap '50s science-fiction flick. At times, the references to Nazi violence are horrifying; in other scenes they're laughable, particularly at the end. The final result is more interesting than good, but the film is never boring. 🎭🎭🎭

much fuss the gang's leader (Richard Boone) takes over. A scared small-time crook (Jess Hahn) and his drug-addicted sister (Rita Moreno) are their accomplices in a scheme that starts going bad as soon as they reach their beachfront hideout. In the existentially "cool" fashion of the late '60s, the characters don't have names. Each is simply playing out his or her role. That's fine, but the film stumbles badly in a few scenes. The weirdest is one in which Brando's character announces that he's getting out of this harebrained scheme, and lists perfectly good reasons for doing so in a long emotional outburst. At moments, the film is reminiscent of other thrillers of that time, notably *Bullitt* and *Point Blank*, but not always in the best ways. And the ending...well, about the best that can be said is that it's pretty screwy. Mistakes not withstanding, this one is recommended for anyone who's interested in the films of those turbulent times. 🎭🎭🎭

Strong language, drug use, violence, brief nudity.

Violence, sexual content, nudity, strong language.

1993 (R) 98m/C Hugh Grant, Malcolm McDowell, Tahnee Welch, Kristina Soderbaum; *D:* Carlo U. Quinterio; *W:* Leo Tichat, Toni Hirtreiter; *M:* Alexander Bubenheim. **VHS, LV** *LIV, WEA*

The Nightman

In the early 1970s, Eve (Joanna Kerns) hires Vietnam vet Tom Wolfe (Ted Marcoux) as the night manager of her resort hotel. Over the course of the hot Georgia summer, her teenaged daughter Maggie (Jenny Robertson) strikes up a friendship with him. Flash forward to the present where Maggie has become a prosperous lawyer, her mother is dead, and Tom has just been released from prison, having served 18 years for her murder. Maggie thinks he's stalking her. But.... Most of the story is set in the past; actor-turned-director Charles Haid lets the proceedings drawl along at a leisurely summertime pace. That's fitting enough, but he let his actors cut loose in big, teary scenes where emotional overindulgence runs amok. Still, this one has a steamy Erskine Caldwell-Tennessee Williams quality that's always kind of fun. *ﾐﾐﾐ*

Sexual content, strong language, brief nudity, some violence.

1993 (R) 96m/C Ted Marcoux, Jenny Robertson, Joanna Kerns; *D:* Charles Haid; *W:* James Poe; *M:* Gary Chang. **VHS, LV** *APX*

Nightscare

Rare horror/comedy actually manages to be frightening, funny, and original. It's obvious from the first shot—an extreme close up of a hypodermic needle entering flesh—that director Vadim Jean is trying to work on a primal level. He's more successful than not. The story concerns Gilmore (Keith Allen), an insane murderer; Dr. Lyell (Elizabeth Hurley), the neurologist who's treating him with an experimental drug which she's testing herself; and detective Hamilton (Craig Fairbrass), the cop who arrested Gilmore and still has reason to hate him. Without giving the game away, the new drug brings the three of them together in a strange nightmare. The bad news is that the British accents are absolutely impossible to decipher at times. It's an irritating though not fatal flaw; the key points are clear enough. More importantly, Jean does a fine job of depicting different states of perception—dream, drugged, memory, sobriety—and making them equally "real" onscreen. Whenever the film threatens to take itself too seriously—a recurring problem in the genre—a wonderfully dry, mordant humor shows up. Don't miss the last little visual joke that's tossed in at the end of the closing credits. *AKA:* Night Scare; Beyond Bedlam. *ﾐﾐﾐﾐ*

Violence, strong language, mature subject matter, brief nudity.

1993 (R) 89m/C *GB* Craig Fairbrass, Elizabeth Hurley, Keith Allen, Jesse Birdsall, Craig Kelly; *D:* Vadim Jean; *W:* Vadim Jean. **VHS, LV** *LIV*

Nina Takes a Lover

In the ever-more-competitive theatrical marketplace, a film like this might not have a chance, but it's one of those neat little sleepers that's perfect for home video. Essentially, it's a San Francisco love story with a twist. Nina (Laura San Giacomo) tells it to a newspaper reporter (Michael O'Keefe) who's working on a feature about affairs. She had one with a nameless photographer (Paul Rhys) while her husband was gone for three weeks. Using that device and title cards between scenes, writer/director Alan Jacobs lets the details of the relationship unfold at an odd, uneven pace. Though the action is talky, it's never dull. About midway through, the film takes a turn that's inexplicable at first—and not completely fair—but it pulls through. Still, a lot of the credit looks to be due to casting. It's a mystery to me why Demi Moore, to pick only one example, can knock down big bucks for turkeys like *The Scarlet Letter* while Laura San Giacomo—who's more interesting and sexier and a better actress—gets comparatively little attention for work this good. That's just the way the business has always been, but this sleeper is well worth seeking out. *ﾐﾐﾐ*

Mature subject matter, sexual content, strong language.

1994 (R) 100m/C Laura San Giacomo, Paul Rhys, Michael O'Keefe, Cristi Conaway, Fisher Stevens; *D:* Alan Jacobs; *W:* Alan Jacobs; *C:* Phil Parmet; *M:* Todd Boekelheide. **VHS, LV** *COL*

9 1/2 Ninjas

The box copy promises "the first erotic martial arts action comedy," and the accent is definitely on comedy. With the exception of one suggestive dance number, this is almost a kids' movie. Most of the humor is broad slapstick, with several parodies of other movies. The plot is properly sophomoric, but any video that makes fun of Jerry Lewis can't be all bad. 🦴🦴 **GPI: 5.1**

Strong language, sex, violence, nudity, etc.

1990 (R) 88m/C Michael Phenicie, Andee Gray, Tiny Lister; *D:* Aaron Worth; *W:* Bill Crounse. **VHS, LV** *REP*

9 1/2 Weeks

Even the unrated "European" video version of this allegedly sizzling "erotic" drama is pretty tame stuff. Director Adrian Lyne is concerned that the characters' clothes match the paint and the wallpaper and that the shine on their shoes is picked up by the shine on the floor and that the light glares through the mini-blinds at precisely the right angle. Forget believable personalities or desire. And the big hubba-hubba scene takes place on a kitchen floor in front of an open refrigerator. Obsessed lovers Mickey Rourke and Kim Basinger waste a lot of power and food, and who's going to clean all that stuff up? In any version, this is a long perfume commercial that tries to pass itself off as a virtually skinless skin flick. 🦴 **GPI: 3.0**

Mature subject matter, sexual content, brief nudity.

1986 (R) 114m/C Mickey Rourke, Kim Basinger, Margaret Whitton, Karen Young, David Margulies, Christine Baranski, Roderick Cook, Dwight Weist; *D:* Adrian Lyne; *W:* Patricia Louisianna Knop, Zalman King; *C:* Peter Biziou; *M:* Jack Nitzsche. **VHS, LV** *MGM*

No More Dirty Deals

Fort Lauderdale speedboat jock (Von VonLindenberg), who has more hair than brains, gets himself hooked up with Sean Halloway (Taimak), the leader of a coed gang of thieves. The story actually generates some complexity toward the end, but it's mostly about chases (on land and water), stick-ups, and such. The young cast is much more attractive than talented, but that's not really a problem with this kind of movie. Filmmaker Andy Sidaris perfected the formula in such memorable video originals as *Hard Ticket to Hawaii* and *Picasso Trigger*. Here, director David Jean Schweitzer puts his own spin on it. 🦴🦴🦴

Violence, strong language, brief nudity, sexual content.

1994 91m/C Von VonLindenberg, Taimak, Jennifer Langdon; *D:* David Jean Schweitzer. **VHS** *NBD*

Nomads

It's difficult to believe that director John McTiernan made his debut with this impressively cast but weak horror flick. Lesley-Anne Down is an L.A. doctor; Pierce Brosnan is a French anthropologist who comes raving into her emergency room, whispers something in her ear, and dies. The titular creatures dress like refugees from a heavy metal concert, play loud rock music, and spray paint garage doors until the good doctor decides to leave California. 🦴🦴

Violence, strong language.

1986 (R) 91m/C Pierce Brosnan, Lesley-Anne Down, Adam Ant, Anna Maria Monticelli, Mary Woronov; *D:* John McTiernan; *M:* Bill Conti. **VHS, LV** *IME, PAR*

Northern Passage

Well-meaning Canadian wilderness adventure is fair entertainment for kids, but most adults will probably be put off by the standard-issue production values and cardboard characters. The central story is about young Nepeese (Neve Campbell) and the wolf-dog she befriends. Lorne Brass is the wicked Taggart who wants to buy her daddy's land and marry her; Jeff Fahey is the hero. The forest looks great and so do the animals, but the film is so grainy, they're less effective than they might have been. Scenic outdoor videos have to look good enough to pull you into their stories. This one doesn't. 🦅

Violence, brief long-distance nudity.

1995 (PG-13) 97m/C Jeff Fahey, Neve Campbell, Lorne Brass; *D:* Arnaud Selignac. **VHS** *VMK*

Not of This Earth

Jim Wynorksi's remake of Roger Corman's original has virtually everything that a B-movie fan could ask for: total lack of seriousness, a silly plot that zips right along, cheesy special effects, and oodles of gratuitous nudity. The overall level of violence is a little too restrained, perhaps, but, hey, nothing is perfect. Alien vampire from the planet Davonna is here to send blood to the folks back home. Traci Lords is the nurse who unwittingly helps him by providing transfusions. But before long, she and her policeman beau realize that something untoward is going on down in the basement. Why is there smoke coming from the furnace when the temperature is close to 100 outside? Could it be that someone is getting rid of the remains of an unlucky door-to-door vacuum cleaner salesman? 🦅🦅🦅

Nudity, sexual scenes, profanity, violence.

1988 (R) 92m/C Traci Lords, Arthur Roberts, Lenny Juliano, Rebecca Perle, Ace Mask, Roger Lodge; *D:* Jim Wynorski; *W:* Jim Wynorski, R.J. Robertson. **VHS** *MGM*

Not of This Earth

B-movie fans everywhere have got to wonder how often producer Roger Corman can make *Not of This Earth*. He did it in 1957 and then in 1987 and now he's done it again. Well, why not? The story of a vampire from another planet is archetypally simple and perfect for a low budget. It's essentially a comedy and this version, like the others, doesn't take itself seriously. The effects range from amateurish to innovative. Michael York is a fine alien. As Nurse Amanda, Elizabeth Barondes is easily the equal of Beverly Garland and Traci Lords, and director Terry Winkless might follow in the footsteps of Corman himself (who directed the original) and schlockmeister Jim Wynorski who handled the first remake. 🦅🦅🦅

Strong language, yucky effects, brief nudity.

1996 (R) 92m/C Michael York, Elizabeth Barondes, Richard Belzer, Parker Stevenson; *D:* Terence H. Winkless. **VHS** *NHO*

Nothing but a Man

Outstanding racial drama was first released in 1964 to serious critical acclaim but only limited commercial success. No surprise there; the film was far ahead of its time, and it's an understated story that probably wouldn't be a big boxoffice hit in any case. But people remembered it, and on tape, this story of a young black man in segregated America will finally find the audience it deserves. In early 1960s Alabama, Duff (Ivan Dixon) is a veteran who wants something more than his job laying railroad track. When he meets Josie (Abbey Lincoln), a preacher's daughter, he begins to think more seriously about settling down. But that's not easy. First, of course, are the insults and indignities of institutionalized racism that he has to endure every day. From thoughtless paternalism to serious threats of lynching and beating, inequality is a fact of life that Duff has to deal with. But how? Should he acquiesce? Stand and fight back? Endure stoically? On a personal level, Duff has to decide what he's going to do about the boy who may or may not be his son. And then there's his father (Julius Harris), an embittered alcoholic who might be a mirror of Duff's own future. There's never a false note in the main characters. As created by Robert Young and director Michael Roemer, they're absolutely believable and they're portrayed with conviction. In telling the story, though, Roemer lets the action move at a slow, halting pace. That's a flaw but it also allows the viewer more time to watch the backgrounds. Today, that part of the film is an engrossing and realistic look back at the deep South of the early 1960s. The black-and-white location photography gives the story a well-aged patina. Finally, the conclusion could not be any better. It's not the big affirmative upbeat that studios demand these days. Instead it's much stronger and much quieter. 🦅🦅🦅

Contains no objectionable material, though the emotional violence is intense.

break it off, the film turns into a fairly standard stalker tale, with crazed villains, stalwart heroes, and a couple of looming plot lapses. It comes close to being much more. For the first half of the film, the antagonists are evenly matched; both are flawed but essentially sympathetic characters. But when the story slides into familiar cliches, Blair becomes one-dimensionally evil and Zane becomes one-dimensionally good. She could have been a woman who's forced to face the conflicts between a glamorous image and the reality behind it. He could have been a real actor, an individual who has adopted other identities because his own character has become shallow and self-centered. But that would have been another movie. As it is, director Jane Simpson makes a credible transition from commercials and videos to feature films. Take a look at whatever she does next. 🦴🦴🦴

Sexual content, nudity, violence, strong language.

1994 **(R)** 93m/**C** Chad McQueen, Catherine Mary Stewart, Renee Ammann, Hoyt Axton, Paul Bartel, Eric Da Re, Charles Matthau; *D:* Jane Simpson; *W:* Anthony Laurence Greene. **VHS** *ORI*

The Nutt House

Timing is everything. This comic misfire about twins (Stephen Kearney) separated as children was made several years ago, and since then has been sitting on a shelf somewhere, not bothering anyone. In the meantime though, Bill and Ted and Wayne and Garth and Ace Ventura appeared and "stupid" comedy became a blight upon the land. An objective observer could argue that this one's no better or worse than *Dumb and Dumber,* and in fact uses many of the same sight gags that appeared there and in *The Mask.* It also boasts the presence of the eminently bankable Traci Lords. So what if it's a terrible movie? So what if the people who made it are embarrassed? Note the variations on the pseudonym "Allan Smithee" that appear in the credits. 🦴🦴

Mild sexual humor, slapstick.

1995 **(PG-13)** 90m/**C** Stephen Kearney, Traci Lords, Amy Yasbeck; *Cameos:* Stella Stevens, Robert Mandan, Catherine Bach; *D:* Adam Rifkin. **VHS, LV** *TRI*

1964 95m/**B** Ivan Dixon, Abbey Lincoln, Gloria Foster, Julius W. Harris, Martin Priest, Yaphet Kotto; *D:* Michael Roemer; *W:* Robert M. Young, Michael Roemer. **VHS** *NEW, BTV, AAE*

Number One Fan

The first rule of reviewing is that you criticize what's on the screen, not what you want to see on the screen. It's hard to remember that with this one because there's so much unrealized potential. Essentially, Anthony Laurence Greene's script is a reworking on *Play Misty for Me* (still one of Hollywood's best thrillers), about Blair Madsen (Renee Ammann), a disturbed young woman who's obsessed with movie star Zane Barry (Chad McQueen). Even though he's about to marry Holly (Catherine Mary Stewart), it doesn't take much for Blair to turn his head, as it were. When he tries to

Oblivion

Producer Charles Band took a fistful of genres, loaded them into his cinematic revolver, and opened fire. The result is your basic s-f/Western/cowboy/comedy/monster flick. As is always the case with Full Moon films, the production values are top-drawer with some nice stop-motion monsters. The characters are colorful; the action is quick; the humor is silly. Despite the unorthodox mixture, the plot elements are familiar. 𝕯𝕯𝖁

Violence, strong language, mature subject matter.

1994 (PG-13) 94m/C Richard Joseph Paul, Andrew Divoff, Jackie Swanson, Meg Foster, Isaac Hayes, Julie Newmar, Carel Struycken, George Takei; **D:** Sam Irvin; **W:** Peter David; **M:** Pino Donaggio. **VHS** *PAR*

Oleanna

The gassy film version of David Mamet's highly touted play really has nothing to add to the public debate about sexual harassment beyond the questions of unfounded character assassination it raises. Mamet stacks the deck in favor of a self-important professor (William Macy) who finds himself opposed by a struggling student (Debra Eisenstadt). There's not a hint of humor to the claustrophobic stagebound proceedings. For a more balanced and informed treatment of the subject, see the soft-core *Improper Conduct*. **WOOF!**

Contains some strong language, violence.

1994 90m/C William H. Macy, Debra Eisenstadt; **D:** David Mamet; **W:** David Mamet; **M:** Rebecca Pidgeon. Nominations: Independent Spirit Awards '95: Best Actor (Macy). **VHS, LV** *HMK*

On the Road with Jack Kerouac

Producer/director John Antonelli combines readings from the author's work, photographs and film footage, interviews with contemporaries, and recreations of key moments to dramatize an eventful life. True, he doesn't get very far beneath the surface of that life, but that's not his point. Penetrating psychological analysis of dead authors is the territory of literary biographers, and they're welcome to it. Antonelli shows us a complex, active man surrounded by colorful characters. Kerouac was the central figure in the "Beat" generation, one of the most boisterous chapters of this country's literary history. Appropriately, his career is presented as a flowing series of images, feelings, and memories; not specific details. Kerouac's literary life began tentatively. His first wife remembers their brief time together in Grosse Pointe; "He lived there with a dog, two cats, my mother, my sister and I. Every single day of his life there he'd go into the bathroom for four hours and read Shakespeare and the Bible. We could never get in." After that imperfect union came the wild times with Neal Cassady, William Burroughs, and Alan Ginzburg; the cross-country drives; the literary scene in San Francisco; the sudden success of *On the Road*. And then the decline, the booze and untimely death. Antonelli isn't blind to Kerouac's faults but he doesn't dwell on them either. This film isn't subtitled "Portrait of a Role Model." Kerouac's life was devoted to words. Whatever else he was or did, the man could write like an angel. The film ends perfectly with a long reading that Kerouac gave on the Steve Allen Show. For students, the film is an excellent and accessible introduction to the Beats. Strongly recommended. 𝕯𝕯𝕯𝖁

Contains some strong language and descriptions of drug use.

1984 73m/C **D:** John Antonelli. **VHS** *WNE*

Once Upon a Time in America

The full-length (227 min.) version of Sergio Leone's gangster masterpiece is available only on tape. The radically edited 143-minute theatrical version misses Leone's central point. The entire film is an opium-fogged memory, an aging criminal's (Robert De Niro) summing up of his violent life in and out of jail. The wealth of detail in the sprawling film is astonishing, from violent sexual encounters to more closely observed moments, like the

famous pastry scene. Economic realities of the business kept the film from its big screen audience. But that's video's gain. For anyone who's missed it, this "premiere" is required viewing. For everyone else, it's worth a second look. ♪♪♪♪

Graphic violence, sexual content, rape, nudity, strong language.

1984 (R) 227m/C Robert De Niro, James Woods, Elizabeth McGovern, Treat Williams, Tuesday Weld, Burt Young, Joe Pesci, Danny Aiello, Darlanne Fluegel, Jennifer Connelly; *D:* Sergio Leone; *C:* Tonino Delli Colli; *M:* Ennio Morricone. **VHS, LV** *WAR*

Once Were Warriors

New Zealand film about domestic violence within a Maori family is very strong stuff—too strong for some viewers. The Maori are an indigenous Polynesian people. As the film puts it, some remain on a protected reservation; others, like the Heke family, have moved to the city. The opening scenes highlight the prison-like conditions of their life there. Beth (Rena Owen) tries to take care of her kids despite her bullying husband Jake's (Temuera Morrison) drunken rages. Director Lee Tamahori makes those scenes so harrowing that they're hard to watch. All of the violence in *Pulp Fiction,* for example, doesn't come close to one scene in a kitchen, not to mention its aftermath. Perhaps it's inevitable that the rest of the film can't measure up to those moments. The key subplot involving Beth's daughter, Grace (subtly and effectively played by Mamaengaroa Kerr-Bell), is somehow out of step—though it certainly doesn't pull any punches either—and in the end, the resolution seems too simple for the problems the film addresses. Still anyone who wants grit, substance, and seriousness of purpose should take a look. ♪♪♪

Mature subject matter, violence, strong language, sexual content.

1994 (R) 102m/C *NZ* Rena Owen, Temuera Morrison, Mamaengaroa Kerr-Bell, Julian (Sonny) Arahanga, Taungaroa Emile,

Rachael Morris, Joseph Kairau, Pete Smith; **D:** Lee Tamahori; **W:** Riwia Brown; **M:** Murray Grindlay, Murray McNabb. Australian Film Institute '95: Best Foreign Film; Montreal World Film Festival '94: Best Actress (Owen), Best Film. **VHS, LV** *NLC*

One False Move

In Los Angeles, Pluto (Michael Beach), Ray (Billy Bob Thornton, who co-wrote the script), and Fantasia (Cynda Williams) pull off an audacious and bloody stick-up. They rob a drug dealer, stealing a huge stash of cocaine and cash. Left behind are several bodies and an odd clue on a camcorder that suggests they may be heading for Star City, Arkansas. It leads the California cops to contact police Chief Dixon (Bill Paxton) in the little town. Flattered that "the big boys" would ask for his help, he agrees to do everything he can when they arrive. The rest of the film follows two plotlines. In one, Pluto's "gang" makes its way east. They are an unstable, unpredictable trio prone to violence and extreme stupidity, depending on the situation. In the second, the city cops learn how things are done in a small town; how people there can know so much about each other and still keep secrets. The two halves of the story meet in a fine Hitchcockian conclusion. The cops-'n'-robbers element is only one side of the film. The other conflicts are much more interesting: urban vs. rural, innocence vs. sophistication, realists vs. dreamers. The script by Thornton and Tom Epperson is filled with fully developed characters. There's not a stereotype or cliche in the bunch, and the cast seems comfortable and natural throughout. Director Carl Franklin, a veteran of several forgettable B-movies, lets the story unfold at a deliberate, suspenseful pace. The violence isn't nearly as graphic as it has been in some recent crime movies, but it's still effective and frightening. And some mention should be made of the strong, understated blues score by Peter Haycock and Derek Holt that sets just the right tone. For comparative purposes, think of an updated *Sugarland Express* with a harder edge. But don't take that too far. 🎬🎬🎬

Violence, strong language.

1991 (R) 105m/C Bill Paxton, Cynda Williams, Michael Beach, Jim Metzler, Earl Billings, Billy Bob Thornton, Natalie Canderday, Robert Ginnaven, Robert Anthony Bell, Kevin Hunter; **D:** Carl Franklin; **W:** Billy Bob Thornton, Tom Epperson; **C:** James L. Carter. Independent Spirit Awards '93: Best Director (Franklin); MTV Movie Awards '93: Best New Filmmaker Award (Franklin). **VHS, LV** *COL, FCT*

One Good Turn

The real key to a good B-movie is unpredictability. Even if you know that it's a horror flick or a dumb comedy or a thriller, the standard formula will be twisted or reversed in enough ways to surprise you. On that level, this one delivers the goods. It's a neatly constructed little mystery that reveals itself through the characters. Matt (Lenny Von Dohlen) is a fast-rising young video executive who's happily—well, fairly happily—married to Laura (Suzy Amis). Then Simon (James Remar) literally bumps into him on an upscale L.A. street. Matt knows him from years before in Panama where Simon saved his life. But Simon, perhaps embarrassed by his shabby clothes, quickly disappears. Matt is compelled to find him, and from that moment on, almost nothing is what it appears to be. Veteran B movie director Tony Randel begins things with a terrific opening montage, and then spices up the tricky plot with a few standard cheap thrills. Again, though, the key is unpredictability, and it's sustained straight through to a satisfying conclusion. 🎬🎬🎬

Violence, sexual content, brief nudity, strong language, drug use.

1995 (R) 90m/C Lenny Von Dohlen, James Remar, Suzy Amis, John Savage, Audie England; **D:** Tony Randel; **W:** Jim Piddock. **VHS** *BMG*

Operation Golden Phoenix

Good locations are virtually all this martial arts flick has going for it. Otherwise, there's nothing to separate it from a hundred others. Producer/director/star Jalal Merhi shot his movie in Montreal and Beirut, Lebanon. The plot has something to do with the theft and retrieval of ancient treasures. The fight scenes are competently choreographed, and the Lebanese locations give the film an exotic

ous, jet-setting youth which she has since renounced to study wildlife in Africa. Assorted poachers, tribesmen, ex-husbands, kidnappers, and villains are tossed into the disjointed mix. The first part, about Donald's normal job, is probably much funnier to people who are directly involved with the entertainment business. The broader physical comedy and slapstick in the jungle will appeal to younger viewers. Throughout, the action loafs along at far too slow a pace. ♫♫♪

Mild violence and profanity.

1988 (PG) 105m/C Matt Salinger, Joanna Pacula, John Kani, James Keach; **Cameos:** Susan Anton, Eric Roberts; **D:** Camilo Vila; **W:** Edward Decter. **VHS, LV** *LIV, VES*

Organized Crime & Triad Bureau

O.K., the title lacks a certain grace, but this is the best Hong Kong action import since John Woo's *Hard-Boiled.* Comparisons between Woo and director Kirk Wong may not be completely fair, but the filmmakers do have similar styles and they certainly know how to spin an entertaining yarn. Wong takes a more lyrical and somewhat less violent approach to crime stories. He can also create moments of incredible beauty, many of those involving rain or water. The good guys here are a squad of cops led by Inspector Lee (Danny Lee, featured in Woo's *The Killer*). He's relentless in his pursuit of gangster Tung (Anthony Wong), who has a highly placed informer in the ranks of the police. Lee's toothless superiors are almost as bad. The film is structured as a chase, with Lee on the trail of Tung and his mistress Cindy (Cecilia Yip), but it's not a simple story. Wong moves back and forth in time without losing any of his narrative drive, and despite the fast pace, he takes time to develop his characters. These are not simple stereotypes. The relationship between Tung and Cindy is so complicated that they become surprisingly sympathetic characters. Perhaps a more useful comparison is Michael Mann's *Heat,* but crank up the speed about three

atmosphere that can't be created on a studio set. ♫♫

Violence, language.

1994 (R) 95m/C Jalal Merhi, James Hong, Al Waxman, Loren Avedon; **D:** Jalal Merhi. **VHS, LV** *MCA*

Options

Satire on Hollywood's deal-making mentality takes its inspiration from the surprise hit *The Gods Must Be Crazy.* Staid, innocent lawyer Donald (Matt Salinger) specializes in acquiring the rights to life stories, the kind that are featured in *People* magazine and then turned into TV movies-of-the-week. He is so good at his job that his boss sends him to Africa to get Princess Nicole (Joanna Pacula) to sign on the dotted line. Nicole, it seems, led a tempestu-

times and give it a great ending. *AKA:* Chun-gon Satluk Linggei. 🦴🦴🦴

Contains strong language, violence, some sexual material.

1993 91m/C *HK* Danny Lee, Anthony Wong, Cecilia Yip; *D:* Kirk Wong. **VHS, LV** *TAI*

The Other Woman

When a reporter (Lee Ann Beaman) finds some curious pictures of her husband (Sam Jones) with a model, she decides to exact marital revenge. But is he guilty of anything? As is always the case in Hippolyte productions, plot and acting are less important than soft-core sexiness and top-drawer production values. Also available in an unrated version. 🦴🦴 **GPI: 8.3**

Violence, strong language, sexual material, nudity.

1992 (R) 90m/C Adrian Zmed, Lee Ann Beaman, Daniel Moriarty, Jenna Persaud, Sam Jones; *D:* Jag Mundhra. **VHS** *IMP*

Out for Blood

This would be a run-of-the-mill martial arts flick if it weren't for the presence of Don "The Dragon" Wilson. There's nothing original about the plot (revenge against drug dealers who killed family) or the characters. The fights are well choreographed and remarkably realistic in a few cases, but that's not too unusual for the genre, either. The key to this one is the star. Wilson has the indefinable screen "presence" that made Bruce Lee so popular. It has something to do with energy. In key scenes, Wilson is reminiscent of a young James Cagney, filled to bursting with adrenaline and fire. He can direct into the camera and share it with the viewer; that's the important part. There are dozens of bigger stars out there, and guys with bulkier muscles who can kick higher and yell louder, but Don Wilson is more fun to watch than any of them. 🦴🦴🦴

Violence, strong language, sexual content.

1993 (R) 90m/C Don "The Dragon" Wilson, Shari Shattuck, Michael Delano, Kenneth McLeod, Todd Curtis, Timothy Baker, Howard Jackson, Bob Schott, Eric Lee; *D:* Richard W. Munchkin; *W:* David S. Green. **VHS** *PMH*

Out of Annie's Past

Formula made-for-cable thriller is something less than thrilling. A good cast led by Catherine Mary Stewart and Dennis Farina is wasted in a poorly written story of a young woman with a guilty secret and the corrupt blackmailer who's tormenting her. At first, the film has some spooky moments, but those are ended by an unintentionally funny hospital scene, and it never recovers. 🦴🦴

Strong language, some violence.

1994 (R) 91m/C Catherine Mary Stewart, Dennis Farina, Scott Valentine; *D:* Stuart Cooper. **VHS** *MCA*

Out of the Rain

Noirish version of the prodigal son story is told at a glacial pace. Though it's attempting to be stylish in its elliptical approach to the material, that's little help. Stars Michael O'Keefe and Bridget Fonda don't have much to work with, but they do manage to strike a few sparks. Again, dedicated moviegoers will feel a sense of deja vu. In terms of setting (a sooty little town that puts the rust back in rustbelt), pace, and characters, this one is strongly reminiscent of Arthur Miller's offbeat *Everybody Wins.* 🦴🦴

Strong language, violence.

1990 (R) 91m/C Bridget Fonda, Michael O'Keefe, John E. O'Keefe, John Seitz, Georgine Hall, Al Shannon; *D:* Gary Winick; *W:* Shem Bitterman. **VHS, LV** *CCB, LIV*

Out There

Alien "abduction" gets the irreverent treatment it so richly deserves. Photographer Delbert Mosley (Bill Campbell) buys an old Kodak Brownie at a yard sale and finds exposed film inside. The developed pictures show what might be a flying saucer, aliens, and two guys in a pickup truck. Turns out they disappeared in 1969. Were they spirited away to outer space? Or did they stumble onto the set of a cheap s-f movie—*Escape from Uranus*—and decide to run away from home? Delbert and Paige (Wendy Schaal), the Nixon-obsessed daughter of one of the missing, set off to find

the truth. They get considerable help from a supporting cast of familiar yet unexpected faces—Jill St. John, Julie Brown, Paul Dooley, P.J. Soles, Bill Cobbs, David Rasche, June Lockhart. The plot has a deceptively disjointed quality and despite some slow moments, the film is brassy and colorful. The humor is generally understated, arriving at a terrific universal-conspiracy conclusion. *X-Files* fans, take a look. 𝄞𝄞𝄞

A little strong language, comic violence.

1995 (PG-13) 98m/C Bill Campbell, Wendy Schaal, Julie Brown, David Rasche, Paul Dooley, Bill Cobbs, Bob(cat) Goldthwait, Rod Steiger, June Lockhart, Jill St. John, Carel Struycken, Billy Bob Thornton, P.J. Soles; *D:* Sam Irvin; *W:* Thomas Strelich, Alison Nigh; *C:* Gary Tieche; *M:* Deborah Holland, Frankie Blue. VHS *PAR*

Outrage

This would have been a radically different movie (and not nearly as good) if it had been made a few years later when the story would have been weighted toward the male lead, not the female. As it is, this 1993 Spanish import is a tightly constructed revenge picture about a circus performer (Francesca Neri) and her reporter boyfriend (Antonio Banderas). The focus is on her, not him, and the structure is unusual. Where most American versions of the plot would end, this one is only half over and is getting better. Writer/director Carlos Saura keeps the pace deliberate and gives the film an inexorable, almost predetermined quality. He's a serious storyteller and he treats his subject as drama, not exploitation. Available in both dubbed and subtitled versions. *AKA:* Dispara. 𝄞𝄞𝄞

Violence, rape, sexual content, nudity, strong language.

1993 (R) 108m/C *SP* Antonio Banderas, Francesca Neri; *D:* Carlos Saura; *W:* Carlos Saura. VHS *APX*

Outrageous Animation, Vols. 1 and 2

As a group, these animated short films are sexual, scatological, sacrilegious, and often, but not always, really funny. There's some-

thing here to offend just about everybody. Many are European and some of the comedy has trouble crossing cultural and national borders. What's going on in "Full of Grace"? "An Inside Job," about dental work, is so effective that I hit the fast-forward button after the first few minutes, and the infamous "Lupo the Butcher" is like nothing you've ever seen. Definitely not for children. 𝄞𝄞𝄞

Contains sexual material, nudity, strong language, and violence.

1990 170m/C VHS, LV *EXP, LUM, TPV*

Outside the Law

Unembarrassed remake of *Basic Instinct* casts Anna Thomson, from *Unforgiven,* in the Sharon Stone role. She's Tanya, the blonde woman of mystery who's at the center of a series of murders. Det. Kingsbury (David Bradley) falls in lust the moment he meets her and spends the rest of the movie proving to his partner Paige (Ashley Laurence) that Tanya had nothing to do with all those murders. The body of the film follows the structure of its predecessor fairly faithfully until the last reel, when it reaches for a "surprise" ending and turns into a bizarre comedy. Throughout, the characters are one-note stereotypes and the acting is equally flat. The exception is Anna Thomson, who looks like Drew Barrymore probably will in about eight or ten years. Her icily cold sexiness is the film's main attraction. Also available in an unrated version. 𝄞𝄞𝄞

GPI: 7.9

Sexual content, nudity, and a little rough language.

1995 (R) 94m/C David Bradley, Anna Thomson, Ashley Laurence; *D:* Boaz Davidson; *W:* Dennis Dimster Denk; *C:* Avi Karpik; *M:* Blake Leyh. VHS, LV *TTC, NLC, IME*

Over the Wire

Standard "erotic thriller" actually has an element of mystery. A telephone repairman (David Christensen) overhears one woman plotting to kill another. When he goes to the address, he finds two sisters (Landon Hall and Shauna O'Brien) with similar voices. Who's up to what? The acting is laughable but that's not exactly the point. Ms. O'Brien is one of the sleekest actresses in the business. Surely it's a joke that the voice actor who plays "the phone sex guy" is Bob Dole. Now, if it were Bill Clinton.... Also available in an unrated version. 🐾🐾 **GPI: 9.3**

Strong sexual content, nudity, strong language, some violence.

1995 (R) 90m/C Shauna O'Brien, Griffin Drew, Tim Abell, David Christensen, Landon Hall; *D:* Nicholas Medina. **VHS** *TRI*

Overexposed

Roger Corman "erotic thriller" is about a soap opera star who may or may not be the target of a crazed fan. Kristin Halsy (Catherine Oxenberg) is the head villainess on *Secrets Kept*. She suffers from nightmares and has been receiving threatening notes in her dressing room. Is she crazy? Is her boyfriend Philip (David Naughton) really a saintly doctor? What about the new neighbor (William Bumiller) who conveniently shows up when she needs help? Karen Black turns in a deranged cameo as a fan who speaks in TV cliches. Catherine Oxenberg has that too-smooth Bo Derek prettiness, but she's a slightly better actress and a first-rate screamer. The clues are trotted out in a fairly conventional manner and the pace is a little slow, but the fractured ending is a real lu-lu. With an honesty that's rarely seen in Hollywood, not one, but two body doubles are given credit for Ms. Oxenberg's love scene. 🐾🐾🐾 **GPI: 6.1**

Sexual scenes, brief nudity, violence, profanity.

1990 (R) 83m/C Catherine Oxenberg, David Naughton, Jennifer Edwards, Karen Black, William Bumiller; *D:* Larry Brand; *W:* Larry Brand. **VHS** *MGM*

Overseas: Three Women with Man Trouble

French mini-epic covers a period of about 20 years from the mid-'40s to the mid-'60s, in the lives of three sisters in French colonial Algeria. The women tell overlapping stories from their separate points of view. The oldest, Zon (Nicole Garcia), is the wife of a naval officer who is seldom at home, and there seems to be trouble between them whenever he is around. Malene (writer/director Brigitte Rouan) is married to a passive intellectual. The youngest, Gritte (Marianne Basler) isn't sure that she wants to be anyone's wife. The opening scene, which will be repeated twice with variations, is a party where all the principal characters wear white. It's impossible to tell who's who or to understand what the various pairings-off mean. As the story progresses, we learn that the women's lives are being changed by the rebellion of the Algerians against the French. Here, though, international politics aren't any more important than sexual politics, and these women have familiar complaints. Men. No matter how nice and promising they start out, they always turn out to be useless. All of the male characters are either incompetent, terrorists, or deceased. You just can't trust 'em. Once you've figured out the odd non-linear narrative structure, the story makes more sense. The scenes of the sisters by themselves ring true, but some of the subtitles have that odd stilted quality that plague all dialogue translations. 🐾🐾🐾

Contains brief nudity, sexual content, some violence.

1990 96m/C *FR* Nicole Garcia, Marianne Basler, Philippe Galland, Pierre Doris, Brigitte Rouan; *D:* Brigitte Rouan; *W:* Brigitte Rouan. Cannes Film Festival '90: Best Film. **VHS** *FXL, BTV, BFV*

Paint It Black

Director Tim Hunter takes Hitchcock as his model for a deliberate throwback. The music by Jurgen Knieper even recalls those wonderful Bernard Herrmann scores. The story revolves around an artist (Rick Rossovich) on the verge of major success and a disturbed young art collector (Jason Bernard) who lets nothing stand in the way of his passion. A gallery owner of dubious honesty (Sally Kirkland) and an important art dealer (Martin Landau) are also involved. The entire production has a highly polished look. The acting is good and the characters have some depth. But the contrived script borrows freely from *Strangers on a Train*, and though the film has some strong moments, it's never quite as suspense-

215

Video Premieres

Mr. Right

It's the question single women ask whenever they meet a new guy: "Is he Mr. Right or a serial murderer?" Video Premieres answer:

THE BABY DOLL MURDERS	LADYKILLER
BLINDFOLD: ACTS OF OBSESSION	LISA
	MR. FROST
BLUE DESERT	THE PAINT JOB
BODY OF INFLUENCE	SKINNER
CRIMINAL PASSION	TRUE CRIME
FATAL CHARM	

in the 'burbs. Wesley (Will Patton) is a painter who works for him. Everything would be fine...except Wesley and Margaret have fallen in love with each other, and Will spends his evenings and weekends murdering old alcoholics. All right, that synopsis does not sound like a knee-slapping laughfest. But, for comparative purposes, imagine what deadpan novelist Thomas Berger might do with those characters in that situation. The locations have a realistic, used-up look, and the actors—including Casey Siemaszko and Mark Boone, Jr., as a chorus in coveralls—make understatement their rule. Almost nothing is overt. The action is so restrained and stylized that most videophiles will either love or loathe it; there's no middle ground. 🦴🦴🦴

Mature subject matter, strong language, some comic violence.

1993 **(R)** 90m/C Will Patton, Bebe Neuwirth, Robert Pastorelli, Casey Siemaszko, Mark Boone; *D:* Micheal Taav; *W:* Micheal Taav; *M:* John Wesley Harding. **VHS** *COL*

---

ful as it's trying to be. The ending, blatantly lifted from *North by Northwest*, is too silly for words. 🦴🦴🦴

Violence, profanity, sexual material.

1989 **(R)** 101m/C Sally Kirkland, Rick Rossovich, Martin Landau, Doug Savant, Peter Frechette, Julie Carmen, Jason Bernard, Monique Van De Ven; *D:* Tim Hunter; *M:* Jurgen Knieper. **VHS, LV** *LIV, VES*

The Paint Job

Though the box copy proclaims a "stark psychological thriller" with "the fury building to a chilling climax," nothing could be farther from the truth. Actually, this is an offbeat comedy about serial murder and adultery. Whatever the cast lacks in star power, it makes up for with professionalism. These are some of the best character actors in the business and they seem to have been perfectly in tune with their material. In a generic, early '60s South, Will (Robert Pastorelli) runs a house painting business. To judge by appearances, he's an average middle-class guy with a loving wife, Margaret (Bebe Neuwirth), and a small tract house

Painted Hero

Curious contemporary Western boasts good characters, some fine performances, and a completely unpredictable plot. Country singer Dwight Yoakam proves that his strong supporting work in *Red Rock West* was no fluke. Here, he's Virgil Kidder, a rodeo clown with a secret in his past. That's why he doesn't want to go back to his Waco, Texas, hometown, but promoter Bo Hopkins persuades him. Virgil runs into his old girlfriend (Michelle Joyner), a bullying sheriff (John Getz) who still holds a grudge, and a young woman (Kiersten Warren) with some peculiar habits. Essentially, it's a return of the prodigal story with a rural setting, but the film has a weird sexual element that's somehow out of step with that world. Still, give writer/director Terry Benedict credit for originality and audacity. This may not be the movie that Yoakam's fans want or expect to see, but they won't be bored. 🦴🦴🦴

Strong language, sexual content, some violence, brief nudity.

1995 **(R)** 105m/C Dwight Yoakam, Bo Hopkins, Cindy Pickett, Michelle Joyner, Kiersten Warren, John Getz; *D:* Terry Benedict; *W:* Terry Benedict. **VHS** *CAF*

The Pamela Principle

Runner-up for the prestigious and coveted Guilty Pleasure of 1992 Award, this story of a married man's seduction into an affair with a free-spirited young model is actually pretty good. Toby Phillips' story captures the embarrassing banality of extramarital sex. At the same time, as a director he knows what fans of "erotic" videos want to see and he delivers the goods with an attractive cast. Also available in an unrated version. ♫♫♫ **GPI: 9.6**

Considerable nudity, strong sexual material, language.

1991 (U) ⁄m/C J.K. Dumont, Veronica Cash, Shelby Lane, Troy Donahue, Frank Pesce; *D:* Toby Phillips. **VHS, LV** *IMP*

Paper Mask

Realistic medical horror story makes Robin Cook's latest tale of medicine-gone-bad look like a walk in the park. Matthew Harris (Paul McGann) is a London hospital aide until a bit of circumstance allows him to fulfill his real ambition—to be a doctor. Simon Hennessy (Dale Rapley) is killed in an accident, Harris takes over his identity and completes his application for a position at a hospital somewhere in the British hinterlands. Harris figures that he has picked up enough experience by watching real doctors and nurses, and he's nervy enough to fake the rest. Given that premise, what follows is logical, possible, and horrifying. Nurse Christine Taylor (Amanda Donohoe) unwittingly helps Harris, and for a time, he pulls it off. But his past and the limits of his knowledge are never far away. John Collee's script is brightened by a droll sense of black humor, and an insider's sure touch with the details of the business. These characters aren't the dedicated, saintly figures of popular entertainment; the doctors, administrators, and nurses are flesh-and-blood people, no better than they have to be and often much much worse. Director Christopher Morahan used his limited budget to its best effect. The acting is up to the high standard we expect from British films, and the sets and locations have an unusually strong sense of reality. The last 30 minutes, when the full implications of Harris's game become clear, are really spooky. ♫♫♫

Mature subject matter, brief nudity, sexual content.

1991 (R) 105m/C *GB* Paul McGann, Amanda Donohoe, Frederick Treves, Barbara Leigh-Hunt, Jimmy Yuill, Tom Wilkinson, Dale Rapley; *D:* Christopher Morahan; *W:* John Collee; *M:* Richard Harvey. **VHS** *ACA*

Parents

Genuinely macabre black satire addresses conformity, obedience, and suburban cannibalism in the 1950s. Director Bob Balaban goes to work in *Blue Velvet/Twin Peaks* territory and comes up with a film that's much more effective and unsettling. Young Michael Lemley (Bryan Madorsky) is moving to a new town with his Dad (Randy Quaid) and Mom (Mary Beth Hurt). Dad develops defoliants to be used in jungle warfare for Toxico; Mom seems to spend most of her time preparing leftovers. They move into a split-level filled with all of the coral and turquoise furniture and appliances we've come to identify with the '50s. But Michael is shy, silent, and basically unlikable. He's troubled by nightmares and visions of his parents with bloodstained mouths. New neighbors and teachers, each bearing some prominent quirk or flaw, become involved with Michael's attempts to "fit in," but nothing seems to help. When his folks give evasive answers about the main course at dinner, he comes to believe that they are cannibals. Is that the truth, or is he a very disturbed child? The script presents no easy answers or escapes. The resolution is too violent and, compared to the body of the film, too conventional. For the most part, Balaban succeeds in making this an unnerving piece of work. All of the colors, for example, are slightly off, slightly too intense. Food, notably meat, has seldom been so revoltingly photographed. The characters are just a notch or two off dead center and a soundtrack of syrupy '50s big band hits like "Cherry Pink and Apple Blossom White" has been poured over these disquieting visual images. Though there is a grimly humorous angle to the story, this is not a comedy. It's the stuff nightmares are made of. ♫♫♫

Mature subject matter, violence, and profanity.

1989 (R) 81m/C Randy Quaid, Mary Beth Hurt, Sandy Dennis, Kathryn Grody, Deborah Rush, Graham Jarvis, Bryan Madorsky, Juno Mills-Cockell; *D:* Bob Balaban; *W:* Christopher Hawthorne; *M:* Angelo Badalamenti, Jonathan Elias. **VHS, LV** *LIV, VES, HHE*

Paris, France

Kinky intellectual comedy earns its NC-17 rating in the first two minutes. Lucy (Leslie Hope) is unhappily married to Michael (Victor Ertmanis), a small-press publisher of serious literature. His homosexual partner (Dan Lett) introduces them to Sloan (Peter Outerbridge), an angry young poet obsessed with sex and mass murderer Ed Gein. Leslie begins an affair with Sloan, and at the same time has vivid memories of another affair she had in Paris years ago. Before it's over, the characters have tried just about every sexual combination imaginable. Between rounds, these libidinal literati indulge in lengthy monologues and soliloquies. I doubt that anyone who is not or has not been an English major could watch *Paris, France* from beginning to end without hitting the fast-forward button. 🦴🦴

Strong sexual content, nudity, language

1994 (NC-17) 96m/C *CA* Leslie Hope, Peter Outerbridge, Victor Ertmanis, Raoul Trujillo, Dan Lett; *D:* Gerard Ciccoritti; *W:* Tom Walmsley; *M:* John McCarthy. **VHS** *APX*

Party Girl

The short review would be "Clueless in New York," but the key ingredient—an engaging, funny young heroine—is missing. Mary (well played by Parker Posey) is a self-centered jerk, and her transformation into something more doesn't wash. Mary's a thief, drunk, and druggie who spends so much time nightclubbing with her gay friends that she can't be bothered with a job. But an unfortunate arrest forces her to seek employment as a librarian with her godmother. She also has a romantic relationship—sort of—with a Turkish immigrant hunk. Writer/director Daisy von Scherler Mayer tries to make Mary's little failings seem cute and endearing, but the character remains little more than a skinny mannequin for a series of trendy/ugly costumes. The entire production has a slick mainstream "stu-

dio" look that doesn't really suit the would-be-hip story. 🦴🦴

Mature subject matter, strong language, sexual material, brief nudity.

1994 (R) 94m/C Parker Posey, Omar Townsend, Anthony De Sando, Guillermo Diaz, Sasha von Scherler, Liev Schreiber; *D:* Daisy von Scherler Mayer; *W:* Harry Birckmayer, Daisy von Scherler Mayer; *C:* Michael Slovis; *M:* Anton Sanko. **VHS, LV** *COL*

Party Incorporated

Marilyn Chambers plays Marilyn Saunders, a woman who becomes a professional party-giver to pay back taxes to the IRS. The gimmick here is one that became popular in the last days of the TV series *Moonlighting*. The actors and crew constantly break the plane between the two sides of the camera. They ask the script supervisor to tell them forgotten lines of dialogue; the camera pans past mirrors to reveal itself and the crew behind it. The joke isn't that funny and it quickly wears thin. The acting is poor, and Marilyn sings two songs which are easy to fast forward through. Overall, the film has a slap-dash quality to it, as if director Chuck Vincent and Chambers invited a bunch of friends over for a long weekend and threw together the movie. *AKA:* Party Girls. 🦴🦴

Nudity, sexual situations, and profanity.

1989 (R) 80m/C Marilyn Chambers, Kurt Woodruff, Christine Veronica, Kimberly Taylor; *D:* Chuck Vincent. **VHS, LV** *VTR, NWV, IME*

Party Plane

Struggling airline turns to mud wrestling and topless stewardesses to find a profit in a spirited little burlesque comedy. This is silly, harmless stuff, along the lines of *The Benny Hill Show*. No, wait a minute, compared to *Party Plane*, *The Benny Hill Show* is *The Merry Wives of Windsor*. 🦴🦴

Contains nudity, sexual humor.

1990 81m/C Kent Stoddard, Karen Annarino, John Goff, Jill Johnson; *D:* Ed Hansen. **VHS, LV** *VES*

Passion Flower

Classy suspense film features absolutely authentic Singapore locations. The story's not bad either. It revolves around a wealthy businessman (Nicol Williamson), his daughter (Barbara Hershey), and a young banker (Bruce Boxleitner). On the minus side are Hershey's idea of a British accent and a plot that gives itself away a little too early. On the plus side is the atmosphere of the Orient, so well realized that it gives the film the quality of a good James Clavell novel. 🗡🗡🗡

Mild sexual content and violence.

1986 (PG-13) 95m/C Bruce Boxleitner, Barbara Hershey, Nicol Williamson; *D:* Joseph Sargent; *M:* Miles Goodman. **VHS** *VMK*

A Passion to Kill

In many ways, this is nothing more than a standard psychological mystery; modestly budgeted, competently produced formula entertainment, but it makes a serious mistake that needs to be addressed. Psychologist David Lawson (Scott Bakula) doesn't know how to react when his best friend, Jerry (John Getz), a long-time bachelor, suddenly gets married. Before long, Jerry is sounding a little weird, and his new wife Diana (Chelsea Field) is making advances on David. Adding the next necessary level of complication is an old flame, Beth Faraday (Sheila Kelly), of uncertain motives. Then someone kills Jerry—stabs him. About now, you're saying to yourself that this sounds like *The Postman Always Rings Twice* by way of *Color of Night,* and you're not far from wrong. What makes this one different is an introduction strongly suggesting—though not showing—that Diana was physically abused by her first husband and fought back by stabbing him. O.K., given the often contentious state of affairs between men and women these days, that's a timely premise for a thriller; it touches a lot of buttons. But when they have to sort things through, the filmmakers chicken out. In the last reel, they make the plot jump through needless hoops, as if the idea of a woman defending herself against a man is unthinkable. At best, the ending has the stench of a committee decision. Perhaps they weren't trying to make anything more ambitious than another "killer babe" imitation, but storytellers can be held accountable,

and when they blatantly cheat, they should be called on it. It would be really interesting to see how a woman—Penelope Spheeris or Kathryn Bigelow—might have handled the same story. Maybe next time. *AKA:* Rules of Obsession. 🗡🗡

Mature subject matter, brief nudity, strong language, violence.

1994 (R) 93m/C Scott Bakula, Chelsea Field, Sheila Kelly, John Getz, Rex Smith, France Nuyen, Michael Warren; *D:* Rick King; *W:* William F. Delligan. **VHS** *APX*

Past Tense

Inventive lightweight thriller manages to sustain a fine premise all the way through to the end. Policeman/novelist Gene Ralston (Scott Glenn) may be going mad. One Sunday, beautiful Tory Bass (Lara Flynn Boyle) moves in across the street. That night she's murdered, and Ralston's partner (Anthony LaPaglia) investigates. The next day, another woman has moved into the house, and no one on the police force remembers either the murder or the investigation. Then bits of physical evidence begin to show up and vanish at random. What's going on? Conspiracy, insanity, or something else? Ralston's psychiatrist (David Ogden Stiers) is no help. It's easy enough to come up with that kind of paranoid concept for a suspense story; it's much more difficult to bring it to a satisfactory conclusion. Writers Scott Frost and Miguel Tejada-Flores are up to the task. There's a terrific twist in the middle and the rest of the story stands up, too. In the first scenes, it looks like director Graeme Clifford doesn't know what he's doing. The pace is flat and he appears to be obsessed with Boyle's cleavage, but eventually the reasons for those curious techniques are made clear. The film is probably too tricky and convoluted for all tastes, but mystery fans with a yen for the (slightly) experimental should give it try. 🗡🗡🗡

Strong language, violence, brief nudity, sexual content.

1994 (R) 91m/C Scott Glenn, Lara Flynn Boyle, Anthony LaPaglia, David Ogden Stiers, Sheree J. Wilson, Marita Geraghty, Stephen Graziano; *D:* Graeme Clifford; *W:* Scott Frost, Miguel Tejada-Flores. **VHS, LV** *REP*

1968 60m/C Pat Paulsen, Henry Fonda; *D:* Bob Collins; *M:* Nelson Riddle. **VHS** *SAN*

Pathfinder

Norwegian film is the best blend of archetype, myth, and adventure put onscreen since the *Star Wars* trilogy. The plot—child escapes peaceful village attacked by barbarians—has been the basis for countless sword-and-sandal flicks, but director Nils Gaup treats it seriously. He presents the complexities of medieval tribal culture and shows how magic, superstition, sacrifice, and prophecy play a part in everyday life. The characters are fully developed individuals, not stereotypes. Under varying circumstances, they're funny, cowardly, brave, wrong-headed, and inspired. Beyond its realistic treatment of Lapp legend, though, the story works as a straightforward adventure filled with chases, hair's-breadth escapes, fancy archery, and a treacherous climb through an icy mountain pass. Those scenes are played out against a brutal, breathtaking backdrop of northern tundra. You can feel the cold. The inherent violence in the story is shocking and effective without being overly graphic. The dialogue is subtitled; it's simple, and the yellow letters are easy to read even against the bright background. Any children old enough to follow the storyline and read the subtitles would be entranced by the film, though the violence might be too strong for younger kids. Forget that this is a foreign film. Like all good movies, *Pathfinder* is told in a universal human language and will appeal to audiences of all ages. 𝄇𝄇𝄇𝄇

Contains some violence.

1987 88m/C *NO* Mikkel Gaup, Nils Utsi, Svein Scharffenberg, Helgi Skulason, Sara Marit Gaup, Sverre Porsanger; *D:* Nils Gaup; *W:* Nils Gaup. Nominations: Academy Awards '87: Best Foreign Language Film. **VHS** *FXL, FCT, INJ*

Payback

Oscar (C. Thomas Howell) is a convict who's given a clue to a hidden fortune's location by fellow con Mack (veteran character actor R.G. Armstrong). But by the time Oscar is released, sadistic guard Gully (Marshall Bell) is already on the trail. He's gone so far as to open a

---

The Hound's Favorite Sleepers: Period Pieces

THE ADVOCATE

HEAVEN & EARTH

KING OF THE HILL

MADAME BOVARY

A NIGHT OF LOVE

NOTHING BUT A MAN

PATHFINDER

PHAROAH'S ARMY

QUEEN MARGOT

TEMPTATION OF A MONK

THERE GOES MY BABY

WHERE THE RIVERS FLOW NORTH

Pat Paulsen for President

Many younger videophiles may not know that back in 1968, comedian Pat Paulsen ran for president. At the time he was writer and occasional guest commentator on the Smothers Brothers' variety show. His official campaign began with this statement to a crowd of his followers: "I did not want this support. I have not desired it. As I said, I'd rather remain, as I am today, a common, ordinary, simple Savior of America's Destiny." This special, wonderfully narrated by Henry Fonda with just the right tone of mock reverence, was first broadcast on CBS in October, 1968. Seen now, almost a quarter century later, it combines a rich sense of nostalgia with sharp political satire that's as fresh, relevant, and funny today as it was then. Paulsen's deader-than-dead-pan delivery was perfectly suited to political impersonation, particularly in a year when the important issues—Vietnam, civil rights—were so divisive. The jibes at then-Governor Ronald Reagan add an ironic subtext. 𝄇𝄇𝄇

No objectionable material.

restaurant in the neighborhood, where he works with his wife Rose (Joan Severance), a button-busting waitress. Of course, there's a catch—several catches before it's all over—and though they're not all successful, they are inventive, leading to a neat twist. Director Anthony Hickox is an old hand at this kind of escapism and he keeps the action moving at a quick pace. He also made good use of Pacific coast locations. Also available in an unrated version. 🗡🗡🗡 **GPI: 8.1**

Mature subject matter, sexual content, brief nudity, violence, strong language.

1994 (R) 92m/C C. Thomas Howell, Joan Severance, Marshall Bell, R.G. Armstrong; **D:** Anthony Hickox. **VHS, LV** KMK

Peacemaker

Modest science-fiction shoot-'em-up contains some pleasant surprises. Writer/director Kevin Tenney's premise is blatantly lifted from *The Terminator* and *Star Man*. A couple of aliens find themselves stranded here. These two guys, played by veteran Robert Forster and Lance Edwards, have remarkable recuperative powers. Shoot them dozens of times and they come back for more; run over them with a car, they don't care; blow them up with dynamite, they sneer. The thing is, one of them is an intergalactic psychotic killer and the other is the cop who's chasing him. Both of them claim to be the good guy. What's a poor pathologist (Hilary Shepard) to do? Overall, the humor isn't as funny as it's trying to be and the pace is a hair too slow at times. But the action picks up smartly during the big chase scenes and the three leads handle the material well enough, even though the real stars are the action sequences and special effects. Note that the closing credits list 20 actors and 56 stunt people in the cast. 🗡🗡🗡

Graphic violence, sexual content, strong language.

1990 (R) 90m/C Robert Forster, Lance Edwards, Hilary Shepard, Bert Remsen, Robert Davi; **D:** Kevin S. Tenney; **W:** Kevin S. Tenney. **VHS, LV** FRH

Peeping Tom

In 1960, Michael Powell's brilliant thriller was decades ahead of its time. Essentially, it's the story of Mark (Karl Boehm), a twisted young film technician driven to murder women as he photographs them. He falls in love with Helen (Anna Massey), but her blind mother (Maxine Audley) seems to know everything about him. The film works on several levels. Of course, voyeurism is a prime subject but it's also about the nature of film, from the perspective of both the creator and the viewer. Seen simply as a thriller, it's Hitchcockian in the very best sense of the term—complex, witty, suspenseful, unpredictable. Still, it was roundly condemned when it was made and was such a critical and commercial failure that it damaged Powell's career. That's a shame, but it's also a tribute to the film's power. Even though it's not explicit by today's standards, it's such a disturbing piece of work that it angered people. Powell is still known best for *The Red Shoes*, but *Peeping Tom* is his real masterpiece. Over the years, it has been poorly distributed, often in a shortened version. This new laser release recreates Powell's vivid use of color, and the sound is remarkably clear and important to the work. It's a rare example of popular filmmaking that needs to be seen twice to be appreciated. 🗡🗡🗡🗡

Contains brief nudity, strong subject matter.

1960 109m/C Karl-Heinz Boehm, Moira Shearer, Anna Massey, Maxine Audley, Esmond Knight, Shirley Anne Field, Brenda Bruce, Pamela Green, Jack Watson, Nigel Davenport, Susan Travers, Veronica Hurst; **D:** Michael Powell. **VHS, LV** HMV, AOV

Phantasm III: Lord of the Dead

For those who might have missed Don Coscarelli's first two horror-comedies, these movies revolve around an ominous Tall Man (Angus Scrimm), evil grave-robbing alien midgets who run around in monk's robes, flying chrome softballs, and a hapless hero named Reg (Reggie Bannister). The films actually predate the *Friday the 13th* and *Elm St.* series, and, like them, they don't follow any internal logic. A character who's killed in one scene reappears in the next without explanation; dream and reality are constantly confused; etc.—you know the drill. The events

onscreen are nothing more than Coscarelli's excuse to trot out special effects of amputations, decapitations, lobotomies, and the like. For better or worse, the gory stuff is played strictly for laughs. Even though the effects have become much more polished, that's not necessarily an improvement. If the overall level of violence had been toned down just a little, and if the same had been done with one dream-sex scene, then the mix of laughs, attitude, and effects might have been recommended for kids. It's not. *AT*

Violence, strong language, brief nudity, sexual content.

1994 **(R)** 91m/C Reggie Bannister, A. Michael Baldwin, Bill Thornbury, Gloria Henry, Kevin Connor, Angus Scrimm; **D:** Don A. Coscarelli; **W:** Don A. Coscarelli. **VHS, LV** *MCA*

Phantom of the Mall: Eric's Revenge

Combine the basic *Phantom of the Opera* storyline with slasher flick overtones and a satiric look at suburban materialism. Not surprisingly, the result is mixed. A shadowy figure lurks in the air conditioning ducts of the new Midwood Mall. Could it be Eric (Derek Rydell), whose house mysteriously burned down on the very site where the mall was built? Overall, the film has a good, crisp look with first-rate production values. The special effects tilt toward the gory and bizarre—severed heads, cobras in commodes, etc.—but they're meant to provoke silly scares, not serious scares. At its best, the film skewers the whole mall mentality of consumerism and mediocrity. While it doesn't have the intensity of George Romero's *Dawn of the Dead* or the unpredictability of *Heathers*, its wicked little heart is in the right place. *AAA*

Graphic violence, nudity, sexual content, profanity.

1989 91m/C Morgan Fairchild, Kari Whitman, Jonathan Goldsmith, Derek Rydell; **D:** Richard S. Friedman. **VHS, LV** *FRH*

Pharoah's Army

Independent production is one of the most accurate portrayals of the Civil War—both visually and psychologically—ever put on film. It's a simple tale, based on a family history, about an isolated incident in the Kentucky mountains, one of those border areas where neighbors and even families are divided by conflicting loyalties. Captain Abston (Chris Cooper), from Ohio, leads a small party of scavenging soldiers onto the Anders' farm. Sarah (Patricia Clarkson) lives there with her son while her husband is fighting for the Confederacy. Her convictions are much more fiercely held than Abston's. What goes on between them is reminiscent of Clint Eastwood's *Unforgiven* with the same sad understated intensity. Director Robby Henson keeps the action and the staging simple. He overuses the hawk-screech sound effect to indicate loneliness, and that's already become a cliche. Much more importantly, though, the film strips away a lot of the romanticism and misinformation that pervades popular ideas about that war, particularly in the South. First rate supporting performances from Kris Kristofferson, Robert Joy, Richard Tyson, and Will Lucas deserve mention, too. *AAA*

Violence, subject matter, language.

1995 **(PG-13)** 90m/C Chris Cooper, Patricia Clarkson, Kris Kristofferson, Richard Tyson, Huckleberry Fox, Will Lucas; **D:** Robby Henson, **W:** Robby Henson, **C:** Doron Schlair. **VHS** *ORI*

Phat Beach

The main attraction in this silly little black-oriented "B" bikini flick is an engaging performance by Jermaine Hopkins as Benny, a shy, overweight, teenaged poet. His pal Durrell (Brian Hooks) has no trouble talking him into a road trip to Venice Beach in Benny's dad's vintage Mercedes convertible. The secondary attractions are Claudia Kaleem as Benny's centerfold-ready dream girl, and Jennifer Lucienne as a fellow sensitive soul who appreciates Benny's better nature. The sketchily plotted action involves a little light hip-hop music, beach volleyball, and colorful California atmosphere. *AA*

Mature subject matter, brief nudity, some strong language

1996 **(R)** 99m/C Jermaine Hopkins, Brian Hooks, Jennifer Lucienne, Claudia Kaleem, Gregg D. Vance, Tiny Lister; ***Cameos:***

Coolio; *D:* Doug Ellin; *W:* Doug Ellin, Brian E. O'Neal, Ben Morris; *C:* Jurgen Baum. **VHS** *LIV*

The Phoenix and the Magic Carpet

No, the title does not refer to the chef's special at your favorite Chinese restaurant. It's a low-budget kid's fantasy that will entertain smallfry but will leave most grown-ups cold. Even the presence of Peter Ustinov (mostly in voiceover) is little help. Three American kids go to England after the death of their grandfather. While their mother (Dee Wallace Stone) works out details of the estate, they complain about the lack of TV and play around in his country house. Hidden away in a box in a closet is an egg whence the golden Phoenix is reborn, though it looks remarkably like one of Monty Python's deceased parrots. And that the ratty old Persian carpet on the floor is actually a flying carpet. Off they go, courtesy of some not-so-special effects. The film is too talky, but the comedy will appeal to some kids and despite the limitations of the budget, it is inventive. 🦴🦴

Mild violence.

1995 (PG) 80m/C Dee Wallace Stone, Timothy Hegeman, Nick Klein, Laura Kamrath, Peter Ustinov; *D:* Zoran Perisic; *W:* Florence Fox; *M:* Alan Parker. **VHS** *PAR*

Picasso Trigger

A modern Olympic video record is set with seven—count 'em, seven!—ex-Playmates in the cast. This is one of auteur Andy Sidaris' more ambitious efforts, with a globe-hopping plot (Paris, Texas, Hawaii, Las Vegas) and a large cast of mostly non-professional actors. These men and women were chosen instead for their suntans and overdeveloped physiques; your screen is filled with bulging biceps and breasts. The gadget-filled story is about a group of villainous drug-selling international assassins who report to their superiors in rhymed couplets. They're trying to kill off a bunch of true-blue American secret agents because their boss, the title character,

has just been rubbed out. Or something; none of it tries to make much sense. Imagine a *Mission: Impossible* plot outline spun out with an MTV sensibility and several hottub scenes and you've got the idea. 🦴🦴🦴 **GPI: 6.0**

Nudity, sexual content, violence, some strong language.

1989 (R) 99m/C Steve Bond, Dona Speir, John Aprea, Hope Marie Carlton, Guich Koock, Roberta Vasquez, Bruce Penhall; *D:* Andy Sidaris. **VHS** *WAR*

Piranha

Producer Roger Corman continues to remake his venerable drive-in hits, but this new version of *Piranha* adds nothing to the early effort from director Joe Dante and writer John Sayles. In fact, it lacks that nice flourish of stop-motion animation and it may even reuse some of the silly little two-dimensional fish "monsters." The rest of the effects are accomplished, as they were before, with red dye and a submerged bubble machine. Alexandra Paul and William Katt are the less-than-dynamic duo who must save the summer camp and the new lakefront development from the titular carnivorous fishies, created by the government as a secret weapon. Bottom line: flat characters, fast pace, no real suspense, some humor, fake violence. 🦴🦴

Violence, strong language, brief nudity.

1996 (R) 76m/C Alexandra Paul, William Katt, Soleil Moon Frye, Monte Markham; *D:* Scott Levy. **VHS** *NHO*

The Pit & the Pendulum

Told in the spirit of those wonderful Roger Corman adaptations of the mid-1960s, this one is a tongue-in-cheek version of several of Poe's stories, with a small tip of the hat to Mel Brooks' *History of the World—Part 1.* Lance Henriksen stars as the mad inquisitor, Torquemada. He is attracted to a baker's wife (Rona De Ricci) mistakenly imprisoned for witchcraft. Even though an Italian Cardinal (Oliver Reed) has come to town to restrain the excesses of the Spanish Inquisition, Torquemada is a slave to his obsession. He tries to torture a confession, and perhaps more, from

the woman. The Cardinal, in his goofy Italian accent, says, "The good lord, you know, padre, he want us to love our neighbor, not roast him." The Grand Guignol torture scenes are inventive and repulsive, though, doubtless, not as inventive and repulsive as the real thing. A shocking streak of sardonic humor keeps the action from becoming sadistic, but this is still a movie for horror fans, and definitely not for kids. 🦴🦴🦴

Torture, violence, brief nudity.

1991 (R) 97m/C Lance Henriksen, Rona De Ricci, Jonathan Fuller, Jeffrey Combs, Tom Towles, Stephen Lee, Francis Bay, Oliver Reed; *D:* Stuart Gordon; *W:* Dennis Paoli; *M:* Richard Band. **VHS, LV** *PAR*

Pizza Man

Political satire-parody was clearly made on a bare-bones budget. Instead of dazzling production values, it's got a savvy, intelligent script and an irreverent attitude. Elmo Bunn (comic Bill Maher) is the best pizza man in the business. He always delivers them hot and he never gets stiffed for the tab. But then one night someone calls from East L.A. and orders an extra large with sausage and anchovies. The last time the guys at Vince's Pizza got that combination, the pizza man, Elmo's best friend, didn't come back. Elmo, unafraid, drives off into the night and into the middle of a conspiracy that eventually involves Ronald Reagan, Geraldine Ferraro, Michael Dukakis, Dan and Marilyn Quayle, and several other real characters, all played by look-alike actors. Maher delivers a fine pseudo-tough voiceover narration. Combined with Daniel May's jazzy score, it's a wicked swipe at *Taxi Driver*. As for the political stuff, any movie that has the guts and imagination to show Ronald Reagan and Geraldine Ferraro in bed together is trying to anger both sides of the spectrum. And when the Quayles show up, director J.F. Lawton (here using the pseudonym J.D. Athens) gets really nasty. Does it go too far? Of course it does and it ought to. 🦴🦴🦴

Contains some strong language and violence.

1991 (PG-13) 90m/C Bill Maher, Annabelle Gurwitch; *D:* J.F. Lawton; *W:* J.F. Lawton; *M:* Daniel May. **VHS** *MNC*

Play Nice

Micro-budget version of *Basic Instinct* actually makes sense, unlike the original. Once again, we've got an unidentified blonde who seduces and kills her male victims at their height of passion. Penucci (Ed O'Ross) is the maverick cop (is there any other kind?) who's out to catch "Rapunzel." Jill (Robey), from the records office, realizes that all of the deceased had been accused of child abuse. You don't have to have seen too many of these flicks to figure out part of the plot right away. But that's not important; there's still one nice twist at the end, making this one a perfectly acceptable little time-waster. Also available in an unrated version. 🦴🦴

Sexual content, nudity, violence, strong language.

1992 (R) 90m/C Ed O'Ross, Robey; *D:* Terri Treas; *W:* Chuck McCollum, Michael Zand. **VHS** *VMK*

Play Time

The new "Emmanuelle" of softcore video premieres is a classy production with realistic characters, glitzy sets, and a hot story of sexual experimentation between two married couples. Eroticism, like beauty, is in the mind of the beholder, but writer Mary Ellen Hanover and director Dale Trevillion push all the right buttons. Also available in an unrated version. 🦴🦴🦴 **GPI: 9.5**

Mature subject matter, nudity, sexual material, language.

1994 90m/C Monique Parent, Craig Stepp, David Elliot, Jennifer Burton; *D:* Dale Trevillion; *W:* Mary Ellen Hanover. **VHS** *TRI*

Playback

Seen as a guilty pleasure, this one's most enjoyable for the casting and outrageous performances. It's a sexy *Executive Suite* about

"*All I do is my characters. I've made the choices before I do them. I know who they are and I know what's going on. All I do is live it through them. I don't try to be sexy because that's a trap. As soon as you try to be sexy, you aren't sexy. The times I've tried it, it hasn't worked. So I just have a good time and do what I'm supposed to do.*"

—ACTRESS SHANNON WHIRRY, STAR OF *PLAYBACK,* ON SCREEN SEXINESS.

CRAIG STEPP AND JENNIFER BURTON IN *PLAY TIME.* ©TRIBORO ENTERTAINMENT GROUP.

ton, Tawny Kitaen, Harry Dean Stanton; **D:** Oley Sassone; **W:** Oley Sassone, David DuBos. **VHS** *PAR*

Plughead Rewired: Circuitry Man 2

Like most sequels, this one's about half as good as the original. It shares most of the same strengths and weaknesses, too, but has a stronger emphasis on comedy. Co-directors Steven and Robert Lovy tell essentially the same futuristic story about a romantic robot (Jim Metzler) and the villainous Plughead (Vernon Wells) who lives to share other people's pain and terror directly. Most of the humor is broad and hammy, with two supporting characters whose appearance and shtick could have come straight from the mad scientists on *Mystery Science Theater 3000*. Recommended for fans of the original only. **AKA:** Circuitry Man 2. 🦴🦴

Strong language, some violence, sexual content, brief nudity.

1994 (R) 97m/C Vernon Wells, Deborah Shelton, Jim Metzler, Dennis Christopher, Nicholas Worth, Traci Lords; **D:** Steven Lovy, Robert Lovy; **W:** Steven Lovy, Robert Lovy. **VHS** *COL*

Poison Ivy

The unrated video of Drew Barrymore's low-budget comeback cult hit contains four minutes of naughtiness that were apparently too hot for the MPAA. She plays an amoral teen temptress who befriends the desperately lonely Sara Gilbert and insinuates herself into the teen's dreary family. Dad (Tom Skerritt) is a burnt-out TV commentator. Mom (Cheryl Ladd) is a bedridden neurotic. Director Katt Shea Ruben can handle low-budget, lurid material with the best of them. (Don't miss her gritty, underrated *Streets.*) The problem here is that these characters are so unattractive and unsympathetic. While the scenes between Barrymore and Gilbert ring true, the rest of the film is so ugly—it looks blue, cold, and grainy—that it's hard to care what happens to these people. Followed by a sequel. 🦴🦴

corporate treachery, lechery, and double-dealing. George Hamilton is terrific as smarmy boss Gil Braman. In fact, he's only a short step away from the self parody that Leslie Nielsen has used to jumpstart his career as a comic star. Our hero is David Burgess (beefy Jimmy Johnson lookalike Charles Grant). While Braman tries to put some none-too-smooth moves on David's wife Sarah (Tawny Kitaen), his wicked co-worker Karen (Shannon Whirry) is undermining his newest project. The final ingredient is unscrupulous private detective Harvey Fontenot (the ever-reliable Harry Dean Stanton). Mix 'em all together and you've got grandly cheesy fun. 🦴🦴🦴 **GPI: 8.0**

Sexual content, brief nudity, strong language, some violence.

1995 (R) 91m/C Charles Grant, Shannon Whirry, George Hamil-

Strong sexual content, language, violence, brief nudity.

1992 (R) 91m/C Drew Barrymore, Sara Gilbert, Tom Skerritt, Cheryl Ladd; *D:* Katt Shea Ruben; *W:* Katt Shea Ruben, Andy Ruben; *C:* Phedon Papamichael. VHS *COL, NLC, PMS*

Poison Ivy 2: Lily

In some ways, this sequel in name only is better than the trashy original. It's beautifully photographed; director Anne Goursaud really knows how to paint with light. If she were as adept at moving the story along it would be a fine sleeper. But the pace is slow and the conclusion is silly. Lily (Alyssa Milano) is an undergraduate who moves from Michigan to L.A. to go to art school and discovers the diaries of Ivy, the bad girl in the first movie. Shazam...shy girl from the sticks becomes a vamp with a ring in her bellybutton and a taste for black lipstick. Overall, the film isn't as successful as the star and director's previous video premiere, *Embrace of the Vampire,* but it is refreshing to see a feminine perspective that presents young men as beautiful brainless himbos. 🦴🦴

Sexual material, brief nudity, strong language, some violence, platform shoes, performance art.

1995 (R) 110m/C Alyssa Milano, Xander Berkeley, Johnathon Schaech, Belinda Bauer; *D:* Anne Goursaud; *W:* Chloe King; *M:* Joseph Williams. VHS, LV *NLC*

The Polar Bear King

Norwegian/Swedish production is, more or less, another variation on the story that was told in *Beauty and the Beast.* It also exists under the titles *East of the Sun, West of the Moon, Cupid and Psyche,* and probably others. This is based on one called *White Bear King Valemon.* It's got all the standard elements: Prince (Tobias Hoesl) turned into beast, in this case a polar bear created by Jim Henson's Creature Shop; the youngest princess (Maria Bonnevie) who agrees to marry him; her envious sisters and their attempts to undermine her. But in this telling of the story, writer/producer Erik Borge has added more, lots more, including a wonderfully wicked witch (Anna-Lotta Larsson), magic

scissors, and an invisible mother-in-law. Director Ola Solum keeps the pace moving so quickly that few kids will be bored by the film, but older kids who appreciate good special effects may be disappointed with the bear. Otherwise, the photography and the Nordic locations are really neat. True, the film has the same problem that plagues all screen versions of the story: the bear/beast is wonderful and lovable; his human incarnation, the prince, is a weenie. That's a quibble. I suspect most grown-ups will enjoy this one as much as younger videophiles. 🦴🦴🦴

Mild violence.

1994 (PG) 87m/C Maria Bonnevie, Jack Fjeldstad, Tobias Hoesl, Anna-Lotta Larsson; *D:* Ola Solum; *W:* Erik Borge. VHS, LV *HMD*

The Pompatus of Love

Comparisons to *The Brothers McMullen* are unavoidable, but this romantic comedy is actually a better, savvier movie. It's the story of four New York friends and their thorny dealings with women. Mark (Jon Cryer) and Nastasha (Kristen Wilson) are thinking of moving in together, but they can't decide where to live. Playwright Runyan (Tim Guinee) can't get over Katherine (Dana Wheeler-Nicholson) who has moved to California. Josh (Adrian Pasdar) is a philanderer who's not-so-secretly in love with Phil's (Adam Oliensis) sister (Paige Turco). Contentedly married Phil is considering a fling with Caroline (Kristin Scott Thomas). Director Richard Schenkman, who co-wrote with Cryer and Oliensis, balances the interrelated stories neatly, mixing in a terrific rock score. (Yes, the title comes from that Steve Miller oldie, "The Joker.") But what really makes the film is its combination of intelligence and freshness. It hasn't been processed through the Hollywood sausage grinder. Highly recommended. 🦴🦴🦴🦴

Mature subject matter, strong language, brief nudity.

1996 (R) 99m/C Jon Cryer, Tim Guinee, Adrian Pasdar, Adam Oliensis, Kristen Wilson, Dana Wheeler-Nicholson, Paige Turco, Mia Sara, Kristin Scott Thomas, Arabella Field, Jennifer Tilly, Roscoe Lee Browne; *D:* Richard Schenkman; *W:* Jon Cryer, Adam Oliensis, Richard Schenkman; *C:* Russell Fine; *M:* John Hill. VHS *BMG*

Portraits of a Killer

It seems that every legal thriller you see these days eventually climbs onto the high board, throws logic away, dives off, and dares you to follow it into the pool. I suspect that's because the work of real lawyers is so tedious. And filmmakers know that it's better to be unbelievable than boring—onscreen, anything's better than boring. So, attorneys hop into the sack with clients, withhold evidence, and wander into threatening places alone late at night. In *Portraits of a Killer*, Elaine Taylor (Jennifer Grey) does all that and much much more to prove that artist George Kendall (Costas Mandylor) didn't kill those young hookers even though his photographs of them are about to be published in a book and this development certainly won't hurt his sales at all. Toss in a politically ambitious D.A. (Patricia Charbonneau) and a tough seen-it-all cop (Michael Ironside), stir vigorously, and boil the pot until it's done to an appropriately nutty turn. This Canadian effort has polished production values and the cast does fine work. Curiously, though, Jennifer Grey's facial features seem somehow to have softened and become less distinct. She doesn't look like the same young woman we saw in *Dirty Dancing*. 🕱🕱

Strong language, violence, subject matter, drug use.

1995 93m/C Jennifer Grey, Costas Mandylor, Michael Ironside, Patricia Charbonneau, Kenneth Welsh, M. Emmet Walsh; **D:** Bill Corcoran. **VHS, LV** *LIV*

Posed for Murder

Thriller seems to be protesting the exploitation of women without being exploitative, but it doesn't quite work. At times, this story of a men's magazine model and actress who is being followed (and perhaps protected) by an anonymous killer is intriguing. More often though, it's just another slasher flick told with a stalking handheld camera and a soundtrack full of heavy breathing. Charlotte J. Helmkamp is effective and sympathetic in the lead, especially when she's trying to land a part in *Meat Cleavers from Mars*. The New Jersey locations have a realistic texture, but the film suffers from a cliched storyline and excessive violence. 🕱🕱

Strong violence, profanity, nudity, sexual situations.

1989 (R) 90m/C Charlotte J. Helmkamp, Carl Fury, Rick Gianisi, Michael Merrins; **D:** Brian Thomas Jones. **VHS** *ACA*

Positive I.D.

Several noir conventions get a sharp feminist twist. The story involves a troubled young woman (Stephanie Rascoe) who's up to something. On the surface, her life is apparently ordinary; she's a wife and mom with two blonde little girls, suburban split-level, and Volvo. But there's a frightening trauma in her past that's revealed by degrees. Exactly what she's doing about it doesn't become clear until the end of writer/producer/director Andy Anderson's story and that's the point. The less you know about what's happening, the more you'll enjoy it. This is one of the better sleepers in your favorite video store. 🕱🕱🕱

Violence, sexual content, strong language.

1987 (R) 96m/C Stephanie Rascoe, John Davies, Steve Fromholz; **D:** Andy Anderson; **W:** Andy Anderson. **VHS** *MCA*

The Power of One

Too-long but well intentioned look at South African apartheid isn't up to the demands of its subject. Based on Bryce Courtenay's novel, the film tells the story of PK (Stephen Dorff), a white South African of English descent, who's bullied by evil Nazi scum from his boyhood during World War II to his teenage years. Along the way, he is guided by a series of wise and patient teachers played by Armin Mueller-Stahl, Morgan Freeman, and Sir John Gielgud. Too much voiceover narration leads to one moment of grand unintentional humor when PK sadly intones, "It seemed that I was to lose everyone I'd ever loved or who had ever loved me—my mother, my chicken, my nanny." 🗡🗡

Strong language, violence.

1992 (PG-13) 126m/C Stephen Dorff, Armin Mueller-Stahl, Morgan Freeman, John Gielgud, Fay Masterson, Marius Weyers, Tracy Brooks Swope, John Osborne, Daniel Craig, Dominic Walker, Alois Mayo, Ian Roberts, Maria Marais; *D:* John G. Avildsen; *W:* Robert Mark Kamen. **VHS, LV** *WAR*

Powwow Highway

What might have been another "buddy" or "road" picture becomes a terrific, low-budget, laugh-out-loud comedy. A week before Christmas, the Cheyenne reservation in Lame Deer, Montana, is a cold, dismal place. As Buddy Red Bow (A. Martinez) puts it, "This ain't the American dream we're living. This here's the Third World." Buddy's cynical and angry. Philbert Bono (Gary Farmer) is his opposite in many ways. He's a mountainous man-child who decides to relearn the ways of his ancestors. Actually, he has a vision while watching a used car commercial in a bar one night, but, hey...whatever works, right? And Philbert's vision is real. He realizes that he must undertake a spiritual journey to transform himself into the warrior, Whirlwind Dreamer. His first step is to acquire his War Pony, a '64 Buick he names Protector. About then Buddy's sister Bonnie (Joanelle Romero) has to be bailed out of a Santa Fe jail, so, like Huck and Jim, they're off. In a series of slow, sweeping shots, director Jonathan Wacks captures the desolation, beauty, and occasional ugliness of the contemporary Western landscape, from sacred mountains to tract houses. But he's more concerned with characters and that's where the

film is at its best. Before Buddy and Philbert reach the end of their journey, you become surprisingly involved with their problems. Wacks was also a co-producer of *Repo Man*, one of the first video premieres to become a genuine cult hit. *Powwow Highway* has the same kind of originality. Here though, it's mixed with warmth, comedy, and adventure. One of the greats. 🗡🗡🗡🗡

Profanity and one naked male backside.

1989 (R) 105m/C Gary Farmer, A. Martinez, Amanda Wyss, Rene Handren-Seals, Joanelle Romero, Graham Greene; *D:* Jonathan Wacks; *M:* Barry Goldberg. Sundance Film Festival '89: Filmmakers Trophy. **VHS, LV** *WAR, OM*

Prehysteria

Take a sure-fire concept—miniature dinosaurs and contemporary kids—and plug it into a simple juvenile plot. A comic villain (Tony Longo) steals some dinosaur eggs from Central America. He brings them back to California where they accidentally fall into the possession of a widowed amateur rockhound (Brett Cullen) and his two kids (Austin O'Brien and Samantha Mills). Under the tender care of Ruby, the family's Golden Retriever, the eggs hatch. The critter effects may not be up to the highest Spielbergian standards, but they're much better than average. Great stuff for kids. Followed by two sequels. 🗡🗡🗡

A little strong language.

1993 (PG) 84m/C Brett Cullen, Austin O'Brien, Samantha Mills, Colleen Morris, Tony Longo, Stuart Fratkin, Stephen Lee; *D:* Albert Band, Charles Band; *W:* Greg Suddeth, Mark Goldstein. **VHS, LV** *PAR*

Priceless Beauty

In a laborious retelling of the genie-in-the-bottle story, Christopher Lambert is Monroe, a rock superstar who blames himself for the death of his brother. He's so distraught that he and his dog move to the beach where Monroe spends his time brooding and, in one truly disgusting moment, mixing beer and granola. But then he stumbles across this urn and out pops a genie (Diane Lane) wrapped in a gossamer sheet so she looks just like the hood ornament on a Rolls Royce. Three wishes, more brood-

"*That wasn't a sermon. It was a political broadcast for the Labour Party.*"

—Father Greg (Linus Roache) to Father Matthew (Tom Wilkinson) in *Priest*.

Protestants have cited it as part of their protests against the Disney company. They're honked off at the film's tolerant acceptance of homosexuality and Disney's corporate decision to extend benefits to same-sex partners of its employees. Happily, the film lives up to all the hoop-la. Writer Jimmy McGovern and director Antonia Bird deal with serious issues in a compelling, entertaining manner. They mean to make people think and to make people angry. The title character is Father Greg (Linus Roache), a young, fairly conservative priest who comes to an innercity parish in Liverpool. His colleague Father Matthew (Tom Wilkinson) is something of a social firebrand who's prone to overstatement, strong drink, and other sins. Father Greg has to face two problems, a case of incest he learns of in the confessional and his own homosexuality. Both cause him to question his faith and his calling. Can he remain silent while a child is being harmed? Is he meant to be celibate? When it's time to answer those questions, the film stacks the deck in favor of certain ideas—so did *On the Waterfront* and *Norma Rae* and *The Green Berets.* This is popular entertainment, not theology. Not all viewers will agree with the conclusions, but even the film's critics will have to admit that it deals with spiritual issues in a serious manner. It neither mocks nor makes light of faith. The filmmakers also depict homosexuality in pretty much the same way that heterosexual relationships are shown in other R-rated films. That part of the story will upset other viewers. 🦴🦴🦴

Mature subject matter, strong language, sexual content.

1994 (R) 98m/C *GB* Linus Roache, Tom Wilkinson, Cathy Tyson, Robert Carlyle, James Ellis, John Bennett, Rio Fanning, Jimmy Coleman, Lesley Sharp, Robert Pugh, Christine Tremarco; *D:* Antonia Bird; *W:* Jimmy McGovern; *C:* Fred Tammes; *M:* Andy Roberts. Nominations: Australian Film Institute '95: Best Foreign Film. **VHS** *TOU*

ing, etc., etc. Italian production is definitely not another *Ghost,* though my fellow members of the Diane Lane Fan Club will find a lot to enjoy. The basic problem is that it takes itself much too seriously. 🦴🦴

Nudity, sexual content, strong language.

1990 (R) 94m/C Christopher Lambert, Diane Lane, Francesco Quinn, J.C. Quinn, Claudia Ohana, Monica Scattini, Joaquin D'Almeida; *D:* Charles Finch. **VHS, LV** *REP*

Priest

Even though it received only a limited theatrical release, this drama has sparked considerable comment, much of it justified, within religious circles. Many Catholics condemned the film for its unapologetic liberal bias and criticism of church hierarchy. Conservative

Primal Secrets

"It's beautiful!" one female or another sighs dreamily about a dozen times in this video chick flick. The made-for-TV roots are visible in the elevator music score and commercial fade-outs. The saving graces are florid performances from Ellen Burstyn and Meg Tilly, really lavish sets, and a soapy Gothic plot based on Jane Stanton Hitchcock's novel, *Trick of the Eye*. Wealthy patron Ellen Burstyn commissions struggling young artist Meg Tilly for a big-bucks sale. But what's the deep dark secret of a death in the past? Moments of unintentional humor—particularly when Burstyn goes ballistic—and a few senseless plot twists add immeasurably. ***AKA:*** Trick of the Eye. 🗡🗡🗡

Contains no objectionable material.

1994 93m/C Meg Tilly, Ellen Burstyn, Barnard Hughes; *D:* Ed Kaplan. **VHS** *HMK*

Private Affairs

Italian sex comedy is wildly complicated and not very funny. Kate Capshaw stars as a woman who's having an affair with a doctor until he dumps her for her son's swimming teacher. At the same time, David Naughton has fallen for his best friend's girl, but she's fooling around with someone else and eventually (I think) she gets hooked up with the doctor. Then Capshaw and Naughton...you get the idea. For a comedy, the pace is all wrong. Part of the story may have been meant to be taken seriously, but it sounds more like a particularly loony letter to Ann Landers. 🗡🗡

GPI: 4.1

Strong language, some violence, brief nudity, sexual situations.

1989 (R) 83m/C *IT* Guiliana de Sio, Kate Capshaw, David Naughton, Luca Barbareschi, Michele Placido; *D:* Francesco Massaro. **VHS** *ACA*

Private Lessons, Another Story

Back in 1981, writer Dan Greenburg translated one of his novels into the flawed but profitable teen fantasy, *Private Lessons*. It's based on a common bit of male wish-fulfillment, the adolescent boy seduced by the beautiful older governess. It's a mess of a movie, in part a half-hearted mystery, but it fit the mood of the day when films like *Porky's* made big

bucks at the boxoffice. Since then, it has become a staple of most video stores, and inevitably generated a sequel, a sequel in title only. This one has nothing to do with the premise of the first. Fashion photographer Mariana Morgan has a fling with chauffeur Ray Garaza in Miami while she's on the rebound from her philandering husband. There's nothing special in the simple story or the wooden acting, but Morgan has an appealingly different kind of thirtysomething warts-and-all glamour. Watchable and, considering the genre, above average. 🗡🗡🗡

Nudity, sexual material.

1994 (R) 86m/C Mariana Morgan, Ray Garaza, Theresa Morris; *D:* Dominique Othenin-Girard; *W:* William Mernit. **VHS** *PAR*

Private Obsession

Reclusive weirdo Michael Christian kidnaps feminist fashion model Shannon Whirry and imprisons her in his house. From that premise, you can predict just about everything else that's going to happen in the two-character drama, though the plot does venture onto some strange side roads. What sets this one apart from your run-of-the-mill video premiere is its rough-edged energy. That comes from drive-in veteran Lee Frost's keep-it-in-the-family philosophy of filmmaking. He wrote, directed, and edited, and he appears onscreen as Jerry the manager. His wife Phyllis produced. Virtually the entire film was shot in his own house. 🗡🗡🗡 **GPI: 8.9**

Nudity, strong sexual material, language.

1994 (R) 93m/C Shannon Whirry, Michael Christian, Bo Svenson, Rip Taylor, Lee Frost; *D:* Lee Frost; *W:* Lee Frost. **VHS** *TRI*

Project: Alien

The best thing about this one is a really neat biplane. The setting is Norway (actually what was then Yugoslavia) and the plot is a crock full of UFO cliches, including but not limited to cattle mutilations, mysterious lights in the sky, and kidnappings. A capable cast gives the flat script its best shot, but there's little anyone can do with this clumsy material. The

story begins well but by the end, it's almost a comedy. ♫♫

Strong language.

1989 (R) 92m/C Michael Nouri, Darlanne Fluegel, Maxwell Caulfield, Charles Durning; **D:** Frank Shields; **W:** Anthony Able. **VHS, LV** *VMK*

Public Access

Director Bryan Singer made quite a splash with his second film, *The Usual Suspects*. His first, *Public Access,* contains some of the same inventiveness and flaws. In some ways, it's more interesting and more serious. But don't expect it to answer all the questions it raises. The film opens in the tranquil town of Brewster where the headline of the local paper reads "Crime and Unemployment Reach Record Low" and, clearly, things are about to go bad. The source is Whiley Pritcher (Ron Marquette), an enigmatic man who walks into town and buys time on the local public access cable channel. He calls his show *Our Town.* Onscreen, he asks one question—"What's wrong with Brewster?"—and waits for his viewers to call in with answers. Like *The Usual Suspects,* the conflicts have to do with talk, with words. But here Singer and co-writer Christopher McQuarrie are also interested in the free floating, often incoherent discontent that's so much a part of today's political landscape. Not surprisingly then, they don't come to a conventional ending. ♫♫♫

Strong language, violence, brief nudity, sexual content.

1993 (R) 90m/C Ron Marquette, Dina Brooks, Burt Williams, Charles Kavanaugh, Larry Maxwell, Brandon Boyce; **D:** Bryan Singer; **W:** Bryan Singer, Christopher McQuarrie, Michael Feit Dougan; **C:** Bruce Douglas Johnson; **M:** John Ottman. Sundance Film Festival '93: Grand Jury Prize. **VHS** *TRI*

Punch the Clock

Overachieving low-budget effort from a no-name cast and crew suffers from a few sound problems, sluggish chases, and stilted action scenes. But those flaws are offset by excellent performances and a refreshingly original script. Eric (Mike Rogen) is a bail interviewer who works with prisoners in a New York jail. Theo (Chris Moore) is a professional car thief. They meet when she's arrested after boosting a BMW, and immediately fall for each other. Besides working on opposite sides of the law, they've got other problems. Their thoughtless bosses don't understand them, and the truth of it is that both of them are suffering from career burn-out. Some moments—notably the bail interview scenes—have a sense of autobiographical realism, and the film captures the dirty side of New York City in all its garish semi-splendor. Both leads are well-drawn and believable, and even if the plot stumbles a time or two, the film ends with a realistic and unexpected conclusion. ♫♫♫

Strong sexual content, profanity, violence.

1990 (R) 88m/C Michael Rogan, Chris Moore, James Lorinz; **D:** Eric L. Schlagman. **VHS** *UAV*

Puppet Master

Despite the title, this one has nothing to do with Robert Heinlein's famous science fiction novel. Instead, it's a slickly made, Stephen King kind of story about a haunted hotel filled with psychics and murderous marionettes. The movie begins well with a suspenseful opening sequence but slides downhill from there. The special effects are acceptable and the production values are high throughout, but the plot is uninvolving and the characters are flat. Even so, it has spawned a fistful of sequels. ♫♫

Graphic violence, grotesque special effects, strong language, brief nudity, sexual content.

1989 (R) 90m/C Paul LeMat, Jimmie F. Skaggs, Irene Miracle, Robin Rates, Barbara Crampton, William Hickey; **D:** David Schmoeller; **M:** Richard Band. **VHS, LV** *PAR*

Puppet Master 2

Inventive sequel is handsomely made but a little slow and mechanical. The critters are

> "*At most screenings, 50 people show up. Half of them leave and the other half stays and loves it.*"
>
> —WILLIAM APPLEGATE, JR., SCREENWRITER OF *PURE DANGER.*

233

> **"I**t's not a 'plotting' movie; it's more an idea.
>
> "This stranger [the main character] is a real stranger. You have no idea what he's doing and why. Chances are he's from outer space...that he fell to Earth. He played with this medium [television], bought this medium, became this sort of metaphor for the political climate at the time.
>
> "As an audience, you've projected assumptions on him. What was his past? Was it this, was it that? It's all about the line that the little boy says at the end, 'My mother told me not to talk to strangers, but you're not a stranger. I've seen you on TV.'
>
> "And that's wrong. You don't know who this person is just because he's the lead in the picture, just because he's the main character...the narrator, just like *The Usual Suspects*. If anyone's reliable it's the narrator. Not in my movie."
>
> —WRITER/DIRECTOR BRYAN SINGER ON HIS DEBUT FILM, *PUBLIC ACCESS*

one black (led by Leon), the other Italian, are after them. Johnny's hyperactive loudmouth friend Dice (Rick Shapiro) is little help. The quickly paced action ranges from confrontations in diners, junkyards, and topless bars to terrific car chases. (This is a PM Entertainment release, after all; if a vehicle doesn't crash and burn every seven minutes, something's wrong.) Throughout, lots of guys in cheap black suits wave pistols in each others' faces and scream vile racial epithets. If the source material is blatantly borrowed, the L.A. locations are well-chosen and the humor is rough, earthy, and original. That's where this one works best. It's a refreshingly unpredictable, tongue-in-cheek approach to the standard video shoot-'em-up. One warning: those who thought the violence was excessive in *Pulp Fiction* won't be any happier with this one. 🦴🦴🦴

Graphic violence, paint-blistering language, brief nudity, sexual content.

1996 **(R)** 99m/C C. Thomas Howell, Teri Ann Linn, Leon, Michael Russo, Rick Shapiro; *D:* C. Thomas Howell; *W:* William Applegate Jr. **VHS** *PMH*

Pushing Hands

To anyone who's seen Ang Lee's *The Wedding Banquet* or *Eat, Drink, Man, Woman,* his first feature will be instantly familiar. He's handling the same themes and conflicts, and his star is the graceful gray-haired Sihung Lung, who was so effective in the other two films. He plays Mr. Chu, a retired tai chi master who moves from Beijing to his son Alex's (Bo Z. Wang) home in suburban New York. It's left to Alex's wife Martha (Deb Snyder) to take care of the non-English-speaking Chu during the day while she's trying to work on her novel. The house is small and, in a deft introduction, Martha and Chu are presented as two people sharing the same physical space but who are, in all other respects, poles apart. Chu's presence does disrupt the family, but his own problems go deeper. His Taoist goal is to attain "carefree nothingness," and he finds himself moving farther and farther away from that as he haltingly adapts to life in America. Lee's story builds to an inevitable confrontation so carefully constructed that when it

murderous puppets created by models, extreme close-up shots, and stop-motion animation. When the atmospheric music kicks in, they're scary enough, but the real star is Charlie Spradling (AKA Charlie) as Wanda, the graduate student. Perhaps the best of the series. 🦴🦴

Violence, brief nudity.

1990 **(R)** 90m/C Elizabeth MacLellan, Collin Bernsen, Greg Webb, Charlie Spradling, Nita Talbot, Steve Welles, Jeff Weston; *D:* David Allen; *W:* David Pabian; *M:* Richard Band. **VHS, LV** *PAR*

Pure Danger

The influence of Quentin Tarantino is slowly spreading throughout the film and video business. This action flick cheerfully recycles elements from *Pulp Fiction, True Romance,* and *Reservoir Dogs.* It's a crime-comedy about ex-con Johnny Dean (director C. Thomas Howell), who finds himself on the run—not altogether unwillingly—with waitress Becky (Teri Ann Linn) and a bag full of diamonds. Two gangs,

occurs, viewers will understand the emotions and actions of all three people involved. That's the mark of a good family story. It's not about heroes and villains; these are sympathetic characters who are trying to work their way through the same problems we all face. The film was made on a limited budget, so it's not as polished as Lee's more recent work, including *Sense and Sensibility*. But Sihung Lung has a confident, crowd-pleasing charm not unlike Paul Newman, and his performance is the key to the film's success. ✄✄✄

Contains some strong language (partially subtitled) and mild martial arts violence.

1992 100m/C Sihung Lung, Deb Snyder, Bo Z. Wang, Lai Wang; *D:* Ang Lee; *W:* Ang Lee; *C:* Jong Lin; *M:* Xiao-Song Qu. **VHS, LV** *TRI*

Queen Margot

Though it's based on a novel by Alexandre Dumas, this adaptation almost could have been the David Lynch version of *The Three Musketeers*. It's that bizarre, overstated, and outlandish. In Paris, 1572, Protestants and Catholics are serious about religious differences—deadly serious. Either to calm the situation or to make it more explosive, the ruthless Catherine de Medici (Virni Lisi) has arranged the marriage of her wild, rebellious daughter Margot (Isabelle Adjani) to the Protestant Henry Bourbon (Daniel Auteuil). Harboring incestuous interests in their sister, Catherine's Catholic sons (Jean-Hugues Anglade and Pascal Greggory) don't take kindly to the new arrangement. Neither does Margot. The ceremony has hardly finished before all concerned are conspiring against each other, and those plots quickly turn to mass slaughter religious cleansing, as it were. The catalyst is LaMole (Vincent Perez), a young Protestant swordsman from the country who comes to the big city for the wedding and winds up being more intimately involved than he ever dreamed. For anyone not already familiar with French history and this story, the

first half is difficult to follow. The film doesn't bother with explanations when there's another palace intrigue to be cooked up, another assassination to be plotted, or another fevered infidelity to be consummated. And all of this is accomplished within a long, lush, extravagant production. The sets and costumes look great, but the cast, not wishing to be upstaged by inanimate objects, gives the hyperbolic plot its full due. No stick of scenery is safe. These people aren't above rolling around on the floor and tearing their clothes when they're upset, and by the end of the story all of them—at least the ones who are still alive—are really pissed off. Again, this kind of deliberately excessive material isn't for everyone. Francophiles of more refined tastes probably won't care for it either. But those who like their history raw, sweaty, rough, and nasty will be hugely entertained. *AKA:* La Reine Margot. 🎬🎬🎬

Graphic violence, strong sexual material, language, nudity.

1994 (R) 153m/C *FR* Isabelle Adjani, Daniel Auteuil, Virna Lisi, Jean-Hugues Anglade, Vincent Perez, Pascal Greggory, Miguel Bose, Dominique Blanc, Claudio Amendola, Asia Argento, Julien Rassam, Jean-Claude Brialy; *D:* Patrice Chereau; *W:* Patrice Chereau, Daniele Thompson; *M:* Goran Bregovic. Cannes Film Festival '94: Special Jury Prize, Best Actress (Lisi); Nominations: Academy Awards '94: Best Costume Design;

British Academy Awards '95: Best Foreign Film; Cesar Awards '95: Best Director (Chereau), Best Film, Best Supporting Actress (Blanc). **VHS, LV** *MAX*

Queens Logic

Ray (Ken Olin) is an artist who's having second and third thoughts about his impending marriage to Patricia (Chloe Webb). His irresponsible and irrepressible big brother Al (Joe Mantegna) is in serious trouble with his wife (Linda Fiorentino). Dennis (Kevin Bacon) has come back to the New York borough from Los Angeles for the event. Their pal Eliot (John Malkovich) can't quite figure out how to deal with his homosexuality. Tom Waits is also on hand as the friendly local fence, and Jamie Lee Curtis is memorable as Grace, a bizarre rich woman who shows up at the bachelor party. The guys in this ensemble take up most of the spotlight, but the women hold their own and have just as much depth. All of these characters are treated with a fond, flattering nostalgia. If their story seems a little too sweet at times, that's easy to forgive. A boisterous, rough-edged charm makes up for a lot of flaws. 🎬🎬🎬

Strong language, subject matter.

1991 (R) 116m/C John Malkovich, Kevin Bacon, Jamie Lee Curtis, Linda Fiorentino, Joe Mantegna, Ken Olin, Tom Waits, Chloe Webb, Ed Marinaro, Kelly Bishop, Tony Spiridakis; *D:* Steve Rash; *W:* Tony Spiridakis; *M:* Joe Jackson. **VHS, LV** *LIV*

Quicker Than the Eye

Magician Ben Norrell (Ben Gazzara) is hired to perform before the leaders of two African countries who are trying to work out a peace settlement in a Swiss hotel. Shady types are planning to assassinate one of the leaders and to frame Norrell, but their hare-brained plot falters because he's a womanizer who's fooling around with his assistant (Mary Crosby) and the hotel manager (Catherine Jarrett). The complete implausibility of the story isn't that big a problem; this kind of thriller doesn't have to make perfect sense. Miscasting Gazzara in a role that calls for a light romantic/comic touch is a much more serious flaw and so is the leaden pace. The film also cheats on the magic; most of the tricks are accomplished through camera cuts, not sleight of hand. 🦴🦴

Violence, subject matter, profanity.

1988 (PG) 94m/C Ben Gazzara, Mary Crosby, Catherine Jarrett, Ivan Desny, Eb Lottimer, Sophie Carle, Wolfram Berger, Dinah Hinz, Jean Yanne; *D:* Nicolas Gessner. **VHS** *ACA*

The Rachel Papers

Updated *Alfie* with a personal computer is the slickly told story of Charles Highway (Dexter Fletcher, who looks like a young Mick Jagger) and his obsession with Rachel (Ione Skye). Charles is an intelligent, slightly nerdy computer whiz who lets nothing stand in the way of his pursuit of this beautiful girl. He often turns to the camera and addresses the audience directly, just as Michael Caine did back in 1966, with glib remarks like "So begins my descent into manhood." At first, this love story is engaging and interesting, but it becomes less and less so as it goes along. When you get to know the two main characters, you realize that beneath their initial attractiveness, they're shallow, manipulative, selfish, faithless, and unpleasant. By the end, you're glad to see them go. By the way, a similar story was told much more effectively and enjoyably in *Getting It Right*. 🦴🦴

Sexual activity, nudity, profanity.

1989 (R) 92m/C Dexter Fletcher, Ione Skye, James Spader, Jonathan Pryce, Bill Paterson, Michael Gambon, Lesley Sharp; *D:* Damian Harris; *W:* Damian Harris; *M:* Chaz Jankel. **VHS** *FOX*

Radio Inside

First-rate love story may not be perfect but it's well worth a look. Our hero and narrator is Matthew (William McNamara), a young man from Indiana who moves to Miami Beach to live with his older brother Michael (Dylan Walsh) after their father dies. Though the two are alike in some ways, their differences are pronounced. Michael is a hard-working ad man who views life as a competition. Matthew just completed a graduate thesis on *Crime and Punishment* and is still grieving for his father. Michael is an unapologetic secularist.

Matthew has personal conversations with Jesus (Ara Madzounian). Michael has a bright, beautiful girlfriend, Natalie (Elisabeth Shue). Matthew is falling in love with her. First-time writer/director Jeffrey Bell makes enough mistakes to ruin a lot of films. A subplot involving a black kid, T.J. (Pee Wee Love) is handled awkwardly. Some of the nostalgic flashbacks verge on the mawkish, and in key scenes, Bell seems at a loss as to where the camera should be. At the same time though, a good heart and honest emotion make up for a lot of technical flaws. These are three believable characters. They have depth, and their conflicts are treated realistically. Beyond that, Bell is one of the few filmmakers in recent years to treat religious belief and spirituality without preaching and to view them as important parts of the protagonist's life. 🦴🦴🦴

Contains mature subject matter, some strong language, fleeting nudity.

1994 91m/C William McNamara, Dylan Walsh, Elisabeth Shue, Gil Goldstein, Ara Madzounian, Pee Wee Love; *D:* Jeffrey Bell; *W:* Jeffrey Bell. **VHS, LV** *MGM*

Raging Angels

Potential alternative classic has all the right ingredients and it makes full use of them. First, there's the crackpot plot that might have come from a religious wacko's nuttier fantasies—one world government led by anti-Christ Michael Pare. Allied against him are a drunken young rocker (Sean Patrick Flanery), his bland blonde girlfriend (Monet Mazur), and his nutty grandmother Shelley Winters...yes, Shelley Winters at her blowsy, scenery-devouring worst. (Her death scene is a real corker, one of the true lowlights in her distinguished career.) As a goofy psychic, veteran co-star Diane Ladd gives Ms. Winters a run for her money with some inspired histrionics. Finally, add in the direction of the infamous Alan Smithee, the pseudonym that filmmakers use when they're too embarrassed by the fruit of their labors. Next stop, *Mystery Science Theater 3000*. 🦴

Strong language, violence, sexual content.

1995 (R) 97m/C Sean Patrick Flanery, Monet Mazur, Michael Pare, Diane Ladd, Shelley Winters, Arielle Dombasle; *D:* Alan

Rated and Unrated

If memory serves, the first film to arrive on cassette in a substantially different form from its theatrical release was a so-so 1984 thriller, *Thief of Hearts*. A few others—among them the first *Star Trek* film and *Blade Runner*—came to video with a few extra minutes, but *Thief of Hearts* broke new ground by using its too-steamy-for-the-MPAA "unrated" footage as a selling point.

Since then, hundreds of B-movies have followed. Mickey Rourke has made a career on the contrived "controversies" of *Wild Orchid, 9 1/2 Weeks,* and *Angel Heart.* The shelves of video stores are packed with "director's cuts," "European" versions, and other euphemistically labeled titles.

Do these movies really have anything different to offer? No and yes. As a rule, they're no more sexually explicit than *Basic Instinct* (which, of course, is also available in two video versions). They're mainstream escapism, not pornography. At the same time, though, some video premieres are more experimental and take more chances than their theatrical counterparts.

In the vocabulary of home video, the word "unrated" carries all sorts of implications. It suggests that the title is racy, too hot for the stodgy old MPAA's rating system; something that carries a faint whiff of the forbidden. Occasionally, the movies in question even deliver on that unspoken promise. More often, the word may mean that no one at the studio or video company took the time and trouble to submit it to the MPAA's ratings board. And in a few cases, it may mean that the material is so unusual and challenging that "PG," "R," and the rest just don't apply.

The above Video Premieres exist in unrated versions that are notably different from their rated forms.

BLADE RUNNER	PEEPING TOM
CAT CHASER	RE-ANIMATOR
COLOR OF NIGHT	SHOWGIRLS
THE GETAWAY *(1993)*	STEALING HEAVEN
INTENT TO KILL	THE STREET FIGHTER
THE LAWNMOWER MAN	A STREETCAR NAMED DESIRE
THE MAN WHO FELL TO EARTH	WHEN NIGHT IS FALLING
ONCE UPON A TIME IN AMERICA	THE WILD BUNCH

Smithee; *W:* Kevin Rock, David Markov, Chris Bittler; *C:* Bryan England; *M:* Terry Plumer. **VHS** *VMK*

Rain Without Thunder

Unapologetic propaganda is for only the most committed partisans in the abortion/choice arena. In 2042, the Supreme Court has so thoroughly chipped away at Roe v. Wade that abortion is essentially illegal. Poor (i.e. black) women are routinely arrested for "fetal murder" while the more affluent fly to Sweden for a "p-term." Then Congress passes the "Unborn Child Kidnapping Act," making it illegal for a pregnant woman to leave the country for that purpose. An ensemble cast builds on the complicated premise through a series of mock-documentary interviews. Nothing really happens in the film. Instead, these people sit around and talk about other things that have already happened, or they make irritating pompous speeches. Despite the subject matter, the action is flat and static, both emotionally and visually. Even those who agree with the film's strong pro-choice stance will find it more irritating than persuasive. ♫♫

Mature subject matter, strong language.

1993 (PG-13) 87m/C Betty Buckley, Jeff Daniels, Ali Thomas, Frederic Forrest, Carolyn McCormick, Linda Hunt, Robert Earl Jones, Graham Greene, Iona Morris, Austin Pendleton; **D:** Gary Bennett; **W:** Gary Bennett; **M:** Randall Lynch, Allen Lynch. **VHS** *ORI*

Rainbow Drive

Police thriller based on Roderick Thorpe's novel is something of a disappointment. It begins well when a Los Angeles detective (Peter Weller) realizes that someone in the police department is covering up details of a multiple murder. A large supporting cast provides fine work, and the production values are top drawer. But the story simply doesn't hold together, the score is pedestrian, and the conclusion is preposterous. Coulda been a contender. ♫♫

Strong language, violence.

1990 (R) 93m/C Peter Weller, Sela Ward, Bruce Weitz, David Caruso, James Laurenson, Chris Mulkey, Kathryn Harrold; **D:** Bobby Roth; **W:** Roderick Thorp, Bill Phillips, Bennett Cohen; **M:** Tangerine Dream. **VHS** *BTV, VMK*

Rampage

Serious but flawed film attempts to examine the complexities of crime, madness, responsibility, and punishment. Michael Biehn is a liberal D.A. whose values are questioned when he has to seek the death penalty against Alex McArthur, a murderer who has killed women and children. The film's mixture of Catholic rituals and religious symbols with ritual murder is disturbing. The characters are unusually well developed and realistic, but the story slips when it attempts to turn certain psychiatrists into conventional, stereotyped villains. ♫♫♫

Extremely strong violence, language.

1987 (R) 92m/C Michael Biehn, Alex McArthur, Nicholas Campbell, Deborah Van Valkenburgh, John Harkins, Art LaFleur; **D:** William Friedkin; **W:** William Friedkin; **M:** Ennio Morricone. **VHS, LV** *PAR, BTV*

Rapa Nui

The title refers to Easter Island and the film is about those big statues—how and why they were created in the years before the island was visited by Europeans. Jason Scott Lee is a prince of the Long Ear tribe, the ruling priest class, who order the Short Ears to construct the statues for religious reasons. Esai Morales is a honcho with the Short Ears. Though they were boyhood friends, they're now in love with the same woman, Sandrine Holt. At the same time, the demands of the chief are becoming more and more outrageous, and the islanders are rapidly running out of food and fuel. Clearly, the filmmakers mean for the film to have an important environmental message for today's audience and they hammer it home with a sledge. When they return to the main story, they follow familiar Hollywood conventions. First, there's the cliched love angle, and then there's a curious competition, complete with Rocky-esque training montages, that leads to an unintentionally hilarious big finish. Actually, there are several moments toward the end that are funnier than they ought to be, but the film still earns a qualified recommendation. It's imaginative, colorful, and never boring—well worth an evening's rental. ♫♫♫

Nudity, sexual material, violence.

1993 (R) 107m/C Jason Scott Lee, Esai Morales, Sandrine Holt; **D:** Kevin Reynolds; **W:** Kevin Reynolds, Tim Rose Price; **M:** Stewart Copeland. **VHS, LV** *WAR*

Raven Hawk

Bodybuilder Rachel McLish makes a credible debut in a weak vehicle. *Raven Hawk* is a crackpot revenge flick that earns the dubious distinction of being named after two birds. Director Albert Pyun gets the most out of tinted Western landscapes. A cast of veteran B-players (including Ed Lauter, Mitch Pileggi, and Mitchell Ryan) does about all anyone could with such an abysmal script full of pseudo-Native American mystical hogwash. Rachel McLish might have what it takes to be an action star—she's certainly strong enough and

attractive enough—but she's going to have to work with better material. ♫

Violence, strong language, brief nudity.

1996 (R) 88m/C Rachel McLish, Ed Lauter, Mitch Pileggi, Mitchell Ryan; **D:** Albert Pyun. **VHS** *COL*

Raw Nerve

Yet another psycho killer story leaves a veteran cast up the proverbial creek with a thankless collection of cliches. There's nothing wrong with wacko B-movies as long as they understand what they are. When the people who make them start to take themselves seriously, all is lost. ♫

Violence, strong language, brief nudity.

1991 (R) 91m/C Glenn Ford, Traci Lords, Sandahl Bergman, Randall "Tex" Cobb, Ted Prior, Jan-Michael Vincent; **D:** David A. Prior; **W:** David A. Prior. **VHS, LV** *AIP*

Re-Animator

THE cult favorite for horror fans with strong stomachs. H.P. Lovecraft's serial novella of a serum that brings back the dead is brought to the screen with all the grotesque inventiveness that the special effects folk can provide. A dense Gothic atmosphere is twisted by a little humor and a lot of sex. The famous "head" scene has never been duplicated. On home video, the film exists in three editions. The R-rated theatrical release is the tamest of three. The unrated tape is more popular. In 1995, the definitive version appeared on videodisk. It contains outtakes, a key deleted scene, and commentary by cast and crew. ♫♫♫

Grotesque special effects, sexual content, nudity.

1984 86m/C Jeffrey Combs, Bruce Abbott, Barbara Crampton, David Gale, Robert Sampson; **D:** Stuart Gordon; **W:** Stuart Gordon, Dennis Paoli, William J. Norris; **C:** Mac Ahlberg; **M:** Richard Band. **VHS, LV** *LIV, VES*

The Real Richard Nixon

Three-volume tape can be seen as a valuable companion piece to Oliver Stone's *Nixon*. The President tells his own story to friendly interviewer and producer Frank Gannon. The first two tapes are focused on his childhood, edu-

cation, early political career, and his marriage to Pat. The third, "28 Days," is about Watergate. It's the central event of his Presidency and Gannon allows Nixon to explain the final stages in his own terms. Gannon doesn't pursue the most questionable aspects of the matter; there's no mention of the infamous 18 and a half minute gap. Instead, Nixon explains what it was like from his point of view. The man is smooth, persuasive, self-serving, and blind to his own flaws. He emerges as a creation of his own power, a political being who never understood what he'd done. Notice, for example, the strange way that he slips in and out of the third-person royal "we" when talking about himself. Near the end, when he's describing the last helicopter ride away from the White House, he says, "I remember Mrs. Nixon was sitting next to us...." Like its subject, the trilogy is fascinating stuff. Recommended for anyone interested in Nixon, but particularly for younger viewers who see the Stone film and need some help sorting out fact, fiction, and interpretation. ♫♫♫

Contains no objectionable material.

1995 201m/C D: Frank Gannon. **VHS** *CPM*

Reason to Die

Ultra-low budget, ultra-violent South African crime movie is notable for a strong early performance from Arnold Vosloo as a mad murderer of prostitutes, and the presence of the always reliable Wings Hauser. Also available in an unrated version. ♫♫

Graphic violence, subject matter, brief nudity.

1990 (R) 86m/C Liam Cundill, Wings Hauser, Anneline Kriel, Arnold Vosloo; **D:** Tim Spring. **VHS, LV** *VMK*

Reckless Kelly

If Buster Keaton had made *'Crocodile' Dundee*, he might well have come up with something like this free-wheeling satire on Hollywood conventions, greed, violence, videos, and beer. The multi-hyphenate Yahoo Serious plays a contemporary descendent of the famous Australian outlaw, Ned Kelly. His headquarters, "Reckless Island," is a peaceable kingdom, complete with a pub/video store, populated by aboriginal Kellys and hundreds of critters. (The kangaroos go "boing, boing" when they hop, and for some reason that simple sound effect is funny all the way through.) Despite the fact that Reckless' motorcycle is in a state of continual self-disassembly, things are going swimmingly until an evil banker (Hugo Weaving) decides that he's had enough of the outlaw. He arranges to sell the island to Japan if Reckless can't come up with a million bucks. Since family tradition demands that money taken from Australian banks go to the poor, Reckless heads to America, "the land of opportunity for bank robbers." But once in Hollywood.... Serious fills the screen with visual jokes and some terrific special effects, particularly at the end. But the best parts of this comedy are based on the same stuff that Chaplin and Keaton used, and Serious deserves to be compared to them. He's telling a story of the ingenious, resourceful little guy pitted against the establishment, and he spins it out with a warmth and sweetness that's seldom seen in comedy these days. If *Reckless* isn't in your local video store, call around and find one that has it. This one's worth an extra effort. 🦴🦴🦴🦴

Comic violence.

1993 (PG) 81m/C *AU* Yahoo Serious, Hugo Weaving, Melora Hardin, Alexei Sayle, Bob Maza, Kathleen Freeman; *D:* Yahoo Serious; *W:* Yahoo Serious. **VHS** *WAR*

Red

Krzysztof Kieslowski's tricolor triology concludes with a complex, unconventional romance about "fraternity." Please see *Blue* for more information. *AKA:* Three Colors: Red; Rouge; Trois Coleurs: Rouge. 🦴🦴🦴🦴

1994 (R) 99m/C *FR PL SI* Irene Jacob, Jean-Louis Trintignant, Frederique Feder, Jean-Pierre Lorit; *Cameos:* Juliette Binoche, Julie Delpy, Benoit Regent, Zbigniew Zamachowski; *D:* Krzysztof Kieslowski; *W:* Krzysztof Kieslowski, Krzysztof Piesiewicz; *C:* Piotr Sobocinski; *M:* Zbigniew Preisner. Cesar Awards '94: Best Score; Independent Spirit Awards '95: Best Foreign Film; Los Angeles Film Critics Association Awards '94: Best Foreign Film; New York Film Critics Awards '94: Best Foreign Film; National Society of Film Critics Awards '94: Best Foreign Film; Nominations: Academy Awards '94: Best Cinematography, Best Director (Kieslowski), Best Original Screenplay; Cesar Awards '94: Best Actor (Trintignant), Best Actress (Jacob), Best Director (Kieslowski), Best Film; Golden Globe Awards '95: Best Foreign Language Film. **VHS, LV** *MAX*

Red Blooded American Girl

This twisted little Grand Guignol shocker is a medical horror comedy. Owen Urban (Andrew Stevens) is a fictionalized Augustus Owsley, the famous outlaw chemist who provided LSD for Ken Kesey and others. Urban gives up his private research into recreational drugs when he is approached by Alcore (Christopher Plummer) to work at his secretive Life Reach Foundation. The subject of his experiments is an AIDS-like blood disease that resembles vampirism The title character is Paula (Heather Thomas), a physical-fitness cutie who is infected with the disease and then runs amok. Most of the scares come from genuinely creepy, skin-crawly stuff involving needles, tubes, plastic bags of blood, and such. Overt, ridiculous special effects are kept to a minimum. Plummer helps things immeasurably with another of his excellent understated supporting performance. In his hands, bad material sounds believable and good material is riveting. 🦴🦴🦴

Strong sexual content, nudity, drug use, violence.

1990 (R) 89m/C *CA* Christopher Plummer, Andrew Stevens, Heather Thomas, Kim Coates; *D:* David Blyth. **VHS, LV** *PSM*

Red Rock West

When we first meet Mike Williams (Nicolas Cage), he's about as down and out as a guy can get: in the middle of Wyoming nowhere, sleeping in his rust bucket Caddy, out of work because of a bad knee, and out of money after he spends his last $5 on gas. From that curious beginning, the film becomes a quirky thriller that's consistently surprising. The other major characters are a suspicious husband (J.T. Walsh), his seemingly faithless wife (Lara Flynn Boyle), and a hitman (Dennis Hopper) with a poor sense of timing. What happens among the four of them is simultaneously so goofy and so inevitable that you really don't want to know anything more about the story. For comparative purposes, think of the Dahl brothers' *Kill Me Again* and the Coens' *Blood*

The Hound's Favorite Sleepers: Road Movies

The Hound views Road Movies in the broadest possible context. In each of these, whether or not there's much actual travel involved, the sense of lonely place and distance is a key element.

BOTTLE ROCKET	NEAR DARK
THE CRUDE OASIS	PATHFINDER
FALL TIME	POWWOW HIGHWAY
FEVER	PUNCH THE CLOCK
HOLD ME, THRILL ME, KISS ME	PURE DANGER
THE INLAND SEA	REMOTE CONTROL
JACK BE NIMBLE	REPO MAN
LITTLE VEGAS	ROMPER STOMPER
MY FAMILY	THE VANISHING
NATURE OF THE BEAST	THE WRONG MAN (1993)

Simple, though this one relies less on the shock effect of individual scenes. Still a fine neo-noir. 🦴🦴🦴

Violence, strong language, sexual content.

1993 (R) 98m/C Nicolas Cage, Dennis Hopper, Lara Flynn Boyle, J.T. Walsh, Timothy Carhart, Dan Shor, Dwight Yoakam, Bobby Joe McFadden; *D:* John Dahl; *W:* John Dahl, Rick Dahl; *M:* William Olvis. Nominations: Independent Spirit Awards '95: Best Director (Dahl), Best Screenplay. VHS, LV COL

Red Wind

Psychological thriller is actually an unintentional comedy so wonderfully bad that it should be watched by large groups of friends who appreciate alternative classics. Kris Morrow (Lisa Hartman Black) is a Miami psychiatrist with quirks of her own. She becomes too close to a client named Lila who has some very serious problems involving fantasies, sexual and otherwise. Is she really going to do in her hubby and stuff him in the wood chipper? It's doubtful that anyone will make it to the end without laughing uncontrollably, loud and often. The key gimmick is so transparent that viewers will get it long before the characters. It's the kind of blunder that makes the movie so much fun. By the way, the film has nothing to do with the famous Raymond Chandler story of the same title. 🦴🦴🦴

Violence, strong language, sexual content.

1991 (R) 93m/C Lisa Hartman Black, Deanna Lund, Philip Casnoff, Christopher McDonald; *D:* Alan Metzger. VHS MCA

Reflections in the Dark

When Regina (Mimi Rogers) is escorted to her cell in the men's penitentiary by her guard Colin (Billy Zane), it's the first trip to death row for both of them. Seven years before, on her seventh anniversary, Regina killed her husband (John Terry). Exactly what she did, how she came to do it, and why are the film's points. Her character and motivation are revealed in a series of flashbacks and conversations with Colin, who has been following her case for years. Nothing is what it first appears to be. Beneath her steel-hard facade, Regina is a complicated, often contradictory individual and her relationship with her husband is as multilayered as any marriage. There's no single moment of revelation, no he-did-this-so-she-did-that balancing of the scales. Because the film is so purposefully ambiguous, it may not satisfy all viewers, but it's a refreshing change from most mainstream entertainment which wraps any and all problems up with neat solutions. The film's main flaw is the clumsy use of a body-double in key love scenes. They're so out of step with the rest of the action that they call attention to themselves. The sexual element is necessary but it could have been handled much more effectively. Even so, writer/director Jon Purdy makes an impressive debut. Producer Roger Corman has based his long and profitable career on two kinds of movies: low-budget, low-brow entertainment and more subtle, more serious foreign films. *Reflections in the Dark* essentially combines the two. Recommended. *AKA:* Reflections on a Crime. *♫♫♫*

Mature subject matter, violence, nudity, sexual content, strong language.

1994 (R) 83m/C Mimi Rogers, Billy Zane, John Terry, Kurt Fuller, Lee Garlington, Nancy Fish; *D:* Jon Purdy; *W:* Jon Purdy. VHS, LV *NHO*

The Refrigerator

Newlyweds David Simonds and Julia McNeal move from Ohio to New York City and find that the titular major appliance is possessed by the devil. Yes, they've got an ancient Norge from hell and there's not much that Caban, the flamenco-dancing Bolivian super, can do about it. It's difficult to mix horror and comedy, and this attempt is successful about half the time. Some moments have an Ira Levin-sort of creepiness while others are just dumb. The lived-in look of a local production made on location is a plus. In the end, it's all quirky enough to rate a recommendation to fans of low-budget horror, but only to them. *♫♫*

Contains violence, strong language, some sexual material.

1993 86m/C David Simonds, Julia McNeal, Angel Caban, Nena Segal, Jaime Rojo, Michelle DeCosta; *D:* Nicholas A.E. Jacobs; *W:* Nicholas A.E. Jacobs. VHS *NO*

Remote Control

Icelandic screwball comedy might have been Ingmar Bergman's version of *Wayne's World*. Axel's (Bjorn Jorundur Fridbjornsson) mother says that if he doesn't return the remote control to the TV set, she'll pull the plug on the bathtub and let all of his tropical fish down the drain. What's Axel to do? His sister's no-good rock 'n' roll boyfriend took the remote and when Axel tracks them down, he discovers that they left it at a friend's house where an armchair caught fire and it sort of melted. That's when the comic gangsters show up wanting to know why they've been getting such poor quality bootleg hooch, and since Axel's sister knows the mysterious bootlegger, and since said bootlegger might also have a spare remote control, Axel agrees to drive her over there in his black *Smokey and the Bandit* Trans Am. Then things really get crazy. Writer/director Oskar Jonasson tells his story with a dry, understated wit that makes the slapstick scenes that much funnier. Young Fridbjornsson has an appealing, hapless Buster Keaton quality. The pace bogs down a little in a long nightclub scene but that's a quibble. The film has the kind of offbeat appeal that's usually associated with film festival sleeper hits, and the suburban Icelandic landscape is probably something new and different for most viewers. *♫♫♫♫*

Strong language (subtitled), comic violence.

1994 85m/C *IC* Bjorn Fridbjornsson, Margret H. Gustavsdottir, Helgi Bjornsson, Soley Eliasdottir; *D:* Oskar Jonasson; *W:* Oskar Jonasson. VHS *COL*

Rented Lips

Despite solid comic credits—director Robert Downey made the 1969 cult masterpiece *Putney Swope*—this one's a full-blown disaster. Writer Martin Mull plays an innocent, incompetent film director who's roped into finishing a porno movie for an unscrupulous producer when he really wants to make a musical documentary on the history of corn. The attempt to parody bad movies falls victim to its own subject matter. Nothing is really done with the idea of the film within a film, either. You might think that any movie that put Edy Williams and June Lockhart (Timmy's mom on *Lassie*) on the same screen would have to have a certain curiosity value, but this one lacks even that dubious virtue. WOOF!

Profanity, brief nudity, sexual content.

1988 (R) 82m/C Martin Mull, Dick Shawn, Jennifer Tilly, Kenneth Mars, Edy Williams, Robert Downey Jr., June Lockhart, Shelley Berman, Mel Welles, Pat McCormick, Eileen Brennan; *D:* Robert Downey; *W:* Martin Mull. VHS, LV *AHV*

Repo Man

Wild, raucous new-wave craziness made this comedy one of the first video premieres to

achieve genuine cult status. A lobotomized scientist is cruising around the scroungier parts of L.A. in a '64 Chevy Malibu with what might be lethally radioactive active aliens from outer space in the trunk. Everyone else is looking for it, including the government and a UFO fan club. So are the guys at the repossession service, Helping Hands—young Otto (Emilio Estevez) and his mentor (Harry Dean Stanton), a principled cynic who takes pride in his work. The sun-blasted decay of Southern California appears almost to be crumbling before the camera, but behind the pessimistic story and the setting, there's a happy anarchy of the Marx brothers variety. *ↄↄↄ*

Strong language and overall weirdness.

1983 (R) 93m/C Emilio Estevez, Harry Dean Stanton, Sy Richardson, Tracey Walter, Olivia Barash, Fox Harris, Jennifer Balgobin, Vonetta McGee, Angelique Pettyjohn; **D:** Alex Cox; **W:** Alex Cox. **VHS, LV** *MCA*

Repossessed

The Exorcist meets *The Naked Gun* in a horror parody. Leslie Nielsen plays Father Mayii; Linda Blair is Nancy, an older version of the character she played in the Friedkin film. She has a family and a house in the suburbs until one night when she gets a strange craving for split pea soup. Yes, the spirit is upon her again. Most of the visual gags are fairly effective and in the other jokes, there are more gems than clunkers. Subjects include people who hold up Bible verse numbers at ball games, Ted Kennedy, aerobics, pro wrestling, MTV, televangelism, and lots of other movies. *ↄↄↄ*

Strong language, religious humor, graphic special effects, brief nudity.

1990 (PG-13) 89m/C Linda Blair, Ned Beatty, Leslie Nielsen, Anthony Starke, Jesse Ventura; **D:** Bob Logan; **W:** Bob Logan; **M:** Charles Fox. Golden Raspberry Awards '90: Worst Song ("He's Comin' Back (The Devil!)"). **VHS, LV** *LIV*

Reservoir Dogs

If not the most famous, then certainly the most influential video premiere, Quentin Tarantino's directorial debut is a shocker. It's not the plot—a simple story about a botched diamond robbery—it's in the elliptical way Tarantino chooses to tell the story. For better and for worse, it's a rough draft of *Pulp Fiction* with more blood-smeared characters in black suits, incessantly profane dialogue, tortuously extended conversations, sudden violence, and that weird mix of emotional intensity and bizarre humor. What's lacking is the final element that made *Pulp Fiction* a hit—redemption by grace. Superb performances from an ensemble cast led by Harvey Keitel. *ↄↄↄ*

Graphic violence, strong language.

1992 (R) 100m/C Harvey Keitel, Tim Roth, Michael Madsen, Steve Buscemi, Christopher Penn, Lawrence Tierney, Kirk Baltz, Quentin Tarantino; **D:** Quentin Tarantino; **W:** Quentin Tarantino. Independent Spirit Awards '93: Best Supporting Actor (Buscemi). **VHS, LV** *LIV, BTV*

Return

Woozy yarn that might have come from Shirley MacLaine's reject file. It's all about souls or spirits or something communicating across time. Diana (Karlene Crockett) is a young women who runs across an innocuous fellow (John Walcutt) who is the reincarnation of her grandfather. Sort of. Whenever he's hypnotized, old granddad speaks through him. Eventually, he tells Diana that her daddy (Frederic Forrest), who's about to run for governor in Arkansas, hasn't been telling her the whole truth about his (granddad's) death. The resolution of this screwball premise is hamfisted, silly, and insulting to any intelligent viewer. *ↄ*

Sexual content, violence, profanity.

1988 (R) 78m/C Frederic Forrest, Anne Francis, Karlene Crockett, John Walcutt, Lisa Richards; **D:** Andrew Silver. **VHS, LV** *ACA*

The Return of Jafar

Sequel to *Aladdin* attempts to repeat all of the elements that made the original so popular. This time, though, the main ingredient of the first film is missing. Dan Castellaneta—the voice of Homer Simpson—takes over for Robin Williams as the Genie, and does a completely respectable job. Much of the action is handled by Gilbert Gottfried as Iago, the irritating parrot. The title pretty much says all that needs to be said of the plot. The animation isn't as detailed as it was in the first, but it's still a cut above most animated videos and it's actually better than a lot of second-rate feature-length cartoons that show up in theatres these days. There's nothing here to match the big action scenes, the elaborate production numbers, or the songs, but that probably won't bother most kids. Will they love it like they love the first film? Of course not. Will they like it? Definitely. Will they want to watch it a dozen times? Probably. Followed by another sequel. 🦴🦴🦴

Contains a little scary stuff.

1994 (G) 66m/C **W:** Kevin Campbell, Mirith J.S. Colao; **V:** Scott Weinger, Linda Larkin, Gilbert Gottfried, Val Bettin, Dan Castellaneta. **VHS, LV** *DIS*

The Return of Swamp Thing

Complete waste of time has none of the quirky, campy energy that made the original so enjoyable. In its place we find two of the worst child actors ever to appear onscreen, an infantile script, and a leaden pace. In a final insult to good movies, villain Louis Jourdan's parrot is named Gigi! *WOOF!*

Profanity and mild violence.

1989 (PG-13) 83m/C Dick Durock, Sarah Douglas, Louis Jourdan, Heather Locklear; **D:** Jim Wynorski. Golden Raspberry Awards '89: Worst Actress (Locklear). **VHS** *COL*

The Return of the Musketeers

Richard Lester's third take on Alexandre Dumas' swashbuckling novels has some of the wit and fun of the first two, but it's not as energetic. Once again, historian, novelist, and screenwriter George MacDonald Fraser has placed our heroes on the wrong side of history. They stoutly defend the French throne against the wily intrigues of Cardinal Mazarin (Phillipe Noiret). The stars of the originals are back with an infusion of young blood by C. Thomas Howell as Athos' son, and Kim Cattrall as Milady's daughter who's out to get the Mus-

keteers. For comparative purposes, this one is about as enjoyable as the Disney *Three Musketeers,* but not nearly as good as the first Lester-Fraser collaboration, one of the best historical adventures ever, and currently unavailable on video. 🦴🦴

Mild violence.

1989 (PG) 103m/C *GB FR SP* Michael York, Oliver Reed, Frank Finlay, Richard Chamberlain, Kim Cattrall, C. Thomas Howell, Geraldine Chaplin, Roy Kinnear, Christopher Lee, Philippe Noiret, Jean-Pierre Cassel, Billy Connolly, Eusebio Lazaro; **D:** Richard Lester; **W:** George MacDonald Fraser. **VHS, LV** *MCA, BTV, FCT*

Riff Raff

Extremely offbeat, extremely British comedy-drama is about poor day laborers doing construction work. Writer/director Ken Loach has given the film a sharply honed leftish edge, but he stops short of propaganda. The cast is unknown on this side of the Atlantic and the characters speak such heavily accented English that much of the dialogue is subtitled. The loose, episodic story has to do with the relationship between Stevie, who's squatting in a London apartment building scheduled for renovation or demolition, and Susie, a singer whose dreams of success are not matched by her voice. A few of the scenes are wildly funny while others are so realistic they look like they could have come from a documentary. Some are driven by a passionate anti-drug message. 🦴🦴

Contains brief nudity, strong language, some violence, drug use.

1992 96m/C *GB* Robert Carlyle, Emer McCourt, Jimmy Coleman, George Moss, Ricky Tomlinson, David Finch, Bill Jesse; **D:** Ken Loach; **W:** Bill Jesse, Ken Loach; **M:** Stewart Copeland. **VHS, LV** *NLC, COL, IME*

Ring of Fire

What might have been just another martial arts flick has become a genuine cult hit. The reasons are simple: 1) Don "The Dragon" Wilson has such an engaging screen presence that he's believable as an updated Romeo to Maria Ford's Juliet; 2) They've got one of the hottest love scenes you'll ever see on video. Followed by sequels. 🦴🦴🦴

Violence, sexual content, nudity, strong language.

1991 (R) 100m/C Don "The Dragon" Wilson, Maria Ford, Vince Murdocco, Dale Jacoby, Michael Delano, Eric Lee; *D:* Richard W. Munchkin. **VHS, LV** *IMP, HMV*

Ring of Fire 2: Blood and Steel

Sequel is a more conventional martial arts/chase genre piece as Don Wilson attempts to rescue kidnapped fiancee from thugs. Not one of the star's best efforts. 🗡🗡

Violence, strong language.

1992 (R) 94m/C Don "The Dragon" Wilson, Maria Ford, Sy Richardson, Michael Delano, Dale Jacoby, Vince Murdocco, Evan Lorie, Gary Robbins, Charlie Ganis, Ron Yuan; *D:* Richard W. Munchkin. **VHS** *PMH*

Ring of Fire 3: Lion Strike

Series has degenerated considerably from the original. Formula fare is notable for the star's likable screen presence and a certain humor, but little else. He plays Dr. Johnny Wu, Dirty Harry with a stethoscope, who's constantly running into bad guys—in the emergency room, on the roof, in the mountains, wherever. The fight choreography is about as convincing as most pro wrestling bouts, though some of the action sequences are so poorly staged they become unintentionally funny. 🗡🗡

Martial arts violence, strong language.

1994 (R) 90m/C Don "The Dragon" Wilson, Bobbie Phillips, Robert Costanzo; *D:* Rick Jacobson. **VHS, LV** *PMH*

Road Lawyers and Other Briefs

Compilation of bare-bones short works may lack glossy production values. Instead, it has humor, high spirits, and bad taste. The title film is a parody of *The Road Warrior* about post-apocalypse attorneys searching for coffee. The cut-rate special effects work well but the result is a mixed bag. The second, "Escape from Heaven," is the real winner of the bunch. It satirizes Catholic beliefs about different levels of sin, purgatory, limbo, the holy trinity, and such. These theological matters are presented as a women-in-prison exploitation flick. The result is deeply sacrilegious, offensive to most Christians, and really really funny. 🗡🗡🗡

Contains some strong language, religious humor.

1989 79m/C *D:* James Desmarais, Tim Doyle, David Lipman, Bert Rhine. **VHS** *AIP*

Road to Ruin

Slick romantic comedy is a deliberate throwback to the world of Rock Hudson and Doris Day. In Paris, zillionaire Jack Sloan (Peter Weller) falls hard for model Jessie Taylor (Carey Lowell). But she'll have nothing to do with him. Jack perseveres—if he didn't, there wouldn't be a movie—and as soon as he has won the object of his affection, he begins to doubt himself: does she love me or my megabucks? He concocts a test, involving his Gallic partner (the wonderfully droll Michael Duchaussoy), and pretends to have lost everything. You don't have to be a film school graduate to figure out the rest, but suspense isn't important. This kind of movie depends on style and atmosphere. Director Charlotte Brandstrom almost hits the bullseye. She sustains a frivolously sophisticated tone throughout, and the Parisian locations look great. Lowell gives an undemanding role all it needs.

Weller seems somehow too focused or intense for this featherweight material. ♫♫♡

Mature subject matter, a little strong language, brief nudity, sexual content.

1991 (R) 94m/C Peter Weller, Carey Lowell, Michael Duchaussoy; *D:* Charlotte Brandstrom. **VHS** *LIV*

Robo-C.H.I.C.

Ultra-low budget comedy is filled with sophomoric humor that's funny enough if you're in the mood. The advertising and the brief presence of star Kathy Shower, from the pages of *Playboy* magazine, suggest that this one is an exploitation picture. But beyond a few seconds of innocent toplessness, it's a kid's movie. The goofy bad guy reads a book with the title *How to Build an Atomic Bomb* and handles plutonium with kitchen tongs. The local motorcycle gang can't get any respect because the lettering on their jackets is wrong. They're not "Satan's Minions"; they're "Satan's Onions." Think Larry, Moe, and Curly without the sophistication. *AKA:* Cyber-Chic. ♫♫

Brief nudity, comic violence, mild profanity.

1989 (R) 90m/C Kathy Shower, Jack Carter, Burt Ward, Lyle Waggoner; *D:* Ed Hansen, Jeffrey Mandel. **VHS** *AIP*

Rockwell: A Legend of the Wild West

Judging by the photographs and copy on the box—pictures of basketball star Karl Malone and a long-haired man with a darkened face over the words "He brought black powder justice to a lawless land"—you'd expect the film to be a black Western along the lines of Mario Van Peebles' *Posse.* It's not. This is a Mormon Western, all about Brigham Young, Joseph Smith, the journey west, and all that. It's an ultra-low-budget production with many nonprofessional actors. Clumsy voiceover narration is used in a transparent attempt to make up for the shortcomings of cast and script. Randy Gleave, who plays the title character, seldom speaks and when he does, his mouth is almost never visible to the camera. Now, there is nothing wrong with a Western having a religious element or a religious point of view. But here, the main Mormon characters are presented as innocent, saintly figures who want only to be left in peace, etc., etc. Those who oppose them are treacherous, lying, cowardly predators. As others have noted in a different context, propaganda that's recognizable as propaganda is third-rate propaganda. *Rockwell* doesn't even rate that high. As entertainment, it may appeal to true believers, but there's nothing to recommend the film to a larger audience. ♫

Contains some violence.

1993 ?m/C Randy Gleave, Karl Malone, Michael Rudd, George Sullivan; *D:* Richard Lloyd Dewey. **VHS, LV** *IMP*

Romero

The true story of the life and assassination of Archbishop Oscar Romero of El Salvador is powerful stuff. As portrayed by Raul Julia, Romero is a complex, bookish man who was appointed to the position of Archbishop as a compromise between activist Jesuit priests and a conservative government. Though he sympathizes with the goals of "liberation theology" and is friendly with some of the more radical priests, Romero is also comfortable among members of the ruling class. He baptizes their children and tries to move the government toward the center. But, as the political situation becomes more and more polarized and violent—the leftist guerrillas kidnap and murder a young man from a wealthy family; rightist death squads do the same to anyone who protests the government's excesses—Romero is unable to maintain his neutrality. That's the central conflict in the film, the archbishop's moral dilemma. Which side should he take? What does God want him to do? The filmmakers' political sympathies are clearly with the revolutionary priests and the poor people of El Salvador. And why not? This is a story of government gone mad, where the most intolerant, brutal elements of the military tortured and murdered anyone—including children—suspected of anything. Romero's spiritual transformation from compromise and conciliation to open defiance is a powerful

story; one scene is clearly based on the story of Christ's driving the moneychangers from the temple. Raul Julia's performance is emotionally restrained and compelling. It's all but impossible to watch the film without sharing its and his growing sense of outrage. ✍✍✍

Violence and profanity.

1989 (PG-13) 108m/C Raul Julia, Richard Jordan, Ana Alicia, Eddie Velez, Alejandro Bracho, Tony Plana, Lucy Reina, Harold Gould, Al Ruscio, Robert Viharo, *D:* John Duigan, *W:* John Sacret Young; *C:* Geoff Burton; *M:* Gabriel Yared. **VHS, LV** *VMK*

Romper Stomper

Comparisons to *A Clockwork Orange* are well taken, particularly in the first half of this loud, raw look at the world of racist Australian skinheads. Hando (Russell Crowe) and Davey (Daniel Pollock) are the leaders of a gang of young thugs. With their swastikas and tattoos, they've bought into the standard Nazi party line, taken straight from Hitler's racist paranoia. When a young woman named Gabe (Jacqueline McKenzie) enters their group, the relationship between the two men changes, but the results of that change don't take hold until later. The first half—by far the strongest—concerns the rising levels of violence between the skinheads and the children of industrious Asian immigrants. There

writer/director Geoffrey Wright really shows his stuff. He uses simple techniques—grainy film, handheld camera, extreme angles, jarringly abrupt edits—to draw you straight into the action. They're the same gimmicks and tricks that are mishandled in music videos all the time, but Wright knows what he's about. He doesn't want you to sympathize with these guys in any way, but he does want you to see the world as they do. And once the Nazi politics and trappings are stripped away, this is simply another story of violent, alienated urban youth. Move the setting to an American city and the characters could belong to just about any racial or ethnic group you choose. In the second half of the film, the action changes; it becomes more focused on the three central characters and loses some steam. Perhaps that's inevitable. Most audiences wouldn't be able to take another 45 minutes of such sustained tension. Though the physical action—both violence and sexual scenes—is graphic, it fits the story and seems more explicit than it really is. Also available in an unrated version at 89 minutes. ✍✍✍✍

Graphic violence, sexual content, nudity, strong language.

1992 (R) 85m/C *AU* Russell Crowe, Jacqueline McKenzie, Daniel Pollock; *D:* Geoffrey Wright; *W:* Geoffrey Wright. Australian Film Institute '92: Best Actor (Crowe), Best Sound, Best Score. **VHS** *ACA, FCT*

Rosalie Goes Shopping

Delightfully off-center comedy gives traditional "family" values and insatiable consumerism a strange, but affectionate treatment. Basically, it's a story about love. At first blush, Rosalie Greenspace (Marianne Saegebrecht) is a typical Stuttgart, Arkansas, housewife with a loving husband Ray (Brad Davis) and six children. But we soon realize what an odd household it is. Ray is a crop duster who plays tapes of his plane's engines during the gourmet dinners that one son cooks for the family. For her part, Rosalie is generous to a fault. She carries 37 credit cards and simply cannot resist anything that her loved ones might want. If she has to sell one daughter's car to buy another one for her son Schatzi (Alex Winter), well, she'll make it up to the girl with a new personal computer. Of course, her creative financing schemes escalate as she tries to juggle payments. The story begins with a strong streak of surrealism, but it becomes more conventional—and less interesting—as the workings of plot details take precedence over mood. Throughout, Percy Adlon tosses in strong experimental touches: unusual editing; goofy camera angles; background filled with odd sounds of bird calls, electronic beeps, and the like; and unrealistic lighting and tinting. The conclusion is predictable and not as satisfying as it might have been, but that's a matter of individual taste. The movie is a warm-hearted fable that smothers harsh criticism with its abundant generosity. 🐾🐾🐾

Mature subject matter.

1989 (PG-13) 94m/C *GE* Marianne Saegebrecht, Brad Davis, Judge Reinhold, Willie Harlander, Alex Winter, Erika Blumberger, Patricia Zehentmayr; *D:* Percy Adlon; *W:* Eleonore Adlon, Percy Adlon; *M:* Bob Telson. **VHS, LV** *VMK, INJ*

Roujin Z

Japanese animated film has an unusually sophisticated premise and enough innovative action for younger viewers. It's about the care of the elderly and the relative roles of government, health care organizations, and individuals. The Z-001 unit is a mobile machine that can do everything for the immobile, incontinent geriatric patient. Literally plugging into the user's brain, it's a super RoboNurse. But when the prototype is tested on an old man, his memories become part of the machine's circuitry. Who's in charge here? As fans of Japanese "manga" expect, the action contains lots of explosions and unexpected transformations. But the film also has a more reflective and gentle side that's rare for the genre. If Katsuhiro Otomo's film isn't as visually powerful and ambitious as his masterpiece *Akira*, it's a solid story with well-written characters and a sometimes childish sense of humor. 🐾🐾🐾

Violence, language, subject matter.

1995 (PG-13) 80m/C *D:* Katsuhiro Otomo. **VHS** *CPM*

Rover Dangerfield

Comedian Rodney Dangerfield provides the voice of his canine alter ego, Rover. Rover does some stand-up routines for his pals in Las Vegas, but still can't get no respect. Then he runs afoul of his mistress's low-life boyfriend and winds up on a farm. Even though this city dog knows nothing about rural life, he falls hard for the pretty collie next door. At first, this tale of con men, chorus girls, and gambling seems ill-suited to a G-rated cartoon, but that changes as soon as the location shifts to the country. Oddly, Dangerfield's brand of comedy makes a smooth transition from adult humor to children's. He doesn't talk down to his young viewers. Jokes about men and women become jokes about various animals. His sense of timing is intact, and Rover's just a funny dog. The animation is no great shakes—it's closer to Saturday morning cartoons than *The Brave Little Toaster*—but again, kids who are more interested in the story and the songs will like it. 🐾🐾🐾

1991 (G) 78m/C *D:* Jim George; *W:* Harold Ramis; *M:* David Newman; *V:* Rodney Dangerfield. **VHS, LV, 8mm** *WAR*

Ruby in Paradise

In the fullest sense of the term, this is a "women's picture" about young Ruby Gissing (Ashley Judd), who leaves her no-account Tennessee husband and takes off on her own. She winds up in Panama City, Florida, the self-described "redneck Riviera." The rest of the story might be summed up as "girl finds job; girl loses job; girl gets job back" or something to that effect. But the plot is less important than pace and sensibility. The story spins itself out in a leisurely way, revealing character slowly. For some tastes, the action will seem slow, but this isn't a movie to hurry through. The performances are first rate all the way through. Bentley Mitchum is a fine bad guy, but the film belongs to Ashley Judd who appears to do an effortless job of non-acting. 🐾🐾🐾

Sexual content, strong language, brief nudity.

1993 (R) 115m/C Ashley Judd, Todd Field, Bentley Mitchum, Allison Dean, Dorothy Lyman, Betsy Dowds; *D:* Victor Nunez; *W:* Victor Nunez; *M:* Charles Engstrom. Independent Spirit Awards '94: Best Actress (Judd); Sundance Film Festival '93: Grand Jury Prize; Nominations: Independent Spirit Awards '94: Best Cinematography, Best Director (Nunez), Best Film, Best Screenplay, Best Supporting Actor (Field). **VHS, LV** *REP*

Rumpelstiltskin

Really good horror movies set up their rules— the monster can be killed by silver, is afraid of fire, cannot cross water, etc.—and then play by them. This one doesn't, though the action scenes are O.K., the characters are colorful, and the mini-creature is properly gross. There's something inherently frightening about squat, quick critters and as played by Max Grodenchik, this Rumpelstiltskin bears a distinct resemblance to Ross Perot. The story has to do with a young widow (Kim Johnston-Ulrich) and her baby, but it really doesn't stick to the basic elements of the fairy tale—social advancement, greed, deal-making, fate. Instead, it's a relatively standard chase/horror movie that makes the most of a low budget. Comedian Tommy Blaze provides scene-stealing support. Considering how popular similarly themed flicks have been on video, this one might well become a series. *ぐぐ*

Graphic violence, strong language, sexual content, eyeball eating.

1996 (R) 91m/C Kim Johnston-Ulrich, Tommy Blaze, Max Grodenchik, Allyce Beasley; *D:* Mark Jones. **VHS** *REP*

The Runnin' Kind

Well-intentioned coming-of-age picture starts well but fades toward the middle. Law student Joey Curtis (David Packer) decides to give up his comfortable suburban life in Akron, Ohio, after he meets a drummer named Thunder (Brie Howard) at a new wave club. When she goes to Los Angeles, he quits his summer job at daddy's law firm and follows her. The main characters are quirky and individualistic, not at all the typical young stereotypes seen in most Hollywood movies. But once the action moves to L.A., the frantic pace of the rock scene takes over and the sharp personalities become members of the crowd. *ぐぐ*

Profanity and sexual situations.

1989 (R) 89m/C David Packer, Pleasant Gehman, Brie Howard, Susan Strasberg; *D:* Max Tash. **VHS** *FOX*

Running Cool

What do you get when you combine motorcycle gangs with wetlands preservation? A biker flick that's environmentally friendly. Self-described "scooter trash" Bone (Andrew Divoff) and Bear (Bubba Baker) are called away from a party in South Dakota when their old pal Ironbutt (grizzled B-movie stalwart James Gammon) needs help. Seems like Mr. Hogg (Paul Gleason) is trying to take away Ironbutt's homestead in the South Carolina wetlands and turn it over to developers. And if that weren't enough, his rotten son is mean to Michelle (Dedee Pfeiffer), the shy, pretty waitress. The working out of this story is about as complex as professional wrestling and, for this kind of movie, it could be a lot trashier than it is, but, hey, the people who made it had their hearts and their heads in the right place. If Earth-firsters and other sober-sided environmentalists don't welcome support from a few hundred tattooed, beer-chugging, Harley-riding biker types, that's their choice. *ぐぐ*

Strong language, mild violence, brief toplessness.

1993 (R) 106m/C Andrew Divoff, Tracy Sebastian, Dedee Pfeiffer, James Gammon, Paul Gleason, Arlen Dean Snyder, Bubba Baker; *D:* Beverly Sebastian, Ferd Sebastian; *W:* Beverly Sebastian, Ferd Sebastian. **VHS** *PAR*

Running Wild

Maddening movie is alternately delightful and atrocious. As soon as it does one thing right, it does something else wrong. Some potentially interesting characters in a possibly comic situation are undone by director Phillipe Blot, who lets his actors wander in and out of the frame. Free-spirited Carlotta (Jennifer Barker) is contemplating suicide, possibly as an alternative to marrying Vince (Mike Kirten). Then his obnoxious son, Frankie (Dan Spector), and

Frankie's pal Miller (Daniel Dupont) show up. Carlotta steals Vince's vintage Impala convertible and runs off, with Frankie and Miller in tow, to find her brother, a priest in Mexico. Before it's all over, a trio of hookers, an ominous stranger, and a severed head in a plastic grocery bag are also involved. In other hands, those motley elements might have been molded into a grand exploitation flick, a south of the border road movie or a feminist adventure/comedy. And, at various times, the film makes passing attempts to be each of them. But Blot, who also co-wrote the script, couldn't settle on a uniform tone. For my money, the film's saving grace is Jennifer Barker. She seems to have identified with Carlotta's willful impulsiveness and makes the most of it. While the rest of the film is disintegrating around her ears, Carlotta rings true, despite a few embarrassingly bad scenes. Even at her worst, she makes Thelma and Louise look like Betty and Wilma. 🦴🦴🦴

Strong language, subject matter, sexual material, brief nudity.

1994 **(R)** 91m/C Jennifer Barker, Daniel Dupont, Daniel Spector, Eliot Keener, Mike Kirten; **D:** Philippe Blot; **W:** Philippe Blot. **VHS, LV** *APX*

Rush Week

Halloween meets *Porky's*. Who is bumping off coeds while all the fraternity guys are getting drunk and disgusting? Could it be the evil dean? About the best that can be said is that the cast is young and attractive, and the violence is restrained. 🦴🦴 **GPI: 4.5**

Strong language, sex, violence, nudity, etc.

1988 **(R)** 93m/C Dean Hamilton, Gregg Allman, Kathleen Kinmont, Roy Thinnes, Pamela Ludwig; **D:** Bob Bravler. **VHS, LV** *COL*

Sacrilege

Hot-to-trot period piece appears to be based on a true story about an intense affair between a cloistered nun and a rapacious Italian nobleman in 1596. It's a handsome production, a bit slow and stiff in the telling—slightly reminiscent of films like *Dangerous Liaisons* and *Stealing Heaven*. But the sexual scenes

become remarkably explicit and at the end, this one turns into a James M. Cain sort of story of betrayal and murder. Even in the slower moments, writer/director Luciano Odorisio will keep your attention. 🦴🦴🦴 **GPI: 9.6**

Contains strong sexual content, nudity, violence.

1986 104m/C IT Myriem Roussel, Alessandro Gassman; **D:** Luciano Odorisio; **W:** Luciano Odorisio. **VHS** *PSM*

Safe

Carol White (Julianne Moore) is a wealthy Southern California homemaker who gradually falls prey to an ill-defined and undiagnosable malady. At length—at tortuous length—she comes to decide that she's a victim of "e.i.," environmental illness. Director Todd Haynes takes perverse delight in keeping viewers off balance. First, Carol is an almost completely passive character. She barely moves. Even at her sickest, when she looks really red-eyed and terrible, she's mostly numb. Haynes further distances her from the viewer by placing her at the edge of long shots, or posing her stiffly in the center of the screen. There are virtually no closeups or reaction shots. Second, the entire film is played out on one even unemotional level. Finally, the action is so slowly paced and understated that the characters seem to be crawling through a thick, clear viscous syrup. Before it's over, you begin to worry that the tape will never end. Instead, it'll just go slower and slower and slower, and will be stuck in your VCR forever, and you'll never get to watch another movie because this one will go on from everlasting to everlasting. 🦴🦴

Mature subject matter, sexual content.

1995 **(R)** 119m/C Julianne Moore, Peter Friedman, Xander Berkeley, Susan Norman, James LeGros, Mary Carver, Kate McGregor Stewart; **D:** Todd Haynes; **W:** Todd Haynes; **C:** Alex Nepomniaschy; **M:** Ed Tomney. Nominations: Independent Spirit Awards '96: Best Actress (Moore), Best Director (Haynes), Best Film, Best Screenplay. **VHS, LV** *COL*

Saints and Sinners

A screwy supercharged energy makes up for a lean budget. Crime drama/buddy flick/romance focuses on two childhood friends and

their adventurous girlfriend. "Big Boy" Baynes (Scott Plank) is a rising star in the illegal drug distribution business despite the opposition of the reigning neighborhood gang; his buddy "Pooch" (Damian Chapa) is a cop whose treacherous boss has forced him undercover to nab "Big Boy." Eva (Jennifer Rubin) has a different story for everyone she meets and mysterious purposes of her own. The details of the innercity drug trade don't ring true but the characters have such a ferocious vitality that compensates. The three leads are really terrific with full-bore performances. Writer/producer/director Paul Mones overdoes some currently popular gimmicks—circling handheld camera, hyperactive editing—but he has still managed to make this one a lot more enjoyable than most crime movies with much bigger budgets. 𝄞𝄞𝄞

Violence, sexual content, strong language, brief nudity.

1995 (R) 99m/C Damian Chapa, Scott Plank, Jennifer Rubin, Damon Whitaker, Panchito Gomez, William Atherton; *D:* Paul Mones; *W:* Paul Mones; *C:* Michael Bonvillain. VHS, LV *LIV*

Satan's Princess

In the introductory scene—"1654, Barcelona, Spain"—the first character we see is a monk played by comedian Jack Carter and that's not the strangest part of this screwloose combination of *Dirty Harry* and *The Picture of Dorian*

Gray. Shift to the present. Cherney (Robert Forster) is a burnt-out ex-cop who agrees to help a man find his runaway daughter. But the girl has fallen under the spell of Nicole St. James (Lydie Denier), an immortal sorceress or something. Nicole has this long-haired sidekick, who looks like he was one of the second string bad guys in *Die Hard,* to do her bidding and bump off anyone who threatens to discover her secret. Stephen Katz's plot lurches drunkenly and is saved by its inventive unpredictability. The big action scenes don't develop much energy, but the rest of the story is about as sexually charged as an R-rated movie can be. That side of the story reaches its strangest point when a sizzling love scene is intercut with a family Christmas reunion that's so saccharine it would nauseate Norman Rockwell. Luckily, the ending is the nuttiest part of a very nutty movie. This is the kind of guilty pleasure that makes home video so enjoyable. 𝄞𝄞𝄞 **GPI: 8.2**

Nudity, strong sexual content, violence, profanity.

1990 (R) 90m/C Robert Forster, Caren Kaye, Lydie Denier, Jack Carter; *D:* Bert I. Gordon; *W:* Steven Katz. VHS *PAR*

Saturday Night Special

Body Heat meets *Urban Cowboy* and the results are mixed at best. Will the wiley Darleen (Maria Ford) seduce ex-con Travis (Billy Burnette) into bumping off the no-account hubby (Rick Dean)? There are no real surprises in the plot and director Dan Golden handles the physical action clumsily. Still, Maria Ford is a sexy, spirited heroine who steals the film from her co-stars. Also available in an unrated version. 𝄞𝄞 **GPI: 9.0**

Nudity and sexual material, some violence.

1992 (R) 75m/C Billy Burnette, Maria Ford, Rick Dean; *D:* Dan Golden; *W:* Jonathan Banks; *M:* Billy Burnette, Nicholas Rivera. VHS *NHO*

Savage Beach

Devotees of cinema Sidaris recognize this as one of the master's finest. It continues the adventures of two federal agents (*Playboy* Playmates Dona Spier and Hope Marie Carlton) in Hawaii and the South Pacific. The plot is a confused mess that revolves around a fortune in gold lost at the end of World War II. Sequel to *Picasso Trigger* and *Hard Ticket to Hawaii* is every bit as enjoyable a guilty pleasure as its predecessors. 🎬🎬🎬 **GPI: 8.8**

Nudity, sexual content, violence.

1989 (R) 90m/C Dona Speir, Hope Marie Carlton, Bruce Penhall, Rodrigo Obregon, John Aprea, Teri Weigel, Lisa London; **D:** Andy Sidaris. **VHS, LV** *COL*

Save Me

Thriller is tasteless and tawdry, but that's the point so criticism is pointless. Harry Hamlin is a stock broker whose work is suffering in direct relationship to his crumbling marriage. Then one day he spies Lysette Anthony as she's shopping for underwear (really!), and is smitten. But is her current beau (Michael Ironside) merely overprotective or abusive? When she passes a note saying "Save Me," he's hooked. Most videophiles will be two or three steps ahead all the way through, but, again, so what? The two stars are so convincing—he as a stud muffin made stupid by testosterone, she as a feral floozy—that the other shortcomings pale. Besides, any video that includes a scene at a monster truck show and then pretends to be superior to it is working on another plane. Credit director Alan Roberts with aiming low and hitting his target. Also available in an unrated version. 🎬🎬 **GPI: 8.5**

Nudity, sexual content, strong language, violence.

1993 (R) 89m/C Harry Hamlin, Lysette Anthony, Michael Ironside, Olivia Hussey, Bill Nunn, Steve Railsback; **D:** Alan Roberts; **W:** Neil Ronco; **M:** Rick Marvin. **VHS, LV** *COL*

Scandal

The R-rated version of Michael Caton-Jones' version of the famous 1963 Profumo-Keeler affair played theatrically, but the original contains ten minutes of footage that inexplicably earned it an X-rating from the MPAA. The offending scene is an orgy. The sexual action takes place in the background and the camera pans over it quickly. Viewers looking for cheap thrills will be disappointed. For a movie that's about sex, this is not a particularly sexy movie. The action revolves around the platonic relationship between Christine Keeler (Joanne Whalley) and Dr. Stephen Ward (John Hurt). It's about real people living messy lives in complicated times when rules were changing. They made a few mistakes and wound up toppling a government. Even though the film winds up becoming a little too moralistic, it is a fascinating, well-told, well-acted story. 🎬🎬🎬

Contains brief nudity, sexual scenes, profanity, adult subject matter.

1989 105m/C *GB* John Hurt, Joanne Whalley, Ian McKellen, Bridget Fonda, Jeroen Krabbe, Britt Ekland, Roland Gift, Daniel Massey, Leslie Phillips; **D:** Michael Caton-Jones; **W:** Michael Thomas; **M:** Carl Davis. **VHS, LV** *HBO*

Scoring

Would-be noirish suspense film follows a faithless composer, Eric Laszlo (Mark Porro), who's being stalked by someone acting out scenes from the movie he's scoring. For my money, the main attraction is the heroine, Abby (Dixie Jayne Beck), who looks like Julia Roberts with a big tattoo of a postage stamp on her butt. Also available in an unrated version. 🎬🎬

Mature subject matter, sexual content, nudity, violence, strong language.

1995 (R) 114m/C Dixie Beck, Mark Porro, Doug Jeffrey, Michele Brin, Wendy Hamilton, Monique Parent; **D:** Toby Phillips; **W:** Penny Antine. **VHS** *ROC*

Scream Dream

This howler deserves a place of honor in the Hall of Shame. Heavy metal rock singer Michelle Shock is everything Tipper Gore hates. Her songs lead good kids down the wrong path because she worships the devil. Sometimes she even turns into a monster, which leads her manager to kill her. But does that stop Michelle? Of course not. She takes over the body of her replacement and goes after everybody who did her dirt. If this video had two consecutive seconds of believability, it would be offensive and repulsive. But director Donald Farmer shows just how little you can do with no money and no talent. This is strictly amateur night in Cookeville, Ten-

nessee, where this shot-on-video epic was made. That's why it's so much fun. The tone is established at the beginning when Michelle seduces this button-down-collar kid from the suburbs. His facial expression, meant to convey blissful heights of sexual ecstasy, is worth the price of a rental all by itself. Overall, the level of non-acting and non-writing is Homeric. Then, toward the middle of the tape, another evil monster shows up, and it's obviously a hand puppet. I could go on, but to tell any more would spoil the fun. This is what bad video is all about. ✍✍✍

Rough language, brief nudity, sexual situations, preposterous violence, facial expressions, hand puppets.

1989 **(R)** 90m/C Melissa Moore, Carole Carr, Nikki Riggins, Jesse Ray; **D:** Donald Farmer; **W:** Donald Farmer. **VHS** *NO*

The Search for One-Eyed Jimmy

Low-budget New York ensemble comedies have become a mini-staple of the video business in recent years. *The Search for One-Eye Jimmy* is a shaggy dog story about a young filmmaker (Holt McCallany) who goes back to his Brooklyn neighborhood and gets caught up with his old buddies—Nicholas Turturro and Michael Badalucco—as they go looking for another missing pal. Anne Meara, Jennifer Beals, John Turturro, and Samuel L. Jackson show up for colorful cameos. Writer/director Sam Henry Kass captures that on-the-fly quality of a good independent production, but this one isn't as enjoyable as *My Life's in Turnaround, Blue in the Face,* or several others that were cut from the same celluloid. ✍✍✍

Strong language.

1996 **(R)** 86m/C Holt McCallany, Nicholas Turturro, Steve Buscemi, Michael Badalucco, Ray "Boom Boom" Mancini, Anne Meara, John Turturro, Samuel L. Jackson, Sam Rockwell, Jennifer Beals; **D:** Sam Henry Kass; **W:** Sam Henry Kass; **C:** Charles Levey; **M:** William Bloom. **VHS** *CAF*

Season of Fear

A son (Michael Bowen) resents his father (Ray Wise), an inventor who deserted his family

years before and went on to become rich. Dad now has a sexy young wife (Clare Wren), and when the grown son comes to visit, smoldering glances are exchanged, fancies are tickled, nostrils flare, temperatures rise. You know the drill. Too often, writer/director Douglas Campbell resorts to MTV visuals and pointless effects that add nothing to the story. But toward the end those flaws become unimportant because the plot flips out. Still, this one does have its moments, particularly when Michael J. Pollard shows up as the world's nuttiest gas station attendant. (In his first scene, he puts a mouse in a vise.) ✍✍✍ **GPI: 8.0**

Mature subject matter, sexual situations, violence, brief nudity, mouse abuse.

1989 **(R)** 89m/C Michael Bowen, Clancy Brown, Clare Wren, Ray Wise, Michael J. Pollard; **D:** Douglas Campbell; **W:** Douglas Campbell. **VHS** *FOX*

The Secret Files of J. Edgar Hoover

This is the stuff of tabloids—sexy, tacky, and probably more accurate than not. The focus here is on the surveillance that the FBI carried out during the Hoover years and the embarrassing material that the director used to maintain his power and control public officials. The scandalous stuff, narrated by actor Mike Connors, was obtained through the Freedom of Information Act and has been broadcast as a syndicated TV program. The writing varies from average to poor. The tales of President Kennedy's sexual escapades before and after his marriage are tawdry and fascinating. ✍✍

Some sexual content.

1991 120m/C **VHS** *FUS, CCP, 3GH*

Secret Games

Michele Brin's husband (Billy Drago) pays more attention to his work than to her. Instead of doing volunteer work or taking a course in introductory auto mechanics at the community college, she decides to become a part-time prostitute. Actually, her best friend talks her into it. Seems she belongs to the "Afternoon

Demitasse," a group of equally bored rich women who supplement their shopping funds. They work out of an ornate mansion where they tart themselves up like refugees from a Madonna music video, showing off their favorite tattoos and thongs, and entertain well-heeled gentleman callers. Everyone is having a fine time until their new client (Martin Hewitt) turns out to be a bit of a psycho. Bummer. Throughout, the production values are first rate. The action tends toward well-lighted, glossy romanticism, and no one involved took this soft-core foolishness seriously. Followed by two sequels to date. Also available in an unrated version at 98 minutes. 𝄇𝄇𝄇 **GPI: 8.3**

Nudity, sexual situations, strong language, no real violence.

1992 (R) 90m/C Martin Hewitt, Michele Brin, Delia Sheppard, Billy Drago; **D:** Alexander Gregory Hippolyte **VHS** *IMP*

Secret Games 2: The Escort

Kyle Lake (Martin Hewitt) makes a dubious career change from critic to performance artist. His wife is not amused, so Kyle records a series of "artistic" tapes with a woman he meets through an escort service. The rest of the plot is based on the differences between men and women that fill the self-help best seller lists and the guest line-ups of Oprah, Montel, et al. Soft-core veteran Hippolyte has given the film a highly polished look with dark gleaming sets, low-key lighting, and a soundtrack filled with classical music and Gregorian chants. Also available in an unrated version at 92 minutes. 𝄇𝄇 **GPI: 8.1**

Strong language, nudity, sexual content, some violence.

1993 (R) ?m/C Martin Hewitt, Amy Rochelle, Sara Suzanne Brown, Marie Leroux; **D:** Alexander Gregory Hippolyte; **W:** Russell Lavalle; **M:** Ashley Irwin. **VHS** *IMP*

Secret Games 3

The plot of the first film is repeated with a new cast. The results are about the same. Also available in an unrated version. 𝄇𝄇 **GPI: 8.2**

Sexual content, nudity, strong language.

1994 (R) 82m/C Woody Brown, Brenda Swanson, Rochelle Swanson; **D:** Alexander Gregory Hippolyte. **VHS** *ACA*

Sensation

Professor Burton (Eric Roberts) enlists co-ed Lyla (Kari Wuhrer) in his "psychometry" experiments. She receives visions of other people from objects they've owned. But the good doctor is giving her stuff that belonged to a girl who was killed a year before. The murder still hasn't been solved, and the girl was Burton's lover. What's going on? Before long, other suspects are popping up everywhere—nerdy student Kieran Mulroney, voyeuristic landlord Paul LeMat, ominous stranger Ed Begley, Jr., detective Ron Perlman, the prof's current girlfriend Claire Stansfield. Director Brian Grant tells the story with some innovative visual flourishes involving paint, ceiling fans, and odd camera angles. Most of the spooky moments are effective and surprising; others are silly. (That's always a possibility when Roberts cuts loose.) Kari Wuhrer could be Marisa Tomei's sexy sister, though her limitations are obvious in the big emotional scenes. That's not a real problem, though. Lightweight thrillers succeed or fail on style and this one has all that it needs. 𝄇𝄇𝄇

Nudity, sexual material, mild violence.

1994 (R) 102m/C Kari Wuhrer, Eric Roberts, Ron Perlman, Ed Begley Jr., Paul LeMat, Claire Stansfield, Kieran Mulroney, Tracey Needham; **D:** Brian Grant; **W:** Doug Wallace; **M:** Arthur Kempel. **VHS, LV** *COL*

Sentinel 2099

Ultra-low-budget science fiction is slowly paced, grainy, and hard to follow. After an introduction that makes full use of black-and-white stock footage, possibly from World War II, director Mike McGee turns his attention to an alien invasion (by blue people) and the crew of a war machine that looks a lot like one of the "walkers" in *Return of the Jedi*. Any other resemblance to George Lucas' films ends right there. The rest involves stop-motion animation and often-repeated flashbacks. The

SGT. KABUKIMAN N.Y.P.D.
©TROMA TEAM VIDEO.

Pressfield and director David Madden aren't as successful or as imaginative with it. For a time, their mystery is engaging and tricky, but at key moments the filmmakers don't get close enough to their characters for the audience to become fully sympathetic. That's a criticism that could be made of many films, both theatrical and video. A more serious flaw is the over-reliance on cheap scares that undercut the stars' usual good work. 🎬🎬

Mature subject matter, strong language, violence, sexual content, brief nudity.

1994 (R) 101m/C Linda Hamilton, James Belushi, Vera Miles, Elissabeth Moss, Drew Snyder, Mark Lindsay Chapman, Marc Poppel, Elizabeth Arlen; **D:** David Madden; **W:** Steven Pressfield; **M:** William Olvis. **VHS** *VMK*

Sgt. Kabukiman N.Y.P.D.

Superhero spoof is the *Citizen Kane* of Troma movies! The budget is still low, the look still grainy—this is still Troma, after all—but the humor has a sharp edge and attitude to burn. Sgt. Harry Griswold (Rick Gianisi) is magically transformed into Kabukiman, with makeup and costume based on a character in the traditional Japanese theatre. The whys and wherefores of Harry's elevation to this new status are not completely clear, but they do involve eating worms. His antagonist is a billionaire who has hatched some sort of astrological plan to rule the world, or something to that effect. This bad guy has enlisted the help of street thugs and a larcenous black preacher in his nefarious scheme. Kabukiman's weapons are flying chopsticks, full-contact sushi, and his slam bang parasol. Unfortunately, Harry doesn't know how to use all of his new Kabuki powers and his Japanese girlfriend (Susan Byun) provides little help. Troma founders and co-directors Lloyd Kaufman and Michael Herz keep the action fast and silly, and they don't let their strong liberal social commentary get in the way. I hope this is the first in a long series. 🎬🎬🎬

Violence, strong language, subject matter.

1994 (PG-13) 104m/C Rick Gianisi, Susan Byun, Brick Bronsky; **D:** Lloyd (Samuel Weil) Kaufman, Michael Herz; **W:** Andrew Osborn, Lloyd (Samuel Weil) Kaufman; **C:** Bob Williams; **M:** Bob Mithoff. **VHS** *TRO*

effects range from relatively crude models to effective explosions and such. 🎬

Violence, strong language.

1995 (PG-13) 62m/C D: Mike McGee. **VHS**

Separate Lives

Well-acted thriller doesn't measure up to its premise. Teaching psychologist Lauren Porter (Linda Hamilton) has a problem—nightly blackouts. She wakes up the next morning with dried blood on her hands and no idea how it got there. That's why she asks a student, ex-cop Tom Beckwith (James Belushi), to follow her when she goes out. Yes, Robert Heinlein chose that situation for his terrific short story "The Unpleasant Profession of Jonathan Hoag." Unfortunately, writer Steven

The Serpent of Death

Archeological adventure was made on location in Europe and the Middle East. The pace is quick throughout, but the plot, as often as not, makes absolutely no sense. I never quite figured it all out, but I'm sure that a semi-shady graduate student (Jeff Fahey), a solar-powered car, a billionaire, his mistress, a piece of ancient Greek pottery, the Egyptian equivalent of Tony Orlando and Dawn, and a bag of snakes were all involved. Flaws and all, this one has the goofy appeal of an old serial. 𝄞𝄞

Strong language, sexual content, brief nudity, violence.

1990 (R) 90m/C Jeff Fahey; *D:* Anwar Kawadri. **VHS, LV** *PAR*

The Seventh Coin

Teen adventure has a slight s-f element—a coin minted by King Herod—and it's the motivation for a long chase set in contemporary Jerusalem. The main characters are bad guy Emil Saber (Peter O'Toole); a Palestinian street kid, Selim (Narin Chowdhry); and Ronnie (Alexandra Powers), an American teenager on vacation. Providing support are John Rhys-Davies as the top cop and Ally Walker as a comic policewoman. The plot won't win any prizes for originality, but writer/director Dror Soref does a good job with the young characters. They're believable enough and likeable. He also made effective use of the locations. Much of the action takes place on rooftops, giving the city an exotic, sun-bleached look. With two onscreen killings, the PG-13 rating is questionable but, on balance, there's nothing here that's too strong for most younger videophiles. 𝄞𝄞𝄞

Violence, brief nudity.

1992 (PG-13) 92m/C Alexandra Powers, Navin Chowdhry, Peter O'Toole, John Rhys-Davies, Ally Walker; *D:* Dror Soref; *W:* Michael Lewis, Dror Soref; *C:* Avi Karpik. **VHS, LV** *HMD*

Sex, Love and Cold Hard Cash

Colson (Anthony John Denison) has served ten years of hard time for armed robbery. He didn't rat on his pals because he knows there's a million waiting for him when he gets out. Sara (Jobeth Williams) is an expensive prostitute who has managed to save $750,000 over ten years and is ready to retire. Each of them gets a nasty surprise. The mechanics of the plot are clumsy, and in that regard, the film is never particularly involving. The slowly developed love story is much more interesting than the crime story. Williams is a good flinty pragmatist. If Denison seems too distant and cold, he gives his character the sense of off-balance uncertainty that must be a part of someone who's just been released from an institution. As these two are getting to know each other, the story has the unpredictability of a good Elmore Leonard novel. If that quality had been carried over to the rest of the film, this one would be a real hit, despite its made-for-cable production values. Still, it rates a qualified recommendation. 𝄞𝄞𝄞

Violence, sexual content.

1993 (PG-13) 86m/C JoBeth Williams, Anthony John Denison; *D:* Harry S. Longstreet; *W:* Harry S. Longstreet. **VHS** *MCA*

Sexual Malice

Despite its title, this erotic thriller also has a certain feminist angle. It's essentially a long-form version of the famous "It's 11:30" Coke commercial where the office women watch the construction worker take off his shirt. The situation: wealthy fast-track lawyer Diana Barton unhappily married to college teacher Edward Albert falls for male stripper John Laughlin. Director Jag Mundhra is a veteran at this kind of soft-core fluff. Roughly the first half of the film keeps to the women's perspective; the second turns to conventional male fantasies. As is so often the case with this genre, the film looks slick—downright gaudy at times—and the acting isn't bad either. 𝄞𝄞𝄞 **GPI: 8.5**

Nudity and sexual material, some violence.

1993 (R) 96m/C Diana Barton, John Laughlin, Chad McQueen, Edward Albert, Don Swayze, Kathy Shower, Samantha Phillips; *D:* Jag Mundhra; *W:* Carl Austin. **VHS** *APX*

Worth a look. Also available in an unrated version. 🦴🦴🦴

Nudity, sexual content, strong language, and mild violence.

1994 (R) 90m/C Mitch Gaylord, Erika West; *D:* Edwin Scott Brown; *W:* Edwin Scott Brown, Summer Brown. **VHS** *MNC*

Sexual Response

The indefatigable Shannon Tweed plays Dr. Robinson, a repressed radio sex therapist who can't follow her own advice. She becomes personally involved with a caller, a suspicious artist-type named Edge (Emile Levisetti) who favors beard stubble and carefully tattered denim. Her domineering husband (Vernon Wells) pays more attention to his hunting rifle than to her. The story has a few neat conspiratorial surprises toward the end and even if the action scenes are weak, the production values are first rate throughout. Richard Berger's music is particularly good. After a slow start, this one's better than the silly title. Also available in an unrated version at 90 minutes. 🦴🦴
GPl: 8.5

Nudity, sexual subject matter, some strong language.

1992 (R) 87m/C Shannon Tweed, Catherine Oxenberg, Vernon Wells, Emile Levisetti; *D:* Yaky Yosha; *M:* Richard Berger. **VHS**, **LV** *COL*

Sexual Outlaws

Conventional guilty pleasure turns out to be pretty good. The main attraction is Olympic gold medalist Mitch Gaylord who turns in an effective performance as Francis, a mute ex-con. Days after his parole he finds himself involved with a couple who publish an erotic magazine. Like Francis, they have trouble with the law. While her husband is busy with the magazine (and other activities), Lisa (Erika West) becomes intrigued with Francis' situation. When the plot focuses on the murder of a prostitute, it becomes standard video stuff. Overall though, the acting is above average, and Edwin Brown, director and co-writer (with Summer Brown), handles the characters well. The conclusion leaves room for a sequel.

S.F.W.

Underachieving teen Cliff Spab (Stephen Dorff, looking for all the world like the winner of the Corey Feldman lookalike contest) is taken hostage by terrorists in a convenience store. He becomes a TV hero for his oft-repeated philosophical statement, "So f—— what?" hence the title. The film's problems are obvious. First, it's almost impossible to parody today's media culture, where nothing exceeds like excess. Second, adolescent nihilism is inherently boring and false. Third, that nihilism turns out to be a smokescreen for your basic dork-loves-cheerleader story, with the innocuous Reese Witherspoon as the object of Spab's affections. **WOOF!**

Strong language, sexual humor and situations, brief nudity.

1994 (R) 92m/C Stephen Dorff, Reese Witherspoon, Jake Busey, Joey Adams, Pamela Gidley, David Barry Gray, Jack Noseworthy, Richard Portnow; *D:* Jefery Levy; *W:* Jefery Levy, James Foley. **VHS** *PGV*

Shadowzone

In a secret underground government facility, something goes wrong with a sleep experiment and a warty creature from another dimension drops in for a visit. He promptly begins making lunch out of anyone who's wearing a lab coat. Among the unlucky few are James Hong, Shawn Weatherly, and Louise Fletcher, who has all the intensity of a woman waiting for a bus. It's obvious that this flick was made on a blue-light special budget, but that's no excuse. This is grade-B material that takes itself seriously, and that's always a fatal combination. **WOOF!**

Violence, bloody special effects, strong language, brief nudity.

1989 (R) 88m/C Louise Fletcher, David Beecroft, James Hong, Shawn Weatherly, Lu Leonard; *D:* J.S. Cardone; *W:* J.S. Cardone. **VHS, LV** *PAR*

Shameless

Model Elizabeth Hurley is surprisingly effective (and realistically unsympathetic) as Antonia, a spoiled upper-class junkie who's mixed up with several shady types. Mike (C. Thomas Howell) is the naive American who falls for her and spends far too much time playing with his hair. The supporting cast—led by the always solid Jeremy Brett, as a snobbish pusher, and Joss Ackland, as a cop with questionable motives—easily lifts the film from the attractive stars. Writer Tim Sewell's story becomes needlessly complicated and confusing at times. Director Henry Cole keeps things moving brightly. He creates a sense of buzzy, drugged-out depravity in a world of pampered luxury that lifts the thriller above the normal level of the genre. *AKA:* Mad Dogs and Englishmen. 🦴🦴🦴

Drug use, violence, sexual content, brief nudity, strong language.

1994 (R) 99m/C *GB* Elizabeth Hurley, C. Thomas Howell, Joss Ackland, Jeremy Brett, Frederick Treves, Claire Bloom, Louise Delamere, Chris Adamson, Paula Hamilton; *D:* Henry Cole; *W:* Tim Sewell; *C:* John Peters; *M:* Barrie Guard. **VHS** *BMG*

Sharon's Secret

Legal/medical/psychological thriller never rises above its uninspired formula roots. Dr. Laurel O'Connor (Mel Harris) is called in by the police when it appears that 16-year-old Sharon (Candace Cameron) has murdered her wealthy parents. Is Sharon's catatonic stupor real? Drug-induced? Faked? And what about the unflattering episode from Dr. O'Connor's past that appears to be replaying itself? The story develops some fitful energy when it moves into family secrets, but throughout it's flatly acted and directed with long scenes focused on characters who stand around and talk. Then in the fiery finish, you can see the safety wire holding one character up. Real mystery fans demand much better. 🦴

Mature subject matter, strong language.

1995 (R) 91m/C Candace Cameron, Mel Harris, Greg Henry, Alex McArthur, Paul Regina, Elaine Kagan, James Pickens Jr.; *D:* Michael Scott; *W:* Mark Homer. **VHS** *MCA*

Shock 'Em Dead

Rock 'n' roll horror flick presents perhaps the most impressive lack of talent ever collected on one tape. It's a terrific unintentional comedy. When Stephen Quadros sells his soul to the devil, he is immediately transformed into a rock star, complete with long black wig, leather britches, excessive jewelry, mascara, mansion, and groupies. The downside is that he's a vampire. Then he falls for band manager Traci Lords. Admittedly, some of the jokes are intentional and many of them are funny, but this one wouldn't suffer from liberal use of the fast-forward button. 🦴🦴 **GPI: 6.0**

Strong language, sex, violence, nudity.

1990 (R) 94m/C Traci Lords, Aldo Ray, Troy Donahue, Stephen Quadros; *D:* Mark Freed; *W:* Andrew Cross. **VHS, LV** *ACA*

Shopping

Stylish thriller is thoroughly watchable despite thoroughly unsympathetic characters—*A Clockwork Orange* with fast cars. In a desolate, nightmarish England, Billy (Jude Law) is a nihilistic thief. Jo (Sadie Frost) picks him up when he gets out of jail and helps him work his way back to the top of their young criminal clique. Writer/director Paul Anderson combines striking action scenes and grubby visuals to create a thin, zippy story. Give this guy a few breaks and he'll be working with much better projects. 🦴🦴🦴

Strong language, violence.

1993 (R) 86m/C *GB* Jude Law, Sadie Frost, Sean Pertwee, Fraser James, Sean Bean, Marianne Faithfull, Jonathan Pryce, Danny Newman; **D:** Paul Anderson; **W:** Paul Anderson; **C:** Tony Imi; **M:** Barrington Pheloung. **VHS** *NHO*

Shotgun

Micro-budget shoot-'em-up is about cops, prostitutes, drug dealers, and kinky lawyers. Logic makes an early exit. This one is trying to be grittily realistic, but it's so amateurish that in the end, it's just gritty. 🦴

Violence, strong language, brief nudity.

1989 90m/C Stuart Chapin, Katie Caple; **D:** Addison Randall. **VHS** *PMH*

Showdown in Little Tokyo

Dolph Lundgren is an American cop who was raised in Japan. Brandon Lee is a cop of Japanese ancestry who's so Americanized he doesn't even know what sushi is. Together they must stop tattooed gangster Cary-Hiroyuki Tagawa from taking over Los Angeles' Little Tokyo. In the process, every buddy-picture cliche and fantasy gets its due. The late Lee demonstrates some good moves and a light touch with dialogue. Lundgren's comedy is harder to define. He's got an uncanny ability to make his face a smooth, expressionless blank slate. Bo Derek can do it too, but Lundgren is a master. He looks like he has completely separated his brain from his central nervous system; it's down right spooky. The bone-crunching fight scenes are comically outlandish. The mixture of sex, violence, and poor taste is so strong that this one deserves a hard R-rating, which is just what fans are looking for. 🦴🦴🦴

Strong language, nudity, violence.

1991 (R) 78m/C Dolph Lundgren, Brandon Lee, Tia Carrere, Cary-Hiroyuki Tagawa; **D:** Mark L. Lester; **W:** Caliope Brattlestreet. **VHS, LV** *WAR*

Showgirl Murders

Bad movie isn't bad enough to be fun. The low-budget faux-noir suspense flick is about the conniving Jessica (Maria Ford) who steals some drug money and runs away to become a stripper at Mitch's (Matt Preston) failing bar. If only she could get Mrs. Mitch (Samantha Carter) out of the way. The plot is as boney as our body-pierced heroine who has never looked more anorexic. The whole film is similar to but not nearly as enjoyable as the so-so *Saturday Night Special*. Also available in an unrated version. 🦴🦴 **GPI: 5.0**

Nudity, sexual content, violence, strong language.

1995 (R) m/C Maria Ford, Matt Preston, Samantha Carter; **D:** Gene Hertel. **VHS** *NHO*

Showgirls

Filmmaker John Waters probably summed it up best on the *Tonight Show* when he told Jay Leno, "It's big budget, it's bad, and it's dirty!" So, what's not to like? For starters, there's the NC-17 rating which bothered Blockbuster Video. Because of that, MGM decided to reverse the trend that we often see with trashy Hollywood movies. Usually, an R-rated version plays in theatres, then six months later, the "unedited director's cut" appears on video. Instead, MGM took the Joe Ezterhas-Paul Verhoeven epic about Las Vegas nude dancing, and cut three minutes from its theatrical NC-17 to a tamer unrated version. They also changed the box art, but Blockbuster still said no. So more cuts were made, the film was resubmitted to the MPAA ratings board and it got an R-rating. Finally, Blockbuster said yes. Is the movie worth all the fuss? Of course not! As Waters said, it's bad and it's dirty, and to see the movie in any form other than its worst and dirtiest misses the point. It's an unintentional comedy about showbiz that has already earned a place beside *Valley of the Dolls* and *Mommie Dearest*. As a movie that you laugh at instead of with, it's wonderful. 🦐🦐 **GPI: 8.6**

Abundant nudity, strong sexual material, language, rape, violence.

1995 (NC-17) 131m/C Elizabeth Berkley, Gina Gershon, Kyle MacLachlan, Glenn Plummer, Alan Rachins, Robert Davi, Gina Ravera; *D:* Paul Verhoeven; *W:* Joe Eszterhas; *C:* Jost Vacano; *M:* David A. Stewart. Golden Raspberry Awards '95: Worst Picture, Worst Actress (Berkley), Worst Director (Verhoeven), Worst Screenplay, Worst Song ("Walk into the Wind"), Worst New Star (Berkley); Nominations: Golden Raspberry Awards '95: Worst Actor (MacLachlan), Worst Supporting Actor (Davi), Worst Supporting Actress (Gershon). **VHS** *MGM*

The Shrimp on the Barbie

Misfired comedy more or less wastes the considerable talents of Cheech Marin. He plays his usual underachiever who opens a Mexican restaurant in Australia. To irritate her domineering father, wealthy Emma Samms pretends to be engaged to him. She's spoiled and stuffy; he's crude and zesty. For a price, he agrees to go along with the joke and to spend a weekend at the family estate. You know exactly how it's going to end. Some of Marin's raunchy humor is spontaneous and bright. Other bits seem forced. Surprisingly, Marin is also effective in the quieter, more realistic moments. But, taken as a whole, the movie is never as good as it should or could be. Note that it was directed by Alan Smithee, the pseudonym that members of the Director's Guild are allowed to adopt when they are dissatisfied with the result of their work. 🦐🦐 **GPI: 4.4**

Strong language, sex, violence, nudity, etc.

1990 (R) 86m/C Richard "Cheech" Marin, Emma Samms, Vernon Wells, Bruce Spence, Carole Davis; *D:* Alan Smithee. **VHS, LV** *MED, VTR*

The Siege of Firebase Gloria

Vietnam film deserves to be ranked with *The Boys in Company C* and *Go Tell the Spartans*, two other underrated films that tried to show the war on a personal level while commenting on the contradictory politics of that time and place. It's based on a true incident: the defense of an outpost by a group of Marines during the Tet Offensive of January, 1968. The main characters are Sgt. Hafner (R. Lee Ermey), Sgt. DiNardo (Wings Hauser), and Cao Van (Robert Arevalo), leader of the Viet Cong attack. Writers William Nagle and Tony Johnston and director Brian Trenchard-Smith base their telling of the story on another great war film, *Zulu*. The central conflict in both is the same: a small number of outsiders try to hold a fort against a much larger force of native attackers who want them to leave. Sgt. Hafner provides voiceover narration to clarify the often confusing action at the firebase and the equally confusing political and military situation in the whole country. At times, the filmmakers fall back on war movie cliches, which is probably inevitable. At other times, the story is too emotional and too simplistic in dealing with the characters, especially one Vietnamese orphan who's meant to symbolize the entire country. But those flaws mean little compared to the clear-eyed view of the war that the film presents. This one isn't about good guys and bad guys. There's more than enough guilt and horror and madness to go around. The sight of American soldiers executing wounded Vietnamese in the field is still chilling. That refusal to take a political point of view gives the film an unusual depth. It also heightens the tension of the battle scenes because it's so difficult for the viewer to take a convenient side. Again, the similarities to *Zulu* are telling. Firebreathers of the left and right will not find much comfort here. For everyone else, *Firebase Gloria* reveals a pivotal moment in history with intelligence, drama, courage, insight, and finally, sadness. 🦐🦐🦐

Graphic violence and profanity.

1989 (R) 95m/C Wings Hauser, R. Lee Ermey, Robert Arevalo; *D:* Brian Trenchard-Smith; *W:* William Nagle, Tony Johnston. **VHS, LV** *FRH*

Silence of the Hams

Horror parody—in part an Italian production financed by ex-President Silvio Berlusconi—is

more silly than funny. When the main characters are FBI agent Jo Dee Fostar (Billy Zane) and Dr. Animal Cannibal Pizza (Dom DeLuise), and the first sight gag involves a flaming toilet, you know you're not dealing with refined material. The high points (if they can be called that) are an extended parody of *Psycho*, with Charlene Tilton in the Janet Leigh role and Martin Balsam repeating his work in the original, and lots of cameo appearances by such second-tier comics as Larry Storch, Rip Taylor, Shelley Winters, and Phyllis Diller looking for all the world like the ghost of Estelle Getty. No one involved took a second of it seriously, giving the entire production a slap-happy, laid back quality. 🎞🎞

Strong language, comic violence, bathroom humor.

1993 **(R)** 85m/C Ezio Greggio, Dom DeLuise, Billy Zane, Joanna Pacula, Charlene Tilton, Martin Balsam; *Cameos:* Stuart Pankin, John Astin, Phyllis Diller, Bubba Smith, Larry Storch, Rip Taylor, Shelley Winters, Mel Brooks, John Landis, John Carpenter, Joe Dante; *D:* Ezio Greggio; *W:* Ezio Greggio; *C:* Jacques Haitkin. **VHS** *CAF*

The Silencer

Fast-paced secret agent spoof has a feminist slant. Writer/director Amy Goldstein was working with an extremely low budget, so at times, her work looks more like an electronic game than a real movie. It's as stylized as a music video and it makes about as much sense. Hitwoman Angel (Lynette Walden), who looks just like the dark-haired Madonna of four or five years ago, comes out of retirement to bump off a bunch of guys who are involved with prostitution. Imagine James Bond in a bustier and you've got the idea. Between jobs, Angel treats stud-muffins just like 007 has always treated bimbos. The action is as silly, hammy, and tasteless as it could possibly be. In fact, the film actually manages to live up (or down) to the copy on the box: "Caress It...Squeeze It...Feel The Kick...." 🎞🎞🎞

GPI: 6.0

Violence, nudity, sexual content, strong language.

1992 **(R)** 85m/C Lynette Walden, Chris Mulkey, Paul Ganus, Morton Downey Jr.; *D:* Amy Goldstein; *W:* Amy Goldstein, Scott Kraft **VHS** *ACA*

The Silencers

PM Entertainment specializes in action films that borrow from big screen, big budget hits. This one retreads *Stargate* and *The Hidden* with surprisingly enjoyable results. It begins with pale-faced, black-haired men in wide brimmed hats and sunglasses. No, they're not Michael Jackson impersonators; they're somehow connected with aliens. Rafferty (Jack Scalia) is a Secret Service agent guarding a Senator these guys want to kill. Rafferty gets help from another alien, Comdor (Dennis Christopher), who spouts quasi-mystical Hollywood claptrap with tongue firmly in cheek. The mad scientists' lab is also handled with a sense of humor. Lots of stuff explodes, and in one bizarre moment a car on the street appears to hit a helicopter in the sky, but so what? It's done with style. 🎞🎞🎞

Violence, strong language.

1995 **(R)** 103m/C Jack Scalia, Dennis Christopher, Clarence Williams III, Carlos Lauchu, Lucinda Weist; *D:* Richard Pepin. **VHS** *PMH*

Silent Fall

An impressive cast is wasted in service of an unbelievable but obvious mystery. Child psychologist Jake Rainer (Richard Dreyfuss) is called in to help a murder investigation where the only witnesses are a young autistic boy, Tim (Ben Faulkner), and his older sister, Sylvie (Liv Tyler). Their parents were stabbed to death in the bedroom of their lakefront estate. Though Jake has one of those cliched secrets in his past, he and his wife Karen (Linda Hamilton) agree to help, treating Tim with personal therapy. His rival (John Lithgow) wants to give the kid a dose of a powerful drug with risky side effects. Director Bruce Beresford handles things competently, but the script depends on such flimsy and improbable psychological motivations and symptoms that it's difficult to become involved with the story. And in the last reel, it all pretty much falls apart. 🎞

Mature subject matter, violence, strong language.

1994 (R) 101m/C Richard Dreyfuss, Ben Faulkner, John Lithgow, Liv Tyler, Linda Hamilton, J.T. Walsh; *D:* Bruce Beresford; *W:* Akiva Goldsman; *M:* Stewart Copeland. **VHS, LV** *WAR*

Silver Strand

In an unashamed carbon copy of *An Officer and a Gentleman*, Gil Bellows takes over for Richard Gere. He's Brian Del Piso, an ensign in the Navy's S.E.A.L. school. Taking over for Debra Winger is pallid Nicolette Sheridan as the commanding officer's wife. Change the marital status of the supporting characters and the subplots are the same, too. Director George Miller (*Les Patterson Saves the World*) brings real energy to the training scenes, and he makes the most of a few well-chosen visual and sound effects. Bellows does good work in the lead, too. So, despite the been-there-done-that familiarity, this one's kind of fun. 🗡🗡🗡

Violence, strong language, sexual content, fleeting nudity.

1995 (R) 104m/C Gil Bellows, Nicolette Sheridan; *D:* George Miller; *W:* Douglas Day Stewart; *C:* David Connell; *M:* Joseph Conlan. **VHS** *MGM*

Sinful Intrigue

Soft-core mystery is nothing more than an excuse to display lots of surgically enhanced young ladies in their lingerie. Beyond that, it's all rather restrained and tasteful, which is not exactly the point. 🗡🗡 **GPI: 7.3**

Nudity, sexual content, strong language, feigned violence.

1995 (R) 88m/C Griffin Drew, Bobby Johnston, Beckie Mullen; *D:* Edward Holzman. **VHS** *PMH*

Sins of the Night

Shameless knockoff of *Basic Instinct* is a lot more fun and a lot sexier than the original. It's a pseudo-noir thriller about ex-con Jack Nietzsche (Nick Cassavetes) who's found a job with an insurance company uncovering fraudulent claims. His corrupt boss (Matt Roe) orders Jack to find Roxy Flowers (Deborah Shelton), an exotic dancer and ex-prostitute who's now married to a big-time gangster (Miles O'Ke-

effe). With a voiceover narration lifted from *Double Indemnity* and oodles of gratuitous sex scenes, Jack works through a none-too-complicated plot involving assorted double- and triple-crosses. There's nothing fancy about any of this, but veteran soft-core director Gregory Hippolyte gives the heavy-breathing action a nice tongue-in-cheek quality and then caps it off with an absolutely right ending. Also available in an unrated version at 90 minutes. 🗡🗡🗡 **GPI: 9.0**

1993 (R) 82m/C Nick Cassavetes, Deborah Shelton, Matt Roe, Miles O'Keeffe; *D:* Alexander Gregory Hippolyte. **VHS** *ACA*

The Sister-in-Law

1970s soft-core drive-in fare is an early work from the director who went on to make the all-time cult fav *The Stepfather* and the theatrical hit *Sleeping With the Enemy*. It's a strange story about familial conflicts and the destructive nature of the drug business. Of course, those staples of the genre—sex, nudity, and fairly graphic violence—are well represented. Most of the filming was done on location and so the sound quality and lighting are less than perfect. The acting is pretty amateurish, too, and the rambling script is pretentious at times. To the film's credit though, it does show us a fairly accurate picture of the way we looked and the things we thought about so many years ago. And the ending is something of a surprise. 🗡🗡

Violence, profanity, brief sexual activity, nudity.

1974 (R) 80m/C John Savage, Anne Saxon, W.G. McMillan, Meredith Baer; *D:* Joseph Rubin. **VHS** *PSM*

Sister, My Sister

Virtually any description or synopsis would make this one sound like pure exploitation. It concerns two women who have an incestuous lesbian relationship and then savagely murder their employers. But in this telling—it's the same true story that inspired Jean Genet's play *The Maids*—the sexual and violent elements are muted. It's a horror film based on emotion. For comparative purposes, imagine a combination of *Upstairs, Downstairs* and

other women? Director Nancy Meckler handles the action deftly, creating tension and suspense in small moments. And the cast handles the claustrophobic material without a single misstep. All that's really lacking is a final unexpected twist, but this is still an engrossing and carefully shaded psychological study. It's also the kind of "little" film that has made a place for itself in the American video market. 𝄞𝄞𝄞𝄞

Sexual material, violence.

1994 (R) 89m/C *GB* Julie Walters, Joely Richardson, Jodhi May, Sophie Thursfield; *D:* Nancy Meckler; *W:* Wendy Kellelman; *C:* Ashley Ropwe; *M:* Stephen Warbeck. **VHS** *APX*

16 Days of Glory: Parts 1 and 2

Bud Greenspan's documentary on the 1984 Los Angeles Olympics focuses on half a dozen or so events. Conventional wins and records are less important than true competition and drama, whether that is a contest between two evenly matched individuals or inner competition. Narration is kept to a minimum. Greenspan uses slow motion, ingenious cutting, and music to enhance the suspense of the games, but for the important moments, he lets the action speak for itself. Yes, he's pushing a lot of the same emotional buttons that beer and soft-drink montage commercials hammer so relentlessly, but his technique is still effective. 𝄞𝄞𝄞

Contains a little strong language.

1984 147m/C *D:* Bud Greenspan. **VHS, LV** *PAR*

Skeeter

'90s version of a '50s drive-in creature feature—*Tarantula, Them,* or any of the big bug movies. Something strange is going on in the little mountain town of Clear Sky and horror fans know that the illegal toxic waste dump has something to do with it. Our hero and heroine are forgettable mannequins. The presence of Charles Napier as the corrupt sheriff and Michael J. Pollard as the town's mad fool do a lot to perk things up. The effects

Roman Polanski's *Repulsion.* It's France, 1932. Christine (Joely Richardson), famous for her needlework, is maid to Madame Danzard (Julie Walters) and her daughter Isabelle (Sophie Thursfield). When Christine asks if her younger sister Lea (Jodhi May) can come to work at their prosperous middle-class house, Madame says yes. At first, Christine is ecstatic. Lea is the only person in the world she cares about. Their relationship with their mother, who left their upbringing to nuns, is ambiguous and troubled. Not nearly as quick or handy as Christine, Lea has trouble with her work. Before long, Madame's petty perfectionism becomes more hateful and the house becomes a prison. From the opening moments, the viewer knows that the story ends in violence. But how does it come to that? What drives two women to murder two

are more silly than scary because it's almost impossible to make flying monsters believable. One interesting change has taken place over the last 40 years. In '50s big bug flicks, the culprit almost always had something to do with nuclear power. The government, working with scientists and/or the military, was able to overcome it. Today, the government is almost always in cahoots with evil capitalists to cause the environmental damage that creates the horror. Back then, the monster came from a new and unknown power. Today, it comes from us. 🦴🦴

Bloody effects, violence, strong language, sexual content, brief nudity.

1993 (R) 95m/C Tracy Griffith, Jim Youngs, Charles Napier, Michael J. Pollard; *D:* Clark Brandon; *W:* Clark Brandon, Lanny Horn; *M:* David Lawrence. **VHS, LV** *COL*

Sketch Artist

Fair little low-budget mystery almost lives up to its premise. Daisy (Drew Barrymore) is a messenger who may have seen the murderess of a fashion designer. The police sketch artist, Jack (Jeff Fahey), carefully coaxes details of the woman's facial features out of Daisy. When he's finished, he has created an accurate portrait of his wife Rayanne (Sean Young). Is she really the killer, or are Jack's financial and marital problems causing him to lead the witness where he wants her to go? For a time, the story manages to balance those two questions. Jack's a shabby, none-too-likable or reliable protagonist. Rayanne might be a scheming liar, or she might be an intelligent, successful woman who's tired of her underachieving husband. When the focus shifts to the supporting characters—the dead man's partner (Tcheky Karyo), the sympathetic cop (Frank McRae), the call girl (Charlotte Lewis)—it becomes much more predictable. Toward the middle it all slides out of control, and the big finish is pure cliche. Followed by a sequel. 🦴🦴🦴

Strong language, brief nudity, sexual content, violence.

1992 (R) 89m/C Jeff Fahey, Sean Young, Drew Barrymore, Frank McRae, Tcheky Karyo, James Tolkan, Charlotte Lewis; *D:* Phedon Papamichael; *W:* Michael Angeli. **VHS, LV** *FXV, VTR*

Sketch Artist 2: Hands That See

Rare sequel breaks most of the rules. Instead of repeating the original, this one builds on and departs from it. And despite the seemingly foolish premise, it tells a fairly realistic story. As the only surviving victim of a serial rapist/murderer, Emmy (Courteney Cox) has problems identifying the man for the police. She's blind. But she did touch the man's face and is able to describe him to sketch artist Jack Whitfield (Jeff Fahey). They work together to create a portrait. Writer Michael Angeli and director Jack Sholder take some care to treat rape and its emotional aftermath with sensitivity. The body of the film is unusual in that it's built on a strong emotional but non-sexual relationship that builds between Emmy and Jack. There's also a neat surprise at the end. 🦴🦴🦴

Contains strong subject matter, violence, strong language, incidental nudity.

1994 95m/C Jeff Fahey, Courteney Cox, Jonathan Silverman, Michael Beach, Brion James, James Tolkan, Leilani Sarelle Ferrer, Michael Nicolosi, Scott Burkholder; *D:* Jack Sholder; *W:* Michael Angeli; *M:* Tim Truman. **VHS, LV** *MGM*

Ski School

Adolescents, overaged and otherwise, can think of this as *Police Academy in the Snow.* Essentially, it's an extended beer commercial with lots of attractive young women dolled up in tight dresses and bikinis, and guys who make fools of themselves in bars and hottubs. The basic level of humor is established by beer burps and lambada jokes intercut with stunt skiing and spectacular Canadian Rockies scenery. No one on either side of the camera paid much attention to the alleged plot. Good move. Followed by a sequel. 🦴🦴 **GPI: 8.1**

Strong language, brief nudity, sexual situations.

1991 (R) 89m/C Ava Fabian, Dean Cameron, Tom Breznahan, Stuart Fratkin; *D:* Damian Lee. **VHS, LV** *HBO*

Ski School 2

Amiable teen sex comedy features lots of brightly lit skiing scenes that are eminently fast-forwardable. Just a few years ago, it would have been easy to dismiss this kind of goofy little movie as forgettable fluff. But considering the popularity of "stupid" comedy—*Dumb and Dumber, Billy Madison, The Jerky Boys,* et al—in theatres, *Ski School 2* is now more comparable to Noel Coward and Moliere. And Wendy Hamilton is certainly easy to watch. 🎬🎬 GPL. 8.0

Brief nudity, strong language, subject matter.

1994 **(R)** 92m/C Dean Cameron, Wendy Hamilton, Heather Campbell, Brent Sheppard, Bill Dwyer; *D:* David Mitchell; *W:* Jay Naples. **VHS** *MNC*

Skinner

Flawed film is about a repellant subject—serial murder and torture—but at times it's exceptionally sharp, similar in some ways to *Henry: Portrait of a Serial Killer,* though not nearly as powerful or frightening. The quirky casting—Ricki Lake as an unsuspecting landlady, Ted Raimi as the killer of the title, and particularly Traci Lords as a woman with several secrets and a mission—helps to counter an ultra-low budget. Director Ivan Nagy creates a Midwestern Gothic atmosphere of dread and horror, particularly at the beginning. When he gets more graphic, the story becomes bloody, sickening, and predictable. The really gory moments—meant to be frightening—could almost have come from a Troma *Toxic Avenger* movie. Also available in an unrated version. 🎬🎬

Subject matter, violence, strong language, brief nudity.

1993 **(R)** 89m/C Theodore (Ted) Raimi, Traci Lords, Ricki Lake; *D:* Ivan Nagy. **VHS, LV** *APX*

Skyscraper

This wonder is video's answer to big-screen alternative classics like *Mommie Dearest* and *Showgirls.* In terms of plot, the film is an attempt to remake *Die Hard* with the lumbering, buxom Anna Nicole Smith in the Bruce Willis role. Talk about a triumph of miscasting—she's too big and clumsy to handle the simple physical action of running and jumping. In the moments that demand emotion, she reaches genuine heights of acting ineptitude. With their silly foreign accents, her male co-stars are just as funny as she is. To fully appreciate this one, invite your most irreverent pals over for an evening of unintentional comedy. 🎬🎬

Graphic violence, strong language, nudity (featuring Ms. Smith's grotesque implants), sexual material.

1996 **(R)** 96m/C Anna Nicole Smith, Richard Steinmetz; *D:* Raymond Martino. **VHS** *PMH*

Slam Dunk Ernest

Jim Varney has taken his Ernest P. Worrell character from TV commercials to feature films and now back to the small screen with video premieres. It's probably the best medium for his particular brand of family-oriented slapstick. Here our intrepid hero works as a janitor in a shopping mall. His boss Barry (Cylk Cozart) still has dreams of an NBA career. Against his better judgment, he lets Ernest join the company basketball team as a benchwarmer. But whenever Ernest hits the hardwood, disaster strikes. Then he is visited by the Archangel of Basketball (Kareem Abdul-Jabbar) and everything changes. At the same time, Barry's young son Quincy (Aaron Joseph) is seriously tempted by a pair of $200 sneakers, thinking that they will make him the star his father never was. This low-budget effort was made by the same production team that's been responsible for most of Varney's films. They know what their audience wants to see and they deliver it. The jokes are silly; the message of hard work and tolerance is never preachy; Ernest is Ernest and Kareem seems completely comfortable with a light but serious role. 🦴🦴🦴

Contains no offensive material.

1995 (PG-13) 93m/C Jim Varney, Kareem Abdul-Jabbar, Joy Brazeau, Cylk Cozart, Aaron Joseph; **D:** John R. Cherry III; **W:** Daniel Butler, John R. Cherry III; **M:** Mark Adler. **VHS, LV** *TOU*

Slamdance

Divorced L.A. cartoonist Drood (Tom Hulce) is involved with enigmatic blonde (Virginia Madsen). When she's killed, the cops suspect him, but he knows she was involved with a political scandal. Writer (and co-star) Don Opper's script is unsatisfyingly cryptic at key points, but the performances are strong throughout and director Wayne Wang creates some evocative visuals. 🦴🦴🦴

Mature subject matter, strong language, violence, nudity, sexual content.

1987 (R) 99m/C Tom Hulce, Virginia Madsen, Mary Elizabeth Mastrantonio, Harry Dean Stanton, Adam Ant, John Doe, Don Opper; **D:** Wayne Wang; **W:** Don Opper. **VHS, LV** *FOX*

Slave Girls from Beyond Infinity

Bikini-clad space babes escape prison ship only to crash on maniac's planet in s-f remake of *The Most Dangerous Game.* This version is pure exploitation with the women's wardrobe consisting entirely of slinky dresses, lingerie, and underwear. Special effects range from fair to good, and the pace is brisk. Fun spoof of '50s movies takes nothing, including itself, seriously. Star Elizabeth Cayton also works as Elizabeth Kaitan. Rumor has it that the video premiere was sold to the producer solely on the basis of the title. 🦴🦴🦴

Sexual material, brief nudity, strong language.

1987 (R) 80m/C Elizabeth Cayton, Cindy Beal, Brinke Stevens; **D:** Ken Dixon; **C:** Thomas Callaway. **VHS, LV** *AFE*

Sleazemania

Compilation brings together lurid previews for some of the tawdriest movies ever made. *Jailbait* is presented as "the shocking story of boy-crazy girls and gun-crazy guys." Bold capital letters splash across the screen telling us that one jungle flick is "WEIRED." The classics are represented by trailers for *Marihuana— The Weed With Roots in Hell* and *Orgy of the Dead.* And, judging by the clips, such unknowns as *Strange Rampage, Young Seducers,* and *Prison Ship* might even be worth watching. But, on second thought...nah...none of the full-length versions could be as much fun as these shorties. 🦴🦴🦴 **GPI: 9.5**

Contains strong language, sex, violence, nudity, etc.

1985 60m/C **VHS** *RHI*

Sleepwalk

The plot elements of a thriller are combined with the sensibility of an experimental film. The pace is leisurely because plot is less important than tone. On one level, this is the story of Nicole (Suzanne Fletcher), who works in a low-rent Manhattan printing office and moonlights as a translator. Her life is boring and uneventful until two strange characters show up at her job and offer her a fat wad of cash to translate and transcribe an ancient Chinese document. Her flighty, greedy roommate (Ann Magnuson) persuades her to take the work and promptly asks to borrow money. As soon as Nicole begins to read the document, strange things happen. She hears voices—perhaps it's the ghost of the Japanese woman, Ecco Ecco (Ako), who said that she knew what the document meant—and even such simple acts as an elevator ride are tinged with mystery. Director Sara Driver's depiction of the less-glamorous side of New York—the decaying buildings and apartments, the streets filled with faces of all nationalities, the pale self-absorbed look of the people who live and work there—is slightly reminiscent of

another cult favorite, *Liquid Sky*. But only in its tone and atmosphere; *Sleepwalk* is not concerned with sex, drugs, and violence. It's about magic, weirdness, coincidence, the power of dreams, and stories. 🦴🦴🦴

Mild profanity.

1988 (R) 78m/C Suzanne Fletcher, Ann Magnuson, Ako; *D:* Sara Driver. **VHS, LV** *NLC, ICA*

Slipping into Darkness

A young retarded man is killed, and his brother (John DiAquino) thinks that three rich girls, led by Michelle Johnson, were somehow responsible. He enlists two biker pals to help find the truth. The first half is by turns clumsy and sharp. Writer/director Eleanor Gaver mixes laughably bad dialogue with some interesting, original visuals. But then in the second half, when we begin to learn who these characters really are and why they're doing what they're doing, the action becomes seriously weird and filled with warped surprises. At the end, the film lives up to its title and becomes a spooky Nebraska Gothic. 🦴🦴🦴

Violence, nudity, sexual situations, profanity.

1988 (R) 86m/C Belle Mitchell, Laslo Papas, Rigg Kennedy, Beverly Ross, T.J. McFadden, Michelle Johnson, John DiAquino; *D:* Eleanor Gaver; *W:* Eleanor Gaver. **VHS, LV** *GHV, HHE*

Slipstream

Big-budget, handsomely made s-f is set in a future where an ecological disaster has destroyed society as we know it. The climate has been radically changed, creating a strong wind current. Mark Hamill is an ill-tempered cop who flies a wild-looking plane. He and partner Kitty Aldridge capture poetry-spouting murderer Bob Peck, but before they can bring him to justice, he's kidnapped by dim-witted bounty hunter Bill Paxton. The chase is on. Unfortunately, the chase is filled with holes. For a time that doesn't matter because director Steven Lisberger captured some stunning aerial footage, and much of the Turkish landscape is exotic and fascinating. Whenever the action moves to ground level, it falters. The characters are poorly drawn and the dia-

logue is amateurish throughout. But when Ben Kingsley shows up in a cameo role, everyone begins to talk in fortune-cookie aphorisms that are apparently meant to pass for wisdom. If that weren't enough, in the second half, the mood shifts abruptly from scene to scene, including one long Fred Astaire/Ginger Rogers-type number that has a demented *Masterpiece Theatre* atmosphere. The ending is appropriately unusual and goofy. 🦴🦴

Violence, profanity, sexual situations.

1989 (PG-13) 92m/C *GB* Mark Hamill, Bill Paxton, Bob Peck, Eleanor David, Kitty Aldridge, Robbie Coltrane, Ben Kingsley, F. Murray Abraham; *D:* Steven Lisberger; *W:* Tony Kayden; *M:* Elmer Bernstein. **VHS, LV** *VTR*

Smooth Talker

You know a movie's in trouble when the executive producer gets the prime credit line. The plot has something do with a serial killer, 976 phone numbers, and D.A. Blair Weickgenant who's having an affair with her opposition. This one doesn't measure up on the most basic level of technical competence. The picture is dark and grainy. The dialogue is sometimes drowned out by the music. The script makes so little sense that key parts of it may have been left out. In the end, the movie is so inept that only the truly masochistic could watch it all the way through without hitting the fast-forward button. **WOOF!**

Violence, strong language, sexual material, and nudity.

1990 (R) 89m/C Joe Guzaldo, Peter Crombie, Stuart Whitman, Burt Ward, Sydney Lassick, Blair Weickgenant; *D:* Tom Milo. **VHS** *ACA*

Snapdragon

Another of those pesky serial killers is loose in L.A. Detective Peckham (Chelsea Field) learns that the victims, all men, have a connection to the Orient, and that the killer is a blonde woman. At the same time, her police psychologist boyfriend (Steven Bauer) has become obsessed with the case of a beautiful tattooed blonde amnesiac (Pamela Anderson Lee) who's suffering nightmares that fit the pattern of the murders. The story manages to mix those outlandish elements with a fair degree of reality in its use of everyday details. The film tends to move slowly and it takes some odd turns en route to a "surprise" ending. Director Worth Keeter has shown his ability to handle this kind of material (sub-genre "psycho-sexual thriller" according to the advertising) with some flair in other video premieres like *Illicit Behavior*. 🦴🦴🦴

Nudity, sexual content, violence, strong language.

1993 (R) 96m/C Steven Bauer, Pamela Anderson, Chelsea Field; *D:* Worth Keeter; *W:* Gene Church. **VHS** *PSM*

A Soldier's Tale

In Normandy, July 1944, Sgt. Saul Scorby (Gabriel Byrne) leads a squad of British infantrymen against the Germans. During a lull in the advance, he finds a farmhouse where beautiful young Isabelle (Marianne Basler) is living by herself. French resistance fighters have already tried and convicted her of collaboration, and demand that she come with them. For the basest of reasons, Saul offers to protect her. What follows is really a story about morality and moral choices. Writer/director Larry Parr makes some good points about fear, innocence, and the realities of occupation and collaboration. They're not clear-cut matters of black and white; to judge them as such is unfair, but, perhaps, unavoidable. The pace could be quicker, though the French countryside is captured so lovingly that it's not a serious problem. Neither are the inaccuracies in period details. Byrne turns in his usual intense performance and Basler looks like a young Brigitte Bardot. 🦴🦴🦴

Violence, subject matter, brief nudity.

1991 (R) 96m/C Gabriel Byrne, Marianne Basler, Judge Reinhold, Paul Wyett; *D:* Larry Parr; *W:* Larry Parr; *M:* John Charles. **VHS** *REP*

Solitaire for 2

The British have a talent for offbeat romantic comedy. From *Alfie* to *Four Weddings and a Funeral*, they've paired up quirky characters with unusual complications. If *Solitaire for Two* isn't as ambitious or polished as the best,

it's still entertaining and intelligent. Katie (Amanda Pays) is a psychic paleontologist who reads the minds of everyone around her. Ergo, she knows what innate pigs men are and usually smacks each one she meets before he can say a word. Daniel (Mark Frankel) is a charmer with a new line for every woman he meets. Writer/director Gary Sinyon knows there's no real suspense in this opposites-attract formula. The key is in the casting and these two are fine. So are the London locations. 🦴🦴🦴

Mature subject matter, strong language, mild violence, brief nudity.

1996 (R) 105m/C GB Mark Frankel, Amanda Pays, Roshan Seth, Maryam D'Abo, Jason Isaacs, Annette Crosbie; *D:* Gary Sinyor; *W:* Gary Sinyor; *C:* Henry Braham; *M:* David A. Hughes, John Murphy. **VHS** *PAR*

Somebody Has to Shoot the Picture

What looks like a conventional murder mystery is really an eloquent and persuasive argument against capital punishment. Roy (Arliss Howard) has been sentenced to the electric chair for his role in the death of a policeman during a drug deal that went bad. He has almost exhausted his appeals and asks that his execution be photographed. Paul Marash (Roy Scheider) is a burnt-out photojournalist. When he arrives in the unnamed Southern state where Roy is held, he realizes that passions are still running high, even though the crime occurred several years before. Why is the dead policeman's brother so upset at his presence? The unraveling of the plot details becomes too convenient toward the end, but that's not serious. When writer Doug Magee and director Frank Pierson focus on the details of state-sponsored killing, the film becomes horribly fascinating and terrifying. Howard seems to become so submerged in his character that in the key scenes you can forget you're watching an actor. Scheider's weary skepticism is a perfect foil for Howard's confusion and despair. And, these days, when our fearless elected officials are falling all over each other to appear tough on crime and proposing the death penalty for all manner of

> **"W**e're not filmmakers, you know. We're just a ragbag bunch of people doing something that is, technologically, almost passe.... It takes too long to make movies. By the time your idea is on the screen, it's already dead."
>
> —ORSON WELLES IN HENRY JAGLOM'S *SOMEONE TO LOVE*

> **"O**rson said, 'I've hidden behind masks in all my work. I'd like to be myself in a movie just once before I die.'"
>
> —HENRY JAGLOM ON ORSON WELLES IN *SOMEONE TO LOVE*

tragedy, women, life, directing. He's sharp, opinionated, smart, unashamed, original, completely captivating. He was clearly a genius and it's good that we have this glimpse of him at his liveliest and most unaffected. The film is a fitting farewell to such an unorthodox, independent talent. 𝄘𝄘𝄘

Profanity.

1987 **(R)** 110m/C Henry Jaglom, Orson Welles, Sally Kellerman, Andrea Marcovicci, Michael Emil, Oja Kodar, Stephen Bishop, Ronee Blakley, Kathryn Harrold, Monte Hellman; **D:** Henry Jaglom; **W:** Henry Jaglom; **C:** Hanania Baer. **VHS, LV** *PAR*

The Sorceress

This rarely seen 1955 black-and-white French film is a modern fairy tale, a variation on *The Little Mermaid* set in a Swedish forest. A French engineer (Maurice Ronet) is hired by a wealthy woman (Nicole Courcel) to cut a road through the wilderness. He's distracted first by his employer and then by a woman-child, Ina (the radiant and sexy Marina Vlady) who lives deep in the woods. With her youthful Kim Novak-Brigitte Bardot blonde glamour, she's the key to the film. The pace may seem slow, because director Andre Michel wraps his story in an atmosphere of inevitability. In look and tone, the film is a lot like Cocteau's *Beauty and the Beast,* but without the bold stylistic flourishes and lush production values. The film's anonymity in this country is really unfair. It is, I suppose, a matter of bad timing. Maybe it will finally find the audience it deserves on tape. 𝄘𝄘𝄘

No objectionable material.

1955 91m/C Maurice Ronet, Nicole Courcel, Marina Vlady; **D:** Andre Michel. **VHS** *IVY*

offenses, the film could hardly be more timely. It probably won't change any minds on this controversial subject, but it will force viewers to examine their beliefs and their motives, and that's important. 𝄘𝄘𝄘

Violence, profanity, sexual situations.

1990 **(R)** 104m/C Roy Scheider, Bonnie Bedelia, Robert Carradine, Andre Braugher, Arliss Howard; **D:** Frank Pierson; **W:** Doug Magee; **C:** Bojan Bazelli. **VHS, LV** *MCA*

Someone to Love

Autobiographical experimental film follows an ensemble cast playing thinly fictionalized versions of themselves as they are brought together by their real-life friend Jaglom for a "party" in an empty theatre. It's to be a film in which they describe their feelings, their loneliness, their hopes, and all that sort of stuff. Predictably, it often boils down to talk talk talk and some silly psychobabble. Orson Welles serves as a sort of Greek Chorus, commenting on the action as we learn that Danny (Henry Jaglom) is having problems in his relationship with Andrea Marcovicci. Even viewers who like this kind of offbeat, improvisational approach will probably think that the central part of the film goes on a little too long. At the end of the film, though, Welles takes over, holding forth on all sorts of subjects: storytelling, comedy,

Sorceress

Wildly complicated, fast-paced, and cheesy horror flick is notable for a veteran cast and some not-so-special effects. It's about a couple of witches competing over the career of a young executive. The filmmakers are professionals in the field. They know how to do a lot on a limited budget and don't try to do things they shouldn't. They don't exactly stretch the limits of the genre, either. Followed by a sequel. Also available in an unrated version. 𝄢𝄢𝄢

Nudity, violence, sexual content.

1994 (R) 93m/C Julie Strain, Larry Poindexter, Linda Blair, Edward Albert; *D:* Jim Wynorski. **VHS** *TRI*

Soultaker

Low-budget, overachieving regional production has become a solid cult hit. Made in Alabama and written by star Vivian Schilling, it's the story of four young people who are killed in a car wreck. Their spirits are thrown clear and the title character, a spooky guy in a long black raincoat, is dispatched to take them to the other side, or wherever. Details and tricky special effects aren't too important here. The action has the senseless energy that makes B-movies so much fun. Example: the kids are running for all they're worth from the guy in black. They're burning up their Reeboks while he just keeps walking with an implacable, determined pace. And, of course, he catches them. Before it's over, the whole thing has become a sort of live-action Pepe LePew cartoon. Now, that's entertainment. 𝄢𝄢𝄢

Contains mild profanity, some violence.

1990 (R) 94m/C Joe Estevez, Vivian Schilling, Gregg Thomsen, David Shark, Jean Reiner, Chuck Williams, Robert Z'Dar; *D:* Michael Rissi; *W:* Vivian Schilling. **VHS, LV** *AIP*

Space Mutiny

S-f comedy appears to be an Italian version of (or sequel to) the television series *Battlestar Galactica*. At least the producers used the same model spaceships and props, and turned that expensive series into high camp silliness. The rewards of alternative classics are difficult to describe, but let's begin with the silver lame spacesuits. Now imagine the most outlandish moments in the old *Batman* series combined with the worst excesses of *Star Trek*. Toss in a disco filled with hula hoops, a villain named Calgon, a heroine who looks (and acts) exactly like a life-sized Barbie doll, and badly overdubbed dialogue that contains such deathless lines as "It's very important

that we not make accusations, so we keep this top classified secret." 𝄢𝄢𝄢

Contains silly violence and a little mild cussing.

1988 (PG) 93m/C Reb Brown, James Ryan, John Phillip Law, Cameron Mitchell; *D:* David Winters; *W:* Maria Dante. **VHS** *AIP*

The Spellbinder

Director Janet Greek is a TV veteran and this one often looks like a slickly produced episode of an expensive series, maybe *Rosemary's Baby Meets L.A. Law.* In a slowly paced introduction, L.A. lawyer Jeff Mills (Timothy Daly) meets and rescues sexy young Miranda (Kelly Preston) from a spooky guy with a knife. Eventually, she tells him that she's trying to escape from a coven of witches. He invites her to move in with him anyway. Things don't get cranked up until the second half and even then the action moves fitfully. The special effects are inventive; some are shocking and effective. The conclusion generates a fair amount of suspense too. 𝄢𝄢

Brief nudity, sexual content, violence, profanity.

1988 (R) 96m/C Timothy Daly, Kelly Preston, Rick Rossovich, Audra Lindley; *D:* Janet Greek; *W:* Tracy Torme; *M:* Basil Poledouris. **VHS** *FOX*

Spitfire

Larky little Bond spoof stars gymnast Kristie Phillips as—natch—a gymnast who has the microdisc with the launch codes that a bunch of semi-comical spies are after. Veteran Albert Pyun directed the globetrotting tale. He made sure that he got lots of local color and energetic action sequences. With her physical grace and athleticism, Phillips could have a real future in films. 𝄢𝄢

Violence, strong language, brief nudity.

1994 (R) 95m/C Lance Henriksen, Kristie Phillips, Tim Thomerson, Sarah Douglas; *D:* Albert Pyun. **VHS** *VMK*

Spy Trap

Five Washington middle school kids decide to raise $100,000 to help their music teacher get an operation. But how? A car wash being out of the question, they decide to trick the Sovi-

ets—the movie was made in 1988 when there were Soviets—into thinking they're spies. Using a computer, they make blueprints of model kits for the Stealth fighter and pass them off as Pentagon originals. Of course, the KGB and the FBI act like Keystone Cops. The whole thing would be nothing more than an after-school special if writer Robert Littell, a veteran espionage novelist, hadn't decided to try to make two of the kids real. Denver (Danielle Du Clos) and Erskine (Jason Kristofer) engage in lengthy and candid conversations about the pubescent changes they're going through. At first, these seem awkwardly funny, but as they progress, they become simply awkward, and they really don't fit comfortably with the slapstick approach that the rest of the story takes. 🦴🦴

Contains some strong language.

1992 96m/C Elya Baskin, Danielle Du Clos, Jason Kristofer, Cameron Johann, Devin Ratray, Kimble Joyner; **D:** Arthur Sherman; **W:** Robert Littell. **VHS** *HMD*

Star Quest

Competently told science fiction has a good cast and a nice O. Henry ending. In an opening lifted straight from *Planet of the Apes*, astronauts en route to the planet Trion are awakened from hibernation. Familiar faces Brenda Bakke, Steven Bauer, Cliff DeYoung, Gregory McKinney, Alan Rachins, Emma Samms, and Ming-Na Wen find that their captain is dead and someone is after them. As they settle on a chain of command, their numbers dwindle and they're forced to face the question that pops up in so many s-f flicks: which of us is the robot? Like his cast, director Rick Jacobson is an old hand with this stuff. The film moves right along with good effects, sets, and characters who have some depth to go along with their funny accents. 🦴🦴🦴

Violence, brief nudity, drug use.

1994 (R) 95m/C Steven Bauer, Emma Samms, Alan Rachins,

Brenda Bakke, Ming-Na Wen, Gregory McKinney, Cliff De-Young; **D:** Rick Jacobson. **VHS, LV** *NHO*

Star Quest: Beyond the Rising Moon

"Hard" s-f is solidly in the *Star Wars* school with obvious references to the fiction of Robert Heinlein and Frederick Pohl. Tracy Davis, as the tough heroine Pentan, is infinitely better than the typical "starlet" who is usually cast in this kind of role. Michael Mack is an intelligent, articulate villain. A 97-minute "director's cut" is scheduled for release. **AKA:** Beyond the Rising Moon; Space 2074. 🦴🦴🦴

Contains some violence and mild sexual material.

1989 84m/C Tracy Davis, Hans Bachman, Michael Mack; **D:** Phillip Cook. **VHS, LV** *NHO*

Starlight

Younger viewers, who have not seen several hundred versions of the "Hey, kids, let's put on a show!" story are the target audience for director Orin Wechsberg's bouncy musical. It's basically *Dirty Dancing* without the dirty dancing, combined with a touch of *Fame*. Camp Starlight is a Catskills theatre camp for aspiring New York kids. But its founder, Uncle Monk, has just died and Louise and Arthur may sell out to the greedy developer (William Hickey). Writer M.J. Wells has tossed in a couple of romantic subplots, but the best moments are musical numbers, notably "Stranded in the Jungle," and solid versions of "God Bless the Child" by Tichina Arnold and "Blues in the Night" by Victor Cook. A test audience of four (three girls and one boy, aged eight to 12 1/2) thought the film was good and would recommend it to their friends. They said the music was the best part and dismissed

TRACY DAVIS AS THE HEROINE PENTAN IN *STAR QUEST: BEYOND THE RISING MOON.* COURTESY OF JOHN ELLIS.

the adult stuff as "boring." They know what they like. 🦴🦴▽

Contains no objectionable material.

1988 78m/C William Hickey, Danny Gerard, Victor Cook, Tichina Arnold, Ricki Lake; *D:* Orin Wechsberg; *W:* M.J. Wells. **VHS** *NO*

Stealing Heaven

Derek De Lint is Abelard, the famous 12th century teacher and philosopher in Paris. Kim Thomson is Heloise, an intelligent, rebellious young woman who continually questions the strict beliefs and conventions of the day. They start falling for each other the day she leaves the convent. The problem is that, like the other university lecturers, Abelard has taken a vow of chastity. Things were indeed different then. Under Clive Donner's direction, this is a slick, polished production; too polished, really. It often looks like a moving cover illustration for a paperback bodice-ripper, lacking the texture and grittiness that give the best historical films their necessary authenticity. And the characters are as wooden and posed as they are in most costume dramas. Still, the film does generate some erotic tension and it earns a footnote in the history of home video for being one of the first releases to appear in two versions, rated and unrated. 🦴🦴▽

Both versions contain nudity, sexual scenes, and violence.

1988 (R) 108m/C *GB YU* Derek De Lint, Kim Thomson, Denholm Elliott, Mark Jax, Bernard Hepton, Kenneth Cranham, Angela Pleasence, Rachel Kempson; *D:* Clive Donner; *W:* Chris Bryant; *M:* Nick Bicat. **VHS, LV** *NO*

Steel Frontier

In the post-World War III wasteland of 2007, an outlaw gang of veterans tries to impose dictatorial authority over the village of New Hope. Then Yuma (Joe Lara) arrives. (In the first few scenes, whenever he shows up, he's introduced by a strange musical signature, a constipated yodel that mimics Ennio Morricone's memorable spaghetti Western scores.) As expected, he's taciturn and good with his inventive s-f weapons. What sets him apart from other heroes is his hair. I mean, these

luxurious tresses are enough to make the Brad Pitt of *Legends of the Fall* jealous. Give this guy a shave, a bath, and some mascara, and you could put him in a Lady Clairol ad. For the most part, the film delivers what fans of the genre want to see. There are lots of neat, goofy vehicles—including a car with an outboard motor—and sets cluttered with broken junk. 🦴🦴

Violence, strong language.

1994 (R) 94m/C Joe Lara, Brion James, Bo Svenson, Stacie Foster; *D:* Paul G. Volk, Jacobsen Hart; *W:* Jacobsen Hart. **VHS, LV** *PMH*

Stormswept

Soft-core Southern Gothic horror comedy begins on a familiar note with six crew members of a film production company trapped by a thunderstorm in a haunted Louisiana mansion. An unspeakable crime occurred there years before. Now, an evil, sexually charged spirit pervades the place and a mysterious blonde (Kathleen Kinmont) has set up housekeeping in the basement. An early establishing shot of a spider walking through an ornate chandelier sets the mood, and the rest of the film pretty much lives up to it. Some of writer/director David Marsh's scares are conventional dark-and-stormy-night stuff, but there are enough inventive moments to keep your interest. The rest of the cast—Justin Carroll, Julie Hughes, Melissa Anne Moore, Lorissa McComas, Ed Wasser, Kim Kopf, Hunt Scarritt—seem to be enjoying the material. The result is a good looking film that's a lot of fun. Horror fans have seen much worse. 🦴🦴🦴
GPI: 9.2

Contains nudity, sexual material, strong language, violence.

1995 94m/C Julie Hughes, Melissa Moore, Kathleen Kinmont, Justin Carroll, Lorissa McComas, Ed Wasser, Kim Kopf, Hunt Scarritt; *D:* David Marsh; *W:* David Marsh. **VHS** *MTH*

Storyville

The youngest member of a Louisiana political family, Cray Fowler (James Spader) is in a longshot campaign for a house seat. His uncle (Jason Robards) is running the show, but that doesn't stop Cray from traipsing off with a fetching young woman (Charlotte Lewis) who sets him up to star in a career-killing videotape. While that side of the plot is being hashed out, Cray learns that his father's death by suicide some years before may be much more complicated than it seems. From that knotty beginning, the story gets even stranger. By the end, it's completely preposterous, but that's not too serious in this case. Writer/director Mark Frost has had a long association with David Lynch and he brings a certain *Twin Peaks* quality to this film. It's long on steamy, humid atmosphere and heavy breathing; deliberately short on substance. It's not imitative, though. Frost's approach to his material is more serious, in some ways more conventional and satisfying than Lynch's. He made fair use of the city's locations and got fine performances from his leads. But perhaps the best things about this one are the terrific supporting roles. Piper Laurie turns in a memorable cameo as Cray's disengaged mother. Two veterans from *Hill St. Blues,* Michael Warren and Charles Haid show up as, respectively, a canny black politician and a plump pornographer. B-movie stalwart Michael Parks, as a cop who may or may not be corrupt, steals all of his scenes, and turns the ending into a real surprise. By the way, despite the title, the film has nothing to do with the city's famous red light district. 🦴🦴🦴🦴

Sexual content, graphic violence, strong language, brief nudity.

1992 **(R)** 112m/C James Spader, Joanne Whalley, Jason Robards Jr., Charlotte Lewis, Michael Warren, Piper Laurie, Michael Parks, Chuck McCann, Woody Strode, Charles Haid; *D:* Mark Frost; *W:* Mark Frost, Lee Reynolds; *M:* Carter Burwell. **VHS, LV** *COL*

The Stranger

Not to be confused with Albert Camus' novel of the same title, this is a feminist action/biker flick. It's also an unembarrassed rip-off of Clint Eastwood's *High Plains Drifter,* but so what? It's still a ton of fun. The title character (Kathy Long) is The Babe With No Name. She rides her Harley into a dying desert town that's run by Angel (Andrew Divoff) and his ruthless motor-cycle gang. In her black bustier and leather jeans, "she looks like a *Cosmo* Don't." That's the opinion of the local badgirl (Ginger Lynn Allen), but anybody who messes with this woman or calls her that famous B-word assumes room temperature within seconds. Fans of the genre will be one step ahead of Gregory Poirer's plot all the way through, but again, that's fine. Director Fritz Kiersch creates a terrific lonely sense of place, and he spent his limited budget wisely. There's hardly a wasted word or frame of film. Kathy Long seems comfortable with the martial arts scenes, but most of the dramatic heavy-lifting is left to Divoff as the scene-stealing villain. 🦴🦴🦴

Violence, strong language, brief nudity, sexual content.

1995 **(R)** 98m/C Kathy Long, Andrew Divoff, Eric Pierpont, Robin Lynn Heath, Ginger Lynn Allen; *D:* Fritz Kiersch; *W:* Gregory Poirier. **VHS** *COL*

A Stranger in Time

Kidvid begins with some strong visuals but loses steam quickly. It's a low-budget time-travel story about young Andie Hopkins (Heather Kottek) who helps Sarah (Amy Seely) after Sarah inexplicably flashes forward 100 years from 1989. For the first half or so, the pioneer-girl-in-suburbia angle keeps things moving but toward the end, writer/director Dennis Rockney lets the action go flat, both emotionally and dramatically. That's also where the lack of a special-effects budget is all too apparent. Still, few films are made for adolescent girls, and any young s-f fan ought to give this one a try. 🦴🦴

No objectionable material.

1995 85m/C Heather Kottek, Amy Seely; *D:* Dennis Rockney; *W:* Dennis Rockney. **VHS** *BPG*

Street Asylum

Another *RoboCop* knockoff posits policemen who are surgically transformed into murderous killing machines. There are no surprises in that part of the story. What sets this one apart from so many others is the presence of right-wing demagogue G. Gordon "the G-Man" Liddy as a sexually perverted sado-maschochistic

right-wing demagogue. The scene in which he slips out of character and starts giggling uncontrollably while Playmate Roberta Vasquez comes after him with a whip is worth the price of a rental all by itself. Also available in an unrated version. �► **GPI: 8.1**

Strong language, some violence, brief nudity, sexual situations.

1990 (R) 94m/C Wings Hauser, Alex Cord, Roberta Vasquez, G. Gordon Liddy, Marie Chambers, Sy Richardson, Jesse Doran, Jesse Aragon, Brion James; *D:* Gregory Brown. **VHS, LV** *NO*

The Street Fighter

Over the years, this martial arts classic has developed quite a reputation. It was made in 1975 and has been seen only in specialty theatres, at festivals, or on tape in an edited, R-rated version. Now available in all its rude, full-length glory, the film lives up to its billing—violent, inventive, excessive, and never boring. Sonny Chiba plays Terry Tsuguri, who will do just about any job for a price. He's an amoral freelancer with no loyalty to any person, group, or cause. Of course his employers—gangsters, corporations, and others of their ilk—seldom keep their word and so Terry is forced to take matters into his own hands. The results are nasty. In this wildly plotted tale, the connections and similarities between Asian martial arts movies and Italian spaghetti Westerns are obvious. They share the same cinematic values and deliver the same visceral kicks. As a star, Chiba is a more expressive and physically powerful Charles Bronson. With his rolling eyeballs and Elvisian sneer, he's a commanding screen presence. And when he goes into his elaborate breathing routine in preparation for most of the big fights—swelling chest, flaring nostrils, lots of snorting—it sounds like he's hawking up the world's biggest loogie. Tasteful? Of course not! And there's a hint of racism to the film, too, but it charges along with such reckless energy that criticism on those points is meaningless. This is an action flick, no more and certainly no less. �► ☑☑☑

Contains graphic violence, implied rape, strong language.

1975 91m/C Sonny Chiba; *D:* Sakae Ozawa. **VHS, LV** *NLC*

A Streetcar Named Desire: The Original Director's Version

Right before the film's 1951 release, three minutes were cut in an attempt to overcome objections by the Hays Office and the Catholic Church's Legion of Decency. Those included the climactic rape of Blanche (Vivian Leigh) by Stanley (Marlon Brando), other bits of dialogue, and references to homosexuality. The most important deletion, though, may well have been something that's less tangible than a single word or act. It's the staircase scene, one of the most famous moments in American film. Everyone knows it: Brando in the torn T-shirt yelling "Stella! Stella!" like a wounded beast; Kim Hunter in her nightgown descending the stairs to comfort him. But director Elia Kazan meant for the focus of the scene to be equally divided between the two. In this version, Kim Hunter does a long, slow, sexy stroll down those stairs, with Alex North's smokey jazz score prominent in the background. The scene was good before. It's so hot now that it'll curl your hair. In this edition, the whole film has been restored with crisp black-and-white photography and a soundtrack to match. Highly recommended. ☑☑☑☑

Mature subject matter, violence, rape.

1951 (PG) 125m/B Vivien Leigh, Marlon Brando, Kim Hunter, Karl Malden; *D:* Elia Kazan; *W:* Tennessee Williams; *C:* Harry Stradling; *M:* Alex North. Academy Awards '51: Best Actress (Leigh), Best Art Direction/Set Decoration (B & W), Best Supporting Actor (Malden), Best Supporting Actress (Hunter); Golden Globe Awards '52: Best Supporting Actress (Hunter); National Board of Review Awards '51: 10 Best Films of the Year; New York Film Critics Awards '51: Best Actress (Leigh), Best Director (Kazan), Best Film; Nominations: Academy Awards '50: Best Actor (Brando), Best Director (Kazan), Best Picture; Academy Awards '51: Best Black and White Cinematography, Best Costume Design (B & W), Best Screenplay, Best Sound, Best Original Score. **VHS, LV** *FOX, WAR, BTV*

Streets

Writer/director Katt Shea Ruben has reworked the standard stuff of B-movies to create an effective thriller with a serious side and believable, unusual characters. Teenaged Sy (David Mendenhall) has a small adventure while his parents are out of town. With vague dreams of rock stardom, he has taken off for Los Angeles on his bicycle with an electronic keyboard strapped to the handlebars. On his first morning out, he is sleeping under a pier at the beach where a young prostitute, Dawn (Christina Applegate), shows up with a client, Lumley (Eb Lottimer), who turns vicious. Sy and Dawn escape, but we soon learn that Lumley is an insane sado-masochistic motorcycle cop. He arms himself with an exotic sawed-off shotgun and stalks the couple. At the same time, Sy is learning who and what Dawn is, and that's where the film is at its best. She's a throwaway (distinct from a runaway) who lives on the street and follows her own rules. Lumley isn't a stereotypical psycho, either. He's a strange, driven figure who's so implacable in his pursuit that he's really frightening. Ruben and co-writer Andy Ruben (who also produced) balance the action well, shifting the focus between life on the streets and Lumley's insane determination. The action is seldom predictable, building to a tense confrontation that's filled with visual quotes from *Blade Runner*. The acting is excellent all the way through, particularly Applegate. True, the film lacks star power and big-budget special effects. It's easily overlooked on the crowded shelves of the video store. But this taut little thriller is worth some extra effort. It's much more engrossing and entertaining than a lot of the theatrical hits and semi-hits that are more heavily promoted. ♫♫♫♪

Profanity, violence, sexual content.

1990 (R) 90m/C Christina Applegate, David Mendenhall, Eb Lottimer; *D:* Katt Shea Ruben; *W:* Katt Shea Ruben, Andy Ruben. **VHS** *MGM*

Streets of Rage

Genre-bender is a two-sided martial-arts movie with a social conscience concerning street kids in Los Angeles. The first side is a standard story of incorruptible would-be reporter Mel Sails (Mimi Lesseos) taking on the leader of a child-prostitution ring and all his henchmen. The fights are generally well-staged with one embarrassing slip where the camera angle reveals that our heroine's kick doesn't come close to the villain's chin. The other side of the film might have come from taped conversations with real runaways. The stories that the kids tell about how they came to be on the street have the sound of barely fictionalized truth. The production values are thin and the acting is uneven. The film's saving grace is its star, who also produced, co-wrote, and -choreographed. Mimi Lesseos has an attractive, likeable screen presence. She seems to be comfortable in the action scenes and if she used a double, I couldn't tell. It's obvious that she's ready to move up the ladder in the genre. ♫♫♪

Martial arts violence, some strong language, brief nudity.

1995 m/C Mimi Lesseos, Oliver Page, Christopher Cass; *D:* Aristide Sumatra; *W:* Mimi Lesseos. **VHS** *MNC*

Strike a Pose

Nick Carter (Robert Eastwick) is a cop on suspension for a questionable shooting during a robbery. His girlfriend Miranda Cross (Michelle LaMothe) is a fashion photographer. His profession provides a plot, of sorts. Hers is an excuse for gobs of gratuitous nudity and hanky-panky. Producer/director Dean Hamilton squeezes every penny out of an obviously low budget. I'm truly ashamed to admit how much I enjoyed this one. Also available in an unrated version. ♫♫♫ **GPI: 8.5**

Nudity and sexual material.

1993 (R) ?m/C Margie Peterson, Robert Eastwick, Michelle LaMothe; *D:* Dean Hamilton. **VHS, LV** *PMH*

Stripshow

As the title indicates, this one contains all the necessary elements for a bonafide guilty pleasure. At the same time, though, it deals more honestly with the realities of stripping and prostitution than many mainstream films. In that respect, it's an extended version of the famous anecdote about George Bernard Shaw. Shaw, the story goes, was seated next to a proper lady at a dress dinner one night. In the

Stripteaser

Curious and mostly serious crime drama masquerades as exploitation. Despite the title, it's a compact well told story about a bad night at Zipper's Clown Palace. At closing time, Neil (Rick Dean, home video's answer to Jack Nicholson) takes over the place, holding Christina (Maria Ford, home video's answer to Michelle Pfeiffer) and the customers hostage. Duane Whitaker's script could almost be a stage play, one of those psychodramas that strips souls bare. Of course, this being home video, it also strips bods bare. But director Dan Golden deliberately destroys the illusions that strippers try to create. This is grim, anti-erotic stuff, similar to *Pulp Fiction* in its talkiness and dark humor, but don't take that as a direct comparison. 🦴🦴🦴

Strong language, violence, nudity, sexual content.

1995 **(R)** **82m/C** Rick Dean, Maria Ford, Lance August; *D:* Dan Golden; *W:* Duane Whitaker. **VHS** *NHO*

course of conversation, he asked her if she'd go to bed with him for a million pounds. She paused and answered yes. Then he asked her if she'd go to bed with him for one pound. "Certainly not," she huffily replied, "what do you think I am?" "We've already established that," said Shaw, "now we're haggling over the price." That's what veteran stripper Raquel (Tane McClure) tries to explain to the neophyte Kara (Monique Parent) in a Death Valley motel. She's got a suitcase full of cash to make the point. Many of the speeches are too long and the exploitation scenes are too short, but director Gary Dean Orona does pretty good work with the characters and the vivid sense of place. 🦴🦴🦴 **GPI: 7.6**

Nudity, sexual material, strong language.

1995 **(R)** **?m/C** Monique Parent, Tane McClure, Steven Tietsort; *D:* Gary Orona; *W:* Gary Orona. **VHS** *MTH*

Subspecies

No-frills vampire story is an updated version of the wonderful Hammer films that starred Christopher Lee and Peter Cushing. The terrific opening scene takes place inside a castle where two really hideous guys (one of whom has a serious problem with drooling) are doing disgusting stuff which will not be described here. Throughout, the Gothic sets and locations are properly atmospheric (the film was shot in Transylvania) with creaking doors and heavy organ music. The plot, revolving around good and bad vampire brothers, is acceptable. The bad guy's makeup is based on the original *Nosferatu* and if the whole thing seems more than a little overdone, that's what the material calls for. This isn't subtle stuff. Followed by sequels. 🦴🦴🦴

Graphic special effects, violence, brief nudity.

1990 **(R)** **90m/C** Laura Tate, Michael Watson, Anders Hove, Michelle McBride, Irina Movila, Angus Scrimm; *D:* Ted Nicolaou. **VHS, LV, 8mm** *PAR, BTV*

Suite 16

Though it's billed as a conventional "erotic" thriller, this one's actually an effective character study, a Pinteresque psychodrama that could be equally at home on the stage. The key players are Chris (Antoine Kamerling), an amoral young hustler who finds himself trapped with the millionaire Glover (Pete Postlethwaite) in a luxurious Monte Carlo hotel. They're a kinky odd couple whose proclivities and cravings come to feed off of each other. Belgian director Dominique Deruddere creates a grainy, sordid atmosphere, and succeeds in deglamorizing the sexual aspects of his story. In fact, that side is downright banal, but the last third of the film becomes increasingly twisted as the mind games intensify. Postlethwaite, nominated for an Oscar for his work in *In the Name of the Father*, is just as believable—if not as sympathetic—here. 🦴🦴🦴

Mature subject matter, strong language, violence, sexual content, brief nudity.

1994 (R) 93m/C *BE GB* Pete Postlethwaite, Antoine Kamerling, Geraldine Pailhas, Tom Jansen; ***D:*** Dominique Deruddere; ***W:*** Charles Higson, Lise Mayer; ***C:*** Jean-Francois Robin; ***M:*** Walter Hus. **VHS** *ARX*

Summer Job

Amiable teen sex comedy is so lightweight and brainless it makes *Porky's* look like *King Lear*. Like *Porky's*, it was filmed in Miami and features sleek, well-tanned young bodies in and out of skimpy bathing suits. The average level of humor is set by whoopee cushions and itching powder in underwear. Video milestone also features what may be the first cinematic treatment of the old frog-in-the-blender joke. 🦴🦴

Nudity, profanity, and poor taste (i.e., the frog bit).

1988 (R) 92m/C Sherrie Rose, Fred Boudin, Dave Clouse, Kirk Earhardt; ***D:*** Paul Madden. **VHS, LV** *COL*

The Summer of Miss Forbes

A writer, his wife, and their two mischievous sons are on vacation at the beach. But the parents want some time to themselves, so they hire German governess Miss Forbes (Hanna Schygulla) to look after the kids and teach them some discipline. Writer Gabriel Garcia Marquez uses *The Turn of the Screw* as his model. The boys rebel against Miss Forbes' hypocritical authoritarianism. She punishes them severely for any disobedience to her arbitrary rules. But at night she breaks into the booze and her interest in the boys' handsome young scuba teacher is anything but platonic. The conclusion is properly surprising and ironic. The humor is often bawdy and childish, especially near the beginning, but the last third is hypnotic as the action moves from objective realism to a child's point of view and then to the reality of dreams. ***AKA:*** El Verano de la Senora Forbes. 🦴🦴🦴

Contains violence, sexual material, brief nudity.

1988 85m/C *SP* Hanna Schygulla, Alexis Castanares, Victor Cesar Villalobos, Guadalupe Sandoval, Fernando Balzaretti, Yuriria Munguia; ***D:*** Jaime Humberto Hermosillo. **VHS, LV** *FXL, FCT, INJ*

Sundown

One more contemporary vampire Western comedy action flick. The shelves of the video store are full of 'em. The inhabitants of the little town of Purgatory are trying to overcome their handicap—vampirism—with UVAB sunglasses, industrial strength sunblock, and synthetic blood. But there are still those who prefer the old ways. The negligible plot is brightened by a few good effects, and the cast is filled with veteran character actors whose faces are more familiar than their names. The comic side of the story is almost as strong as the horror. When things start to drag, feel free to use the fast-forward button. Recommended to those who appreciate subgenius humor. 🦴🦴

Violence, strong language.

1991 (R) 104m/C David Carradine, Bruce Campbell, Deborah Foreman, Maxwell Caulfield, Morgan Brittany; ***D:*** Anthony Hickox. **VHS** *VES*

Sunset Grill

Mystery mixes old cliches—the hard drinking, hard smoking detective who does divorce

work, with new cliches—the apartment that can only be reached by a freight elevator, the big slow-turning fan in the wall, lots of smoky light. Ryder Hart (Peter Weller) sorts through an overly complex story that involves crooked cops, a series of murders, illegal immigrants, gangs, and many of the other standard elements of the genre. Lori Singer provides the love interest and Stacy Keach is all right as the wealthy and powerful bad guy. Similar material has been handled much more deftly in other movies, so this one comes across as a rehash of the familiar with a noticeable lack of chemistry among the leads. *Chinatown* it ain't, and it doesn't have anything to do with the Don Henley song, either. Also available in an unrated version. 🎬🎬

Contains sexual material, nudity, strong language, violence.

1992 (R) 103m/C Peter Weller, Lori Singer, Alexandra Paul, John Rhys-Davies, Michael Anderson Jr., Stacy Keach; **D:** Kevin Connor. **VHS** *NLC, PMS*

Sunset Heat

Confection of style, slickness, and attitude without a gram of substance is *Miami Vice* in L.A. Eric (Michael Pare) is a drug dealer who got out of the business four years ago and left the west coast. His ex-partner Carl (Dennis Hopper) has prospered, while Eric's old flame (Daphne Ashbrook) hasn't gotten over him. But his pal Danny (Adam Ant, in a dandy cameo) gets him involved with a good-time girl (Tracy Tweed) and a drug deal that goes bad. After the requisite bedroom scenes, car chases, party sequences, and confrontations, an arsenal of fully automatic weapons is hauled out. The remaining principals then blaze away at each other for what seems like 20 minutes. The action has a glossy music-video patina, and it's hard to tell whether the humor is intentional, but it's still often very funny. Hopper is not, alas, at his crazed best. Also available in an unrated version. *AKA:* Midnight Heat. 🎬🎬🎬 **GPI: 8.4**

Nudity, strong sexual content, violence, language.

1992 (R) 94m/C Michael Pare, Dennis Hopper, Adam Ant, Daphne Ashbrook, Tracy Tweed, Charlie Schlatter; **D:** John Nicolella. **VHS** *NLC*

The Surgeon

In a dandy little medical horror/comedy, the title character (Sean Haberle) is the proverbial mad scientist—actually he's a little madder than most—who's out to get everyone who has thwarted his research into "pituitary extract." Those include Malcolm McDowell and Charles Dance. Isabel Glasser and James Remar are the good doctors. Peter Boyle is the cop on the case. Director Carl Schenkel and special effects co-ordinator Steve Johnson have come up with some genuinely creepy moments, most of them infused with strong humor. It's difficult to maintain an effective ratio of laughs and scares, but they manage it all the way through. *AKA:* Exquisite Tenderness. 🎬🎬🎬

Mature subject matter, violence, graphic effects, strong language, brief nudity, sexual content.

1994 (R) 100m/C *GE* Isabel Glasser, James Remar, Sean Haberle, Charles Dance, Peter Boyle, Malcolm McDowell, Charles Bailey-Gates, Gregory West, Mother Love; **D:** Carl Schenkel; **W:** Patrick Cirillo; **C:** Thomas Burstyn; **M:** Christopher Franke. **VHS** *APX*

Suspect Device

Three Days of the Condor goes to *The Twilight Zone*. Dan Jerico (C. Thomas Howell) works for a government intelligence outfit, and suffers from vivid, violent dreams of mass slaughter. When those visions become real, his friends' reactions make no sense. Though the story won't stand up to much scrutiny, video veteran Rick Jacobson handles things with a sense of humor. He also got good performances from Howell and co-star Jonathan Fuller as an unreconstructed half-mad hippie doctor. For a sci-fi shoot-'em-up, you could do worse. *AKA:* Roger Corman Presents: Suspect Device. 🎬🎬🎬

Graphic violence, strong language, brief nudity, sexual content.

1995 (R) 90m/C C. Thomas Howell, Stacy Travis, Jed Allan, John Beck, Marcus Aurelius, Jonathan Fuller; **D:** Rick Jacobson; **W:** Alex Simon; **C:** John Aronson; **M:** Christopher Lennertz. **VHS** *NHO*

Suture

Some viewers are going to love this offbeat thriller; others will be thoroughly frustrated by it. The reason's simple. It's a piece of popular entertainment told with the techniques of an experimental film. And at the center, where more movies provide an answer or resolution, filmmakers Scott McGehee and David Siegel leave an enigmatic question mark. Clay Arlington (Dennis Haysbert) arrives in Phoenix, Arizona, on a bus. Vincent Towers (Michael Harris) meets him. Clay's a construction worker—dusty jeans and work boots. Vincent drives a Bentley. They met only recently at their father's funeral and both comment on their resemblance. The thing is...Clay's black; Vincent's white. The police suspect that Vincent may have had something to do with his wealthy father's death, and that's the beginning of a carefully paced Hitchcockian suspense tale. The other important characters are Dr. Renee Descartes (Mel Harris), a plastic surgeon, and Max Shinoda (Sab Shimono), a psychiatrist. To reveal almost anything else would spoil things. McGehee and Siegel give the story a dreamlike fluidity. Greg Gardiner's richly textured black-and-white photography adds immensely to that suspended reality. Haysbert handles a difficult role with some of the most restrained and subtle work you'll see. It's the kind of performance that can turn a character actor into a star. As for the story and the racial issues—that's where the questions come in. *Suture* is challenging, inventive, and different in the finest sense of the word. 🎬🎬🎬🎬

Contains some strong language, violence, sexual material.

1993 96m/B Dennis Haysbert, Sab Shimono, Mel Harris, Michael Harris, Dina Merrill, David Graf, Fran Ryan; *D*: Scott McGehee, David Siegel; *W*: Scott McGehee, David Siegel; *C*: Greg Gardiner; *M*: Cary Berger. Sundance Film Festival '94: Best Cinematography; Nominations: Independent Spirit Awards '95: Best Cinematography, Best First Feature. **VHS** *HMK*

Sweet Bird of Youth

Screenwriter Gavin Lambert based this version on Tennessee Williams' own "rethinking of the material." It's different from the play and from the 1962 Paul Newman-Geraldine Page film. Mark Harmon and Elizabeth Taylor take on the roles of Chance, the hustling beach boy, and Alexandra Delago, the once

and future screen legend. Fueled by ambition and hashish, they breeze into Chance's Gulf-coast hometown, and find themselves in the middle of Boss Finlay's (Rip Torn) crusade to maintain segregation. (The setting is a vague, generic 1950s with a vague, generic pop soundtrack and vague, generic Southern accents.) The rest of the plot has to do with the dark secret in young Heavenly Finlay's (Cheryl Paris) past, and considerable soul-searching for all concerned. Director Nicolas Roeg lets the action drag along at an unusually slow and predictable pace. While it's always fun to listen to Liz handling Williams' overripe dialogue, this is far from her best work. She was in one of her plumper phases when the film was made, a long way from her svelte days as Maggie the Cat. The central problem, though, is that this story remains a play. The stage was Williams' medium and his strengths there—vivid, emotional characters; charged personal conflicts; long, carefully constructed scenes—don't necessarily lend themselves to the screen. Some of the "big" moments here are misfires, and the ending, while faithful to the source, lacks clarity and logic. Still, even when Williams and Roeg aren't at their best, they're more interesting than a lot of people who are making movies these days. For their fans, this *Sweet Bird* earns a qualified recommendation. 🎬🎬🎬

Brief nudity, sexual content, subject matter.

1989 (R) 95m/C Elizabeth Taylor, Mark Harmon, Rip Torn, Valerie Perrine, Ruta Lee, Seymour Cassel, Kevin Geer, Michael Wilding Jr., Cheryl Paris; *D*: Nicolas Roeg; *W*: Gavin Lambert; *M*: Ralph Burns. **VHS** *TRI*

Sweet Killing

Canadian crime story is jazzed up with a strong streak of black humor. Outwardly normal bank executive Adam Cross (Anthony Higgins) plans to murder his wife. And why not? Louise (Andrea Ferreol) calls him at the office, gets drunk on her birthday, talks too loud, and spills cake in his lap. Those might be forgivable sins, but one night at dinner, she says that the red wine Adam has chosen, an expensive Bordeaux, is too strong, so she thins it with half a glass of milk! Inventing an imaginary character

named Zargo to cover his tracks, Adam concocts a Rube Goldberg scheme to do her in. Right in the middle of it, he meets the fetching Eva (Leslie Hope), who becomes an unwitting part of his plan. None of it fools detective Garcia (Michael Ironside) for a minute, but then, in his own way, he's almost as nutty as Adam. Fairly late in the game, Zargo appears in the person of F. Murray Abraham. What could have been a run-of-the-mill exercise in formula suspense is saved by a comic sense that's hard to describe. Be warned, whenever you think this one is going to settle into the conventions of the genre, it surprises you—particularly in the last reel. 🦴🦴🦴

Brief nudity, sexual content, mild violence.

1993 (R) 87m/C Anthony Higgins, F. Murray Abraham, Leslie Hope, Michael Ironside, Andrea Ferreol; **D:** Eddy Matalon; **W:** Eddy Matalon. **VHS** *PAR*

Sweet Poison

Escaped convict Steven Bauer kidnaps Milquetoast husband Edward Herrmann and his restless wife Patricia Healy. You know the drill. The story sticks to the well-worn formula most of the way through, but it does arrive at a couple of nice turns toward the end. Fans will like it more than others. 🦴🦴

Violence, strong language, brief nudity, sexual activity.

1991 (R) 101m/C Steven Bauer, Patricia Healy, Edward Herrmann; **D:** Brian Grant. **VHS** *MCA*

Sweet Talker

Conman Harry Reynolds (Bryan Brown) comes up with his scheme the old-fashioned way; he steals it from his cellmate. As soon as he's released from prison, he heads for the sleepy little South Australian resort town of Beachport. He persuades the locals that he knows the location of the legendary Duneship, a Portuguese galleon that ran aground centuries before and is buried beneath the sand. He's such a silver-tongued rascal that everyone but his landlady (Karen Allen) falls for his line. Before long the locals are begging Harry to take their money. But what about the greedy businessman whose credit cards Harry stole? And his old cellmate? There aren't many surprises, but that's all right. The leads handle the light material deftly; the scenery is gorgeous, even on the small screen, and the soundtrack contains a few minutes of Billie Holiday's "I Cried for You." No, it isn't another *'Crocodile' Dundee*, but it's a lot of fun and the kids will like it. 🦴🦴🦴

Strong language.

1991 (PG) 91m/C *AU* Bryan Brown, Karen Allen, Chris Haywood, Bill Kerr, Bruce Spence, Bruce Myles, Paul Chubb, Peter Hehir, Justin Rosniak; **D:** Michael Jenkins; **W:** Tony Morphett; **M:** Richard Thompson, Peter Filleul. **VHS, LV** *LIV*

Swift Justice

Aspiring actress Cindy Rome gets lost on the way to Las Vegas and her VW conks out in the desert. After being helped by a survivalist Vietnam vet, she goes into a little town and is raped by the local good old boys. Vet gets even. Rome is a Pia Zadora wannabe, and hero Jon Greene is all profile and pecs. Neither of them is called upon to deliver many lines of dialogue. Most of the speaking is done by veteran character actors Aldo Ray and Cameron

Mitchell. Overall, the film is surprisingly well made with good production values and a gritty look. Its finest moment comes when Greene disguises himself as a rhododendron and sneaks up on one of the bad guys. 🦴🦴

Contains violence, graphic though unconvincing special effects, profanity, brief nudity, shrubbery impersonation.

1988 90m/C Jon Greene, Cindy Rome, Cameron Mitchell, Aldo Ray, Chuck "Porky" Mitchell, Wilson Dunster, Ted Leplat; *D:* Harry Hope. **VHS** *TWE*

Swimming with Sharks

For anyone who's interested in the film business, this sharp satire may be the best sleeper in the video store. It gives Oscar-winner Kevin Spacey a meaty role as Buddy Ackerman, maniacal Hollywood studio executive. The primary target of Buddy's many abuses is his young assistant Guy (Frank Whaley), who may be every bit as cold and ambitious as Buddy. Between them is Dawn Lockhard (Michelle Forbes), one of Buddy's ex-girlfriends and a player herself in the movie game. Essentially, writer/director George Huang's story is a three-character psychodrama, and while Whaley and Forbes hold their own, the film is Spacey's. He commands the big scenes with long, intense monologues. His work here is every bit as effective and carefully shaded as it was in *The Usual Suspects.* Like the film the three are discussing throughout, this one has the wrong ending. It's a curious flaw that could have been fixed easily with a few slight changes, and it really doesn't detract from the rest. Like Robert Altman's *The Player,* it's funny, acerbic, and maybe more accurate than we'd care to know. *AKA:* The Buddy Factor. 🦴🦴🦴

Strong language, some violence.

1994 (R) 93m/C Kevin Spacey, Frank Whaley, Michelle Forbes, Benicio Del Toro; *D:* George Huang; *W:* George Huang; *C:* Steven Firestone. New York Film Critics Awards '95: Best Supporting Actor (Spacey); Nominations: Independent Spirit Awards '96: Best Actor (Spacey). **VHS, LV** *VMK*

Sword of Honor

Like a good Hong Kong martial arts flick, this one has a cartoonish comic book quality, with speeded-up fight scenes and semi-pro acting. Las Vegas gangsters duke it out over a mystical Mongol sword. A cop (Steven Leigh), called a "wild koomakazee" by his boss, and a martial arts teacher (Sophia Crawford) are the good guys. Under Robert Tiffe's direction and Jeff Pruitt's choreography, the big action scenes are nutty constructions filled with spontaneous gunfights, bazookas, and such, but the movie's heartfelt cheesiness is the main attraction. 🦴🦴

Violence, strong language, brief nudity, sexual content.

1994 (R) 90m/C Steven Leigh, Sophia Crawford, Angelo Tiffe, Jerry Tiffe, Jeff Pruitt, Debbie Scofield; *D:* Robert Tiffe; *W:* Robert Tiffe, Clay Ayers; *M:* David Rubinstein. **VHS, LV** *PMH*

Synapse

Entertaining feminist science fiction begins shakily in one of those near-futures where wicked capitalist greedheads run everything. The top executives will do anything to maintain their power, and those who rebel are subject to summary justice resulting in confiscation of their bodies. That, more or less, is the situation Celeste (Karen Duffy) finds herself in, though it's really more complicated than that. The plot, screwy as it is, takes precedence over the poorly staged action scenes, and the acting is a cut above average for the genre. Unfortunately, the scene in which a woman performs brain surgery on herself isn't as neat or as gross as it could have been. 🦴🦴🦴

Mature subject matter, violence, brief nudity, sexual content.

1995 (R) 89m/C Karen Duffy, Saul Rubinek, Matt McCoy, Chris Makepeace; *D:* Allan Goldstein. **VHS** *AVE*

T-Force

Low-budget *Terminator* knockoff focuses on a cop (Jack Scalia) who's teamed up with a bland blond cyborg (Bobby Johnston) against rogue cyborgs with aluminum breastplates and bad hair. The pace is quick, the explosions multitudinous. 🦴🦴

Violence, brief nudity, sexual content.

"You can't do a good film or video without well-paid, talented actors; good locations; attention paid to set design and costumes; enough shooting days; enough editing to do something decent. And you have to start with a good story. Even a good educational film on cataracts or glaucoma has to start with a decent story.

"Box art is so important. We had to change the box for *The Voyeur* so it would stand out. It was much more pastel colored, appealing, we thought, to women. But if it doesn't stand out on a shelf, people don't pick it up.

"If you don't have name talent—and this can be people who were in TV sitcoms in the '60s—you're lost in this country. You're especially lost in any foreign distribution.

"Men buy the videotapes and promote them, even the ones that appeal to women. So, you have to make sure that men understand your message and that's not always easy. Women understand character devel-opment, storyline, romance. Men want to know what kind of sex is in it.

"Most of the distributors of videotape operate at such a small profit margin that if you don't give them kickbacks or incentives to sell your independent film, they're going to go with whatever project can make them the most money. So even though they make like your film more and think that the other one is brainless and inane, they're going to sell the brainless inane one if the profit margin is higher.

"Big studios do a huge marketing and advertising push to sell their entire inventory or what they need to break even and make a profit in the first three to six months. Smaller independents don't have that luxury. Most of us can't man a big advertising campaign. We can't get it out to our markets in the first three to six months. So what happens is that as you spend a year to three years to get your product out, your monthly expenses, your overhead eats you alive."

—DEBORAH SHAMES, PRODUCER, DIRECTOR, AND HEAD OF DEBORAH FILMS

1994 (R) 101m/C Jack Scalia, Erin Gray, Evan Lurie, Daron McBee, Bobby Johnston; *D*: Richard Pepin. **VHS, LV** *PMH*

Tainted Love

Tough cop Lee Ann Beaman transforms herself into a knockout model to snare a millionaire who may be a serial killer. See review of *Irresistible Impulse* for more. 🗡🗡

Sexual scenes, nudity, violence, strong language.

1996 93m/C Lee Ann Beaman, Doug Jeffrey, Granville Ames; *D*: Jag Mundhra. **VHS** *YHV*

The Takeover

Low-octane gangster movie attempts to do more than its budget will allow. The central problem here is pace; it's so slow you may wonder if there's something wrong with your VCR. Maybe the belts need tightening. Ex-cons Jonathan (David Amos) and Mickey (Gene Mitchell) are caught in the middle when Chicago gangsters (Billy Drago and John Savage) move in on the L.A. cocaine business, and the local boss (Nick Mancuso) objects. Though its debts to John Woo are obvious, the plot is still fairly inventive, but unlike Woo, director Troy Cook shows no affinity for physical action. ⚡⚡

Violence, strong language, brief nudity.

1994 (R) 91m/C Billy Drago, Nick Mancuso, John Savage, Eric Da Re, Cali Timmins, David Amos, Gene Mitchell; **D:** Troy Cook; **W:** Gene Mitchell; **M:** Jimmy Lifton. **VHS, LV** *LIV*

Tales of Erotica

Four veteran filmmakers tell short low-budget bawdy stories. Mira Sorvino is a dental technician who finds her way into an oil painting in Susan Seidelman's Felliniesque "The Dutch Master." Melvin Van Peebles spins out a sexy variation on the three-wishes theme with "Vrooom, Vrooom, Vrooom." Ken Russell's "The Insatiable Mrs. Kirsh" is about a writer's misunderstanding of a mysterious hotel guest. The best of the bunch is Bob Rafelson's "Wet," about a salesman (Arliss Howard), a canny young woman (Cynda Williams), and the hot-tub she wants to buy. In all four, the production values are acceptable, the acting's better, and the humor is rowdy. ⚡⚡⚡

Mature subject matter, a little strong language, brief nudity.

1996 (R) 103m/C Mira Sorvino, Arliss Howard; **D:** Susan Seidelman, Melvin Van Peebles, Ken Russell, Bob Rafelson. **VHS** *VMK*

Tales of the Unknown

Poorly written short films share supernatural themes and odd, out-of-place comic elements. "The Big Garage" is a Kafka-esque story about car trouble. Another concerns a man who meets Death. These look like they were made for TV, with the addition of fairly strong violence and a few dirty words. ⚡

Contains some violence, profanity.

1990 87m/C **D:** Roger Nygard, John Kim, Fred Gallo, Greg Beeman; **W:** Roger Nygard, Greg Beeman, Jeff Copeland. **VHS** *AIP*

Talkin' Dirty After Dark

The plot of this loose-jointed movie is little more than an excuse to display the work of young black stand-up comedians. At Dukie's Club, mostly unknown stand-ups develop their routines in front of a loud, raucous crowd that's ready to laugh, but is also ready to hound an unfunny routine off the stage. Aretha (Phyllis Stickney) has the hottest act, but young Terry (Martin Lawrence) is a rising star. Dukie (John Witherspoon) has his eye on Aretha; his wife Ruby (Jedda Jones) feels the same about Terry and that's only the beginning of the romantic entanglements of the staff and patrons. Writer/director Topper Carew doesn't follow through on all the subplots and jokes that he sets up, but overall, this is a fast-moving and entertaining little low-budget comedy. What it lacks in sophistication (and that's a lot), it makes up for in earthy, bawdy humor and good spirits. ⚡⚡⚡

Strong sexual humor and language, mild violence.

1991 (R) 89m/C Martin Lawrence, Jedda Jones, Phyllis Stickney, Darryl Sivad, John Witherspoon; **D:** Topper Carew; **W:** Topper Carew. **VHS** *NLC, FCT*

The Tall Guy

This slapstick romantic comedy may be the funniest sleeper in your favorite video store. Jeff Goldblum is the title character, Dexter King, straightman to an obnoxious British comedian (Rowan Atkinson) in a long-running stage show. The pay stinks but the work is steady and Dexter is only vaguely dissatisfied with his lot until he meets Kate Lebon (Emma Thompson), and falls hopelessly in love. Eventually, they engage in the wildest love scene ever put on film. It couldn't have been any funnier if it had been choreographed by the Three Stooges. The second half shifts gears slightly, becoming a wicked satire of contemporary British drama when Dexter takes part in a musical version of *The Elephant Man*, called simply *Elephant*. At times, you'll be reminded of those fine British comedies from the 1960s like *The Knack, and How to Get It*. The filmmakers take chances with some

inventive visual tricks and a breezy sense of fun. Again, the casting is letter-perfect. Goldblum is believable and Thompson is as radiant as ever. 🦴🦴🦴🦴

Brief nudity, sexual content, strong language.

1989 (R) 92m/C Jeff Goldblum, Emma Thompson, Rowan Atkinson, Geraldine James, Kim Thomson, Anna Massey; *D:* Mel Smith; *W:* Richard Curtis; *M:* Peter Brewis. **VHS, LV** *COL, FCT*

Tammy and the T-Rex

As the title suggests, this one's aimed at the same teen audience that made *Buffy the Vampire Slayer* a modest hit. The silly plot has to do with a cute high school girl (Denise Richards) whose boyfriend (Paul Walker) has his brain transplanted into a robot T-Rex by yet another mad scientist (Terry Kiser). The tone of the film doesn't quite match the story. It's about as violent and sexually suggestive as it could be this side of an R rating. The low-budget effects are all right. The same critter was featured in *Carnosaur* and *Dinosaur Island,* so the proceedings have a certain familiarity. 🦴🦴

Language, violence, some sexual material.

1994 (PG-13) 82m/C Paul Walker, Denise Richards, Terry Kiser, John Franklin; *D:* Stewart Raffill. **VHS, LV** *IMP*

Target: Favorite Son

If you thought this one was lewd, lurid, trashy, and salacious in its first incarnation as a TV mini-series, wait till you get a look at the video version. It's condensed cream of sleaze. The thriller is a Byzantine conspiracy that makes little sense during the truncated exposition. That's understandable; they cut six hours to two, and they weren't about to lose any of the steamy stuff. It all has to do with a corrupt senator, Washington nastiness, and kinky sex. No, this is not a documentary or a campaign ad. The bizarre humor is intact, particularly when the script delves into false sanctimony. Interestingly, there's nothing in this tape that wasn't broadcast on network television, but the MPAA felt that it deserved an R rating. 🦴🦴🦴

Violence, implied sexual content, general principle.

1987 (R) 115m/C Linda Kozlowski, Harry Hamlin, Robert Loggia, Ronny Cox, James Whitmore. **VHS** *VMK*

TC 2000

In another post-apocalyptic future, humans live underground with clean air and water while the surface mutants try to break in. Billy Blanks is a guard who questions his role and is kicked upstairs for punishment. Director T.J. Scott mishandles some of the fight scenes and once even lets a microphone boom swing into the shot through a mirror, but he's saved by his cast. Blanks, as usual, is excellent. He gets solid support from Bobbie Philips and the incredible Bolo Yeung who's usually cast as villain. With his commanding screen presence, Yeung may be the most graceful and impressive martial artist in the business, and he's at his best here. 🦴🦴🦴

Martial arts violence, strong language.

1993 (R) 92m/C Billy Blanks, Bobbie Phillips, Jalal Merhi, Bolo Yeung, Matthias Hues; *D:* T.J. Scott; *W:* T.J. Scott. **VHS, LV** *MCA, SGE*

Ted & Venus

When Ted (Bud Cort) meets Linda (Kim Adams), he thinks she is the vision he once saw or imagined rising from the Venice, California, surf. As he puts it in verse, she is his "tube-top Venus who undulates my soul and my shorts." The fact that she already has a live-in beau (Brian Thompson) doesn't dissuade Ted. His best friend Max (James Brolin), a free-spirited artist, advises him to take it easy, but Ted's in love. He'll do anything to win Linda, and that's the point of the film. But when does love become something else? Does infatuation excuse everything? Can expressions of eternal devotion turn to terrorism? Is Ted a fool for love, or has he crossed a line into true madness? Those aren't simple questions and director Cort keeps viewers off balance, unsure of their reactions. The comedy-drama-romance doesn't end with expected answers either. 🦴🦴🦴

Strong language, sexual themes, brief nudity.

1993 (R) 100m/C Bud Cort, Kim Adams, Rhea Perlman, James Brolin, Carol Kane, Brian Thompson; *Cameos:* Gena Rowlands, Martin Mull, Woody Harrelson, Andrea Martin, Timothy Leary, Cassandra Peterson; *D:* Bud Cort; *W:* Paul Ciotti, Bud Cort. **VHS** *COL*

Temptation

So-so little thriller benefits from a Caribbean setting. Ex-con Eddie Lanarsky (Jeff Fahey) sets out to exact revenge on Michael Reddick (Philip Casnoff), the conman who set him up and has since married a wealthy socialite (Alison Doody). With his prison pal Bone (David Keith, sporting a ridiculous Aussie accent), Lanarsky manages to finagle his way into the captaincy of Reddick's yacht. The overwrought plot is fueled by tempestuous affairs, murder schemes, and bomb threats. Somehow, it's never quite as suspenseful or as trashy as it might have been, and the story falls apart at the end. But the sense of place is strong, and the pace moves so quickly that this is a completely adequate potboiler. ✄✄✓

Strong language, violence, sexual content, brief nudity.

1994 **(R)** 91m/C Jeff Fahey, Alison Doody, Philip Casnoff, David Keith, Patricia Durham, W. Paul Bodie; *D:* Strathford Hamilton. **VHS, LV** *LIV*

Temptation of a Monk

In 7th century China, the dynastic succession is in question. Hoping to ensure a peaceful transition, General Shi (Wu Hsin-Kuo), agrees to hold his men back when another faction makes a bid for power. When the moment comes, he is betrayed. He retires in shame to a monastery where his men chaff at monastic life and the idea of taking orders from a ten-year-old monk who's completely full of himself. Shi is torn between a desire to exact whatever revenge he can find, thereby regaining some self-respect, and an equally strong desire to surrender to religious discipline. He returns to the pleasures of the flesh in a partially allegorical sequence set in a brothel, and then finds that the outside world isn't yet finished with him. The other key character is Joan Chen, who plays both Princess Scarlet and a temptress who appears late in the story. She figures prominently in a head-shaving scene that's as intensely sensual as anything

you're likely to see on film. It's a long, carefully photographed sequence, and director Clara Law wrings every molecule of emotion out of it. She seems equally comfortable with the large-scale battle scenes. One that's set in a narrow rocky canyon could have come straight from Peckinpah, and the climactic confrontation in a burning monastery is just terrific. In the end, the film is too unusual and too deliberately paced to recommend to all videophiles, but it's so well made with such strong, memorable images that anyone who has a taste for the exotic and challenging should give it a try. ✄✄✄✓

Graphic violence, strong sexual material, brief nudity.

1994 118m/C *CH* Wu Hsin-kuo, Joan Chen, Zhang Fengyi, Michael Lee; *D:* Clara Law; *C:* Andrew Lesnie. **VHS** *FXL*

Temptress

Photographer Karin Swann (Kim Delaney) returns from India with a suggestive new tattoo to remind her of the "spiritual reawakening" she found when she tapped into her "goddess energy" on the long trip. Actually, she tapped into a little more than she realized and her goddess is one mean mother. Her live-in boyfriend (Chris Sarandon) is not amused. A mysterious stranger (Ben Cross) says that he understands. What follows is, in essence, a possession story, extremely well told. Writer Melissa Mitchell and director Lawrence Lanoff manage to combine the supernatural with everyday reality and psychological reality remarkably well. They also use the conventions of the genre to show both the creative and destructive aspects of sex. ✄✄✄

Nudity, sexual content, strong language, violence.

1995 **(R)** 93m/C Kim Delaney, Chris Sarandon, Corbin Bernsen, Dee Wallace Stone, Jessica Walter, Ben Cross; *D:* Lawrence Lanoff; *W:* Melissa Mitchell; *M:* Michael Stearns. **VHS** *PAR*

Teresa's Tattoo

Uneven screwball comedy is notable for engaging performances from the stars and a carload of cameo appearances. The titular Teresa (Adrienne Shelly) is a grad student

Guilty Pleasures

If there's a difference between big screen, big budget guilty pleasures, and their more modest video cousins, it's violence. Such theatrical hits as *Basic Instinct* and *Single White Female* carry an R-rating to its bloody limit.

But video premieres, which these days are almost always both R- and un-rated, are moving away from violence and toward a more romantic eroticism. That is, by no means, an absolute rule—there are a lot of disgustingly violent tapes out there—but it is a definite and, to my thinking, healthy trend in mainstream video.

Here are some of the best examples:

ANIMAL INSTINCTS	OVER THE WIRE
BEACH BABES FROM BEYOND	PLAY TIME
BODY OF INFLUENCE	STRIPSHOW
FEMALIEN	TEST TUBE TEENS FROM THE YEAR 2000
FRIEND OF THE FAMILY	VIRTUAL ENCOUNTERS
I LIKE TO PLAY GAMES	
MERIDIAN: KISS OF THE BEAST	

between actors and stars. Unfortunately, the rest of the film isn't as good as she is. 🐾🐾

Strong language, comic violence.

1994 88m/C Adrienne Shelly, C. Thomas Howell, Nancy McKeon, Lou Diamond Phillips, Casey Siemaszko, Jonathan Silverman; **Cameos:** Majel Barrett, Anthony Clark, Nanette Fabray, Tippi Hedren, k.d. lang, Joe Pantoliano, Mary Kay Place, Mare Winningham, Kiefer Sutherland; **D:** Julie Cypher; **W:** Georgie Huntington; **M:** Melissa Etheridge. **VHS** *VMK*

Terminal Exposure

Low-budget California comedy is a weird combination of Michelangelo Antonioni's *Blowup* and *Beach Blanket Bingo*. While they're out taking photos of women's bottoms on Venice Beach, Lenny (Mark Hennessy) and Bruce (Scott King) manage to capture a murder on film. They think they have shots of a dead man, and a woman (Hope Marie Carlton) with a pistol in her hand and a tattoo of a black rose on her left cheek. Inquiring minds want to know more, so Lenny and Bruce (yes, there are lots of interesting names here) investigate. Conspiracies, capos, criminals, chases, corpses, and countless cuties come into play before the conclusion. The young cast is attractive. Everyone onscreen handles this featherweight material with the right light touch. The pace is quick and the tone is breezy throughout. 🐾🐾🐾

Profanity, nudity, sexual situations, comic violence.

1989 (R) 105m/C Steve Donmyer, John Vernon, Ted Lange, Joe Phelan, Hope Marie Carlton, Mark Hennessy, Scott King; **D:** Nico Mastorakis. **VHS, LV** *LIV, VES*

Terminal Impact

As a general rule, avoid generic titles like *Terminal Impact*, though in this case, it is an accurate moniker for a *Terminator* retread. Max and Sam (Bryan Genesse and Frank Zagarino) are the toughest federal marshals in all Iowa (actually South Africa). They've got big biceps and big guns. Between explosions and chases, the plot deals with indestructible robots created by mad corporate scientists. It's all long, lively and senseless with been-there-seen-those stunts and effects. 🐾🐾

Violence, language.

1995 (R) 94m/C Bryan Genesse, Frank Zagarino, Jennifer Miller; **D:** Yossi Wein. **VHS, LV** *NLC*

who's a dead ringer for Gloria (ditto), who's being held hostage by three bumbling crooks. It all has to do with Gloria's "holographic" earrings which have the key to the code for the secret formula, or something like that. Whatever.... Shelly has developed a following in such offbeat independent comedies as *The Unbelievable Truth* and *Hold Me, Thrill Me, Kiss Me*, and this may be her best role to date. She brings a real sense of energy and spontaneity to her work. It's a cliche but it's true: the camera loves her. And that "likability," for want of a better word, is the difference

Terrified

Quirky suspense film defies easy categorization or review. It's a guessing game. The audience knows that Olive (Heather Graham) is a troubled young woman. With good reason. But when she claims that she's being stalked by a stranger and is attacked in her apartment, is she fantasizing or telling the truth? Are director James Merendino and co-writer Megan Heath taking *Repulsion* as their model? Or is it *Psycho*? Or are they up to something else entirely? Balancing that elliptical uncertainty, much of the dialogue seems absolutely authentic. Despite some narrative lapses and a conclusion that won't sit well with all viewers, this one still earns a strong recommendation for fans of psychological puzzles. 🦴🦴🦴

Mature subject matter, violence, strong language, sexual content, brief nudity.

1994 **(R)** 90m/C Heather Graham, Lisa Zane, Rustam Branaman, Tom Breznahan; *Cameos:* Max Perlich, Balthazar Getty, Richard Lynch, Don Calfa; *D:* James Merendino; *W:* Megan Heath. **VHS** *APX*

Test Tube Teens from the Year 2000

The opening titles, presented over the silhouette of a naked dancing woman, could have come straight from the mid-'60s. The fast-forwardable plot concerns the title characters' (Ian Abercrombie and Brian Bremer) efforts to go back in time and stop Morgan Fairchild from banning conventional reproduction. The rest of the movie is set in a girls' boarding school. Production designer Arlan Jay Vetter and art director Matthew Kern Atzenhoffer took their cue from the deliberately cheesy sets and props used on television's *Mystery Science Theater 3000*. Don't miss the apple corer that's glued to the front of the time machine and the white "boots" made of cardboard sleeves over tennis shoes. This, folks, is what low-budget video is all about. *AKA:* Virgin Hunters. 🦴🦴 **GPI:** 7.4

Nudity, sexual content.

1993 **(R)** 74m/C Morgan Fairchild, Ian Abercrombie, Brian Bremer, Christopher Wolf, Michelle Matheson, Sara Suzanne Brown, Don Dowe; *D:* Ellen Cabot; *W:* Kenneth J. Hall; *M:* Reg Powell. **VHS, LV** *PAR*

Tetsuo: The Iron Man

One morning, a Japanese fellow looks in the mirror and finds an aluminum zit on his cheek. He pops it and blood spurts everywhere. Then before you know it, he's being chased around a subway station by a woman who's got metal goop on her forehead and hand, which she may have got by touching a second guy. When guy number one goes back home to his girlfriend, more metallic accoutrements pop up, and unless you're into some very kinky stuff, that's all you want to know. What follows is more comic than shocking. Yes, it's all grotesque, violent, and sexual but it's handled like an exaggerated silent comedy. The film was made in grainy black and white and the special effects aren't particularly special. Imagine a fast-paced MTV version of that alternative classic *Robot Monster*, the B-movie featuring a guy in a gorilla suit and a diving helmet, and you're close to the mark. Silly and inventive, yes. Shocking and memorable, not really. 🦴🦴

Contains graphic special effects, sexual material.

1992 67m/B *JP* Tomoroh Taguchi, Kei Fujiwara, Shinya Tsukamoto; *D:* Shinya Tsukamoto; *W:* Shinya Tsukamoto. **VHS** *FXL*

Texas Payback

Action flick is a poorly made celebration of firearms. The fight scenes are clumsy and slow, and the more dramatic moments are downright embarrassing. The opening shot of chaingang convicts weeding desert scrub brush is a tip-off that this one's scraping the bottom of the low-budget barrel. After that, raving bad guy Gary Hudson escapes and sets off for vengeance against ex-Texas Rangers Sam Jones and Bo Hopkins, who has plumped up to become novelist Tom Clancy's lost twin. Lots of weapons are fired and junkyard wrecks crash and explode on Las Vegas locations. 🦴

Violence, language, brief nudity.

Video Premieres

1995 (R) 96m/C Sam Jones, Gary Hudson, Kathleen Kinmont, Bo Hopkins; **D:** Richard W. Munchkin; **W:** Brian Page; **C:** Mark Morris; **M:** Jim Halfpenny. **VHS** *CAF*

That's Action!

Compilation of stunts and fight scenes from several low-budget action movies on the A.I.P. label is an exercise in video recycling. It's competent material lightened by humor, most of it intentional. But when all of the crashes and shoot-outs and martial artistry are removed from any narrative context, they become boring. For an action movie to work effectively, the viewer has to believe in the context. Whether the conflict is set in feudal Japan, an office building on Christmas Eve, or a galaxy far far away, we have to accept that world as real. If not, even the most compelling action is meaningless. 🦴🦴

Brief nudity, profanity, violence.

1990 78m/C David Carradine, Robert Ginty, Oliver Reed, Reb Brown. **VHS** *AIP*

That's Black Entertainment

Writer, director, and narrator William Greaves says, "If you didn't see these films, and you happen to be white, maybe it's because you weren't supposed to." He's right. Under the institutionalized segregation of the 1930s and '40s, black people weren't allowed in many white establishments, including theatres. There was a chain of about 1,100 theatres across the country that showed movies made by black filmmakers for black audiences. Economic realities being what they were, these films were made on extremely low budgets and so they lack the slickness of mainstream studio films. But they told the same kinds of stories—Westerns, musicals, dramas, mysteries—from a black perspective. Hundreds were made but only a few have survived. This collection contains clips from 29 of them, including two black newsreels. At a time when Hollywood films were routinely racist and patronizing toward black characters—if they were included at all—these films presented a more accurate reflection of their audience. And they gave the few established black stars an opportunity to work outside the system. Bessie Smith, Lena Horn, Paul Robeson, Eubie Blake, Cab Calloway, Nat "King" Cole, Ethel Waters, Cicely Tyson, and a very young Sammy Davis Jr. had roles. It's impossible to judge the quality of the filmmaking from these brief clips, but that's not really important. The major directors, Oscar Micheaux and Spencer Williams, seem to have been the Roger Cormans of their day, economizing wherever they could and telling human-scale stories that fit their budgets. The most intriguing clips are from Williams' version of Somerset Maugham's story, "Rain," retitled *Dirty Gertie from Harlem, U.S.A,* Micheaux's *Murder in Harlem,* and Powell Lindsey's *Souls of Sin.* Befitting its subject, the film is told simply, without tricky effects or editing. It's a fine introduction to a particular kind of American movie that many of us know nothing about. 🦴🦴🦴

Contains no objectionable material.

1985 60m/C Ethel Waters, Sammy Davis Jr., Lena Horne, Spencer Williams Jr., Nat King Cole, Bessie Smith, Cab Calloway, Eubie Blake, Paul Robeson, Cicely Tyson; **D:** William Greaves; **W:** William Greaves. **VHS** *VCI, FCT, BTV*

Theodore Rex

S-f comedy is probably the most expensive studio production to go directly to video and it really doesn't deserve that dubious distinction. Not it's that great—it isn't—but many movies that are even worse have shown up in theatres. As a fantasy for kids it's every bit as good as *Super Mario Bros., Lawnmower Man 2,* or any number of recent releases. It's set in a near future when cute dinosaurs have been recreated by a scientist (Armin Mueller-Stahl) and partially integrated into human society. The parallels between racism and "speciesism" are heavy handed at best, but that won't bother the target audience. They'll enjoy seeing Whoopi Goldberg as a tough cop whose new partner is Theodore "Teddy" Rex, a cookie-craving, vegetarian touchy-feely dinosaur. Writer/director Jonathan Betuel tones down the shoot-'em-up violence and tones up the potty humor. The make-up effects have the simplicity and obvious emotions that kids like. ✂✂

Mild violence and bathroom humor.

1995 (PG) 92m/C Whoopi Goldberg, Armin Mueller-Stahl, Richard Roundtree, Juliet Landau; **D:** Jonathan Betuel; **W:** Jonathan Betuel; **C:** David Tattersall; **M:** Robert Folk. **VHS, LV** *NLC*

There Goes My Baby

1965 is a pivotal year for a group of Los Angeles high school seniors. Stick (Rick Schroder) is a surfer who's about to go to Vietnam. Finnegan (Noah Wyle) is the straight-arrow honor student headed for Harvard. His equally respectable girlfriend Tracy (Kristin Minter)—"a perfect 34-C at age 12"—isn't sure what she'll do. Calvin (Kenny Ransom), their black friend, doesn't know which world he belongs in when Watts erupts in riots. Babette (Jill Schoelen) dreams of being a rock star. Free spirits Pirate (Dermot Mulroney) and Sunshine (Kelli Williams) are about ten minutes ahead of the hippie movement. Mary Beth (Lucy Deakins) is our narrator, who explains what these young men and women are up to. Mirroring the larger domestic and international upheavals going on around them, their favorite hang-out, Pop's Paradise, is about to be bulldozed to make room for a shopping center. Writer/director Floyd Mutrux, who was also responsible for the cult hit *American Hot Wax,* divides the action fairly evenly among his large ensemble cast, and he got fine performances from them. His script may not be one hundred percent true in terms of historical fact, but he gets the emotions absolutely right. For teenagers, those were heady days of conflict and uncertainty, and the film captures that instability. Though there is a certain unavoidable *American Graffiti* nostalgia to the film, Mutrux also borrows a more hardheaded sensibility from *Medium Cool.* It's an unusual combination, but one that finally works well and winds up at just the right ending. ✂✂✂✇

Strong language, violence, sexual content.

1992 (R) 99m/C Dermot Mulroney, Rick Schroder, Kelli Williams, Jill Schoelen, Noah Wyle, Kristin Minter, Lucy Deakins, Kenny Ransom, Seymour Cassel, Paul Gleason, Frederick Coffin, Andrew (Andy) Robinson, Shon Greenblatt, J.E. Freeman; **D:** Floyd Mutrux; **W:** Floyd Mutrux. **VHS, LV** *ORI*

There Goes the Neighborhood

Comedy of fits and starts doesn't get the most out of a high-powered cast but still has its moments. The plot hinges on $8.5 million in cash buried beneath a suburban house. Normally, prison psychiatrist Jeff Daniels would dismiss the tale as a convict's fantasy. But when he learns that it could be true, he heads for the 'burbs. The loot is supposed to be under Catherine O'Hara's place. She's in the middle of a nasty divorce, and her nosy neighbors are more than a little interested. So are the three ex-cons who have already tried to kill Daniels. As far as production values go, this one is a medium-budget, back-lot exercise. Even if the film isn't a *Home Alone* for adults, it's got enough laughs to earn a recommendation. ✂✂

Language, comic violence.

1992 (PG-13) 88m/C Jeff Daniels, Catherine O'Hara, Dabney Coleman, Hector Elizondo, Judith Ivey, Rhea Perlman, Harris Yulin, Jonathan Banks, Chazz Palminteri, Mary Gross; **D:** Bill Phillips; **M:** David Bell. **VHS** *PAR*

They Bite

The legitimate cinematic heir to *Frankenstein Meets the Space Monster* is the funniest low-budget horror satire to show up since the demise of the drive-in. The setting is Florida and the subject, appropriately, is the making of a low-budget horror movie. While the schlockmeisters (including porn star Ron Jeremy) are making their flick, real fish monsters and other weird guys are invading the beaches. Ichthyologist Melody Duncan (Donna Frotscher) is on the case. It's obvious that writer/director Brett Piper loves his subject matter. (True cognoscenti will catch his arcane reference to another low-budget epic, *The Boogens.*) The effects range from really silly rubber suits to good model work. The acting (both professional and non-) is fine but it's the humor that makes this one so much fun. Required viewing for fans. Also available in an unrated version. ✂✂✂

Consumer VCR Smarts

Consumer VCR Smarts (JDM Communications; $14.95, trade paper) is a fine reference book. Authors David Scott and Jason MacZura run a VCR and TV repair shop in Tulsa, Oklahoma, and if they're not memorable prose stylists, they know their business.

They make no recommendations on individual models or brand names. The book is filled with solid advice on the equipment features that consumers should look for and those they should avoid. It also has more esoteric knowledge that most of us probably don't know. For example, the powerful electric motors in most vacuum cleaners can damage video tapes and distort the color on floor-level TV screens. Low-cost blank tapes that don't display the letters "VHS" inside the rectangular logo box don't meet the minimum quality standards of the company that holds the patent, and should be avoided.

The book also covers cable and antenna connections, camcorders, and video games. Laserdisc players and interactive video are not included.

Nudity, comic violence, strong language.

1995 (R) 96m/C Donna Frotscher, Nick Baldasare, Charlie Barnett, Ron Jeremy; *D:* Bret Piper; *W:* Bret Piper. **VHS** *MTH*

Thieves of Fortune

Silly adventure combines the sensibility of *Romancing the Stone* with a dash of *Tootsie*. Shawn Weatherly has to disguise herself as a man to claim an inheritance in South America. She and Michael Nouri dash through a series of cliff-hangers involving plane crashes, shoot-outs, and such. When Weatherly is decked out in her macho duds and fake beard, she's a dead ringer for William Hurt in *I Love You to Death*. The leads have a light touch. 🦴🦴 **GPI: 6.2**

Strong language, some violence, brief nudity, sexual situations.

1989 (R) 100m/C Michael Nouri, Lee Van Cleef, Shawn Weatherly; *D:* Michael McCarthy. **VHS, LV** *ACA*

32 Short Films about Glenn Gould

For those who may be only casually familiar with the name, Glenn Gould was a Canadian pianist who decided not to perform publicly at the height of his career. He devoted the rest of his professional life to recording until he died of a stroke at age 50, leaving half his estate to the Society for the Prevention of Cruelty to Animals and half to the Salvation Army. A child prodigy, he grew up to be a true genius, albeit an eccentric, completely self-involved genius with a taste for arrowroot cookies and ketchup. Here he's presented as a man for whom all sound—from conversations overheard in a truck stop to a Bach prelude—was pure abstraction. As the title suggests, his story is told in vignettes. Some, featuring actor Colm Feore, dramatize moments in Gould's life; others are interviews with people who knew and worked with him; some are experimental pieces. One of those examines the inner workings of a piano during a Gould performance. Another is made of moving X-rays of living people. Director Francois Girard has placed Gould's music at the center of each of these short films, sometimes fading into the background but more often overpowering the visual aspects. Think of this one as a long-form music video for grown-ups. 🦴🦴🦴

Contains no objectionable material.

1993 94m/C CA Colm Feore, Gale Garnett, David Hughes; *D:* Francois Girard; *W:* Don McKellar, Francois Girard. Genie Awards '93: Best Cinematography, Best Director (Girard), Best Film, Best Film Editing; Nominations: Independent Spirit Awards '95: Best Foreign Language Film. **VHS, LV** *COL*

This Gun for Hire

Only the bare bones of the plot remain the same in this low-octane adaptation of Graham Greene's fine suspense novel. Robert Wagner turns in a lethargic performance as a hitman betrayed by his employers. Nancy Everhard is much brighter as a stripper he kidnaps, and character actor John Harkins steals the film as a duplicitous go-between. He looks and sounds like a Southern Sidney Greenstreet. The setting is New Orleans and director Lou Antonio gets as much mileage as he can out of the locations. 🎻🎻

Brief nudity, violence, strong language.

1990 (R) 89m/C Robert Wagner, Nancy Everhard, Frederic Lehne, John Harkins; **D:** Lou Antonio. **VHS** *MCA*

Three of Hearts

New York phone sex hustler Joey (William Baldwin) finds himself caught in the middle of a serious lovers' quarrel between Connie (Kelly Lynch) and Ellen (Sherilyn Fenn), who has walked out of their relationship. But Connie still loves her. When Joey boasts, "Any woman, any time, any place, guaranteed," Connie hires him to seduce and abandon Ellen, thereby winning her back. As a romantic comedy, the film has some good moments. An uneven tone is balanced against three good performances by the leads. Perhaps because the filmmakers were a little uncertain about how to handle these unusual characters, they made two endings. Before the movie was released on tape, video retailers and distributors saw both endings and voted on their favorite. They did the right thing and retained the original, despite the fact that it contains a blatant continuity error. Note how Baldwin's T-shirt miraculously changes color during the last scene. 🎻🎻🎻

Mature subject matter, strong language, some violence.

1993 (R) 102m/C Kelly Lynch, William Baldwin, Sherilyn Fenn, Joe Pantoliano, Gail Strickland, Cec Verrell, Claire Callaway, Tony Amendola; **D:** Yurek Bogayevicz; **W:** Philip C. Epstein, Adam Greenman; **M:** Richard Gibbs. **VHS, LV** *COL, IME, FCT*

Thunderground

Action movie about hobos and bare-knuckle boxing is cut from the same cloth as Clint Eastwood's *Every Which Way* comedies and Walter Hill's first film, *Hard Times.* The plot is standard stuff. Burt (Paul Coufos) is a down-on-his-luck

fighter; Casey (Margaret Langrick) is the tough-talking gamin who becomes his manager. Together, they make their way from Hobo Junction, Tennessee, to New Orleans for a fight with The Man (professional wrestler Jesse Ventura), a legendary and eccentric rich guy. The only real surprises in the story come from the characters themselves. The film is carefully paced so we have time to get to know them. Burt and Casey are flawed, likable, and sympathetic, and, in the end, they have remarkable depth. The violence is strictly bare-knuckle fantasy, and the fights are well-choreographed. 🎻🎻🎻

Violence and profanity.

1989 (R) 92m/C Paul Coufos, Margaret Langrick, Jesse Ventura, M. Emmet Walsh; **D:** David Mitchell. **VHS, LV** *IME*

Tiger Warsaw

Tiger (Patrick Swayze), a man with a secret in his past, comes back home to a small Pennsylvania town, but virtually no one wants to see him—not his dad (Lee Richardson), not his sister (Mary McDonnell). Only an old sort-of-girlfriend (Barbara Williams), who's now divorced, and his mother (Piper Laurie) are at all glad he's back. Tiger says that he's kicked a serious drug habit, and now wants to atone for the mysterious sins of his youth. The cast is excellent. Even when the story gets a bit far-fetched, the characters maintain believability. The film as a whole stands or falls on Swayze's performance and he's very good. Perhaps he overdoes it somewhat, but his character is edgy, nervous, full of barely controlled emotions, and that seems right for a recovering addict who could go either way. But even Swayze's most ardent fans will probably admit that it all gets a little overwrought toward the end. **AKA:** The Tiger. 🎻🎻🎻

Profanity, violence, sexual situations.

1987 (R) 92m/C Patrick Swayze, Barbara Williams, Piper Laurie, Bobby DiCicco, Kaye Ballard, Lee Richardson, Mary McDonnell; **D:** Amin Q. Chaudhri. **VHS, LV** *COL*

The Tigress

Underfed European production seems to be set in the 1920s. Perhaps the producers couldn't

The Hound's Favorite Sleepers: Unclassifiable

The Hound understands that some may quibble with an "unclassifiable" classification, but such contradictions make life more interesting. Besides, several of these titles also appear on other Favorite Sleeper lists, so they're *not* unclassifiable, after all. But each is nutty and/or odd enough to deserve inclusion here.

DIAL HELP	MIRACLE MILE
FATALLY YOURS	MR. FROST
IN A MOMENT OF PASSION	SLEEPWALK
LOVE IS A GUN	

afford to fill all of the sets so there are large dark areas in many of the early scenes. The plot has something to do with a con man (James Remar) and a conwoman (Valentina Vargas) attempting to swindle an astonishingly plump George Peppard who wears a tux and a silly cowboy hat. Also available in an unrated version. 🐾

Strong language, brief nudity, sexual activity, some violence.

1993 (R) 89m/C Valentina Vargas, James Remar, George Peppard; *D:* Karin Howard. **VHS, LV** *VMK*

Till the End of the Night

Young architect John Davenport (Scott Valentine) and his wife Diana (Katherine Kelly Lang) are on the verge of financial and personal success when evil parolee Drew Darcy (John Enos) shows up to stalk the couple and their two young children. He's the ex- that Diana has neglected to mention, and his years in the pen have made him a tad jealous. Yes, it's *Cape Fear Lite.* To their credit, the cast handles the material with more professionalism than it sometimes deserves. In key scenes the dialogue is tediously repetitive, with characters explaining over and over what the audience already knows. And a major subplot involving David Keith is too transparent. Solid production values and performances, particularly from Enos, are the main attractions. 🐾🐾

Violence, strong language, sexual material, brief nudity.

1994 (R) 90m/C John Enos, Katherine Kelly Lang, Scott Valentine, David Keith; *D:* Larry Brand; *W:* Larry Brand. **VHS** *COL*

The Time Guardian

Australian s-f borrows liberally from *The Terminator* near the beginning, but soon establishes its own style. It opens in the future where a domed city is being attacked by robot-like critters who look like they're AWOL from a Saturday morning kids' show. They are the Jen-Diki, half human, half machine, all nasty. But the city can travel in time and manages to escape. After more confusing exposition, two of the city's residents—Ballard (Tom Burlinson), a hard-case Jen-Diki fighter, and Petra (Carrie Fisher)—are dispatched to the 20th century outback to prepare for the damaged city's arrival. A pretty geologist, Annie (Nikki Coghill), agrees to help them, though the thick-headed local police do nothing but get in the way. Of course, the Jen-Diki are lurking about, too. Oddly, the big battle scenes, filled with smoke and laser blasts and such, are the least engaging parts of the story. 🐾🐾🐾

Violence, profanity, brief nudity.

1987 (PG) 105m/C Tom Burlinson, Carrie Fisher, Dean Stockwell, Nikki Coghill; *D:* Brian Hannant; *W:* Brian Hannant, John Baxter; *C:* Geoff Burton. **VHS, LV** *COL, NLC*

Time Indefinite

Ross McElwee continues his meditations on family, marriage, aging, children, dogs, reli gion, race relations, death, and fish begun in *Sherman's March.* He opens with the announcement of his engagement to a pleasant woman named Marilyn. She's a fellow filmmaker who doesn't seem to mind McElwee's compulsion to turn his own life into a movie, even when it involves his accompanying her to the gynecologist's office. Many familiar characters from his earlier films reappear: Charleen, Lucille, Melvin, and others. And though McElwee is dealing with the most serious subjects and the most powerful emotions, his sense of humor is intact. So is his light touch. 🦴🦴🦴🦴

Contains some graphic medical scenes, brief nudity.

1993 117m/C *D:* Ross McElwee; *W:* Ross McElwee. **VHS** *ICA*

A Time to Die

Three things separate this one from the dozens of shoot-'em-ups that show up on tape every month: first, its attention to characters; second, a plot that revolves around the relationship between a divorced mother and her five-year-old son; and finally, unusually sharp production values for a low-budget film. Jackie Swanson (Traci Lords) is a divorced photographer. Because she's the victim of a trumped up cocaine charge, her ex- has custody of the boy. She's involved in community service work, and a possible romance with a cop, when she discovers a police conspiracy. Writer/director Charles Kanganis is more comfortable with characters than action, and the first part of the film is stronger than the conclusion. 🦴🦴🦴

Violence, strong language, brief nudity and sexual content.

1991 (R) 93m/C Traci Lords, Jeff Conaway, Richard Roundtree, Bradford Bancroft, Nitchie Barrett; *D:* Charles Kanganis; *W:* Charles Kanganis; *M:* Louis Febre. **VHS, LV** *PMH*

Time to Kill

Imagine a spaghetti Western version of a particularly grim Albert Camus existential novel about fate, death, and fascism. Got that? Now put Nicolas Cage in the lead and dress him in outfits from Banana Republic. He's Enrico, an Italian soldier in Africa some time before World War II. After a strange encounter with an African woman, he is wracked with guilt and spends the rest of the movie trying to atone for his many sins. Sort of. The story is very slow in the telling and at times unintentionally funny. Cage has never avoided outrageous, overstated characterizations and this one is no exception. **AKA:** Tempo di Uccidere. 🦴

Sexual content, brief nudity, pretentious cinematic philosophy.

1989 (R) 110m/C Nicolas Cage, Giancarlo Giannini, Robert Liensol; *D:* Guiliano Montaldo; *W:* Furio Scarpelli; *M:* Ennio Morricone. **VHS, LV** *REP*

Timebomb

Tricky s-f suspense story is the kind of thing that Dean R. Koontz and Stephen King handle so well in fiction. Though it slips from time to time, the pace is quick and the plot takes enough unexpected twists to smooth over the rough stretches. Eddy Kay (Michael Biehn) lives an ordinary life as a watchmaker. But that changes when he rescues a woman and her baby from a burning building. His heroism is captured on the local TV news, bringing him to the attention of a shady government type (Richard Jordan) and a team of assassins, led by Tracy Scoggins doing a grand Dragon-Lady turn. At the same time, he begins to suffer from hallucinations so vivid that they lead him to psychiatrist Patsy Kensit. Then he realizes that he can speak and understand Hungarian. Viewers familiar with the structure that Koontz and King employ will probably figure out some of the plot twists before they should. But judged by just about any standard you care to apply, this one is as good as most films that come through the theatres every week. (By the way, comedienne Julie Brown makes an uncredited cameo as a waitress.) 🦴🦴🦴

Graphic violence, strong language, nudity, sexual content.

1991 (R) 96m/C Michael Biehn, Patsy Kensit, Tracy Scoggins, Robert Culp, Richard Jordan, Raymond St. Jacques, Jim Maniaci, Billy Blanks, Ray "Boom Boom" Mancini, Steven J. Oliver; *Cameos:* Julie Brown; *D:* Avi Nesher; *W:* Avi Nesher; *M:* Patrick Leonard. **VHS, LV** *MGM*

Tina Turner: The Girl from Nutbush

Generally praiseful video biography doesn't over-glamorize its subject. At the same time, it neither probes too deep nor shows Tina Turner in anything but a favorable light. All of the controversies and troubles in her life are presented as things that happened to her, not things she was responsible for. By now, everyone who's interested in her music must know the bare facts of her life: how she came from a small town, met band leader Ike Turner in St. Louis, became a singer and then the star of the show and then his wife. From there, the story gets ugly but this examination of the singer's life gives the bad years only an indirect glance. It's more focused on her second musical career after she met Roger Davies, who returned her to stardom. Her pals Mick Jagger, David Bowie, and Mark Knopfler show up to say even more nice things about her, and all that's just fine. This tape is an appreciation, not an expose. There's no reason to be too critical. 𝄞𝄞𝄞

Contains no objectionable material.

1993 103m/C **VHS, LV** *VTR, FCT*

To Die For

This is the umpteenth version of the vampire in contemporary L.A. plot, but it's told with solid production values, good acting, and relatively restrained effects. What really sets this one apart, though, is the feminine point of view. They could have called Leslie King's script *Designing Women Meet Dracula*. Realtor Kate Wooten (Sydney Walsh) meets Vlad (Brendan Hughes) at a party and is immediately smitten. He, you understand, is the dark, passionate, Byronic sort of vampire who could have come straight from the cover of a paperback bodice-ripper. Her friends become involved, and there's also a "bad" vampire hanging around to complicate matters. Followed by a sequel. 𝄞𝄞𝄞

Strong sexual content, violent special effects, profanity.

1989 (R) 99m/C Brendan Hughes, Scott Jacoby, Duane Jones, Steve Bond, Sydney Walsh, Amanda Wyss, Ava Fabian; *D:* Deran Sarafian; *W:* Leslie King; *M:* Cliff Eidelman. **VHS, LV** *ACA*

To Die For 2: Son of Darkness

Horror fans will remember that in the first film, a pretty L.A. realtor fell in love with a "good" Byronic vampire and ran afoul of his "bad" brother. Here the situation is the same but the location has moved to the rural Lake Serenity. When Nina's (Rosalind Allen) adopted baby becomes mysteriously ill, she takes him to Dr. Max Schreck (Michael Praed). He "cures" the boy by increasing his red cell count. Before long, she's visiting Max's estate for dinner and whatever. At the same time, his evil, cigar-smoking brother Tom (Steve Bond) and Celia (Amanda Wyss) are terrorizing the local population. The sheriff (Vince Edwards) blames coyote attacks. The sensual and romantic aspects of the story can be traced to Anne Rice's vampire novels. The film also has a strong streak of humor. The acting, stunt work, and special effects are first rate, and though the film is a bit violent, it's actually restrained by contemporary standards. 𝄞𝄞𝄞

Violence, nudity, strong sexual content.

1991 (R) 95m/C Rosalind Allen, Steve Bond, Scott Jacoby, Michael Praed, Jay Underwood, Amanda Wyss, Remy O'Neill, Vince Edwards; *D:* David F. Price. **VHS** *VMK*

To Sleep with a Vampire

Despite the title and some grimy settings, this is a remarkably intelligent and well made low-budget movie. The main characters are a sensitive, nameless vampire (Scott Valentine) and Nina (Charlie Spradling), a suicidal stripper. She desperately wants to see her estranged young son before she ends her life; he wants to know what the sun feels like. In Patricia Harrington's script, eventually they come to an understanding. In places, the story is too talky, but director Adam Friedman makes the most of limited special effects (including switchblade fingernails) and got moving performances from his leads. Though they sound like cliches, these two become sympathetic, fully believable characters before it's over. 🐾🐾🐾

Violence, nudity, sexual content, strong language.

1992 (R) 90m/C Scott Valentine, Charlie Spradling, Richard Zobel, Ingrid Vold, Stephanie Hardy; **D:** Adam Friedman; **W:** Patricia Harrington. **VHS** *NHO*

To the Limit

Purposefully bad action flick is made watchable through liberal use of the fast-forward button. The only attraction is *Playboy* and Guess Jeans model Anna Nicole Smith as a buxom CIA hitperson involved with spies, rogue Vietnam vets, and the Mafia. The film appears to have been made on the fly and/or rushed into release to capitalize on the tabloid goddess' widowhood from an aging Texas millionaire. 🐾🐾

Violence, sexual material, nudity, strong language.

1995 (R) 96m/C Anna Nicole Smith, Joey Travolta, Michael Nouri, Branscombe Richmond, John Aprea, Kathy Shower, Rebecca Ferratti, David Proval; **D:** Raymond Martino; **W:** Joey Travolta, Raymond Martino; **M:** Jim Halfpenny. **VHS** *PMH*

Tokyo Decadence

Fascinating but grim film examines the life of a prostitute. Ai (Miho Nikaido) caters to the sadistic sexual proclivities of upscale clients. She's superstitious, none-too-bright and, despite her profession, naive. Ryu Murakami based the screenplay on his own novel and directed the film. It's slowly paced and Felliniesque at times, but throughout, he manages to tell a story about the most serious kinds of exploitation without ever being exploitative. With this kind of material, it's difficult to say what individual viewers will judge to be erotic. From my point of view, it didn't appear that Murakami was trying to excite or titillate his audience. Instead, he presents this young woman without making value judgments. He neither condemns nor glorifies her. Once the shock value of her profession has worn off, she's really uninteresting and banal. Her clients are shown as wealthy, dangerous, and deeply flawed. Comparisons to *In the Realm of the Senses* are inevitable but while

this one isn't nearly as explicit, it isn't nearly as passionate either. 🐾🐾🐾

Nudity and sexual material.

1991 (NC-17) 92m/C *JP* Miho Nikaido, Tenmei Kano, Yayoi Kusama, Sayoko Amano; **D:** Ryu Murakami; **W:** Ryu Murakami; **M:** Ryuichi Sakamoto. **VHS, LV** *TRI, FCT*

Tollbooth

Funky comedy revels in its own ugliness. Writer/director Salome Breziner's shapeless script often stops cold to focus on roadkill and dismembered body parts. What story there is revolves around the rocky romance between dimbulb tollbooth attendant Jack (Lenny Von Dohlen) and gas jockey Doris (Fairuza Balk) who's waiting for her long-gone daddy to return to their Florida Keys mobile home. Meanwhile, she's also carrying on with a baitshop owner (Will Patton). The good moments look like ideas borrowed from writer Harry Crews' reject file. Despite the glaring flaws, the film has enough unpredictably and quirkiness to earn a qualified recommendation for fans of the offbeat. 🐾🐾

Mature subject matter, overall tone, strong language, fleeting nudity.

1994 (R) 108m/C Fairuza Balk, Lenny Von Dohlen, Will Patton, Seymour Cassel, James Wilder, Louise Fletcher, William Katt; **D:** Salome Breziner; **W:** Salome Breziner; **C:** Henry Vargas; **M:** Adam Gorgoni. **VHS, LV** *NLC*

Tomcat: Dangerous Desires

Richard Grieco becomes the title character after scientist Maryam D'Abo does a little Frankenstein number on him to cure a genetic disorder. He gets quick reflexes, an affinity for high places, and loose morals. The low-budget Canadian film has a certain grotesque humor that helps it over the rough spots. Considering the formulaic nature of the material, the acting's not bad either. The main problem here is that the story is over about 15 minutes before the movie is, so the conclusion is needlessly padded. 🐾🐾

extensively tested with young audiences to ensure maximum popularity across the targeted age ranges. But they make grown-up reviewers nauseous because they're so cliched and saccharine. On this side of the video landscape, however, the opinions of grown-up reviewers don't mean squat. 🦴🦴

Contains no objectionable material.

1996 85m/C D: Stephen Anderson, Tom Decker, Rhoydon Shishido; **V:** Jonathan Taylor Thomas, Bradley Michael Pierce, Benjamin Salisbury. **VHS** *PAR*

Tough and Deadly

Amnesiac spy Billy Blanks and hustling bounty hunter Roddy Piper team up against bad government guys. It's standard stuff, but the stars have that elusive "chemistry" in the comic scenes. Good action, too. 🦴🦴🦴

Violence, strong language.

1994 (R) 92m/C Billy Blanks, Roddy Piper; **D:** Steve Cohen. **VHS** *MCA*

The Toxic Avenger

Made on a tiny, tiny budget and apparently filmed on location in New Jersey, Troma's alternative superhero is a *Mad* magazine/ Three Stooges sort of horror comedy. Melvin is a weakling who's dumped into an open vat of toxic waste and emerges as Toxie the monstrous Avenger, a rough cross between Arnold Schwarzenegger and Mr. Potato-Head, who proceeds to fight injustice wherever he finds it. That includes bad guys (and bad girls) who like to go out and drive drunk and run down kids on bikes. We're not talking subtlety here. And if you think those guys are bad, just wait until you see what Toxie does to the thieves who try to rob Tromaville's finest Mexican restaurant. Followed by sequels. Also available in an unrated version. 🦴🦴🦴

Violence, strong language, nudity, sexual content.

1986 (R) 90m/C Mitchell Cohen, Andree Maranda, Jennifer Baptist, Robert Prichard, Cindy Manion; **D:** Michael Herz, Lloyd (Samuel Weil) Kaufman; **W:** Joe Ritter. **VHS, LV** *VES, LIV*

Strong language, nudity, sexual content, some violence.

1993 (R) 96m/C Richard Grieco, Maryam D'Abo, Natalie Radford; **D:** Paul Donovan. **VHS, LV** *REP*

Toto: Lost in New York

Following one lamentable trend in animated entertainment, characters from a proven favorite—*The Wizard of Oz* here—are recast as contemporary kids with lame results. The animation, writing, and music are substandard but the bright colors will appeal to children who like Saturday morning fare. A comparatively small part of this story actually takes place in Oz. Following episodes (and there will be more) will probably change that. All of these "recycled" cartoons have probably been

Tracks of a Killer

Hard-nosed businessman Hawk (James Brolin) invites his protege Patrick (Wolf Larson) to his mountaintop retreat for a winter vacation. Little does Hawk know that his ultra-competitive management philosophy has turned Patrick into a raving psychotic! Tough luck for their wives Clair (Kelly LeBrock) and Bella (Courtney Taylor). Obvious and repetitive dialogue and unconventional plotting lead to some screwy torture scenes that might be offensive if they were at all believable. As it is, director Harvey Frost has created a film that looks terrific even at its silliest. 𝄢𝄢𝄢

Violence, language, brief nudity, sexual material.

1995 **(R)** 100m/C Kelly Le Brock, James Brolin, Wolf Larson, Courtney Taylor, George Touliatos; **D:** Harvey Frost; **W:** Michael Cooney; **C:** Bruce Worrall; **M:** Barron Abramovitch. **VHS, LV** *LIV*

Trade Off

Yet another attempt to remake *Double Indemnity* and *Body Heat* meets with a notable lack of success. Thomas (Adam Baldwin) is unhappily married to Karen (Megan Gallagher) when he meets Jackie (Theresa Russell) in a bar. As luck would have it, she's got an inconvenient husband she'd like to be rid of and suggests that they help each other out. Thomas is reluctant but persuadable. Yes, fans of the genre have seen it all before, but they've seldom seen it handled so transparently. It's easy to stay one or two steps ahead of director Andrew Lane's script. The performances are so-so, and the "passionate" affair at the heart of the story is pretty timid. Virtually the same stuff was handled with much more trashy elan a couple of years ago in *Dead On,* a fine sleeper. 𝄢

Mature subject matter, violence, strong language, brief nudity, sexual content.

1995 **(R)** 92m/C Theresa Russell, Adam Baldwin, Megan Gallagher, Barry Primus, Pat Skipper; **D:** Andrew Lane; **W:** Andrew Lane. **VHS, LV** *REP*

Transmutations

Genre-bender begins well with lots of action setting up the conflict virtually without dialogue. As it goes along, the story mixes the detective and horror genres fairly well, but the ending is a letdown. A solid cast of character actors does good work. The special effects are relatively restrained because the aim is a certain thoughtfulness. **AKA:** Underworld. 𝄢𝄢

Violence, strong language.

1985 **(R)** 103m/C *GB* Denholm Elliott, Steven Berkoff, Miranda Richardson, Nicola Cowper, Larry Lamb, Art Malik, Ingrid Pitt, Irina Brook, Paul Brown; **D:** George Pavlou; **W:** James Caplin, Clive Barker. **VHS, LV** *LIV, VES*

Transylvania Twist

Director Jim Wynorski makes good bad movies (*The Lost Empire*) and rotten bad movies (*The Return of Swamp Thing*). This is one of the good ones. It borrows footage from several of Roger Corman's old films and tosses in screwy quotes from such disparate sources as *Night of the Living Dead* and *Taxi Driver*. It's even got a few seconds of music that sounds like Spike Jones' version of *Bolero*. 𝄢𝄢 **GPI: 6.4**

Strong language, some violence, brief nudity, and sexual situations.

1989 **(PG-13)** 90m/C Robert Vaughn, Teri Copley, Steve Altman, Ace Mask, Angus Scrimm, Jay Robinson, Brinke Stevens; **D:** Jim Wynorski; **W:** R.J. Robertson. **VHS** *MOM*

Treacherous

Mexico is the setting for writer/director Kevin Brodie's tale of interlocking double-crosses. Mickey (C. Thomas Howell) and Tommy (Adam Baldwin) got out of the auto racing business when Tommy was paralyzed from the waist down. Now they own a luxurious resort and they're in hock up to their earlobes. That's how the situation stands when Mickey's girlfriend Jessica (Tia Carrere) comes for a visit, and finds that one of Mickey's old girlfriends, Lisa (Randi Ingerman), has shown up too. The other key elements are a bad guy who wants Mickey to race cars for him, an evil industrialist (there aren't any other kinds of industrialists in this kind of movie), and a suitcase with $2 million in cash. From that basis, the plot flips itself into all sorts of contortions which make about as much sense as they have to. In the end, it's fun if you're in the mood. The

299

LaPaglia), but still hasn't got over her. Tommy hangs out at Trees and is slowly coming to realize what a total screw-up he's made of his life. Eventually Tommy stumbles into a job but it also introduces him to Debbie (Chloe Sevigny), who's 17 and far too tempting. Much of the action concerns Tommy's equally besotted and aimless pals, played without a false step by Mark Boone Junior, Debi Mazar, and Bronson Dudley. The action is off beat, episodic, and slow, but Buscemi knows these people so well that he makes their world an interesting place to visit. The film's strengths are its intuitive understanding of flawed characters and realistically lived-in locations. Those same qualities don't play well in today's theatrical market, but they're well suited to the intimacy of video. In fact, *Trees Lounge* gains a lot on the small screen. 🦴🦴🦴

Mature subject matter, strong language, sexual material, drug use.

1996 (R) 94m/C Steve Buscemi, Chloe Sevigny, Daniel Baldwin, Elizabeth Bracco, Anthony LaPaglia, Debi Mazar, Carol Kane, Seymour Cassel, Mimi Rogers, Mark Boone Jr., Bronson Dudley; *Cameos:* Samuel L. Jackson; *D:* Steve Buscemi; *W:* Steve Buscemi; *C:* Lisa Rinzler; *M:* Evan Lurie. **VHS** *LIV*

Tremors 2: Aftershocks

Fine sequel recreates the 1990 original's sense of humor and builds on the inventive special effects that were so much fun before. Fred Ward and Michael Gross reprise their roles as cowboy and survivalist. Writer/director S.S. Wilson co-wrote the first film, so this one retains its offbeat sensibility. The monster earthworms, called "Graboids," have returned to the oilfields of Chiapis, Mexico. Since Earl Bassett (Ward) has frittered away the wealth and fame that came from his earlier triumph over the monsters, he accepts an offer from the Mexican government to hunt down this new infestation. Off he goes with new sidekick Grady (Christopher Gartin). Not surprisingly, this one isn't as lively or as explosive as the first film—sequels almost never are—but it's still enjoyable because the characters are treated seriously, and the violence isn't excessive. Fine fare for younger audiences. 🦴🦴🦴

oddest thing about the film is the way Randi Ingerman is made up to look like a combination of Loni Anderson and Lani Guinier. 🦴🦴🦴

Violence, strong language, brief nudity.

1995 (R) 96m/C C. Thomas Howell, Adam Baldwin, Tia Carrere, Randi Ingerman; *D:* Kevin Brodie; *W:* Kevin Brodie. **VHS** *FXV*

Trees Lounge

Steve Buscemi is best known as "that funny looking guy" from *Reservoir Dogs* and *Fargo*. In his feature writing/directing/starring debut, he does for Long Island barflies what Danny Boyle did for Scottish junkies in *Trainspotting*. That is, he makes their lives real, sad, funny, and bleak. Buscemi plays Tommy Basilio, an unemployed mechanic who's lost his girlfriend (Elizabeth Bracco) to his ex-boss (Anthony

Violence, a little strong language, suggestive sexual material.

1996 (PG-13) 100m/C Fred Ward, Michael Gross, Helen Shaver, Christopher Gartin, Marcelo Tubert; *D:* S.S. Wilson; *W:* S.S. Wilson, Brent Maddock. **VHS, LV** *MCA*

Tromeo & Juliet

"Tromatic" is an adjective created to describe that incomparable mixture of rude audacity and on-the-fly production values that characterize the best work of the Troma studio. No film has ever been more Tromatic than *Tromeo and Juliet,* a contemporary version of the tragic romance that's told with unbelievably poor taste. Any videophile who can't find something to be offended by really isn't trying. Excessive body piercing, child abuse, monstrous transformations, sexual perversion of every stripe—all of them are part of the story of Tromeo Que (Will Keenan) and Juliet Capulet (Jane Jensen). They're a couple of New York teens whose fathers hate each other. Why? It all has to do with a film studio scam and other betrayals hidden deep in the past. As for the rest of the plot, it's about as faithful to the Bard as it needs to be, but that's not the point with Troma. Writer/director Lloyd Kaufman (also the studio boss) is trying to be funny and provocative. It's a telling comment on our time that it takes a close-up nipple-piercing to shock today's audiences. I, for one, was truly Tromatized. By the way, be sure to watch the closing credits. That's where some of the best jokes are. Also available unrated. 🦴🦴🦴

Graphic comic violence, strong subject matter, nudity, sexual material, raw language.

1995 (R) 102m/C Will Keenan, Jane Jensen, Debbie Rochon, Lemmy; *D:* Lloyd (Samuel Weil) Kaufman; *W:* Lloyd (Samuel Weil) Kaufman, James Gunn; *C:* Brendan Flynt. **VHS** *TRO*

Trouble Bound

Harry (Michael Madsen), a gambler, and Kit (Patricia Arquette), an heiress-turned-waitress, find themselves crossing the high desert in a Continental convertible with a body in the trunk. Drug dealers are after Harry, and Kit, for unknown reasons, is trying to kill a gang-ster (Seymour Cassell). The story has that refreshing anything-can-happen quality you look for in a good road movie. Overall, the film is well cast and exceptionally well acted. The two leads are terrific. Unfortunately, the big finish is marred by lots of continuity errors. 🦴🦴🦴

Strong language, violence, incidental nudity.

1992 (R) 90m/C Michael Madsen, Patricia Arquette, Florence Stanley, Seymour Cassel, Sal Jenco; *D:* Jeff Reiner; *W:* Darrell Fetty, Francis Delia; *M:* Vinnie Golia. **VHS, LV** *FXV*

Trouble in Paradise

Light romantic comedy is reminiscent of the glossy Rock Hudson-Doris Day entertainments. It takes a proven comic premise—opposites stranded on a desert island—and handles it with a deft touch. Recently widowed Rachel Baxley (Racquel Welch) accompanies her husband's coffin from Hong Kong to the States on a freighter. Jake La Fontaine (Jack Thompson) is a crude, drunken sailor who has stashed his Stoli in with the dear departed. They're caught in a storm and you can take it from there. Even if there aren't many surprises in the script, Welch and Thompson are more than adequate, and in her little black dress and sexily tattered outfits, she is very easy on the eyes. 🦴🦴🦴

Contains some sexual material.

1988 92m/C *AU* Raquel Welch, Jack Thompson, Nicholas Hammond, John Gregg; *D:* Di Drew. **VHS** *CAF*

Troublemakers

What a curious title for a Christmas Western. This one's a throwback to the early days of spaghetti Westerns—stars Terrence Hill and Bud Spencer have been in the business since the 1960s—but without the violence and killings. Instead, the action is old-fashioned fist fights, shooting guns out of hands, and such. The light humor will remind older viewers of Jerry Lewis and Dean Martin. Hill (who directed) and Spencer are feuding brothers whose Mom (fellow '60s survivor Ruth Buzzi) wants them to come home for Christmas. The complications involve comic outlaws, a pretty

> "'**B**ody-piercing, kinky sex, dismemberment—the things that made Shakespeare great!' Well, they have a point. I'll be interested to see that.... 'Manic rock 'n' roll with Motorhead and the Ass Ponys.' Maybe we can get Ass Ponys to do the soundtrack for Hamlet."
>
> —KENNETH BRANAGH READING FROM AND COMMENTING ON A TROMA PRESS RELEASE FOR *TROMEO & JULIET.*

veterinarian, and a bear. The New Mexico locations look terrific but the whole thing goes on too long. 🦴🦴

Comic violence.

1994 (PG) 98m/C Terence Hill, Bud Spencer, Ruth Buzzi; *D:* Terence Hill. **VHS** *TRI*

True Colors

At law school, Pete (John Cusack), who's poor but dishonest, finds himself rooming with Tim (James Spader), rich but ethical. In fact, he's a bit too ethical for his girlfriend, Diana (Imogen Stubbs). When the three find themselves in Washington, D.C., Tim decides to work for the Justice Dept. while Pete goes to work for Diana's father, Sen. Stiles (Richard Widmark). The characters are more interesting than the high-road/low-road story. At various times, the movie will remind you of *The Paper Chase, St. Elmo's Fire,* and *The Candidate.* 🦴🦴🦴

Profanity, subject matter.

1991 (R) 111m/C John Cusack, James Spader, Imogen Stubbs, Mandy Patinkin, Richard Widmark; *D:* Herbert Ross. **VHS, LV** *PAR*

True Crime

On one hand, this disturbing little crime movie is a fairly well-constructed mystery based on too-familiar cliches—think Nancy Drew Meets Ted Bundy. At the same time, it deals frankly with teenaged sexuality without exploiting either the characters or the subject. Mary Giordino (Alicia Silverstone), daughter of a slain policeman, is fascinated by her father's work. She pores over articles she reads and re-reads in copies of *True Crime* magazine. When a classmate at her Catholic high school is brutally murdered, she suspects a serial killer. Police cadet Tony Campbell (Kevin Dillon) thinks she's right. Neither of them can do anything officially, but of course that doesn't stop them. As their "investigation" progresses, she comes to believe that Tony might not be all he seems. All that is familiar stuff and nothing really new or innova-

tive is done with it. But the performances by the two leads are remarkably good. Kevin Dillon makes a curious role seem believable and Alicia Silverstone proves that there's some substance behind her sudden popularity. No, this film isn't another *Clueless* but she has her moments. *AKA:* Dangerous Kiss. 🦴🦴🦴

Sexual content, violence, subject matter, strong language.

1995 (R) 94m/C Alicia Silverstone, Kevin Dillon; *D:* Pat Verducci. **VHS** *VMK*

Truly, Madly, Deeply

Nina (Juliet Stevenson) is devastated by the death of her lover Jamie (Alan Rickman). The loss is almost more than she can bear. Simple household maintenance exhausts her. Then Jamie's spirit returns. Why? How? Those really aren't important. The supernatural and religious aspects are of less interest than the more concrete human emotions of grief, love, and loneliness. Just because one half of a couple is dead, that doesn't mean that things don't get complicated. There are still jealousy and petty irritations to be dealt with. How, for example, is she to react when he invites a group of his friends over to watch videos? More importantly, can she be faithful to a spirit when she meets a fully animate man (Michael Maloney) and is attracted to him? This synopsis makes the film sound unusual (it is) and confusing (it isn't). The characters are engaging and interesting, and the performances are first rate. 🦴🦴🦴🦴

Mature subject matter, some strong language.

1991 (PG) 107m/C Juliet Stevenson, Alan Rickman, Bill Paterson, Michael Maloney, Christopher Rozycki, Keith Bartlett, David Ryall, Stella Maris; *D:* Anthony Minghella; *W:* Anthony Minghella; *C:* Remi Adefarasin. Australian Film Institute '92: Best Foreign Film; British Academy Awards '91: Best Original Screenplay. **VHS** *TOU*

The Tunnel

Spanish-Argentine production is about an artist (Peter Weller) who falls in love with a

JULIET (JANE JENSEN) AND DIRECTOR LLOYD KAUFMAN IN *TROMEO & JULIET.* ©TROMA TEAM VIDEO.

married woman (Jane Seymour). We know from the evocative opening scene that this affair will end badly. At times the action becomes much more blatantly romantic and overblown than American audiences are used to seeing. Initially, the two leads seem stiff and far too rational for these driven, obsessive characters. Then later, the action bogs down in long neurotic discussions about truth, lies, art, memory, and the nature of love that sound like bad Woody Allen. But you'll also hear echoes of Hitchcock, James M. Cain, and Jorge Luis Borges. ♫♫

Contains mature subject matter.

1989 (R) 99m/C Jane Seymour, Peter Weller, Fernando Rey; *D:* Antonio Drove. VHS, LV *VES, IME*

Tunnel Vision

First-rate Aussie mystery is a tricky tale filled with crosscurrents of conflicting stories, jealousies, and hidden motives. Detectives Wheatstone (Patsy Kensit) and Yankovitch (Robert Reynolds) are hunting for a killer who's into the SGM club scene. But Yankovitch is consumed with suspicion that his new wife Helena (Rebecca Rigg) is having an affair. Writer/director Clive Fleury isn't completely successful in juggling the two plotlines, but he manages to keep viewers guessing all the way through. For fans, this one is better than nine out of ten suspense films that show up in theatres. ♫♫♫♫

Violence, strong language, sexual material, brief nudity.

1995 (R) 100m/C *AU* Patsy Kensit, Robert Reynolds, Rebecca Rigg; *D:* Clive Fleury. VHS *TRI*

The Turn On

The premise—a gizmo that makes women sexually insatiable—is an adolescent fantasy, and the action never rises above that level. The production values are fine with a distinctly European cast to the softcore humor based on the work of Italian comic/erotic artist Milo Manara. ♫♫ GPI: 8.1

Contains nudity, sexual content, strong language.

1995 (R) 80m/C Florence Guerin, Jean-Pierre Kelfon, Bernie Kuby, Crofton Hardester; *D:* Jean-Louis Richard; *W:* Jean-Louis Richard. VHS *NHO*

Twenty-One

"Frank" confessional story of a promiscuous girl tells all about Kate (Patsy Kensit) and her lovers. Those include but are not limited to a heroin addict and a married man, and the whole lot of them are the most irritating, useless, and uninteresting bunch you're ever likely to meet in a movie. Kate spends much of her time talking to the audience, recalling *Alfie,* but there's no resemblance. Where Alfie was flawed, likable, and moving, Kate is shallow, self-centered, and too glamorous to be believed. ♫

Strong language, strong sexual content, brief nudity.

1991 (R) 92m/C Patsy Kensit, Jack Shepherd, Patrick Ryecart, Maynard Eziashi, Rufus Sewell, Sophie Thompson, Susan Wooldridge, Julia Goodman; *D:* Don Boyd; *W:* Don Boyd; *M:* Michael Berkeley. VHS, LV *NO*

29th Street

Would-be warm-hearted comedy about a father and son (Danny Aiello and Anthony LaPaglia) and a potentially valuable lottery ticket never quite clicks. The setting is New York and the main characters belong to one of those stereotypical families where the women spend all their time screaming profanities at the guys who sit around in their undershirts. ♫♫

Language.

1991 (R) 101m/C Danny Aiello, Anthony LaPaglia, Lainie Kazan, Frank Pesce, Donna Magnani, Rick Aiello, Vic Manni, Ron Karabatsos, Robert Forster, Joe Franklin, Pete Antico; *D:* George Gallo; *W:* George Gallo; *M:* William Olvis. VHS *FXV, CCB*

Twice Upon a Time

Delightful animated film has to be one of the best kept secrets in kidvid. Full animation, collage, and live action are combined in a process called "Lumage" to tell a wild story about dreams and nightmares. It's probably too complex for some younger viewers. But in terms of style, detail, and craftsmanship, this movie can't be compared to the usual Saturday morning fare. The humor is equal parts Stan Freeberg and Monty Python. Visually, director John Korty's work recalls *Yellow Submarine* and Ralph Steadman's cartoons and drawings. 🎬🎬🎬

A little strong humor.

1983 (PG) 75m/C **D:** Charles Swenson, John Korty; **W:** Bill Couturie; **V:** Lorenzo Music, Marshall Efron, Paul Frees, Hamilton Camp. **VHS, LV** *WAR, FCT*

Twilight of the Dogs

Low-budget post-apocalypse s-f tale has some good, thoughtful ideas but it's given little help by largely untrained actors. The special effects are pretty good and so are some of the performances. The main problems are a weak supporting cast, some unintentional humor, and too-obvious budgetary limitations. Sam Asgarde (Tim Sullivan, who also wrote the script) is your basic loner who's surrounded by assorted plague-ridden scavengers (the "dogs" of the title) and religious fanatics led by Rev. Zerk (Ralph Carl Bluemke). A cow named Gertrude and Karuy (Gage Sheridan), a mysterious and powerful woman, are the other key players. Producer/director John Ellis (*Star Quest, Invader*) tries to pump some energy into a genre that's seen little originality since *The Road Warrior*. He succeeds with Gage Sheridan. She's a good actress playing an interesting multi-dimensional character. Sullivan has his moments, too, but the film's ambitions are undercut by barebones sets, props, and costumes. 🎬🎬🎬

Violence, subject matter.

1996 (R) 114m/C Tim Sullivan, Gage Sheridan, Ralph Bluemke; **D:** John Ellis; **W:** Tim Sullivan. **VHS** *RVN*

Twin Sisters

Stephanie Kramer plays the title roles, Carol Mallory, a wealthy Beverly Hills matron, and Lynn Cameron, a Montreal call girl who has disappeared under ominous circumstances. Carol goes to Canada to find her, and becomes involved in an improbable but predictable plot. A police detective (Frederic Forrest) says that Lynn is dead. To help find the killer, Carol picks out one of her sister's slinkiest dresses, slaps on the mascara with a trowel, and impersonates the allegedly dead floozie. You'll predict part of the "trick" ending, but this engaging little mystery does kick in with a surprise or two before it's over. Also available in an unrated version. 🎬🎬🎬

Nudity, sexual situations, strong language, no real violence.

1991 (R) 92m/C Stephanie Kramer, Susan Almgren, Frederic Forrest, James Brolin; **D:** Tom Berry; **M:** Lou Forestieri. **VHS** *VMK*

Twist

Appropriately irreverent and loose-jointed video looks at the craze that swept over America like no dance before or since in the early 1960s. Producer/director Ron Mann uses most of the familiar techniques of fact-based filmmaking. He combines archival film and TV footage with the testimony of key "witnesses" who were there when it happened. Hank Ballard, who appears with his dog, wrote and recorded the original song "The Twist." Chubby Checker made a hit out of it a few months later. Joey Dee's "Peppermint Twist" brought the dance to the attention of New York society folk. And of course there were the American Bandstand dancers who took it to television. They're all older and most of them are more comfortably padded now, and they seem happy to recall those heady days. Mann also provides some background on post-World War II dances from the creation of the exuberant Lindy Hop in Harlem, through Arthur Murray's more restrained teachings and the gyrations of Elvis, to the Twist and its many followers. It's impossible to say exactly why something like the Twist becomes so overwhelmingly popular. Chubby Checker credits his own unthreatening, friendly personality and the simplicity of the dance itself. The dance's popularity began with young people, but many who willingly participated in this craze, including Marshall McLuhan, were old enough to know better. For those who remember the times, the film is the best kind of nostalgia. For kids, it'll be grand comedy. 🎬🎬🎬

Contains a lot of "vulgar" dancing.

1993 (PG) 78m/C **D:** Ron Mann. **VHS, LV** *COL, IME, MVD*

Twisted Love

Inventive variation on Stephen King's *Misery* is almost a low-budget masterpiece. Janna (Lisa Dean Ryan) is the emotionally unstable new girl at a California high school. Bo (Sasha Jenson) is the BMOC; Sharon (Soleil Moon Frye) is his girlfriend. Without giving too much away, an accident puts a seriously injured Bo in Janna's care at an isolated mansion. Mark Evan Schwartz's script veers between conventional B-movie cliches and absolutely accurate observations of teenaged characters and their insecurities. Lisa Dean Ryan and Sasha Jenson handle most of the dramatic action, and they do excellent work, even in scenes that stretch credibility. Some credit for their work must go to director Eb Lottimer (*Love Matters*). He also gave the film a cold, grungy, rainy look that serves the story well. So does Amotz Plessner's simple music. All those elements fit together smoothly. Most of the film's flaws occur early on, and so the conclusion is really tense and effective—really, more tense and effective than the big-budget adaptation of King's novel. Another overachiever from Roger Corman's organization. 🎬🎬🎬

Violence, subject matter, strong language, brief nudity.

1995 (R) 80m/C Lisa Dean Ryan, Mark Paul Gosselaar, Soleil Moon Frye, Sasha Jenson; **D:** Eb Lottimer; **W:** Mark Evan Schwartz; **M:** Amotz Plessner. **VHS** *NHO*

Twisted Passion

Police sketch artist suspects her husband is a psycho killer, but it could be her ex-boyfriend. See review of *Irresistible Impulse* for more. 🎬🎬

Sexual scenes, nudity, violence, strong language.

1996 101m/C Kelly Burns, Tom Reilly, Granville Ames; **D:** Jag Mundhra. **VHS** *YHV*

Under Lock and Key

In your basic babes-behind-bars exploitation flick, an undercover policewoman (Wendi Westbrook) tries to finagle information from a drug boss' incarcerated moll (Stephanie Smith). Director Henri Charr knows the drill—shower scenes, fights, vicious guards—and he manages to provide about as many intentional laughs as un-. O.K. for fans. 🎬🎬 **GPI: 5.2**

Violence, nudity, sexual content, strong language.

1995 (R) 90m/C Wendi Westbrook, Stephanie Smith; **D:** Henri Charr. **VHS** *IMP*

Under Suspicion

Due to a loophole in the British divorce laws of the late 1950s, Brighton private detective Tony Aaron (Liam Neeson) is able to make a living by arranging fake assignations for prosperous businessmen. He helps them to end their marriages by photographing them with his wife in hotel rooms. He's not proud of his work. The pay is rotten—his car is about to be repossessed—and his relationship with his wife has virtually disintegrated. Then a routine job goes wrong. A famous artist and Tony's wife are murdered before he can snap the incriminating pictures. There's no shortage of suspects. The man's mistress Angeline (Laura San Giacomo) stands to inherit the bulk of his life's work. His wife Selena (Alphonsia Emmanuel) is bitter and jealous enough to have done it, and the cops keep finding clues that seem to point to Tony. Seasoned mystery fans may think that they've got things figured out, but writer/director Simon Moore will keep you guessing all the way through. Toward the middle, the action does become a bit muddled, but not fatally so. Strong acting in the leads helps, and so does Christopher Gunning's terrific score, even if it does borrow liberally from John Barry's music for *The Ipcress File*. Genuine sleeper in the Hitchcock tradition is strongly recommended. 🎬🎬🎬

cameos are ex-surfer Corky Carroll and Rep. Sonny Bono as two old guys who are stuck in the 1960s. They form a sort of disengaged Greek Chorus that never quite understands what's going on. To them, everything was better, faster, neater, whatever, "back then." 🦴🦴🦴

Profanity and mature subject matter.

1989 (R) 102m/C Keith Coogan, Danielle von Zerneck, Richard Joseph Paul, Hunter von Leer, Tracey Walter, Roxana Zal, Dick Miller, Sonny Bono, Corky Carroll; **D:** Fritz Kiersch; **C:** Don Burgess. **VHS, LV** *VTR, NWV*

Undercover

In a polished soft-core video premiere, beautiful young policewoman (Athena Massey) bravely infiltrates an upscale bordello to solve the murder of a prostitute. Her boss assures her that he will rig her client list with men who know who she is. They'll just go up to her room "and play canasta." Yeah, right. As always, director Gregory Hippolyte stresses glamour and romantic images over explicit action. The script, by the euphoniously named Oola Bloome and Lalo Wolf, takes the same approach. 🦴🦴🦴 **GPI: 8.9**

Nudity and sexual content.

1994 (R) 93m/C Athena Massey, Tom Tayback, Anthony Guidera, Rena Riffel, Jeffrey Dean Morgan, Meg Foster; **D:** Alexander Gregory Hippolyte; **W:** Lalo Wolf, Oola Bloome. **VHS** *4PY*

The Underneath

It's easy to see why this one didn't catch on in its limited theatrical release. First, it takes a harshly critical look at one of America's favorite pastimes—gambling—in all of its most popular forms, from illegal sports betting to government-sponsored lotteries. Second, though it's a crime film—a remake of the 1949 Robert Siodmak/Burt Lancaster film noir *Criss Cross*—director Steven Soderbergh downplays conventionally suspenseful and violent elements in favor of a more elliptical, stylized approach. There's also some questionable casting. The opening shots establish a mood of inevitable failure and loss as Michael Chambers (Peter Gallagher) returns home to Austin, Texas, for his mother's (Anjanette Comer) marriage. On the bus he meets Susan (Elisabeth

Mature subject matter, violence, strong language, brief nudity, sexual content.

1992 (R) 99m/C GB Liam Neeson, Laura San Giacomo, Alphonsia Emmanuel, Kenneth Cranham, Maggie O'Neill, Martin Grace, Stephen Moore; **D:** Simon Moore; **W:** Simon Moore; **M:** Christopher Gunning. **VHS, LV** *COL*

Under the Boardwalk

Fine little beach movie is a mish-mash of elements—from *Romeo and Juliet, Beach Blanket Bingo,* and every surfing cliche ever filmed. But the characters are interesting and amazingly well developed. More importantly, they're treated seriously, the women as well as the men. The thin plot concerns the trials of two pairs of mismatched young lovers, ending with the good guys vs. the bad guys in the big surfing tournament. Also on hand in significant

Shue), and though there's something between them, he's still in love with an old girlfriend, Rachel (Alison Elliott). Michael's new stepfather (Paul Dooley) gets him a job at the armored car service where he works, but Michael hasn't overcome the problems that got him in trouble years before. That's where Soderbergh does his best work. He mixes past and present fluidly, spinning out a story with strong psychological roots. He also makes effective use of colors, often washing the screen with solid tints. The two female leads are problematic. Shue has the range and screen presence to play a bad woman who'd make a man do the wrong thing. But in that role, Elliott is hardly a femme fatale. She looks like she'd be more at home at a Cub Scout meeting. The film would have been served better if the two had been reversed. Even so, this is a crime story with substance and style. 🦴🦴🦴

Strong language, violence, sexual content.

1995 (R) 99m/C Peter Gallagher, Alison Elliott, William Fichtner, Elisabeth Shue, Adam Trese, Paul Dooley, Anjanette Comer; *D:* Steven Soderbergh; *W:* Daniel Fuchs, Sam Lowry; *C:* Elliot Davis; *M:* Cliff Martinez. Nominations: Independent Spirit Awards '96: Best Cinematography. **VHS** *MCA*

Understudy: The Graveyard Shift 2

In a sequel to the cult hit video premiere, vampire Silvio Oliviero returns to the set of a horror film that's in production and becomes the star. Writer/director Gerard Ciccoritti has a genuine flair for this kind of story. He treats the genre seriously, avoiding campy outrageousness on one side and overly serious artiness on the other. The film doesn't hold up all the way through—toward the end, plot is sacrificed to stylishness—but it's much better than *Friday the 13th* or the other formula series. 🦴🦴

Graphic violence, grotesque special effects, strong language, brief nudity, sexual content.

1988 (R) 88m/C Wendy Gazelle, Mark Soper, Silvio Oliviero; *D:* Gerard Ciccoritti; *W:* Gerard Ciccoritti. **VHS, LV** *NO*

The Universal Story

A cynic would say that this collection of clips

is nothing but pure self-promotion, and it's true that the studio takes an uncritical, congratulatory look at itself in the retrospective. But, like most moviegoers, I'm a sucker for this kind of anthology, particularly when the clips are as varied as these. After all, Universal's hits range from *Creature from the Black Lagoon* to *Schindler's List* with *To Kill a Mockingbird* and *Touch of Evil* in between. Richard Dreyfuss is an agreeable host and narrator. Keep a notepad handy to make a list for your next trip to the video store. 🦴🦴🦴

Some rough language.

1996 119m/C *D:* David Heeley. **VHS** *MCA*

Unknown Origin

Throwback s-f looks like it might have been made in the 1950s even though it's an *Alien* retread that also borrows freely from *The Thing*. Futuristic miners in an underwater installation are attacked by a parasitic little alien beastie. Dime store sets, props, and costumes, and a tongue-in-cheek script complete the effect. To their credit, the cast members are professionals who give it their best shot. The result is still a strong candidate for a future episode of *Mystery Science Theater 3000*. **AKA:** The Alien Within. 🦴🦴

Violence, strong language, brief nudity.

1995 (R) 95m/C Roddy McDowall, Melanie Shatner, Alex Hyde-White, Don Stroud; *D:* Scott Levy. **VHS** *NHO*

Until the End of the World

Just your basic apocalyptic-spy-detective-road-comedy-science-fiction romantic epic. In 1999, a nuclear satellite may or may not be about to crash into the Earth. Claire (Solveig Dommartin) is driving across Europe when a series of accidents, coincidents, and/or synchronicities brings her into contact with Trevor McPhee (William Hurt). Trevor is a mysterious man with a mission, and an alias. He's really Sam Farber, possibly an industrial spy, certainly on the run from an Australian bounty hunter. When he meets Claire, he steals her heart, her money, and her car. Actually, the car belongs to her ex-lover Eugene (Sam Neill), a

RODDY MCDOWALL AND
ALEX HYDE-WHITE IN
UNKNOWN ORIGIN.
©NEW HORIZONS HOME VIDEO.

novelist. The three of them, followed and accompanied by about a dozen other characters, set off on a chase — or perhaps it should be called a quest—that leads them across eight countries and 15 cities. The story, concocted by Wim Wenders and Dommartin, is a free-wheeling series of surprises. It has such a capricious sense of chance that they might have been guided by the *I Ching*. For almost two hours, the film is a refreshing, unpredictable delight. Then the wheels fall off. With about 20 minutes to go, the action comes to a virtual stop. The purpose of the earlier action is revealed when Farber's parents (Max von Sydow and Jeanne Moreau) show up, and then Wenders begins to experiment with curious special effects involving high-definition video. These long, slow scenes have several important symbolic points to make involving dreams and the power of images. But they're completely out of step with the earlier action. Some viewers may find that the conclusion works on an intellectual level. Emotionally, it's an unsatisfactory

ending to a film that could have been a masterpiece. Don't let that reservation keep you away. Hurt is well cast in an intelligent, difficult role, and Dommartin is as intriguing as she was in *Wings of Desire*. As long as his story is on the road, Wenders directs it brilliantly, capturing the spirit and flavor of his wide-ranging locales—from Berlin, to Tokyo to San Francisco to the Australian wilderness. 🦴🦴🦴

Brief nudity, strong language.

1991 **(R)** 158m/C William Hurt, Solveig Dommartin, Sam Neill, Max von Sydow, Ruediger Vogler, Ernie Dingo, Jeanne Moreau; *D:* Wim Wenders; *W:* Wim Wenders, Peter Carey; *M:* Graeme Revell. **VHS, LV** *WAR*

Urotsukidoji 1: Legend of the Overfiend

The box copy for this Japanese animated horror film states "WARNING: ABSOLUTELY NOT FOR CHILDREN" and it isn't kidding. Many key scenes attempt to recreate the hellish nightmares of Hieronymus Bosch. They often succeed in stomach-churning fashion. As is often the case with "Japanimation," the plot doesn't make much sense. It mixes "realistic" and supernatural elements without any real differentiation. A brief prologue explains that every 3,000 years the three levels of reality—the human world, the demon world, and the world of the man-beasts—will be united when a savior, or "overfiend," is born to a human woman. The woman in question is a young college student who is pursued and ravished by a variety of beings, human and otherwise, from those various levels. Lovecraftian monsters are insinuated into and then burst forth from human bodies in graphically bloody scenes. The threat of complete destruction looms over the individual characters. Director Hideki Takayama spins it all out with the fast pace and raw energy of an early Godzilla film. If the whole thing didn't go so far beyond the bounds of good taste, *Overfiend* could be dismissed as misogynist porn. But this is Grand Guignol on a grand scale. Intentionally offensive and provocative, it will shock many viewers, including this one, and that's its point. *AKA:* The Wandering Kid. 🦴🦴🦴

Graphic violence, strong sexual content, nudity.

1993 (NC-17) 108m/C JP D: Hideki Takayama. **VHS** CPM, MOV

Urotsukidoji 2: Legend of the Demon Womb

Like the first film, this one tells a mad story that pinballs from one impossible event to another that's even more outlandish. The plot begins with a stomach-churning introduction in Nazi Germany, 1944, and moves to contemporary Japan. The rest involves humans, demons, and supernatural creatures that are forever transforming themselves into something else, usually something revolting. The quality of the animation isn't up to the highest standards—this is no *Akira*—and it's all so senseless that even the most disgusting perversions seem detached. Beyond the cultural differences and the unexplained supernatural

aspects of the story, the plot is impossible to follow. 🦴🦴

Contains nudity and violent sexual material. (Not for children.)

1993 88m/C JP D: Hideki Takayama. **VHS** CPM, MOV

Urotsukidoji 3: Return of the Overfiend

Part 3 continues the bizarre combination of a supernatural Saturday-morning cartoon with politics, sex, post-apocalyptic destruction, Christianity, and the Faust legend. Curiously, it makes more sense than most parts of this crazed comic-book epic. 🦴🦴🦴

Contains violence, strong language, nudity, sexual material.

1995 60m/C JP D: Hideki Takayama. **VHS** CPM

Urotsukidoji Perfect Collection

These five full-length tapes are even more violent, excessive, and explicit in their Grand Guignol horrors than the individual volumes of the series. This is very strong stuff that goes so far beyond the limits of most American movies, live action or animated, that it's in an indescribable class by itself. 🦴🦴🦴

Unrated and unratable for graphic violence, horror, nudity, sexual content.

1994 250m/C D: Hideki Takayama. **VHS**

Vampire at Midnight

Loony cross-genre blend mixes the traditional vampire flick with a contemporary urban cop thriller and a New Age self-help tape. A low budget, inept writing, and bad acting don't help. A possible vampire (Gustav Vintas) with an accent not heard since the heyday of Bela Lugosi works the lecture circuit with a "realize your full potential through visualization" routine. The object of his affection (or whatever) is a mediocre concert pianist (Leslie Milne, who looks more comfortable with a swimsuit

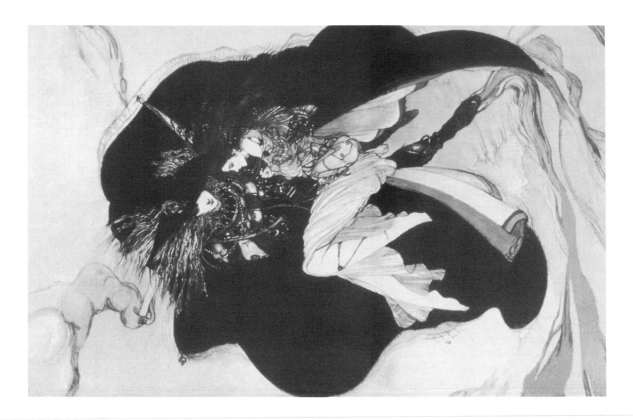

than a Steinway). Similar material was handled best by George Romero in his moody and largely unknown 1978 horror film, *Martin*. More recently, Kathryn Bigelow's brilliant *Near Dark* worked some of this same territory much more effectively. Still, for cheap thrills.... ♫♫

Contains profanity, violence, sexual content, nudity.

1988 93m/C Jason Williams, Gustav Vintas, Jeanie Moore, Christina Whitaker, Leslie Milne; *D:* Gregory McClatchy. **VHS** *FOX*

Vampire Hunter D

From a foreword that says the film is set "in a distant future when mutants and demons slither through a world of darkness," fans of Japanese *anime* know what to expect—grotesque transformations, characters who can suddenly fly, bloody violence. With his cape and hat, the title character looks like The Shadow, but the story borrows freely from other sources,

including *Yojimbo*, conventional horror films, and classical myths. The plot is simplicity itself with the laconic D taking on the vampire Magnus Lee and his monstrous gang. The visual inventions are wildly imaginative and some of the artwork is stylized. Though the supernatural violence isn't as strong as it's been in some recent Grand Guignol animation, it's still too strong for kids. ♫♫♪

Graphic violence, brief nudity.

1985 80m/C *JP D:* Toyoo Ashida. **VHS** *STP, TPV*

The Vanishing

A young couple, Rex (Gene Bervoets) and his girlfriend Saskia (Johanna Ter Steege) are on their way to a vacation in France. After a curious quarrel, she disappears. Also involved is a middle-class family man, Raymond Lemorne (Bernard Pierre Donnadieu). That's all anyone should know about the plot. Director George Sluizer lets events unfold at their own pace, using completely ordinary settings and situations to study the nature of evil. Though *The Vanishing* does have some thematic similarities to *Silence of the Lambs,* it's working on an entirely different, more subtle and frightening level. Without showing a single drop of blood or overt physical violence, this one will scare you in a way that movies almost never attempt, much less succeed at. It's an unsettling experience that you'll find yourself remembering at odd moments. And when you do, you'll feel a deep chill. Subtitled; Sluizer remade the film in English in 1993. **AKA:** Spoorloos. 🏵🏵🏵🏵

Contains no graphic violence or sexual content but is still too strong for younger viewers.

1988 107m/C *NL FR* Barnard Pierre Donnadieu, Johanna Ter Steege, Gene Bervoets; **D:** George Sluizer. **VHS** *FXL, INJ*

Venus Rising

So-so sci-fi gets off to a rocky start, wobbles along for 90 minutes, and collapses at a weak conclusion. Although it's technically science fiction, the film lacks special effects or a strong vision of the near future (in this case Hawaii). It also lacks a decent plot and interesting characters. Toss in continuity mistakes, a non-exploitative approach to what might have been pure exploitation, and you've got a real mess. In the early 21st century, Eve (Audie England) escapes from a prison island and tries to make a place for herself in an amorphously authoritarian society. Billy Wirth is the ex-con who's hired to capture her. Another escapee, a murder, a suicide, and some cliched virtual reality stuff fill out the running time. 🏵🏵

Violence, strong language, sexual content, brief nudity.

1995 (R) 91m/C Audie England, Costas Mandylor, Billy Wirth, Morgan Fairchild, Joel Grey; **D:** Leora Barish; **W:** Leora Barish. **VHS** *COL*

Vibrations

Imagine the frankly dubious combination of a youth-oriented sitcom like *Friends* grafted onto a disease-of-the-week, based-on-a-true-story TV movie. For openers, teen musician TJ (stone-faced James Marshall) loses his hands in an indescribably screwy scene. He promptly bottoms out, becoming a squeegee-teen in the Big Apple. But he's pulled out of the gutter by Ananeeka (Christina Applegate), an entrepreneur who sells T-shirts at raves. The rest of the predictable plot comes to a bizarre and largely inexplicable "happy" ending. Though the music is hypnotic, the whole rave phenomenon deserves better treatment. 🏵🏵

Strong language, violence, mild sexual content.

1994 (R) 114m/C James Marshall, Christina Applegate, Faye Grant, Paige Turco, Bruce Altman, David Burke, Scott Cohen, Shane Butterworth; **D:** Michael Paseornek; **W:** Michael Paseornek; **M:** Bob Christianson. **VHS, LV** *TOU*

Vicious

Australian thriller begins in a Spielbergian suburb. Bored Craig (Tamblyn Lord) is about to go off to college when he falls in with a gang of housebreakers led by Terry (Damon Kennedy). What begins as innocent wild oats turns into a nightmare with overtones of *In Cold Blood* and *Straw Dogs.* Director Karl Zwicky builds the key scenes to frightening levels of intensity. And in the last third of the film, when you'd expect the action to be resolved, it takes some unexpected turns. The film is not to all tastes (and definitely not for younger viewers), but fans of Peckinpah and George Miller (*The Road Warrior*) won't be bored. 🏵🏵🏵

Contains extreme violence, strong language, sexual content.

1988 88m/C *AU* Tamblyn Lord, Craig Pearce, Tiffany Dowe, Damon Kennedy; **D:** Karl Zwicky. **VHS, LV** *COL*

Virtual Combat

In the near future, as envisioned by home video, Las Vegas turns away from its "family-friendly" image to promote full-body-cybersex and cyberfighting martial arts matches, in which average men and women fulfill their various fantasies with the partners or enemies of their choice. Of course, a scientist (the venerable Turhan Bey!) takes the next step and

brings the lovely Lana (Athena Massey) and the nasty Dante (Michael Bernardo) from virtual reality to everyday reality. Gridrunner cop Quarry (Don "The Dragon" Wilson) has to bring them back. If it all sounds pretty derivative, well, it is. But director Andrew Stevens is a practiced hand at this material. He uses effects sparingly and keeps the camera on his stars who actually do pretty good work. And, as he's done in the past, he finds a nice role for his mom, Stella Stevens. 𝄢𝄢𝄢

Violence, nudity, sexual content, strong language.

1995 (R) 97m/C Don "The Dragon" Wilson, Athena Massey, Loren Avedon, Kenneth McLeod, Turhan Bey, Stella Stevens, Michael Bernardo; *D:* Andrew Stevens. **VHS** *APX*

Virtual Encounters

Top-drawer soft-core fluff follows a busy executive (Elizabeth Kaitan) whose birthday present is a session of virtual wish fulfillment at a high-tech fantasyland. The fantasies involve masks, leather, desks, broccoli...well, O.K., the broccoli is an exaggeration. This is sexy and kinky, not sick. The action is slickly staged and well photographed by director Cybil Richards. Also available in an unrated version at 84 minutes. 𝄢𝄢𝄢 **GPI: 8.5**

Nudity, strong sexual content.

1996 (R) 80m/C Elizabeth Kaitan, Taylore St. Claire, Rob Lee; *D:* Cybil Richards. **VHS** *AFE*

Visions of Light: The Art of Cinematography

If you love movies, or even like movies, you really have to see this documentary. Besides being a fine tribute to dozens of Hollywood's best efforts, it will also show you how those films have worked on you, manipulating your emotions and thoughts in ways you may never have imagined. When people outside the industry try to analyze films, they think first of directors, writers, producers, and studios. The person who's so often overlooked is the cinematographer, or d.p.—director of photography. The importance of these men (so far there have been almost no women d.p.'s) to the cre-

ative collaboration is hard to overstate. All of us have seen the results of their contributions, but the men who work behind the camera have remained largely anonymous. Until now—the film goes a long way toward correcting that mistake. It's essentially a series of interviews with living cinematographers who talk about their work, and remember those who came before them. It's also a collection of memorable moments from great and not-so-great films that illustrate their points. (Keep a pad of paper at hand; you'll want to make a list of the titles to pick up again, or for the first time, on your next visit to the video store.) Some of the conversation is technical, concerning changes brought about by sound, new cameras, film stocks, lights, and other equipment. But the filmmakers are always quick to demonstrate exactly how those technical changes are translated onto the screen. You may not care about the details of a shot lit by candles, but when you can see the difference the lighting makes, then you have a better understanding of how it works, and how it works on you. The clips from *Citizen Kane*, *In Cold Blood*, *The Long Voyage Home*, *The Big Combo*, *McCabe and Mrs. Miller*, *Goodfellas*, *Days of Heaven*, *Chinatown*, *Sweet Smell of Success*, *Hud*, *Raging Bull*, and so many more are the real point, and they're terrific. But what makes the film so enjoyable and instructive is the fact that these men are so articulate about their craft. They can explain what they're doing and why they're doing it much more effectively than many directors who are household names. 𝄢𝄢𝄢𝄢

Contains no objectionable material.

1993 95m/C *D:* Arnold Glassman, Stuart Samuels, Todd McCarthy; *W:* Todd McCarthy. New York Film Critics Awards '93: Best Feature Documentary; National Society of Film Critics Awards '93: Best Feature Documentary. **VHS, LV** *FXV*

Volere Volare

Slapstick Italian love story mixes live action and animation as well as any movie has since *Who Framed Roger Rabbit?* Maurizio (Maurizio Nichetti) is a sound effects man who dubs noises onto cartoons. With his bushy mustache, childlike manner, and delight in odd sounds, he's almost a cartoon character him-

self. Martina (Angela Finocchiaro), on the other hand, is a cynical woman who's not exactly a prostitute. She fulfills her clients' curious fantasies and predilections without ever becoming physical or intimate with them. She's far too calculating and detached for that. Clearly, there's no way these two could ever get together, but, of course, that's just what happens. But when Maurizio falls in love with Martina, he starts to become a cartoon version of himself. As various parts of his body become animated, he loses control over them. That premise is developed at a leisurely pace and doesn't really become important to the story until late in the second half. Most of the film is a playful examination of these two characters who are polar opposites in every way. It's told with lively wit and a real sense of fun. ♫♫♫

Comic nudity, sexual content.

1992 (R) 92m/C *IT* Maurizio Nichetti, Angela Finocchiaro, Mariella Valentini, Patrizio Roversi, Remo Remotti, Renato Scarpa; *D:* Maurizio Nichetti, Guido Manuli; *W:* Maurizio Nichetti, Guido Manuli. Montreal World Film Festival '92: Best Director (Nichetti). **VHS, LV** *COL, FCT*

Voodoo

When young Andy (Corey Feldman) transfers to a new college, he needs a place to stay and decides to join a frat. He could've gone with the local party boys or the computer geeks, but no, Andy innocently opts for the fraternity of the walking dead. Zombie House! Bummer! The chapter prez (Joel J. Edwards) has a scheme for eternal life. He needs just one more human sacrifice...er, pledge. Director Rene Eram creates a few good atmospheric scenes, but the pace drags too often. O.K. low-budget genre piece. ♫♫

Violence, strong language, brief nudity, raw liver.

1995 (R) 91m/C Corey Feldman, Sarah Douglas, Jack Nance, Joel J. Edwards; *D:* Rene Eram; *W:* Brian DiMuccio, Dino Vindeni; *M:* Keith Bilderbeck. **VHS, LV** *APX*

The Voyeur

Subtitled "an erotic spoof," this one manages, for the most part, to be both sexy and funny. A married couple (Kim Dawson and Al Sapienza) try to get through their ten-year-itch with a weekend vacation at a wine country inn. If the production values aren't lavish, they're certainly slick enough, and the cast is really attractive. Writer Udana Power's script is sharp. She's given the story a real sense of humor and her dialogue sounds realistic when it ought to be. Deborah Shames tells the story with straight-forward direction that doesn't call attention to itself. Some of the comic bits misfire, and the plot moves too slowly in places. Though the filmmakers are careful with the sexual material, their treatment of the story may seem too racy for some tastes, too tame for others. That's the nature of the genre, particularly when it's meant for both men and women. The real key to the film is star Kim Dawson, a platinum blonde with Kim Basinger-Sharon Stone looks and a livelier, funnier screen presence than either of them. ♫♫♫

Contains nudity, sexual material.

1994 80m/C Al Sapienza, Kim Dawson; *D:* Deborah Shames; *W:* Udana Power. **VHS** *TPV, DEB*

Warm Summer Rain

One of the screwiest movies ever made will remind you of an avant-garde one-act play that somehow escaped from a theatre and overpowered a film company. In the opening scene, Kate (Kelly Lynch) tries to commit suicide by slicing her wrists. Later she manages to get out of the hospital (still in her bandages and backless hospital nightgown) and catch a bus which takes her into the middle of the desert. That's where she meets Guy (Barry Tubb, winner of the Dennis Quaid look alike contest), a college kid with a convertible and a tuxedo. They get drunk in a bar and wake up in a little shack, one of those tastefully squalid places you see only in movies. What happens after that is ridiculous. It boils down to end-less talk about the meaning of life and sanity and such, with a lot of nakedness tossed in to keep all the inquiring minds in the audience from falling asleep. Several key incidents are described in long tedious soliloquies, not shown. Whatever guilty-pleasure value the film might have had is undercut by Kelly

Lynch's all-too-convincing portrayal of severe emotional problems. 🦴🦴

Sexual content, nudity, profanity, violence.

1989 (R) 85m/C Kelly Lynch, Barry Tubb; *D:* Joe Gayton. **VHS, LV** COL

The Warrior & the Sorceress

In the grand tradition of Hercules and other gladiator pictures, this sword-and-sorcery fantasy is yet another remake of *Yojimbo*. David Carradine, acting even more comatose than usual, wanders into a little place run by rival magicians and predictably chops up scores of bad guys. The titular sorceress is topless. 🦴🦴

Nudity, violence, sexual material.

1984 (R) 81m/C David Carradine, Luke Askew, Maria Socas, Harry Townes; *D:* John Broderick; *W:* John Broderick. **VHS, LV** LIV, VES

Warrior Spirit

Canadian film combines a coming-of-age story with snow-covered adventure. At a private academy in Detroit, 1890, young Rod Elliott (Lukas Haas) meets Wabi Dray (Allan Musy), who's half-Indian. They're both outsiders at the school, and circumstances soon take them to Wabi's home on the Canadian frontier. The conflicts there revolve around an ongoing feud between a particular group of Indians and Wabi's father, who runs a trading post. These Indians want Wabi and his pretty sister Mondagee (Jessica Welch) to return to their tribe. Rod thinks she should stay, but he and Wabi are off to hunt wolves. (An ecologically correct fig leaf of a reason for their hunt is provided to accommodate contemporary sensibilities.) The body of the film, then, follows three plotlines: the boys with their sagacious guide, the villains' kidnapping plot and, just to keep the pot boiling, a lost gold mine. The yarn zips right along like a good Louis L'Amour novel, and the Indians are never treated as stereotypes. The locations look believably remote and icy. The only real flaw in the film is some stiff, amateurish acting in supporting roles. Older kids may enjoy it more than their parents, but there's nothing wrong with that. 🦴🦴🦴

Some violence, strong language.

1994 (PG-13) 94m/C Lukas Haas, Jimmy Herman, Allan Musy, Jessica Welch; *D:* Rene Manzor. **VHS** VMK

Watch Me

You know a movie is in trouble when one character refers to "the wind off the East River," presumably referring to New York, and that's followed by a shot of the Los Angeles skyline. And that's the least important flaw in this "erotic thriller" filled with anorexic women and equally undernourished production values. Also available in an unrated version. 🦴🦴

Mature subject matter, nudity, sexual content, strong language.

1996 (R) 90m/C Jennifer Burton; *D:* Lipo Ching. **VHS** TRI

Watchers

Extremely violent horror movie based on Dean R. Koontz's novel is your basic science-run-amok material. A miraculously intelligent dog and a mean, nasty, slobbering monster have escaped from the proverbial Top Secret Government Lab. Both were created through genetic engineering. The toothy critter is trying to kill the dog and anyone else he meets. Corey Haim is the kid who befriends superpooch, played by Sandy, possibly the world's most photogenic Golden Retriever. Michael Ironside, who's never looked more like Jack Nicholson's twin, is the evil government agent. Even judged by the relaxed standards of the genre, some of the overacting here is excessive and so is the violence. It borders on sadism at times and it's often aimed at children. Followed by two sequels. **WOOF!**

Graphic, bloody violence and profanity.

1988 (R) 99m/C Barbara Williams, Michael Ironside, Corey Haim; *D:* Jon Hess; *M:* Joel Goldsmith. **VHS, LV** *LIV*

Waterlogged

In 1962, Bruce Brown decided to make the *Citizen Kane* of surf movies. To raise the money, he put together the greatest moments from his first films and released that as this feature. It was a success and allowed him to make the cult favorite *The Endless Summer.* Brown's documentaries are essentially ambitious home movies. He filmed surfers practicing their sport, added simple voiceover narration and lots of hokey humor. Seen now, the films have a wonderful innocence and friendliness. It's clear that they were made out of a genuine love of surfing. And remember, in those days the sport wasn't nearly as popular or as fashionable as it is now. The honest emotion that Brown and his subjects bring to the film is refreshing. It's also infinitely more important than slick production values or special effects. 🦴🦴🦴

Rated O for Old; contains no objectionable material.

1962 83m/C VHS *FCT*

Wavelength

If you're looking for a story of quantum physics and lust among the dreaming spires of Oxford, *Wavelength* is your movie. Jeremy Piven is an American physicist who's having an affair with a grad student (Liza Walker) while he claims to love his wife (Kelli Williams). Equally vexing to him is the nature

of light as both wave and particle. Writer/director Benjamin Fry resolves the issues in a cliched denouement lifted from *The Graduate,* followed by an impassioned, grammatically challenged, touchy-feely explanation of that wave-particle business. The personal side is much stronger than the scientific, though they don't fit together as well as they should. This isn't another *Frankie Starlight.* **AKA:** EMC2. 🦴🦴🦴

Strong language, subject matter, sexual content, brief nudity.

1996 (R) 94m/C Jeremy Piven, Kelli Williams, Liza Walker, James Villiers, James Faulkner, Richard Attenborough, Byrne Piven, Nicholas Marco, Dominic West; *D:* Benjamin Fry; *W:* Benjamin Fry; *C:* Chris Middleton; *M:* Michael Storey. **VHS** *PAR*

Waxwork

Bizarre horror/comedy is almost an anthology of stories set in a wax museum and involving exhibits that come to life (what other kind are there?): werewolves, cannibal vampires, mummies, and such. The film has a few good moments, but, as often as not the ultra-gory special effects preclude any humor, and the big finale is very poorly edited. For no apparent reason, it ends with Leslie Gore singing "It's My Party and I'll Cry If I Want To" over the closing credits. Recommended for hard-core horror fans only. Followed by a sequel. 🦴🦴

Graphic violence, strong sexual content, and profanity in both the R-rated and an unrated version.

1988 (R) 97m/C Zach Galligan, Deborah Foreman, Michelle Johnson, Dana Ashbrook, Miles O'Keeffe, Patrick Macnee, David Warner; *D:* Anthony Hickox; *M:* Roger Bellon. **VHS, LV** *LIV, VES*

Welcome to Spring Break

Has Diablo, the leader of a vicious motorcycle gang, come back to life after his execution in the electric chair to terrorize a beach town during spring break? Or was he framed by the crooked police chief (John Saxon) and the drunken doctor (Michael Parks)? Do the beer-swilling college louts care? It's up to intrepid heroes, Skip and Gail (Nicolas DeToth and Sarah Buxton, who may have been recruited from the legions of actual revelers) to find

out. The violence is so silly and predictable that this one is more humorous than offensive. ♫♫

Profanity, silly violence, one wet T shirt contest.

1988 **(R)** 92m/**C** John Saxon, Michael Parks, Nicolas DeToth, Sarah Buxton; *D:* Harry Kirkpatrick. **VHS, LV** *AHV*

The Wharf Rat

Interesting crime film gets off to a strong start but runs into the usual cliches and never recovers. Petey (Lou Diamond Phillips) is the boss waterfront smuggler in an unnamed city. Doc (Judge Reinhold) is a corrupt cop who's trying to steal the same stuff Petey moves. Dexter (Rachel Ticotin) is a reporter looking for a story. For a time, the characters' moral ambiguity and conflicting goals make for an interesting, unpredictable story. What are they going to do? Who's going to be betrayed? The second half turns into a moderately engaging caper flick. Overall, the perfor-

mances are good and writer/director Jimmy Huston has created colorful characters. He also keeps the pace quick, even when his plot is retracing familiar territory. ♫♫♫

Violence, strong language.

1995 **(R)** 88m/**C** Lou Diamond Phillips, Rachel Ticotin, Judge Reinhold, Rita Moreno, Scott Cohen; *D:* Jimmy Huston; *W:* Jimmy Huston; *C:* Levie Isaacks; *M:* Mervyn Warren. **VHS** *PAR*

When Dinosaurs Ruled the Earth

Late '60s rarity is still a nutty delight. The cast of cave people speak a cinematic primitive language without benefit of subtitles, and apparently it's meant to be taken seriously— at least in part—but it's often hard to tell the difference between intended and unintended humor. How seriously can you take a movie that features blondes in rawhide bikinis and guys wearing alligator heads? Is it a joke when our heroine, played by *Playboy*'s Playmate of the Year Victoria Vetri, calls to her pet dinosaur by saying "Neitzsche! Neitzsche!" or is it a clever reference to a German philosopher? Whatever, Jim Danforth's special effects are good, though limited. 🦴🦴🦴

Contains some violence.

1970 (G) 96m/C *GB* Victoria Vetri, Robin Hawdon, Patrick Allen, Drewe Henley, Sean Caffrey, Magda Konopka, Imogen Hassall, Patrick Holt, Jan Rossini; *D:* Val Guest; *W:* Val Guest. VHS, LV *WAR, FCT, MLB*

When Night Is Falling

Since two of the key figures in this unapologetically erotic lesbian love story are Protestant theologians, it's obvious that writer/director Patricia Rozema isn't trying to avoid controversy. Camille (Pascale Bussieres) teaches mythology at a seminary. She and fellow professor Martin (Henry Czerny) have been involved for several years, and their superiors think that if they married, they'd be an ideal choice for a dual promotion to campus chaplain. But when Camille meets Petra (Rachael Crawford), a "performance magician" who works in a circus, her calm academic world is turned upside down. Petra is attracted to Camille and pursues her. Though the plot works through a fairly conventional love triangle (conventional in one sense), Patricia Rozema gives the film a strong, almost hypnotic lyricism. The neat and tidy ending is less successful. Viewers uncomfortable with female homosexuality will certainly have a hard time with this intense portrayal. For everyone else, it's recommended as a beautifully realized, graphic approach to sensational material. Also available in an unrated version. 🦴🦴🦴

Mature subject matter, nudity, strong sexual content, rough language.

1995 (R) 96m/C *CA* Pascale Bussieres, Rachael Crawford, Henry Czerny, David Fox, Don McKellar, Tracy Wright; *D:* Patricia Rozema; *W:* Patricia Rozema; *C:* Douglas Koch; *M:* Lesley Barber. VHS *NYR*

When the Bullet Hits the Bone

A B-movie that arrives at a moment where a corrupt Senator is forced to do push-ups for a drug dealer is on the right track. Unfortunately, this one's is a little too slow and, in some places, too clumsy to rise to B-greatness. It's your basic revenge story about an E.R. doctor (Jeff Wincott) who decides to kick butt and take names after the violence he deals with every day becomes too much and he's wounded himself. The best moment: kitchen surgery conducted with table knives and oven mitts. 🦴🦴

Violence, language.

1996 (R) 92m/C Jeff Wincott, Michelle Johnson; *D:* Damian Lee. VHS *NHO*

Where the Rivers Flow North

Based on Howard Frank Mosher's novel, this story of fiercely individualistic characters confronting the establishment is reminiscent of Ken Kesey's early work. In Kingdom County, Vermont, 1927, Noel Lourdes (Rip Torn) refuses to give up the lease on his land when the power company wants to flood it for a hydroelectric dam. The grizzled one-handed logger and his housekeeper/companion/wife Bangor (Tantoo Cardinal) prefer instead to produce cedar oil and to fish for trout. Actually, they spend most of their time bickering and sniping at each other in the film's best scenes. The power company people, led by Michael J. Fox, aren't really evil or greedy. They simply want to bring electricity to rural New England and Canada. What Lourdes wants isn't quite so clear, and it changes. That's where director Jay Craven runs into problems. The film unfolds in such a curious way that audience reaction will be mixed. For my money, the good outweighs the bad because of the filmmakers' obvious commitment to tell a story they believe in. That kind of passion has been pretty much eliminated from mainstream films. But it's still more important than all the

special effects and slickness that Hollywood loves. ♫♫♫

Violence, strong language.

1994 (PG-13) 104m/C Rip Torn, Tantoo Cardinal, Bill Raymond, Mark Margolis, John Griesemer, Amy Wright, Dennis Mientka, Jusef Bulos; *Cameos:* Michael J. Fox, Treat Williams; *D:* Jay Craven; *W:* Jay Craven, Don Bredos. **VHS** *APX*

A Whisper to a Scream

Quirky, serious thriller/slasher parody opens with a quote from Ovid's *Metamorphoses*. The gimmick here is that a young actress (Nadia Capone) takes a job in a phone sex operation to research a role she's going to play. The "service" is run out of the back room of a flashy nightclub. But the dial-a-porn angle is less important than the contrasts between the reality of women's appearance and the illusion of beauty they create—the illusion that the callers accept. The screen is also filled with religious imagery and quotes from the Song of Solomon. Toward the end, the plot becomes far too intricate, but throughout, this one gets full points for audacity. ♫♫♫

One strong sexual scene, graphic violence, brief nudity, profanity.

1988 (R) 96m/C CA Nadia Capone, Yaphet Kotto, Lawrence Bayne, Silvio Oliviero; *D:* Robert Bergman; *W:* Robert Bergman, Gerard Ciccoritti. **VHS, LV** *NO*

The Whispering

Serious, often interesting but unfocused movie wanders all over the genre landscape and never fully resolves its vague premise. The story seems to be about a mysterious pale woman who may be death or some sort of spirit who encourages potential suicides. A cop turned insurance investigator (Leif Garrett) involves himself in a series of suicides after he meets a pretty girl (Leslie Danon) who has even less to do with the matter than he does. Some effective tricks and atmospherics don't make up for long pointless philosophical discussions and other loud scenes that go nowhere. The conclusion is equally unsatisfactory. ♫♫

Mature subject matter, violence, strong language, brief nudity, sexual content.

1994 (R) 88m/C Leif Garrett, Leslie Danon, Tom Patton, Maxwell Rutherford, Mette Holt; *D:* Gregory Gieras; *W:* Leslie Danon. **VHS** *APX*

White

The recent political and social history of Poland is reflected in a hairdresser's (Ziebigniew Zamachowski) divorce from his French wife (Julie Delpy) in the second entry in Krzysztof Kieslowski's *Three Colors* triology. See *Blue* for more complete information. *AKA:* Blanc; Three Colors: White; Trois Coleurs: Blanc. ♫♫♫

1994 (R) 92m/C FR SI PL Zbigniew Zamachowski, Julie Delpy, Janusz Gajos, Jerzy Stuhr; *Cameos:* Juliette Binoche, Florence Pernel; *D:* Krzysztof Kieslowski; *W:* Krzysztof Piesiewicz. Berlin International Film Festival '94: Best Director (Kieslowski). **VHS, LV** *MAX*

White Hot

Cautionary tale about drug use and abuse thoroughly deglamorizes its subject. Robby Benson (who also directed) and Tawny Kitaen are a Manhattan couple who descend from recreational cocaine-snorting to crack addiction. That descent also involves their manufacturing and selling the drugs, and their selling themselves, both physically and morally. The film has an appropriately grainy, nasty texture and highly contrasted colors. It's probably realistic in its way, as a portrait of people who are so intent on rewiring their brains that nothing else matters to them. The main flaw is the ending, which undercuts the body of the film. ♫♫♫

Mature subject matter, nudity, strong sexual content, graphic violence, profanity.

1988 (R) 95m/C Robby Benson, Tawny Kitaen, Danny Aiello, Sally Kirkland, Judy Tenuta; *D:* Robby Benson. **VHS, LV** *ACA*

White Light

A cop (Martin Kove) "meets" a beautiful woman (Allison Hossack) during a near-death experience and then becomes obsessed with finding her. But is she alive or dead? The film lacks that final layer of Hollywood polish that made *Ghost* look so slick, though the production values here are more than adequate. The leads are attractive and talented enough for the material. Most important, the two films share the same unabashed romanticism. 🦴🦴🦴

Violence, strong language, one soft-focus love scene.

1990 (R) 96m/C Martin Kove, Allison Hossack, Martha Henry, Heidi von Palleske, James Purcell, Bruce Boa; *D:* Al Waxman. VHS, LV *ACA*

The Wicked

Campy, micro-budget Australian horror comedy is *The Rocky Horror Picture Show* without the songs (or the wit). The obligatory plot has to do with two lamebrained guys and a girl who are trapped first in a spooky little desert town and then in a spooky house. The film does have a few imaginative special effects and some nice jokes on such movie cliches as the heroine on the conveyor belt, but those wear thin quickly. Even the most devoted horror fans won't find much to hold their interest. 🦴🦴

Contains strong comic violence.

1989 87m/C *AU* Brett Cumo, Richard Morgan, Angela Kennedy, Maggie Blinco, John Doyle; *D:* Colin Eggleston. VHS *HMD*

Wicked City

Wild and woolly Japanese animated feature is similar in tone to a James Bond movie. In fact, the whole production has a mid-'60s look. A young man named Taki allows himself to be picked up by a sexy woman and immediately regrets his decision. Big time. She's a visitor from the parallel Black World of monsters. He's an agent of the Black Guard, a secret intelligence organization that protects the Earth from these supernatural bad guys. The story revolves around Guiseppi Mayart, a strange little character who looks (and acts!) like an oversexed E.T., and is the key to a

WICKED CITY.
©ORION HOME VIDEO.

treaty between the two worlds. Taki and his reluctant female partner Makea are assigned to guard the debauched diplomat. Unlike so much current Japanese *anime,* this one actually makes sense within its loose limits. It's a lot of fun for fans who appreciate the glorious excesses of the genre. *♫♫♫*

Contains graphic violence, sexual material, nudity, strong language.

1992 88m/C *HK* Jacky Cheung, Leon Lai, Michelle Li; *D:* Peter Mak. **VHS** *FXL*

The Wild Bunch

From the first image of happy, smiling children torturing ants and scorpions, the viewer is on unsteady moral ground. That's what Sam Peckinpah wanted. Nothing about *The Wild Bunch* is easy. It was recut right after its first release in 1969, restored in 1995 for another limited theatrical run, and now is available to most viewers as it was meant to be seen only on tape or disc. In any form, it has aged well. To be fair, some moments do seem dated— much of the macho humor is forced—and the film is still strikingly misogynistic, perhaps because Peckinpah's marriage had just come apart and much of the fault was his. But it's also brilliant, passionate, and as emotionally powerful as it ever was. The film has become so familiar by now that most people know the story of a gang of outlaws who agree to steal guns for a Mexican general in 1913. It begins with a bank robbery that turns into a massacre more deadly to bystanders than participants, and ends in an extended shoot-out that's often been copied but never surpassed. In the middle is a train robbery that's another brilliantly staged cinematic set-piece. Actually, the restored footage, about ten minutes, has been available on tape for some time, but the additional work on the film—made from a seemingly pristine negative, reproduced in the original widescreen ratio, and with remixed stereo soundtrack—makes the newer version the best available. It looks and sounds terrific. The deletions were made at the order of studio executives for various commercial reasons. The scenes fill in background about character relationships, and don't really add

that much to the story. Ironically, though, the new executives at Warner Bros. didn't realize that the version they were planning to re-release theatrically had already been rated by the MPAA. The studio resubmitted it to the board and was horrified to receive an "NC-17" for violence. But before this new controversy went too far, someone realized what had happened and the film has its original "R." *The Wild Bunch* is a masterpiece. Ideally, it should be seen in a theatre—a 70mm. print projected onto a big screen with great stereo sound— but most of us don't have 70mm. projectors in our living rooms. For purists, Warner Home Video tape #1014 is 144 minutes long. It's the older pan-and-scan version. Tape #14034, at 145 min., is the restored letterboxed version with Dolby Surround stereo sound. Tape #14416 is the restored pan-and-scan. Yes, this material will be on the final exam. *♫♫♫♫*

Violence, strong language, brief nudity.

1969 (R) 145m/C William Holden, Ernest Borgnine, Robert Ryan, Warren Oates, Strother Martin, L.Q. Jones, Albert Dekker, Bo Hopkins, Edmond O'Brien, Ben Johnson, Jaime Sanchez, Emilio Fernandez, Dub Taylor; *D:* Sam Peckinpah; *W:* Walon Green, Sam Peckinpah; *C:* Lucien Ballard. National Society of Film Critics Awards '69: Best Cinematography; Nominations: Academy Awards '69: Best Story & Screenplay, Best Original Score. **VHS, LV** *WAR*

Wild Cactus

This spicy little number contains an edge of sexual violence that some viewers will find troubling. It begins as a standard convict vs. wimpy husband formula. The bad guy (creepily played by Gary Hudson) enjoys hurting women. He's been locked up for abusing his girlfriend (Kathy Shower) and goes looking for her when he's released. On the way, he picks up a kinky hitchhiker (Michelle Moffett) who's about as twisted as he is. Out in the desert, they run across a college professor (David Naughton) and his wife (India Allen). That's when it all turns into a low-budget *Straw Dogs.* Of course, there are plenty of coincidences, and at key moments the characters do incredibly stupid things to keep the plot going. Viewers who aren't turned off by the violence will not be bored. *♫♫♫* **GPI: 9.0**

Mature subject matter, nudity, strong sexual content, violence, language.

1992 **(R)** 92m/C David Naughton, India Allen, Gary Hudson, Michelle Moffett, Kathy Shower, Robert Z'Dar, Paul Gleason, Anna Karin, David Wells; *D:* Jag Mundhra; *W:* Carl Austin. **VHS** *IMP*

Wild Orchid

Mickey Rourke's howler is, without question, one of the silliest films ever made. From its screwball beginning to the pseudo-sizzling conclusion, it's a monument to unintentional humor. Model-turned-actress Carre Otis feebly impersonates an international lawyer who has never left home. Actor-turned-statue Rourke is a mumbling man of mystery who introduces her to temptations of the flesh in Brazil. Jacqueline Bisset, apparently the only member of the cast who realized this is a comedy, is Otis' boss. Their tale has to do with real estate, motorcycles, voyeurism, and sex. The film might not even have had a theatrical release if it hadn't been for the carefully constructed "controversy" surrounding it. In 1990, the MPAA gave this version of the film an X-rating. It was recut to an R for theatres. Around the same time, Mickey Rourke stated publicly that he and his real-life girlfriend Otis actually "did it" on camera. The scene is about as explicit as soft-core gets, but it's no more believable than anything else in this glossy potboiler. Throughout, Rourke is a cipher; no matter what's going on around him, he hits one flat, unemotional note. By the end of the tape, you begin to wonder if perhaps the electroshock treatments didn't have quite the desired effect. In the end, this "international" version has an undeniable guilty pleasure appeal for fans of alternative video, but Rourke is still a monotonous old drudge. Followed by a sequel. *♪♪* **GPI: 8.1**

Contains considerable nudity, graphic sexual scenes, profanity, Mickey Rourke without a shirt.

1990 112m/C Mickey Rourke, Jacqueline Bisset, Carre Otis, Assumpta Serna, Bruce Greenwood; *D:* Zalman King; *W:* Zalman King. **VHS, LV** *COL, FCT*

Wild Orchid 2: Two Shades of Blue

Sequel in title only is actually better than the original, but only in that it doesn't have Mickey Rourke in it. Like all of Zalman King's soft-core, it's glossy, slow, pretentious, cliched, and unintentionally funny. In California, 1958, Blue (Nina Siemaszko) is the daughter of jazz trumpeter and junkie Tom Skerrit. To support his habit, or something, she agrees to become a call girl, but then she falls for one of her fellow high school students. If the plot weren't so ridiculous it would be offensive, but there's no danger of that. Siemaszko wears one petulant expression for the whole movie. *♪♪* **GPI: 8.2**

Both the R-rated and an unrated versions contain violence, strong language, sexual material, and nudity.

1992 **(R)** 105m/C Nina Siemaszko, Wendy Hughes, Brent Fraser, Robert Davi, Tom Skerritt, Joe Dallesandro, Christopher McDonald, Liane Curtis; *D:* Zalman King; *W:* Zalman King. **VHS** *COL*

The Wild World of Batwoman

Children may not be the intended audience but older kids will find a lot to laugh at in this nutty exercise in camp nostalgia. The ultra-cheap B-movie was made in 1966 to capitalize on the original *Batman* television craze. The title character wears a mask and a low-cut Merry Widow outfit and she sports a picture of a bat on her chest. The overall level of silliness is a notch or two below the old *Monkees* TV series. Kids who like to watch adults making idiots out of themselves will be hugely entertained. **AKA:** She Was a Hippy Vampire. *♪♪*

Contains some comic violence.

1966 70m/C Katherine Victor, George Andre, Steve Brodie, Lloyd Nelson; *D:* Jerry Warren. **VHS** *RHI, SNC, DVT*

Wildest Dreams

Trifling variation on the old three-wishes-from-the-genie-in-the-bottle plot is combined with a *Risky Business* premise. When a young

lonely outpost where one man doubles as undertaker and saloon-keeper, the suspicious nature of cowboys toward strangers—all of them are drawn with the same kind of careful clarity found in Louis L'Amour's best novels. The second half becomes more sentimental and overly dramatic with intrusive, sugary music. But it's not enough to drain the power of Heston's impressive work. Tom Gries died of a heart attack in 1977. This was unquestionably his finest film. 🐾🐾🐾

Contains some violence.

1967 109m/C Charlton Heston, Joan Hackett, Donald Pleasence, Lee Majors, Bruce Dern, Anthony Zerbe, Ben Johnson, Clifton James; *D:* Tom Gries; *W:* Tom Gries; *M:* Elmer Bernstein. **VHS, LV** *PAR*

A Wind Named Amnesia

Apocalyptic Japanese animated film opens in "San Francisco, 199X," two years after a wind swept across the planet and caused people everywhere to forget everything they know. Speech, technology, religion, family, civilization—all gone. Humanity is ignorant, innocent, and brutal. One young man, Wataru, has been re-educated through a curious plot device. He wanders a mostly deserted landscape searching for anyone else who might have retained or regained intelligence. He finds Sophia, a woman who can speak, and a lethal robot (reminiscent of the Walkers in *Return of the Jedi*) that seems driven to attack him. While that could be the basis for any number of B-movies, writer Hideyuki Kikuchi, animator Satoru Nakamura, and director Kazuo Yamazaki are also interested in some more serious ideas. The curious pace suggests that the film might have been condensed from a longer episodic work. But the filmmakers still take time to speculate on the larger questions raised by the story: the philosophical implications of pure innocence, the nature of men and women, the evolution of religion. The animation is excellent; more subdued and pastoral than *Akira*, but detailed and interesting. 🐾🐾🐾

Contains violence, brief nudity, sexual content.

1993 80m/C *JP D:* Kazuo Yamazaki; *W:* Hideyuki Kikuchi. **VHS** *CPM*

man is left in charge of the family antique business for the weekend, he discovers a magic bottle and asks the genie to find the perfect woman for him. His misadventures are familiar but they're handled with wildly overacted spirit. *AKA:* Bikini Genie. 🐾🐾 **GPI: 8.2**

Strong language, some violence, brief nudity, sexual situations.

1990 (R) 84m/C James Davies, Heidi Paine, Deborah Blaisdell, Ruth Collins, Jane Hamilton, Jill Johnson; *D:* Chuck Vincent. **VHS, LV** *LIV, VES*

Will Penny

Charlton Heston's best acting work found only a limited audience in theatres but it's been rediscovered on tape. This is a flawed film, but Heston's low-key and touching performance and a first-rate supporting cast make up for a lot of mistakes. Will Penny is an illiterate cowboy who knows that his way of life is dying. After an encounter with a group of psychotic "rawhiders" (led by Donald Pleasence, who devours every stick of scenery in sight), he finds himself helping a woman (Joan Hackett) and her young son make it through the winter in a remote mountain shack. The first half is far stronger than the second. Writer/director Tom Gries paid attention to authentic details of situation and character. A cattle drive, a

Wing Chun

Wild Hong Kong martial-arts feminist fantasy has a plot as convoluted as a Shakespearian comedy with women disguised as men and general confusion as to who's in love with whom and how various marriages should be arranged. But those matters are less important than the action sequences—elaborately chore-ographed fights staged with dance-like grace and soaring acrobatics. In medieval China, Wing Chun (Michelle Yeoh) sells great bean curd and defends her village from marauding bandits. She dresses as a man, leading to great confusion when a childhood sweetie drops by. The film's violence is so stylized, exaggerated, and cartoonish that conventional "realism" isn't a consideration. And Wing Chun is careful never to kill her opponents; she even smacks them with the flat side of her sword, when she uses one. A little silly sexual banter will proba-bly generate embarrassed giggles from younger audiences, but this is still a good choice for older kids who are looking for something more advanced than Power Rangers or Turtles. Available in dubbed or subtitled versions. 𝄞𝄞𝄞

Contains some sexual humor and lots of balletic violence.

1994 93m/C *HK* Michelle Yeoh, Donnie Yan, Waise Lee; *D:* Yuen Woo Ping. **VHS, LV** *TAI*

Wings of Fame

Struggling writer Smith (Colin Firth) shoots movie star Valentin (Peter O'Toole) and then is killed himself. The two men awaken (if that's the right word) in a boat crossing the River Styx. On the other side, they find that the afterlife is a huge art deco hotel, one that might serve as the setting for a really spacey perfume ad. It is, as one of the residents puts it, a place of "jealousy, vanity, and boredom." In this purgatory, religious beliefs and good works count for nothing. The departed are ranked according to their fame on Earth. Smith and Valentin get good rooms while seri-ous composers are moved to cramped garrets. Writer/director Otakar Votocek aims for a Felliniesque quality and sometimes achieves it. At other times, the influence of Terry Gilliam is apparent. The real key is Firth's assured performance. His sense of wonder and curiosity carries the story over the rough spots. The finish is weaker than the first half of the film, but this one is still a serious attempt to tell a good story. 𝄞𝄞𝄞

Strong language, subject matter, brief nudity, sexual content.

1993 (R) 109m/C Peter O'Toole, Colin Firth; *D:* Otakar Votocek; *W:* Herman Koch, Otakar Votocek. **VHS** *PAR*

Winter People

In a generic Appalachia, circa 1930, a clock-maker (Kurt Russell) and his daughter happen upon an unmarried mom (Kelly McGillis) and her daughter. When their truck breaks down, they wind up spending the winter together. What follows involves feuding families—civi-lized townsfolk vs. brutish Neanderthals—a drunken bear hunt, and several long commit-tee meetings. The cliched characters spout ridiculous purple speeches in perhaps the worst Southern accents ever collected in one movie. The filmmakers do not demonstrate even the most superficial understanding of the people, the region, the times, or the basics of storytelling. **WOOF!**

Strong language, subject matter, violence.

1989 (PG-13) 109m/C Kurt Russell, Kelly McGillis, Lloyd Bridges, Mitchell Ryan, Jeffrey Meek, Eileen Ryan, Amelia Burnette; *D:* Ted Kotcheff; *W:* Carol Sobieski; *M:* John Scott. **VHS, LV** *NLC*

Wisecracks

Collection of routines and musings from female performers and comediennes is, as you might expect, a mixed bag—some of the mate-rial is really sharp and funny; some of it's flat; some is whiny and complaining. On balance, the good outweighs the bad, though the con-tent is so varied in tone and subject that there's something to offend or to delight just about everyone. Perhaps the most interesting single performer is veteran Phyllis Diller. Her appeal isn't so much her comedy itself, but her insights into the mechanics of stagecraft:

"From the beginning [when] Michael Herz and I founded the studio, we believed the 'brand name' was the way to go. We couldn't compete with the majors. The guys who tried to challenge the establishment—the battlefield is littered with their bodies."

—LLOYD KAUFMAN, PRODUCER, DIRECTOR, AND CO-FOUNDER OF TROMA FILMS

how different physical arrangements affect the relationship between audience and performer; what distracts the crowd and what draws it in. For comedians and actors, it's probably the stuff they learn in Drama 101. For the rest of us, it's a fascinating peek behind the curtain. 🦴🦴🦴

Contains some strong language and sexual humor.

1993 93m/C *D:* Gail Singer; *Performed by:* Whoopi Goldberg, Paula Poundstone, Ellen DeGeneres, Kim Wayans, Pam Stone, Joy Behar, Maxine Lapidus, Phyllis Diller, Jenny Jones. **VHS** *MNC*

Wishful Thinking

Daydreaming writer's (Murray Langston) scribbles somehow come true. This one's a slow starter. The comedy is so forced and so poorly paced that it's best appreciated with a well-oiled fast-forward button. 🦴

Strong language, brief nudity, sexual activity, some violence.

1992 94m/C Murray Langston, Michelle Johnson, Ruth Buzzi, Billy Barty, Johnny Dark, Ray "Boom Boom" Mancini, Vic Dunlop, Kip Addotta; *D:* Murray Langston. **VHS** *HMD*

Witchboard 3: The Possession

This is what a horror movie is supposed to be: inventive, spooky, well made, and with a nasty little sense of humor. The story begins with a tip of the hat to *Rosemary's Baby* and then goes on to tell a story of demonic possession via Ouija board. It lures newlywed stockbroker Brian Fields (David Nerman) into all sorts of nastiness. His wife Julie (Locky Lambert) doesn't know what Brian and their creepy landlord (Cedric Smith) are up to, but when Brian brings home a new Miata, she doesn't ask too many questions. The script by Kevin S. Tenney and Jon Ezrine doesn't really depend on the first two *Witchboard* films, and director Peter Svatek moves things along at a nice clip. Though he's not above a few moments of Grand Guignol yuckiness, he doesn't over-rely on effects. Great stuff for fans. 🦴🦴🦴

Violence, nudity, sexual material, strong language.

1995 (R) 93m/C David Nerman, Locky Lambert, Cedric Smith, Donna Sarrasin; *D:* Peter Svatek; *W:* Kevin S. Tenney, Jon Ezrine; *C:* Barry Gravelle. **VHS** *REP*

Witchcraft

Supernatural tale borrows liberally from *Rosemary's Baby*, *The Exorcist*, and *The Amityville Horror*. It lacks the grotesque special effects and overall nastiness so prevalent in many big-budget horror films. The plot concerns a young woman's worries about her husband and creepy mother-in-law after the birth of her first child. The weird opening juxtaposes the Lamaze method with burning at the stake. Horror fans have seen better and much, much worse. Amazingly, this slender reed has been the basis for seven—count 'em, seven!—sequels to date. 🦴🦴

Violence, subject matter, strong language.

1988 (R) 90m/C Anat "Topol" Barzilai, Gary Sloan, Lee Kisman, Deborah Scott; *D:* Robert Spera. **VHS, LV** *ACA*

Witchcraft 2: The Temptress

Exploitative fluff is an odd mixture of the very good and the very bad. The small-town setting and characters are believably realistic. The erotic elements, concerning a witch's attempt to seduce a teenager, produce unintentional laughs. If overacting were a crime, most of the cast would be in jail. But it would be unfair to leave it at that. Even though this one is no *Rosemary's Baby*, it has some unsettling moments. Part of the credit goes to the make-up and costume people who dolled up the witch (Delia Sheppard) to look like a combination of Madonna and Brigitte Nielsen. Now, that is frightening. 🦴🦴🦴

Nudity, sexual content, violence, profanity.

1990 **(R)** 88m/C Charles Solomon, Mia Ruiz, Delia Sheppard; **D:** Mark Woods. **VHS, LV** *ACA*

Witchcraft 3: The Kiss of Death

By *3*, the formula for the series is set—lawyers vs. vampires. The plot is really silly, and so is the acting, but then this is one of those B-movies that's served better by bad acting than by good. What might have been just another goofy horror flick is brightened considerably by the presence of Lisa Toothman as our heroine. She may or may not be much of an actress—given the material it's impossible to tell—but she projects a feeling of vitality and she looks like a busty Julia Roberts. 🦴🦴🦴

Violence, nudity, sexual content.

1990 **(R)** 85m/C Charles Solomon, Lisa Toothman, William L. Baker, Lena Hall; **D:** R.L. Tillmanns. **VHS** *ACA*

Witchcraft 4: Virgin Heart

Series star Will Spanner (Charles Solomon), the son of Satan, is a California lawyer by day, warlock by night. Hopeless cynics might say there's no difference. This is one of those movies that's so ridiculously bad that it sinks to the bottom, then breaks through the bottom and enters another video dimension. 🦴

Contains brief nudity, violence, strong language.

1992 92m/C Charles Solomon, Julie Strain, Clive Pearson, Jason O'Gulihar, Lisa Jay Harrington, Barbara Dow; **D:** James Merendino. **VHS, LV** *ACA*

Witchcraft 5: Dance with the Devil

5 continues to break new ground in alternative entertainment. For those who haven't kept up with these films, they're about a fellow named Will Spanner (Marklen Kennedy) who's the son of Satan, but he's still a good guy. In this one, the bad guy is Cain (David Huffman), some sort of evil angel who looks like Richard Simmons and slaps people on the head like Ernest Aingley. When he really turns it on, no piece of scenery is safe. For alternative horror fans, though, the memorable combination of bad writing and over emoting makes this a grand exercise in unintentional humor. 🦴🦴🦴

Both the R-rated and unrated versions contain graphic violence, strong language, nudity, sexual content.

1992 **(R)** 94m/C Marklen Kennedy, Carolyn Taye-Loren, Nicole Sassaman, Aysha Hauer, David Huffman; **D:** Talun Hsu. **VHS** *ACA*

Witchcraft 6: The Devil's Mistress

By this number, hero Spanner's character has evolved into Los Angeles divorce lawyer by day, supernatural troubleshooter by night. Someone is sacrificing young women up in the hills, so the police call on him for help. There's nothing unusual in the off-the-shelf plot or in the various love scenes that move this one into the "erotic horror" subgenre. But co-writer/director Julie Davis handles things with a fair sense of humor and she got a terrific performance from Bryan Nutter as Savanti, the bad guy with heavy-duty press-on nails. She also made the most of a small budget and limited special effects. 🦴🦴🦴

Both the unrated and R-rated versions contain sexual content, nudity, strong language, some violence.

1994 **(R)** 86m/C Kurt Alan, John E. Holiday, Bryan Nutter, Jerry Spicer, Shannon Lead; **D:** Julie Davis; **W:** Julie Davis. **VHS** *ACA*

Witchcraft 7: Judgement Hour

Could this be the final chapter in the remarkably long-lived series about Will Spanner (David Byrnes), California lawyer by day, warlock by night, and full-time son of Satan? This installment is a softcore vampire story that begins with a party for the undead out at the Polytechnic Institute. Somebody in the casting or make-up department must have had a wicked sense of humor because a key supporting character belongs to the Kato Kaelin hair club, and Will's girlfriend (April Breneman) is a ringer for Hillary Clinton. 🗡🗡

Both the unrated and R-rated versions contain violence, nudity, sexual content, and strong language.

1995 (R) 91m/C David Byrnes, April Breneman, Alisa Christensen, John Cragen, Loren Schmalle; **D:** Michael Paul Girard; **W:** Peter Fleming; **C:** Denis Maloney; **M:** Miriam Cutler. **VHS** *APX*

Witchcraft 8: Salem's Ghost

Not even the demise of its central character can kill off this incredibly resilient series. Yes, the cheap horror continues, unabashed, into its eighth installment in title only. The budget is so low that you can actually see the wires in one special effects scene. And where else could you expect to find such wonderful dialogue as this: "A vile warlock, a wretched and evil man by the name of Simon Renfro, accused of murdering and ingesting countless children and raping more than a dozen women and forcing them into black witchery, was desecrated on this very ground and buried in what you know to be the room off your basement!" *AKA:* Witchcraft 8; Salem's Ghost. 🗡🗡

Both the R-rated and unrated versions contain violence, ridiculous effects, nudity, sexual content, strong language.

1995 (R) 90m/C Lee Grober, Kim Kopf, David Weilis, Anthoni Stuart, Tom Overmyer; **D:** Joseph John Barmettler Jr. **VHS** *APX*

WitchTrap

Amateurish effort from filmmakers and cast who have worked with the same material—people trapped in a haunted house and graphically slaughtered by supernatural forces—much more effectively in other horror films. The unrated version scores high on the Yuck-scale. 🗡

Graphic violence, grotesque special effects, strong language, brief nudity, and sexual content.

1989 (R) 87m/C James W. Quinn, Kathleen Bailey, Linnea Quigley; **D:** Kevin S. Tenney. **VHS, LV** *IME*

Without Mercy

Wacko action flick makes no sense, but that's not to say it isn't enjoyable. Frank Zagarino is a Rambo-esque soldier who's traumatized in Somalia and then goes to some unnamed Asian place where he becomes a prize fighter and gets hooked up with bad guy Martin Kove, who's doing something nasty, apparently involving slavery, but I couldn't figure it out. The dialogue is no help there. It contains such inscrutable lines as, "Be careful, little Tonya, you're sitting on too many edges of the fence." I'm not sure what that means either but it doesn't sound comfortable. The shoot-out scenes are clumsy. The martial arts choreography is better. 🗡🗡

Violence, strong language, sexual content.

1995 (R) 88m/C Frank Zagarino, Martin Kove, Ayu Azhari, Frans Tumbuan; **D:** Robert Anthony; **W:** Robert Anthony; **C:** Gerry Lively. **VHS, LV** *LIV*

Wizards of the Demon Sword

Fred Olen Ray has a reputation for making movies quickly and cheaply, and they don't get much quicker and cheaper than this. Feeble humor along the lines of a character called "the Seer of Robuck" does nothing to elevate uninspired sword and sorcery. Cult figures Michael Berryman, Lawrence Tierney, and Russ Tamblyn show up in support. 🗡🗡

Violence, profanity, brief nudity.

1994 (R) 90m/C Lawrence Tierney, Michael Berryman, Russ Tamblyn, Lyle Waggoner, Blake Bahner, Heidi Paine, Dan Speaker, Jay Richardson, Dawn Wildsmith; *D:* Fred Olen Ray; *W:* Dan Golden, Ernest Farino. **VHS** *TTV*

A Woman, Her Men and Her Futon

Despite the title, this is a serious, flawed story about a young woman, Helen (Jennifer Rubin), who's trying to put her life back together after a divorce. Once she's on her own, Helen has to make certain compromises. She's trying to write and sell a screenplay, but when men show interest, do they want her work or her? Before long, the story turns into a movie about movies, about making movies, about love and sex, lies and hope, and individual responsibility. It gets better and more complicated as it goes along. The characters aren't sugar-coated, and director Mussef Sibay is especially good at showing the uncomfortable moments between people. Overall, the writing is better than the direction or the acting. *♫♫♫*

Nudity, sexual subject matter, some strong language

1992 (R) 90m/C Jennifer Rubin, Lance Edwards, Grant Show, Michael Ceveris, Delaune Michel, Robert Lipton; *D:* Mussef Sibay; *W:* Mussef Sibay, *M.* Joel Goldsmith. **VHS** *REP*

Woman of Desire

In a tepid South African thriller, Steven Bauer plays Ted and Jonathan, good and bad millionaires. Christina (Bo Derek) is married to one of them and fooling around with the other. She's also fooling around with yacht captain Jack Lynch (Jeff Fahey). When one of the brothers is bumped off on the boat, she tells the police that Jack did it. His lawyer (Robert Mitchum) smells a rat. It all becomes much too complicated. The entire cast wisely sleepwalks through the action, but even so, this is the kind of movie you laugh at, not with, which is not altogether bad. *♫♪*

Both the unrated and R-rated versions contain sexual material, nudity, strong language, and violence.

1993 (R) 97m/C Bo Derek, Jeff Fahey, Steven Bauer, Robert Mitchum; *D:* Robert Ginty. **VHS, LV** *VMK*

Wrestling Ernest Hemingway

An unlikely friendship is born between two Florida retirees. Frank (Richard Harris) is a garrulous braggart who loves to spin wild stories about his past and himself. Walter (Robert Duvall) is a Cuban barber who's carrying a small torch for a friendly waitress (Sandra Bullock). These two old guys are opposites in almost every way, but they're both lonely. That's more than enough to bring them together. The pace is slow and almost all the big scenes are swamped by syrupy music. The two stars are up to their usual standard and they're given fine support by Shirley MacLaine and Piper Laurie. *♫♫♫*

Salty language and Richard Harris doing naked push-ups.

1993 (PG-13) 123m/C Robert Duvall, Richard Harris, Piper Laurie, Shirley MacLaine, Sandra Bullock; *D:* Randa Haines; *W:* Steve Conrad; *C:* Lajos Koltai; *M:* Michael Convertino. **VHS, LV** *WAR*

The Wrong Man

If crime novelist Jim Thompson and Tennessee Williams had ever collaborated on a spicy potboiler, they might well have come up with something like this south-of-the-border thriller. Sailor Alex Walker (Kevin Anderson) is falsely accused of the murder of a smuggler in Tampico, Mexico. On the run from the law, he accepts a lift from Phillip Mills (John Lithgow) and his wife Missy (Rosanna Arquette), the most wonderfully bizarre married couple in recent memory. Their relationship is impossible to describe and a joy to discover. He's a complex, drunken, bigoted salesman with more than a few secrets. She's a mercurial flirt who loves to taunt her older husband. The three of them form a shifting, unstable romantic triangle that finally reaches a conclusion, of sorts, in an extended booze-soaked confrontation in a hotel room. It's the high point of the movie—a long scene that careens from suspense to bawdy humor to sexual tension in less time than it takes to toss back a shot of mescal. Give equal credit to writers Roy Carl-

son and Michael Thoma and to the actors, particularly Lithgow, for playing these screwloose characters with absolute conviction. And give director Jim McBride credit for tying it all together into a tight package with the right ending. 🦴🦴🦴▿

Sexual content, nudity, strong language, violence.

1993 (R) 98m/C Kevin Anderson, John Lithgow, Rosanna Arquette, Robert Harper; *D:* Jim McBride; *W:* Roy Carlson, Michael Thoma; *C:* Alfonso Beato. VHS, LV *REP*

The Wrong Trousers

British filmmaker Nick Park won a well-deserved Oscar for this delightful short film. He uses cartoon-like clay figures of Wallace and his dog Gromit to tell a comic caper tale worthy of Hitchcock. It's filled with visual jokes and ends with one of the wildest chases you'll ever see. Highly recommended for kids and adults. 🦴🦴🦴🦴

Contains no objectionable material.

1993 30m/C *GB D:* Nick Park. Academy Awards '93: Best Animated Short Film. VHS *TVC*

Xtro

Sci-fi fans might want to see this relentlessly weird slasher/horror flick simply for the woman-giving-birth-to-a-fully grown-man scene, or for that indescribable movie moment when the dwarf drops the big green jelly eggs into the refrigerator full of guacamole. Or not. The muddled plot concerns alien abduction, the abductee's return, his wife's unfaithfulness, and other even less edifying sexual goings-on. Followed by a sequel. 🦴🦴▿

Graphic violence, nudity, sexual content, strong language.

1983 (R) 80m/C *GB* Philip Sayer, Bernice Stegers, Danny Brainin, Simon Nash, Maryam D'Abo, David Cardy, Anna Wing, Peter Mandell, Robert Fyfe; *D:* Harry Bromley Davenport. VHS, LV *NLC*

The Year My Voice Broke

Australian film follows three young people (two boys and a girl) making the difficult transitions through adolescence in 1962. Danny (Noah Taylor) is a smart, cocky kid who's been friends with a slightly older girl, Freya (Leone Carmen), for years. Recently, he's fallen hopelessly in love with her. But, Freya, who has an unearned reputation among the girls as a "nymphoniac," has just become interested in an older boy. Trevor (Ben Mendelsohn) is wild, unpredictable, and unstable. He stands up for Danny when school bullies attack him. Danny, who narrates the story, is understandably confused and unsure of himself. Yes, the story's been told before, but it has universal appeal. Like *The Last Picture Show*, it's a strong evocation of a small town in the middle of a vast, lonely landscape, and the desires of these kids to escape from it. The young leads are unaffected, and they lack the slick superficial attractiveness that mainstream Hollywood entertainment imposes on teenage characters. They seem as real and as overly emotional as most of us are during those rough times. Followed by the excellent sequel, *Flirting*. 🦴🦴🦴▿

Profanity, mild violence and mature subject matter.

1987 (PG-13) 103m/C *AU* Noah Taylor, Leone Carmen, Ben Mendelsohn, Graeme Blundell, Lynette Curran, Malcolm Robertson, Judi Farr; *D:* John Duigan; *W:* John Duigan; *C:* Geoff Burton; *M:* Christine Woodruff. Australian Film Institute '87: Best Film. VHS, LV *LIV*

The Young Americans

Harvey Keitel's confident screen presence and star power add a lot to this lyrically paced and sometimes muddy story of crime and generational conflicts. He plays a cynical DEA agent who helps London cops against American drug kingpin Viggo Mortensen. At its best, the story works in the gray areas where characters are neither completely good nor bad. The young British supporting actors are excellent, and even if things are sometimes difficult to follow, the film is worth watching. Comparisons to such cult favorites as *The Long Good Friday* and *The Krays* aren't out of place. Director Danny Cannon makes an impressive debut. 🦴🦴🦴

Graphic violence, strong language, drug use, brief nudity.

1993 (R) 108m/C *GB* Harvey Keitel, Viggo Mortensen, Iain Glen, John Wood, Keith Allen, Craig Kelly, Thandie Newton, Terence

Rigby; **D:** Danny Cannon; **W:** Danny Cannon, David Hilton; **M:** David Arnold. **VHS, LV** *LIV*

Young Lady Chatterley

Classy British soft-core '70s skin flick may have lacked the star power for theatrical success when it was made, but a decade or so later, it became one of the first cult hits on video, and set the tone for the genre. The reasons: polished production values, a romantic approach to the material, an attractive star (Harlee MacBride), and a title that combines respectability with prurience. The formula has been copied thousands of times since. Followed by a sequel. 🗡🗡🗡 **GPI: 9.0**

Contains strong sexual material, considerable nudity.

1985 100m/C Harlee MacBride, Peter Ratay, William Beckley, Anne Michelle, Joi Staton; **D:** Alan Roberts. **VHS** *LIV*

Young Lady Chatterley 2

Soft-core sequel is really more of a remake with the addition of Sybil Danning as a repressed, straitlaced widow. The basic elements are the same—attractive sets, attractive people, minimal wardrobe. Also available in an unrated version at 100 minutes. 🗡🗡 **GPI: 8.3**

Mature subject matter, sexual content, nudity.

1985 87m/C Sybil Danning, Adam West, Harlee MacBride; **D:** Alan Roberts. **VHS, LV** *LIV*

Young Nurses in Love

So-so little hospital farce trots out the predictable medical jokes—sperm banks, plastic surgery, etc.—and the going is slow at the beginning. By the end, all of the doctors, nurses, and patients are running around being chased by assorted hit men and old guys in drag. Director Chuck Vincent was a veteran of adult films. He knew how to make low-budget movies effectively, but he couldn't sustain the comic pace with this sketchy material. The throw-away gags are the funniest. 🗡🗡

Profanity and brief comic nudity.

1989 (R) 82m/C Jeanne Marie, Alan Fisher, Barbra Robb, James Davies; **D:** Chuck Vincent. **VHS, LV** *LIV, VES*

Younger & Younger

Jonathan Younger (Donald Sutherland) starts each day with a fresh silk shirt, ice cream suit, and a generous splash of cologne. Thus prepared, he sets out to charm the customers, particularly the women, of Younger Self Storage in Los Angeles. Actually, his wife Penelope (Lolita Davidovich) does the work. Jonathan's life is powered by charm and he's running on cruise control. He dotes on his son Winston (Brendan Fraser), and whenever the realities of business threaten to intrude, he hops on his motorcycle and rides over to a glittery disco. Rounding out the cast are our narrator Francis (Linda Hunt), and the enigmatic and glamorous Mrs. Zig Zag (Sally Kellerman), and her daughter Melody (Julie Delpy). They're in the middle of an O.J.-esque celebrity murder case that's treated as a throwaway subplot. Things are going along swimmingly for all concerned—except the overworked and underappreciated Penny—until Penny dies. In death, she finds new life, and that's when this curious film really gets started. Viewers will catch overtones of *Ghost* and *Truly, Madly, Deeply*, along with a bit of Fellini. Director/writer Percy Adlon gives his world the same kind of tacky-glamorous circus sensuality. This charming fantasy will probably appeal most to fans of his *Bagdad Cafe* and *Rosalie Goes Shopping*. 🗡🗡🗡

Mature subject matter, some strong language.

1994 (R) 97m/C Donald Sutherland, Brendan Fraser, Lolita Davidovich, Sally Kellerman, Julie Delpy, Linda Hunt; **D:** Percy Adlon; **W:** Percy Adlon, Felix Adlon; **C:** Bernd Heinl; **M:** Hans Zimmer. **VHS, LV** *PAR*

Zandalee

Overwrought and overripe romantic drama combines the worst elements of *Wild Orchid* and *sex, lies and videotape* with a quarter-baked religious sensibility. The subject, sort of, is an adulterous affair between Zandalee (Erika Anderson) and artist Johnny Collins (Nicolas Cage) in New Orleans' French Quarter. The problem is her husband (Judge Reinhold). Given the diverse but universally unconvincing Southern accents that the actors

adopt, it's hard to tell exactly what his name is. At various times, it sounds like Tree, Twee, and Tureen, but the credits list it as Thierry and that's good enough for me. Thierry, an ex-poet and part-time drunk, is undergoing a severe midlife crisis. He can't write, he detests his job, and he's impotent. Bummer. Zandalee's reaction: "I wish you were a paraplegic because at least I'd understand then." The steamy love scenes are mostly notable for their use of wet paint and canvas. Given the breathless quality of the writing, Reinhold and Anderson don't really embarrass themselves too much, but Cage indulges in yet another display of inspired histrionics. Whenever director Sam Pillsbury lets the camera loose on the streets of New Orleans, he finds religious symbolism everywhere. Presumably, he is attempting to add a layer of Catholic guilt to this hyperventilating tale, but it doesn't work because the dialogue is so funny. The film really comes into its own toward the end. The characters begin to indulge in all kinds of self-destructive behavior, and the unintentional humor reaches an alternative crescendo. Just when you think it couldn't possibly become any more ridiculous, it goes straight over the deep end. And after that, it really gets crazy. Also available in an unrated version at 100 minutes. 𝄞𝄞𝄞 GPI: 9.3

Graphic sexual content, nudity, strong language.

1991 (R) 97m/C Nicolas Cage, Judge Reinhold, Erika Anderson, Viveca Lindfors, Aaron Neville, Joe Pantoliano, Ian Abercrombie, Marisa Tomei, Zach Galligan; **D:** Sam Pillsbury; **W:** Mari Kornhauser. **VHS, LV** *LIV*

Zarkorr! The Invader

What is it that makes some of us enjoy movies about guys in silly rubber suits knocking down miniature cities? Maybe our folks wouldn't let us be destructive enough with our blocks. In any case, there's something about the giant lizard creature feature that's innately appealing, and this one pushes all the right buttons. Actually, it has distilled the formula down to the essentials. In the opening scene, Zarkorr! The Irrepressible bursts out of a mountain and goes amuck. Presently, an alien being disguised as a "tiny teenaged mall tramp"

appears to postal worker Tommy Ward (Rhys Christian Pugh). She says that it's up to him to save the world, explaining why he's been chosen, what the ground rules are, etc., etc. Then it's up to Tommy. Whenever Zarkorr! The Industrial isn't squashing buildings or knocking down power lines, the story tends to drag but the filmmakers' sense of humor is in tune with their target audience, and they have fun with the material. So, why quibble about shortcomings? Perhaps a sequel, *Zarkorr! The Interpositional* is on the way. 𝄞𝄞𝄞

Comic violence, strong language.

1996 (PG) 80m/C Rhys Pugh, Deprise Grossman, Mark Hamilton, Charles Schneider, Eileen Wesson; **D:** Aaron Osborne; **W:** Benjamin Carr; **C:** Joe C. Maxwell; **M:** Richard Band. **VHS, LV** *AFE*

Zentropa

Hypnotic tale of intrigue in post-war Europe is told in a non-realistic style that's almost impossible to describe. If the Coen brothers had made a new version of *The Third Man* from a script by Ingmar Bergman they might have come up with something like this. American pacifist, Leo Kessler (Jean-Marc Barr) comes to Germany in 1945, naively believing he can help rebuild the country he refused to fight against. To that dubious end, he finds work as a conductor on the monolithic Zentropa Railways and becomes involved with the owner, Max Hartmann (Jorgen Reenberg), and his beautiful daughter Katherina (Barbara Sukowa). Their interest in Leo is mirrored by Col. Harris (Eddie Constantine), an American who suspects that the Hartmanns are part of a Nazi underground, the Werewolves. He wants Leo to keep tabs on the family. Leo complies, and he finds that there are no moral absolutes in this world. Guilt and innocence are matters of subtle shadings of gray. Good intentions count for nothing as Leo becomes more deeply enmeshed in romantic and political conflicts. But the plot is less important than the visual dream that director Lars von Trier has created. Onscreen, it's a night-world of rain and railroad tracks, the constant rhythm of the steel wheels and Max von Sydow's lulling, monotone voiceover narration. (Warning: if you try to watch this film late at night after a large dinner, you'll be asleep in five minutes.) He uses some astonishing visual tricks—bright selective colors within a black-and-white film, back projection, layers and still more layers of images—to give the story a pervasive surrealistic ambience. 🦴🦴🦴

Violence, strong language, brief nudity.

1992 **(R)** 112m/**C** *GE* Jean-Marc Barr, Barbara Sukowa, Udo Kier, Eddie Constantine, Jorgen Reenberg; *N:* Max von Sydow; *D:* Lars von Trier; *W:* Lars von Trier, Niels Vorsel. **VHS, LV** *TOU*

Zeram

Science-fiction fans will catch elements of *Wonder Woman, Godzilla,* and *Alien* in this Japanese video comic book. The title charac-ter looks like a guy in a gorilla suit and an old bathrobe who has a giant shitake mushroom growing on top of his head. He's an intergalac-tic criminal. Hot on his trail are bounty hunter Delia (Yuko Moriyama) and her computer, Bob. They manage to trap Zeram in an indus-trial suburb of Tokyo, but a couple of electri-cal workers—imagine a Japanese Laurel and Hardy—are caught with the critter. Most of the action is commonplace s-f martial arts stuff: lots of explosions, fighting, running, and jumping about. Some of the effects are fairly inventive, notably some monstrous little mucus babies that Zeram creates. 🦴🦴🦴

Contains violence and some strong language.

1991 92m/**C** *JP* Yuko Moriyama, Yukihiro Hotaru, Kunihiko Ida; *D:* Keita Amemiya; *W:* Hajime Matsumoto. **VHS** *FXL, FCT*

O.K., videos are sometimes hard enough to find without having to look under a different title, but it does happen. Luckily, we've got all the bases covered here. Sometimes they're foreign language translations; sometimes they're the original theatrical titles; sometimes they're just *slightly* different...but enough to trip you up; sometimes they're deliberate attempts to fool you into thinking that something old is new. We're here to help.

Acts of Love *See* Carried Away (1995)

Alexa *See* Alexa: A Prostitute's Own Story (1988)

The Alien Within *See* Unknown Origin (1995)

American Rickshaw *See* American Tiger (1989)

Ami de Mon Ami *See* Boyfriends & Girlfriends (1988)

Beyond Bedlam *See* Nightscare (1993)

Beyond the Rising Moon *See* Star Quest: Beyond the Rising Moon (1989)

Bikini Genie *See* Wildest Dreams (1990)

Blanc *See* White (1994)

Bleu *See* Blue (1993)

Bohemian Life *See* La Vie de Bohème (1993)

Bound by Honor *See* Blood In...Blood Out: Bound by Honor (1993)

Bram Stoker's Burial of the Rats *See* Burial of the Rats (1995)

The Buddy Factor *See* Swimming with Sharks (1994)

California Hot Wax *See* The Bikini Car Wash Company (1990)

Children of the Dust *See* A Good Day to Die (1995)

Chinchero *See* The Last Movie (1971)

Chungon Satluk Linggei *See* Organized Crime & Triad Bureau (1993)

Circuitry Man 2 *See* Plughead Rewired: Circuitry Man 2 (1994)

Clean Slate *See* Coup de Torchon (1981)

Crazy Horse *See* Friends, Lovers & Lunatics (1989)

Cyber-Chic *See* Robo-C.H.I.C. (1989)

Dance of the Vampires *See* The Fearless Vampire Killers (1967)

Dangerous Kiss *See* True Crime (1995)

Deranged *See* Idaho Transfer (1973)

Die Xue Shuang Xiong *See* The Killer (1990)

Dispara *See* Outrage (1993)

Edgar Allen Poe's House of Usher *See* The House of Usher (1988)

El Verano de la Senora Forbes *See* The Summer of Miss Forbes (1988)

Elke *See* Friend of the Family (1995)

EMC2 *See* Wavelength (1996)

Exquisite Tenderness *See* The Surgeon (1994)

Fabula de la Bella Palomera *See* The Fable of the Beautiful Pigeon Fancier (1988)

Falltime *See* Fall Time (1994)

Fatal Woman *See* Femme Fatale (1990)

Federico Fellini's Intervista *See* Intervista (1987)

Follow Your Dreams *See* Independence Day (1983)

Freddie as F.R.O.7 *See* Freddie the Frog (1992)

Gnaw: Food of the Gods 2 *See* Food of the Gods: Part 2 (1988)

Ham Ham *See* Jamon, Jamon (1993)

Heartstone *See* Demonstone (1989)

Hidden Vision *See* Night Eyes (1990)

High Finance Woman *See* The Loves of a Wall Street Woman (1989)

Highlander 3: The Magician *See* Highlander: The Final Dimension (1994)

Highlander 3: The Sorcerer *See* Highlander: The Final Dimension (1994)

The Hour of the Pig *See* The Advocate (1993)

335

Hunchback *See* The Hunchback of Notre Dame (1982)

If He Hollers, Let Him Go *See* Dead Right (1968)

Il Diavolo in Corpo *See* Devil in the Flesh (1987)

Io Speriamo Che Me La Cavo *See* Ciao, Professore! (1994)

Istanbul, Keep Your Eyes Open *See* Istanbul (1990)

Je Vous Salue Marie *See* Hail Mary (1985)

Killer *See* Bulletproof Heart (1995)

La Grieta *See* Endless Descent (1990)

La Reine Margot *See* Queen Margot (1994)

Lashou Shentan *See* Hard-Boiled (1992)

Les Liens de Sang *See* Blood Relatives (1977)

Machine Gun Blues *See* Black Rose of Harlem (1995)

Mad Dogs and Englishmen *See* Shameless (1994)

Manifesto *See* A Night of Love (1987)

Marilyn Chambers' Bikini Bistro *See* Bikini Bistro (1994)

Midnight Heat *See* Sunset Heat (1992)

My Girlfriend's Boyfriend *See* Boyfriends & Girlfriends (1988)

My Love Letters *See* Love Letters (1983)

Necronomicon *See* H. P. Lovecraft's Necronomicon: Book of the Dead (1996)

Ned Blessing: The Story of My Life and Times *See* Lone Justice 2 (1993)

Night Scare *See* Nightscare (1993)

Oblivion 2 *See* Backlash: Oblivion 2 (1995)

Pardon Me, Your Teeth Are in My Neck *See* The Fearless Vampire Killers (1967)

Party Girls *See* Party Incorporated (1989)

Passion Play *See* Love Letters (1983)

Reflections on a Crime *See* Reflections in the Dark (1994)

Roger Corman Presents Burial of the Rats *See* Burial of the Rats (1995)

Roger Corman Presents: Suspect Device *See* Suspect Device (1995)

Rouge *See* Red (1994)

Rules of Obsession *See* A Passion to Kill (1994)

Salem's Ghost *See* Witchcraft 8: Salem's Ghost (1995)

Shadows of the Peacock *See* Echoes of Paradise (1986)

She Drives Me Crazy *See* Friends, Lovers & Lunatics (1989)

She Was a Hippy Vampire *See* The Wild World of Batwoman (1966)

Space 2074 *See* Star Quest: Beyond the Rising Moon (1989)

Spoorloos *See* The Vanishing (1988)

Spotswood *See* The Efficiency Expert (1992)

Stepfather *See* Beau Pere (1981)

Subspecies 2 *See* Bloodstone: Subspecies 2 (1992)

Subspecies 3 *See* Bloodlust: Subspecies 3 (1993)

Summer with Monika *See* Monika (1952)

Sylvia Kristel's Beauty School *See* Beauty School (1993)

Tempo di Uccidere *See* Time to Kill (1989)

Three Colors: Blue *See* Blue (1993)

Three Colors: Red *See* Red (1994)

Three Colors: White *See* White (1994)

The Tiger *See* Tiger Warsaw (1987)

Tower of Terror *See* Hard to Die (1990)

The Tree of Hands *See* Innocent Victim (1990)

Trick of the Eye *See* Primal Secrets (1994)

Trois Coleurs: Blanc *See* White (1994)

Trois Coleurs: Bleu *See* Blue (1993)

Trois Coleurs: Rouge *See* Red (1994)

Underworld *See* Transmutations (1985)

Urga *See* Close to Eden (1990)

Virgin Hunters *See* Test Tube Teens from the Year 2000 (1993)

The Wandering Kid *See* Urotsukidoji 1: Legend of the Overfiend (1993)

Witchcraft 8 *See* Witchcraft 8: Salem's Ghost (1995)

Yingxiong Bense *See* A Better Tomorrow (1986)

The following index lists all actors listed in the main review section (including cameos and voiceovers), alphabetically by said actors' last names. Don't let the fact that the names are presented first name/last name fool you—it really is alphabetical by last name ("Well of course it is," I can hear you saying. "Why would they do it any other way?"). Directors get the same treatment in the aptly named "Director Index."

Bruce Abbott
Bride of Re-Animator '89
Re-Animator '84

Kareem Abdul-Jabbar
Slam Dunk Ernest '95

Tim Abell
Masseuse '95
Over the Wire '95

Ian Abercrombie
Test Tube Teens from the Year 2000 '93
Zandalee '91

F. Murray Abraham
Dillinger and Capone '95
Slipstream '89
Sweet Killing '93

Ken Abraham
Deadly Embrace '88

James Acheson
Body Language '92

Forrest J. Ackerman
Hard to Die '90

Joss Ackland
Jekyll and Hyde '90
Shameless '94

David Ackroyd
Dead On '93
Love, Cheat & Steal '93

Jay Acovone
Doctor Mordrid: Master of the Unknown '90

Deborah Adair
Endless Descent '90

Brooke Adams
The Last Hit '93

Joey Adams
S.F.W. '94

Julie Adams
The Last Movie '71

Kim Adams
Ted & Venus '93

Lynne Adams
Blood Relations '87

Trudy Adams
The American Angels: Baptism of Blood '89

Chris Adamson
Shameless '94

Kip Addotta
Wishful Thinking '92

Wesley Addy
Kiss Me Deadly '55

Isabelle Adjani
Queen Margot '94

John Agar
Miracle Mile '89

Kris Aguilar
Bloodfist '89

Danny Aiello
Once Upon a Time in America '84
29th Street '91
White Hot '88

Rick Aiello
29th Street '91

Andrew Airlie
Hard Evidence '94

Ako
Sleepwalk '88

Kurt Alan
Witchcraft 6: The Devil's Mistress '94

Jamie Alba
Ice '93

Kevin Alber
Alien Terminator '95
Burial of the Rats '95

Eddie Albert
Brenda Starr '86

Edward Albert
Body Language '92
Broken Trust '93

Demon Keeper '95
Mind Games '89
Sexual Malice '93
Sorceress '94

Kitty Aldridge
American Roulette '88
Slipstream '89

Barbara Lee Alexander
Illegal Entry: Formula for Fear '93

Jason Alexander
I Don't Buy Kisses Anymore '92

Alvin Alexis
Night of the Demons '88

Kristian Alfonso
Blindfold: Acts of Obsession '94

Ana Alicia
Romero '89

Jed Allan
Suspect Device '95

Peter Allas
Iron Maze '91

Ginger Lynn Allen
Bound and Gagged: A Love Story '93
The Stranger '95

337

India Allen
Almost Hollywood '95
Wild Cactus '92

Karen Allen
King of the Hill '93
Sweet Talker '91

Keith Allen
Nightscare '93
The Young Americans '93

Patrick Allen
When Dinosaurs Ruled the Earth '70

Rosalind Allen
To Die for 2: Son of Darkness '91

Gregg Allman
Rush Week '88

Susan Almgren
Twin Sisters '91

John Altamura
Bikini Bistro '94

Bruce Altman
Vibrations '94

Steve Altman
Transylvania Twist '89

Bayoko Amano
Tokyo Decadence '91

Claudio Amendola
Queen Margot '94

Tony Amendola
Three of Hearts '93

Granville Ames
Tainted Love '96
Twisted Passion '96

Madchen Amick
The Courtyard '95
Dream Lover '93
I'm Dangerous Tonight '90
Love, Cheat & Steal '93

Suzy Amis
Fandango '85
One Good Turn '95

Renee Ammann
Number One Fan '94

David Amos
The Takeover '94

John Amos
Hologram Man '95

Avalon Anders
Great Bikini Off-Road Adventure '94

Cole Andersen
Dragon Fury 2 '96

Dana Anderson
Ginger Ale Afternoon '89

Erika Anderson
Zandalee '91

Isa Anderson
Night Angel '90

Kevin Anderson
Liebestraum '91
The Wrong Man '93

Manon Anderson
Hail Mary '85

Melody Anderson
Final Notice '89
Landslide '92

Michael Anderson, Jr.
Sunset Grill '92

Pamela Anderson
Naked Souls '95
Snapdragon '93

Richard Anderson
The Glass Shield '95

Harriet Andersson
Monika '52

George Andre
The Wild World of Batwoman '66

Simon Andrew
Blood and Sand '89

Anthony Andrews
Haunted '95

David Andrews
Deconstructing Sarah '94

Edward Andrews
Avanti! '72

James Andronica
Mirage '94

Vanessa Angel
Another Chance '88
Homicidal Impulse '92

Jean-Hugues Anglade
Queen Margot '94

Philip Anglim
Haunted Summer '88

Franco Angrisano
Avanti! '72

Christien Anholt
Class of '61 '92

Amina Annabi
The Advocate '93

Karen Annarino
Party Plane '90

Frank Annese
Another Chance '88

Imogen Annesley
Howling III: The Marsupials '87

Susan Anspach
Into the Fire '88

Adam Ant
Nomads '86
Slamdance '87
Sunset Heat '92

Lysette Anthony
The Advocate '93
Dead Cold '96
Save Me '93

Pete Antico
29th Street '91

Gabrielle Anwar
Body Snatchers '93
Innocent Lies '95
A Night of Love '87

Scott Apel
Almost Hollywood '95

Apollonia
Black Magic Woman '91

Christina Applegate
Across the Moon '94
Streets '90
Vibrations '94

John Aprea
Cyber-Tracker '93
Picasso Trigger '89
Savage Beach '89
To the Limit '95

Amy Aquino
Descending Angel '90

Jesse Aragon
Street Asylum '90

Julian (Sonny) Arahanga
Once Were Warriors '94

Armando Araiza
Johnny 100 Pesos '96

Julie Araskog
In a Moment of Passion '93

Richard Arbolino
Mirror Images '91

Anne Archer
The Man in the Attic '94

Robert Arevalo
The Siege of Firebase Gloria '89

Asia Argento
Queen Margot '94

Victor Argo
Blue in the Face '95
King of New York '90

David Arkin
The Long Goodbye '73

Allen Arkus
A Matter of Honor '95

Elizabeth Arlen
Separate Lives '94

Bess Armstrong
Dream Lover '93

Jack Armstrong
The Guyver '91

Jerry Armstrong
Gator Bait 2: Cajun Justice '88

Kerry Armstrong
The Hunting '92

Melinda Armstrong
Bikini Summer '91

R.G. Armstrong
Payback '94

Ronald K. Armstrong
Bugged! '96

Eva Arnaz
Ferocious Female Freedom Fighters '88

Tichina Arnold
Starlight '88

Tracy Arnold
Henry: Portrait of a Serial
Killer '90

**Eduardo
Arozamena**
Dracula (Spanish Version) '31

Alexis Arquette
Don't Do It '94
Jack Be Nimble '94

David Arquette
Fall Time '94

Patricia Arquette
Trouble Bound '92

Rosanna Arquette
Black Rainbow '91
The Wrong Man '93

Michael Artura
Killer Looks '94

Atsuko Asano
Heaven & Earth '90

Dana Ashbrook
Waxwork '88

Daphne Ashbrook
Sunset Heat '92

Linda Ashby
Night Angel '90

John Ashton
Fast Money '96

Luke Askew
The Warrior & the Sorceress
'84

Armand Assante
Eternity '90

Fred Astaire
George Stevens: A
Filmmaker's Journey '84

William Atherton
Saints and Sinners '95

Christopher Atkins
Dracula Rising '93
Fatal Charm '92
Guns of Honor '95

Eileen Atkins
Jack and Sarah '96

Jayne Atkinson
Capone '89

Rowan Atkinson
The Tall Guy '89

**Richard
Attenborough**
Wavelength '96

Rene Auberjonois
The Feud '90

Maxine Audley
Peeping Tom '60

Stephane Audran
Blood Relatives '78
Coup de Torchon '81

Lance August
Stripteaser '95

Jean-Pierre Aumont
Jefferson in Paris '94

Marcus Aurelius
A.P.E.X. '94
Suspect Device '95

Julie Austin
Elves '89

Karen Austin
Far from Home '89

Daniel Auteuil
Queen Margot '94

Luis Avalos
Lone Justice 2 '93

Loren Avedon
Operation Golden Phoenix
'94
Virtual Combat '95

Joe Mari Avellana
Bloodfist 2 '90

Margaret Avery
Blueberry Hill '88

Val Avery
Faces '68

Nina Axelrod
Cross Country '83

Hoyt Axton
Number One Fan '94

Ayu Azhari
Without Mercy '95

Barbara Babcock
Happy Together '89

Lauren Bacall
Innocent Victim '90

Hans Bachman
Invader '91

Star Quest: Beyond the
Rising Moon '89

Kevin Bacon
Queens Logic '91

Michael Badalucco
The Search for One-Eyed
Jimmy '96

Badema
Close to Eden '90

Meredith Baer
The Sister-in-Law '74

Blake Bahner
Wizards of the Demon Sword
'94

Blake Bailey
Head of the Family '96
Lurking Fear '94

Kathleen Bailey
WitchTrap '89

**Charles Bailey-
Gates**
The Surgeon '94

Kirk Baily
Alexa: A Prostitute's Own
Story '88

Scott Baio
I Love N.Y. '87

Blanche Baker
Dead Funny '94

Bubba Baker
Running Cool '93

Dylan Baker
Love Potion #9 '92

Kathy Baker
Mr. Frost '89

Timothy Baker
Bloodfist 2 '90
Out for Blood '93

William L. Baker
Witchcraft 3: The Kiss of
Death '90

Brenda Bakke
Dangerous Love '87
Death Spa '87
Lone Justice 2 '93
Star Quest '94

Brigitte Bako
Dark Tide '93

Scott Bakula
Color of Night '94
My Family '94
A Passion to Kill '94

Nick Baldasare
They Bite '95

A. Michael Baldwin
Phantasm III: Lord of the
Dead '94

Adam Baldwin
Cold Sweat '93
Digital Man '94
Trade Off '95
Treacherous '95

Alec Baldwin
The Getaway '93

Daniel Baldwin
Trees Lounge '96

Stephen Baldwin
Fall Time '94

William Baldwin
Three of Hearts '93

Jennifer Balgobin
Repo Man '83

Fairuza Balk
Tollbooth '94

Kaye Ballard
Eternity '90
Fate '90
Tiger Warsaw '87

**Jean-Francois
Balmer**
Madame Bovary '91

Martin Balsam
Silence of the Hams '93

Kirk Baltz
Reservoir Dogs '92

Fernando Balzaretti
The Summer of Miss Forbes
'88

Bradford Bancroft
A Time to Die '91

Antonio Banderas
Outrage '93

Jonathan Banks
Dark Breed '96
Last Man Standing '95
There Goes the
Neighborhood '92

Cast Index

Diana Bellamy
The Nest '88

Ned Bellamy
Carnosaur '93

Cynthia Belliveau
The Dark '94

Sara Bellomo
Beach Babes from Beyond '93
Bikini Drive-In '94

Gil Bellows
Black Day Blue Night '95
Silver Strand '95

Robert Beltran
Kiss Me a Killer '91
La Pastorela '92

James Belushi
Separate Lives '94

Richard Belzer
Not of This Earth '96

Brian Benben
Mortal Sins '90

Michael C. Bendetti
Amanda and the Alien '95
Netherworld '90

Dirk Benedict
Demon Keeper '95

John Bennes
Black Rainbow '91

John Bennett
Priest '94

Marjorie Bennett
Kiss Me Deadly '55

Nigel Bennett
Back in Action '94
Darkman 3: Die Darkman Die '95

Ray Bennett
Lovers' Lovers '94

Amber Benson
King of the Hill '93

Robby Benson
White Hot '88

Fabrizio Bentivoglio
Apartment Zero '88

Kevin Benton
Intent to Kill '92

Luca Bercovici
Mirror Images 2 '93
Mortal Passions '90

Tom Berenger
At Play in the Fields of the Lord '91
Eddie and the Cruisers '83
Last Rites '88

Marisa Berenson
Night of the Cyclone '90

Peter Berg
Across the Moon '94
A Case for Murder '93
A Midnight Clear '92
Never on Tuesday '88

Wolfram Berger
Quicker Than the Eye '88

Patrick Bergin
Highway to Hell '92

Sandahl Bergman
Body of Influence '93
Lipstick Camera '93
Raw Nerve '91

Xander Berkeley
The Gun in Betty Lou's Handbag '92
Poison Ivy 2: Lily '95
Safe '95

Elizabeth Berkley
Showgirls '95

Steven Berkoff
Transmutations '85

Warren Berlinger
The Long Goodbye '73

Shelley Berman
Rented Lips '88

Jason Bernard
Paint It Black '89

Michael Bernardo
Virtual Combat '95

Daniel Bernhardt
Bloodsport 2: The Next Kumite '95

Kevin Bernhardt
Beauty School '93

Collin Bernsen
Puppet Master 2 '90

Corbin Bernsen
Baja '95
Cover Me '95

Final Mission '93
The New Age '94
Temptress '95

Elizabeth Berridge
Five Corners '88

Stephanie Berry
The Incredibly True Adventure of Two Girls in Love '95

Michael Berryman
The Guyver '91
Wizards of the Demon Sword '94

Gene Bervoets
The Vanishing '88

Bibi Besch
Kill Me Again '89

Ariel Besse
Beau Pere '81

Leigh Betchley
Knock Outs '92

Turhan Bey
Virtual Combat '95

Richard Beymer
Cross Country '83

Didier Bezace
L.627 '92

Michael Biehn
Deep Red '94
In the Kingdom of the Blind the Man with One Eye Is King '94
Rampage '87
Timebomb '91

Lynn Bieler
The Crude Oasis '95

Roxann Biggs-Dawson
Darkman 3: Die Darkman Die '95

Tom Billett
Lurkers '88

Earl Billings
One False Move '91

Peter Billingsley
Arcade '93

Edward Binns
After School '88

Juliette Binoche
Blue '93
Hail Mary '85

Leigh Biolos
Howling III: The Marsupials '87

Veronica Bird
Moral Code '96

Jesse Birdsall
Nightscare '93

Lori Birdsong
Blood Salvage '90

Matt Birman
Back in Action '94

Kelly Bishop
Queens Logic '91

Stephen Bishop
Someone to Love '87

Jacqueline Bisset
Crimebroker '95
The Maid '90
Wild Orchid '90

Joel Bissonnette
Boulevard '94

Helgi Bjornsson
Remote Control '94

Craig Black
Flirting '89

James Black
The Man with the Perfect Swing '95

Karen Black
Bound and Gagged: A Love Story '93
Mirror, Mirror '90
Night Angel '90
Overexposed '90

Ryan Black
Dance Me Outside '95

Steven Blade
Alien Seed '89

Ruben Blades
Color of Night '94
The Josephine Baker Story '90

Dasha Blahova
Howling III: The Marsupials '87

Kevin Blair
Bloodlust: Subspecies 3 '93
Bloodstone: Subspecies 2 '92

Linda Blair
Bedroom Eyes 2 '89
Repossessed '90
Sorceress '94

Deborah Blaisdell
Wildest Dreams '90

Eubie Blake
That's Black Entertainment '85

Ronee Blakley
Someone to Love '87

Dominique Blanc
Queen Margot '94

Mel Blanc
Kiss Me, Stupid! '64

Billy Blanks
Back in Action '94
Bloodfist '89
TC 2000 '93
Timebomb '91
Tough and Deadly '94

Tommy Blaze
Rumpelstiltskin '96

Jonah Blechman
Full Time '94

Maggie Blinco
The Wicked '89

Claire Bloom
Shameless '94

Lisa Blount
Femme Fatale '90

Ralph Bluemke
Invader '91
Twilight of the Dogs '96

Erika Blumberger
Rosalie Goes Shopping '89

Graeme Blundell
The Year My Voice Broke '87

John Bluthal
Leapin' Leprechauns! '95

Bruce Boa
Murder Story '89
White Light '90

Michael Boatman
The Glass Shield '95

Hart Bochner
Apartment Zero '88
A Good Day to Die '95

Lloyd Bochner
Landslide '92

W. Paul Bodie
Temptation '94

Wolfgang Bodison
The Expert '95

Jenna Bodnar
Cellblock Sisters: Banished
    Behind Bars '95

Karl-Heinz Boehm
Peeping Tom '60

Dumitri Bogmaz
Forbidden Zone: Alien
    Abduction '96

Kelley Bohanan
Idaho Transfer '73

Richard Bohringer
The Cook, the Thief, His Wife
    & Her Lover '90

Cynthia Bond
Def by Temptation '90

James Bond, III
Def by Temptation '90

Steve Bond
Picasso Trigger '89
To Die for '89
To Die for 2: Son of Darkness
    '91

Vivian Bonnell
The Josephine Baker Story
    '90

Frank Bonner
The Colony '95

Maria Bonnevie
The Polar Bear King '94

Sonny Bono
Under the Boardwalk '89

Brian Bonsall
Lily in Winter '94

Mark Boone
The Paint Job '93

Mark Boone, Jr.
Trees Lounge '96

Richard Boone
The Night of the Following
    Day '69

Ernest Borgnine
The Wild Bunch '69

Katherine Borowitz
Men of Respect '91

Jesse Borrego
Blood In...Blood Out: Bound
    by Honor '93

Miguel Bose
Queen Margot '94

Jackson Bostwick
A Matter of Honor '95

Charles Boswell
Kiss Me a Killer '91

Jean Both
The Girl in a Swing '89

Sara Botsford
The Gunrunner '84

Joseph Bottoms
Inner Sanctum '91

Sam Bottoms
After School '88

Timothy Bottoms
Digger '94
Hourglass '96
Istanbul '90

Fred Boudin
Summer Job '88

Jim Bouton
The Long Goodbye '73

Michael Bowen
Mortal Passions '90
Season of Fear '89

David Bowie
The Man Who Fell to Earth
    '76

Riley Bowman
Bloodfist '89

Bruce Boxleitner
Diplomatic Immunity '91
Passion Flower '86

Brandon Boyce
Public Access '93

Todd Boyce
Jefferson in Paris '94

Cameron Boyd
King of the Hill '93

Guy Boyd
Kiss Me a Killer '91

Lara Flynn Boyle
Past Tense '94
Red Rock West '93

Lisa Boyle
Friend of the Family '95
I Like to Play Games '95

Peter Boyle
Bulletproof Heart '95
Men of Respect '91
The Surgeon '94

Elizabeth Bracco
Trees Lounge '96

Alejandro Bracho
Romero '89

Jesse Bradford
King of the Hill '93

Richard Bradford
The Crossing Guard '94

David Bradley
Hard Justice '95
Outside the Law '95

Richard Bradshaw
The Man with the Perfect
    Swing '95

Danny Brainin
Xtro '83

Rustam Branaman
Terrified '94

Marlon Brando
The Night of the Following
    Day '69
A Streetcar Named Desire:
    The Original Director's
    Version '51

Rikki Brando
The Bikini Car Wash
    Company 2 '92

Clark Brandon
Fast Food '89

Marjorie Bransfield
Easy Wheels '89

Lorne Brass
Northern Passage '95

Ellen Burstyn
Primal Secrets '94

Jennifer Burton
Play Time '94
Watch Me '96

Kate Burton
Love Matters '93

Stephen Burton
Cyber-Tracker 2 '95

Steve Buscemi
Ed and His Dead Mother '93
Floundering '94
King of New York '90
Reservoir Dogs '92
The Search for One-Eyed
    Jimmy '96
Trees Lounge '96

Gary Busey
Carried Away '95
Man with a Gun '95

Jake Busey
S.F.W. '94

Chuck Bush
Fandango '85

Pascale Bussieres
When Night Is Falling '95

Holly Butler
Desperate Prey '94

William Butler
Inner Sanctum '91

Yancy Butler
Fast Money '96

Merritt Butrick
Death Spa '87

Shane Butterworth
Vibrations '94

Sarah Buxton
Welcome to Spring Break '88

Ruth Buzzi
Troublemakers '94
Wishful Thinking '92

Bill Byrge
Ernest Goes to School '94

Gabriel Byrne
A Dangerous Woman '93
A Soldier's Tale '91

David Byrnes
Witchcraft 7: Judgement
    Hour '95

Susan Byun
Crime Lords '91
Sgt. Kabukiman N.Y.P.D. '94

James Caan
Bottle Rocket '95

Scott Caan
A Boy Called Hate '95

Katia Caballero
Beyond Innocence '87

Angel Caban
The Refrigerator '93

Sean Caffrey
When Dinosaurs Ruled the
    Earth '70

Nicolas Cage
Red Rock West '93
Time to Kill '89
Zandalee '91

Michael Caine
Jekyll and Hyde '90

Don Calfa
Chopper Chicks in
    Zombietown '91

Claire Callaway
Three of Hearts '93

Cab Calloway
That's Black Entertainment
    '85

John Calvin
Dragonworld '94

Candace Cameron
Sharon's Secret '95

Dean Cameron
Ski School '91
Ski School 2 '94

Rod Cameron
The Last Movie '71

Joseph Campanella
Body Chemistry '90
The Glass Cage '96
Last Call '90

Bill Campbell
Out There '95

Bruce Campbell
Moontrap '89
Sundown '91

Chip Campbell
Driven to Kill '90

Heather Campbell
Ski School 2 '94

Neve Campbell
Northern Passage '95

Nicholas Campbell
Rampage '87

Rob Campbell
Lone Justice 2 '93

Natalie Canderday
One False Move '91

Stephen J. Cannell
Identity Crisis '90

Dyan Cannon
Based on an Untrue Story '93

Antonio Cantafora
Intervista '87

Katie Caple
Shotgun '89

Nadia Capone
A Whisper to a Scream '88

Kate Capshaw
Private Affairs '89

Tantoo Cardinal
Where the Rivers Flow
    North '94

David Cardy
Xtro '83

Timothy Carhart
Red Rock West '93

Gia Carides
Bad Company '94

Len Cariou
Class of '61 '92
The Man in the Attic '94

Sophie Carle
Quicker Than the Eye '88

Catherine Carlen
Chopper Chicks in
    Zombietown '91

Lynn Carlin
Faces '68

Joel Carlson
Communion '89

Veronica Carlson
Freakshow '95

Hope Marie Carlton
Hard Ticket to Hawaii '87

Picasso Trigger '89
Savage Beach '89
Terminal Exposure '89

Robert Carlyle
Priest '94
Riff Raff '92

Julie Carmen
Kiss Me a Killer '91
Paint It Black '89

Leone Carmen
The Year My Voice Broke '87

Bridget Carney
Hard to Die '90

Veronica Carothers
Fatal Skies '90

Bret Carr
The Girl with the Hungry
    Eyes '94

Carole Carr
Scream Dream '89

Lindsay Carr
Glitch! '88

David Carradine
Animal Instincts '92
Future Force '89
Night Rhythms '92
Sundown '91
That's Action! '90
The Warrior & the Sorceress
    '84

John Carradine
Jack-O '95
Killer Inside Me '76

Keith Carradine
Capone '89
Idaho Transfer '73

Robert Carradine
Somebody Has to Shoot the
    Picture '90

Tia Carrere
Hostile Intentions '95
Showdown in Little Tokyo '91
Treacherous '95

Tonia Carrero
The Fable of the Beautiful
    Pigeon Fancier '88

Elpidia Carrillo
My Family '94

Corky Carroll
Under the Boardwalk '89

Justin Carroll
Stormswept '95

Justine Carroll
Dark Secrets '95

Crystal Carson
Cartel '90

Alex Carter
The Man in the Attic '94

Alice Carter
Dangerous Heart '93

Bruce Carter
Laser Moon '92

Jack Carter
Deadly Embrace '88
Robo-C.H.I.C. '89
Satan's Princess '90

Jason Carter
The Dark Dancer '95

Jim Carter
The Advocate '93

Samantha Carter
Showgirl Murders '95

Veronica Cartwright
Dead Air '94
Mirror, Mirror 2: Raven
   Dance '94

David Caruso
King of New York '90
Rainbow Drive '90

Brent Carver
Cross Country '83

Mary Carver
Safe '95

Fernando Carzon
Glitch! '88

Eloy Casados
A Climate for Killing '91

Nicholas Cascone
84 Charlie Mopic '89

Bernie Casey
The Man Who Fell to Earth
   '76

Veronica Cash
The Pamela Principle '91

Philip Casnoff
Red Wind '91
Temptation '94

Christopher Cass
Streets of Rage '95

Nick Cassavetes
Backstreet Dreams '90
Black Rose of Harlem '95
Body of Influence '93
Broken Trust '93
Sins of the Night '93

Jean-Pierre Cassel
The Maid '90
Mr. Frost '89
The Return of the
   Musketeers '89

Seymour Cassel
Adventures in Spying '92
Bad Love '95
Dark Side of Genius '94
Faces '68
Sweet Bird of Youth '89
There Goes My Baby '92
Tollbooth '94
Trees Lounge '96
Trouble Bound '92

Joanna Cassidy
Blade Runner '82
Landslide '92

Alexis Castanares
The Summer of Miss Forbes
   '88

Mel Castelo
Crime Lords '91

Enrique Castillo
Blood In...Blood Out: Bound
   by Honor '93
My Family '94

Kim Cattrall
The Return of the
   Musketeers '89

Maxwell Caulfield
Alien Intruder '93
Animal Instincts '92
Backlash: Oblivion 2 '95
Empire Records '95
In a Moment of Passion '93
Mind Games '89
Project: Alien '89
Sundown '91

Victor Cavallo
Dial Help '88

Lumi Cavazos
Bottle Rocket '95

Dick Cavett
After School '88

Patricia Cavoti
The American Angels:
   Baptism of Blood '89

Elizabeth Cayton
Slave Girls from Beyond
   Infinity '87

Henry Cele
The Last Samurai '90

Nicholas Celozzi
Hidden Obsession '92

Brian Cesak
Fandango '85

Michael Ceveris
A Woman, Her Men and Her
   Futon '92

Feodor Chaliapin, Jr
The Inner Circle '91

**Richard
Chamberlain**
The Return of the
   Musketeers '89

Marie Chambers
Street Asylum '90

Marilyn Chambers
Bikini Bistro '94
Party Incorporated '89

Michael Champion
Dead Cold '96

Philip Chan
Hard-Boiled '92

Stephen Chang
Double Happiness '94

Carissa Channing
Lurkers '88

Damian Chapa
Blood In...Blood Out: Bound
   by Honor '93
Saints and Sinners '95

Robert Chapin
Dragon Fury 2 '96

Stuart Chapin
Shotgun '89

Geraldine Chaplin
The Return of the
   Musketeers '89

Judith Chapman
And God Created Woman
   '88

**Mark Lindsay
Chapman**
Separate Lives '94

Crystal Chappell
Lady in Waiting '94

Lisa Chappell
Desperate Remedies '93

**Patricia
Charbonneau**
Portraits of a Killer '95

Gilles Charmant
La Vie de Boheme '93

**Emmanuelle
Chaulet**
Boyfriends & Girlfriends '88

Richard Chaves
Night Eyes 2 '91

Maury Chaykin
Cold Comfort '90
George's Island '91

Joan Chen
Golden Gate '93
Temptation of a Monk '94

Jacky Cheung
Wicked City '92

Leslie Cheung
A Better Tomorrow '86
The Bride with White Hair
   '93

Maggie Cheung
The Executioners '93
The Heroic Trio '93

Hank Cheyne
Bad Blood '94

Sonny Chiba
The Street Fighter '75

Joey Chin
King of New York '90

Florin Chiriac
Forbidden Zone: Alien
   Abduction '96

Alina Chivulescu
Forbidden Zone: Alien
   Abduction '96

Paris Chong
Far Out Man '89

Rae Dawn Chong
Boulevard '94
Far Out Man '89

Video Premieres

Shelby Chong
Far Out Man '89

Thomas Chong
Far Out Man '89

Navin Chowdhry
The Seventh Coin '92

Ranjit Chowdhry
Lonely in America '90

Joseph Chrest
King of the Hill '93

Alisa Christensen
Witchcraft 7: Judgement
Hour '95

David Christensen
Over the Wire '95

Keith Christensen
Little Heroes '91

Claudia Christian
Never on Tuesday '88

Michael Christian
Private Obsession '94

Dennis Christopher
Circuitry Man '90
H. P. Lovecraft's
Necronomicon: Book of
the Dead '96
Plughead Rewired: Circuitry
Man 2 '94
The Silencers '95

Melissa Christopher
Lonely in America '90

Paul Chubb
Sweet Talker '91

Jennifer Ciesar
Lovers' Lovers '94

Rony Clanton
Def by Temptation '90

Anthony Clark
Hourglass '95

Brett Clark
Inner Sanctum '91

Candy Clark
The Man Who Fell to Earth
'76

Corrie Clark
Deadly Sins '95

Dane Clark
Last Rites '88

Liddy Clark
Deadly Possession '88

Matt Clark
Love Letters '83

Andrew Clarke
Les Patterson Saves the
World '90

David Clarke
The Great St. Louis Bank
Robbery '59

J. Jerome Clarke
Luther the Geek '90

Richard Clarke
Identity Crisis '90

Helene Clarkson
Blood & Donuts '96

Patricia Clarkson
Pharoah's Army '95

Andrew Dice Clay
National Lampoon's Favorite
Deadly Sins '95

Debra Clein
My Life's in Turnaround '94

Renee Clinc
Lock 'n' Load '90

Dave Clouse
Summer Job '88

Jason Clow
Bikini Summer '91

Kim Coates
The Club '94
Red Blooded American Girl
'90

Julie Cobb
Lisa '90

Randall "Tex" Cobb
Raw Nerve '91

Bill Cobbs
Man with a Gun '95
Out There '95

Rory Cochrane
Empire Records '95

Scott Coffey
Dream Lover '93

Frederick Coffin
There Goes My Baby '92

Anne Coffrey
Death Magic '92

Nikki Coghill
The Time Guardian '87

Alex Cohen
CyberSex Kittens '95

Mitchell Cohen
The Toxic Avenger '86

Scott Cohen
Vibrations '94
The Wharf Rat '95

Diane Colazzo
Head of the Family '96

Dallas Cole
Glitch! '88

Nat King Cole
That's Black Entertainment
'85

Natalie Cole
Lily in Winter '94

Dabney Coleman
There Goes the
Neighborhood '92

Jimmy Coleman
Priest '94
Riff Raff '92

Renee Coleman
After School '88

Signy Coleman
H. P. Lovecraft's
Necronomicon: Book of
the Dead '96

Toni Collette
The Efficiency Expert '92
Muriel's Wedding '94

Ruth Collins
Alexa: A Prostitute's Own
Story '88
Wildest Dreams '90

Robbie Coltrane
Slipstream '89

Jean-Paul Comart
L.627 '92

Jeffrey Combs
Bride of Re-Animator '89
Castle Freak '95
Doctor Mordrid: Master of
the Unknown '90
From Beyond '86
The Guyver '91

H. P. Lovecraft's
Necronomicon: Book of
the Dead '96
Lurking Fear '94
The Pit & the Pendulum '91
Re-Animator '84

Anjanette Comer
Netherworld '90
The Underneath '95

Cristi Conaway
Nina Takes a Lover '94

Jeff Conaway
Almost Pregnant '91
The Banker '89
L.A. Goddess '92
Mirror Images '91
A Time to Die '91

Darlene Conley
Faces '68

Jennifer Connelly
Once Upon a Time in
America '84

Billy Connolly
The Return of the
Musketeers '89

Kevin Connor
Phantasm III: Lord of the
Dead '94

Eddie Constantine
Zentropa '92

Keith Coogan
Under the Boardwalk '89

Carole Cook
Fast Money '96

Penny Cook
Deadly Possession '88

Roderick Cook
9 1/2 Weeks '86

Victor Cook
Starlight '88

John Cooke
Invader '91

Chris Cooper
Pharoah's Army '95

Gary Cooper
Dark Before Dawn '89

Teri Copley
Transylvania Twist '89

Alex Cord
Street Asylum '90

Jeff Corey
Color of Night '94

Bud Cort
Love Letters '83
Ted & Venus '93

Joe Cortese
Illicit Dreams '94

Robert Costanzo
Lady in Waiting '94
Ring of Fire 3: Lion Strike '94

John Costelloe
Me and the Mob '94

George Costigan
The Hawk '93

Kevin Costner
Fandango '85
The Gunrunner '84

Tina Cote
Nemesis 2: Nebula '94

Ralph Cotterill
Howling III: The Marsupials '87

Paul Coufos
Food of the Gods: Part 2 '88
Thunderground '89

Bernie Coulson
Adventures in Spying '92
Eddie and the Cruisers 2: Eddie Lives! '89

Nicole Courcel
The Sorceress '55

Nicola Cowper
Transmutations '85

Alex Cox
Dead Beat '94

Courteney Cox
Blue Desert '91
Sketch Artist 2: Hands That See '94

Mitchell Cox
A.P.E.X. '94

Ronny Cox
Target: Favorite Son '87

Peter Coyote
Exposure '91
Heart of Midnight '89

Cylk Cozart
Slam Dunk Ernest '95

Debra Crable
How U Like Me Now? '92

John Cragen
Witchcraft 7: Judgement Hour '95

Daniel Craig
The Power of One '92

Grant Cramer
Leapin' Leprechauns! '95

Barbara Crampton
Castle Freak '95
From Beyond '86
Puppet Master '89
Re-Animator '84

Kenneth Cranham
Stealing Heaven '88
Under Suspicion '92

Matt Craven
Bulletproof Heart '95

Mimi Craven
Midnight Heat '95

Rachael Crawford
When Night Is Falling '95

Sophia Crawford
Sword of Honor '94

Wayne Crawford
Crime Lords '91

Missy Crider
A Boy Called Hate '95

Karlene Crockett
Return '88

Peter Crombie
Smooth Talker '90

Gail Cronauer
Carried Away '95

Annette Crosbie
Solitaire for 2 '96

Denise Crosby
Miracle Mile '89

Mary Crosby
Body Chemistry '90
Quicker Than the Eye '88

Norm Crosby
Amore! '93

Ben Cross
Cold Sweat '93

The Criminal Mind '93
Live Wire '92
Temptress '95

Lindsay Crouse
Communion '89

Emilia Crow
Grand Tour: Disaster in Time '92

Russell Crowe
The Efficiency Expert '92
Romper Stomper '92

Rosalie Crutchley
The Hunchback of Notre Dame '82

Penelope Cruz
Jamon, Jamon '93

Jon Cryer
The Pompatus of Love '96

Brett Cullen
Prehysteria '93

Robert Culp
Timebomb '91

Ji Tu Cumbuka
Glitch! '88

Gregory Scott Cummins
Lone Justice 2 '93

Brett Cumo
The Wicked '89

Liam Cundill
Reason to Die '90

Ceri Cunnington
Hedd Wyn '92

Lynette Curran
The Year My Voice Broke '87

Gordon Currie
Blood & Donuts '96

Clifford Curtis
Desperate Remedies '93

Jamie Lee Curtis
Love Letters '83
Queens Logic '91

Liane Curtis
Hard Choices '84
Wild Orchid 2: Two Shades of Blue '92

Robin Curtis
Dark Breed '96

Todd Curtis
Out for Blood '93

Tony Curtis
Lobster Man from Mars '89

John Cusack
Floundering '94
True Colors '91

Lise Cutter
Fleshtone '94

Henry Czerny
When Night Is Falling '95

Eric Da Re
Number One Fan '94
The Takeover '94

Lara Daans
Electra '95

Maryam D'Abo
Solitaire for 2 '96
Tomcat: Dangerous Desires '93
Xtro '83

Olivia D'Abo
Into the Fire '88

Liza D'Agostino
Bar Girls '95

Elizabeth Daily
Fandango '85

Joe Dallesandro
Bad Love '95
Wild Orchid 2: Two Shades of Blue '92

Joaquin D'Almeida
Priceless Beauty '90

Abby Dalton
Cyber-Tracker '93

Kristen Dalton
Digital Man '94

Timothy Dalton
Brenda Starr '86

Timothy Daly
Caroline at Midnight '93
Dangerous Heart '93
The Spellbinder '88

Leo Damian
Ghosts Can't Do It '90

Gabriel Damon
Iron Maze '91

Cast Index

347

Video Premieres

Charles Dance
Century '94
China Moon '91
Hidden City '87
The Surgeon '94

Isa Danieli
Ciao, Professore! '94

Alex Daniels
Meridian: Kiss of the Beast
'90

Gary Daniels
Fist of the North Star '96

J.D. Daniels
Beanstalk '94

Jeff Daniels
Grand Tour: Disaster in Time
'92
Rain Without Thunder '93
There Goes the
Neighborhood '92

Shell Danielson
Blindfold: Acts of Obsession
'94

Eli Danker
Impulse '90

Sybil Danning
Howling II:Your Sister Is a
Werewolf '85
Malibu Express '85
Young Lady Chatterley a '85

Leslie Danon
The Whispering '94

Niki Dantine
Malibu Express '85

Catherine Dao
Femme Fontaine: Killer Babe
for the C.I.A. '95

Patrika Darbo
Fast Money '96

Debra Dare
Hard to Die '90

Johnny Dark
Wishful Thinking '92

Tony Darrow
Me and the Mob '94

Stacey Dash
Illegal in Blue '95

Alex Datcher
The Expert '95

Kristin Datillo
Mirror, Mirror '90

Harry Davenport
December 7th: The Movie '91

Nigel Davenport
Peeping Tom '60

Robert Davi
The Dangerous '95
The Dogfighters '95
Illicit Behavior '91
Peacemaker '90
Showgirls '95
Wild Orchid 2: Two Shades of
Blue '92

Eleanor David
Slipstream '89

Keith David
Blue in the Face '95

Lolita Davidovich
The Inner Circle '91
Younger & Younger '94

Eileen Davidson
Easy Wheels '89
Eternity '90

James Davies
Wildest Dreams '90
Young Nurses in Love '89

John Davies
Positive I.D. '87

Stephen Davies
Dillinger and Capone '95
The Nest '88

Brad Davis
Rosalie Goes Shopping '89

Carole Davis
The Shrimp on the Barbie '90

Judy Davis
The New Age '94

Sammy Davis, Jr.
That's Black Entertainment
'85

Traci Davis
Nemesis 2: Nebula '94

Tracy Davis
Star Quest: Beyond the
Rising Moon '89

Viveka Davis
A Dangerous Woman '93

Kim Dawson
Lap Dancing '95
The Voyeur '94

Matt Day
Muriel's Wedding '94

Patrick Day
Hollywood Hot Tubs 2:
Educating Crystal '89

Yvonne De Carlo
Mirror, Mirror '90

Danny De La Paz
Miracle Mile '89

John de Lancie
Arcade '93
Deep Red '94

Derek De Lint
Mascara '87
Stealing Heaven '88

Robert De Niro
Once Upon a Time in
America '84

Rona De Ricci
The Pit & the Pendulum '91

Larry De Russy
The Bikini Car Wash
Company 2 '92

Anthony De Sando
Party Girl '94

Guiliana de Sio
Private Affairs '89

**Jose-Luis De
Villalonga**
Blood and Sand '89

Lucy Deakins
There Goes My Baby '92

Allison Dean
Ruby in Paradise '93

Rick Dean
Bloodfist 7: Manhunt '94
Cheyenne Warrior '94
New Crime City: Los Angeles
2020 '94
Saturday Night Special '92
Stripteaser '95

Xavier DeClie
Nemesis 3: Time Lapse '95

Michelle DeCosta
The Refrigerator '93

Eddie Deezen
Mob Boss '90

Keith DeGreen
Death Magic '92

John Dehner
Killer Inside Me '76

Albert Dekker
Kiss Me Deadly '55
The Wild Bunch '69

Laura Del Sol
The Crew '95

Benicio Del Toro
China Moon '91
Swimming with Sharks '94

Louise Delamere
Shameless '94

Kim Delaney
Darkman 2: The Return of
Durant '94
The Force '94
Temptress '95

Michael Delano
Out for Blood '93
Ring of Fire '91
Ring of Fire 2: Blood and
Steel '92

Debra Deliso
Iced '88

**Michael
DellaFemina**
Bloodlust: Subspecies 3 '93

Jennifer Delora
Bedroom Eyes 2 '89

Julie Delpy
White '94
Younger & Younger '94

Dom DeLuise
Almost Pregnant '91
Silence of the Hams '93

Alex Demir
Killing for Love '95

Rebecca DeMornay
And God Created Woman
'88

Darcy Demoss
Forbidden Zone: Alien
Abduction '96
Living to Die '91

Patrick Dempsey
Bloodknot '95

Happy Together '89

Jeffrey DeMunn
Eyes of an Angel '91

Judi Dench
Jack and Sarah '96

Lydie Denier
Blood Relations '87
Satan's Princess '90

Michael Denish
Bloodstone: Subspecies 2 '92

Alexis Denisof
Murder Story '89

Anthony John Denison
Little Vegas '90
Men of War '94
Sex, Love and Cold Hard Cash '93

Sandy Dennis
Parents '89

Chris Denton
Bound and Gagged: A Love Story '93

Graham Denton
The Great St. Louis Bank Robbery '59

Johnny Depp
Arizona Dream '94

Bo Derek
Ghosts Can't Do It '90
Woman of Desire '93

Bruce Dern
Into the Badlands '92
A Mother's Prayer '95
Will Penny '67

Laura Dern
Haunted Summer '88

Lamya Derval
Howling IV: The Original Nightmare '88

Ivan Desny
Quicker Than the Eye '88

Maruschka Detmers
Devil in the Flesh '87

Nicolas DeToth
Welcome to Spring Break '88

William Devane
Lady in Waiting '94

Nathaniel DeVeaux
Hard Evidence '94

Dean Devlin
Moon 44 '90

Patrick Dewaere
Beau Pere '81

Cliff DeYoung
Carnosaur 2 '94
Forbidden Sun '89
Independence Day '83
Star Quest '94

John DiAquino
Slipping into Darkness '88

Chico Diaz
The Fable of the Beautiful Pigeon Fancier '88

Guillermo Diaz
Party Girl '94

Vic Diaz
Caged Heat 2: Stripped of Freedom '94

Bobby DiCicco
The Baby Doll Murders '92
Frame Up '91
The Last Hour '91
Tiger Warsaw '87

Andy Dick
...And God Spoke '94

Angie Dickinson
The Maddening '95

Evelyne Didi
La Vie de Boheme '93

Robert Diedermann
Invader '91

Juan Diego
Jamon, Jamon '93

John Diehl
Almost Dead '94
A Climate for Killing '91

Kevin Dillon
Criminal Hearts '95
A Midnight Clear '92
True Crime '95

Matt Dillon
Golden Gate '93

Paul Dillon
Kiss Daddy Goodnight '87

Dyanne DiMarco
Electra '95

Ernie Dingo
Until the End of the World '91

Kelly Dingwall
The Custodian '94

Andrew Divoff
Backlash: Oblivion 2 '95
Dangerous Touch '94
Interceptor '92
Oblivion '94
Running Cool '93
The Stranger '95

Ivan Dixon
Nothing but a Man '64

Gosia Dobrowolska
The Custodian '94

Peter Dobson
Dead Cold '96

Vernon Dobtcheff
M. Butterfly '93

Jack Dodson
A Climate for Killing '91

John Doe
Slamdance '87

Shannen Doherty
Almost Dead '94
Blindfold: Acts of Obsession '94

Damon D'Oliveira
Back in Action '94

Jessica Dollarhide
Castle Freak '95

Arielle Dombasle
Raging Angels '95

Solveig Dommartin
Until the End of the World '91

Linda Dona
Delta Heat '92

Troy Donahue
Dr. Alien '88
The Pamela Principle '91
Shock 'Em Dead '90

Len Donato
Killer Looks '94

Steve Donmyer
Glitch! '88
Terminal Exposure '89

Barnard Pierre Donnadieu
The Vanishing '88

Vincent D'Onofrio
Desire '93
Fires Within '91

Amanda Donohoe
Paper Mask '91

Tate Donovan
Love Potion #9 '92

Alison Doody
Temptation '94

James Doohan
Amore! '93

Paul Dooley
A Dangerous Woman '93
Last Rites '88
Out There '95
The Underneath '95

Robert DoQui
Miracle Mile '89

Jesse Doran
Street Asylum '90

Stephen Dorff
Innocent Lies '95
The Power of One '92
S.F.W. '94

Antonia Dorian
Dinosaur Island '93

Pierre Doris
Overseas: Three Women with Man Trouble '90

Cody Dorkin
The Colony '95

Michael Dorn
Amanda and the Alien '95

Sarah Douglas
The Art of Dying '90
The Return of Swamp Thing '89
Spitfire '94
Voodoo '95

Brad Dourif
Color of Night '94
Dead Certain '92
Death Machine '95

Barbara Dow
Witchcraft 4: Virgin Heart '92

Betsy Dowds
Ruby in Paradise '93

Video Premieres

Don Dowe
Test Tube Teens from the
Year 2000 '93

Tiffany Dowe
Vicious '88

Lesley-Anne Down
The Hunchback of Notre
Dame '82
Nomads '86

Brian Downey
George's Island '91

Morton Downey, Jr.
Body Chemistry 2: Voice of a
Stranger '91
The Silencer '92

Robert Downey, Jr.
Heart and Souls '93
Rented Lips '88

John Doyle
Contagion '87
The Wicked '89

Brian Doyle-Murray
The Experts '89

Pamella D'Pella
Caged Heat 2: Stripped of
Freedom '94

Billy Drago
Dark Before Dawn '89
Diplomatic Immunity '91
Never Say Die '94
Secret Games '92
The Takeover '94

Larry Drake
Darkman 2: The Return of
Durant '94
The Journey of August King
'95

Fred Draper
Faces '68

Polly Draper
A Million to Juan '94

Griffin Drew
Dinosaur Island '93
Friend of the Family '95
Masseuse '95
Over the Wire '95
Sinful Intrigue '95

Richard Dreyfuss
Silent Fall '94

Deborah Driggs
Night Rhythms '92

Jeanie Drynan
Muriel's Wedding '94

Danielle Du Clos
Spy Trap '92

Kristie Ducati
The Bikini Car Wash
Company '90
The Bikini Car Wash
Company 2 '92

Michael Duchaussoy
Road to Ruin '91

Bronson Dudley
Trees Lounge '96

Denice Duff
Bloodlust: Subspecies 3 '93
Bloodstone: Subspecies 2 '92

Karen Duffy
Synapse '95

Quinn Duffy
In the Kingdom of the Blind
the Man with One Eye Is
King '94

Thomas F. Duffy
Eye of the Stranger '93

Olympia Dukakis
Digger '94

James Dukas
The Great St. Louis Bank
Robbery '59

David Dukes
The Josephine Baker Story
'90

Denise Dumont
Heart of Midnight '89

J.K. Dumont
The Pamela Principle '91

Jose Dumont
At Play in the Fields of the
Lord '91

Faye Dunaway
Arizona Dream '94

Adrian Dunbar
Innocent Lies '95

Jack Dunlap
Death Magic '92

Vic Dunlop
Wishful Thinking '92

Griffin Dunne
Love Matters '93

Judd Dunning
Cabin Fever '93

Wilson Dunster
Swift Justice '88

Daniel Dupont
Running Wild '94

John Durbin
King of the Hill '93

Patricia Durham
Temptation '94

Charles Durning
Brenda Starr '86
Cat Chaser '90
Project: Alien '89

Dick Durock
The Return of Swamp Thing
'89

Michael Durrell
Illegal in Blue '95

Joe Dusic
The Bikini Car Wash
Company '90

Robert Duvall
Wrestling Ernest Hemingway
'93

Kill Dwyor
Ski School 2 '94

Rachel Dyer
Almost Hollywood '95

Bob Dylan
Hearts of Fire '87

George Dzundza
Impulse '90

Kirk Earhardt
Summer Job '88

Jeff East
Another Chance '88

Steve Eastin
Last Man Standing '95

Robert Eastwick
Strike a Pose '93

Roberta Eaton
The Crude Oasis '95

Dagmar Ebbesen
Monika '52

Bonnie Ebson
Black Magic Woman '91

Richard Edson
Bad Love '95
Joey Breaker '93
Love, Cheat & Steal '93

Anthony Edwards
Delta Heat '92
Landslide '92
Miracle Mile '89

Barbara Edwards
Another Chance '88
Malibu Express '85

Charles Edwards
The Loves of a Wall Street
Woman '89

Jennifer Edwards
Overexposed '90

Joel J. Edwards
Voodoo '95

Lance Edwards
Peacemaker '90
A Woman, Her Men and Her
Futon '92

Vince Edwards
To Die for 2: Son of Darkness
'91

Will Egan
Glitch! '88

Nicole Eggert
Amanda and the Alien '95
Blown Away '93

Stan Egi
Come See the Paradise '90
Golden Gate '93

Lisa Eichhorn
King of the Hill '93
Moon 44 '90

Lisa Eilbacher
The Last Samurai '90
Live Wire '92

Sten Eirik
Electra '95

Debra Eisenstadt
Oleanna '94

Anita Ekberg
Intervista '87

Lars Ekborg
Monika '52

Donna Ekholdt
Dangerous Touch '94

Britt Ekland
Scandal '89

Jack Elam
Kiss Me Deadly '55

Dana Elcar
Inside Out '91

Soley Eliasdottir
Remote Control '94

Hector Elizondo
There Goes the
Neighborhood '92

David Elliot
Play Time '94

Alison Elliott
The Underneath '95

Denholm Elliott
Stealing Heaven '88
Transmutations '85

Shawn Elliott
Impulse '90

James Ellis
Leapin' Leprechauns! '95
Priest '94

Rehekah Elmaloglou
In Too Deep '90

Jonathon Emerson
84 Charlie Mopic '89

David Emge
Dawn of the Dead '78

Michael Emil
Adventures in Spying '92
Someone to Love '87

Taungaroa Emile
Once Were Warriors '94

Alphonsia Emmanuel
Under Suspicion '92

Audie England
One Good Turn '95
Venus Rising '95

Takaai Enoki
Heaven & Earth '90

John Enos
Till the End of the Night '94

Brenda Epperson
Amore! '93

R. Lee Ermey
Body Snatchers '93
Demonstone '89
Endless Descent '90
I'm Dangerous Tonight '90
Love Is a Gun '94
The Siege of Firebase Gloria
'89

Krista Errickson
Mortal Passions '90

Victor Ertmanis
Paris, France '94

Johnnie Saiko Espiritu
Kung Fu Rascals '90s

Ciro Esposito
Ciao, Professore! '94

Giancarlo Esposito
Blue in the Face '95
King of New York '90

Michael Esposito
Fatal Skies '90

Emilio Estevez
Repo Man '83

Joe Estevez
Beach Babes from Beyond
'93
Eye of the Stranger '93
In a Moment of Passion '93
L.A. Goddess '92
The Mosaic Project '95
Soultaker '90

Renee Estevez
Forbidden Sun '89

Erik Estrada
Alien Seed '89
Do or Die '91
Guns '90

John Evans
Long Road Home '91

Rupert Everett
Hearts of Fire '87

Nancy Everhard
Demonstone '89
This Gun for Hire '90

Jason Evers
Basket Case 2 '90

Maynard Eziashi
Twenty-One '91

Ava Fabian
Last Man Standing '95
Ski School '91
To Die for '89

Jeff Fahey
Darkman 3: Die Darkman Die
'95
Impulse '90
Iron Maze '91
The Lawnmower Man '92
Northern Passage '95
The Serpent of Death '90
Sketch Artist '92
Sketch Artist 2: Hands That
See '94
Temptation '94
Woman of Desire '93

Craig Fairbrass
Nightscare '93

Max Fairchild
Howling III: The Marsupials
'87

Morgan Fairchild
Based on an Untrue Story '93
Body Chemistry 3: Point of
Seduction '93
Criminal Hearts '95
Mob Boss '90
Phantom of the Mall: Eric's
Revenge '89
Test Tube Teens from the
Year 2000 '93
Venus Rising '95

Matthew Faison
Lily in Winter '94

Marianne Faithfull
Shopping '93

Richard Fancy
Identity Crisis '90

Rio Fanning
Priest '94

Debrah Farentino
Capone '89
Dead Air '94
Mortal Sins '90

James Farentino
A Cop for the Killing '94

Dennis Farina
Men of Respect '91
Out of Annie's Past '94

Gary Farmer
Blown Away '93
Powwow Highway '89

Ken Farmer
Another Pair of Aces: Three
of a Kind '91

Richard Farnsworth
Highway to Hell '92
Independence Day '83

Felicia Farr
Kiss Me, Stupid! '64

Jamie Farr
Curse 2: The Bite '88

Judi Farr
The Year My Voice Broke '87

Belinda Farrell
Cabin Fever '93

Sharon Farrell
Arcade '93
Beyond Desire '94

Ben Faulkner
Silent Fall '94

James Faulkner
The Maid '90
Wavelength '96

Farrah Fawcett
A Good Day to Die '95

Angela Featherstone
Dark Angel: The Ascent '94

Frederique Feder
Red '94

Corey Feldman
Blown Away '93
Lipstick Camera '93
Voodoo '95

Tovah Feldshuh
Blue Iguana '88

Federico Fellini
Intervista '87

Freddy Fender
La Pastorela '92

Zhang Fengyi
Temptation of a Monk '94

Tanya Fenmore
Lisa '90

Sherilyn Fenn
Backstreet Dreams '90
Meridian: Kiss of the Beast
'90
Three of Hearts '93

351

Video Premieres

Lance Fenton
Night of the Demons '88

Colm Feore
32 Short Films about Glenn Gould '93

Matthew Ferguson
The Club '94

Tom Ferguson
Biohazard: The Alien Force '95

Robert J. Ferilli
Caged Heat 3000 '95

Emilio Fernandez
The Wild Bunch '69

Juan Fernandez
Cat Chaser '90

Rebecca Ferratti
To the Limit '95

Andrea Ferreol
Sweet Killing '93

Leilani Sarelle Ferrer
Sketch Artist 2: Hands That See '94

Miguel Ferrer
Incident at Deception Ridge '94

Lou Ferrigno
...And God Spoke '94

Debra Feuer
Night Angel '90

William Fichtner
The Underneath '95

John Fiedler
Kiss Me, Stupid! '64

Arabella Field
The Pompatus of Love '96

Chelsea Field
Dust Devil '93
A Passion to Kill '94
Snapdragon '93

Shirley Anne Field
Peeping Tom '60

Todd Field
Ruby in Paradise '93

Christopher John Fields
The Gun in Betty Lou's Handbag '92

Holly Fields
Moral Code '96

Tony Fields
Across the Moon '94
Backstreet Dreams '90

Kaisa Figura
Fatal Past '94

David Finch
Riff Raff '92

Jon Finch
Lurking Fear '94

Frank Finlay
The Return of the Musketeers '89

Angela Finocchiaro
Volere Volare '92

Fiona
Hearts of Fire '87

Linda Fiorentino
Queens Logic '91

Colin Firth
The Advocate '93
Apartment Zero '88
Femme Fatale '90
Wings of Fame '93

Peter Firth
Burndown '89
Innocent Victim '90

Nancy Fish
Reflections in the Dark '94

Laurence "Larry" Fishburne
Bad Company '94
King of New York '90

Alan Fisher
Young Nurses in Love '89

Carrie Fisher
The Time Guardian '87

Frances Fisher
Frame Up '91

Tricia Leigh Fisher
Arizona Dream '94
Hostile Intentions '95

Annie Fitzgerald
Fatally Yours '95

Jack Fjeldstad
The Polar Bear King '94

Sean Patrick Flanery
Raging Angels '95

John Flaus
Bootleg '89
In Too Deep '90

Noah Fleiss
A Mother's Prayer '95

Dexter Fletcher
The Rachel Papers '89

Louise Fletcher
Final Notice '89
Shadowzone '89
Tollbooth '94

Page Fletcher
Friends, Lovers & Lunatics '89

Suzanne Fletcher
Sleepwalk '88

Holly Floria
Netherworld '90

Darlanne Fluegel
Darkman 3: Die Darkman Die '95
Once Upon a Time in America '84
Project: Alien '89

Colleen Flynn
Incident at Deception Ridge '94

Michael Foley
Intent to Kill '92

Bridget Fonda
Iron Maze '91
Out of the Rain '90
Scandal '89

Henry Fonda
Pat Paulsen for President '68

Peter Fonda
The Last Movie '71

Phil Fondacaro
Dollman Vs. Demonic Toys '93
Meridian: Kiss of the Beast '90

Fred Fondren
Joey Breaker '93

Michelle Forbes
Black Day Blue Night '95
Swimming with Sharks '94

Glenn Ford
Raw Nerve '91

Harrison Ford
Blade Runner '82

Lita Ford
Highway to Hell '92

Maria Ford
Alien Terminator '95
Angel of Destruction '94
Black Rose of Harlem '95
Burial of the Rats '95
The Glass Cage '96
Masque of the Red Death '89
Night Hunter '95
Ring of Fire '91
Ring of Fire 2: Blood and Steel '92
Saturday Night Special '92
Showgirl Murders '95
Stripteaser '95

Mick Ford
How to Get Ahead in Advertising '89

Ken Foree
Dawn of the Dead '78
From Beyond '86

Deborah Foreman
The Experts '89
Friends, Lovers & Lunatics '89
Lobster Man from Mars '89
Sundown '91
Waxwork '88

Farrah Forke
National Lampoon's Favorite Deadly Sins '95

Frederic Forrest
Cat Chaser '90
Rain Without Thunder '93
Return '88
Twin Sisters '91

Robert Forster
The Banker '89
Body Chemistry 3: Point of Seduction '93
Diplomatic Immunity '91
Peacemaker '90
Satan's Princess '90
29th Street '91

William Forsythe
Beyond Desire '94
The Gun in Betty Lou's Handbag '92

Isabelle Fortea
Bikini Bistro '94

Eric Foster
Grandma's House '88

Gloria Foster
Nothing but a Man '64

Jodie Foster
Five Corners '88

Kimberly Foster
Broken Trust '93

Meg Foster
Backlash: Oblivion 2 '95
Backstab '90
Diplomatic Immunity '91
Jezebel's Kiss '90
Lady in Waiting '94
Oblivion '94
Undercover '94

Stacie Foster
Cyber-Tracker 2 '95
Steel Frontier '94

Rich Foucheux
Invader '91

David Fox
When Night Is Falling '95

Huckleberry Fox
Pharoah's Army '95

Michael J. Fox
Blue in the Face '95

Anthony (Tony) Franciosa
Backstreet Dreams '90

Anne Francis
Little Vegas '90
Return '88

Ramon Franco
Kiss Me a Killer '91

Dan Frank
Great Bikini Off-Road Adventure '94

Mark Frankel
Solitaire for 2 '96

Joe Franklin
29th Street '91

John Franklin
Tammy and the T-Rex '94

Pamela Franklin
The Night of the Following Day '69

Mary Frann
Fatal Charm '92
I'm Dangerous Tonight '90

Brendan Fraser
Dark Side of Genius '94
Younger & Younger '94

Brent Fraser
Wild Orchid 2: Two Shades of Blue '92

Stuart Fratkin
Dr. Alien '88
Prehysteria '93
Ski School '91

Rupert Frazer
The Girl in a Swing '89

Peter Frechette
Paint It Black '89

Vicki Frederick
Chopper Chicks in Zombietown '91

J.E. Freeman
There Goes My Baby '92

Kathleen Freeman
Reckless Kelly '93

Morgan Freeman
The Power of One '92

Matt Frewer
Far from Home '89

Bjorn Fridbjornsson
Remote Control '94

Peter Friedman
Safe '95

Steve Fromholz
Positive I.D. '87

Troy Fronin
Kung Fu Rascals '90s

Danielle Frons
Death Magic '92

Susan Fronsoe
Biohazard: The Alien Force '95

Lee Frost
Private Obsession '94

Lindsay Frost
Monolith '93

Sadie Frost
Shopping '93

Donna Frotscher
They Bite '95

Kevin Fry
Femme Fontaine: Killer Babe for the C.I.A. '95

Soleil Moon Frye
Piranha '96
Twisted Love '95

Tatsuya Fuji
In the Realm of the Senses '76

John Fujioka
The Last Samurai '90

Kei Fujiwara
Tetsuo: The Iron Man '92

Jonathan Fuller
Arcade '93
Castle Freak '95
Last Man Standing '95
The Pit & the Pendulum '91
Suspect Device '95

Kurt Fuller
Miracle Mile '89
Reflections in the Dark '94

Samuel Fuller
La Vie de Boheme '93
The Last Movie '71

Christina Fulton
The Girl with the Hungry Eyes '94

Carl Fury
Posed for Murder '89

Dan Futterman
Class of '61 '92

Catrin Fychan
Hedd Wyn '92

Robert Fyfe
Xtro '83

Richard Gabai
Bikini Drive-In '94
Dinosaur Island '93

June Gable
Brenda Starr '86

Nathy Gaffney
Contagion '87

Jenny Gago
My Family '94

Janusz Gajos
White '94

David Gale
Bride of Re-Animator '89
The Guyver '91
Re-Animator '84

Anna Galiena
Jamon, Jamon '93

Megan Gallagher
Trade Off '95

Peter Gallagher
The Underneath '95

Philippe Galland
Overseas: Three Women with Man Trouble '90

Zach Galligan
Caroline at Midnight '93
Ice '93
Mortal Passions '90
Waxwork '88
Zandalee '91

Vincent Gallo
Arizona Dream '94

William Gallo
Night of the Demons '88

Michael Gambon
The Cook, the Thief, His Wife & Her Lover '90
The Rachel Papers '89

James Gammon
Running Cool '93

Charlie Ganis
Ring of Fire 2: Blood and Steel '92

Paul Ganus
The Silencer '92

Ray Garaza
Private Lessons, Another Story '94

Andy Garcia
American Roulette '88

Nicole Garcia
Overseas: Three Women with Man Trouble '90

Stenio Garcia
At Play in the Fields of the Lord '91

Cecile Garcia-Fogel
L.627 '92

Cathleen Ann Gardner
Dragon Fury 2 '96

Daniel Gardner
How U Like Me Now? '92

Lee Garlington
Reflections in the Dark '94

Huw Garmon
Hedd Wyn '92

Gale Garnett
32 Short Films about Glenn
Gould '93

Eliza Garrett
Love Is a Gun '94

Leif Garrett
The Banker '89
The Whispering '94

Christopher Gartin
Tremors 2: Aftershocks '96

Alessandro Gassman
Sacrilege '86

Ed Gate
Lifepod '93

Mikkel Gaup
Pathfinder '87

Sara Marit Gaup
Pathfinder '87

Dan Gauthier
Excessive Force 2: Force on
Force '95
Illegal in Blue '95

Dick Gautier
Glitch! '88

Lisa Gaye
Class of Nuke 'Em High 2:
Subhumanoid Meltdown '91
Class of Nuke 'Em High 3:
The Good, the Bad and the
Subhumanoid '94

Mitch Gaylord
American Tiger '89
Animal Instincts '92
Sexual Outlaws '94

Wendy Gazelle
Understudy: The Graveyard
Shift 2 '88

Ben Gazzara
The Dogfighters '95
Quicker Than the Eye '88

Anthony Geary
Dangerous Love '87

Jason Gedrick
The Force '94

Kevin Geer
Sweet Bird of Youth '89

Pleasant Gehman
The Runnin' Kind '89

Sarah Gellar
High Stakes '89

Francois-Eric Gendron
Boyfriends & Girlfriends '88

Bryan Genesse
Live Wire: Human Timebomb '95
Terminal Impact '95

Sabryn Gene't
Illegal Entry: Formula for
Fear '93

Denise Gentile
Netherworld '90

Minnie Gentry
Def by Temptation '90

Stephen Geoffreys
Moon 44 '90

Marita Geraghty
Past Tense '94

Danny Gerard
Starlight '88

Gil Gerard
Final Notice '89

Joan Gerardi
Bikini Bistro '94

Gerardo
A Million to Juan '94

Louise Germaine
Lipstick on Your Collar '94

Savina Gersak
Curse 2: The Bite '88

Gina Gershon
Joey Breaker '93
Love Matters '93
Showgirls '95

Lisa Gerstein
My Life's in Turnaround '94

Balthazar Getty
Dead Beat '94
Don't Do It '94

John Getz
Painted Hero '95
A Passion to Kill '94

Louis Giambalvo
Illegal in Blue '95

Rick Gianisi
Posed for Murder '89
Sgt. Kabukiman N.Y.P.D. '94

Giancarlo Giannini
Time to Kill '89

Marla Gibbs
Lily in Winter '94

Henry Gibson
Brenda Starr '86
Kiss Me, Stupid! '64
The Long Goodbye '73

Sonny Gibson
Dark Before Dawn '89

Pamela Gidley
Bad Love '95
Blue Iguana '88
The Crew '95
Highway to Hell '92
Liebestraum '91
S.F.W. '94

John Gielgud
The Hunchback of Notre
Dame '82
The Power of One '92

Roland Gift
Scandal '89

Sara Gilbert
Dead Beat '94
Poison Ivy '92

Jeremy Gilley
Nexus '96

Seth Gilliam
Jefferson in Paris '94

Rebecca Gilling
The Naked Country '85

Robert Ginnaven
One False Move '91

Robert Ginty
That's Action! '90

Roland Giraud
Mr. Frost '89

Isabel Glasser
The Surgeon '94

Paul Gleason
Digital Man '94
Running Cool '93
There Goes My Baby '92
Wild Cactus '92

Randy Gleave
Rockwell: A Legend of the
Wild West '93

Iain Glen
The Young Americans '93

Scott Glenn
Past Tense '94

John Glover
Ed and His Dead Mother '93
Meet the Hollowheads '89

Julian Glover
Hearts of Fire '87

Kara Glover
Caribe '87

Trevor Goddard
Fast Money '96
Men of War '94
Moral Code '96

Alexander Godunov
The Dogfighters '95

John Goff
Party Plane '90

Joanna Going
A Good Day to Die '95

Whoopi Goldberg
Theodore Rex '95

Jeff Goldblum
Mr. Frost '89
The Tall Guy '89

Ricky Paull Goldin
Mirror, Mirror '90

Jonathan Goldsmith
Phantom of the Mall: Eric's
Revenge '89

Gil Goldstein
Radio Inside '94

Jenette Goldstein
Near Dark '87

Bob(cat) Goldthwait
Little Vegas '90
Out There '95

Tony Goldwyn
The Last Word '95
Love Matters '93

Nemesis '93
Night Hunter '95

Anthony Guidera
Undercover '94

Paul Guilfoyle
Class of '61 '92

Robert Guillaume
A Good Day to Die '95

Tim Guinee
Men of War '94
The Pompatus of Love '96

Lara Guirao
L.627 '92

Dorothy Gulliver
Faces '68

Annabelle Gurwitch
Pizza Man '91

Margret H. Gustavsdottir
Remote Control '94

Joe Guzaldo
Smooth Talker '90

Lukas Haas
Warrior Spirit '94

Sean Haberle
The Surgeon '94

Joan Hackett
Will Penny '67

Jonathan Hadary
The New Age '94

Ross Hagen
Bikini Drive-In '94
Dinosaur Island '93
Midnight Tease 2 '95

Dan Haggerty
Cheyenne Warrior '94
Elves '89

Jess Hahn
The Night of the Following
    Day '69

Charles Haid
A Cop for the Killing '94
Storyville '92

Ion Haiduc
Bloodlust: Subspecies 3 '93
Bloodstone: Subspecies 2 '92

Stacy Haiduk
Luther the Geek '90

Corey Haim
Blown Away '93
Watchers '88

Anthony Michael Hall
Into the Sun '92
Me and the Mob '94

Georgine Hall
Out of the Rain '90

Kevin Peter Hall
Highway to Hell '92

Landon Hall
Over the Wire '95

Lena Hall
Witchcraft 3: The Kiss of
    Death '90

Philip Baker Hall
Blue Desert '91

Edmund Halley
Midnight Tease '94

Rodger Halstead
Alien Terminator '95

Mark Hamill
Black Magic Woman '91
The Guyver '91
Slipstream '89

Antony Hamilton
Howling IV: The Original
    Nightmare '88

Dean Hamilton
Rush Week '88

George Hamilton
Amore! '93
Playback '95

Jane Hamilton
Beauty School '93
Bedroom Eyes 2 '89
Wildest Dreams '90

Linda Hamilton
A Mother's Prayer '95
Separate Lives '94
Silent Fall '94

Mark Hamilton
Zarkorr! The Invader '96

Paula Hamilton
Shameless '94

Tony Hamilton
Fatal Instinct '92

Wendy Hamilton
The Dallas Connection '94
Scoring '95
Ski School 2 '94

Harry Hamlin
Ebbtide '94
Save Me '93
Target: Favorite Son '87

Nicholas Hammond
Trouble in Paradise '88

Olivia Hamnett
Deadly Possession '88

Ong Soo Han
Bloodsport 2: The Next
    Kumite '95

Lou Hancock
Miracle Mile '89

Tres Handley
Grim '95

Rene Handren-Seals
Powwow Highway '89

Larry Hankin
Black Magic Woman '91

Adam Hann-Byrd
Digger '94

Daryl Hannah
At Play in the Fields of the
    Lord '91
Blade Runner '71

Page Hannah
After School '88

Gunnar Hansen
Freakshow '95

Mitch Hara
The Art of Dying '90

Crofton Hardester
The Turn On '95

Kate Hardie
Innocent Victim '90

Ian Hardin
Cannibal! The Musical '96

Melora Hardin
Chameleon '95
Reckless Kelly '93

Kadeem Hardison
Def by Temptation '90

Stephanie Hardy
To Sleep with a Vampire '92

John Harkins
Rampage '87
This Gun for Hire '90

Willie Harlander
Rosalie Goes Shopping '89

Mark Harmon
Long Road Home '91
Sweet Bird of Youth '89

Jessica Harper
Blue Iguana '88

Robert Harper
The Wrong Man '93

Laura Harrington
Dead Air '94
Linda '93

Lisa Jay Harrington
Witchcraft 4: Virgin Heart '92

Ed Harris
China Moon '91

Fox Harris
Repo Man '83

Gail Harris
Cellblock Sisters: Banished
    Behind Bars '95

Jared Harris
Blue in the Face '95

Julie Harris
Carried Away '95

Julius W. Harris
Nothing but a Man '64

Kathryn Harris
Broken Trust '93

Lara Harris
The Dogfighters '95

Mel Harris
Sharon's Secret '95
Suture '93

Michael Harris
Dead Air '94
Mr. Stitch '95
Suture '93

Neil Patrick Harris
The Man in the Attic '94

Richard Harris
Wrestling Ernest Hemingway
    '93

Robin Harris
Hard to Die '90

Anthony Higgins
Sweet Killing '93

Clare Higgins
Fatherland '94

Michael Higgins
Crusoe '89

Torri Higginson
Jungleground '95

Lauryn Hill
King of the Hill '93

Leslie Hill
Flirting '89

Richard Hill
Bloodfist 2 '90

Terence Hill
Troublemakers '94

Art Hindle
Into the Fire '88

Gregory Hines
Dead Air '94

Darby Hinton
Malibu Express '85

Dinah Hinz
Quicker Than the Eye '88

Chanel Akiko Hirai
Caged Heat 2: Stripped of
Freedom '94

Kate Hodge
Desire '95
The Hidden 2 '94

Tom Hodges
The Baby Doll Murders '92

Tobias Hoesl
The Polar Bear King '94

Basil Hoffman
Communion '89

Philip S. Hoffman
Joey Breaker '93

Thom Hoffman
Lily Was Here '89

Cecil Hoffmann
Lily in Winter '94

Pato Hoffmann
Cheyenne Warrior '94

Hal Holbrook
Carried Away '95

Frankie J. Holden
Ebbtide '94

Marjean Holden
Ballistic '94

William Holden
The Wild Bunch '69

John E. Holiday
Witchcraft 6: The Devil's
Mistress '94

Kene Holliday
The Josephine Baker Story
'90

Laurel Holloman
The Incredibly True
Adventure of Two Girls in
Love '95

Lauren Holly
Dangerous Heart '93

Ian Holm
The Advocate '93

Meredyth Holmes
Forbidden Zone: Alien
Abduction '96

Jim Holt
Fever '88

Mette Holt
The Whispering '94

Patrick Holt
When Dinosaurs Ruled the
Earth '70

Sandrine Holt
Rapa Nui '93

Mark Holton
Easy Wheels '89

Evander Holyfield
Blood Salvage '90

Arabella Holzbog
Carnosaur 2 '94
The Last Samurai '90

James Hong
Bad Company '94
Bloodsport 2: The Next
Kumite '95
Crime Lords '91
Femme Fontaine: Killer Babe
for the C.I.A. '95
L.A. Goddess '92
Operation Golden Phoenix
'94
Shadowzone '89

Brian Hooks
Phat Beach '96

Jan Hooks
A Dangerous Woman '93

William Hootkins
Death Machine '95
Dust Devil '93

Leslie Hope
First Degree '95
Paris, France '94
Sweet Killing '93

Margot Hope
Femme Fontaine: Killer Babe
for the C.I.A. '95

Anthony Hopkins
The Efficiency Expert '92
The Hunchback of Notre
Dame '82

Bo Hopkins
Blood Ties '92
Cheyenne Warrior '94
Painted Hero '95
Texas Payback '95
The Wild Bunch '69

Jermaine Hopkins
Phat Beach '96

Dennis Hopper
Carried Away '95
The Last Movie '71
Red Rock West '93
Sunset Heat '92

Lena Horne
That's Black Entertainment
'85

Adam Horovitz
Long Road Home '91

Shizuko Hoshi
Come See the Paradise '90
M. Butterfly '93

Bob Hoskins
The Inner Circle '91

Allison Hossack
White Light '90

Yukihiro Hotaru
Zeram '91

Joey House
Fist of Honor '92

Thelma Houston
And God Created Woman
'88

Anders Hove
Bloodlust: Subspecies 3 '93
Bloodstone: Subspecies 2 '92
Subspecies '90

Alan Howard
The Cook, the Thief, His Wife
& Her Lover '90

Arliss Howard
Somebody Has to Shoot the
Picture '90
Tales of Erotica '96

Brie Howard
Android '82
The Runnin' Kind '89

Clint Howard
Carnosaur '93
Cheyenne Warrior '94
Dillinger and Capone '95

Rance Howard
Dark Before Dawn '89

C. Thomas Howell
Dangerous Indiscretion '94
Far Out Man '89
Hourglass '95
Jailbait '93
Payback '94
Pure Danger '96
The Return of the
Musketeers '89
Shameless '94
Suspect Device '95
Teresa's Tattoo '94
Treacherous '95

Carol Hoyt
Illegal Entry: Formula for
Fear '93

**Brigitte Lin Ching
Hsia**
The Bride with White Hair
'93

Wu Hsin-kuo
Temptation of a Monk '94

Cooper Huckabee
Night Eyes '90

Gary Hudson
The Force '94
Texas Payback '95
Wild Cactus '92

Laura Hudspeth
Great Bikini Off-Road
Adventure '94

Matthias Hues
Cyberzone '95
Digital Man '94
TC 2000 '93

David Huffman
Witchcraft 5: Dance with the
Devil '92

Daniel Hugh-Kelly
Bad Company '94

Barnard Hughes
Primal Secrets '94

Brendan Hughes
To Die for '89

David Hughes
32 Short Films about Glenn
Gould '93

Finola Hughes
Dark Side of Genius '94

Julie Hughes
Stormswept '95

Wendy Hughes
Echoes of Paradise '86
Wild Orchid 2: Two Shades of
Blue '92

Tom Hulce
Black Rainbow '91
The Inner Circle '91
Slamdance '87

Renee Humphrey
Jailbait '93

Barry Humphries
Les Patterson Saves the
World '90

Helen Hunt
Into the Badlands '92

Linda Hunt
Rain Without Thunder '93
Younger & Younger '94

Marsha Hunt
Howling II:Your Sister Is a
Werewolf '85

**William Dennis
Hunt**
Flesh Gordon 2: Flesh
Gordon Meets the Cosmic
Cheerleaders '90

Bill Hunter
The Custodian '94
Fever '88
Muriel's Wedding '94

Kevin Hunter
One False Move '91

Kim Hunter
A Streetcar Named Desire:
The Original Director's
Version '51

Isabelle Huppert
Coup de Torchon '81
Madame Bovary '91

Elizabeth Hurley
Nightscare '93
Shameless '94

Michael Hurst
Desperate Remedies '93

Veronica Hurst
Peeping Tom '60

John Hurt
Monolith '93
Scandal '89

Mary Beth Hurt
Parents '89

William Hurt
Until the End of the World
'91

Olivia Hussey
Save Me '92

Anjelica Huston
The Crossing Guard '94

Walter Huston
December 7th: The Movie '91

Lauren Hutton
Forbidden Sun '89

Timothy Hutton
The Last Word '95

Alex Hyde-White
Unknown Origin '95

Ice Cube
The Glass Shield '95

Hiroki Ida
Cyber Ninja '94

Kunihiko Ida
Zeram '91

Randi Ingerman
Treacherous '95

Kathy Ireland
Amore! '93
Backfire! '94

Floyd Irons
Great Bikini Off-Road
Adventure '94

Jeremy Irons
M. Butterfly '93

Michael Ironside
Cross Country '83
Fortunes of War '94
The Glass Shield '95
Mindfield '89
Portraits of a Killer '95
Save Me '93
Sweet Killing '93
Watchers '88

Amy Irving
Carried Away '95

Tom Irwin
Ladykiller '92

Jason Isaacs
Solitaire for 2 '96

Binpachi Ito
Heaven & Earth '90

Dana Ivey
Class of '61 '92

Judith Ivey
There Goes the
Neighborhood '92

Chona Jackson
Knock Outs '92

Howard Jackson
Out for Blood '93

John M. Jackson
Ginger Ale Afternoon '89

Joshua Jackson
Digger '94

Samuel L. Jackson
Def by Temptation '90
The New Age '94
The Search for One-Eyed
Jimmy '96

Victoria Jackson
Based on an Untrue Story '93

Irene Jacob
Red '94

Derek Jacobi
The Hunchback of Notre
Dame '82

Lou Jacobi
I Don't Buy Kisses Anymore
'92

Andre Jacobs
Curse of the Crystal Eye '93

Jake Jacobs
Driven to Kill '90

Steve Jacobs
Echoes of Paradise '86

Billy Jacoby
Dr. Alien '88

Dale Jacoby
Ring of Fire '91
Ring of Fire 2: Blood and
Steel '92

Scott Jacoby
To Die for '89
To Die for 2: Son of Darkness
'91

Sheila Jaffe
My Life's in Turnaround '94

Henry Jaglom
Someone to Love '87

Brion James
Blade Runner '82
The Dark '94
Future Shock '93
Hong Kong '97 '94
Nature of the Beast '94
Sketch Artist 2: Hands That
See '94
Steel Frontier '94
Street Asylum '90

Clifton James
Will Penny '67

Fraser James
Shopping '93

Geraldine James
The Tall Guy '89

Godfrey James
Leapin' Leprechauns! '95
Magic in the Mirror '96

Ken James
Landslide '92

Milton James
Dark Angel: The Ascent '94

Malcom Jamieson
Meridian: Kiss of the Beast
'90

Oleg Jankowskij
Mute Witness '95

Tom Jansen
Suite 16 '94

Jim Jarmusch
Blue in the Face '95

Catherine Jarrett
Quicker Than the Eye '88

Graham Jarvis
Parents '89

Peter Jason
Deconstructing Sarah '94

Mark Jax
Stealing Heaven '88

Doug Jeffrey
Irresistible Impulse '95
Scoring '95
Tainted Love '96

Lionel Jeffries
Jekyll and Hyde '90

Todd Jeffries
The Colony '95

Sal Jenco
Trouble Bound '92

Richard Jenkins
Descending Angel '90

Sam Jenkins
The Crew '95
Ed and His Dead Mother '93
Fortunes of War '94

David Jonson
King of the Hill '93

Jane Jensen
Tromeo & Juliet '95

Todd Jensen
Never Say Die '94

Sasha Jenson
Twisted Love '95

Ron Jeremy
They Bite '95

Bill Jesse
Riff Raff '92

Falco Jimenez
La Pastorela '92

Cameron Johann
Spy Trap '92

Stratford Johns
A Demon in My View '92

Alan Johnson
Iced '88

Ben Johnson
Dark Before Dawn '89
The Wild Bunch '69
Will Penny '67

Bobby Johnson
Body Strokes '95

Brad Johnson
Lone Justice 2 '93

Derek C. Johnson
Bugged! '96

Jill Johnson
Party Plane '90
Wildest Dreams '90

Laura Johnson
Fatal Instinct '92

Lynn-Holly Johnson
The Criminal Mind '93
Fugitive X '96

Michelle Johnson
Blood Ties '92
Body Shot '93
Incident at Deception
    Ridge '94
The Last Word '95
Slipping into Darkness '88
Waxwork '88
When the Bullet Hits the
    Bone '96
Wishful Thinking '92

**Ryan Thomas
Johnson**
Carnosaur 2 '94

Bobby Johnston
Sinful Intrigue '95
T-Force '94

Kim Johnston-Ulrich
Blood Ties '92
Rumpelstiltskin '96

Andras Jones
Far from Home '89

Chuck Jones
Chuck Amuck: The Movie '91

Claude Earl Jones
Bride of Re-Animator '89

Clyde Jones
Delta Heat '92

Duane Jones
Fright House '89
To Die for '89

Gillian Jones
Echoes of Paradise '86

James Jones
Head of the Family '96

James Earl Jones
Excessive Force '93
Freddie the Frog '92
Jefferson in Paris '94

Jedda Jones
Talkin' Dirty After Dark '91

L. Q. Jones
The Wild Bunch '69

Robert Earl Jones
Rain Without Thunder '93

Sam Jones
Ballistic '94
Fist of Honor '92
Night Rhythms '92
The Other Woman '92
Texas Payback '95

Sharon Lee Jones
Leapin' Leprechauns! '95

**Joanne Moore
Jordan**
Faces '68

Richard Jordan
Romero '89
Timebomb '91

Aaron Joseph
Slam Dunk Ernest '95

Todd Joseph
Midnight Tease '94

Larry Joshua
A Midnight Clear '92

Louis Jourdan
The Return of Swamp Thing
    '89

Mark Joy
Black Rainbow '91

Kimble Joyner
Spy Trap '92

Michelle Joyner
Painted Hero '95

Ashley Judd
Ruby in Paradise '93

Raul Julia
Romero '89

Janet Julian
King of New York '90

Lenny Juliano
Not of This Earth '88

Roger Kabler
Alligator Eyes '90

Charlotte Kady
L.627 '92

Elaine Kagan
Sharon's Secret '95

David Kagen
Body Chemistry '90

Joseph Kairau
Once Were Warriors '94

Joel Kaiser
Dead Certain '92

Elizabeth Kaitan
Virtual Encounters '96

Claudia Kaleem
Phat Beach '96

Rob Kaman
Bloodfist '89

Antoine Kamerling
Suite 16 '94

Dan Kamin
Another Pair of Aces: Three
    of a Kind '91

Laura Kamrath
The Phoenix and the Magic
    Carpet '95

Carol Kane
Ted & Venus '93
Trees Lounge '96

John Kani
Options '88

Tenmei Kano
Tokyo Decadence '91

Ivar Kants
The Naked Country '85

Ron Karabatsos
29th Street '91

May Karasun
Lake Consequence '92

Anna Karin
Body of Influence '93
Wild Cactus '92

Sergei Karlenkov
Mute Witness '95

Claudia Karvan
Desperate Prey '94

Tcheky Karyo
Exposure '91
Husbands and Lovers '91
Sketch Artist '92

Linda Kash
Ernest Goes to School '94

Kimberley Kates
Bad Blood '94

Massaya Kato
Crimebroker '95

Andreas Katsulas
Communion '89

William Katt
Last Call '90
Piranha '96
Tollbooth '94

Charles Kavanaugh
Public Access '93

Hanbel Kawai
Cyber Ninja '94

Caren Kaye
Satan's Princess '90

Lila Kaye
Dragonworld '94

Fred Kaz
...And God Spoke '94

Lainie Kazan
Eternity '90
I Don't Buy Kisses Anymore '92
29th Street '91

James Keach
The Experts '89
Love Letters '83
Options '88

Stacy Keach
Amanda and the Alien '95
Killer Inside Me '76
New Crime City: Los Angeles 2020 '94
Sunset Grill '92

Staci Keanan
Lisa '90

Stephen Kearney
The Nutt House '95

Ele Keats
Lipstick Camera '93

Richard Keats
A.P.E.X. '94

Steven Keats
Eternity '90

Will Keenan
Tromeo & Juliet '95

Eliot Keener
Running Wild '94

Andrew Keir
Dragonworld '94

Harvey Keitel
Blue in the Face '95
Reservoir Dogs '92
The Young Americans '93

Brian Keith
National Lampoon's Favorite Deadly Sins '95

David Keith
Deadly Sins '95
The Further Adventures of Tennessee Buck '88
Independence Day '83
Temptation '94
Till the End of the Night '94

Jean-Pierre Kelfon
The Turn On '95

Mary Page Keller
The Colony '95

Sally Kellerman
Mirror, Mirror 2: Raven Dance '94
Someone to Love '87
Younger & Younger '94

Kimberly Kelley
Hard Bounty '94
Midnight Tease 2 '95

Sheila Kelley
Deconstructing Sarah '94
Mortal Passions '90

Brian D. Kelly
Freakshow '95

Craig Kelly
Nightscare '93
The Young Americans '93

Rae'ven Kelly
Lily in Winter '94

Robyn Kelly
Flesh Gordon 2: Flesh Gordon Meets the Cosmic Cheerleaders '90

Sheila Kelly
A Passion to Kill '94

Martin Kemp
Desire '95
Embrace of the Vampire '95
Fleshtone '94

Will Kempe
Hit the Dutchman '92

Rachel Kempson
Stealing Heaven '88

Angela Kennedy
The Wicked '89

Damon Kennedy
Vicious '88

Jonelle Kennedy
How U Like Me Now? '92

Marklen Kennedy
Witchcraft 5: Dance with the Devil '92

Merele Kennedy
Nemesis '93

Rigg Kennedy
Slipping into Darkness '88

Sarah Kennedy
Jack Be Nimble '94

Patsy Kensit
Timebomb '91
Tunnel Vision '95
Twenty-One '91

Brad Kepnick
Gator Bait 2: Cajun Justice '88

Nicholas Kepros
Identity Crisis '90

Joanna Kerns
The Nightman '93

Bill Kerr
Sweet Talker '91

Mamaengaroa Kerr-Bell
Once Were Warriors '94

Robert Kessler
Lonely in America '90

Orville Ketchum
Hard to Die '90

Elizabeth Key
Blondes Have More Guns '95

Irwin Keyes
Backlash: Oblivion 2 '95

Margot Kidder
Beanstalk '94
Bloodknot '95

Nicole Kidman
Flirting '89

Udo Kier
Zentropa '92

Val Kilmer
Kill Me Again '89

Erik King
Joey Breaker '93

Scott King
Terminal Exposure '89

Ben Kingsley
Slipstream '89

Mimi Kinkade
Night of the Demons '88

Kathleen Kinmont
The Art of Dying '90
Bride of Re-Animator '89
Final Impact '91
Rush Week '88
Stormswept '95
Texas Payback '95

Roy Kinnear
The Return of the Musketeers '89

Terry Kinney
Body Snatchers '93

Klaus Kinski
Android '82

Bruno Kirby
Golden Gate '93

Jean Kirkland
The American Angels: Baptism of Blood '89

Sally Kirkland
Eye of the Stranger '93
High Stakes '89
Hit the Dutchman '92
Love Letters '83
Paint It Black '89
White Hot '88

Oona Kirsch
Nexus '96

Mike Kirten
Running Wild '94

John Lennon
The Beatles: The First U.S.
Visit '91

Leon
Pure Danger '96

Lu Leonard
Circuitry Man '90
A Climate for Killing '91
Shadowzone '89

Ted Leplat
Swift Justice '88

Marie Leroux
Secret Games 2: The Escort
'93

Mimi Lesseos
The American Angels:
Baptism of Blood '89
Final Impact '91
Streets of Rage '95

Jeff Lester
In the Cold of the Night '89

Dan Lett
Paris, France '94

Tony Leung
Hard-Boiled '92

Annabel Leventon
M. Butterfly '93

Floyd Levine
Ice '93

Emile Levisetti
Alien Terminator '95
Sexual Response '92

Al Lewis
Fright House '89

Charlotte Lewis
Dial Help '88
Embrace of the Vampire '95
Excessive Force '93
The Glass Cage '96
Men of War '94
Sketch Artist '92
Storyville '92

Geoffrey Lewis
The Lawnmower Man '92

Jenifer Lewis
Deconstructing Sarah '94

Jerry Lewis
Arizona Dream '94

Juliette Lewis
Meet the Hollowheads '89

Johan Leysen
Hail Mary '85

Michelle Li
Wicked City '92

G. Gordon Liddy
Adventures in Spying '92
Street Asylum '90

Robert Liensol
Time to Kill '89

Marilyn Lightstone
Grand Tour: Disaster in Time
'92

Paola Liguori
Intervista '87

Sandy Lillingston
Dangerous Game '90

Abbey Lincoln
Nothing but a Man '64

Hal Linden
The Colony '95

Viveca Lindfors
Zandalee '91

Audra Lindley
The New Age '94
The Spellbinder '88

Delroy Lindo
Blood In...Blood Out: Bound
by Honor '93

Teri Ann Linn
Pure Danger '96

Laura Linney
Class of '61 '92

Kent Lipham
Bikini Summer '91

Peggy Lipton
Fatal Charm '92

Robert Lipton
A Woman, Her Men and Her
Futon '92

Joe Lisi
Come See the Paradise '90

Virna Lisi
I Love N.Y. '87
Queen Margot '94

Tiny Lister
Hologram Man '95
Men of War '94
9 1/2 Ninjas '90

Phat Beach '96

John Lithgow
At Play in the Fields of the
Lord '91
Love, Cheat & Steal '93
Silent Fall '94
The Wrong Man '93

Carolyn Liu
Do or Die '91

Barry Livingston
Easy Wheels '89

Amy Locane
Carried Away '95
Criminal Hearts '95

June Lockhart
The Colony '95
Out There '95
Rented Lips '88

Heather Locklear
Body Language '92
The Return of Swamp Thing
'89

Gary Lockwood
The Magic Sword '62

David Lodge
Edge of Sanity '89

Roger Lodge
Not of This Earth '88

Kristina Loggia
Chopper Chicks in
Zombietown '91

Robert Loggia
Lifepod '93
Man with a Gun '95
Target: Favorite Son '87

Donal Logue
Baja '95
The Crew '95

Leigh Lombardi
Moontrap '89

Jason London
Blood Ties '92
Fall Time '94

Lisa London
Savage Beach '89

John Lone
Echoes of Paradise '86
M. Butterfly '93

Kathy Long
The Stranger '95

Tony Longo
Prehysteria '93

Jennifer Lopez
My Family '94

Tamblyn Lord
Vicious '88

Traci Lords
Fast Food '89
Ice '93
Intent to Kill '92
Laser Moon '92
Not of This Earth '88
The Nutt House '95
Plughead Rewired: Circuitry
Man 2 '94
Raw Nerve '91
Shock 'Em Dead '90
Skinner '93
A Time to Die '91

Tray Loren
The American Angels:
Baptism of Blood '89
Gator Bait 2: Cajun Justice
'88

Evan Lorie
Ring of Fire 2: Blood and
Steel '92

James Lorinz
Frankenhooker '90
Me and the Mob '94
Punch the Clock '90

Jean-Pierre Loril
Red '94

Eb Lottimer
Quicker Than the Eye '88
Streets '90

Justin Louis
Blood & Donuts '96

Mother Love
The Surgeon '94

Pee Wee Love
Radio Inside '94

Jacqueline Lovell
Femalien '96
Head of the Family '96

Alex Lowe
Haunted '95

Chad Lowe
Highway to Hell '92

Rob Lowe
First Degree '95

Carey Lowell
Road to Ruin '91

Curt Lowens
A Midnight Clear '92

Andrew Lowery
Color of Night '94

Jennifer Lowry
Brain Damage '88

Joshua Lucas
Class of '61 '92

Will Lucas
Pharoah's Army '95

Jennifer Lucienne
Phat Beach '96

Pamela Ludwig
Rush Week '88

Joanna Lumley
Innocent Lies '95

Deanna Lund
Elves '89
Red Wind '91

Dolph Lundgren
Men of War '94
Showdown in Little Tokyo '91

Jeff Lundy
The American Angels:
   Baptism of Blood '89

Sihung Lung
Pushing Hands '92

Ti Lung
A Better Tomorrow '86

Cherie Lunghi
Jack and Sarah '96

Robert LuPone
High Stakes '89

Federico Luppi
Cronos '94

Evan Lurie
Hologram Man '95
T-Force '94

Gloria Lusiak
Blondes Have More Guns '95

Franc Luz
The Nest '88

Dorothy Lyman
Ruby in Paradise '93

Kelly Lynch
Three of Hearts '93
Warm Summer Rain '89

Richard Lynch
H. P. Lovecraft's
   Necronomicon: Book of
   the Dead '96
High Stakes '89

Cheryl Lynn
Fate '90

Susan Lyons
Ebbtide '94

Tzi Ma
Golden Gate '93

Harlee MacBride
Young Lady Chatterley '85
Young Lady Chatterley 2 '85

Gordon MacDonald
Brain Damage '88

James Michael
   MacDonald
Criminal Hearts '95

Wendy MacDonald
Broken Trust '93

Sarah MacDonnell
Fatally Yours '95

Jack MacGowran
The Fearless Vampire Killers
   '67

Michael Mack
Star Quest: Beyond the
   Rising Moon '89

John MacKay
Alligator Eyes '90

Jan MacKenzie
The American Angels:
   Baptism of Blood '89
Gator Bait 2: Cajun Justice
   '88

Sam Mackenzie
Dragonworld '94

Allison Mackie
Lurking Fear '94

Kyle MacLachlan
Showgirls '95

Shirley MacLaine
Wrestling Ernest Hemingway
   '93

Elizabeth MacLellan
Puppet Master 2 '90

Patrick Macnee
Lobster Man from Mars '89
Masque of the Red Death '89
Waxwork '88

William H. Macy
Oleanna '94

Amy Madigan
Love Letters '83

Madonna
Blue in the Face '95

Bryan Madorsky
Parents '89

Michael Madsen
Fatal Instinct '92
The Getaway '93
Kill Me Again '89
Man with a Gun '95
Reservoir Dogs '92
Trouble Bound '92

Virginia Madsen
Caroline at Midnight '93
Linda '93
Slamdance '87

Ara Madzounian
Radio Inside '94

Donna Magnani
29th Street '91

Ann Magnuson
Sleepwalk '88

Johnny Mah
Double Happiness '94

Redge Mahaffey
Moral Code '96

Bill Maher
Cannibal Women in the
   Avocado Jungle of Death
   '89
Pizza Man '91

Joseph Maher
Bulletproof Heart '95

Michael C. Mahon
Dark Angel: The Ascent '94

Lee Majors
Will Penny '67

Chris Makepeace
Synapse '95

Mako
Highlander: The Final
   Dimension '94

Christophe MaLavoy
Madame Bovary '91

Karl Malden
A Streetcar Named Desire:
   The Original Director's
   Version '51

Laurent Malet
Blood Relatives '78

Art Malik
Transmutations '85

Tirlok Malik
Lonely in America '90

Sam Malkin
Caribe '87

John Malkovich
Queens Logic '91

Korey Mall
Mirror Images '91

Louis Malle
La Vie de Boheme '93

Karl Malone
Rockwell: A Legend of the
   Wild West '93

Michael Maloney
Truly, Madly, Deeply '91

Ray "Boom Boom"
   Mancini
Backstreet Dreams '90
The Search for One-Eyed
   Jimmy '96
Timebomb '91
Wishful Thinking '92

Nick Mancuso
The Takeover '94

Peter Mandell
Xtro '83

Costas Mandylor
Almost Dead '94
Fatal Past '94
Fist of the North Star '96
Portraits of a Killer '95
Venus Rising '95

Jim Maniaci
Timebomb '91

Cindy Manion
The Toxic Avenger '86

Vic Manni
29th Street '91

Paul Mantee
Lurking Fear '94

Joe Mantegna
National Lampoon's Favorite
    Deadly Sins '95
Queens Logic '91

Michael Mantell
Dead Funny '94

Mary Mara
Love Potion #9 '92

Maria Marais
The Power of One '92

Andree Maranda
The Toxic Avenger '86

Peter Marc
Dangerous Love '87

Dominique Marcas
La Vie de Boheme '93

Jane March
Color of Night '94

Guy Marchand
Coup de Torchon '81

Nicholas Marco
Wavelength '96

Ted Marconi
The Nightman '93

Andrea Marcovicci
Someone to Love '87

Mark Margolis
Descending Angel '90
Where the Rivers Flow
    North '94

Miriam Margolyes
Ed and His Dead Mother '93

David Margulies
9 1/2 Weeks '86

Constance Marie
My Family '94

Jeanne Marie
Young Nurses in Love '89

Jean-Pierre Marielle
Coup de Torchon '81

Jacques Marin
The Night of the Following
    Day '69

Richard "Cheech" Marin
The Courtyard '95
Far Out Man '89
La Pastorela '92
The Shrimp on the Barbie '90

Ed Marinaro
Queens Logic '91

Stella Maris
Truly, Madly, Deeply '91

Daniel Markel
Dark Angel: The Ascent '94

Monte Markham
Piranha '96

Ben Marley
The Mosaic Project '95

Cedella Marley
Joey Breaker '93

John Marley
Faces '68

Ron Marquette
Public Access '93

Kenneth Mars
Rented Lips '88

Jean Marsh
Fatherland '94

James Marshall
Don't Do It '94
Vibrations '94

Joshua Marshall
Flirting '89

Lee Marshall
The American Angels:
    Baptism of Blood '89

Paula Marshall
The New Age '94

Dean Martin
Kiss Me, Stupid! '64

Helen Martin
Night Angel '90

John Martin
Dark Before Dawn '89

Strother Martin
Kiss Me Deadly '55
The Wild Bunch '69

Tina Martin
Leapin' Leprechauns! '95

W.T. Martin
High Stakes '89

A. Martinez
Deconstructing Sarah '94
Powwow Highway '89

Ace Mask
Not of This Earth '88
Transylvania Twist '89

Hilary Mason
Meridian: Kiss of the
    Beast '90

Anna Massey
Haunted '95
Peeping Tom '60
The Tall Guy '89

Athena Massey
Undercover '94
Virtual Combat '95

Daniel Massey
Scandal '89

Chase Masterson
In a Moment of Passion '93
Married People, Single
    Sex '93

Fay Masterson
The Power of One '92

Rod Masterson
Delta Heat '92

Mary Elizabeth Mastrantonio
Slamdance '87

Marcello Mastroianni
Intervista '87

Richard Masur
Far from Home '89

Michelle Matheson
Test Tube Teens from the
    Year 2000 '93

Tim Matheson
Midnight Heat '95

Samantha Mathis
Jack and Sarah '96

John Matshikiza
Dust Devil '93

Eiko Matsuda
In the Realm of the Senses
    '76

Charles Matthau
Number One Fan '94

James Matthew
Animal Instincts 3: The
    Seductress '95

Al Matthews
American Roulette '88

Dennis Matthews
The Hottest Bid '95

Sarah Maur-Thorp
Edge of Sanity '89

Larry Maxwell
Public Access '93

Jodhi May
Sister, My Sister '94

John Maynard
Biohazard: The Alien
    Force '95

Ferdinand "Ferdy" Mayne
The Fearless Vampire
    Killers '67
Howling II: Your Sister Is a
    Werewolf '85

Alois Mayo
The Power of One '92

Gale Mayron
The Feud '90
Heart of Midnight '89

Bob Maza
Reckless Kelly '93

Debi Mazar
Bad Love '95
Empire Records '95
Trees Lounge '96

Monet Mazur
Raging Angels '95

Alex McArthur
Rampage '87
Sharon's Secret '95

Cathy McAuley
Beanstalk '94

Daron McBee
T-Force '94

Michelle McBride
Subspecies '90

Holt McCallany
The Search for One-Eyed
    Jimmy '96

Jeffrey Meek
Night of the Cyclone '90
Winter People '89

Ralph Meeker
Kiss Me Deadly '55

Maurizio Mein
Intervista '87

Kathryn Meisle
Basket Case 2 '90

Nicholas Mele
Impulse '90

Stephen Mendel
Midnight Heat '95

Ben Mendelsohn
The Efficiency Expert '92
The Year My Voice Broke '87

David Mendenhall
Streets '90

Alex Meneses
Amanda and the Alien '95

Jon Menick
Easy Wheels '89

Doro Merande
Kiss Me, Stupid! '64

Burgess Meredith
Across the Moon '94

Jalal Merhi
Operation Golden Phoenix
    '94
TC 2000 '93

**S. Epatha
    Merkerson**
A Mother's Prayer '95

Dina Merrill
Suture '93

Michael Merrins
Posed for Murder '89

John Mese
Excessive Force 2: Force on
    Force '95

Laurie Metcalf
A Dangerous Woman '93

Art Metrano
Malibu Express '85

Nancy Mette
Meet the Hollowheads '89

Jim Metzler
Circuitry Man '90

One False Move '91
Plughead Rewired: Circuitry
    Man 2 '94

Bess Meyer
H. P. Lovecraft's
    Necronomicon: Book of
    the Dead '96
The Inner Circle '91

Vittorio Mezzogiorno
The Conviction '95

Delaune Michel
A Woman, Her Men and Her
    Futon '92

Anne Michelle
Young Lady Chatterley '85

Shelley Michelle
Bikini Summer '91
Married People, Single Sex
    '93

David Michie
A Matter of Honor '95

Dale Midkiff
Love Potion #9 '92

Dennis Mientka
Where the Rivers Flow
    North '94

Nikita Mikhalkov
Close to Eden '90

Alyssa Milano
Deadly Sins '95
Embrace of the Vampire '95
Poison Ivy 2: Lily '95

Sylvia Miles
The Last Movie '71

Vera Miles
Separate Lives '94

Tomas Milian
Cat Chaser '90

David Millburn
Bikini Summer '91

Adelaide Miller
Lonely in America '90

C.T. Miller
Friend of the Family '95
Lap Dancing '95

Dick Miller
Far from Home '89
Under the Boardwalk '89

Jennifer Miller
Never Say Die '94
Terminal Impact '95

Joshua Miller
Near Dark '87

Larry Miller
Dream Lover '93

Penelope Ann Miller
The Gun in Betty Lou's
    Handbag '92

Juliet Mills
Avanti! '72

Kiri Mills
Desperate Remedies '93

Samantha Mills
Prehysteria '93

Tom Mills
Luther the Geek '90

Juno Mills-Cockell
Parents '89

Leslie Milne
Vampire at Midnight '88

Jean-Roger Milo
L.627 '92

Kelly Jo Minter
Miracle Mile '89

Kristin Minter
There Goes My Baby '92

Irene Miracle
Puppet Master '89

Robert Miranda
Desire '95

Helen Mirren
The Cook, the Thief, His Wife
    & Her Lover '90
The Hawk '93

Karen Mistal
Cannibal Women in the
    Avocado Jungle of Death
    '89

Belle Mitchell
Slipping into Darkness '88

Cameron Mitchell
Jack-O '95
Space Mutiny '88
Swift Justice '88

**Chuck "Porky"
    Mitchell**
Swift Justice '88

Eddy Mitchell
Coup de Torchon '81

Gene Mitchell
The Takeover '94

Ilan Mitchell-Smith
Identity Crisis '90

Bentley Mitchum
Ruby in Paradise '93

Chris Mitchum
Biohazard: The Alien Force
    '95
Fugitive X '96

Robert Mitchum
Backfire! '94
Woman of Desire '93

Matt Mitler
Basket Case 2 '90

Teresa Mo
Hard-Boiled '92

Marcello Modugno
Dial Help '88

Donald Moffat
Love, Cheat & Steal '93

D.W. Moffett
Lisa '90

Michelle Moffett
Wild Cactus '92

Harry Mok
Femme Fontaine: Killer Babe
    for the C.I.A. '95

Zakes Mokae
Dust Devil '93

Alfred Molina
A Night of Love '87

Richard Moll
Beanstalk '94
The Glass Cage '96

Jordi Molla
Jamon, Jamon '93

Marjorie Monaghan
Nemesis '93

Samuel Mongiello
Married People, Single Sex
    '93

Lawrence Monoson
Black Rose of Harlem '95
Dangerous Love '87

Lee Montague
Jekyll and Hyde '90

Karla Montana
La Pastorela '92

Lee Montgomery
Into the Fire '88

Anna Maria Monticelli
Nomads '86

Chris Moore
Punch the Clock '90

Christine Moore
Alexa: A Prostitute's Own Story '88
Lurkers '88

Deborah Maria Moore
Into the Sun '92

Frank Moore
Blood & Donuts '96

Jeanie Moore
Vampire at Midnight '88

Julianne Moore
The Gun in Betty Lou's Handbag '92
Safe '95

Melissa Moore
Hard to Die '90
Scream Dream '89
Stormswept '95

Stephen Moore
Under Suspicion '92

Esai Morales
Don't Do It '94
My Family '94
Rapa Nui '93

Patrick Moran
Biohazard: The Alien Force '95

Jeanne Moreau
Until the End of the World '91

Nathaniel Moreau
George's Island '91

Elizabeth Morehead
Interceptor '92

Rita Moreno
The Night of the Following Day '69
The Wharf Rat '95

Chesty Morgan
Deadly Weapons '70

Jeffrey Dean Morgan
Undercover '94

Mariana Morgan
Private Lessons, Another Story '94

Nancy Morgan
The Nest '88

Richard Morgan
The Wicked '89

Shelley Taylor Morgan
Malibu Express '85

Cathy Moriarty
Burndown '89
The Gun in Betty Lou's Handbag '92

Daniel Moriarty
The Other Woman '92

Michael Moriarty
A Good Day to Die '95

Noriyuki "Pat" Morita
Bloodsport 2: The Next Kumite '95
Do or Die '91

Yuko Moriyama
Zeram '91

Robert Morley
Istanbul '90

Colleen Morris
Prehysteria '93

Garrett Morris
Black Rose of Harlem '95

Iona Morris
Rain Without Thunder '93

John Morris
Beyond Innocence '87

Rachael Morris
Once Were Warriors '94

Theresa Morris
Private Lessons, Another Story '94

Temuera Morrison
Once Were Warriors '94

David Morse
The Crossing Guard '94
The Getaway '93

Glen Morshower
84 Charlie Mopic '89

Viggo Mortensen
American Yakuza '94
The Crew '95
The Young Americans '93

Josh Mosby
Backfire! '94

Bill Moseley
Fair Game '89

William R. Moses
Almost Dead '94

Elissabeth Moss
Separate Lives '94

George Moss
Riff Raff '92

Ron Moss
Hard Ticket to Hawaii '87

Irina Movila
Subspecies '90

Maureen Mueller
The New Age '94

Armin Mueller-Stahl
The Power of One '92
Theodore Rex '95

Debbie Muggli
Nemesis 3: Time Lapse '95

Anita Mui
The Executioners '93
The Heroic Trio '93

Chris Mulkey
Bound and Gagged: A Love Story '93
Dead Cold '96
Rainbow Drive '90
The Silencer '92

Martin Mull
Far Out Man '89
Rented Lips '88

Beckie Mullen
Sinful Intrigue '95

Patty Mullen
Frankenhooker '90

Terry David Mulligan
Deadly Sins '95

Rod Mullinar
Echoes of Paradise '86

Dermot Mulroney
There Goes My Baby '92

Kieran Mulroney
Sensation '94

Yuriria Munguia
The Summer of Miss Forbes '88

Hiroaki Murakami
Iron Maze '91

Vince Murdocco
Flesh Gordon 2: Flesh Gordon Meets the Cosmic Cheerleaders '90
L.A. Wars '94
Ring of Fire '91
Ring of Fire 2: Blood and Steel '92

George Murdock
Grand Tour: Disaster in Time '92

Christine Murillo
La Vie de Boheme '93

Peter Murnik
Golden Gate '93

Kayla Murphy
Dragon Fury 2 '96

Reilly Murphy
Body Snatchers '93

Don Murray
Ghosts Can't Do It '90

Robert Musgrave
Bottle Rocket '95

Allan Musy
Warrior Spirit '94

Paul Muzzcat
Gator Bait 2: Cajun Justice '88

Bruce Myles
Sweet Talker '91

Lycia Naff
Chopper Chicks in Zombietown '91

Jimmy Nail
Crusoe '89

369
Video Premieres

Aio Nakajima
In the Realm of the Senses '76

Naomi Nakano
Come See the Paradise '90

Jack Nance
Across the Moon '94
Voodoo '95

Neriah Napaul
The Bikini Car Wash
Company '90
The Bikini Car Wash
Company 2 '92

Charles Napier
Ballistic '94
Body Shot '93
Hard Justice '95
Skeeter '93

Toni Naples
Dinosaur Island '93

Andrea Naschak
Hold Me, Thrill Me, Kiss Me
'93

Simon Nash
Xtro '83

**Francesca "Kitten"
Natividad**
Inside Out 2 '92

David Naughton
Beanstalk '94
Overexposed '90
Private Affairs '89
Wild Cactus '92

Edwin Neal
Neurotic Cabaret '90

Claire Nebout
The Conviction '95

Tracey Needham
Sensation '94

Liam Neeson
Under Suspicion '92

Taylor Negron
Mr. Stitch '95

Richard Neil
Blondes Have More Guns '95

Sam Neill
Until the End of the World
'91

Kate Nelligan
A Mother's Prayer '95

Allen Nelson
Criminal Passion '94

Craig T. Nelson
The Josephine Baker Story
'90

Danny Nelson
Blood Salvage '90

Ed Nelson
Brenda Starr '86

Judd Nelson
Blindfold: Acts of Obsession
'94
Caroline at Midnight '93
Fandango '85
Far Out Man '89

Lloyd Nelson
The Wild World of
Batwoman '66

Willie Nelson
Another Pair of Aces: Three
of a Kind '91

Francesca Neri
Outrage '93

David Nerman
Witchboard 3: The
Possession '95

Lois Nettleton
Mirror, Mirror 2: Raven
Dance '94

Bebe Neuwirth
The Paint Job '93

Aaron Neville
Zandalee '91

Danny Newman
Shopping '93

Julie Newmar
Backlash: Oblivion 2 '95
Oblivion '94

Thandie Newton
Flirting '89
Jefferson in Paris '94
The Journey of August King
'95
The Young Americans '93

Haing S. Ngor
Fortunes of War '94

Maurizio Nichetti
Volere Volare '92

Stephen Nichols
The Glass Cage '96

Jack Nicholson
The Crossing Guard '94

Michael A. Nickles
Baja '95

Julia Nickson-Soul
Glitch! '88

Michael Nicolosi
Sketch Artist 2: Hands That
See '94

Leslie Nielsen
Digger '94
Repossessed '90

Miho Nikaido
Tokyo Decadence '91

Yvette Nipar
Doctor Mordrid: Master of
the Unknown '90

Akemi Nishino
Come See the Paradise '90

Alexis Nitzer
La Vie de Boheme '93

Felix Nobis
Flirting '89

Philippe Noiret
Coup de Torchon '81
The Return of the
Musketeers '89

Nick Nolte
Jefferson in Paris '94

Jeffrey Nordling
Dangerous Heart '93

Matt Norero
Mind Games '89

Nicole Norman
Inside Out '91

Susan Norman
Safe '95

Dean Norris
The Lawnmower Man '92

Mike Norris
Dragon Fury 2 '96

Alex Norton
Hidden City '87

Barry Norton
Dracula (Spanish Version) '31

Richard Norton
Cyber-Tracker '93
Fugitive X '96

Jack Noseworthy
S.F.W. '94

Michael Nouri
American Yakuza '94
Fortunes of War '94
The Hidden 2 '94
Hologram Man '95
Lady in Waiting '94
Little Vegas '90
Project: Alien '89
Thieves of Fortune '89
To the Limit '95

Kim Novak
Kiss Me, Stupid! '64
Liebestraum '91

Don Novello
La Pastorela '92

Bruce Nozick
Hit the Dutchman '92

Winston Ntshona
Night of the Cyclone '90

Bill Nunn
Def by Temptation '90
Save Me '93

Bryan Nutter
Witchcraft 6: The Devil's
Mistress '94

France Nuyen
A Passion to Kill '91

Warren Oates
The Wild Bunch '69

Rodrigo Obregon
L.A. Wars '94
Savage Beach '89

Austin O'Brien
Prehysteria '93

Edmond O'Brien
The Wild Bunch '69

Niall O'Brien
Class of '61 '92

Shauna O'Brien
Friend of the Family '95
Over the Wire '95

Kevin J. O'Connor
Color of Night '94

Renee O'Connor
Darkman 2: The Return of
Durant '94

Jason O'Gulihar
Witchcraft 4: Virgin Heart '92

Sandra Oh
Double Happiness '94

Jack O'Halloran
Mob Boss '90

Claudia Ohana
The Fable of the Beautiful
    Pigeon Fancier '88
Priceless Beauty '90

Catherine O'Hara
Little Vegas '90
There Goes the
    Neighborhood '92

Jenny O'Hara
A Mother's Prayer '95

Dan O'Herlihy
Love, Cheat & Steal '93

John O'Hurley
Mirror Images '91

John E. O'Keefe
Out of the Rain '90

Michael O'Keefe
Incident at Deception Ridge
    '94
Nina Takes a Lover '94
Out of the Rain '90

Miles O'Keeffe
Cartel '90
Sins of the Night '93
Waxwork '88

Yuji Okumoto
Hard Justice '95
Nemesis '93

Ken Olandt
Digital Man '94

Adam Oliensis
The Pompatus of Love '96

Ken Olin
Queens Logic '91

Steven J. Oliver
Timebomb '91

Laurence Olivier
Ebony Tower '86

Silvio Oliviero
Understudy: The Graveyard
    Shift 2 '88
A Whisper to a Scream '88

Edward James
    Olmos
Blade Runner '82
A Million to Juan '94

Mirage '94
My Family '94

Jason O'Malley
Backstreet Dreams '90

Jennifer O'Neill
Bad Love '95
Discretion Assured '93
I Love N.Y. '87

Maggie O'Neill
Under Suspicion '92

Michael O'Neill
The Gun in Betty Lou's
    Handbag '92

Remy O'Neill
Hollywood Hot Tubs 2:
    Educating Crystal '89
To Die for 2: Son of Darkness
    '91

Walter O'Neill
Dragon Fury 2 '96

Alannah Ong
Double Happiness '94

Lupe Ontiveros
My Family '94

Don Opper
Android '82
Slamdance '87

Terry O'Quinn
Don't Talk to Strangers '94
The Forgotten One '89
Lipstick Camera '93

Gerald Orange
A Fool and His Money '88

Jerry Orbach
I Love N.Y. '87

Michael Ornstein
Man of the Year '96

Ed O'Ross
Play Nice '92

Marina Orsini
Eddie and the Cruisers 2:
    Eddie Lives! '89

Humberto Ortiz
Arcade '93

John Osborne
The Power of One '92

Cliff Osmond
Kiss Me, Stupid! '64

Jeffery Osterhage
Dark Before Dawn '89
Masque of the Red Death '89

Carre Otis
Wild Orchid '90

Annette O'Toole
Love Matters '93

Peter O'Toole
The Seventh Coin '92
Wings of Fame '93

Nadia Ottaviani
Intervista '87

Barry Otto
The Custodian '94
Howling III: The Marsupials
    '87

Peter Outerbridge
Paris, France '94

Tom Overmyer
Witchcraft 8: Salem's Ghost
    '95

Clive Owen
Century '94
Class of '61 '92
Close My Eyes '91

Rena Owen
Once Were Warriors '94

Catherine Oxenberg
Overexposed '90
Sexual Response '92

Carlo Pacchi
Last Rites '88

David Packer
The Runnin' Kind '89

Joanna Pacula
Deep Red '94
Husbands and Lovers '91
Options '88
Silence of the Hams '93

Harrison Page
Carnosaur '93

Oliver Page
Streets of Rage '95

Geraldine Pailhas
Suite 16 '94

Heidi Paine
Alien Seed '89
Wildest Dreams '90
Wizards of the Demon Sword
    '94

Ron Palillo
Hellgate '89

Joseph Pallister
Bikini Bistro '94

Chazz Palminteri
The Last Word '95
There Goes the
    Neighborhood '92

Gwyneth Paltrow
Jefferson in Paris '94

Stuart Pankin
Beanstalk '94

Joe Pantoliano
Dangerous Heart '93
Eddie and the Cruisers '83
The Last Word '95
Three of Hearts '93
Zandalee '91

Laslo Papas
Slipping into Darkness '88

Kiri Paramore
Flirting '89

Michael Pare
The Dangerous '95
Eddie and the Cruisers '83
Eddie and the Cruisers 2:
    Eddie Lives! '89
Into the Sun '92
The Last Hour '91
Moon 44 '90
Raging Angels '95
Sunset Heat '92

Monique Parent
Dark Secrets '95
Masseuse '95
Play Time '94
Scoring '95
Stripshow '95

Cheryl Paris
Sweet Bird of Youth '89

Blair Parker
The Forgotten One '89

Cindy Parker
Lovers' Lovers '94

Corey Parker
I'm Dangerous Tonight '90
A Mother's Prayer '95

Jameson Parker
Curse of the Crystal Eye '93

Nicole Parker
The Incredibly True
Adventure of Two Girls in
Love '95

Trey Parker
Cannibal! The Musical '96

Catherine Parks
Body of Influence '93

Michael Parks
Storyville '92
Welcome to Spring Break '88

Max Parrish
Hold Me, Thrill Me, Kiss Me
'93

**Shannon Michelle
Parsons**
Freakshow '95

Adrian Pasdar
Near Dark '87
The Pompatus of Love '96

Cyndi Pass
The Force '94

Robert Pastorelli
The Paint Job '93

Michael Pate
Howling III: The Marsupials
'87

Bill Paterson
Hidden City '87
The Rachel Papers '89
Truly, Madly, Deeply '91

Mandy Patinkin
True Colors '91

Jason Patric
The Journey of August King
'95

Randal Patrick
Fast Food '89

Robert Patrick
Body Shot '93
Hong Kong '97 '94

Jay Patterson
Excessive Force 2: Force on
Force '95

Tom Patton
The Whispering '94

Will Patton
Deadly Desire '91
The Paint Job '93
Tollbooth '94

Adrian Paul
Masque of the Red Death '89

Alexandra Paul
Piranha '96
Sunset Grill '92

Richard Paul
Beanstalk '94

Richard Joseph Paul
Oblivion '94
Under the Boardwalk '89

Stuart Paul
Fate '90

Pat Paulsen
Pat Paulsen for President '68

Bill Paxton
Future Shock '93
Monolith '93
Near Dark '87
One False Move '91
Slipstream '89

Vivian Paxton
Man of the Year '96

David Paymer
Heart and Souls '93

Bruce Payne
H. P. Lovecraft's
Necronomicon: Book of
the Dead '96

Amanda Pays
Exposure '91
Solitaire for 2 '96

E.J. Peaker
The Banker '89

Craig Pearce
Vicious '88

Guy Pearce
The Hunting '92

Clive Pearson
Witchcraft 4: Virgin Heart '92

Patsy Pease
Improper Conduct '94

Bob Peck
Slipstream '89

J. Eddie Peck
Curse 2: The Bite '88

Tony Peck
Brenda Starr '86

Nia Peeples
I Don't Buy Kisses Anymore
'92
Improper Conduct '94
Mr. Stitch '95

Lisa Pelikan
Into the Badlands '92

Matti Pellonpaa
La Vie de Boheme '93

Elizabeth Pena
Across the Moon '94
Dead Funny '94

Austin Pendleton
Rain Without Thunder '93

Thaao Penghlis
Les Patterson Saves the
World '90

Bruce Penhall
The Dallas Connection '94
Do or Die '91
Picasso Trigger '89
Savage Beach '89

Christopher Penn
Fist of the North Star '96
Reservoir Dogs '92

Jonathan Penner
Bloodfist 7: Manhunt '94
A Fool and His Money '88

George Peppard
The Tigress '93

Barbara Pepper
Kiss Me, Stupid! '64

Marco Perella
The Man with the Perfect
Swing '95

Vincent Perez
Queen Margot '94

Anthony Perkins
A Demon in My View '92
Edge of Sanity '89
I'm Dangerous Tonight '90

Rebecca Perle
Not of This Earth '88

Max Perlich
Dead Beat '94

Rhea Perlman
Ted & Venus '91
There Goes the
Neighborhood '92

Ron Perlman
Cronos '94
Mr. Stitch '95
Sensation '94

Florence Pernel
Blue '93

J.W. Perra
Head of the Family '96

Valerie Perrine
Sweet Bird of Youth '89

Jenna Persaud
The Other Woman '92

Lisa Jane Persky
Dead Funny '94

Sean Pertwee
Shopping '93

Frank Pesce
The Pamela Principle '91
29th Street '91

Joe Pesci
Once Upon a Time in
America '84

Lisa Pescia
Body Chemistry '90
Body Chemistry 2: Voice of a
Stranger '91
The Dark Dancer '95

William L. Petersen
In the Kingdom of the Blind
the Man with One Eye Is
King '94

Amanda Peterson
Fatal Charm '92

Margie Peterson
Strike a Pose '93

Robert Peterson
The Crude Oasis '95

Christopher Pettiet
Carried Away '95

Lori Petty
The Glass Shield '95

Angelique Pettyjohn
Biohazard '85
Repo Man '83

Dedee Pfeiffer
A Climate for Killing '91
Running Cool '93

Jean Pflieger
Ice '93

Joe Phelan
Terminal Exposure '89

Michael Phenicie
9 1/2 Ninjas '90

John Philbin
The Crew '95

Bobbie Phillips
Back in Action '94
Ring of Fire 3: Lion Strike '94
TC 2000 '93

Kristie Phillips
Spitfire '94

Leslie Phillips
Scandal '89

Lou Diamond
  Phillips
Boulevard '94
Dangerous Touch '94
Teresa's Tattoo '94
The Wharf Rat '95

Michelle Phillips
The Last Movie '71

Samantha Phillips
The Dallas Connection '94
Sexual Malice '93

Robert Picardo
Frame Up '91

Alexandra Picatto
The Colony '95

James Pickens, Jr.
Lily in Winter '94
Sharon's Secret '95

Josh Picker
Flirting '89

Cindy Pickett
Painted Hero '95

Ronald Pickup
Jekyll and Hyde '90

Linda Pierce
Black Rainbow '91

Eric Pierpont
The Stranger '95

Tim Pigott-Smith
The Hunchback of Notre
  Dame '82

Joseph Pilato
Married People, Single Sex
  '93

Mitch Pileggi
Raven Hawk '96

Roddy Piper
Back in Action '94
Jungleground '95
Moral Code '96
Tough and Deadly '94

Ingrid Pitt
Transmutations '85

Federico Pitzalis
Devil in the Flesh '87

Byrne Piven
Wavelength '96

Jeremy Piven
Wavelength '96

Michele Placido
Private Affairs '89

Tony Plana
Romero '89

Scott Plank
Saints and Sinners '95

Angela Pleasence
Stealing Heaven '88

Donald Pleasence
The Advocate '93
American Tiger '89
Blood Relatives '78
The House of Usher '88
Will Penny '67

John Pleshette
Eye of the Stranger '93

George Plimpton
Easy Wheels '89
A Fool and His Money '88

Eve Plumb
...And God Spoke '94

Christopher
  Plummer
I Love N.Y. '87
Mindfield '89
Red Blooded American Girl
  '90

Glenn Plummer
Showgirls '95

Cathy Podewell
Night of the Demons '88

Tanya Pohlkotte
National Lampoon's Favorite
  Deadly Sins '95

Larry Poindexter
Body Chemistry 4: Full
  Exposure '95
Sorceress '94

Priscilla Pointer
Carried Away '95

Sidney Poitier
A Good Day to Die '95

Roman Polanski
The Fearless Vampire Killers
  '67

Kevin Pollak
Chameleon '95

Michael J. Pollard
The Art of Dying '90
Fast Food '89
Season of Fear '89
Skeeter '93

Daniel Pollock
Romper Stomper '92

Teri Polo
Golden Gate '93

John Polson
Dangerous Game '90

Jim Ponds
Bottle Rocket '95

Antonella Ponziani
Intervista '87

Marc Poppel
Separate Lives '94

Paulina Porizkova
Arizona Dream '94

Mark Porro
Scoring '95

Sverre Porsanger
Pathfinder '87

Richard Portnow
Meet the Hollowheads '89
S.F.W. '94

Nicole Posey
Beach Babes from Beyond
  '93

Parker Posey
Party Girl '94

Pete Postlethwaite
Suite 16 '94

Ely Pouget
Death Machine '95

Endless Descent '90

CCH Pounder
Lifepod '93

Brittney Powell
Dragonworld '94

Charles Powell
Cheyenne Warrior '94

Robert Powell
The Hunchback of Notre
  Dame '82

Alexandra Powers
The Seventh Coin '92

Michael Praed
To Die for 2: Son of Darkness
  '91

Paula Prentiss
Dead Right '68

Santha Press
In Too Deep '90

Kelly Preston
Cheyenne Warrior '94
The Experts '89
Love Is a Gun '94
The Spellbinder '88

Matt Preston
Showgirl Murders '95

Sue Price
Nemesis 2: Nebula '94
Nemesis 3: Time Lapse '95

Robert Prichard
The Toxic Avenger '86

Martin Priest
Nothing but a Man '64

Barry Prima
Ferocious Female Freedom
  Fighters '88

Barry Primus
Cannibal Women in the
  Avocado Jungle of Death
  '89
Trade Off '95

Ted Prior
Raw Nerve '91

Juergen Prochnow
Guns of Honor '95
Interceptor '92

Phil Proctor
Lobster Man from Mars '89

Victoria Prouty
American Tiger '89

David Proval
To the Limit '95

Harrison Pruett
Embrace of the Vampire '95

Jeff Pruitt
Sword of Honor '94

Jonathan Pryce
The Rachel Papers '89
Shopping '93

Robert Pucci
The Last Hour '91

Rhys Pugh
Zarkorr! The Invader '96

Robert Pugh
Priest '94

Bill Pullman
Liebestraum '91

James Purcell
White Light '90

Lee Purcell
Long Road Home '91

Carolyn Purdy-Gordon
From Beyond '86

Linda Purl
Body Language '92
Incident at Deception Ridge '94

Stephen Quadros
Shock 'Em Dead '90

Dennis Quaid
Come See the Paradise '90

Randy Quaid
Parents '89

Jonathan Ke Quan
Breathing Fire '91

Iain Quarrier
The Fearless Vampire Killers '67

James Quarter
In the Kingdom of the Blind the Man with One Eye Is King '94

Linnea Quigley
Beach Babes from Beyond '93

Deadly Embrace '88
Jack-O '95
Murder Weapon '90
Night of the Demons '88
WitchTrap '89

Kathleen Quinlan
Independence Day '83

Aidan Quinn
At Play in the Fields of the Lord '91
Crusoe '89
Haunted '95

Anthony Quinn
Ghosts Can't Do It '90

Francesco Quinn
The Dark Dancer '95
Dead Certain '92
Priceless Beauty '90

James W. Quinn
WitchTrap '89

J.C. Quinn
Priceless Beauty '90

Martha Quinn
Chopper Chicks in Zombietown '91

Elie Raab
Eyes of an Angel '91

Hugo Race
In Too Deep '90

Alan Rachins
Showgirls '95
Star Quest '94

Natalie Radford
Tomcat: Dangerous Desires '93

Cassidy Rae
National Lampoon's Favorite Deadly Sins '95

William Ragsdale
National Lampoon's Favorite Deadly Sins '95

Steve Railsback
Final Mission '93
Save Me '93

Theodore (Ted) Raimi
Skinner '93

Pam Raines
Bar Girls '95

Charlotte Rampling
Mascara '87

Bruce Ramsay
Dead Beat '94
The New Age '94

Anne Ramsey
Another Chance '88
Meet the Hollowheads '89

Addison Randall
Coldfire '90

Ethan Randall
Empire Records '95

Stacie Randall
Excessive Force 2: Force on Force '95
Moral Code '96

John Randolph
Iron Maze '91

Ty Randolph
Deadly Embrace '88

Kenny Ransom
There Goes My Baby '92

Anna Rapagna
Future Force '89

Dale Rapley
Paper Mask '91

Anthony Rapp
Far from Home '89

Stephen Rappaport
...And God Spoke '94

David Rasche
Out There '95

Stephanie Rascoe
Positive I.D. '87

Julien Rassam
Queen Margot '94

Peter Ratay
Young Lady Chatterley '85

Robin Rates
Puppet Master '89

Basil Rathbone
The Magic Sword '62

Devin Ratray
Spy Trap '92

Heather Rattray
Basket Case 2 '90

Gina Ravera
Showgirls '95

Aldo Ray
Biohazard '85
Drug Runners '88
Shock 'Em Dead '90
Swift Justice '88

Jesse Ray
Scream Dream '89

Greg Raye
The Bikini Car Wash Company 2 '92

Bill Raymond
Where the Rivers Flow North '94

Lou Reed
Blue in the Face '95

Oliver Reed
Dragonard '88
The House of Usher '88
The Pit & the Pendulum '91
The Return of the Musketeers '89
That's Action! '90

Rachel Reed
Midnight Tease '94

Shanna Reed
The Banker '89
Don't Talk to Strangers '94

Harry Reems
Deadly Weapons '70

Jorgen Reenberg
Zentropa '92

Roger Rees
Ebony Tower '86

Saskia Reeves
Close My Eyes '91

Mary Regan
Fever '88

Duncan Regehr
The Banker '89
The Last Samurai '90

Benoit Regent
Blue '93

Paul Regina
Sharon's Secret '95

Fiona Reid
Blood & Donuts '96

Perry Roberts
Lock 'n' Load '90

Tanya Roberts
Almost Pregnant '91
Inner Sanctum '91
Night Eyes '90

Jenny Robertson
The Nightman '93

Malcolm Robertson
The Year My Voice Broke '87

Robbie Robertson
The Crossing Guard '94

Paul Robeson
That's Black Entertainment '85

Robey
Play Nice '92

Andrew (Andy) Robinson
Fatal Charm '92
Into the Badlands '92
There Goes My Baby '92

Jay Robinson
Transylvania Twist '89

Wayne Robson
Love & Murder '91

Eugene Roche
Eternity '90

Amy Rochelle
Secret Games 2: The Escort '93

Debbie Rochon
Broadcast Bombshells '95
Tromeo & Juliet '95

Sam Rockwell
The Search for One-Eyed Jimmy '96

Thierry Rode
Hail Mary '85

Serge Rodnunsky
Lovers' Lovers '94

Paul Rodriguez
La Pastorela '92
A Million to Juan '94

Matt Roe
Last Call '90
Sins of the Night '93

Michael Rogan
Punch the Clock '90

Ginger Rogers
George Stevens: A Filmmaker's Journey '84

Mimi Rogers
Bulletproof Heart '95
Ladykiller '92
Reflections in the Dark '94
Trees Lounge '96

Tristan Rogers
Night Eyes 3 '93

Clayton Rohner
Caroline at Midnight '93
Naked Souls '95

Eduardo Lopez Rojas
My Family '94

Jaime Rojo
The Refrigerator '93

Andy Romano
Fast Money '96

Rino Romano
The Club '94

Cindy Rome
Knock Outs '92
Swift Justice '88

Joanelle Romero
Powwow Highway '89

Maurice Ronet
Beau Pere '81
The Sorceress '55

Linda Ronstadt
La Pastorela '92

Michael Rooker
Henry: Portrait of a Serial Killer '90

Bert Rosario
A Million to Juan '94

Bartholomew Rose
Flirting '89

Jamie Rose
Chopper Chicks in Zombietown '91

Sherrie Rose
New Crime City: Los Angeles 2020 '94
Summer Job '88

Roseanne
Blue in the Face '95

Alan Rosenberg
After Midnight '89
Impulse '90

Ron Rosenthal
Black Rainbow '91

Justin Rosniak
Sweet Talker '91

Ace Ross
Cellblock Sisters: Banished Behind Bars '95

Annie Ross
Basket Case 2 '90

Beverly Ross
Slipping into Darkness '88

Gaylen Ross
Dawn of the Dead '78

Katharine Ross
A Climate for Killing '91

Mary Ella Ross
Bound and Gagged: A Love Story '93

Frank Rossi
The Criminal Mind '93

Leo Rossi
Beyond Desire '94
In the Kingdom of the Blind the Man with One Eye Is King '94

Jan Rossini
When Dinosaurs Ruled the Earth '70

Rick Rossovich
Cover Me '95
Fatally Yours '95
New Crime City: Los Angeles 2020 '94
Paint It Black '89
The Spellbinder '88

Andrea Roth
The Club '94

Joan Roth
Luther the Geek '90

Tim Roth
The Cook, the Thief, His Wife & Her Lover '90
Reservoir Dogs '92

Brigitte Rouan
Overseas: Three Women with Man Trouble '90

Richard Roundtree
Ballistic '94
The Banker '89
Body of Influence '93
Theodore Rex '95
A Time to Die '91

Mickey Rourke
Fall Time '94
9 1/2 Weeks '86
Wild Orchid '90

Myriem Roussel
Hail Mary '85
Sacrilege '86

Patrizio Roversi
Volere Volare '92

Misty Rowe
Goodnight, Sweet Marilyn '89

Leesa Rowland
Class of Nuke 'Em High 2: Subhumanoid Meltdown '91

Gena Rowlands
Faces '68

Gregory Rozakis
Five Corners '88

Christopher Rozycki
Truly, Madly, Deeply '91

Jan Rubes
Blood Relations '87
Descending Angel '90

Jennifer Rubin
Blueberry Hill '88
Saints and Sinners '95
A Woman, Her Men and Her Futon '92

Saul Rubinek
Synapse '95

Sergio Rubini
Intervista '87

Pablo Alvarez Rubio
Dracula (Spanish Version) '31

Michael Rudd
Rockwell: A Legend of the Wild West '93

Dennis Rudge
Lily Was Here '89

Vyto Ruginis
Descending Angel '90

Mia Ruiz
Witchcraft 2: The Temptress
'90

Jennifer Runyon
Carnosaur '93

RuPaul
A Mother's Prayer '95

Al Ruscio
Romero '89

Deborah Rush
Parents '89

Joseph Ruskin
The Criminal Mind '93
Cyber-Tracker '93

Tim Russ
Night Eyes 2 '91

Betsy Russell
Amore! '93
Delta Heat '92

Karen Russell
Dead Certain '92
Easy Wheels '89
Murder Weapon '90

Kurt Russell
Winter People '89

Lisa Ann Russell
A.P.E.X. '94

Monte Russell
Lily in Winter '94

Theresa Russell
Impulse '90
Trade Off '95

James Russo
Blue Iguana '88
Illicit Behavior '91

Michael Russo
Pure Danger '96

Leon Russom
Long Road Home '91

Maxwell Rutherford
The Whispering '94

David Ryall
Truly, Madly, Deeply '91

Eileen Ryan
Winter People '89

Fran Ryan
Suture '93

James Ryan
The Last Samurai '90
Space Mutiny '88

John P. Ryan
Eternity '90

John T. Ryan
Bad Blood '94

Lisa Dean Ryan
Hostile Intentions '95
Twisted Love '95

Mitchell Ryan
Raven Hawk '96
Winter People '89

Robert Ryan
The Wild Bunch '69

Christopher Rydell
Blood and Sand '89

Derek Rydell
Phantom of the Mall: Eric's
Revenge '89

Mark Rydell
The Long Goodbye '73

Patrick Ryecart
Twenty-One '91

Adrienne Sachs
In the Cold of the Night '89

**Marianne
Saegebrecht**
Dust Devil '93
Rosalie Goes Shopping '89

Taylore St. Claire
Virtual Encounters '96

**Raymond St.
Jacques**
Dead Right '68
Timebomb '91

Jill St. John
Out There '95

Meredith Salenger
Dead Beat '94

Soupy Sales
...And God Spoke '94

Carlos Salgado
La Vie de Boheme '93

Matt Salinger
Fortunes of War '94
Options '88

Elizabeth Saltarelli
Bound and Gagged: A Love
Story '93

Emma Samms
The Shrimp on the Barbie '90
Star Quest '94

Chris Samples
King of the Hill '93

Robert Sampson
Re-Animator '84

Laura San Giacomo
Nina Takes a Lover '94
Under Suspicion '92

Jaime Sanchez
The Wild Bunch '69

Brandy Sanders
Killing for Love '95

William Sanderson
Blade Runner '82
Hologram Man '95
Mirror, Mirror '90
Mirror, Mirror 2: Raven
Dance '94

Elizabeth Sandifer
Animal Instincts 2 '94

**Guadalupe
Sandoval**
The Summer of Miss Forbes
'88

Stefania Sandrelli
Jamon, Jamon '93

Julian Sands
Husbands and Lovers '91

**Carmen Santa
Maria**
Bikini Summer '91

Joe Santos
Deadly Desire '91

Ade Sapara
Crusoe '89

Al Sapienza
Animal Instincts 2 '94
The Voyeur '94

Mia Sara
Black Day Blue Night '95
Caroline at Midnight '93
A Climate for Killing '91
The Maddening '95
The Pompatus of Love '96

Chris Sarandon
Dark Tide '93
Temptress '95

Dick Sargent
Frame Up '91

Donna Sarrasin
Witchboard 3: The
Possession '95

Michael Sarrazin
Mascara '87

Nicole Sassaman
Witchcraft 5: Dance with the
Devil '92

Jason Saucier
The Crawlers '93

John Savage
Caribe '87
Carnosaur 2 '94
The Crossing Guard '94
The Dangerous '95
The Hunting '92
One Good Turn '95
The Sister-in-Law '74
The Takeover '94

Telly Savalas
Backfire! '94

Doug Savant
Paint It Black '89

Suzanne Savoy
The Man with the Perfect
Swing '95

Anne Saxon
The Sister-in-Law '74

John Saxon
Animal Instincts '92
The Baby Doll Murders '92
Blood Salvage '90
The Last Samurai '90
Welcome to Spring Break '88

Philip Sayer
Xtro '83

Alexei Sayle
Reckless Kelly '93

John Sayles
Hard Choices '84
Little Vegas '90

Raphael Sbarge
Carnosaur '93
The Hidden 2 '94

Cast Index

Mattia Sbragia
Dial Help '88

Greta Scacchi
Desire '93
Ebony Tower '86
Fires Within '91
Jefferson in Paris '94

Jack Scalia
Amore! '93
Dark Breed '96
Deadly Desire '91
Endless Descent '90
Illicit Behavior '91
The Silencers '95
T-Force '94

Michelle Scarabelli
The Colony '95

Renato Scarpa
Volere Volare '92

Hunt Scarritt
Stormswept '95

Diana Scarwid
Brenda Starr '86

Monica Scattini
Priceless Beauty '90

Wendy Schaal
Out There '95

Sam Schacht
Heart of Midnight '89

Johnathon Schaech
Poison Ivy 2: Lily '95

Eric Schaeffer
My Life's in Turnaround '94

Svein Scharffenberg
Pathfinder '87

Roy Scheider
Somebody Has to Shoot the
  Picture '90

Vincent Schiavelli
The Courtyard '95
Lurking Fear '94

Stephanie Schick
Do or Die '91

Vivian Schilling
Future Shock '93
In a Moment of Passion '93
Soultaker '90

Charlie Schlatter
Sunset Heat '92

Loren Schmalle
Witchcraft 7: Judgement
  Hour '95

Monika Schnarre
Bulletproof Heart '95

Charles Schneider
Zarkorr! The Invader '96

Dan Schneider
Happy Together '89

Jill Schoelen
Adventures in Spying '92
Curse 2: The Bite '88
There Goes My Baby '92

Annabel Schofield
Dragonard '88

Bob Schott
Head of the Family '96
Out for Blood '93

Lisa Schrage
Food of the Gods: Part 2 '88

Liev Schreiber
Party Girl '94

Rick Schroder
There Goes My Baby '92

Matt Schuc
Femalien '96

Wendy Schumacher
Animal Instincts 3: The
  Seductress '95
Fugitive Rage '96

Juan Schwartz
Cannibal! The Musical '96

Rusty Schwimmer
Lone Justice 2 '93

Hanna Schygulla
The Summer of Miss Forbes
  '88

Annabella Sciorra
National Lampoon's Favorite
  Deadly Sins '95

Debbie Scofield
Sword of Honor '94

Tracy Scoggins
Alien Intruder '93
Dead On '93
Dollman Vs. Demonic Toys
  '93
Timebomb '91

Andren Scott
Even Hitler Had a Girlfriend
  '91

Deborah Scott
Witchcraft '88

Donna W. Scott
Dark Breed '96

George C. Scott
Descending Angel '90

Gregg Scott
Almost Hollywood '95

Lisa Marie Scott
The Glass Cage '96

Timothy Scott
Inside Out '91

**Kristin Scott
Thomas**
The Pompatus of Love '96

Angus Scrimm
Phantasm III: Lord of the
  Dead '94
Subspecies '90
Transylvania Twist '89

Sandra Seacat
The New Age '94

Ben Sebastian
Gator Bait 2: Cajun Justice
  '88

Tracy Sebastian
Running Cool '93

Kyra Sedgwick
Heart and Souls '93

Amy Seely
A Stranger in Time '95

Nena Segal
The Refrigerator '93

Pamela Segall
After Midnight '89

John Seitz
Five Corners '88
Hard Choices '84
Out of the Rain '90

Mary Sellers
The Crawlers '93

Willy Semler
Johnny 100 Pesos '96

Meika Seri
In the Realm of the Senses
  '76

Yahoo Serious
Reckless Kelly '93

Assumpta Serna
Wild Orchid '90

Pepe Serna
Fandango '85
A Million to Juan '94

Nestor Serrano
Brenda Starr '86

Roshan Seth
Solitaire for 2 '96

Joan Severance
Almost Pregnant '91
Another Pair of Aces: Three
  of a Kind '91
Criminal Passion '94
Dangerous Indiscretion '94
Hard Evidence '94
Illicit Behavior '91
Lake Consequence '92
Payback '94

Susanne Severeid
Howling IV: The Original
  Nightmare '88

Chloe Sevigny
Trees Lounge '96

Rufus Sewell
Twenty-One '91

Andrzej Seweryn
The Conviction '95

Susan Sexton
The American Angels:
  Baptism of Blood '89

Jane Seymour
The Tunnel '89

Glenn Shadix
Dark Side of Genius '94

Dirk Shafer
Man of the Year '96

Matt Shakman
Meet the Hollowheads '89

Victoria Shalet
Haunted '95
The Maid '90

Tamara Shanath
Cronos '94

Michael Shaner
Bloodfist '89
The Expert '95

Al Shannon
Out of the Rain '90

Rick Shapiro
Pure Danger '96

David Shark
Femme Fontaine: Killer Babe
    for the C.I.A. '95
Soultaker '90

Billy Ray Sharkey
After Midnight '89

Ray Sharkey
Capone '89

Lesley Sharp
Priest '94
The Rachel Papers '89

Melanie Shatner
Unknown Origin '95

Shari Shattuck
Body Chemistry 3: Point of
    Seduction '93
Dead On '93
Out for Blood '93

Helen Shaver
Innocent Victim '90
Tremors 2: Aftershocks '96

Crystal Shaw
Laser Moon '92

Stan Shaw
Lifepod '93

Dick Shawn
Rented Lips '88

John Shea
Ladykiller '92

Moira Shearer
Peeping Tom '60

Allison Sheehy
Invader '91

Martin Sheen
Dillinger and Capone '95
Fortunes of War '94
Guns of Honor '95
The Maid '90

Craig Sheffer
Bloodknot '95
Blue Desert '91

Tom Shell
Dinosaur Island '93

Adrienne Shelly
Hold Me, Thrill Me, Kiss Me
    '93
Teresa's Tattoo '94

Deborah Shelton
Desire '95
Plughead Rewired: Circuitry
    Man 2 '94
Sins of the Night '93

Hilary Shepard
Peacemaker '90

Jewel Shepard
Caged Heat 2: Stripped of
    Freedom '94
Hollywood Hot Tubs 2:
    Educating Crystal '89

Jack Shepherd
Twenty-One '91

Brent Sheppard
Ski School 2 '94

Delia Sheppard
Animal Instincts '92
Mirror Images '91
Night Rhythms '92
Secret Games '92
Witchcraft 2: The Temptress
    '90

Gage Sheridan
Moral Code '96
Twilight of the Dogs '96

Nicolette Sheridan
Silver Strand '95

David Sherwood
Curse of the Crystal Eye '93

Aaron Shields
The Crude Oasis '95

Brooke Shields
Backstreet Dreams '90
Brenda Starr '86

Sab Shimono
Come See the Paradise '90
Suture '93

Sofia Shinas
Hourglass '95

William Shockley
Dream Lover '93

Dan Shor
Red Rock West '93

Grant Show
A Woman, Her Men and Her
    Futon '92

Kathy Shower
Bedroom Eyes 2 '89
The Further Adventures of
    Tennessee Buck '88
Improper Conduct '94
Irresistible Impulse '95
L.A. Goddess '92
Robo-C.H.I.C. '89
Sexual Malice '93
To the Limit '95
Wild Cactus '92

John Shrapnel
Fatherland '94
How to Get Ahead in
    Advertising '89

Elisabeth Shue
Heart and Souls '93
Radio Inside '94
The Underneath '95

Mussef Sibay
The Crude Oasis '95

Casey Siemaszko
The Paint Job '93
Teresa's Tattoo '94

Nina Siemaszko
Wild Orchid 2: Two Shades of
    Blue '92

Tusse Silberg
Hidden City '87

Judith Silinsky
Minute Movie Masterpieces
    '89

Geno Silva
Night Eyes 2 '91

Borah Silver
Elves '89

Ron Silver
Lifepod '93
Live Wire '92

Jonathan Silverman
Sketch Artist 2: Hands That
    See '94
Teresa's Tattoo '94

Alicia Silverstone
True Crime '95

Llio Silyn
Hedd Wyn '92

David Simonds
The Refrigerator '93

Raeanin Simpson
Little Heroes '91

Warwick Sims
Night Eyes '90

Lori Singer
Sunset Grill '92

Marc Singer
Body Chemistry '90
Cyberzone '95
In the Cold of the Night '89

Gary Sinise
A Midnight Clear '92

Jeremy Sisto
The Crew '95

Darryl Sivad
Talkin' Dirty After Dark '91

Frank Sivero
Fist of Honor '92

Tom Sizemore
Bad Love '95
Heart and Souls '93

Jimmie F. Skaggs
Backlash: Oblivion 2 '95
Puppet Master '89

Georg Skarstedt
Monika '52

Tom Skerritt
Poison Ivy '92
Wild Orchid 2: Two Shades of
    Blue '92

Pat Skipper
Trade Off '95

Helgi Skulason
Pathfinder '87

Ione Skye
The Rachel Papers '89

Jeremy Slate
Goodnight, Sweet Marilyn
    '89
The Lawnmower Man '92

Helen Slater
Happy Together '89

Justine Slater
Bar Girls '95

379

Video Premieres

381

Video Premieres

Claudette Sutherland
Man of the Year '96

Donald Sutherland
Blood Relatives '78
Long Road Home '91
Younger & Younger '94

Bo Svenson
Curse 2: The Bite '88
Private Obsession '94
Steel Frontier '94

Brenda Swanson
Secret Games 3 '94

Gary Swanson
Coldfire '90

Jackie Swanson
Oblivion '94

Kristy Swanson
Highway to Hell '92

Rochelle Swanson
Cyberzone '95
Hard Bounty '94
Secret Games 3 '94

Rufus Swart
Dust Devil '93

Don Swayze
Beach Babes from Beyond
'93
Body of Influence '93
Broken Trust '93
Eye of the Stranger '93
Sexual Malice '93

Patrick Swayze
Tiger Warsaw '87

D.B. Sweeney
Blue Desert '91

Dominic Sweeney
In Too Deep '90

Gary Sweet
Fever '88

Tracy Brooks Swope
The Power of One '92

Harold Sylvester
A Cop for the Killing '94

Grazyna Szapolowska
The Conviction '95

Joe Tab
Electra '95

Jon Tabler
The Mosaic Project '95

Cary-Hiroyuki Tagawa
Nemesis '93
Showdown in Little Tokyo '91

Tomoroh Taguchi
Tetsuo: The Iron Man '92

Taimak
No More Dirty Deals '94

George Takei
Backlash: Oblivion 2 '95
Oblivion '94

Nita Talbot
Puppet Master 2 '90

Russ Tamblyn
The Last Movie '71
Wizards of the Demon Sword
'94

Jeffrey Tambor
Brenda Starr '86
Lisa '90

Quentin Tarantino
Reservoir Dogs '92

Laura Tate
Subspecies '90

Sharon Tate
The Fearless Vampire Killers
'67

Nils Tavernier
L.627 '92

Tom Tayback
Undercover '94

Carolyn Taye-Loren
Witchcraft 5: Dance with the
Devil '92

Courtney Taylor
Cover Me '95
Tracks of a Killer '95

Dub Taylor
The Wild Bunch '69

Elizabeth Taylor
Sweet Bird of Youth '89

Jennifer Taylor
The Crude Oasis '95

Kelli Taylor
The Club '94

Kimberly Taylor
Beauty School '93
Party Incorporated '89

Lili Taylor
Arizona Dream '94

Lindsay Taylor
Hard to Die '90

Marina Taylor
Lurkers '88

Meshach Taylor
Inside Out '91

Noah Taylor
Flirting '89
The Year My Voice Broke '87

Regina Taylor
A Good Day to Die '95

Rip Taylor
Private Obsession '94

Vanessa Taylor
Femalien '96

Marshall Teague
The Colony '95

Owen Teale
The Hawk '93

Blair Tefkin
Dream Lover '93

Julius Tennon
Lone Justice 2 '93

Judy Tenuta
White Hot '88

Johanna Ter Steege
The Vanishing '88

Edward Terry
Luther the Geek '90

John Terry
A Dangerous Woman '93
Reflections in the Dark '94

Robert Tessier
Future Force '89

Eric Thal
The Gun in Betty Lou's
Handbag '92

Lynne Thigpen
Impulse '90

Roy Thinnes
Rush Week '88

Ali Thomas
Rain Without Thunder '93

Byron Thomas
84 Charlie Mopic '89

Dave Thomas
Cold Sweat '93

Giles Thomas
Lipstick on Your Collar '94

Heather Thomas
Hidden Obsession '92
Red Blooded American Girl
'90

Jay Thomas
Little Vegas '90

Richard Thomas
Linda '93

Tim Thomerson
Dollman Vs. Demonic Toys
'93
Fleshtone '94
Hong Kong '97 '94
Near Dark '87
Nemesis '93
Nemesis 3: Time Lapse '95
Spitfire '94

Alina Thompson
Dead Cold '96

Brian Thompson
Doctor Mordrid: Master of
the Unknown '90
Moon 44 '90
Ted & Venus '93

Emma Thompson
The Tall Guy '89

Jack Thompson
Trouble in Paradise '88

Sophie Thompson
Twenty-One '91

Teri Thompson
Married People, Single Sex
'93

Gregg Thomsen
Soultaker '90

Anna Thomson
Outside the Law '95

Kim Thomson
Jekyll and Hyde '90
Stealing Heaven '88
The Tall Guy '89

Nicholas Turturro
The Search for One-Eyed
　Jimmy '96

Shannon Tweed
Body Chemistry 4: Full
　Exposure '95
Cannibal Women in the
　Avocado Jungle of Death
　'89
Cold Sweat '93
The Dark Dancer '95
Electra '95
Illicit Dreams '94
In the Cold of the Night '89
Last Call '90
The Last Hour '91
Night Eyes 2 '91
Night Eyes 3 '93
Sexual Response '92

Terry Tweed
Night Rhythms '92

Tracy Tweed
Night Eyes 3 '93
Sunset Heat '92

Twiggy
Istanbul '90

Anne Twomey
Last Rites '88

Liv Tyler
Empire Records '95
Silent Fall '94

Susan Tyrrell
Far from Home '89
Killer Inside Me '76

Cathy Tyson
Priest '94

Cicely Tyson
That's Black Entertainment
　'85

Richard Tyson
Dark Tide '93
The Glass Cage '96
Pharoah's Army '95

Fabiana Udenio
Bride of Re-Animator '89

Jay Underwood
To Die for 2: Son of Darkness
　'91

Deborah Unger
Highlander: The Final
　Dimension '94

Peter Ustinov
The Phoenix and the Magic
　Carpet '95

Nils Utsi
Pathfinder '87

Kari Vaananen
La Vie de Boheme '93

Brenda Vaccaro
Heart of Midnight '89

Justina Vail
Naked Souls '95

Kim Valentine
Grandma's House '88

Scott Valentine
Homicidal Impulse '92
Out of Annie's Past '94
Till the End of the Night '94
To Sleep with a Vampire '92

Mariella Valentini
Volere Volare '92

Nick Vallelonga
In the Kingdom of the Blind
　the Man with One Eye Is
　King '94

Frankie Valli
Eternity '90

Lee Van Cleef
Thieves of Fortune '89

**Monique Van De
Ven**
Paint It Black '89

**Sylvie van den
Elsen**
La Vie de Boheme '93

**Nadine Van Der
Velde**
After Midnight '89

**Kelley Van Der
Velden**
I Love N.Y. '87

**Kevin Van
Hentenryck**
Basket Case 2 '90

Brant Van Hoffman
The Further Adventures of
　Tennessee Buck '88

Nina Van Pallandt
The Long Goodbye '73

Nels Van Patten
Mirror Images '91

Mario Van Peebles
Highlander: The Final
　Dimension '94
Identity Crisis '90

Melvin Van Peebles
Fist of the North Star '96

Marion Van Thijn
Lily Was Here '89

**Deborah Van
Valkenburgh**
Rampage '87

Gregg D. Vance
Phat Beach '96

Musetta Vander
Backlash: Oblivion 2 '95

Jacob Vargas
My Family '94

Valentina Vargas
The Tigress '93

Jim Varney
Ernest Goes to School '94
The Expert '95
Fast Food '89
Slam Dunk Ernest '95

Roberta Vasquez
Do or Die '91
Easy Wheels '89
Picasso Trigger '89
Street Asylum '90

Peter Vaughan
Fatherland '94

Robert Vaughn
Transylvania Twist '89

Ron Vawter
King of the Hill '93

Eddie Velez
Romero '89

Chick Vennera
Body Chemistry 3: Point of
　Seduction '93
Last Rites '88

Harley Venton
Blood Ties '92

Jesse Ventura
Repossessed '90
Thunderground '89

John Vernon
Terminal Exposure '89

Kate Vernon
Bloodknot '95
Dangerous Touch '94

Christine Veronica
Party Incorporated '89

Cec Verrell
Three of Hearts '93

Charlotte Very
Blue '93

Victoria Vetri
When Dinosaurs Ruled the
　Earth '70

John Vickery
Deconstructing Sarah '94

Katherine Victor
The Wild World of
　Batwoman '66

Eric Viellard
Boyfriends & Girlfriends '88

Abadah Viera
Black Magic Woman '91

Gregory Vignolle
Illegal Entry: Formula for
　Fear '93

Abe Vigoda
Fist of Honor '92

Robert Viharo
Coldfire '90
Romero '89

Joey Villa
Eternity '90

Paolo Villaggio
Ciao, Professore! '94

**Victor Cesar
Villalobos**
The Summer of Miss Forbes
　'88

Carlos Villarias
Dracula (Spanish Version) '31

James Villiers
Wavelength '96

Pruitt Taylor Vince
Come See the Paradise '90

**Jan-Michael
Vincent**
Animal Instincts '92
Deadly Embrace '88
Demonstone '89
Hidden Obsession '92

Cast Index

Video Premieres

Naomi Watts
The Custodian '94

Al Waxman
Operation Golden Phoenix '94

Shawn Weatherly
Mind Games '89
Shadowzone '89
Thieves of Fortune '89

Hugo Weaving
The Custodian '94
Reckless Kelly '93

Chloe Webb
A Dangerous Woman '93
Queens Logic '91

Greg Webb
Puppet Master 2 '90

Catherine Weber
Body Strokes '95

Steven Weber
A Cop for the Killing '94

Blair Weickgenant
Smooth Talker '90

Teri Weigel
The Banker '89
Glitch! '88
Savage Beach '89

David Weilis
Witchcraft 8: Salem's Ghost '95

Michael T. Weiss
Howling IV: The Original Nightmare '88

Morgan Weisser
Long Road Home '91

Norbert Weisser
Arcade '93
Nemesis 3: Time Lapse '95

Dwight Weist
9 1/2 Weeks '86

Lucinda Weist
The Silencers '95

Bruce Weitz
Rainbow Drive '90

Jessica Welch
Warrior Spirit '94

Raquel Welch
Trouble in Paradise '88

Tahnee Welch
The Criminal Mind '93
Improper Conduct '94
Night Train to Venice '93

Tuesday Weld
Once Upon a Time in America '84

Peter Weller
Cat Chaser '90
The New Age '94
Rainbow Drive '90
Road to Ruin '91
Sunset Grill '92
The Tunnel '89

Mel Welles
Rented Lips '88

Orson Welles
Someone to Love '87

Steve Welles
Puppet Master 2 '90

David Wells
Wild Cactus '92

Tracy Wells
Mirror, Mirror 2: Raven Dance '94

Vernon Wells
Circuitry Man '90
Hard Justice '95
Plughead Rewired: Circuitry Man 2 '94
Sexual Response '92
The Shrimp on the Barbie '90

Kenneth Welsh
Portraits of a Killer '95

Ming-Na Wen
Hong Kong '97 '94
Star Quest '94

Lara Wendell
Intervista '87

Gary Werntz
The Art of Dying '90

Doug Wert
Dracula Rising '93

Eileen Wesson
Zarkorr! The Invader '96

Adam West
The New Age '94
Young Lady Chatterley 2 '85

Dominic West
Wavelength '96

Erika West
Sexual Outlaws '94

Gregory West
The Surgeon '94

Red West
The Expert '95

Wendi Westbrook
Married People, Single Sex '93
Under Lock and Key '95

Jeff Weston
Puppet Master 2 '90

Marius Weyers
Happy Together '89
The Power of One '92

Frank Whaley
A Midnight Clear '92
Swimming with Sharks '94

Joanne Whalley
Kill Me Again '89
Scandal '89
Storyville '92

Wil Wheaton
Mr. Stitch '95

Dana Wheeler-Nicholson
Circuitry Man '90
My Life's in Turnaround '94
The Pompatus of Love '96

Shannon Whirry
Animal Instincts '92
Animal Instincts 2 '94
Body of Influence '93
Lady in Waiting '94
Mirror Images 2 '93
Playback '95
Private Obsession '94

Christina Whitaker
Vampire at Midnight '88

Damon Whitaker
Saints and Sinners '95

Forest Whitaker
Body Snatchers '93

Earl White
Nemesis 2: Nebula '94

Ron White
Love & Murder '91

Raymond Whitefield
How U Like Me Now? '92

Lynn Whitfield
The Josephine Baker Story '90

Kari Whitman
Phantom of the Mall: Eric's Revenge '89

Stuart Whitman
Improper Conduct '94
Mob Boss '90
Smooth Talker '90

James Whitmore
Target: Favorite Son '87

Margaret Whitton
9 1/2 Weeks '86

Johnny Whitworth
Empire Records '95

Richard Widmark
True Colors '91

David Wieland
Flirting '89

Dianne Wiest
Independence Day '83

Toyah Wilcox
Ebony Tower '86

James Wilder
Tollbooth '94

Michael Wilding, Jr.
Sweet Bird of Youth '89

Valerie Wildman
Inner Sanctum '91

Dawn Wildsmith
Jack-O '95
Wizards of the Demon Sword '94

Ed Wiley
Class of '61 '92

Kathleen Wilhoite
Color of Night '94

Tom Wilkinson
Paper Mask '91
Priest '94

Barbara Williams
Digger '94
Tiger Warsaw '87
Watchers '88

Billy Dee Williams
Alien Intruder '93

Amy Wright
Where the Rivers Flow
North '94

Jenny Wright
The Lawnmower Man '92
Near Dark '87

Robin Wright
The Crossing Guard '94

Steven Wright
Men of Respect '91

Tom Wright
Men of War '94

Tracy Wright
When Night Is Falling '95

Vivian Wu
The Guyver '91

Kari Wuhrer
Beyond Desire '94
Boulevard '94
The Crossing Guard '94
Sensation '94

Paul Wyett
A Soldier's Tale '91

Noah Wyle
There Goes My Baby '92

Joel Wyner
The Club '94

Keenan Wynn
Killer Inside Me '76

Dana Wynter
Dead Right '68

Amanda Wyss
Black Magic Woman '91
Powwow Highway '89
To Die for '89
To Die for 2: Son of Darkness
'91

Nelson Xavier
At Play in the Fields of the
Lord '91

Emmanuel Xuereb
Grim '95

Salvator Xuereb
Blood Ties '92

Ronald Yamamoto
Come See the Paradise '90

Donnie Yan
Wing Chun '94

Edward Yang
Kung Fu Rascals '90s

Jean Yanne
Madame Bovary '91
Quicker Than the Eye '88

Amy Yasbeck
The Nutt House '95

Sally Yeh
The Killer '90

Michelle Yeoh
The Executioners '93
The Heroic Trio '93
Wing Chun '94

Bolo Yeung
Breathing Fire '91
TC 2000 '93

Mechmed Yilmaz
Moon 44 '90

Cecilia Yip
Organized Crime & Triad
Bureau '93

Dwight Yoakam
Painted Hero '95
Red Rock West '93

Malik Yoba
Blue in the Face '95

Kathleen York
Dream Lover '93

Michael York
Discretion Assured '93
Not of This Earth '96
The Return of the
Musketeers '89

Susannah York
American Roulette '88
Fate '90

Frances You
Double Happiness '94

Burt Young
Backstreet Dreams '90

Excessive Force '93
Once Upon a Time in
America '84

Karen Young
9 1/2 Weeks '86

Sean Young
Blade Runner '82
Hold Me, Thrill Me, Kiss Me
'93
Mirage '94
Sketch Artist '92

Jim Youngs
Skeeter '93

Ron Yuan
Ring of Fire 2: Blood and
Steel '92

Jimmy Yuill
Paper Mask '91

Harris Yulin
The Last Hit '93
There Goes the
Neighborhood '92

Chow Yun-Fat
A Better Tomorrow '86
Hard-Boiled '92
The Killer '90

Grace Zabriskie
Blood Ties '92
The Crew '95

Robert Zachar
Married People, Single Sex
'93

Ramy Zada
After Midnight '89

Frank Zagarino
Never Say Die '94
Terminal Impact '95
Without Mercy '95

Naomi Zaizen
Heaven & Earth '90

Roxana Zal
Under the Boardwalk '89

**Zbigniew
Zamachowski**
White '94

Billy Zane
Femme Fatale '90
Lake Consequence '92
Reflections in the Dark '94
Silence of the Hams '93

Lisa Zane
Femme Fatale '90
Floundering '94
Terrified '94

Moon Zappa
Dark Side of Genius '94

Alexandre Zbruev
The Inner Circle '91

Robert Z'Dar
Fugitive X '96
In a Moment of Passion '93
Soultaker '90
Wild Cactus '92

**Patricia
Zehentmayr**
Rosalie Goes Shopping '89

Renee Zellweger
Empire Records '95

Anthony Zerbe
Will Penny '67

Mary Zilba
L.A. Wars '94

William Zipp
Future Force '89

Adrian Zmed
Improper Conduct '94
The Other Woman '92

Richard Zobel
To Sleep with a Vampire '92

Daphne Zuniga
Last Rites '88

Jahi JJ Zuri
Nemesis 2: Nebula '94

Steve Zurk
Biohazard: The Alien Force
'95

Brad Zutaut
Knock Outs '92

This index lists all directors credited in the main review section, alphabetically by their last names. Because some directors can't keep their mugs *behind* the cameras, you might check out the "Cast Index" for your favorite directors to see if they had a gratuitous cameo in their own (or their best friend's) movie. It's worth a look.

Jon Acevski
Freddie the Frog '92

Daniel Adams
A Fool and His Money '88

Percy Adlon
Rosalie Goes Shopping '89
Younger & Younger '94

Carlton J. Albright
Luther the Geek '90

Robert Aldrich
Kiss Me Deadly '55

Don Allan
Jungleground '95

David Allen
Puppet Master 2 '90

James Allen
Burndown '89

Robert Altman
The Long Goodbye '73

Keita Amemiya
Cyber Ninja '94
Zeram '91

Andy Anderson
Positive I.D. '87

Kurt Anderson
Dead Cold '96

Paul Anderson
Shopping '93

Stephen Anderson
Toto: Lost in New York '96

Wes Anderson
Bottle Rocket '95

Len Anthony
Fright House '89

Robert Anthony
Without Mercy '95

John Antonelli
On the Road with Jack
    Kerouac '84

Lou Antonio
This Gun for Hire '90

Daniel Appleby
Bound and Gagged: A Love
    Story '93

Mats Arehn
Istanbul '90

Gillian Armstrong
Fires Within '91

Ronald K. Armstrong
Bugged! '96

Eddie Arno
Murder Story '89

Toyoo Ashida
Vampire Hunter D '85

Paul Auster
Blue in the Face '95

Roger Roberts Avary
Mr. Stitch '95

Rick Avery
The Expert '95

John G. Avildsen
The Power of One '92

Meiert Avis
Far from Home '89

Hector Babenco
At Play in the Fields of the
    Lord '91

Phillip Badger
The Forgotten One '89

John Bailey
China Moon '91

Bob Balaban
Parents '89

Albert Band
Doctor Mordrid: Master of
    the Unknown '90
Prehysteria '93

Charles Band
Doctor Mordrid: Master of
    the Unknown '90
Dollman Vs. Demonic Toys
    '93
Meridian: Kiss of the Beast
    '90
Prehysteria '93

Leora Barish
Venus Rising '95

Joseph John Barmettler, Jr.
Witchcraft 8: Salem's Ghost
    '95

Bruno Barreto
Carried Away '95

Zelda Barron
Forbidden Sun '89

Ian Barry
Crimebroker '95

Kim Bass
Ballistic '94

Bradley Battersby
Blue Desert '91

Craig R. Baxley
Deconstructing Sarah '94
Deep Red '94

Dixie Beck
Body Strokes '95

Greg Beeman
Tales of the Unknown '90

A. Dean Bell
Backfire! '94

Jeffrey Bell
Radio Inside '94

Donald P. Bellisario
Last Rites '88

Marco Bellocchio
The Conviction '95
Devil in the Flesh '87

Jack Bender
Lone Justice 2 '93

Terry Benedict
Painted Hero '95

Gary Bennett
Rain Without Thunder '93

Robby Benson
White Hot '88

Luca Bercovici
Dark Tide '93

Bruce Beresford
Silent Fall '94

Ingmar Bergman
Monika '52

Robert Bergman
A Whisper to a Scream '88

Joe Berlinger
Brother's Keeper '92

Brigitte Berman
Bix '90

Tom Berry
Twin Sisters '91

Jonathan Betuel
Theodore Rex '95

Kathryn Bigelow
Near Dark '87

Tony Bill
Five Corners '88

Antonia Bird
Priest '94

Andrew Birkin
Desire '93

Alan Birkinshaw
The House of Usher '88

Bill Bixby
Another Pair of Aces: Three
of a Kind '91

Bertrand Blier
Beau Pere '81

Philippe Blot
Running Wild '94

Andy Blumenthal
Bloodfist 2 '90

David Blyth
Red Blooded American Girl
'90

Yurek Bogayevicz
Three of Hearts '93

Mauro Bolognini
Husbands and Lovers '91

James Bond, III
Def by Temptation '90

Mike Bonifer
Lipstick Camera '93

Lizzie Borden
Inside Out '92

Arthur Borman
...And God Spoke '94

John Bowen
Dark Secrets '95
Knock Outs '92

Kirk Bowman
CyberSex Kittens '95

Don Boyd
Twenty-One '91

Gianni Bozzacchi
I Love N.Y. '87

Larry Brand
Masque of the Red Death '89
Overexposed '90
Till the End of the Night '94

Clark Brandon
Skeeter '93

**Charlotte
Brandstrom**
Road to Ruin '91

Bob Bravler
Rush Week '88

Salome Breziner
Tollbooth '94

John Broderick
The Warrior & the Sorceress
'84

Kevin Brodie
Treacherous '95

Nick Broomfield
Heidi Fleiss: Hollywood
Madam '95

Barry Brown
Lonely in America '90

Edwin Scott Brown
Sexual Outlaws '94

Gregory Brown
Street Asylum '90

Larry Buchanan
Goodnight, Sweet Marilyn
'89

**Penelope
Buitenhuis**
Boulevard '94

Robert Burge
The Dark Dancer '95

Tom Burman
Meet the Hollowheads '89

Jopi Burnama
Ferocious Female Freedom
Fighters '88

Charles Burnett
The Glass Shield '95

Tim Burstall
The Naked Country '85

Steve Buscemi
Trees Lounge '96

Ellen Cabot
see also David DeCoteau
Beach Babes from Beyond
'93
Deadly Embrace '88
Murder Weapon '90
Test Tube Teens from the
Year 2000 '93

Douglas Campbell
Season of Fear '89

Graeme Campbell
Blood Relations '87
Into the Fire '88
The Man in the Attic '94

Danny Cannon
The Young Americans '93

Frank Cappello
American Yakuza '94

J.S. Cardone
Black Day Blue Night '95
A Climate for Killing '91
Shadowzone '89

Topper Carew
Talkin' Dirty After Dark '91

Lucille Carra
The Inland Sea '93

Bruce Carter
Laser Moon '92

John Cassavetes
Faces '68

Nardo Castillo
The Gunrunner '84

**Michael Caton-
Jones**
Scandal '89

Claude Chabrol
Blood Relatives '78
Madame Bovary '91

Matthew Chapman
Heart of Midnight '89

Henri Charr
Cellblock Sisters: Banished
Behind Bars '95
Illegal Entry: Formula for
Fear '93
Under Lock and Key '95

Amin Q. Chaudhri
Tiger Warsaw '87

Patrice Chereau
Queen Margot '94

John R. Cherry, III
Slam Dunk Ernest '95

Lipo Ching
Watch Me '96

Thomas Chong
Far Out Man '89

Lyndon Chubbuck
Naked Souls '95

Gerard Ciccoritti
Paris, France '94
Understudy: The Graveyard
Shift 2 '88

Graeme Clifford
Past Tense '94

Paul E. Clinco
Death Magic '92

Craig Clyde
Little Heroes '91

Steve Cohen
Tough and Deadly '94

Michael Cohn
Interceptor '92

Henry Cole
Shameless '94

Bob Collins
Pat Paulsen for President '68

Carl Colpaert
The Crew '95

Kevin Connor
Sunset Grill '92

Patrick Conrad
Mascara '87

Phillip Cook
Invader '91
Star Quest: Beyond the
   Rising Moon '89

Troy Cook
The Takeover '94

William Cooke
Freakshow '95

Stuart Cooper
Out of Annie's Past '94

Bill Corcoran
Portraits of a Killer '95

Hubert Cornfield
The Night of the Following
   Day '69

Charles Correll
Deadly Desire '91

Bud Cort
Ted & Venus '93

Don A. Coscarelli
Phantasm III: Lord of the
   Dead '94

Hil Covington
Adventures in Spying '92

Alex Cox
Repo Man '83

Ronnie Cramer
Even Hitler Had a Girlfriend
   '91

Jay Craven
Where the Rivers Flow
   North '94

Wayne Crawford
Crime Lords '91

David Cronenberg
M Butterfly '93

William Curran
Love, Cheat & Steal '93

Julie Cypher
Teresa's Tattoo '94

Catherine Cyran
Hostile Intentions '95

John Dahl
Kill Me Again '89
Red Rock West '93

Holly Dale
Blood & Donuts '96

Joe D'Amato
The Loves of a Wall Street
   Woman '89

Mel Damski
Happy Together '89

Maria Dante
The Dangerous '95

**Harry Bromley
Davenport**
Xtro '83

Boaz Davidson
Outside the Law '95

Martin Davidson
Eddie and the Cruisers '83

Julie Davis
Witchcraft 6: The Devil's
   Mistress '94

Michael Paul Davis
Beanstalk '94

Ate De Jong
Highway to Hell '92

Marcus De Leon
Kiss Me a Killer '91

Tom Decker
Toto: Lost in New York '96

David DeCoteau
see also Ellen Cabot
Dr. Alien '88

Steve DeJarnatt
Miracle Mile '89

Guillermo Del Toro
Cronos '94

Sean Delgado
Alexa: A Prostitute's Own
   Story '88

Bill D'Elia
The Feud '90

Michael DeLuise
Almost Pregnant '91

Ruggero Deodato
Dial Help '88

John Derek
Ghosts Can't Do It '90

**Dominique
Deruddere**
Suite 16 '94

Caleb Deschanel
Crusoe '89

James Desmarais
Road Lawyers and Other
   Briefs '89

**Richard Lloyd
Dewey**
Rockwell: A Legend of the
   Wild West '93

Patrick Dewolf
Innocent Lies '95

Lucian S. Diamonde
Forbidden Zone: Alien
   Abduction '96

Nigel Dick
Inside Out 2 '92

Donna Dietch
Criminal Passion '94

Steve DiMarco
Back in Action '94

John Dingwall
The Custodian '94

John Dirlam
Fatal Instinct '92

Ken Dixon
Slave Girls from Beyond
   Infinity '87

Martin Dolman
American Tiger '89

Roger Donaldson
The Getaway '93

Clive Donner
Stealing Heaven '88

Martin Donovan
Apartment Zero '88
Inside Out 2 '92

Paul Donovan
George's Island '91
Tomcat: Dangerous Desires
   '93

Lorenzo Doumani
Amore! '93

Robert Downey
Rented Lips '88

Tim Doyle
Road Lawyers and Other
   Briefs '89

Jim Drake
Based on an Untrue Story '93

Di Drew
Trouble in Paradise '88

Sara Driver
Sleepwalk '88

Antonio Drove
The Tunnel '89

Adam Dubov
Dead Beat '94

Thomas Dugan
Fatal Skies '90

Christian Duguay
Live Wire '92

John Duigan
Flirting '89
The Journey of August King
   '95
Romero '89
The Year My Voice Broke '87

Patrick Duncan
84 Charlie Mopic '89

Robert Dyke
Moontrap '89

Colin Eggleston
The Wicked '89

Jan Egleson
The Last Hit '93

Rafael Eisenman
Lake Consequence '92

Larry Elikann
A Mother's Prayer '95

Doug Ellin
Phat Beach '96

John Ellis
Twilight of the Dogs '96

Javier Elorrieta
Blood and Sand '89

Roland Emmerich
Moon 44 '90

Rene Eram
Voodoo '95

Tim Everitt
Fatally Yours '95

John Eyres
Monolith '93

Donald Farmer
Scream Dream '89

John Feldman
Alligator Eyes '90
Dead Funny '94

Federico Fellini
Intervista '87

Abel Ferrara
Body Snatchers '93
Cat Chaser '90
King of New York '90

Brian Ferren
Funny '92

Mike Figgis
Liebestraum '91

Charles Finch
Priceless Beauty '90

Roberta Findlay
Lurkers '88

Michael Fischa
Death Spa '87
Delta Heat '92

Clive Fleury
Fatal Past '94
Tunnel Vision '95

Peter Fonda
Idaho Transfer '73

John Ford
December 7th: The Movie '91

Jose Maria Forque
Nexus '96

Giles Foster
Innocent Victim '90

Carl Franklin
One False Move '91

Mark Freed
Shock 'Em Dead '90

William Friedkin
Rampage '87

Adam Friedman
Inside Out '92
To Sleep with a Vampire '92

Richard S. Friedman
Phantom of the Mall: Eric's Revenge '89

Harvey Frost
Midnight Heat '95
Tracks of a Killer '95

Lee Frost
Private Obsession '94

Mark Frost
Storyville '92

Roy Frumkes
Document of the Dead '90

Benjamin Fry
Wavelength '96

Ricardo Jacques Gale
Alien Intruder '93

Fred Gallo
Black Rose of Harlem '95
Dracula Rising '93
Lady in Waiting '94
Tales of the Unknown '90

George Gallo
29th Street '91

Frank Gannon
The Real Richard Nixon '95

Christophe Gans
H. P. Lovecraft's Necronomicon: Book of the Dead '96

Nils Gaup
Pathfinder '87

Eleanor Gaver
Slipping into Darkness '88

Joe Gayton
Warm Summer Rain '89

John Gazarian
Driven to Kill '90

Jim George
Rover Dangerfield '91

Nicolas Gessner
Quicker Than the Eye '88

Duncan Gibbins
A Case for Murder '93

Brian Gibson
The Josephine Baker Story '90

Gregory Gieras
The Whispering '94

Lewis Gilbert
Haunted '95

Robert Ginty
Woman of Desire '93

Marita Giovanni
Bar Girls '95

Francois Girard
32 Short Films about Glenn Gould '93

Michael Paul Girard
Witchcraft 7: Judgement Hour '95

Arnold Glassman
Visions of Light: The Art of Cinematography '93

Jean-Luc Godard
Hail Mary '85

Menahem Golan
Hit the Dutchman '92

Dan Golden
Burial of the Rats '95
Saturday Night Special '92
Stripteaser '95

Jill Goldman
Bad Love '95

Allan Goldstein
Synapse '95

Amy Goldstein
The Silencer '92

Fred Goodwin
Curse 2: The Bite '88

Bert I. Gordon
The Magic Sword '62
Satan's Princess '90

Keith Gordon
A Midnight Clear '92

Stuart Gordon
Castle Freak '95
From Beyond '86
The Pit & the Pendulum '91
Re-Animator '84

Lisa Gottlieb
Across the Moon '94

Anne Goursaud
Embrace of the Vampire '95
Poison Ivy 2: Lily '95

Gustavo Graef-Marino
Johnny 100 Pesos '96

Brian Grant
Sensation '94
Sweet Poison '91

Julian Grant
Electra '95

Alex Graves
The Crude Oasis '95

William Greaves
That's Black Entertainment '85

Janet Greek
The Spellbinder '88

Peter Greenaway
The Cook, the Thief, His Wife & Her Lover '90

David Greene
A Good Day to Die '95

Bud Greenspan
16 Days of Glory: Parts 1 and 2 '84

Ezio Greggio
Silence of the Hams '93

Tom Gries
Will Penny '67

Mark Griffiths
Cheyenne Warrior '94

Ruy Guerra
The Fable of the Beautiful Pigeon Fancier '88

Val Guest
When Dinosaurs Ruled the Earth '70

Charles Guggenheim
The Great St. Louis Bank Robbery '59

Nathaniel Gutman
Linda '93

Andre Guttfreund
Femme Fatale '90

Stephen Gyllenhaal
A Dangerous Woman '93

Taylor Hackford
Blood In...Blood Out: Bound
by Honor '93

Petra Haffter
A Demon in My View '92

Charles Haid
The Nightman '93

Randa Haines
Wrestling Ernest Hemingway
'93

Dean Hamilton
Strike a Pose '93

Strathford
Hamilton
Blueberry Hill '88
Temptation '94

Brian Hannant
The Time Guardian '87

Ed Hansen
The Bikini Car Wash
Company '90
Party Plane '90
Robo-C.H.I.C. '89

Robert Harmon
Eyes of an Angel '91

Damian Harris
Bad Company '94
The Rachel Papers '89

Jacobsen Hart
Steel Frontier '94

David Hartwell
Love Is a Gun '94

Gail Harvey
Cold Sweat '93

Linda Hassani
Dark Angel: The Ascent '94
Inside Out '92
Inside Out 2 '92

Maurice Hatton
American Roulette '88

Wings Hauser
The Art of Dying '90
Coldfire '90

Living to Die '91

David Hayman
The Hawk '93

Todd Haynes
Safe '95

Robert Heath
Hugh Hefner: Once Upon a
Time '92

David Heavener
Eye of the Stranger '93
Fugitive X '96

Rob Hedden
The Colony '95

David Heeley
The Universal Story '96

Ralph Hemecker
Dead On '93

Frank Henenlotter
Basket Case 2 '90
Brain Damage '88
Frankenhooker '90

Robby Henson
Pharoah's Army '95

Jaime Humberto
Hermosillo
The Summer of Miss Forbes
'88

Joel Hershman
Hold Me, Thrill Me, Kiss Me
'93

Gene Hertel
Showgirl Murders '95

Michael Herz
Sgt. Kabukiman N.Y.P.D. '94
The Toxic Avenger '86

Eugene Hess
Don't Do It '94

Jon Hess
Excessive Force '93
Watchers '88

Gordon Hessler
The Girl in a Swing '89

Rod Hewitt
The Dangerous '95

Anthony Hickox
Payback '94
Sundown '91
Waxwork '88

Terence Hill
Troublemakers '94

Alexander Gregory
Hippolyte
Animal Instincts '92
Animal Instincts 2 '94
Animal Instincts 3: The
Seductress '95
Body of Influence '93
Mirror Images '91
Mirror Images 2 '93
Night Rhythms '92
Secret Games '92
Secret Games 2: The Escort
'93
Secret Games 3 '94
Sins of the Night '93
Undercover '94

Rupert Hitzig
Backstreet Dreams '90

Gregory Hoblit
Class of '61 '92

Mike Hodges
Black Rainbow '91

P.J. Hogan
Muriel's Wedding '94

Edward Holzman
Friend of the Family '95
Sinful Intrigue '95

Tobe Hooper
I'm Dangerous Tonight '90

Harry Hope
Swift Justice '88

Margot Hope
Femme Fontaine: Killer Babe
for the C.I.A. '95

Stephen Hopkins
Dangerous Game '90

Dennis Hopper
The Last Movie '71

Dan Hoskins
Chopper Chicks in
Zombietown '91

John Hough
Howling IV: The Original
Nightmare '88

Michael Hovis
The Man with the Perfect
Swing '95

Karin Howard
The Tigress '93

C. Thomas Howell
Hourglass '95
Pure Danger '96

Frank Howson
The Hunting '92

Talun Hsu
Witchcraft 5: Dance with the
Devil '92

George Huang
Swimming with Sharks '94

P.I. Huemer
Kiss Daddy Goodnight '87

Tim Hunter
Paint It Black '89

Harry Hurwitz
Fleshtone '94

Danny Huston
The Maddening '95

Jimmy Huston
The Wharf Rat '95

Markus Innocenti
Murder Story '89

Sam Irvin
Backlash: Oblivion 2 '95
Oblivion '94
Out There '95

David Irving
Night of the Cyclone '90

Koichi Ishiguro
The Guyver '89

James Ivory
Jefferson in Paris '94

David Jablin
National Lampoon's Favorite
Deadly Sins '95

Peter Jackson
Meet the Feebles '89

Alan Jacobs
Nina Takes a Lover '94

Jon Jacobs
The Girl with the Hungry
Eyes '94

Nicholas A.E. Jacobs
The Refrigerator '93

Rick Jacobson
Night Hunter '95
Ring of Fire 3: Lion Strike '94
Star Quest '94

Walter Lima, Jr.
The Dolphin '87

David Lipman
Road Lawyers and Other
Briefs '89

Aaron Lipstadt
Android '82

Steven Lisberger
Slipstream '89

David Lister
Guns of Honor '95

Ken Loach
Riff Raff '92

Moctezuma Lobato
I Like to Play Games '95

Sondra Locke
Impulse '90

Bob Logan
Repossessed '90

Dimitri Logothetis
Body Shot '93

Harry S. Longstreet
Sex, Love and Cold Hard
Cash '93

Jean-Claude Lord
Eddie and the Cruisers 2:
Eddie Lives! '89
Landslide '92
Mindfield '89

Eb Lottimer
Love Matters '93
Twisted Love '95

Eric Louzil
Class of Nuke 'Em High 2:
Subhumanoid Meltdown
'91
Class of Nuke 'Em High 3:
The Good, the Bad and the
Subhumanoid '94

Robert Lovy
Plughead Rewired: Circuitry
Man 2 '94

Steven Lovy
Circuitry Man '90
Plughead Rewired: Circuitry
Man 2 '94

Dick Lowry
A Cop for the Killing '94

Bigas Luna
Jamon, Jamon '93

Paul Lynch
Cross Country '83

Adrian Lyne
9 1/2 Weeks '86

Rodney MacDonald
Desire '95

David Madden
Separate Lives '94

John Madden
Golden Gate '93

Paul Madden
Summer Job '88

Maria Maggenti
The Incredibly True
Adventure of Two Girls in
Love '95

Redge Mahaffey
Moral Code '96

Stewart Main
Desperate Remedies '93

Peter Mak
Wicked City '92

Dusan Makavejev
A Night of Love '87

Mark Malone
Bulletproof Heart '95

David Mamet
Oleanna '94

Jeffrey Mandel
Elves '89
Robo-C.H.I.C. '89

Robert Mandel
Independence Day '83

Delbert Mann
Lily in Winter '94

Ron Mann
Twist '93

Guido Manuli
Volere Volare '92

Rene Manzor
Warrior Spirit '94

Robert Marcarelli
I Don't Buy Kisses Anymore
'92

Mitch Marcus
A Boy Called Hate '95

Peter Maris
Diplomatic Immunity '91

Richard Marquand
Hearts of Fire '87

David Marsh
Stormswept '95

Charles Martin
Dead Right '68

Raymond Martino
Skyscraper '96
To the Limit '95

Francesco Massaro
Private Affairs '89

Nico Mastorakis
Glitch! '88
In the Cold of the Night '89
Terminal Exposure '89

Eddy Matalon
Sweet Killing '93

Paul Matthews
Grim '95

Garth Maxwell
Jack Be Nimble '94

Bradford May
Darkman 2: The Return of
Durant '94
Darkman 3: Die Darkman Die
'95

Daisy von Scherler
Mayer
Party Girl '94

Paul Mayersberg
The Last Samurai '90

Al Maysles
The Beatles: The First U.S.
Visit '91

David Maysles
The Beatles: The First U.S.
Visit '91

Jim McBride
Blood Ties '92
The Wrong Man '93

Michael McCarthy
Thieves of Fortune '89

Peter McCarthy
Floundering '94

Todd McCarthy
Visions of Light: The Art of
Cinematography '93

Gregory McClatchy
Vampire at Midnight '88

Bruce McDonald
Dance Me Outside '95

Rodney McDonald
Night Eyes 2 '91

Ross McElwee
Charleen and Backyard '78
Time Indefinite '93

Mike McGee
Sentinel 2099 '95

Scott McGehee
Suture '93

Scott McGinnis
Caroline at Midnight '93

John McNaughton
Henry: Portrait of a Serial
Killer '90

John McPherson
Incident at Deception Ridge
'94
Incident at Deception Ridge
'94

John McTiernan
Nomads '86

Nancy Meckler
Sister, My Sister '94

Nicholas Medina
Over the Wire '95

Leslie Megahey
The Advocate '93

Alan Mehrez
Bloodsport 2: The Next
Kumite '95

Bill Melendez
The Lion, the Witch and the
Wardrobe '79

George Melford
Dracula (Spanish Version) '31

Christopher Menaul
Fatherland '94

Odorico Mendes
Discretion Assured '93

James Merendino
Terrified '94
Witchcraft 4: Virgin Heart '92

Jalal Merhi
Operation Golden Phoenix '94

Joseph Merhi
Final Impact '91
Last Man Standing '95

George Merriweather
Blondes Have More Guns '95

Alan Metzger
Red Wind '91

Andre Michel
The Sorceress '55

Nikita Mikhalkov
Close to Eden '90

George Miller
Les Patterson Saves the World '90

George Miller
Silver Strand '95

Robert Ellis Miller
Brenda Starr '86

Tom Milo
Smooth Talker '90

Anthony Minghella
Truly, Madly, Deeply '91

Emilio P. Miraglio
Night Eyes '90

Bob Misiorowski
Beyond Forgiveness '94

David Mitchell
Ski School 2 '94
Thunderground '89

Paul Mones
Saints and Sinners '95

Guiliano Montaldo
Time to Kill '89

Jorge Montesi
Bloodknot '95

Charles Philip Moore
Angel of Destruction '94

Simon Moore
Under Suspicion '92

Philippe Mora
Communion '89
Howling II: Your Sister Is a Werewolf '85

Howling III: The Marsupials '87

Andrew Morahan
Highlander: The Final Dimension '94

Christopher Morahan
Paper Mask '91

Louis Morneau
Carnosaur 2 '94

Martin Morris
L.A. Wars '94

Allan Moyle
Empire Records '95
The Gun in Betty Lou's Handbag '92

Richard W. Munchkin
Out for Blood '93
Ring of Fire '91
Ring of Fire 2: Blood and Steel '92
Texas Payback '95

Jag Mundhra
Improper Conduct '94
Irresistible Impulse '95
L.A. Goddess '92
Last Call '90
The Other Woman '92
Sexual Malice '93
Tainted Love '96
Twisted Passion '96
Wild Cactus '92

Ryu Murakami
Tokyo Decadence '91

Scott Murray
Beyond Innocence '87

Floyd Mutrux
There Goes My Baby '92

Ivan Nagy
Skinner '93

Gregory Nava
My Family '94

John Needham
Chuck Amuck: The Movie '91

Hiroshi Negishi
Judge '91

Avi Nesher
Timebomb '91

Martin Newlin
The Crawlers '93

Ted Newsom
Ed Wood: Look Back in Angora '94

Maurizio Nichetti
Volere Volare '92

Ted Nicolaou
Bloodlust: Subspecies 3 '93
Bloodstone: Subspecies 2 '92
Dragonworld '94
Leapin' Leprechauns! '95
Magic in the Mirror '96
Subspecies '90

John Nicolella
Sunset Heat '92

Stephen Norrington
Death Machine '95

Thierry Notz
Fortunes of War '94

Phillip Noyce
Echoes of Paradise '86

Victor Nunez
Ruby in Paradise '93

Roger Nygard
Tales of the Unknown '90

Luciano Odorisio
Sacrilege '86

Marty Ollstein
Dangerous Love '87

William Olsen
After School '88

David O'Malley
Easy Wheels '89

Mario Orfini
Fair Game '89

Gary Orona
The Bikini Car Wash Company 2 '92
Great Bikini Off-Road Adventure '94
Stripshow '95

Aaron Osborne
Caged Heat 3000 '95
Zarkorr! The Invader '96

Mamoru Oshii
Ghost in the Shell '95

Nagisa Oshima
In the Realm of the Senses '76

Dominique Othenin-Girard
Beyond Desire '94
Night Angel '90
Private Lessons, Another Story '94

Katsuhiro Otomo
Akira '87
Roujin Z '95

Sakae Ozawa
The Street Fighter '75

Anders Palm
Dead Certain '92

Phedon Papamichael
Dark Side of Genius '94
Sketch Artist '92

Nick Park
The Wrong Trousers '93

Alan Parker
Come See the Paradise '90

Trey Parker
Cannibal! The Musical '96

Eric Parkinson
Future Shock '93

Larry Parr
A Soldier's Tale '91

Michael Paseornek
Vibrations '94

Ivan Passer
Haunted Summer '88

Steven Paul
Eternity '90

Stuart Paul
Fate '90

George Pavlou
Transmutations '85

Michael Pavone
Chameleon '95

Alexander Payne
Inside Out '92

Dave Payne
Alien Terminator '95
Criminal Hearts '95

Sam Peckinpah
The Wild Bunch '69

Sean Penn
The Crossing Guard '94

Victor Salva
Nature of the Beast '94

Coke Sams
Ernest Goes to School '94

Stuart Samuels
Visions of Light: The Art of
Cinematography '93

Cirio H. Santiago
Caged Heat 2: Stripped of
Freedom '94

Deran Sarafian
To Die for '89

Joseph Sargent
Passion Flower '86

Marina Sargenti
Mirror, Mirror '90

Vic Sarin
Cold Comfort '90

Oley Sassone
Future Shock '93
Playback '95

Ernest G. Sauer
Beauty School '93
Bikini Bistro '94
Broadcast Bombshells '95

Carlos Saura
Outrage '93

Eric Schaeffer
My Life's in Turnaround '94

Carl Schenkel
The Surgeon '94

Richard Schenkman
The Pompatus of Love '96

Eric L. Schlagman
Punch the Clock '90

David Schmoeller
Netherworld '90
Puppet Master '89

Michael Schroeder
Cover Me '95
The Glass Cage '96

**David Jean
Schweitzer**
No More Dirty Deals '94

George C. Scott
Descending Angel '90

Michael Scott
Dangerous Heart '93

Ladykiller '92
Sharon's Secret '95

Ridley Scott
Blade Runner '82

T.J. Scott
TC 2000 '93

**Screaming Mad
George**
The Guyver '91

Beverly Sebastian
The American Angels:
Baptism of Blood '89
Gator Bait 2: Cajun Justice
'88
Running Cool '93

Ferd Sebastian
The American Angels:
Baptism of Blood '89
Gator Bait 2: Cajun Justice
'88
Running Cool '93

Mike Sedan
Lap Dancing '95
Married People, Single Sex
'93

Stu Segall
Illegal in Blue '95

Arthur Seldelman
Body Language '92

Susan Seidelman
Tales of Erotica '96

Arnaud Selignac
Northern Passage '95

Yahoo Serious
Reckless Kelly '93

Phillip Setbon
Mr. Frost '89

Dirk Shafer
Man of the Year '96

Deborah Shames
Cabin Fever '93
The Hottest Bid '95
The Voyeur '94

Richard Shepard
Inside Out '92

Arthur Sherman
Spy Trap '92

Gary Sherman
Lisa '90

Frank Shields
Project: Alien '89

Stanley Shiff
Lobster Man from Mars '89

Rhoydon Shishido
Toto: Lost in New York '96

Jack Sholder
Sketch Artist 2: Hands That
See '94

Mina Shum
Double Happiness '94

Mussef Sibay
A Woman, Her Men and Her
Futon '92

Andy Sidaris
Do or Die '91
Guns '90
Hard Ticket to Hawaii '87
Malibu Express '85
Picasso Trigger '89
Savage Beach '89

Drew Sidaris
The Dallas Connection '94

David Siegel
Suture '93

Andrew Silver
Return '88

Ron Silver
Litepod '93

**Lawrence L.
Simeone**
Blindfold: Acts of Obsession
'94

Adam Simon
Body Chemistry 2: Voice of a
Stranger '91
Carnosaur '93

J. Piquer Simon
Endless Descent '90

Jane Simpson
Number One Fan '94

Michael A. Simpson
Fast Food '89

Bryan Singer
Public Access '93

Gail Singer
Wisecracks '93

Bruce Sinofsky
Brother's Keeper '92

Gary Sinyor
Solitaire for 2 '96

Yuri Sivo
Inside Out 2 '92
Mortal Sins '90

John Sjogren
The Mosaic Project '95

George Sluizer
The Vanishing '88

Mel Smith
The Tall Guy '89

Roy Allen Smith
The Land Before Time 2: The
Great Valley Adventure
'94
The Land Before Time 3: The
Time of the Great Giving
'95
The Land Before Time 4:
Journey Through the Mists
'96

Alan Smithee
Fatal Charm '92
I Love N.Y. '87
Raging Angels '95
The Shrimp on the Barbie '90

Stephen Smoke
Final Impact '91

Steven Soderbergh
King of the Hill '93
The Underneath '95

Ola Solum
The Polar Bear King '94

Dror Soref
The Seventh Coin '92

Colin South
In Too Deep '90

Benton Spencer
Blown Away '93
The Club '94

Robert Spera
Witchcraft '88

Tony Spiridakis
The Last Word '95

Tim Spring
Reason to Die '90

Peter Spry-Leverton
Mysteries of Peru '93

Richard Stanley
Dust Devil '93

Video Premieres

399

Video Premieres

Terminal Impact '95

Peter Wells
Desperate Remedies '93

Wim Wenders
Until the End of the World '91

John Wentworth
Inside Out 2 '92

Lina Wertmuller
Ciao, Professore! '94

Jim Wheat
After Midnight '89

Ken Wheat
After Midnight '89

David Wickes
Jekyll and Hyde '90

Billy Wilder
Avanti! '72
Kiss Me, Stupid! '64

Paul W. Williams
Mirage '94

S.S. Wilson
Tremors 2: Aftershocks '96

Jonathan Winfrey
Bloodfist 7: Manhunt '94
Excessive Force 2: Force on
Force '95
New Crime City: Los Angeles
2020 '94

Gary Winick
Out of the Rain '90

Terence H. Winkless
Bloodfist '89
The Nest '88
Not of This Earth '96

David Winters
Space Mutiny '88

Doris Wishman
Deadly Weapons '70

Stephen Withrow
Friends, Lovers & Lunatics '89

Kirk Wong
Organized Crime & Triad
Bureau '93

John Woo
A Better Tomorrow '86
Hard-Boiled '92
The Killer '90

Mark Woods
Witchcraft 2: The Temptress
'90

John Woodward
Neurotic Cabaret '90

Jeff Woolnough
First Degree '95

Aaron Worth
9 1/2 Ninjas '90

Alexander Wright
Fast Money '96

Geoffrey Wright
Romper Stomper '92

David Wyles
Man with a Gun '95

Jim Wynorski
Body Chemistry 3: Point of
Seduction '93
Body Chemistry 4: Full
Exposure '95
Dinosaur Island '93
Hard Bounty '94
Hard to Die '90
Not of This Earth '88
The Return of Swamp Thing
'89
Sorceress '94
Transylvania Twist '89

Greg Yaitanes
Hard Justice '95

Kazuo Yamazaki
A Wind Named Amnesia '93

Bob Yari
Mind Games '89

Brook Yeaton
Ice '93

Yaky Yosha
Sexual Response '92

Hiroaki Yoshida
Iron Maze '91

Ronny Yu
The Bride with White Hair
'93

Brian Yuzna
Bride of Re-Animator '89
H. P. Lovecraft's
Necronomicon: Book of
the Dead '96

Rafal Zeilinski
Ginger Ale Afternoon '89

Barry Zetlin
The Dogfighters '95

Howard Ziehm
Flesh Gordon 2: Flesh
Gordon Meets the Cosmic
Cheerleaders '90

Rafal Zielinksi
Jailbait '93

Paul Ziller
Back in Action '94

Karl Zwicky
Contagion '87
Vicious '88

Some dogs play fetch, some bury bones...the VideoHound spends his time thinking up new and unusual ways to categorize movies. In addition to classifications you'd expect, like "Action Adventure," "Comedy," and "Erotic Thrillers," the Hound offers categories such as "Bad Hair Days," "John Woo Wannabes," and "Snakes in the Toilet." You were looking for a movie (or two) that had snakes in a toilet, weren't you? The Hound knew you were.

Video Premieres

Category Index

How to Get Ahead in
Advertising
Meet the Feebles
Miracle Mile
Muriel's Wedding
Parents
Repo Man
Riff Raff
Swimming with Sharks
Transylvania Twist
White

Blindness
See also Physical Problems
Alligator Eyes
The Killer
Sketch Artist 2: Hands That
See
Until the End of the World

Bloody Mayhem
See also Horror
The Art of Dying
The Banker
Basket Case 2
Cannibal! The Musical
Dangerous Game
Dawn of the Dead
Death Magic
Death Spa
Dollman Vs. Demonic Toys
Hard-Boiled
The Hidden 2
Howling IV: The Original
Nightmare
The Killer
The Lawnmower Man
Masque of the Red Death
Meet the Feebles
Night of the Demons
Overexposed
Phantom of the Mall: Eric's
Revenge
Queen Margot
Re-Animator
Shadowzone
Skinner
TC 2000
The Toxic Avenger
Tromeo & Juliet
Vicious
Welcome to Spring Break
The Wicked
The Wild Bunch
Xtro

Boating
See Sail Away

Bringing Up Baby
See also Parenthood;
Pregnant Pauses
Almost Pregnant

Cheyenne Warrior
Jack and Sarah
Monika

Buddies
A Better Tomorrow
Crime Lords
Digger
Dragonworld
Galaxies Are Colliding
The Mosaic Project
Once Upon a Time in
America
Phat Beach
The Pompatus of Love
The Return of the
Musketeers
Saints and Sinners
The Search for One-Eyed
Jimmy
Showdown in Little Tokyo
Trees Lounge
True Colors
Warrior Spirit
Wrestling Ernest Hemingway

Buses
Heart and Souls
Incident at Deception Ridge

Campus Capers
See also Hell High School;
School Daze
Adventures in Spying
American Tiger
Deadly Possession
I Don't Buy Kisses Anymore
Knock Outs
Oleanna
Rush Week
Sensation
Slipping into Darkness
Voodoo
Wavelength

Canada
See also Cold Spots
Blood Relations
Cold Comfort
Cross Country
Dance Me Outside
Eddie and the Cruisers 2:
Eddie Lives!

Cannibalism
See also Edibles; Horror
Cannibal! The Musical
Cannibal Women in the
Avocado Jungle of Death
The Cook, the Thief, His Wife
& Her Lover
Dawn of the Dead

The Further Adventures of
Tennessee Buck
Parents
Slave Girls from Beyond
Infinity

Carnivals &
Circuses
Freakshow
Luther the Geek
Outrage
When Night Is Falling

Cave People
After School
Dinosaur Island
When Dinosaurs Ruled the
Earth

Central
America/South
America
At Play in the Fields of the
Lord
Diplomatic Immunity
Discretion Assured
The Dolphin
Exposure
The Fable of the Beautiful
Pigeon Fancier
Johnny 100 Pesos
The Last Movie
Romero
The Summer of Miss Forbes
Wild Orchid

Chases
See also Road Trip
Criminal Hearts
Fast Money
The Getaway
Hard Bounty
No More Dirty Deals
Sex, Love and Cold Hard
Cash
Trouble Bound
Until the End of the World

Childhood Visions
Digger
Jack Be Nimble
King of the Hill
Parents

Children
See Animation & Cartoons;
Childhood Visions

China
See also Asia
The Killer
M. Butterfly
Temptation of a Monk

Christmas
See also Holidays
Elves
La Pastorela
Lily in Winter
A Midnight Clear

CIA
See Feds; Spies & Espionage

Circuses
See Carnivals & Circuses

City Lights
See Berlin; L.A.; London;
Miami; New Orleans; New
York, New York; Paris; San
Francisco; Tokyo; Urban
Drama; Viva Las Vegas!

Classic Horror
See also Horror; Horror
Anthologies
Cronos
Dracula (Spanish Version)
Haunted Summer
The House of Usher
Masque of the Red Death
The Pit & the Pendulum

Cold Spots
Pathfinder
Winter People

Cold War
See Red Scare

Comedy
See also Black Comedy;
Comedy Drama; Comic
Adventure; Horror
Comedy; Musical Comedy;
Romantic Comedy; Satire
& Parody; Slapstick
Comedy; Sports Comedies;
Western Comedy
Across the Moon
Amanda and the Alien
...And God Spoke
Android
Based on an Untrue Story
Beauty School
Bikini Bistro
The Bikini Car Wash
Company 2
Bikini Drive-In
Bikini Summer
Blondes Have More Guns
Bottle Rocket
Bound and Gagged: A Love
Story
Ciao, Professore!
Dead Funny

Sweet Poison
Temptation of a Monk
There Goes My Baby
32 Short Films about Glenn
    Gould
Tiger Warsaw
The Tigress
Time to Kill
Tokyo Decadence
Tollbooth
Treacherous
Trees Lounge
True Colors
The Vanishing
The Voyeur
The Wharf Rat
Where the Rivers Flow
    North
White
Wild Orchid
Wild Orchid 2: Two Shades of
    Blue
A Woman, Her Men and Her
    Futon
Wrestling Ernest Hemingway
The Young Americans
Zandalee

Dream Girls

Beauty School
Bikini Bistro
The Bikini Car Wash
    Company
The Bikini Car Wash
    Company 2
Bikini Drive In
Bikini Summer
Blondes Have More Guns
Burial of the Rats
Cover Me
Deadly Weapons
Do or Die
Dr. Alien
Fate
Femme Fontaine: Killer Babe
    for the C.I.A.
Forbidden Zone: Alien
    Abduction
Ghosts Can't Do It
Great Bikini Off-Road
    Adventure
Guns
Masseuse
Mirror Images
Mirror Images 2
Naked Souls
Party Incorporated
Phat Beach
Posed for Murder
Priceless Beauty
Private Affairs
Savage Beach

Ski School 2
Thieves of Fortune
To the Limit
Undercover
When Dinosaurs Ruled the
    Earth
Wishful Thinking
Young Nurses in Love

Drugs
See Pill Poppin'

Eating
See Cannibalism; Edibles

Eco-Vengeance!
See also Killer Bugs & Slugs
Body Snatchers
The Crawlers
Idaho Transfer
The Toxic Avenger

Edibles
See also Cannibalism
Bikini Bistro
The Cook, the Thief, His Wife
    & Her Lover
9 1/2 Weeks

Erotic Thrillers
See also Sex & Sexuality
Animal Instincts 2
Animal Instincts 3: The
    Seductress
Beyond Desire
Blindfold: Acts of Obsession
Blown Away
Body Chemistry 3: Point of
    Seduction
Body Chemistry 4: Full
    Exposure
Body of Influence
Body Shot
Body Strokes
Broken Trust
Caroline at Midnight
Cold Sweat
Color of Night
Criminal Passion
The Dangerous
Dangerous Indiscretion
Dangerous Touch
The Dark Dancer
Dark Secrets
Dark Tide
Dead Cold
Dead On
Desire
Discretion Assured
Ebbtide
Embrace of the Vampire
Fatal Instinct
Fatal Past

Hourglass
I Like to Play Games
Illegal in Blue
Illicit Behavior
Illicit Dreams
Improper Conduct
In a Moment of Passion
Killer Looks
Killing for Love
Lady in Waiting
Lipstick Camera
Love Is a Gun
The Man in the Attic
Midnight Tease
Midnight Tease 2
Mirror Images
Mirror Images 2
Night Eyes
Night Eyes 2
Night Eyes 3
The Nightman
Outside the Law
Over the Wire
Payback
Playback
Poison Ivy 2: Lily
Private Obsession
Running Wild
Saturday Night Special
Save Me
Secret Games
Secret Games 2: The Escort
Secret Games 3
Sexual Malice
Showgirl Murders
Sinful Intrigue
Sins of the Night
Snapdragon
Stormswept
Strike a Pose
Suite 16
Sunset Grill
Sweet Killing
Temptation
Temptress
Terrified
Trade Off
Undercover
Wild Cactus

Ethics & Morals
A Dangerous Woman
Fortunes of War
Twenty-One

Evil Doctors
See also Doctors & Nurses;
    Mad Scientists
Dr. Alien
Jekyll and Hyde
Paper Mask
The Surgeon

Experimental
See Avant-Garde

Exploitation
See also Sexploitation
Last Call
Malibu Express
Overexposed
Party Incorporated
Sleazemania
Suite 16
Young Lady Chatterley
Young Lady Chatterley 2

Family Ties
See also Fractured Family
    Values; Moms; Parenthood
Almost Dead
Angel of Destruction
Avanti!
Bad Blood
Based on an Untrue Story
Basket Case 2
Beau Pere
Blood In...Blood Out: Bound
    by Honor
Blood Relations
Blood Ties
Bloodknot
Blue
Breathing Fire
The Bride with White Hair
Broken Trust
Brother's Keeper
Castle Freak
Cellblock Sisters: Banished
    Behind Bars
Class of '61
Close to Eden
Cold Comfort
Communion
The Criminal Mind
The Crossing Guard
Demonstone
Desperate Remedies
Digger
Double Happiness
Ed and His Dead Mother
Electra
The Expert
Eyes of an Angel
The Feud
Friend of the Family
Ghosts Can't Do It
Golden Gate
The Hawk
Innocent Lies
Jack Be Nimble
Jamon, Jamon
King of the Hill
The Last Hit
Leapin' Leprechauns!

Category Index

Body Chemistry 3: Point of
    Seduction
Chuck Amuck: The Movie
Document of the Dead
Ed Wood: Look Back in
    Angora
84 Charlie Mopic
George Stevens: A
    Filmmaker's Journey
In a Moment of Passion
Intervista
Mute Witness
My Life's in Turnaround
Swimming with Sharks
Understudy: The Graveyard
    Shift 2
Visions of Light: The Art of
    Cinematography

Flashback
Carried Away
Liebestraum
Nina Takes a Lover
Reservoir Dogs
The Underneath
The Wild Bunch

Flight
See Airborne

Flower Children
Dead Beat
There Goes My Baby

Flying Saucers
See also Alien Beings—
    Benign; Alien Beings—
    Vicious
Moral Code
Invader
Out There

Folklore &
    Mythology
Leapin' Leprechauns!
Pathfinder
The Phoenix and the Magic
    Carpet

Food
See Edibles

Foreign Intrigue
See also Spies & Espionage
American Roulette
The Experts
Exposure

Fractured Family
    Values
Jack Be Nimble
Meet the Feebles
Meet the Hollowheads
Parents

Frame-Ups
Another Pair of Aces: Three
    of a Kind
Fleshtone
Linda
Sunset Heat
The Wrong Man

France
See also Paris
The Advocate
Jefferson in Paris
La Vie de Boheme
Madame Bovary
Queen Margot
Sister, My Sister
Suite 16

Friendship
See Buddies

Front Page
See also Mass Media;
    Shutterbugs
Brenda Starr
Caroline at Midnight
Dark Side of Genius
Dead Air
Demonstone
Eternity
Fatherland
Istanbul
The Last Word
Night Hunter
Nina Takes a Lover
The Other Woman
The Wharf Rat

Fugitives
See also Lovers on the Lam
Bloodfist 7: Manhunt
A Boy Called Hate
Cyber-Tracker 2
Hold Me, Thrill Me, Kiss Me
Suspect Device
The Wrong Man

Gambling
See also Viva Las Vegas!
Eyes of an Angel
Inside Out
Little Vegas
Living to Die
Showgirls
29th Street
The Underneath

Gangs
See also Crime & Criminals;
    Organized Crime
A Better Tomorrow
Blood In...Blood Out: Bound
    by Honor

The Gunrunner
Jungleground
Men of Respect
Mob Boss
Showdown in Little Tokyo

Gays
See also AIDS; Bisexuality;
    Gender Bending; Lesbians
Joey Breaker
Man of the Year
Priest

Gender Bending
See also Gays; Lesbians; Role
    Reversal
M. Butterfly
Mascara

Generation X
Bottle Rocket
Don't Do It
Floundering
Party Girl
S.F.W.

Genetics
See also Mad Scientists
Biohazard: The Alien Force
Tomcat: Dangerous Desires

Genies
Aladdin and the King of
    Thieves
Priceless Beauty
The Return of Jafar
Wildest Dreams

Genre Spoofs
See also Satire & Parody
Based on an Untrue Story
Blondes Have More Guns
Cannibal! The Musical
Ferocious Female Freedom
    Fighters
Mob Boss
Repossessed
Tromeo & Juliet

Ghosts, Ghouls, &
    Goblins
See also Death & the
    Afterlife; Demons &
    Wizards; Occult
The Club
Cold Sweat
The Dark
Death Magic
Fatally Yours
The Forgotten One
Ghosts Can't Do It
Haunted
Heart and Souls
Lurking Fear

Phantasm III: Lord of the
    Dead
Soultaker
Stormswept
Younger & Younger

Giants
See also Monsters, General
Beanstalk
Kung Fu Rascals
Tremors 2: Aftershocks

Grand Hotel
The Girl with the Hungry
    Eyes
Suite 16
Wings of Fame

Great Britain
See also London
Haunted
Lipstick on Your Collar
Riff Raff
Scandal
Shopping
The Young Americans

Great Depression
King of the Hill
Long Road Home
Winter People

Great Escapes
See also Men in Prison; War,
    General; Women in Prison
Hostile Intentions
The Last Samurai
Sweet Poison
Teresa's Tattoo
Texas Payback
Venus Rising

Growing Older
See also Death & the
    Afterlife; Late Bloomin'
    Love
Ebony Tower
Pushing Hands
Queens Logic
The Wild Bunch
Wrestling Ernest Hemingway

Guilty Pleasures
Animal Instincts
The Banker
Beach Babes fro Beyond
Body of Influence
Dial Help
Femalien
Friend of the Family
Hard Ticket to Hawaii
I Like to Play Games
In a Moment of Passion
Meridian: Kiss of the Beast

411

Video Premieres

Mad Scientists

See also Inventors &
  Inventions; Science &
  Scientists
Alien Terminator
Brenda Starr
Bride of Re-Animator
Darkman 2: The Return of
  Durant
Darkman 3: Die Darkman Die
Deep Red
Frankenhooker
Jekyll and Hyde
The Lawnmower Man
Mr. Stitch
The Mosaic Project
Naked Souls
Re-Animator
Red Blooded American Girl
Tammy and the T-Rex
Transmutations

Made for Television

See TV Movies

Mafia

See Organized Crime

Magic

See also Genies; Occult
Death Magic
Doctor Mordrid: Master of
  the Unknown
Quicker Than the Eye
Wizards of the Demon Sword

Marriage

See also Divorce; Otherwise
  Engaged; War Between the
  Sexes; Wedding Bells;
  Wedding Hell
Backstreet Dreams
Bedroom Eyes 2
Blindfold: Acts of Obsession
Blue in the Face
Body Chemistry
China Moon
Dead On
Desperate Remedies
Don't Talk to Strangers
Dream Lover
Faces
Femme Fatale
Fever
The Hawk
Husbands and Lovers
Linda
Love, Cheat & Steal
Love Matters
Madame Bovary
Muriel's Wedding
The New Age

Nina Takes a Lover
One Good Turn
The Paint Job
Paris, France
A Passion to Kill
Pushing Hands
Queen Margot
Red Rock West
Season of Fear
Sexual Malice
Sketch Artist
Sweet Poison
Till the End of the Night
Trade Off
The Tunnel
Younger & Younger

Martial Arts

Back in Action
Bloodfist
Bloodfist 2
Bloodfist 7: Manhunt
Bloodsport 2: The Next
  Kumite
Breathing Fire
The Bride with White Hair
Cyber Ninja
The Executioners
Ferocious Female Freedom
  Fighters
Final Impact
The Heroic Trio
Kung Fu Rascals
The Mosaic Project
Night Hunter
9 1/2 Ninjas
Operation Golden Phoenix
Out for Blood
Ring of Fire
Ring of Fire 2: Blood and
  Steel
Ring of Fire 3: Lion Strike
Showdown in Little Tokyo
The Street Fighter
Sword of Honor
Wing Chun
Without Mercy

Mass Media

See also Front Page; Radio
Dennis Potter: The Last
  Interview
Eternity
Lipstick Camera
S.F.W.

Medieval Romps

See also Historical Drama;
  Period Piece
The Magic Sword
Stealing Heaven
The Warrior & the Sorceress

Wizards of the Demon Sword

Meltdown

Miracle Mile
TC 2000
Young Lady Chatterley 2

Men

See Macho Men; War
  Between the Sexes

Men in Prison

See also Fugitives; Great
  Escapes; Women in Prison
Bloodsport 2: The Next
  Kumite
Caged Heat 2: Stripped of
  Freedom
Dead Right
Hard Justice
Mr. Frost
Moon 44
New Crime City: Los Angeles
  2020
Payback

Mental Retardation

See also Physical Problems
A Dangerous Woman
Slipping into Darkness

Miami

See also American South
American Tiger
Fires Within
The Girl with the Hungry
  Eyes
Radio Inside

Miners & Mining

Backlash: Oblivion 2
Cannibal! The Musical
Unknown Origin

Missing Persons

See also Hostage!;
  Kidnapped!
Night of the Cyclone
The Search for One-Eyed
  Jimmy
The Vanishing

Mistaken Identity

See also Gender Bending;
  Role Reversal
Amore!
Body Snatchers
Deconstructing Sarah
The Gun in Betty Lou's
  Handbag
Landslide
Lisa
The Nutt House
Paper Mask

Red Rock West
Suture

Mr. Right

The Baby Doll Murders
Blindfold: Acts of Obsession
Blue Desert
Body of Influence
Criminal Passion
Fatal Charm
Ladykiller
Lisa
Mr. Frost
The Paint Job
Skinner
True Crime

Modern Cowboys

See also Western Comedy;
  Westerns
Another Pair of Aces: Three
  of a Kind
Powwow Highway
Texas Payback

Modern
Shakespeare

Men of Respect
Ring of Fire
Tromeo & Juliet

Moms

See also Bad Dads;
  Parenthood
A Mother's Prayer
Rumpelstiltskin

Monsters, General

See also Ghosts, Ghouls, &
  Goblins; Giants; Killer
  Bugs & Slugs; Killer Plants;
  Killer Reptiles; Killer
  Rodents; Killer Sea
  Critters; Killer Toys; Mad
  Scientists; Robots &
  Androids; Vampires;
  Werewolves; Zombies
The Dark
Demonstone
Dragonworld
Mirror, Mirror
Scream Dream
Shadowzone
Subspecies
Transmutations
Watchers

Motor Vehicle Dept.

See also Bikers
Fast Money
Punch the Clock
Repo Man

413

Video Premieres

The Glass Cage
Storyville
A Streetcar Named Desire:
    The Original Director's
    Version
Thunderground

New York, New York
Blue in the Face
Dead Funny
King of New York
Lonely in America
9 1/2 Weeks
Once Upon a Time in
    America
Party Girl
The Pompatus of Love
29th Street

New Zealand
See Down Under

Newspapers
See Front Page

Nightclubs
Animal Instincts
Bar Girls
Black Rose of Harlem
Dark Secrets
Party Girl
Showgirls

Ninjitsu
See Martial Arts

Nuclear Disaster
See Meltdown

Nuns & Priests
See also Religion
After School
Last Rites
Priest

Nursploitation!
See also Doctors & Nurses;
    Sexploitation
Inner Sanctum
Young Nurses in Love

Occult
See also Demons & Wizards;
    Satanism; Witchcraft
Black Magic Woman
Fright House
The Girl in a Swing
I'm Dangerous Tonight
Into the Badlands
Judge
Mirror, Mirror
Mirror, Mirror 2: Raven
    Dance

Phantasm III: Lord of the
    Dead
Puppet Master
Repossessed
Return
Satan's Princess
Sensation
Shock 'Em Dead
The Spellbinder
Temptress
Witchboard 3: The
    Possession
Witchcraft
Witchcraft 2: The Temptress
Witchcraft 3: The Kiss of
    Death
Witchcraft 4: Virgin Heart
Witchcraft 5: Dance with the
    Devil
Witchcraft 6: The Devil's
    Mistress
Witchcraft 7: Judgement
    Hour
Witchcraft 8: Salem's Ghost

Oldest Profession
See also Women in Prison
Alexa: A Prostitute's Own
    Story
Beyond Desire
Boulevard
Cross Country
Frankenhooker
Hard Bounty
Heidi Fleiss: Hollywood
    Madam
High Stakes
Impulse
Jamon, Jamon
Lady in Waiting
Reason to Die
Secret Games
Sex, Love and Cold Hard
    Cash
The Silencer
Tokyo Decadence
Twin Sisters
Wild Orchid 2: Two Shades of
    Blue

The Olympics
See also Sports Dramas
16 Days of Glory: Parts 1
    and 2

On the Rocks
See also Pill Poppin'
The Crossing Guard
Jack and Sarah
Once Were Warriors
Trees Lounge

Only the Lonely
Even Hitler Had a Girlfriend
The Gun in Betty Lou's
    Handbag
Inside Out
Luther the Geek
Primal Secrets
The Rachel Papers
Someone to Love
Wildest Dreams

Order in the Court
See also Justice Prevails...?;
    Law & Lawyers
Body Chemistry 4: Full
    Exposure
The Conviction
Rampage

Organized Crime
See also Crime & Criminals;
    Disorganized Crime; Gangs
American Yakuza
Ballistic
Black Rose of Harlem
Capone
The Criminal Mind
Darkman 3: Die Darkman Die
Deadly Weapons
Excessive Force
Fatal Past
Fatally Yours
Fist of Honor
Hard-Boiled
High Stakes
Hit the Dutchman
Ice
In the Kingdom of the Blind
    the Man with One Eye Is
    King
Kill Me Again
The Killer
L.A. Wars
Last Rites
The Last Word
Little Vegas
Man with a Gun
Me and the Mob
Men of Respect
Mob Boss
Once Upon a Time in
    America
Organized Crime & Triad
    Bureau
Remote Control
Ring of Fire 3: Lion Strike
Sex, Love and Cold Hard
    Cash
The Takeover
To the Limit

Otherwise Engaged
See also Romantic Triangles;
    Wedding Bells; Wedding
    Hell
Fandango
Running Wild

Painting
See Art & Artists

Parenthood
See also Bad Dads; Bringing
    Up Baby; Moms
Innocent Victim
Jack and Sarah
Parents

Paris
See also France
Jefferson in Paris
La Vie de Boheme

Party Hell
See also Horror
The Club
Night of the Demons

Peculiar Partners
See also Buddies; Cops
The Hidden 2
Theodore Rex

Period Piece
See also Historical Drama;
    Medieval Romps; Royalty
The Advocate
Bix
Brenda Starr
Century
Dead Beat
Desperate Remedies
Dillinger and Capone
Fall Time
Fatherland
Five Corners
Golden Gate
Haunted
Haunted Summer
Hit the Dutchman
Innocent Lies
The Journey of August King
King of the Hill
Lily in Winter
M. Butterfly
Madame Bovary
The Man in the Attic
Once Upon a Time in
    America
The Power of One
Rapa Nui
The Return of the
    Musketeers
Sister, My Sister

415

Video Premieres

Temptation of a Monk
The Tigress
Where the Rivers Flow
  North

Phone Terror
Dial Help
Lisa
Smooth Talker

Photography
See Shutterbugs

Physical Problems
See also Blindness; Mental
  Retardation
Mute Witness
Suite 16
Treacherous
Vibrations

Pill Poppin'
See also On the Rocks
Adventures in Spying
Back in Action
Baja
Blood In...Blood Out: Bound
  by Honor
Caroline at Midnight
Cartel
Coldfire
A Cop for the Killing
Dangerous Heart
Darkman 3: Die Darkman Die
Delta Heat
Edge of Sanity
Exposure
Fever
Hard Evidence
Haunted Summer
Intent to Kill
Jekyll and Hyde
L.627
L.A. Wars
Mindfield
One False Move
Out of the Rain
Red Blooded American Girl
Saints and Sinners
Shameless
Shotgun
Showdown in Little Tokyo
Sunset Heat
Tough and Deadly
Transmutations
Trouble in Paradise
Twenty-One
The Young Americans

**Books to Film: Edgar
  Allan Poe**
The House of Usher
Masque of the Red Death

The Pit & the Pendulum

Politics
See also Presidency
Animal Instincts
Demonstone
Eye of the Stranger
Fires Within
Jefferson in Paris
M. Butterfly
Pizza Man
Rain Without Thunder
The Real Richard Nixon
The Secret Files of J. Edgar
  Hoover
Storyville
Temptation of a Monk

Post Apocalypse
See also Technology—
  Rampant
Circuitry Man
Nemesis
Plughead Rewired: Circuitry
  Man 2
Star Quest
Steel Frontier

Pregnant Pauses
See also Bringing Up Baby
Almost Pregnant
Lily Was Here

Presidency
See also Politics
Four Days in November
In the Blood
Jefferson in Paris
The Real Richard Nixon

Price of Fame
See also Rags to Riches
Eddie and the Cruisers
Eddie and the Cruisers 2:
  Eddie Lives!
Goodnight, Sweet Marilyn
True Colors

Prison
See Great Escapes; Men in
  Prison; Women in Prison

Prostitutes
See Oldest Profession

Psychiatry
See Shrinks

Psycho-Thriller
See also Mystery & Suspense
After Midnight
Alligator Eyes
Almost Dead
Apartment Zero

The Art of Dying
Black Day Blue Night
Bloodknot
Body Chemistry 2: Voice of a
  Stranger
The Courtyard
The Crew
Dangerous Touch
Deconstructing Sarah
Desperate Prey
Don't Talk to Strangers
Dream Lover
Fair Game
Fatally Yours
Haunted
Jack Be Nimble
Killer Inside Me
Lady in Waiting
Laser Moon
Love, Cheat & Steal
Love Is a Gun
The Maddening
Midnight Tease
Mind Games
Mortal Sins
Nature of the Beast
The Night of the Following
  Day
Night Train to Venice
Number One Fan
One Good Turn
Outrage
The Paint Job
A Passion to Kill
Peeping Tom
Poison Ivy
Posed for Murder
Reason to Die
Secret Games
Secret Games 2: The Escort
Secret Games 3
Sensation
Separate Lives
Sharon's Secret
Snapdragon
Stripteaser
Suture
Sweet Killing
Terrified
Till the End of the Night
Timebomb
Tunnel Vision
Twisted Love
The Vanishing

**Psychotics/
  Sociopaths**
Don't Talk to Strangers
Killer Inside Me
Live Wire
One Good Turn
Play Nice

Poison Ivy
Rampage
Reservoir Dogs
The Silencer
Skinner
Stripteaser
Ted & Venus
Tetsuo: The Iron Man

Puppets
See also Killer Toys
Meet the Feebles
Puppet Master
Puppet Master 2

Queens
See Royalty

Race Against Time
Grand Tour: Disaster in Time
Somebody Has to Shoot the
  Picture

Radio
See also Mass Media
Dead Air
Laser Moon
Night Rhythms
Sexual Response

Rags to Riches
See also Price of Fame;
  Wrong Side of the Tracks
A Million to Juan
The Tall Guy
White

Rape
Blue Desert
Caged Heat 2: Stripped of
  Freedom
Forbidden Sun
Outrage
Positive I.D.
Showgirls
Sketch Artist 2: Hands That
  See
Streets
Time to Kill

**Ready for Mystery
  Science Theater
  3000**
Girl with the Hungry Eyes
Plughead Rewired: Circuitry
  Man 2
Raging Angels
Rapa Nui
Shadowzone
Shock 'Em Dead
Skyscraper
Space Mutiny
Unknown Origin

417

Video Premieres

Category Index

Category Index

Video Premieres

Mr. Frost
Mr. Stitch
A Passion to Kill
Red Wind
Sharon's Secret
Silent Fall

Shutterbugs
See also Front Page
Adventures in Spying
Body Shot
Lipstick Camera
Love & Murder
Love Is a Gun
Out There
Peeping Tom
Portraits of a Killer
Private Lessons, Another
    Story
Somebody Has to Shoot the
    Picture
Sunset Heat
Temptress
A Time to Die
Under Suspicion
Until the End of the World

Sixties
See Flower Children

Slapstick Comedy
See also Comedy
Ernest Goes to School
The Feud
Reckless Kelly

Slavery
Dragonard
Jefferson in Paris
The Journey of August King
The Silencer

Slice of Life
See also America's
    Heartland; True Stories
Arizona Dream
Blueberry Hill
Dance Me Outside
A Dangerous Woman
Double Happiness
Five Corners
How U Like Me Now?
I Don't Buy Kisses Anymore
My Family
The New Age
Once Were Warriors
Priest
Queens Logic
Riff Raff
Rosalie Goes Shopping
The Search for One-Eyed
    Jimmy
Trees Lounge

29th Street

Snakes
See also Snakes in the Toilet;
    Wild Kingdom
Curse 2: The Bite
Hard Ticket to Hawaii
Phantom of the Mall: Eric's
    Revenge

Snakes in the Toilet
Hard Ticket to Hawaii
Phantom of the Mall: Eric's
    Revenge

Special FX
Extravaganzas
Aliens, Dragons, Monsters &
    Me: The Fantasy Film
    World of Ray Harryhausen
Blade Runner
Darkman 2: The Return of
    Durant
Darkman 3: Die Darkman Die
Dawn of the Dead
Highlander: The Final
    Dimension

Spies & Espionage
See also Feds; Foreign
    Intrigue; Terrorism
Adventures in Spying
Bad Company
The Emporte
Hard Ticket to Hawaii
Lipstick Camera
M. Butterfly
Mindfield
Picasso Trigger
Spitfire
Spy Trap
Young Nurses in Love

Sports
See also The Olympics;
    Sports Comedies
A Matter of Honor
The Power of One
Thunderground

Sports Comedies
The Man with the Perfect
    Swing
Ski School
Ski School 2
Slam Dunk Ernest

Books to Film: Bram
Stoker
Burial of the Rats
Dracula (Spanish Version)

Strained Suburbia
Adventures in Spying

The Crude Oasis
Don't Talk to Strangers
Parents

Strippers
The Dark Dancer
The Glass Cage
Lap Dancing
The Last Word
Midnight Tease
Midnight Tease 2
Showgirl Murders
Showgirls
Stripshow
Stripteaser

Struggling
Musicians
See also Music
Bikini Summer
Eddie and the Cruisers
Eddie and the Cruisers 2:
    Eddie Lives!
Vibrations

Suicide
See also Death & the
    Afterlife
The Crude Oasis
Golden Gate
Peeping Tom
Warm Summer Rain

Super Heroes
Freddie the Frog
Sgt. Kabukiman N.Y.P.D.
The Wild World of
    Batwoman

Supernatural
Comedies
See also Comedy
Heart and Souls
Wishful Thinking

Supernatural
Horror
See also Classic Horror;
    Horror
Def by Temptation
Demon Keeper
Demonstone
Dust Devil
Edge of Sanity
Embrace of the Vampire
Fright House
Howling II: Your Sister Is a
    Werewolf
Howling III: The Marsupials
Howling IV: The Original
    Nightmare
Lurkers
Meridian: Kiss of the Beast
Mirror, Mirror

Near Dark
Netherworld
Night of the Demons
Nomads
Sorceress

Supernatural
Martial Arts
The Bride with White Hair
The Heroic Trio
Kung Fu Rascals
Sgt. Kabukiman N.Y.P.D.

Supernatural
Westerns
Into the Badlands
Sundown

Technology—
Rampant
See also Computers; Killer
    Appliances; Robots &
    Androids
Blade Runner
Circuitry Man
Cyber-Tracker 2
Digital Man
Final Mission
Hologram Man
Live Wire: Human Timebomb
The Mosaic Project
New Crime City: Los Angeles
    2020
Plughead Rewired: Circuitry
    Man 2
Shadowzone
Terminal Impact

Teen Angst
See also Coming of Age; Hell
    High School
Backstreet Dreams
Beyond Innocence
Body Snatchers
A Boy Called Hate
Carried Away
The Club
Dance Me Outside
Dead Beat
Empire Records
Fall Time
Flirting
The Incredibly True
    Adventure of Two Girls in
    Love
Johnny 100 Pesos
Lisa
The Man in the Attic
Mirror, Mirror
Monika
Pathfinder
Poison Ivy
The Seventh Coin

S.F.W.
Sharon's Secret
Streets
Tammy and the T-Rex
There Goes My Baby
True Crime
Twisted Love
Under the Boardwalk
The Year My Voice Broke

Television
See Mass Media; TV Movies

Terror in Tall Buildings
See also Mystery & Suspense
Hard to Die
Skyscraper

Terrorism
See also Crime & Criminals;
   Foreign Intrigue; Spies &
   Espionage
The Dogfighters
Hologram Man
Live Wire
Project: Alien

This Is Your Life
The Beatles: The First U.S.
   Visit
Bix
Crime Lords
Ed Wood: Look Back in
   Angora
George Stevens: A
   Filmmaker's Journey
Goodnight, Sweet Marilyn
Haunted Summer
Hugh Hefner: Once Upon a
   Time
Jefferson in Paris
The Josephine Baker Story
Kovacs!
The Real Richard Nixon
Romero
32 Short Films about Glenn
   Gould
Tina Turner: The Girl from
   Nutbush

Books to Film: Jim Thompson
Coup de Torchon
The Getaway

Time Travel
A.P.E.X.
Doctor Mordrid: Master of
   the Unknown
Grand Tour: Disaster in Time
Highlander: The Final
   Dimension

Idaho Transfer
A Stranger in Time
Test Tube Teens from the
   Year 2000
The Time Guardian

Tokyo
See also Japan
Akira
Tokyo Decadence

Torn in Two (or More)
Edge of Sanity
Jekyll and Hyde
Mirage
Separate Lives

Torrid Love Scenes
See also Sex & Sexuality;
   Sexploitation
Cat Chaser
Close My Eyes
The Cook, the Thief, His Wife
   & Her Lover
Deadly Desire
The Dolphin
The Hunting
In the Realm of the Senses
Kiss Me a Killer
The Lawnmower Man
Night Eyes 2
Night Eyes 3
9 1/2 Weeks
The Pamela Principle
Sexual Response
Wild Orchid
Wild Orchid 2: Two Shades of
   Blue
Zandalee

Trains
Night Train to Venice
Zentropa

Transvestites & Transsexuals
See Gender Bending

Trapped with a Killer!
See also
   Psychotics/Sociopaths
Alien Terminator
Lifepod
The Maddening
Mute Witness
Tracks of a Killer

Treasure Hunt
Curse of the Crystal Eye
Operation Golden Phoenix
There Goes the
   Neighborhood

Thieves of Fortune
Warrior Spirit

Troma Films
Blondes Have More Guns
Cannibal! The Musical
Chopper Chicks in
   Zombietown
Class of Nuke 'Em High 2:
   Subhumanoid Meltdown
Class of Nuke 'Em High 3:
   The Good, the Bad and the
   Subhumanoid
Ferocious Female Freedom
   Fighters
Sgt. Kabukiman N.Y.P.D.
The Toxic Avenger
Tromeo & Juliet
Wizards of the Demon Sword

True Crime
See also Crime & Criminals;
   This Is Your Life; True
   Stories
The Great St. Louis Bank
   Robbery
Johnny 100 Pesos
The Man in the Attic
Rampage
Sister, My Sister

True Stories
See also This Is Your Life;
   True Crime
Communion
Hard Choices
Hedd Wyn
Henry: Portrait of a Serial
   Killer
The Inner Circle
Little Heroes
M. Butterfly
A Mother's Prayer
Rainbow Drive
Scandal
Stealing Heaven
29th Street

TV Movies
Amanda and the Alien
Another Pair of Aces: Three
   of a Kind
Based on an Untrue Story
Blood Ties
Bloodknot
Burial of the Rats
Capone
Class of '61
Cold Comfort
Dead Air
Deconstructing Sarah
Don't Talk to Strangers
Ebony Tower

Fatherland
First Degree
A Good Day to Die
Grand Tour: Disaster in Time
The Hunchback of Notre
   Dame
Incident at Deception Ridge
Into the Badlands
Jekyll and Hyde
Kovacs!
Lifepod
Lily in Winter
Live Wire
Lone Justice 2
Long Road Home
The Man in the Attic
A Mother's Prayer
National Lampoon's Favorite
   Deadly Sins
The Nightman
Out of Annie's Past
Out There
Passion Flower
Past Tense
Priest
Primal Secrets
Radio Inside
Rainbow Drive
Sharon's Secret
Sketch Artist
Sketch Artist 2: Hands That
   See
Suspect Device
Sweet Bird of Youth
Target: Favorite Son
Trouble in Paradise
The Wharf Rat
The Wrong Man

Twins
See also Family Ties
Basket Case 2
The Bride with White Hair
Class of Nuke 'Em High 3:
   The Good, the Bad and the
   Subhumanoid
Man with a Gun
Mirror Images
Mirror Images 2
The Nutt House
Twin Sisters

UFOs
See Alien Beings—Benign;
   Alien Beings—Vicious;
   Flying Saucers

Unashamed Trash
Bikini Drive-In
Hold Me, Thrill Me, Kiss Me
The House of Usher
In the Cold of the Night

Murder Weapon
Sgt. Kabukiman N.Y.P.D.

Underground
See Avant-Garde

Unexplained Phenomena
Black Rainbow
Grandma's House
Lurkers
Nomads
Out There
Truly, Madly, Deeply

Urban Drama
Jungleground
Once Were Warriors

Vacations
Dead Cold
Far from Home
Phat Beach
Ring of Fire 3: Lion Strike
Tracks of a Killer
Welcome to Spring Break

Vampire Babes
See also Vampires
The Fearless Vampire Killers
The Girl with the Hungry
  Eyes

Vampire Spoof
See also Horror Comedy;
  Vampires
The Fearless Vampire Killers
Near Dark

Vampires
See also Vampire Babes;
  Vampire Spoof
Blood & Donuts
Blood Ties
Bloodlust: Subspecies 3
Bloodstone: Subspecies 2
Cronos
Dracula (Spanish Version)
Dracula Rising
Embrace of the Vampire
Near Dark
Night Hunter
Not of This Earth '88
Not of This Earth '96
Red Blooded American Girl
Subspecies
Sundown
To Die for
To Die for 2: Son of Darkness
To Sleep with a Vampire
Transylvania Twist
Understudy: The Graveyard
  Shift 2
Vampire at Midnight

Vampire Hunter D
The Wicked
Witchcraft 7: Judgement
  Hour

Vietnam War
84 Charlie Mopic
The Siege of Firebase Gloria

Viva Las Vegas!
See also Gambling
Beyond Desire
Kiss Me, Stupid!
Nature of the Beast
Showgirl Murders
Showgirls
Stripshow
Sword of Honor
Texas Payback

Voodoo
See also Occult
Black Magic Woman
Caribe
Voodoo

War Between the Sexes
See also Divorce; Marriage
Cannibal Women in the
  Avocado Jungle of Death
Easy Wheels
Solitaire for 2
Ted & Venus
Three of Hearts

War, General
See also Big Battles;
  Terrorism; Vietnam War;
  World War I; World War II
Heaven & Earth
Lipstick on Your Collar
Project: Alien
Time to Kill

Wedding Bells
See also Marriage; Otherwise
  Engaged; Wedding Hell
Jack and Sarah
Muriel's Wedding

Wedding Hell
See also Marriage; Otherwise
  Engaged; Wedding Bells
Bride of Re-Animator
The Bride with White Hair
Highway to Hell

Werewolves
Howling II: Your Sister Is a
  Werewolf
Howling III: The Marsupials
Howling IV: The Original
  Nightmare

Meridian: Kiss of the Beast
Zentropa

Western Comedy
See also Comedy; Westerns
Powwow Highway
Troublemakers

Westerns
See also Western Comedy
Another Pair of Aces: Three
  of a Kind
Backlash: Oblivion 2
Cheyenne Warrior
A Good Day to Die
Guns of Honor
Hard Bounty
Into the Badlands
Lone Justice 2
Northern Passage
Oblivion
Rockwell: A Legend of the
  Wild West
The Wild Bunch
Will Penny

Wild Kingdom
See also Dinosaurs; Killer
  Bugs & Slugs; Killer Sea
  Critters; King of Beasts
  (Dogs)
Food of the Gods: Part 2
The Further Adventures of
  Tennessee Buck
The Polar Bear King

Witchcraft
See also Demons & Wizards;
  Occult
The Bride with White Hair
Netherworld
The Polar Bear King
Sorceress
Witchcraft
Witchcraft 2: The Temptress
Witchcraft 3: The Kiss of
  Death
Witchcraft 4: Virgin Heart
Witchcraft 5: Dance with the
  Devil
Witchcraft 6: The Devil's
  Mistress
Witchcraft 7: Judgement
  Hour
Witchcraft 8: Salem's Ghost
WitchTrap

Women
See also Dream Girls; Femme
  Fatale; Moms; Women in
  Prison; Wonder Women
Bar Girls
Black Day Blue Night

Boulevard
Cabin Fever
The Dallas Connection
A Dangerous Woman
The Heroic Trio
Jamon, Jamon
Madame Bovary
Murder Weapon
Overseas: Three Women
  with Man Trouble
Ruby in Paradise
Snapdragon
The Stranger
Twenty-One
Wing Chun

Women in Prison
See also Exploitation; Men in
  Prison; Sexploitation
Caged Heat 2: Stripped of
  Freedom
Caged Heat 3000
Cellblock Sisters: Banished
  Behind Bars
Reflections in the Dark

Wonder Women
See also Dream Girls
The American Angels:
  Baptism of Blood
Backfire!
Chopper Chicks in
  Zombietown
Deadly Weapons
Do or Die
Dragon Fury 2
The Executioners
Savage Beach
Skyscraper
The Wild World of
  Batwoman

John Woo Wannabes
American Yakuza
Bad Blood
Drug Runners
Hard Justice
Hong Kong '97
Never Say Die
The Takeover

World War I
Hedd Wyn

World War II
Come See the Paradise
December 7th: The Movie
A Midnight Clear
A Soldier's Tale

Wrestling
The American Angels:
  Baptism of Blood

You read the book, you want the movie, it's not at your video store. What to do? The tiny three-letter codes at the end of each review indicate distributors for each video. This list tells what those codes mean, and if you flip the page to the "Distributor Guide," you can even get the address, phone number, and sometimes even the fax number for each company. Fair warning: studio distributors do not sell to the general public; they act as wholesalers, selling only to retail outlets. Many video stores provide an ordering service; you can also check out the sidebar on page 72 entitled "How to Find 'Em" for more hints on obtaining your Video Premieres.

3GH—3-G Home Video
AAE—A & E Home Video
ACA—Academy Entertainment
ACD—Academy Videos
AFE—Amazing Fantasy Entertainment
AHV—Avid Home Video
AIP—A.I.P. Home Video, Inc
AOV—Admit One Video
APX—A-PIX Entertainment Inc.
ATS—Acorn Media Publishing
AVE—WarnerVision
AVI—Arrow Video, Inc.
BAR—Barr Films
BFV—Best Film & Video Corporation
BMG—BMG
BPG—Bridgestone Multimedia
BTV—Baker & Taylor Video
CAF—Cabin Fever Entertainment
CAN—Cannon Video
CCB—Critics' Choice Video, Inc.
CCP—Cambridge Educational
COL—Columbia Tristar Home Video
CPM—Central Park Media/U.S. Manga Corps

CRC—Criterion Collection
CVC—Connoisseur Video Collection
DAP—Dead Alive Productions
DEB—Deborah Films
DIS—Walt Disney Home Video
DVT—Discount Video Tapes, Inc.
EXP—Expanded Entertainment
FCT—Facets Multimedia, Inc.
FEI—FM Entertainment, Inc.
FHS—Films for the Humanities & Sciences
FLL—Full Moon Home Video
FOX—CBS/Fox Video
FRH—Fries Home Video
FUS—Fusion Video
FXL—Fox/Lorber Home Video
FXV—FoxVideo
GHV—Genesis Home Video
HBO—HBO Home Video
HEG—Horizon Entertainment
HHE—Hollywood Home Entertainment
HMD—Hemdale Home Video
HMK—Hallmark Home Entertainment
HMV—Home Vision Cinema

HPH—Hollywood Pictures Home Video
HTV—Hen's Tooth Video
HVL—Home Video Library
ICA—First Run/Icarus Films
IME—Image Entertainment
IMP—Imperial Entertainment Corp.
ING—Ingram Entertainment
INJ—Ingram International Films
IVY—Ivy Film/Video
KIT—Kit Parker Video
KIV—Kino on Video
LIV—Live Entertainment
LUM—Lumivision Corporation
MAX—Miramax Pictures Home Video
MCA—MCA/Universal Home Video
MED—Media Home Entertainment
MGM—MGM/UA Home Entertainment
MLB—Mike LeBell's Video
MNC—Monarch Home Video
MOV—Movies Unlimited
MPI—MPI Home Video

MRV—Moore Video

MTH—MTI Home Video

MTX—MNTEX Entertainment, Inc.

MVD—Music Video Distributors

NBD—No-Bull Distribution

NEW—New Video Group

NHO—New Horizons Home Video

NLC—New Line Home Video

NWV—New World Entertainment

NYR—Not Yet Released

OM—On Moratorium

ORI—Orion Home Video

ORP—Orphan Entertainment

PAR—Paramount Home Video

PBY—Playboy Home Entertainment

PGV—Polygram Video (PV)

PME—Public Media Video

PMH—PM Entertainment Group, Inc.

PMS—Professional Media Service Corp.

PSM—Prism Entertainment

REP—Republic Pictures Home Video

RHI—Rhino Home Video

RIN—Rincon Children's Entertainment/BMG Kidz

ROC—Rocket Pictures

ROM—Romance Home Video

RVN—Raven International

SAN—Sanro Entertainment

SEP—Scorched Earth Productions

SGE—Amsell Entertainment

SHA—Shaffer Travis Productions

SHE—Showcase Entertainment

SLI—Silver Lake International

SLZ—Sleaziest Movies in the History of the World

SNC—Sinister Cinema

STP—Streamline Pictures

TAI—Tai Seng Video Marketing

TCE—Third Coast Entertainment

TOU—Buena Vista Home Video

TPV—Tapeworm Video Distributors

TRI—Triboro Entertainment Group

TRO—Troma Inc.

TSR—3-Star Releasing

TTC—Turner Home Entertainment Company

TTV—Troma Team Video

TVC—The Video Catalog

TWE—Trans-World Entertainment

UAV—UAV Corporation

UND—Uni Distribution

USR—U.S. Renditions

VCI—VCI Home Video

VES—Vestron Video

VMK—Vidmark Entertainment

VTR—Anchor Bay

VYY—Video Yesteryear

WAR—Warner Home Video, Inc.

WAX—Waxworks/Videoworks, Inc.

WEA—Warner/Elektra/Atlantic (WEA) Corporation

WNE—WNET/Thirteen Non-Broadcast

YHV—York Home Video

Video Premieres

The following listings offer the addresses, phone numbers, and fax numbers for distributors cited in the main review section. Those listings with the code OM are on moratorium (distributed at one time, although not currently). Don't lose hope though—videos can linger on a store's shelves for a long time, so if don't find the movie you're looking for at your regular video haus, mosey on down the road to the next one.

A-PIX ENTERTAINMENT INC.
(APX)
500 5th Ave., 46th Fl.
New York, NY 10110
Ph: 212-764-7171

A & E HOME VIDEO (AAE)
c/o New Video Group
126 5th Ave., 15th Fl.
New York, NY 10011
Ph: 212-206-8600
To: 800-423-1212 Fax: 212-206-9001

ACADEMY ENTERTAINMENT
(ACA)
9250 Wilshire Blvd., Ste. 400
Beverly Hills, CA 90212
Ph: Fax: 310-275-2195

ACADEMY VIDEOS (ACD)
Box 5224
Sherman Oaks, CA 91423-5224
Ph: 818-788-6662
To: 800-423-2397
Fx: 818-788-1580

ACORN MEDIA PUBLISHING
(ATS)
7910 Woodmont Ave., Ste. 350
Bethesda, MD 20814
Ph: 301-907-0030
To: 800-999-0212
Fx: 301-907-9049

ADMIT ONE VIDEO (AOV)
PO Box 66, Sta. O

Toronto, ON, Canada M4A 2M8
Ph: 416-463-5714
Fx: 416-463-5714

A.I.P. HOME VIDEO, INC.
(AIP)
10726 McCune Ave.
Los Angeles, CA 90034
Ph: Fax: 213-559-8849

AMAZING FANTASY
ENTERTAINMENT (AFE)
3061 Fletcher Dr.
Los Angeles, CA 90065
Ph: 213-550-4530

AMSELL ENTERTAINMENT
(SGE)
12001 Ventura Pl., 4th Fl., Ste. 404
Studio City, CA 91604
Ph: 818-766-8500
Fx: 818-766-7873

ANCHOR BAY (VTR)
500 Kirts Blvd.
Troy, MI 48084
Ph: 810-362-9660
To: 800-786-8777
Fx: 810-362-4454

ARROW VIDEO, INC. (AVI)
135 W. 50th St., Ste. 1925
New York, NY 10020
Ph: 212-258-2200
Fx: 212-245-1252

AVID HOME VIDEO (AHV)
c/o Live Home Video
15400 Sherman Way
PO Box 10124
Van Nuys, CA 91406
Ph: 818-908-0303
To: 800-423-7455

BAKER & TAYLOR VIDEO
(BTV)
501 S. Gladiolus
Momence, IL 60954
Ph: 815-472-2444
To: 800-775-2300
Fx: 800-775-3500

BARR FILMS (BAR)
12801 Schabarum
Irwindale, CA 91706
Ph: 818-338-7878
To: 800-234-7878
Fx: 818-814-2672

BEST FILM & VIDEO
CORPORATION (BFV)
108 New South Rd.
Hicksville, NY 11801-5223
Ph: 516-931-6969
To: 800-527-2189
Fx: 516-931-5959

BMG (BMG)
6363 Sunset Blvd., 6th Fl.
Hollywood, CA 90028-7318

427

BRIDGESTONE MULTIMEDIA
(BPG)
300 N. McKemy Ave.
Chandler, AZ 85226
Ph: 602-940-5771
To: 800-523-0988
Fx: 602-940-8924

BUENA VISTA HOME VIDEO
(TOU)
350 S. Buena Vista St.
Burbank, CA 91521-7145
Ph: 818-562-3568

CABIN FEVER
ENTERTAINMENT *(CAF)*
100 W. Putnam Ave.
Greenwich, CT 06830
Ph: 203-661-1100
Fx: 203-863-5258

CAMBRIDGE EDUCATIONAL
(CCP)
PO Box 2153
Charleston, WV 25328-2153
Ph: 304-744-9323
To: 800-468-4227
Fx: 304-744-9351

CANNON VIDEO *(CAN)*
PO Box 17198
Beverly Hills, CA 90290
Ph: 310-772-7765

CBS/FOX VIDEO *(FOX)*
PO Box 900
Beverly Hills, CA 90213
Ph: 562-373-4800
To: 800-800-2369
Fx: 562-373-4803

CENTRAL PARK MEDIA/U.S.
MANGA CORPS *(CPM)*
250 W. 57th St., Ste. 317
New York, NY 10107
Ph: 212-977-7456
To: 800-833-7456
Fx: 212-977-8709

COLUMBIA TRISTAR HOME
VIDEO *(COL)*
Sony Pictures Plz.
10202 W. Washington Blvd.
Culver City, CA 90232
Ph: 310-280-8000
Fx: 310-280-2485

CONNOISSEUR VIDEO
COLLECTION *(CVC)*
1575 Westwood Blvd., Ste. 305
Los Angeles, CA 90024
Ph: 310-231-1350
To: 800-529-2300

Fx: 310-231-1359

CRITERION COLLECTION
(CRC)
c/o The Voyager Company
1 Bridge St.
Irvington, NY 10533-1543

CRITICS' CHOICE VIDEO, INC.
(CCB)
PO Box 749
Itasca, IL 60143-0749
Ph: 708-775-3300
To: 800-367-7765
Fx: 708-775-3355

DEAD ALIVE PRODUCTIONS
(DAP)
111 W. Main St.
Mesa, AZ 85201

DEBORAH FILMS *(DEB)*
1750 Bridgeway, Ste. 103B
Sausalito, CA 94965
To: 800-338-3711

DISCOUNT VIDEO TAPES,
INC. *(DVT)*
PO Box 7122
Burbank, CA 91510
Ph: 818-843-3366
Fx: 818-843-3821

EXPANDED ENTERTAINMENT
(EXP)
28024 Dorothy Dr.
Agoura Hills, CA 91301-2635
Ph: 818-991-2884
To: 800-996-TOON
Fx: 818-991-3773

FACETS MULTIMEDIA, INC.
(FCT)
1517 W. Fullerton Ave.
Chicago, IL 60614
Ph: 312-281-9075
To: 800-331-6197
Fx: 312-929-5437

FILMS FOR THE HUMANITIES
& SCIENCES *(FHS)*
PO Box 2053
Princeton, NJ 08543-2053
Ph: 609-275-1400
To: 800-257-5126
Fx: 609-275-3767

FIRST RUN/ICARUS FILMS
(ICA)
153 Waverly Pl.
New York, NY 10014
Ph: 212-727-1711
To: 800-876-1710

Fx: 212-989-7649

FM ENTERTAINMENT, INC.
(FEI)
10551 W. Pico Blvd.
Los Angeles, CA 90064
Ph: 310-441-4417
Fx: 310-446-9791

FOX/LORBER HOME VIDEO
(FXL)
419 Park Ave. S., 20th Fl.
New York, NY 10016
Ph: 212-532-3392
Fx: 212-685-2625

FOXVIDEO *(FXV)*
2121 Avenue of the Stars, 25th Fl.
Los Angeles, CA 90067
Ph: 310-369-3900
To: 800-800-2FOX
Fx: 310-369-5811

FRIES HOME VIDEO *(FRH)*
6922 Hollywood Blvd., 12th Fl.
Hollywood, CA 90028
Ph: 213-466-2266
Fx: 213-466-2126

FULL MOON HOME VIDEO
(FLL)
8721 Santa Monica Blvd., Ste. 526
West Hollywood, CA 90069
Ph: 213-341-5959

FUSION VIDEO *(FUS)*
100 Fusion Way
Country Club Hills, IL 60478
Ph: 708-799-2073
Fx: 708-799-8375

GENESIS HOME VIDEO *(GHV)*
15820 Arminta St.
Van Nuys, CA 91406

HALLMARK HOME
ENTERTAINMENT *(HMK)*
6100 Wilshire Blvd., Ste. 1400
Los Angeles, CA 90048
Ph: 213-634-3000
Fx: 213-549-3760

HBO HOME VIDEO *(HBO)*
1100 6th Ave.
New York, NY 10036
Ph: 212-512-7400
Fx: 212-512-7498

HEMDALE HOME VIDEO
(HMD)
7966 Beverly Blvd.
Los Angeles, CA 90048
Ph: 213-966-3700

Fx: 213-653-5452

HEN'S TOOTH VIDEO *(HTV)*
2805 E. State Blvd.
Fort Wayne, IN 46805
Ph: 219-471-4332
Fx: 219-471-4449

**HOLLYWOOD HOME
ENTERTAINMENT** *(HHE)*
6165 Crooked Creek Rd., Ste. B
Norcross, GA 30092-3105

**HOLLYWOOD PICTURES
HOME VIDEO** *(HPH)*
Fairmont Bldg. 526
500 S. Buena Vista St.
Burbank, CA 91505-9842

HOME VIDEO LIBRARY *(HVL)*
Better Homes & Gardens Books
PO Box 10670
Des Moines, IA 50336
Ph: 800-678-2665
Fx: 515-237-4765

HOME VISION CINEMA *(HMV)*
5547 N. Ravenswood Ave.
Chicago, IL 60640-1199
Ph: 312-878-2600
To: 800-826-3456

HORIZON ENTERTAINMENT
(HEG)
45030 Trevor Ave.
Lancaster, CA 93534
Ph: 805-940-1040
To: 800-323-2061
Fx: 805-940-8511

IMAGE ENTERTAINMENT
(IME)
9333 Oso Ave.
Chatsworth, CA 91311
Ph: 818-407-9100
To: 800-473-3475
Fx: 818-407-9111

**IMPERIAL ENTERTAINMENT
CORP.** *(IMP)*
4640 Lankershim Blvd., Ste. 201
North Hollywood, CA 91602
Ph: 818-762-0005
To: 800-888-5826
Fx: 818-762-0006

INGRAM ENTERTAINMENT
(ING)
2 Ingram Blvd.
La Vergne, TN 37086-7006
Ph: 615-287-4000
To: 800-759-5000
Fx: 615-287-4992

**INGRAM INTERNATIONAL
FILMS** *(INJ)*
7900 Hickman Rd.
Des Moines, IA 50322
Ph: 515-254-7000
To: 800-621-1333
Fx: 515-254-7021

IVY FILM/VIDEO *(IVY)*
PO Box 18376
Asheville, NC 28814
Ph: 704-285-9995
To: 800-669-4057
Fx: 704-285-9997

KINO ON VIDEO *(KIV)*
333 W. 39th St., Ste. 503
New York, NY 10018
Ph: 212-629-6880
To: 800-562-3330
Fx: 212-714-0871

KIT PARKER VIDEO *(KIT)*
c/o Central Park Media
250 W. 57th St., Ste. 317
New York, NY 10107
Ph: 212-977-7456
Fx: 212-977-8709

LIVE ENTERTAINMENT *(LIV)*
15400 Sherman Way
PO Box 10124
Van Nuys, CA 91410-0124
Ph: 818-988-5060

LUMIVISION CORPORATION
(LUM)
877 Federal Blvd.
Denver, CO 80204-3212
Ph: 303-446-0400
To: 800-776-LUMI
Fx: 303-446-0101

**MCA/UNIVERSAL HOME
VIDEO** *(MCA)*
100 Universal City Plz.
Universal City, CA 91608-9955
Ph: 818-777-1000
Fx: 818-866-1483

**MEDIA HOME
ENTERTAINMENT** *(MED)*
510 W. 6th St., Ste. 1032
Los Angeles, CA 90014
Ph: 213-236-1336
Fx: 213-236-1346

**MGM/UA HOME
ENTERTAINMENT** *(MGM)*
2500 Broadway
Santa Monica, CA 90404-6061
Ph: 310-449-3000
Fx: 310-449-3100

MIKE LEBELL'S VIDEO *(MLB)*
75 Freemont Pl.
Los Angeles, CA 90005
Ph: 213-938-3333
Fx: 213-938-3334

**MIRAMAX PICTURES HOME
VIDEO** *(MAX)*
500 S. Buena Vista St.
Burbank, CA 91521

**MNTEX ENTERTAINMENT,
INC.** *(MTX)*
500 Kirts Dr.
Troy, MI 48084-5225

MONARCH HOME VIDEO
(MNC)
Two Ingram Blvd.
La Vergne, TN 37086-7006
Ph: 615-287-4632
Fx: 615-287-4992

MOORE VIDEO *(MRV)*
PO Box 5703
Richmond, VA 23220
Ph: 804-745-9785
Fx: 804-745-9785

MOVIES UNLIMITED *(MOV)*
3015 Darnell Rd.
Philadelphia, PA 19154
Ph: 215-637-4444
To: 800-466-8437
Fx: 215-637-2350

MPI HOME VIDEO *(MPI)*
16101 S. 108th Ave.
Orland Park, IL 60462
Ph: 708-460-0555
Fx: 708-873-3177

MTI HOME VIDEO *(MTH)*
14216 SW 136th St.
Miami, FL 33186
Ph: 305-255-8684
To: 800-821-7461
Fx: 305-233-6943

MUSIC VIDEO DISTRIBUTORS
(MVD)
O'Neill Industrial Center
1210 Standbridge St.
Norristown, PA 19401
Ph: 610-272-7771
To: 800-888-0486
Fx: 610-272-6074

**NEW HORIZONS HOME
VIDEO** *(NHO)*
2951 Flowers Rd., S., Ste. 237
Atlanta, GA 30341
Ph: 404-458-3488

429

To: 800-854-3323
Fx: 404-458-2679

**NEW LINE HOME VIDEO
(NLC)**
116 N. Robertson Blvd.
Los Angeles, CA 90048
Ph: 310-967-6670
Fx: 310-854-0602

NEW VIDEO GROUP (NEW)
126 5th Ave., 15th Fl.
New York, NY 10011
Ph: 212-206-8600
To: 800-423-1212
Fx: 212-206-9001

**NEW WORLD
ENTERTAINMENT (NWV)**
1440 S. Sepulveda Blvd.
Los Angeles, CA 90025
Ph: 310-444-8100
Fx: 310-444-8101

**NO-BULL DISTRIBUTION
(NBD)**
1 E. Broward Blvd., Ste. 620
Fort Lauderdale, FL 33301
Ph: 800-643-1471

ORION HOME VIDEO (ORI)
1888 Century Park E.
Los Angeles, CA 90067
Ph: 310-282-0550
Fx: 310-282-9902

**ORPHAN ENTERTAINMENT
(ORP)**
6930 Sunset Blvd.
Hollywood, CA 90028
Ph: 213-962-6280

**PARAMOUNT HOME VIDEO
(PAR)**
Bluhdorn Bldg.
5555 Melrose Ave.
Los Angeles, CA 90038
Ph: 213-956-3952

**PLAYBOY HOME
ENTERTAINMENT (PBY)**
9242 Beverly Blvd.
Beverly Hills, CA 90210
Ph: 310-246-4000

**PM ENTERTAINMENT GROUP,
INC. (PMH)**
9450 Chivers Ave.
Sun Valley, CA 91352
Ph: 818-504-6332
To: 800-934-2111
Fx: 818-504-6380

POLYGRAM VIDEO (PV) (PGV)
825 8th Ave.
New York, NY 10019
Ph: 212-333-8000
To: 800-825-7781
Fx: 212-603-7960

**PRISM ENTERTAINMENT
(PSM)**
1888 Century Park, E., Ste. 350
Los Angeles, CA 90067
Ph: 310-277-3270
Fx: 310-203-8036

**PROFESSIONAL MEDIA
SERVICE CORP. (PMS)**
19122 S. Vermont Ave.
Gardena, CA 90248
Ph: 310-532-9024
To: 800-223-7672
Fx: 800-253-8853

PUBLIC MEDIA VIDEO (PME)
5547 N. Ravenswood Ave.
Chicago, IL 60640-1199
Ph: 312-878-2600
To: 800-826-3456
Fx: 312-878-8406

**RAVEN INTERNATIONAL
(RVN)**
859 Hollywood Way, Ste. 273
Burbank, CA 91505
Ph: 818-508-4785

**REPUBLIC PICTURES HOME
VIDEO (REP)**
5700 Wilshire Blvd., Ste. 525 North
Los Angeles, CA 90036-3659
Ph: 213-965-6900
Fx: 213-965-6963

RHINO HOME VIDEO (RHI)
10635 Santa Monica Blvd., 2nd Fl.
Los Angeles, CA 90025-4900
Ph: 310-828-1980
To: 800-843-3670
Fx: 310-453-5529

**RINCON CHILDREN'S
ENTERTAINMENT/BMG
KIDZ (RIN)**
1525 Crossroads of the World
Hollywood, CA 90028

ROCKET PICTURES (ROC)
9536 Wilshire Blvd., Ste. 410
Beverly Hills, CA 90212
Ph: 310-550-3300

**ROMANCE HOME VIDEO
(ROM)**
2532 Lincoln Blvd., Ste. 180

Marina del Ray, CA 90291-5798
Ph: 310-305-7178

**SANRO ENTERTAINMENT
(SAN)**
PO Box 10
Tujunga, CA 91042

**SCORCHED EARTH
PRODUCTIONS (SEP)**
PO Box 101083
Denver, CO 80250

**SHAFFER TRAVIS
PRODUCTIONS (SHA)**
1527 Mark West Springs Rd.
Santa Rose, CA 95404
Ph: 707-576-8115

**SHOWCASE ENTERTAINMENT
(SHE)**
Warner Center
21800 Oxnard St., Ste. 150
Woodland Hills, CA 91387
Ph: 818-715-7005

**SILVER LAKE INTERNATIONAL
(SLI)**
18840 Ventura Blvd., Ste. 210
Tarzana, CA 91356
Ph: 818-757-0007
Fx: 818-757-0038

SINISTER CINEMA (SNC)
PO Box 4369
Medford, OR 97501-0168
Ph: 503-773-6860
Fx: 503-779-8650

**SLEAZIEST MOVIES IN THE
HISTORY OF THE WORLD
(SLZ)**
3350 Ocean Park Blvd.
Santa Monica, CA 90405

STREAMLINE PICTURES (STP)
2908 Nebraska Avenue
Santa Monica, CA 90404-4109
Ph: 310-998-0070
To: 800-846-1453
Fx: 310-998-1145

**TAI SENG VIDEO MARKETING
(TAI)**
170 S. Spruce Ave., Ste. 200
San Francisco, CA 94080
Ph: 415-871-8118
To: 800-888-3836
Fx: 415-871-2392

**TAPEWORM VIDEO
DISTRIBUTORS (TPV)**
27833 Hopkins Ave., Unit 6

Valencia, CA 91355
Ph: 805-257-4904
Fx: 805-257-4820

**THIRD COAST
ENTERTAINMENT** *(TCE)*
12750 Ventura Blvd., Ste. 102
Studio City, CA 91604
Ph: 818-769-9986

3-G HOME VIDEO *(3GH)*
8025 Deering Ave.
Canoga Park, CA 91304
Ph: 818-888-6563
To: 800-345-5855
Fx: 818-888-6576

3-STAR RELEASING *(TSR)*
15745 Stagg St.
Van Nuys, CA 91406
Ph: 818-997-1174
To: 800-257-3777
Fx: 818-376-8505

**TRANS-WORLD
ENTERTAINMENT** *(TWE)*
8899 Beverly Blvd., 8th Fl.
Los Angeles, CA 90048-2412

**TRIBORO ENTERTAINMENT
GROUP** *(TRI)*
12 W. 27th St., 15th Fl.
New York, NY 10001
Ph: 212-606-0116
Fx: 212-686-6178

TROMA INC. *(TRO)*
733 9th St.
New York, NY 10019
Ph: 212-757-4555
To: 800-83-TROMA
Fx: 212-399-9885

TROMA TEAM VIDEO *(TTV)*
1501 Broadway, Ste. 2605
New York, NY 10036
Ph: 212-997-0595
Fx: 212-997-0968

**TURNER HOME
ENTERTAINMENT COMPANY
(TTC)**
Box 105366
Atlanta, GA 35366
Ph: 404-827-3066
To: 800-523-0823

Fx: 404-827-3266

UAV CORPORATION *(UAV)*
PO Box 5497
Fort Mill, SC 29715
Ph: 803-548-7300
To: 800-486-6782
Fx: 803-548-3335

UNI DISTRIBUTION *(UND)*
60 Universal City Plz.
Universal City, CA 91608
Ph: 818-777-4400
Fx: 818-766-5740

U.S. RENDITIONS *(USR)*
1123 Domingues St., Ste. K
Carson, CA 90746

VCI HOME VIDEO *(VCI)*
11333 E. 60th Pl.
Tulsa, OK 74146
Ph: 918-254-6337
To: 800-331-4077
Fx: 918-254-6117

VESTRON VIDEO *(VES)*
c/o Live Home Video
15400 Sherman Way
PO Box 10124
Van Nuys, CA 91410-0124
Ph: 818-988-0303
To: 800-367-7765
Fx: 818-778-3194

THE VIDEO CATALOG *(TVC)*
7000 Westgate Dr.
St. Paul, MN 55114
Ph: 612-659-3700
To: 800-733-6656
Fx: 612-659-0083

VIDEO YESTERYEAR *(VYY)*
Box C
Sandy Hook, CT 06482
Ph: 203-426-2476
To: 800-243-0987
Fx: 203-797-0819

**VIDMARK ENTERTAINMENT
(VMK)**
2644 30th St.
Santa Monica, CA 90405-3009
Ph: 310-314-2000
Fx: 310-392-0252

**WALT DISNEY HOME VIDEO
(DIS)**
500 S. Buena Vista St.
Burbank, CA 91521
Ph: 818-562-3560

**WARNER/ELEKTRA/ATLANTIC
(WEA) CORPORATION
(WEA)**
9451 LBJ Fwy., Ste. 107
Dallas, TX 75243
Ph: 214-234-6200
Fx: 214-699-9343

**WARNER HOME VIDEO, INC.
(WAR)**
4000 Warner Blvd.
Burbank, CA 91522
Ph: 818-954-6000

WARNERVISION *(AVE)*
A Time Warner Company
75 Rockefeller Plz.
New York, NY 10019
Ph: 212-275-2900
To: 800-95-WARNER
Fx: 212-765-0899

**WAXWORKS/VIDEOWORKS,
INC. (WAX)**
325 E. 3rd St.
Owensboro, KY 42303
Ph: 502-926-0008
To: 800-825-8558
Fx: 502-685-0563

**WNET/THIRTEEN NON-
BROADCAST** *(WNE)*
356 W. 58th St.
New York, NY 10019
Ph: 212-560-2000
Fx: 212-582-3297

YORK HOME VIDEO *(YHV)*
4733 Lankershim Blvd.
North Hollywood, CA 91602
Ph: 310-278-1034
To: 800-84-MOVIE
Fx: 818-505-8290